Perspectives on American Politics

Perspectives on American Politics

THIRD EDITION

William Lasser

Clemson University

Houghton Mifflin Company

Boston New York

Sponsoring Editor: Melissa Mashburn
Editorial Associate: Vikram Mukhija
Senior Project Editor: Julie Lane
Editorial Assistant: Jennifer O'Neill
Production/Design Coordinator: Jennifer Meyer Dare
Senior Cover Design Coordinator: Deborah Azerrad Savona
Senior Manufacturing Coordinator: Marie Barnes
Senior Marketing Manager: Sandra McGuire
Marketing Assistant: Ivan Chan

Cover Design: Walter Kopec

Cover Image: John Skowronski Photography

Printed in the U.S.A.

Library of Congress Catalog Card Number: 99-71942

ISBN: 0-395-96102-5

123456789-XX-03   02   01   00   99

To Susan J. S. Lasser, with love

Contents

Chapter 1 **The Constitution**   **1**

I Foundations   2

1.1 *Federalist* No. 10   4
James Madison
"A zeal for different opinions concerning religion, concerning government, and many other points . . . have, in turn, divided mankind into
parties, [and] inflamed them with mutual animosity."

1.2 *Federalist* No. 47   9
James Madison
"In the extent and proper structure of the Union . . . we behold a republican remedy for the diseases most incident to republican government."

1.3 *Federalist* No. 48   12
James Madison
"Will it be sufficient to mark, with precision, the boundaries of these
departments in the constitution of the government, and to trust to
parchment barriers against the encroaching spirit of power?"

1.4 *Federalist* No. 51   14
James Madison
"Ambition must be made to counteract ambition."

1.5 The Address and Reason of Dissent of the Minority of the
Convention of Pennsylvania to Their Constituents   18
"We entered on the examination of the proposed system of government, and found it to be such as we could not adopt, without, as we
conceived, surrendering up your dearest rights."

II American Politics Today   27

1.6 Second Thoughts on the Second Amendment   27
Wendy Kaminer
"The tension at the heart of the Second Amendment, which makes it
so difficult to construe, is the tension between republicanism and liberal individualism."

III The Comparative Context   33

1.7 How Ideas Travel: Rights at Home and Abroad   34
A. E. Dick Howard

"Americans have good cause to celebrate two hundred years of the Bill of Rights. They likewise have every reason to hope for the principles of that document to take root in the lands now free of tyrannical rule."

IV View from the Inside   39

1.8 The Founding Fathers: A Reform Caucus in Action   39
John P. Roche
"There is a common rumor that the Framers divided their time between philosophical discussions of government and reading the classics in political theory. Perhaps this is as good a time as any to note that their concerns were highly practical . . . ."

Chapter 2 **Federalism**   **48**

I Foundations   49

2.1 What the Antifederalists Were For   51
Herbert Storing
"Federalism means that the states are primary . . . and that they possess the main weight of political power. The defense of the federal character of the American union was the most prominent article of Anti-Federalist conservative doctrine."

2.2 *Federalist* No. 39   56
James Madison
"The proposed Constitution . . . is, in strictness, neither a national nor a federal Constitution, but a combination of both."

2.3 *Federalist* No. 45   61
James Madison
"The powers delegated by the proposed Constitution to the federal government are few and defined. Those which are to remain in the State governments are numerous and indefinite."

II American Politics Today   65

2.4 The War Between the States . . . and Washington   65
Garry Wills
"On a whole range of . . . issues, the states have been out ahead of Federal programs, reversing a long-term trend. . . . [P]eople with new ideas and a passion for public policy are turning away from Washington and attacking social issues at the state and local levels. This shift raises deep questions about the virtues of direct democracy, the merits of federalism and the possibility of isolating states from the national society."

III The Comparative Context   73

2.5 If You Sincerely Want to Be a United States . . .   73
The Economist

"[The job of] the people now charged with trying to create a political union in Europe . . . is not different in kind from that which faced America's constitutional convention [in 1787] . . . . Might the most mature and successful constitutional settlement in the world have some lessons for those European parvenus?"

IV View from the Inside   79

2.6 The Taming of Texas   79
Jonathan Walters

"Ask George W. Bush how hard it is to govern Texas, and he's glad to tell you. He swings his arms wide to denote the vastness of the domain that he can't control. 'You don't get everything you want,' he says, understating the case considerably. 'A dictatorship would be a lot easier.'"

Chapter 3 Civil Liberties   85

I Foundations   86

3.1 On Liberty   86
John Stuart Mill

"The object 'towards which every human being must ceaselessly direct his efforts . . . is the individuality of power and development' . . . for this there are two requisites, 'freedom and variety of situations.'"

II American Politics Today   93

3.2 *Roe* v. *Wade*   94
Justice Harry A. Blackmun

"We do not agree that, by adopting one theory of life, Texas may override the rights of the pregnant woman that are at stake."

3.3 *Planned Parenthood of Southeastern Pennsylvania* v. *Casey*   98
Justice Sandra Day O'Connor

"A decision to overrule *Roe*'s essential holding would address error, if error there was, at the cost of both profound and unnecessary damage to the Court's legitimacy, and to the Nation's commitment to the rule of law. It is therefore imperative to adhere to the essence of *Roe*'s original decision. . . ."

III The Comparative Context   102

3.4 The Universal Declaration and the U.S. Constitution   103
Louis Henkin

"The U.S. Constitution, and the constitutional culture it engendered, were a principal conduit for the idea of rights later espoused by the Universal Declaration [of Human Rights], and a principal source of many—not all—of the rights recognized in the Declaration."

IV View from the Inside   108

3.5 Is the Criminal Trial a Search for Truth?   109
Alan Dershowitz
*"The term 'search for truth' was repeatedly invoked by both sides of
the [O. J.] Simpson case. . . . The prosecutors claimed they were
searching for truth and justice. . . . The defense also claimed the mantle of truth and accused the prosecution of placing barriers in its path.
And throughout the trial, the pundits observed that neither side was
really interested in truth, only winning. They were right—and
wrong."*

Chapter 4 **Civil Rights**   **117**

I Foundations   118

4.1 *Plessy* v. *Ferguson*   119
Justice Henry B. Brown
Justice John Marshall Harlan, dissenting
*"The object of the [Fourteenth] Amendment was undoubtedly to en-
force the absolute equality of the two races before the law, but . . . it
could not have been intended to abolish distinctions based upon color,
or to enforce social . . . equality."*

4.2 *Brown* v. *Board of Education*   123
Chief Justice Earl Warren
*"In the field of education the doctrine of 'separate but equal' has no
place. Separate educational facilities are inherently unequal."*

4.3 *Bolling* v. *Sharpe*   126
Chief Justice Earl Warren
*"In view of our decision that the Constitution prohibits the states from
maintaining racially segregated public schools, it would be unthinkable
that the same Constitution would impose a lesser duty on the Federal
Government."*

II American Politics Today   127

4.4 *Meritor Savings Bank* v. *Vinson*   128
Chief Justice William H. Rehnquist
*"Without question, when a supervisor sexually harasses a subordinate
because of the subordinate's sex, that supervisor discriminate[s] on the
basis of sex."*

4.5 Tales From the Front Line of Sexual Harassment   131
Margot Slade
*"Sexual harassment laws have always been notoriously confusing, so
there was much cheering when the Supreme Court clarified things by
issuing new rulings [in 1998]. . . . Here are case studies drawn from
the files of consultants and interpreted in light of the Supreme Court's
new rulings."*

III The Comparative Context   135

   4.6 Multicultural Citizenship   135
        Will Kymlicka
        "I believe it is legitimate, and indeed unavoidable, to supplement tradi-
        tional human rights with minority rights. A comprehensive theory of
        justice in a multicultural state will include both universal rights, assigned
        to individuals regardless of group membership, and certain group-differ-
        entiated rights or 'special status' rights for minority cultures."

IV View from the Inside   143

   4.7 Serving in Silence   144
        Margarethe Cammermeyer
        "I took a breath; a little moment passed. Up to a few years before, I
        wouldn't have been hesitant. I would have affirmed my heterosexual-
        ity and the interview would have proceeded without a hitch. But I
        had changed. . . . I said, 'I am a lesbian.'"

Chapter 5 **Political Culture and Public Opinion   149**

   I Foundations   150

   5.1 Democracy in America   151
        Alexis de Tocqueville
        "The social condition of the Americans is entirely democratic."

   II American Politics Today   160

   5.2 A Question of Values   160
        David S. Broder and Richard Morin
        "The sharply divided public reaction to the impeachment of President
        Clinton has provided a dramatic showcase of a struggle for American
        values that goes back to the 1960s and remains unresolved today."

   III The Comparative Context   165

   5.3 American Exceptionalism: A Double-Edged Sword   166
        Seymour Martin Lipset
        "Other countries' senses of themselves are derived from a common
        history. . . . In Europe, nationality is related to community, and thus
        one cannot become un-English or un-Swedish. Being an American,
        however, is an ideological commitment. It is not a matter of birth.
        Those who reject American values are un-American."

   IV View from the Inside   172

   5.4 The Power of the Presidents' Pollsters   172
        Michael Barone
        "Polling is a tool, not magic; and political pollsters at their best are in-
        spired mechanics. . . . They are not—certainly they are not yet—our
        masters."

Chapter 6 **Interest Groups   178**

  I Foundations   179

   6.1 The Scope and Bias of the Pressure System   179
   E. E. Schattschneider
   *"Pressure politics is essentially the politics of small groups. . . . [I]t is a
   selective process ill designed to serve diffuse interests. The system is
   skewed, loaded, and unbalanced in favor of a fraction of a minority."*

  II American Politics Today   186

   6.2 Interest Groups, PACs, and Campaigns   187
   Paul S. Herrnson
   *"Individual citizens . . . are not the only ones who use the electoral
   connection to express their views about politics. Businesses, labor
   unions, professional associations, and a variety of other groups—
   some of which are at best only loosely organized—also use elections
   to influence public policy."*

  III The Comparative Context   198

   6.3 The Japanese Lobby in Washington   199
   Ronald J. Hrebenar and Clive S. Thomas
   *"The Japan lobby has become a symbol of 150 years of distrust and
   misunderstanding between Japan and the United States. In fact,
   however, Japan's lobbying efforts appear to be commensurate to the
   stakes it holds in its relations with the United States."*

  IV View from the Inside   206

   6.4 A New Form of Lobbying Puts Public Face
   on Private Interest   207
   Alison Mitchell
   *"In their million-dollar costs and in their reliance on television, polling
   and grass-roots constituency building . . . [modern lobbying efforts]
   most resemble Presidential campaigns. And they are now so pervasive and sophisticated that it has become difficult to distinguish between a lobbying effort, an issue advocacy campaign and a citizens'
   movement."*

Chapter 7 **The Media   214**

  I. Foundations   215

   7.1 *New York Times Co.* v. *United States*   216
   Justice Hugo L. Black
   *"In the First Amendment the Founding Fathers gave the free press the
   protection it must have to fulfill its essential role in a democracy. The
   press was to serve the governed, not the governors. The Government's power to censor the press was abolished so that the press would
   remain forever free to censure the Government."*

II American Politics Today   218

7.2 Monicanomics   219
John Cassidy
"[In early 1998] the big media companies launched a new product that they were enormously excited about—the Monica Lewinsky story—only to run into a lack of enthusiasm from customers."

III The Comparative Context   223

7.3 Foreign News: Who Gives a Damn?   224
James F. Hoge, Jr.
"Except for the collapse of the Soviet Union in 1989–90, the coverage of . . . international news in American media has steadily declined since the late seventies, when the cold war lost its sense of imminent danger."

IV View from the Inside   229

7.4 The Master of Spin   230
Howard Kurtz
"One thing about [White House Press Secretary] Mike McCurry, he knew how to play the game . . . . McCurry was a spinmeister extraordinaire, deflecting questions with practiced ease, sugar-coating the ugly messes into which the Clintonites seemed repeatedly to stumble. . . . He was walking the tightrope, struggling to maintain credibility with both the press and the president, to serve as an honest broker between the antagonists."

Chapter 8 **Parties and Elections   238**

I Foundations   239

8.1 Towards a More Responsible Two-Party System   239
The APSA Committee on Political Parties
"In brief, our view is this: The party system that is needed must be democratic, responsible and effective—a system that is accountable to the public, respects and expresses differences of opinion, and is able to cope with the great problems of modern government."

II American Politics Today   245

8.2 The Mighty Middle   246
John B. Judis
"[In 1998, the] Democrats did much better than expected precisely because the public identified them with a cautious, liberal centrism. Those Republicans who did particularly well . . . were also identified with this kind of political approach. The real losers in the election were right-wing Republicans."

8.3 The Southern Captivity of the GOP   250
Christopher Caldwell

"The Republican Party is increasingly a party of the South and the mountains. . . . There is a big problem with having a southern, as opposed to a midwestern or a California, base. Southern interests diverge from those of the rest of the country, and the southern presence in the Republican Party has passed a 'tipping point,' at which it began to alienate voters from other regions."

III The Comparative Context   256

8.4 Breaking the Two-Party Monopoly   257
Douglas J. Amy
"Americans have suffered under our two-party system for so long that we tend to view its problems and limitations as unfortunate but inevitable. . . . In reality, . . . the adoption of proportional representation in the United States would go a long way toward addressing many of these shortcomings."

IV View from the Inside   263

8.5 Trail Fever   264
Michael Lewis
"I watch [Steve] Forbes deliver the same speech half a dozen times before I get close enough to find evidence to support my hunch—or perhaps my hope—that a perfectly strict routine is not as straightforward as it appears . . . I assumed that he read from the same written text but to my amazement see that he actually uses loose notes, as if he had just thought up his speech in the car on the way over."

Chapter 9 **The Congress**   **269**

I Foundations   270

9.1 *Federalist* No. 55   271
James Madison
"Had every Athenian citizen been born a Socrates, every Athenian assembly would still have been a mob."

9.2 *Federalist* No. 57   274
James Madison
"Such will be the relation between the House of Representatives and their constituents. Duty, gratitude, interest, ambition itself, are the cords by which they will be bound to fidelity and sympathy with the great mass of the people."

II American Politics Today   276

9.3 Party Leaders and the New Legislative Process   277
Barbara Sinclair
"[T]he how-a-bill-becomes-a-law diagram that is a staple of American government textbooks in reality describes the legislative process on fewer and fewer of the major measures Congress considers."

III The Comparative Context   283

9.4   Changing Perceptions of the British System   284
Leon D. Epstein
"Since the development of their academic discipline over a century ago, American political scientists have treated British parliamentary democracy as a benchmark in evaluating the American system. . . . My perspective combines respect for the British political system with a disbelief in the suitability of its parliamentary institutions for the United States."

IV View from the Inside   288

9.5   Women on the Hill   289
Clara Bingham
"In the House . . . the congresswomen dominated the family-leave debate. . . . Their speaking styles were personal and powerful. Patricia Ireland, president of the National Organization for Women, applauded them, noting that their performances were emblematic of the difference women were making on the Hill: 'Women bring a different set of priorities,' she said."

Chapter 10 **The Presidency**   295

I Foundations   296

10.1   *Federalist* No. 68   297
Alexander Hamilton
"Talent for low intrigue, and the little arts of popularity, may alone suffice to elevate a man to the first honors of a single State; but it will require other talents . . . to establish him in the esteem and confidence of the whole Union."

10.2   *Federalist* No. 70   299
Alexander Hamilton
"Energy in the executive is a leading characteristic of good government."

10.3   Presidential Power   302
Richard Neustadt
"A President's authority and status give him great advantages in dealing with the men he would persuade . . . . [A] President may need them all."

II American Politics Today   304

10.4   Presidential Paradoxes   305
Thomas E. Cronin and Michael Genovese
"Our expectations of, and demand on, the president are frequently so contradictory as to invite two-faced behavior by our presidents. Presidential powers are often not as great as many of us believe, and the president gets unjustly condemned as ineffective. Or a president

will overreach or resort to unfair play while trying to live up to our demands."

III The Comparative Context 314

10.5 Presidents and Prime Ministers 315
Richard Rose
"There are diverse ways of organizing the direction of government, not only between democracies and authoritarian regimes, but also among democracies. Switzerland stands at one extreme, with collective direction provided by a federal council whose president rotates from year to year. At the other extreme are countries that claim to centralize authority, under a . . . parliamentary system or in a . . . presidential system."

IV View from the Inside 325

10.6 Public Acts, Private Moments 326
Robert D. McFadden, John Kifner, and N. R. Kleinfield
"It was not a routine Wednesday for Mr. Clinton because a budget impasse with Congress had shut down the Federal government. . . . The President . . . had meetings with aides, as well as with three Senators and a group of farmers. He had an appropriations bill and several proclamations to sign and an interview with a television network. . . . At 1:30 P.M . . . . [Monica] Lewinsky entered the White House."

Chapter 11 **The Bureaucracy** 333

I Foundations 334

11.1 Bureaucracy 335
Max Weber
"Bureaucracy offers above all the optimum possibility for carrying through the principle of specializing administrative functions according to purely objective considerations."

II American Politics Today 338

11.2 Bureaucracy: What Government Agencies Do and Why They Do It 339
James Q. Wilson
"When we denounce bureaucracy for being inefficient we are saying something that is half true. . . . The only way to decide whether an agency is truly inefficient is to decide which of the constraints affecting its action ought to be ignored or discounted."

III The Comparative Context 347

11.3 The Distinctive Nature of American Public Administration 347
Gerald E. Caiden, Richard A. Lovard, Thomas J. Pavlak, Lynn F. Sipe, and Molly M. Wong

"The scope of American public administration is distinct [from that of Europe] in at least ten ways."

IV View from the Inside   351

11.4 Locked in the Cabinet   351
Robert Reich
"I take the elevator to floors I've never visited. I wander to places in the department I've never been. I have a spontaneous conversation with employees I'd never otherwise see. Free at last. . . . Kitty discovers I'm missing. . . . The alarm is sounded: Secretary loose! Secretary escapes from the bubble! Find the Secretary!"

Chapter 12 **The Judiciary**   **360**

I Foundations   361

12.1 *Federalist* No. 78   362
Alexander Hamilton
"The judiciary . . . has no influence over either the sword or the purse; no direction either of the strength or the wealth of society; and can take no active resolution whatever. It may truly be said to have neither FORCE nor WILL but merely judgment."

12.2 *Marbury* v. *Madison*   367
Chief Justice John Marshall
"If an act of the legislature, repugnant to the constitution, is void, does it, notwithstanding its invalidity, bind the courts, and oblige them to give it effect?"

II American Politics Today   371

12.3 The Jurisprudence of the Rehnquist Court   371
Kathleen M. Sullivan
"[T]he Rehnquist Court, while it has undoubtedly turned rightward, has never turned as starkly rightward as predicted . . . even though Presidents Reagan and Bush between them filled five seats on the Court. . . . Why might this be so?"

III The Comparative Context   380

12.4 Judicial Activism in Canada and the United States   381
Mark C. Miller
"The legal systems of Canada and the United States share many common characteristics. Both have their roots in British Common Law. Legal training is similar, and both countries draw their judges primarily from the practicing bar. But despite their similarities, Canadian and U.S. judges have approached their policy-making roles quite differently."

IV View from the Inside   387

12.5 Closed Chambers   387
Edward Lazarus
*"In the Blackmun chambers, each outgoing clerk designated two
days to train his or her successor. I remember that time as a giant
blur, a jumble of shorthand explanations of procedures I couldn't
quite grasp, mixed in with a number of don't worry, you'll figure it
out as you go alongs."*

Chapter 13 **Public Policy   395**

I Foundations   396

13.1 Domestic Policymaking   396
Roger H. Davidson and Walter J. Oleszek
*"Policies can be regarded as reflecting 'who gets what, when, and
how in society.' A more serviceable definition of policy [is that] . . .
policy is what the government says and does about perceived problems."*

II American Politics Today   401

13.2 Nine Misconceptions About Social Security   402
Dean Baker
*"In fact the demographics of the Baby Boom have very little to do
with the long-range problems of Social Security. The main reason
the fund will run into deficits in future years is that people are living
longer."*

III The Comparative Context   408

13.3 Ideas, Institutions, and the Policies of Government:
A Comparative Analysis   409
Anthony King
*"The State plays a more limited role in America than elsewhere be-
cause Americans, more than other people, want it to play a limited
role."*

IV View from the Inside   416

13.4 "Mr. Chairman, We've Got a Problem"   417
Colin Powell
*"George Bush sat like a patron on a bar stool coolly observing a
brawl while his advisors went hard at it. [National Security Adviser]
Brent Skowcroft . . . wanted to leave the President with no comfortable illusions: 'There are going to be casualties. People are going to
die,' Skowcroft said. . . . The questions continued. . . . [T]hen
Bush, after everyone had had his say, gripped the arms of his chair
and rose. 'Okay, let's do it,' he said. 'The hell with it.'"*

Readings by Perspective

Foundations

1.1 James Madison, *Federalist* No. 10
1.2 James Madison, *Federalist* No. 47
1.3 James Madison, *Federalist* No. 48
1.4 James Madison, *Federalist* No. 51
1.5 *The Address and Reason of Dissent of the Minority of the Convention of Pennsylvania to Their Constituents*

2.1 Herbert Storing, *What the Antifederalists Were For*
2.2 James Madison, *Federalist* No. 39
2.3 James Madison, *Federalist* No. 45

3.1 John Stuart Mill, *On Liberty*

4.1 Justices Henry B. Brown and John Marshall Harlan, *Plessy v. Ferguson*
4.2 Chief Justice Earl Warren, *Brown v. Board of Education*
4.3 Chief Justice Earl Warren, *Bolling v. Sharpe*

5.1 Alexis de Tocqueville, *Democracy in America*

6.1 E. E. Schattschneider, *The Scope and Bias of the Pressure System*

7.1 Justice Hugo L. Black, *New York Times Co. v. United States*

8.1 The APSA Committee on Political Parties, *Towards a More Responsible Two-Party System*

9.1 James Madison, *Federalist* No. 55
9.2 James Madison, *Federalist* No. 57

10.1 Alexander Hamilton, *Federalist* No. 68
10.2 Alexander Hamilton, *Federalist* No. 70

11.1 Max Weber, *Bureaucracy*

12.1 Alexander Hamilton, *Federalist* No. 78
12.2 Chief Justice John Marshall, *Marbury v. Madison*

13.1 Roger H. Davidson and Walter J. Oleszek, *Domestic Policymaking*

American Politics Today

1.6 Wendy Kaminer, *Second Thoughts on the Second Amendment*

2.4 Garry Wills, *The War Between the States . . . and Washington*

3.2 Justice Harry A. Blackmun, *Roe v. Wade*
3.3 Justice Sandra Day O'Connor, *Planned Parenthood of Southeastern Pennsylvania v. Casey*

4.4 Chief Justice William H. Rehnquist, *Meritor Savings Bank v. Vinson*
4.5 Margot Slade, *Tales from the Front Line of Sexual Harassment*

5.2 David S. Broder and Richard Morin, *A Question of Values*

6.2 Paul S. Herrnson, *Interest Groups, PACs, and Campaigns*

7.2 John Cassidy, *Monicanomics*

8.2 John B. Judis, *The Mighty Middle*
8.3 Christopher Caldwell, *The Southern Captivity of the GOP*

9.3 Barbara Sinclair, *Party Leaders and the New Legislative Process*

10.3 Richard Neustadt, *Presidential Power*
10.4 Thomas E. Cronin and Michael Genovese, *Presidential Paradoxes*

11.2 James Q.Wilson, *Bureaucracy: What Government Agencies Do and Why They Do It*

12.3 Kathleen M. Sullivan, *The Jurisprudence of the Rehnquist Court*

13.2 Dean Baker, *Nine Misconceptions About Social Security*

The Comparative Context

1.7 A. E. Dick Howard, *How Ideas Travel: Rights at Home and Abroad*

2.5 *The Economist, If You Sincerely Want to Be a United States . . .*

3.4 Louis Henkin, *The Universal Declaration and the U.S. Constitution*

4.6 Will Kymlicka, *Multicultural Citizenship*

5.3 Seymour Martin Lipset, *American Exceptionalism: A Double-Edged Sword*

6.3 Ronald J. Hrebenar and Clive S. Thomas, *The Japanese Lobby in Washington*

7.3 James F. Hoge, Jr., *Foreign News: Who Gives a Damn?*

8.4 Douglas J. Amy, *Breaking the Two-Party Monopoly*

9.4 Leon D. Epstein, *Changing Perceptions of the British System*

10.5 Richard Rose, *Presidents and Prime Ministers*

11.3 Gerald E. Caiden, Richard A. Lovard, Thomas J. Pavlak, Lynn F. Sipe, and Molly M. Wong, *The Distinctive Nature of American Public Administration*

12.4 Mark C. Miller, *Judicial Activism in Canada and the United States*

13.3 Anthony King, *Ideas, Institutions, and the Policies of Government: A Comparative Analysis*

View from the Inside

1.8 John P. Roche, *The Founding Fathers: A Reform Caucus in Action*

2.6 Jonathan Walters, *The Taming of Texas*

3.5 Alan Dershowitz, *Is the Criminal Trial a Search for Truth?*

4.7 Margarethe Cammermeyer, *Serving in Silence*

5.4 Michael Barone, *The Power of the President's Pollsters*

6.4 Alison Mitchell, *A New Form of Lobbying Puts Public Face on Private Interest*

7.4 Howard Kurtz, *The Master of Spin*

8.5 Michael Lewis, *Trail Fever*

9.5 Clara Bingham, *Women on the Hill*

10.6 Robert D. McFadden, John Kifner, and N. R. Kleinfield, *Public Acts, Private Moments*

11.4 Robert Reich, *Locked in the Cabinet*

12.5 Edward Lazarus, *Closed Chambers*

13.4 Colin Powell, *"Mr. Chairman, We've Got a Problem"*

Federalist Papers

1.1 James Madison, *Federalist* No. 10
1.2 James Madison, *Federalist* No. 47
1.3 James Madison, *Federalist* No. 48
1.4 James Madison, *Federalist* No. 51

2.2 James Madison, *Federalist* No. 39
2.3 James Madison, *Federalist* No. 45

9.1 James Madison, *Federalist* No. 55
9.2 James Madison, *Federalist* No. 57

10.1 Alexander Hamilton, *Federalist* No. 68
10.2 Alexander Hamilton, *Federalist* No. 70

12.1 Alexander Hamilton, *Federalist* No. 78

Supreme Court Decisions

3.2 Justice Harry A. Blackmun, *Roe v. Wade*
3.3 Justice Sandra Day O'Connor, *Planned Parenthood of Southeastern Pennsylvania* v. *Casey*

4.1 Justices Henry B. Brown and John Marshall Harian, *Plessy* v. *Ferguson*

4.2 Chief Justice Earl Warren, *Brown* v. *Board of Education*

4.3 Chief Justice Earl Warren, *Bolling* v. *Sharpe*

4.4 Chief Justice William H. Rehnquist, *Meritor Savings Bank* v. *Vinson*

7.1 Justice Hugo L. Black, *New York Times Co.* v. *United States*

12.2 Chief Justice John Marshall, *Marbury* v. *Madison*

Preface

The third edition of *Perspectives on American Politics* presents a collection of interesting and important readings on matters of fundamental concern to students and professors of American government. Like its predecessors, the third edition is organized in a manner that provides a variety of perspectives on these issues, from classic works in American politics to contemporary accounts and analyses by academics and nonacademics alike. The third edition has been fully updated; over sixty percent of the selections reflect recent developments in American politics. But the third edition is not simply an updated version of previous editions. The selections are now organized around four essential perspectives—Foundations, American Politics Today, The Comparative Context, and View from the Inside. Every chapter now includes a selection providing a comparative or international perspective on American politics.

The Purpose of This Reader

My goal in *Perspectives on American Politics* has been to develop a collection of readings that is clearly organized; that can be easily integrated into an American government course and actually help in teaching the course; and that will hold the students' (and professor's) attention by presenting a wide variety of viewpoints, writing styles, and approaches. Above all, I have endeavored to create a reader that shows students just why I—and all other professors of American government—find this subject so meaningful and important.

The challenge in compiling an American government reader is to maintain structure and coherence without sacrificing the extraordinary eclecticism that marks the enormous body of writings about American government. The solution incorporated here is to begin each chapter with certain key questions in mind and then to present a set of readings designed to provide various perspectives on those questions. This approach allows students to focus in on a relatively narrow range of critical issues, while at the same time giving them a variety of perspectives on those issues. All of the readings, however diverse they might be, revolve around the central chapter questions and thus maintain a clear and cohesive relationship with each other, and with the readings in earlier and later chapters.

Another key goal has been to produce a reader that professors and students alike will find easy to use. The thirteen chapters of this book correspond to the most frequently assigned chapters of most American government textbooks, so they should fit neatly into any standard syllabus. Furthermore, many of the chapter and reading questions can serve as essay assignments, and the selections can be used as a starting point for class discussions of controversial or important issues.

The readings in this book should help students develop critical thinking skills along with providing a deeper and clearer appreciation for the complexities of American politics.

Finally, as in earlier editions, I have avoided excessive editing, especially of important classic works. With minor exceptions, individual numbers of the *Federalist Papers* are presented in full. Where editing of the selections was required, I have focused on preserving large portions of the originals.

The Third Edition

In preparing the third edition, I carefully scrutinized each selection for readability, usefulness, and timeliness. The following changes and new features are worthy of note.

- *Four essential perspectives in every chapter.* To make the third edition easier to use and to provide a consistent chapter structure, the number of perspectives has been reduced to four: Foundations, American Politics Today, The Comparative Context, and View from the Inside. Reducing the number of perspectives allows for consistency from chapter to chapter, making the reader easier to use for students and professors alike. At the same time, however, these perspectives are diverse enough to give students a wide range of vantage points on American politics. These four perspectives appear in the same order in every chapter.
- *Over 60 percent new selections reflect recent developments in American politics.* It was obviously necessary to include new selections to cover developments in American politics since the publication of the second edition. These include the Clinton impeachment, the 1996 and 1998 elections, new trends in federalism, a series of Supreme Court decisions on sexual harassment, and the rapidly changing face of the American media. These selections are especially prominent in the chapters on federalism, civil rights, the media, political parties and elections, Congress, and the Presidency.
- *New comparative emphasis.* As described in detail below, each chapter now includes a reading designed to put American politics into comparative and international perspective. These new readings reflect increasing interest in exposing students to global issues, and also allow students to place developments in the United States in a broader context.

The Perspectives

All of the readings are grouped into four perspectives that are presented in every chapter in the order listed here:

- **Foundations.** The first perspective presents either a classic work in American politics, an important theoretical reading, or a seminal work in American political science. Examples include selections from the *Federalist Papers;* important Supreme Court cases, such as *Brown v. Board of Education* or *Marbury v. Madison;* and excerpts from works such as John Stuart Mill's *On Liberty* and E. E. Schattschneider's *The Semisovereign People.*

- **American Politics Today.** The second perspective provides a snapshot of the current state of American politics. This section often comprises works by political scientists and others who do not merely describe the current state of affairs, but seek to analyze and understand it. These selections may also include contemporary Supreme Court cases or other works that present new developments in American politics. Examples include a scholarly account of the "new legislative process," by the political scientist Barbara Sinclair; an analysis of the Rehnquist Court; contemporary cases on abortion and sexual harassment; and articles dealing with the Clinton impeachment and, more broadly, the modern presidency.
- **The Comparative Context.** Each chapter now includes a reading chosen to provide a global or comparative perspective on American politics. Choosing the selections for this category was not easy, particularly since I could not presume that the students would have preexisting knowledge of international affairs or other political systems. In every case my aim was to choose a reading that cast light on key issues in the United States; purists may note that some of the readings deal more with international affairs than comparative politics. Examples include a comparison of American and European federalism; an analysis of the activities of the Japanese lobby in the United States; a comparison of presidential and parliamentary systems; and an argument in favor of proportional representation in American elections.
- **View from the Inside.** This popular perspective from earlier editions appears now in every chapter. These readings provide an inside view of American politics and government—often, but not always, in the first person. Examples include accounts by former Labor Secretary Robert Reich and former Joint Chiefs of Staff Chairman Colin Powell, a journalist's view of modern campaign politics, and an inside look at the Supreme Court from the perspective of a former clerk.

Pedagogy

Like earlier editions, the third edition of *Perspectives on American Politics* includes pedagogical devices designed to make life easier for students and professors alike. These include chapter, category, and reading introductions as well as questions that orient students to the key themes, promote critical thinking, and make essential background information available. The questions can also be used by students for review purposes and by instructors for generating class discussion. Outlines for difficult readings, such as the *Federalist Papers*, provide some help to students approaching these works for the first time. Finally, I have provided a separate Instructor's Resource Manual, which features teaching hints for each chapter and each selection; ideas for assignments and class discussions; additional readings; and Internet links.

Some Technical Notes

I have used several standard conventions throughout the text. The omission of large amounts of material is indicated by centered bullets (• • •); smaller omissions are indicated by ellipses (. . .). In general I have not corrected antique spellings, nor have I modified older styles of punctuation or capitalization. I have eliminated virtually all footnotes; readers who are interested in source notes and other references should go directly to the originals. Where necessary, I have inserted explanatory or additional matter within brackets. For the sake of clarity, I have frequently shortened selection titles, and in some cases I have modified them substantially.

An Apology, More or Less

No anthology can contain everything. Undoubtedly there will be some who are dismayed or scandalized at the omission or inclusion of a particular article, case, or essay. To some extent the third edition reflects the criticisms, compliments, or suggestions offered by particular readers. All such communications are welcome and appreciated; my e-mail address is william.lasser@hubcap.clemson.edu.

Acknowledgments

I am grateful for the advice and assistance of editors, colleagues, and friends both in the preparation of the original manuscript and in the revisions for the third edition. Above all, I would like to thank Vik Mukhija at Houghton Mifflin, who consistently provided excellent advice, was patient when I (frequently) missed deadlines, and who, in general, kept this project in focus and on track. I am grateful as well to Melissa Mashburn, who helped set the tone and direction for the third edition, and has provided much-appreciated support and guidance on this and other projects. It was also a pleasure to work with the production and marketing staff at Houghton Mifflin Company, particularly Julie Lane, who had overall responsibility for turning my manuscript into a finished book, and Sandra McGuire, senior marketing manager for political science. I am also grateful for the production and manufacturing expertise of Jennifer Meyer Dare and Marie Barnes.

My colleagues at Clemson University—particularly Laura Olson, Marty Slann, and Steve Wainscott—gave much helpful advice, and did not openly object when I forgot to return their books after six or seven months. I also appreciate the suggestions of Robert Vipond of the University of Toronto, particularly on the comparative selections. A number of others read and critiqued various parts of this manuscript or otherwise gave helpful suggestions:

Manley Elliott Banks, Virginia Commonwealth University
Stephen Bennett, University of Cincinnati
Cary Covington, University of Iowa
Jack Citrin, University of California, Berkeley
Louis DeSipio, University of Illinois, Urbana
Robert Dion, Wabash College
R. Shep Melnick, Brandeis University
David L. Paletz, Duke University
Robert Scigliano, Boston College
Mark Silverstein, Boston University

Finally, I thank my children—Max, who has grown up with this book, and Adina Rose, who is just beginning the process. Their very existence is a constant delight. Most of all, I thank my wife, Susan J. S. Lasser, who—after twenty years, two children, and three editions—remains a constant inspiration. As with the earlier editions, this remains, with love and gratitude, her book.

W. L.

Perspectives on American Politics

 Chapter 1

The Constitution

The U.S. Constitution forms the basis of the American political system. Despite extraordinary changes in the American economy and in the nation's role and responsibilities in the world, the Constitution remains essentially the same document as written in Philadelphia in the summer of 1787. Over the years, several amendments have made it more inclusive and extended the "blessings of liberty" to previously excluded groups, including blacks and women. At the same time, countless decisions of the U.S. Supreme Court have altered the nuances and interpretations of the original text. Still, the original document and the political philosophy that lies behind it are well worth studying.

The political philosophy of the Constitution is largely that of the Federalists, its primary supporters. The Federalists were less than a political party; they were a loosely organized group of individuals who shared a commitment to the proposed Constitution and the ideas it represented. Because they won and because they counted among their number such leading figures as Alexander Hamilton and James Madison, the Federalists are far better known than their opponents, who went by the unfortunately negative-sounding name "Antifederalists." To understand the Federalists and their political philosophy, however, it is essential to understand the views and opinions of the opposition.

This chapter begins with a presentation of the major ideas of the Federalists and Antifederalists (selections 1.1 through 1.5). It then provides a modern example—drawn from the debates over the meaning of the Second Amendment—which suggests that the ideas of the Founding Generation still have relevance today (selection 1.6). It concludes with articles on the influence of the United States Constitution abroad, particularly with respect to the developments in Eastern Europe (selection 1.7), and with an inside view of the political realities of the Constitutional Convention of 1787 (selection 1.8).

Chapter Questions

1. In what senses are the Federalists properly described as "aristocrats" and the Antifederalists as "democrats"? Consider both the social standing of the two groups and their ideas about politics.
2. Did the Federalists believe in democracy? What evidence is there that they did? that they did not? How can these two views be reconciled?

3. Were the Antifederalists correct in at least some of their charges against the Constitution? Which of their complaints look more reasonable after two hundred years? Which look less so?

 Foundations

There is no better way to understand the political philosophy of the Federalists than to read the *Federalist Papers*. Originally a selection of newspaper columns written during the debate over the ratification of the Constitution in New York State, the *Federalist Papers* are a compendium of eighty-five essays explaining, defending, and elaborating on the proposed Constitution. The *Federalist*, as it is known, is widely regarded as the definitive statement of the Federalists' views on the Constitution and thus is a frequent reference point for those (federal judges, for example) who seek to know the intent of those who wrote the Constitution. The essays that make up the *Federalist* were written by three prominent proponents of the Constitution: John Jay, Alexander Hamilton, and James Madison. Following the style of the day, the articles were signed by the pseudonym Publius, a name that perhaps sought to imply that the authors spoke for the public interest.

Federalist No. 10, written by James Madison, is concerned with the problem of factions. Frequently it appears in a textbook chapter on interest groups, and it might profitably be reread along with the selections in Chapter 9. Its real importance, however, lies in Publius's discussion of human nature and representative government. Publius believes that in a free society, there will soon arise factions, or groups of individuals motivated by a common interest or passion adverse to the interests of other citizens or to the public interest. These factions arise because individuals are free to think for themselves about "religion . . . government, and many other points" and because they have different abilities for acquiring property. Once factions arise, it is in the nature of human beings that they will attempt to use the government to advance their own interests, even at the expense of others. In a pure democracy, the majority faction will pursue its own interest at the expense of the minority, with the result that rational government is impossible. The solution is to construct a representative government covering a large area, so that each representative will represent many diverse interests, and no one faction will be able to dominate.

Notice the consequences of Publius's theory: representative government is not merely a means of approximating a direct democracy but an improvement on it, and representatives are expected not merely to echo the interests of their constituents but to refine and filter those interests and balance them against the interest of others and against the public interest.

In *Federalist* Nos. 47–51, James Madison lays out his theory of the separation of powers. Contrary to the assumption of most other Americans, Madison did not believe that legislative, executive, and judicial power should be rigidly constrained, each to its own branch of government. In fact, *Federalist* No. 47 was written explicitly to challenge the assumption that the separation of powers means that the three departments of government "ought to have no *partial agency* in, or no *control* over, the acts of each other." Quite the opposite is true, in Madison's opinion: each branch should be given a share of the others' powers. It is only if "the *whole* power of one department is exercised by the same hands which possess the whole power of another department" that liberty is threatened.

Having demonstrated that the separation of powers does not demand a strict separation of functions, Madison then lays out the psychological basis for the separation of powers. Put simply, human beings are not angels; they are and will always be ambitious and power hungry. The only security against such individuals (and politicians are especially likely to possess such qualities) is to make sure that ambition checks ambition. By dividing power among ambitious people and then making them compete for power among themselves, liberty is protected.

All of this may be a sad commentary on human nature, as Madison suggests, but "what is government itself but the greatest of all reflections on human nature?" Madison's political theory here tracks the Scottish economist Adam Smith's theory of capitalism: we rely for bread not on the assumption that the baker will want to feed his fellow human beings but on his personal desire for money. Similarly, Madison relies for the protection of liberty not on politicians' love of the people but on their desire to protect their own power.

Also included here is a selection from the Antifederalists, who opposed the Constitution. That they lost their battle does not mean that their arguments were without merit. The Antifederalists were in general educated and intelligent men, whose ideas on politics presented a viable alternative to that presented by the Federalists. In fact, the Antifederalists' views typically represented the conventional eighteenth-century wisdom as compared to the much more innovative—and therefore controversial—ideas of the Federalists.

The Antifederalists produced no such book as the *Federalist Papers*. Their writings were diverse, uncoordinated, and of uneven quality. One example—the report of the minority of the Pennsylvania ratifying convention of 1787—is given below. This report presents one of the most systematic statements of the Antifederalists' arguments. Notice in particular the minority's fearful and suspicious tone—justifiable, considering the way they were treated by the majority—along with their objections to a large republic: the mixing of legislative, executive, and judicial power; the lack of limits to federal authority over the states; and the absence of a Bill of Rights.

Other selections from the *Federalist Papers* are contained in chapters 2, 9, 10, and 12.

Questions

1. What is a faction? Why are majority factions more dangerous than minority factions, according to Madison?
2. According to Madison, what advantages does a large republic have over a smaller one? How might the Antifederalists respond to Madison's position?
3. How does Madison respond to the Antifederalists' charge that the Constitution impermissibly blends executive, legislative, and judicial power? Why, in Madison's view, is it necessary to blend the three types of power?
4. Compare and contrast the Federalists' and Antifederalists' views on human nature. Pay particular attention to Madison's argument in *Federalist* No. 51.

1.1 *Federalist* No. 10 (1787)

James Madison

Outline

I. Republican governments are prone to the disease of *factions;* protecting against factions is critical to the success of any design for republican government.

II. Definition of faction.

III. The problem of factions can be cured by removing the causes of factions or by controlling their effects.

  A. It is impractical and unwise to try to remove the causes of factions; they are "sown in the nature of man."

  B. Therefore factions must be controlled.

   1. Minority factions can be controlled by the principle of majority rule.

   2. Minority factions can be controlled by creating a large republic and by creating a system of representation to "refine and enlarge" the views of the public.

Among the numerous advantages promised by a well-constructed Union, none deserves to be more accurately developed than its tendency to break and control the violence of faction. The friend of popular governments never finds himself so much alarmed for their character and fate as when he contemplates their propensity to this dangerous vice. He will not fail, therefore, to set a due value on any plan which, without violating the principles to which he is attached, provides a proper cure for it. The instability, injustice, and confusion introduced into the public councils have, in truth, been the mortal diseases under which popular governments have everywhere perished, as they continue to be the favorite and fruitful topics from which the adversaries to liberty derive their most specious declamations. The valuable improvements made by the American constitutions on the popular models, both ancient and modern, cannot certainly be too much admired; but it would be an unwarrantable partiality to contend that they have as effectually obviated the danger on this side, as was wished and expected. Complaints are everywhere heard from our most considerate and virtuous citizens, equally the friends of public and private faith and of public and personal liberty, that our governments are too unstable, that the public good is disregarded in the conflicts of rival parties, and that measures are too often decided, not according to the rules of justice and the rights of the minor party, but by the superior force of an interested and overbearing majority. However anxiously we may wish that these complaints had no foundation, the evidence of known facts will not permit us to deny that they are in some degree true. It will be found, indeed, on a candid review of our situation, that some of the distresses under which we labor have been erroneously charged on the operation of our governments; but it will be found, at the same time, that other causes will not alone account for many of our heaviest misfortunes; and, particularly, for that prevailing and increasing distrust of public engagements and alarm for private rights which are echoed from one end of the continent to the other. These must be chiefly, if not wholly, effects of the unsteadiness and injustice with which a factious spirit has tainted our public administration.

By a faction I understand a number of citizens, whether amounting to a majority or minority of the whole, who are united and actuated by some common impulse of passion, or of interest, adverse to the rights of other citizens, or to the permanent and aggregate interests of the community.

There are two methods of curing the mischiefs of faction: the one, by removing its causes; the other, by controlling its effects.

There are again two methods of removing the causes of faction: the one, by destroying the liberty which is essential to its existence; the other, by giving to every citizen the same opinions, the same passions, and the same interests.

It could never be more truly said than of the first remedy that it was worse than the disease. Liberty is to faction what air is to fire, an aliment without which it instantly expires. But it could not be a less folly to abolish liberty, which is essential to political life, because it nourishes faction than it would be to wish the annihilation of air, which is essential to animal life, because it imparts to fire its destructive agency.

The second expedient is as impracticable as the first would be unwise. As long as the reason of man continues fallible, and he is at liberty to exercise it, different opinions will be formed. As long as the connection subsists between his reason and his self-love, his opinions and his passions will have a reciprocal influence on each other; and the former will be objects to which the latter will attach themselves. The diversity in the faculties of men, from which the rights of property originate, is not less an insuperable obstacle to a uniformity of interests. The protection of these faculties is the first object of government. From the protection of different and unequal faculties of acquiring property, the possession of different degrees and kinds of property immediately results; and from the influence of these on the sentiments and views of the respective proprietors ensues a division of the society into different interests and parties.

The latent causes of faction are thus sown in the nature of man; and we see them everywhere brought into different degrees of activity, according to the different circumstances of civil society. A zeal for different opinions concerning religion, concerning government, and many other points, as well of speculation as of practice; an attachment to different leaders ambitiously contending for preeminence and power; or to persons of other descriptions whose fortunes have been interesting to the human passions, have, in turn, divided mankind into parties, inflamed them with mutual animosity, and rendered them much more disposed to vex and oppress each other than to cooperate for their common good. So strong is this propensity of mankind to fall into mutual animosities that where no substantial occasion presents itself the most frivolous and fanciful distinctions have been sufficient to kindle their unfriendly passions and excite their most violent conflicts. But the most common and durable source of factions has been the various and unequal distribution of property. Those who hold and those who are without property have ever formed distinct interests in society. Those who are creditors, and those who are debtors, fall under a like discrimination. A landed interest, a manufacturing interest, a mercantile interest, a moneyed interest, with many lesser interests, grow up of necessity in civilized nations, and divide them into different classes, actuated by different sentiments and views. The regulation of these various and interfering interests forms the principal task of modern legislation and involves the spirit of party and faction in the necessary and ordinary operations of government.

No man is allowed to be a judge in his own cause, because his interest would certainly bias his judgment, and, not improbably, corrupt his integrity. With equal, nay with greater reason, a body of men are unfit to be both judges and parties at the same time; yet what are many of the most important acts of legislation but so many judicial determinations, not indeed concerning the rights of single persons, but concerning the rights of large bodies of citizens? And what are the different classes of legislators but advocates and parties to the causes which they determine? Is a law proposed concerning private debts? It is a question to which the creditors are parties on one side and the debtors on the other. Justice ought to hold the balance between them. Yet the parties are, and must be, themselves the judges; and the most numerous party, or in other words, the most powerful faction must be expected to prevail. Shall domestic manufacturers be encouraged, and in what degree, by restrictions on foreign manufacturers? are questions which would be differently decided by the landed and the manufacturing classes, and probably by neither with a sole regard to justice and the public good. The apportionment of taxes on the various descriptions of property is an act which seems to require the most exact impartiality; yet there is, perhaps, no legislative act in which greater opportunity and temptation are given to a predominant party to trample on the rules of justice. Every shilling with which they overburden the inferior number is a shilling saved to their own pockets.

It is in vain to say that enlightened statesmen will be able to adjust these clashing interests and render them all subservient to the public good. Enlightened statesmen will not always be at the helm. Nor, in many cases, can such an adjustment be made at all without taking into view indirect and remote considerations, which will rarely prevail over the immediate interest which one party may find in disregarding the rights of another or the good of the whole.

The inference to which we are brought is that the *causes* of faction cannot be removed and that relief is only to be sought in the means of controlling its *effects*.

If a faction consists of less than a majority, relief is supplied by the republican principle, which enables the majority to defeat its sinister views by regular vote. It may clog the administration, it may convulse the society; but it will be unable to execute and mask its violence under the forms of the Constitution. When a majority is included in a faction, the form of popular government, on the other hand, enables it to sacrifice to its ruling passion or interest both the public good and the rights of other citizens. To secure the public good and private rights against the danger of such a faction, and at the same time to preserve the spirit and the form of popular government, is then the great object to which our inquiries are directed. Let me add that it is the great desideratum by which alone this form of government can be rescued from the opprobrium under which it has so long labored and be recommended to the esteem and adoption of mankind.

By what means is this object attainable? Evidently by one of two only. Either the existence of the same passion or interest in a majority at the same time must be prevented, or the majority, having such coexistent passion or interest, must be rendered, by their number and local situation, unable to concert and carry into effect schemes of oppression. If the impulse and the opportunity be suffered to coincide, we well know that neither moral nor religious motives can be relied on as an adequate control. They are not found to be such on the injustice and violence of individuals, and lose their efficacy in proportion to the number combined together, that is, in proportion as their efficacy becomes needful.

From this view of the subject it may be concluded that a pure democracy, by which I mean a society consisting of a small number of citizens, who assemble and administer the government in person, can admit of no cure for the mischiefs of faction. A common passion or interest will, in almost every case, be felt by a majority of the whole; a communication and concert results from the form of government itself; and there is nothing to check the inducements to sacrifice the weaker party or an obnoxious individual. Hence it is that such democracies have ever been spectacles of turbulence and contention; have ever been found incompatible with personal security or the rights of property; and have in general been as short in their lives as they have been violent in their deaths. Theoretic politicians, who have patronized this species of government, have erroneously supposed that by reducing mankind to a perfect equality in their political rights, they would at the same time be perfectly equalized and assimilated in their possessions, their opinions, and their passions.

A republic, by which I mean a government in which the scheme of representation takes place, opens a different prospect and promises the cure for which we are seeking. Let us examine the points in which it varies from pure democracy, and we shall comprehend both the nature of the cure and the efficacy which it must derive from the Union.

The two great points of difference between a democracy and a republic are: first, the delegation of the government, in the latter, to a small number of citizens elected by the rest; secondly, the greater number of citizens and greater sphere of country over which the latter may be extended.

The effect of the first difference is, on the one hand, to refine and enlarge the public views by passing them through the medium of a chosen body of citizens, whose wisdom may best discern the true interest of their country and whose patriotism and love of justice will be least likely to sacrifice it to temporary or partial considerations. Under such a regulation it may well happen that the public voice, pronounced by the representatives of the people, will be more consonant to the public good than if pronounced by the people themselves, convened for the purpose. On the other hand, the effect may be inverted. Men of factious tempers, of local prejudices, or of sinister designs, may, by intrigue, by corruption, or by other means, first obtain the suffrages, and then betray the interests of the people. The question resulting is, whether small or extensive republics are most favorable to the election of proper guardians of the public weal; and it is clearly decided in favor of the latter by two obvious considerations.

In the first place it is to be remarked that however small the republic may be the representatives must be raised to a certain number in order to guard against the cabals of a few; and that however large it may be they must be limited to a certain number in order to guard against the confusion of a multitude. Hence, the number of representatives in the two cases not being in proportion to that of the constituents, and being proportionally greatest in the small republic, it follows that if the proportion of fit characters be not less in the large than in the small republic, the former will present a greater option, and consequently a greater probability of a fit choice.

In the next place, as each representative will be chosen by a greater number of citizens in the large than in the small republic, it will be more difficult for unworthy candidates to practise with success the vicious arts by which elections are too often carried; and the suffrages of the people being more free, will be more likely to center on men who possess the most attractive merit and the most diffusive and established characters.

It must be confessed that in this, as in most other cases, there is a mean, on both sides of which inconveniences will be found to lie. By enlarging too much the number of electors, you render the representative too little acquainted with all their local circumstances and lesser interests; as by reducing it too much, you render him unduly attached to these, and too little fit to comprehend and pursue great and national objects. The federal Constitution forms a happy combination in this respect; the great and aggregate interests being referred to the national, the local and particular to the State legislatures.

The other point of difference is the greater number of citizens and extent of territory which may be brought within the compass of republican than of democratic government; and it is this circumstance principally which renders factious combinations less to be dreaded in the former than in the latter. The smaller the society, the fewer probably will be the distinct parties and interests composing it; the fewer the distinct parties and interests, the more frequently will a majority be found of the same party; and the smaller the number of individuals composing a majority, and the smaller the compass within which they are placed, the more easily will they concert and execute their plans of oppression. Extend the sphere and you take in a greater variety of parties and interests; you make it less probable that a majority of the whole will have a common motive to invade the rights of other citizens; or if such a common motive exists, it will be more difficult for all who feel it to discover their own strength and to act in unison with each other. Besides other impediments, it may be remarked that, where there is a consciousness of unjust or dishonorable purposes, communication is always checked by distrust in proportion to the number whose concurrence is necessary.

Hence, it clearly appears that the same advantage which a republic has over a democracy in controlling the effects of faction is enjoyed by a large over a small republic—is enjoyed by the Union over the States composing it. Does this advantage consist in the substitution of representatives whose enlightened views and virtuous sentiments render them superior to local prejudices and to schemes of injustice? It will not be denied that the representation of the Union will be most likely to possess these requisite endowments. Does it consist in the greater security afforded by a greater variety of parties, against the event of any one party being able to outnumber and oppress the rest? In an equal degree does the increased variety of parties comprised within the Union increase this security. Does it, in fine, consist in the greater obstacles opposed to the concert and accomplishment of the secret wishes of an unjust and interested majority? Here again the extent of the Union gives it the most palpable advantage.

The influence of factious leaders may kindle a flame within their particular States but will be unable to spread a general conflagration through the other States. A religious sect may degenerate into a political faction in a part of the Confederacy; but the variety of sects dispersed over the entire face of it must secure the national councils against any danger from that source. A rage for paper money, for an abolition of debts, for an equal division of property, or for any other improper or wicked project, will be less apt to pervade the whole body of the Union than a particular member of it, in the same proportion as such a malady is more likely to taint a particular county or district than an entire State.

In the extent and proper structure of the Union, therefore, we behold a republican remedy for the diseases most incident to republican government. And according to the degree of pleasure and pride we feel in being republicans ought to be our zeal in cherishing the spirit and supporting the character of federalists. ∎

1.2 *Federalist* No. 47 (1787)

James Madison

Outline

I. The charge that the Constitution violates the separation of powers principle is based on a misinterpretation of the separation of powers.

  A. The Constitution is consistent with Montesquieu's view of the separation of powers.

    1. Montesquieu's view based on the British Constitution.

    2. Discussion of Montesquieu's theory.

  B. The Constitution is consistent with the implementation of the separation of powers in the constitutions of the several states.

. . . One of the principal objections inculcated by the more respectable adversaries to the Constitution is its supposed violation of the political maxim that the legislative, executive, and judiciary departments ought to be separate and distinct. In the structure of the federal government no regard, it is said, seems to have been paid to this essential precaution in favor of liberty. The several departments of power are distributed and blended in such a manner as at once to destroy all symmetry and beauty of form, and to expose some of the essential parts of the edifice to the danger of being crushed by the disproportionate weight of other parts.

No political truth is certainly of greater intrinsic value, or is stamped with the authority of more enlightened patrons of liberty than that on which the objection is founded. The accumulation of all powers, legislative, executive, and judiciary, in the same hands, whether of one, a few, or many, and whether hereditary, self-appointed, or elective, may justly be pronounced the very definition of tyranny.

Were the federal Constitution, therefore, really chargeable with this accumulation of power, or with a mixture of powers, having a dangerous tendency to such an accumulation, no further arguments would be necessary to inspire a universal reprobation of the system. I persuade myself, however, that it will be made apparent to everyone that the charge cannot be supported, and that the maxim on which it relies has been totally misconceived and misapplied. In order to form correct ideas on this important subject it will be proper to investigate the sense in which the preservation of liberty requires that the three great departments of power should be separate and distinct.

The oracle who is always consulted and cited on this subject is the celebrated Montesquieu. If he be not the author of this invaluable precept in the science of politics, he has the merit at least of displaying and recommending it most effectually to the attention of mankind. Let us endeavor, in the first place, to ascertain his meaning on this point.

The British Constitution was to Montesquieu what Homer has been to the didactic writers on epic poetry. As the latter have considered the work of the immortal bard as the perfect model from which the principles and rules of the epic art were to be drawn, and by which all similar works were to be judged, so this great political critic appears to have viewed the Constitution of England as the standard, or to use his own expression, as the mirror of political liberty; and to have delivered, in the form of elementary truths, the several characteristic principles of that particular system. That we may be sure, then, not to mistake his meaning in this case, let us recur to the source from which the maxim was drawn.

On the slightest view of the British Constitution, we must perceive that the legislative, executive, and judiciary departments are by no means totally separate and distinct from each other. The executive magistrate forms an integral part of the legislative authority. He alone has the prerogative of making treaties with foreign sovereigns which, when made, have, under certain limitations, the force of legislative acts. All the members of the judiciary department are appointed by him, can be removed by him on the address of the two Houses of Parliament, and form, when he pleases to consult them, one of his constitutional councils. One branch of the legislative department forms also a great constitutional council to the executive chief, as, on another hand, it is the sole depositary of judicial power in cases of impeachment, and is invested with the supreme appellate jurisdiction in all other cases. The judges, again, are so far connected with the legislative department as often to attend and participate in its deliberations, though not admitted to a legislative vote.

From these facts, by which Montesquieu was guided, it may clearly be inferred that in saying "There can be no liberty where the legislative and executive powers are united in the same person, or body of magistrates," or, "if the power of judging be not separated from the legislative and executive powers," he did not mean that these departments ought to have no *partial agency* in, or no *control* over, the acts of each other. His meaning, as his own words import, and still more conclusively as illustrated by the example in his eye, can amount to no more than this, that where the *whole* power of one department is exercised by the same hands which possess the *whole* power of another department, the fundamental principles of a free constitution are subverted. This would have been the case in the constitution examined by him, if the king, who is the sole executive magistrate, had possessed also the complete legislative power, or the supreme administration of justice; or if the entire legislative body had possessed the supreme judiciary, or the supreme executive authority. This, however, is not among the vices of that constitution. The magistrate in whom the whole executive power resides cannot of himself make a law, though he can put a negative on every law; nor administer justice in person, though he has the appointment of those who do administer it. The judges can exercise no executive prerogative, though they are shoots from the executive stock; nor any legislative function, though they may be advised by the legislative councils. The entire legislature can perform no judiciary act, though by the joint act of two of its branches the judges may be removed from their offices, and though one of its branches is possessed of the judicial power in the last resort. The entire legislature, again, can exercise no executive prerogative, though one of its branches constitutes the supreme executive magistracy, and another, on the impeachment of a third, can try and condemn all the subordinate officers in the executive department.

The reasons on which Montesquieu grounds his maxim are a further demonstration of his meaning. "When the legislative and executive powers are united in the same person or body," says he, "there can be no liberty, because apprehensions may arise lest *the same* monarch or senate should *enact* tyrannical laws to *execute* them in a tyrannical manner." Again: "Were the power of judging joined with the legislative, the life and liberty of the subject would be exposed to arbitrary control, for *the judge* would then be *the legislator*. Were it joined to the executive power, *the judge* might behave with all the violence of *an oppressor*." Some of these reasons are more fully explained in other passages; but briefly stated as they are here they sufficiently establish the meaning which we have put on this celebrated maxim of this celebrated author.

If we look into the constitutions of the several States we find that, notwithstanding the emphatical and, in some instances, the unqualified terms in which this axiom has been laid down, there is not a single instance in which the several departments of power have been kept absolutely separate and distinct. New Hampshire, whose constitution was the last formed, seems to have been fully aware of the impossibility and inexpediency of avoiding any mixture whatever of these departments, and has qualified the doctrine by declaring "that the legislative, executive, and judiciary powers ought to be kept as separate from, and independent of, each other *as the nature of a free government will admit; or as is consistent with that chain of connection that binds the whole fabric of the constitution in one indissoluble bond of unity and amity*." Her constitution accordingly mixes these departments in several respects. The Senate, which is a branch of the legislative department, is also a judicial tribunal for the trial of impeachments, The President, who is the head of the executive department, is the presiding member also of the Senate; and, besides an equal vote in all cases, has a casting vote in case of a tie. The executive head is himself eventually elective every year by the legislative department, and his council is every year chosen by and from the members of the same department. Several of the officers of state are also appointed by the legislature. And the members of the judiciary department are appointed by the executive department.

The constitution of Massachusetts has observed a sufficient though less pointed caution in expressing this fundamental article of liberty. It declares "that the legislative department shall never exercise the executive and judicial powers, or either of them; the executive shall never exercise the legislative and judicial powers, or either of them; the judicial shall never exercise the legislative and executive powers, or either of them." This declaration corresponds precisely with the doctrine of Montesquieu, as it has been explained, and is not in a single point violated by the plan of the convention. It goes no farther than to prohibit any one of the entire departments from exercising the powers of another department. In the very Constitution to which it is prefixed, a partial mixture of powers has been admitted. The executive magistrate has a qualified negative on the legislative body, and the Senate, which is a part of the legislature, is a court of impeachment for members both of the executive and judiciary departments. The members of the judiciary department, again, are appointable by the executive department, and removable by the same authority on the address of the two legislative branches. Lastly, a number of the officers of government are annually appointed by the legislative department. As the appointment to offices, particularly executive offices, is in its nature an executive function, the compilers of the Constitution have, in this last point at least, violated the rule established by themselves. . . . *[Publius next reviews other state constitutions.]*

In citing these cases, in which the legislative, executive, and judiciary departments have not been kept totally separate and distinct, I wish not to be regarded as an advocate for the particular organizations of the several State governments. I am fully aware that among the many excellent principles which they exemplify they carry strong marks of the haste, and still stronger of the inexperience, under which they were framed. It is but too obvious that in some instances the fundamental principle under consideration has been violated by too great a mixture, and even an actual consolidation of the different powers; and that in no instance has a competent provision been made for maintaining in practice the separation delineated on paper. What I have wished to evince is that the charge brought against the proposed Constitution of violating the sacred maxim of free government is warranted neither by the real meaning annexed to that maxim by its author, nor by the sense in which it has hitherto been understood in America. This interesting subject will be resumed in the ensuing paper. ■

1.3 *Federalist* No. 48 (1787)

James Madison

Outline

I. The separation of powers requires that the three departments be connected and blended, giving each control over the others.

   A. Encroaching nature of political power.

   B. Inadequacy of "parchment (or paper) barriers."

II. Preeminent danger of legislative power makes it necessary to give the other two branches some control.

I t was shown in the last paper that the political apothegm there examined does not require that the legislative, executive, and judiciary departments should be wholly unconnected with each other. I shall undertake, in the next place, to show that unless these departments be so far connected and blended as to give to each a constitutional control over the others, the degree of separation which the maxim requires, as essential to a free government, can never in practice be duly maintained.

It is agreed on all sides that the powers properly belonging to one of the departments ought not to be directly and completely administered by either of the other departments. It is equally evident that none of them ought to possess, directly or indirectly, an overruling influence over the others in the administration of their respective powers. It will not be denied that power is of an encroaching nature and that it ought to be effectually restrained from passing the limits assigned to it. After discriminating, therefore, in theory, the several classes of power, as they may in their nature be legislative, executive, or judiciary, the next and most difficult task is to provide some practical security for each, against the invasion of the others. What this security ought to be is the great problem to be solved.

Will it be sufficient to mark, with precision, the boundaries of these departments in the constitution of the government, and to trust to these parchment barriers against the encroaching spirit of power? This is the security which appears to have been principally relied on by the compilers of most of the American constitutions. But experience assures us that the efficacy of the provision has been greatly overrated; and that some more adequate defense is indispensably necessary for the more feeble against the more powerful members of the government. The legislative department is everywhere extending the sphere of its activity and drawing all power into its impetuous vortex.

The founders of our republics have so much merit for the wisdom which they have displayed that no task can be less pleasing than that of pointing out the errors into which they have fallen. A respect for truth, however, obliges us to remark that they seem never for a moment to have turned their eyes from the danger, to liberty, from the overgrown and all-grasping prerogative of an hereditary magistrate, supported and fortified by an hereditary branch of the legislative authority. They seem never to have recollected the danger from legislative usurpations, which, by assembling all power in the same hands, must lead to the same tyranny as is threatened by executive usurpations.

In a government where numerous and extensive prerogatives are placed in the hands of an hereditary monarch, the executive department is very justly regarded as the source of danger, and watched with all the jealousy which a zeal for liberty ought to inspire. In a democracy, where a multitude of people exercise in person the legislative functions and are continually exposed, by their incapacity for regular deliberation and concerted measures, to the ambitious intrigues of their executive magistrates, tyranny may well be apprehended, on some favorable emergency, to start up in the same quarter. But in a representative republic where the executive magistracy is carefully limited, both in the extent and the duration of its power; and where the legislative power is exercised by an assembly, which is inspired by a supposed influence over the people with an intrepid confidence in its own strength; which is sufficiently numerous to feel all the passions which actuate a multitude, yet not so numerous as to be incapable of pursuing the objects of its passions by means which reason prescribes; it is against the enterprising ambition of this department that the people ought to indulge all their jealousy and exhaust all their precautions.

The legislative department derives a superiority in our governments from other circumstances. Its constitutional powers being at once more extensive, and less susceptible of precise limits, it can, with the greater facility, mask, under complicated and indirect measures, the encroachments which it makes on the co-ordinate departments. It is not unfrequently a question of real nicety in legislative bodies whether the operation of a particular measure will, or will not, extend beyond the legislative sphere. On the other side, the executive power being restrained within a narrower compass and being more simple in its nature, and the judiciary being described by landmarks still less uncertain, projects of usurpation by either of these departments would immediately betray and defeat themselves. Nor is this all; as the legislative department alone has access to the pockets of the people, and has in some constitutions full discretion, and in all a prevailing influence, over the pecuniary rewards of those who fill the other departments, a dependence is thus created in the latter, which gives still greater facility to encroachments of the former. . . .

The conclusion which I am warranted in drawing from these observations is that a mere demarcation on parchment of the constitutional limits of the several departments is not a sufficient guard against those encroachments which lead to a tyrannical concentration of all the powers of government in the same hands. ∎

1.4 *Federalist* No. 51 (1787)

James Madison

Outline

I. Maintaining the separation of powers in practice requires giving each branch the means of checking the others.

    A. Members of one branch should not appoint members of the other branches, but an exception is made in the case of the judiciary.

    B. Members of one branch should not be dependent on the other branches for pay and perks.

    C. Above all, each branch must have the *means* and the *motive* to check and balance the others.

    D. Overwhelming power of the legislature requires dividing it into two parts and strengthening the executive branch.

II. Protection of liberty further enhanced by dividing power between the national and state governments and by diluting the influence of majority factions.

To what expedient, then, shall we finally resort, for maintaining in practice the necessary partition of power among the several departments as laid down in the Constitution? The only answer that can be given is that as all these exterior provisions are found to be inadequate the defect must be supplied by so contriving the interior structure of the government as that its several constituent parts may, by their mutual relations, be the means of keeping each other in their proper places. Without presuming to undertake a full development of this important idea I will hazard a few general observations which may perhaps place it in a clearer light, and enable us to form a more correct judgment of the principles and structure of the government planned by the convention.

In order to lay a due foundation for that separate and distinct exercise of the different powers of government, which to a certain extent is admitted on all hands to be essential to the preservation of liberty, it is evident that each department should have a will of its own; and consequently should be so constituted that the members of each should have as little agency as possible in the appointment of the members of the others. Were this principle rigorously adhered to, it would require that all the appointments for the supreme executive, legislative, and judiciary magistracies should be drawn from the same fountain of authority, the people, through channels having no communication whatever with one another. Perhaps such a plan of constructing the several departments would be less difficult in practice than it may in contemplation appear. Some difficulties, however, and some additional expense would attend the execution of it. Some deviations, therefore, from the principle must be admitted. In the constitution of the judiciary department in particular, it might be inexpedient to insist rigorously on the principle: first, because peculiar qualifications being essential in the members, the primary consideration ought to be to select that mode of choice which best secures these qualifications; second, because the permanent tenure by which the appointments are held in that department must soon destroy all sense of dependence on the authority conferring them.

It is equally evident that the members of each department should be as little dependent as possible on those of the others for the emoluments annexed to their offices. Were the executive magistrate, or the judges, not independent of the legislature in this particular, their independence in every other would be merely nominal.

But the great security against a gradual concentration of the several powers in the same department consists in giving to those who administer each department the necessary constitutional means and personal motives to resist encroachments of the others. The provision for defense must in this, as in all other cases, be made commensurate to the danger of attack. Ambition must be made to counteract ambition. The interest of the man must be connected with the constitutional rights of the place. It may be a reflection on human nature that such devices should be necessary to control the abuses of government. But what is government itself but the greatest of all reflections on human nature? If men were angels, no government would be necessary. If angels were to govern men, neither external nor internal controls on government would be necessary. In framing a government which is to be administered by men over men, the great difficulty lies in this: you must first enable the government to control the governed; and in the next place oblige it to control itself. A dependence on the people is, no doubt, the primary control on the government; but experience has taught mankind the necessity of auxiliary precautions.

This policy of supplying, by opposite and rival interests, the defect of better motives, might be traced through the whole system of human affairs, private as well as public. We see it particularly displayed in all the subordinate distributions of power, where the constant aim is to divide and arrange the several offices in such a manner as that each may be a check on the other—that the private interest of every individual may be a sentinel over the public rights. These inventions of prudence cannot be less requisite in the distribution of the supreme powers of the State.

But it is not possible to give to each department an equal power of self-defense. In republican government, the legislative authority necessarily predominates. The remedy for this inconveniency is to divide the legislature into different branches; and to render them, by different modes of election and different principles of action, as little connected with each other as the nature of their common functions and their common dependence on the society will admit. It may even be necessary to guard against dangerous encroachments by still further precautions. As the weight of the legislative authority requires that it should be thus divided, the weakness of the executive may require, on the other hand, that it should be fortified. An absolute negative on the legislature appears, at first view, to be the natural defense with which the executive magistrate should be armed. But perhaps it would be neither altogether safe nor alone sufficient. On ordinary occasions it might not be exerted with the requisite firmness, and on extraordinary occasions it might be perfidiously abused. May not this defect of an absolute negative be supplied by some qualified connection between this weaker department and the weaker branch of the stronger department, by which the latter may be led to support the constitutional rights of the former, without being too much detached from the rights of its own department?

If the principles on which these observations are founded be just, as I persuade myself they are, and they be applied as a criterion to the several State constitutions, and to the federal Constitution, it will be found that if the latter does not perfectly correspond with them, the former are infinitely less able to bear such a test.

There are, moreover, two considerations particularly applicable to the federal system of America, which place that system in a very interesting point of view.

First. In a single republic, all the power surrendered by the people is submitted to the administration of a single government; and the usurpations are guarded against by a division of the government into distinct and separate departments. In the compound republic of America, the power surrendered by the people is first divided between two distinct governments, and then the portion allotted to each subdivided among distinct and separate departments. Hence a double security arises to the rights of the people. The different governments will control each other, at the same time that each will be controlled by itself.

Second. It is of great importance in a republic not only to guard the society against the oppression of its rulers, but to guard one part of the society against the injustice of the other part. Different interests necessarily exist in different classes of citizens. If a majority be united by a common interest, the rights of the minority will be insecure. There are but two methods of providing against this evil: the one by creating a will in the community independent of the majority—that is, of the society itself; the other, by comprehending in the society so many separate descriptions of citizens as will render an unjust combination of a majority of the whole very improbable, if not impracticable. The first method prevails in all governments possessing an hereditary or self-appointed authority. This, at best, is but a precarious security; because a power independent of the society may as well espouse the unjust views of the major as the rightful interests of the minor party, and may possibly be turned against both parties. The second method will be exemplified in the federal republic of the United States. Whilst all authority in it will be derived from and dependent on the society, the society itself will be broken into so many parts, interests and classes of citizens, that the rights of individuals, or of the minority, will be in little danger from interested combinations of the majority. In a free government the security for civil rights must be the same as that for religious rights. It consists in the one case in the multiplicity of interests, and in the other in the multiplicity of sects. The degree of security in both cases will depend on the number of interests and sects; and this may be presumed to depend on the extent of country and number of people comprehended under the same government. This view of the subject must particularly recommend a proper federal system to all the sincere and considerate friends of republican government, since it shows that in exact proportion as the territory of the Union may be formed into more circumscribed Confederacies, or States, oppressive combinations of a majority will be facilitated; the best security, under the republican forms, for the rights of every class of citizen, will be diminished; and consequently the stability and independence of some member of the government, the only other security, must be proportionally increased. Justice is the end of government. It is the end of civil society. It ever has been and ever will be pursued until it be obtained, or until liberty be lost in the pursuit. In a society under the forms of which the stronger faction can readily unite and oppress the weaker, anarchy may as truly be said to reign as in a state of nature, where the weaker individual is not secured against the violence of the stronger; and as, in the latter state, even the stronger individuals are prompted, by the uncertainty of their condition, to submit to a government which may protect the weak as well as themselves; so, in the former state, will the more powerful factions or parties be gradually induced, by a like motive, to wish for a government which will protect all parties, the weaker as well as the more powerful. It can be little doubted that if the State of Rhode Island was separated from the Confederacy and left to itself, the insecurity of rights under the popular form of government within such narrow limits would be displayed by such reiterated oppressions of factious majorities that some power altogether independent of the people would soon be called for by the voice of the very factions whose misrule had proved the necessity of it. In the extended republic of the United States, and among the great variety of interests, parties, and sects which it embraces, a coalition of a majority of the whole society could seldom take place on any other principles than those of justice and the general good; whilst there being thus less danger to a minor from the will of a major party, there must be less pretext, also, to provide for the security of the former, by introducing into the government a will not dependent on the latter, or, in other words, a will independent of the society itself. It is no less certain than it is important, notwithstanding the contrary opinions which have been entertained, that the larger the society, provided it lie within a practicable sphere, the more duly capable it will be of self-government. And happily for the *republican cause*, the practicable sphere may be carried to a very great extent by a judicious modification and mixture of the *federal principle*. ∎

1.5 The Address and Reasons of Dissent of the Minority of the Convention of Pennsylvania to Their Constituents (1788)

It was not until after the termination of the late glorious contest, which made the people of the United States, an independent nation, that any defect was discovered in the present confederation. It was formed by some of the ablest patriots in America. It carried us successfully through the war; and the virtue and patriotism of the people, with their disposition to promote the common cause, supplied the want of power in Congress. . . .

It was at the end of the war . . . that the want of an efficient federal government was first complained of, and that the powers vested in Congress were found to be inadequate to the procuring of the benefits that should result from the union. . . . [Many states refused to grant Congress the funds it needed to carry out its responsibilities.] . . . It was found that our national character was sinking in the opinion of foreign nations. The Congress could make treaties of commerce, but could not enforce the observance of them. We were suffering from the restrictions of foreign nations, who had shackled our commerce, while we were unable to retaliate: and all now agreed that it would be advantageous to the union to enlarge the powers of Congress; that they should be enabled in the amplest manner to regulate commerce, and to lay and collect duties on the imports throughout the United States. With this view a convention was first proposed by Virginia, and finally recommended by Congress for the different states to appoint deputies to meet in convention, "for the purposes of revising and amending the present articles of confederation, so as to make them adequate to the exigencies of the union." This recommendation the legislatures of twelve states complied with so hastily as not to consult their constituents on the subject; and though the different legislatures had no authority from their constituents for the purpose, they probably apprehended the necessity would justify the measure; and none of them extended their ideas at that time further than "revising and amending the present articles of confederation." Pennsylvania by the act appointing deputies expressly confined their powers to this object; and though it is probable that some of the members of the assembly of this state had at that time in contemplation to annihilate the present confederation, as well as the constitution of

Pennsylvania, yet the plan was not sufficiently matured to communicate it to the public.

The majority of the legislature of this commonwealth, were at that time under the influence of the members from the city of Philadelphia. They agreed that the deputies sent by them to convention should have no compensation for their services, which determination was calculated to prevent the election of any member who resided at a distance from the city. It was in vain for the minority to attempt electing delegates to the convention, who understood the circumstances, and the feelings of the people, and had a common interest with them. They found a disposition in the leaders of the majority of the house to chuse themselves and some of their dependants. The minority attempted to prevent this by agreeing to vote for some of the leading members, who they knew had influence enough to be appointed at any rate, in hopes of carrying with them some respectable citizens of Philadelphia, in whose principles and integrity they could have more confidence; but even in this they were disappointed, except in one member: the eighth member was added at a subsequent session of the assembly.

The Continental convention met in the city of Philadelphia at the time appointed. It was composed of some men of excellent characters; of others who were more remarkable for their ambition and cunning, than their patriotism; and of some who had been opponents to the independence of the United States. The delegates from Pennsylvania were, six of them, uniform and decided opponents to the constitution of this commonwealth. The convention sat upwards of four months. The doors were kept shut, and the members brought under the most solemn engagements of secrecy. Some of those who opposed their going so far beyond their powers, retired, hopeless, from the convention, others had the firmness to refuse signing the plan altogether; and many who did sign it, did it not as a system they wholly approved, but as the best that could be then obtained, and notwithstanding the time spent on this subject, it is agreed on all hands to be a work of haste and accommodation.

Whilst the gilded chains were forging in the secret conclave, the meaner instruments of despotism without, were busily employed in alarming the fears of the people with dangers which did not exist, and exciting their hopes of greater advantages from the expected plan than even the best government on earth could produce.

The proposed plan had not many hours issued forth from the womb of suspicious secrecy, until such as were prepared for the purpose, were carrying about petitions for people to sign, signifying their approbation of the system, and requesting the legislature to call a convention. While every measure was taken to intimidate the people against opposing it, the public papers teemed with the most violent threats against those who should dare to think for themselves, and *tar and feathers* were liberally promised to all those who would not immediately join in supporting the proposed government be it what it would. Under such circumstances petitions in favour of calling a convention were signed by great numbers in and about the city, before they had leisure to read and examine the system, many of whom, now they are better acquainted with it, and have had time to investigate its principles, are heartily opposed to it. The petitions were speedily handed into the legislature. . . .

In this situation of affairs were the subscribers elected members of the convention of Pennsylvania. A convention called by a legislature in direct violation of their duty, and composed in part of members, who were compelled to attend for that purpose, to consider of a constitution proposed by a convention of the United States, who were not appointed for the purpose of framing a new form of government, but whose powers were expressly confined to altering and amending the present articles of confederation.—Therefore the members of the continental convention in proposing the plan acted as individuals, and not as deputies from Pennsylvania. The assembly who called the state convention acted as individuals, and not as the legislature of Pennsylvania; nor could they or the convention chosen on their recommendation have authority to do any act or thing, that can alter or annihilate the constitution of Pennsylvania (both of which will be done by the new constitution) nor are their proceedings in our opinion, at all binding on the people.

The election for members of the convention was held at so early a period and the want of information was so great, that some of us did not know of it until after it was over, and we have reason to believe that great numbers of the people of Pennsylvania have not yet had an opportunity of sufficiently examining the proposed constitution.—We apprehend that no change can take place that will affect the internal government or constitution of this commonwealth, unless a majority of the people should evidence a wish for such a change; but on examining the number of votes given for members of the present state convention, we find that of upwards of *seventy thousand* freemen who are intitled to vote in Pennsylvania, the whole convention has been elected by about *thirteen thousand* voters, and though *two thirds* of the members of the convention have thought proper to ratify the proposed constitution, yet those *two thirds* were elected by the votes of only *six thousand and eight hundred* freemen.

In the city of Philadelphia and some of the eastern counties, the junto that took the lead in the business agreed to vote for none but such as would solemnly promise to adopt the system in *toto*, without exercising their judgment. In many of the counties the people did not attend the elections as they had not an opportunity of judging of the plan. Others did not consider themselves bound by the call of a set of men who assembled at the statehouse in Philadelphia, and assumed the name of the legislature of Pennsylvania; and some were prevented from voting by the violence of the party who were determined at all events to force down the measure. To such lengths did the tools of despotism carry their outrage, that in the night of the election for members of convention, in the city of Philadelphia, several of the subscribers (being then in the city to transact your business) were grossly abused, ill-treated and insulted while they were quiet in their lodgings, though they did not interfere, nor had any thing to do with the said election, but as they apprehend, because they were supposed to be adverse to the proposed constitution, and would not tamely surrender those sacred rights, which you had committed to their charge.

The convention met, and the same disposition was soon manifested in considering the proposed constitution, that had been exhibited in every other stage of the business. We were prohibited by an express vote of the convention, from taking any question on the separate articles of the plan, and reduced to the necessity of adopting or rejecting *in toto*.—'Tis true the majority permitted us to debate on each article, but restrained us from proposing amendments.—They also determined not to permit us to enter on the minutes our reasons of dissent against any of the articles, nor even on the final question our reasons of dissent against the whole. Thus situated we entered on the examination of the proposed system of government, and found it to be such as we could not adopt, without, as we conceived, surrendering up your dearest rights. We offered our objections to the convention, and opposed those parts of the plan, which, in our opinion, would be injurious to you, in the best manner we were able; and closed our arguments by offering the following propositions to the convention.

1. The right of conscience shall be held inviolable; and neither the legislative, executive nor judicial powers of the United States shall have authority to alter, abrogate, or infringe any part of the constitution of the several states, which provide for the preservation of liberty in matters of religion.

2. That in controversies respecting property, and in suits between man and man, trial by jury shall remain as heretofore, as well in the federal courts, as in those of the several states.

3. That in all capital and criminal prosecutions, a man has a right to demand the cause and nature of his accusation, as well in the federal courts, as in those of the several states; to be heard by himself and his counsel; to be confronted with the accusers and witnesses; to call for evidence in his favor, and a speedy trial by an impartial jury of his vicinage, without whose unanimous consent, he cannot be found guilty, nor can he be compelled to give evidence against himself; and that no man be deprived of his liberty, except by the law of the land or the judgment of his peers.

4. That excessive bail ought not to be required, nor excessive fines imposed, nor cruel nor unusual punishments inflicted.

5. That warrants unsupported by evidence, whereby any officer or messenger may be commanded or required to search suspected places, or to seize any person or persons, his or their property, not particularly described, are grievous and oppressive, and shall not be granted either by the magistrates of the federal government or others.

6. That the people have a right to the freedom of speech, of writing and publishing their sentiments, therefore, the freedom of the press shall not be restrained by any law of the United States.

7. That the people have a right to bear arms for the defence of themselves and their own state, or the United States, or for the purpose of killing game; and no law shall be passed for disarming the people or any of them, unless for crimes committed, or real danger of public injury from individuals; and as standing armies in the time of peace are dangerous to liberty, they ought not to be kept up; and that the military shall be kept under strict subordination to and be governed by the civil powers.

8. The inhabitants of the several states shall have liberty to fowl and hunt in seasonable times, on the lands they hold, and on all other lands in the United States not inclosed, and in like manner to fish in all navigable waters, and others not private property, without being restrained therein by any laws to be passed by the legislature of the United States.

9. That no law shall be passed to restrain the legislatures of the several states from enacting laws for imposing taxes, except imposts and duties on goods imported or exported, and that no taxes, except imposts and duties upon goods imported and exported, and postage on letters shall be levied by the authority of Congress.

10. That the house of representatives be properly increased in number; that elections shall remain free; that the several states shall have power to regulate the elections for senators and representatives, without being controuled either directly or indirectly by any interference on the part of the Congress; and that elections of representatives be annual.

11. That the power of organizing, arming and disciplining the militia (the manner of disciplining the militia to be prescribed by Congress) remain with the individual states, and that Congress shall not have authority to call or march any of the militia out of their own state, without the consent of such state, and for such length of time only as such state shall agree.

That the sovereignty, freedom and independency of the several states shall be retained, and every power, jurisdiction and right which is not by this constitution expressly delegated to the United States in Congress assembled.

12. That the legislative, executive, and judicial powers be kept separate; and to this end that a constitutional council be appointed, to advise and assist the president, who shall be responsible for the advice they give, hereby the senators would be relieved from almost constant attendance; and also that the judges be made completely independent.

13. That no treaty which shall be directly opposed to the existing laws of the United States in Congress assembled, shall be valid until such laws shall be repealed, or made conformable to such treaty; neither shall any treaties be valid which are in contradiction to the constitution of the United States, or the constitutions of the several states.

14. That the judiciary power of the United States shall be confined to cases affecting ambassadors, other public ministers and consuls; to cases of admiralty and maritime jurisdiction; to controversies to which the United States shall be a party; to controversies between two or more states—between a state and citizens of different states—between citizens claiming lands under grants of different states; and between a state or the citizen thereof and foreign states, and in criminal cases, to such only as are expressly enumerated in the constitution, and that the United States in Congress assembled, shall not have power to enact laws, which shall alter the laws of descents and distribution of the effects of deceased persons, the titles of lands or goods, or the regulation of contracts in the individual states.

After reading these propositions, we declared our willingness to agree to the plan, provided it was so amended as to meet these propositions, or something similar to them; and finally moved the convention to adjourn, to give the people of Pennsylvania time to consider the subject, and determine for themselves; but these were all rejected, and the final vote was taken, when our duty to you induced us to vote against the proposed plan, and to decline signing the ratification of the same.

During the discussion we met with many insults, and some personal abuse; we were not even treated with decency, during the sitting of the convention, by the persons in the gallery of the house; however, we flatter ourselves that in contending for the preservation of those invaluable rights you have thought proper to commit to our charge, we acted with a spirit becoming freemen, and being desirous that you might know the principles which actuated our conduct, and being prohibited from inserting our reasons of dissent on the minutes of the convention, we have subjoined them for your consideration, as to you alone we are accountable. It remains with you whether you will think those inestimable privileges, which you have so ably contended for, should be sacrificed at the shrine of despotism, or whether you mean to contend for them with the same spirit that has so often baffled the attempts of an aristocratic faction, to rivet the shackles of slavery on you and your unborn posterity.

Our objections are comprised under three general heads of dissent, viz.

We dissent, first, because it is the opinion of the most celebrated writers on government, and confirmed by uniform experience, that a very extensive territory cannot be governed on the principles of freedom, otherwise than by a confederation of republics, possessing all the powers of internal government; but united in the management of their general, and foreign concerns.

• • •

We dissent, secondly, because the powers vested in Congress by this constitution, must necessarily annihilate and absorb the legislative, executive, and judicial powers of the several states, and produce from their ruins one consolidated government, which from the nature of things will be *an iron handed despotism*, as nothing short of the supremacy of despotic sway could connect and govern these United States under one government.

• • •

. . . We dissent, Thirdly, Because if it were practicable to govern so extensive a territory as these United States includes, on the plan of a consolidated government, consistent with the principles of liberty and the happiness of the people, yet the construction of this constitution is not calculated to attain the object, for independent of the nature of the case, it would of itself, necessarily, produce a despotism, and that not by the usual gradations, but with the celerity that has hitherto only attended revolutions effected by the sword.

To establish the truth of this position, a cursory investigation of the principles and form of this constitution will suffice.

The first consideration that this review suggests, is the omission of a BILL of RIGHTS, ascertaining and fundamentally establishing those unalienable and personal rights of men, without the full, free, and secure enjoyment of which there can be no liberty, and over which it is not necessary for a good government to have the controul. The principal of which are the rights of conscience, personal liberty by the clear and unequivocal establishment of the writ of *habeas corpus*, jury trial in criminal and civil cases, by an impartial jury of the vicinage or county, with the common-law proceedings, for the safety of the accused in criminal prosecutions; and the liberty of the press, that scourge of tyrants, and the grand bulwark of every other liberty and privilege; the stipulations heretofore made in favor of them in the state constitutions, are entirely superceded by this constitution.

• • •

We will now bring the legislature under this constitution to the test of the foregoing principles, which will demonstrate, that it is deficient in every essential quality of a just and safe representation.

The house of representatives is to consist of 65 members; that is one for about every 50,000 inhabitants, to be chosen every two years. Thirty-three members will form a quorum for doing business; and 17 of these, being the majority, determine the sense of the house.

The senate, the other constituent branch of the legislature, consists of 26 members being *two* from each state, appointed by their legislatures every six years—fourteen senators make a quorum; the majority of whom, eight, determines the sense of that body; except in judging on impeachments, or in making treaties, or in expelling a member, when two thirds of the senators present, must concur.

The president is to have the controul over the enacting of laws, so far as to make the concurrence of *two* thirds of the representatives and senators present necessary, if he should object to the laws.

Thus it appears that the liberties, happiness, interests, and great concerns of the whole United States, may be dependent upon the integrity, virtue, wisdom, and knowledge of 25 or 26 men—How unadequate and unsafe a representation! Inadequate, because the sense and views of 3 or 4 millions of people diffused over so extensive a territory comprising such various climates, products, habits, interests, and opinions, cannot be collected in so small a body; and besides, it is not a fair and equal representation of the people even in proportion to its number, for the smallest state has as much weight in the senate as the largest, and from the smallness of the number to be chosen for both branches of the legislature; and from the mode of election and appointment, which is under the controul of Congress; and from the nature of the thing, men of the most elevated rank in life, will alone be chosen. The other orders in the society, such as farmers, traders, and mechanics, who all ought to have a competent number of their best informed men in the legislature, will be totally unrepresented.

The representation is unsafe, because in the exercise of such great powers and trusts, it is so exposed to corruption and undue influence, by the gift of the numerous places of honor and emoluments at the disposal of the executive; by the arts and address of the great and designing; and by direct bribery.

The representation is moreover inadequate and unsafe, because of the long terms for which it is appointed, and the mode of its appointment, by which Congress may not only controul the choice of the people, but may so manage as to divest the people of this fundamental right, and become self-elected.

The number of members in the house of representatives *may* be increased to one for every 30,000 inhabitants. But when we consider, that this cannot be done without the consent of the senate, who from their share in the legislative, in the executive, and judicial departments, and permanency of appointment, will be the great efficient body in this government, and whose weight and predominancy would be abridged by an increase of the representatives, we are persuaded that this is a circumstance that cannot be expected. On the contrary, the number of representatives will probably be continued at 65, although the population of the country may swell to treble what it now is; unless a revolution should effect a change.

• • •

The next consideration that the constitution presents, is the undue and danger-ous mixture of the powers of government; the same body possessing legislative, ex-ecutive, and judicial powers. The senate is a constituent branch of the legislature, it has judicial power in judging on impeachments, and in this case unites in some measure the characters of judge and party, as all the principal officers are ap-pointed by the president-general, with the concurrence of the senate and there-fore they derive their offices in part from the senate. This may bias the judgments of the senators and tend to screen great delinquents from punishment. And the senate has, moreover, various and great executive powers, viz. in concurrence with the president-general, they form treaties with foreign nations, that may con-troul and abrogate the constitutions and laws of the several states. Indeed, there is no power, privilege or liberty of the state governments, or of the people, but what may be affected by virtue of this power. For all treaties, made by them, are to be the "supreme law of the land, any thing in the constitution or laws of any state, to the contrary notwithstanding."

And this great power may be exercised by the president and 10 senators (being two-thirds of 14, which is a quorum of that body). What an inducement would this offer to the ministers of foreign powers to compass by bribery *such concessions* as could not otherwise be obtained. It is the unvaried usage of all free states, whenever treaties interfere with the positive laws of the land, to make the inter-vention of the legislature necessary to give them operation. This became neces-sary, and was afforded by the parliament of Great-Britain. In consequence of the late commercial treaty between that kingdom and France—As the senate judges on impeachments, who is to try the members of the senate for the abuse of this power! And none of the great appointments to office can be made without the consent of the senate.

Such various, extensive, and important powers combined in one body of men, are inconsistent with all freedom; the celebrated Montesquieu tells us, that "when the legislative and executive powers are united in the same person, or in the same body or magistrates, there can be no liberty, because apprehensions may arise, lest the same monarch or *senate* should enact tyrannical laws, to execute them in a tyrannical manner."

"Again, there is no liberty, if the power of judging be not separated from the legislative and executive powers. Were it joined with the legislative, the life and liberty of the subject would be exposed to arbitrary controul; for the judge would then be legislator. Were it joined to the executive power, the judge might behave with all the violence of an oppressor. There would be an end of every thing, were the same man, or the same body of the nobles, or of the people, to exercise those three powers; that of enacting laws; that of executing the public resolutions; and that of judging the crimes or differences of individuals."

The president general is dangerously connected with the senate; his coincidence with the views of the ruling junto in that body, is made essential to his weight and importance in the government, which will destroy all independency and purity in the executive department, and having the power of pardoning without the concurrence of a council, he may skreen from punishment the most treasonable attempts that may be made on the liberties of the people, when instigated by his coadjutors in the senate. Instead of this dangerous and improper mixture of the executive with the legislative and judicial, the supreme executive powers ought to have been placed in the president, with a small independent council, made personally responsible for every appointment to office or other act, by having their opinions recorded; and that without the concurrence of the majority of the quorum of this council, the president should not be capable of taking any step.

• • •

From the foregoing investigation, it appears that the Congress under this constitution will not possess the confidence of the people, which is an essential requisite in a good government; for unless the laws command the confidence and respect of the great body of the people, so as to induce them to support them, when called on by the civil magistrate, they must be executed by the aid of a numerous standing army, which would be inconsistent with every idea of liberty; for the same force that may be employed to compel obedience to good laws, might and probably would be used to wrest from the people their constitutional liberties. The framers of this constitution appear to have been aware of this great deficiency; to have been sensible that no dependence could be placed on the people for their support; but on the contrary, that the government must be executed by force. They have therefore made a provision for this purpose in a permanent STANDING ARMY, and a MILITIA that may be subjected to as strict discipline and government.

• • •

As this government will not enjoy the confidence of the people, but be executed by force, it will be a very expensive and burthensome government. The standing army must be numerous, and as a further support, it will be the policy of this government to multiply officers in every department: judges, collectors, tax gatherers, excisemen and the whole host of revenue officers will swarm over the land, devouring the hard earnings of the industrious. Like the locusts of old, impoverishing an desolating all before them.

We have not noticed the smaller, nor many of the considerable blemishes, but have confined our objections to the great and essential defects; the main pillars of the constitution; which we have shewn to be inconsistent with the liberty and happiness of the people, as its establishment will annihilate the state governments, and produce one consolidated government that will eventually and speedily issue in the supremacy of despotism. ■

American Politics Today

Because the Supreme Court plays such a key role in interpreting the United States Constitution (see Chapter 12), constitutional debates in the United States can quickly become mired in legal details and technicalities. The debate over the Second Amendment—which protects the right of the people to "keep and bear arms"—is in this regard the exception that proves the rule. Because the Court has been largely silent on the meaning and application of the Second Amendment, both supporters and opponents of gun control make arguments that more closely reflect the debates of the Founding Generation than the thinking of modern justices. As Wendy Kaminer points out, the Second Amendment debate brings out "the fundamental tension between republicanism and individualism" in the American constitutional system.

Questions

1. What are the meanings of "republicanism" and "individualism," particularly in the context of the Second Amendment debate?
2. What are the strongest points in favor of those who argue that the Second Amendment should be interpreted to guarantee the right *of the individual* to keep and bear arms? What are the strongest points in favor of those who argue that the amendment protects the right of the people to bear arms collectively?

1.6 Second Thoughts on the Second Amendment (1996)

Wendy Kaminer

Debates about gun ownership and gun control are driven more by values and ideology than by pragmatism—and hardly at all by the existing empirical research, which is complex and inconclusive. . . . As for legal debates about the existence of constitutional rights, empirical data is irrelevant, or at best peripheral. But the paucity of proof that gun controls lessen crime is particularly galling to people who believe that they have a fundamental right to bear arms. In theory, at least, we restrict constitutional rights only when the costs of exercising them seem unbearably high. In fact we argue continually about what those costs are: Does violence in the media cause violence in real life? Did the release of the Pentagon Papers

Excerpted from Wendy Kaminer, "Second Thoughts on the Second Amendment," *The Atlantic Monthly* (March 1996), Volume 277, pp. 32–45—abridged. A longer version of this article first appeared in *The Atlantic Monthly,* March 1995. Copyright Wendy Kaminer. Reprinted with permission.

endanger the national security? Does hate speech constitute discrimination? In the debate about firearms, however, we can't even agree on the principles that should govern restrictions on guns, because we can't agree about the right to own them.

How could we, given the importance of the competing values at stake—public safety and the right of self-defense—and the opacity of the constitutional text? The awkwardly drafted Second Amendment doesn't quite make itself clear: "A well regulated Militia, being necessary to the security of a free State, the right of the people to keep and bear Arms, shall not be infringed." Is the reference to a militia a limitation on the right to bear arms or merely an explanation of an armed citizenry's role in a government by consent? There is little dispute that one purpose of the Second Amendment was to ensure that the people would be able to resist a central government should it ever devolve into despotism. But there is little agreement about what that capacity for resistance was meant to entail— armed citizens acting under the auspices of state militias or armed citizens able to organize and act on their own. And there is virtually no consensus about the con- stitutional right to own a gun in the interests of individual self-defense against crime, rather than communal defense against tyranny. Is defense of the state, and of the common good, the *raison d'être* of the Second Amendment or merely one use of it?

The Supreme Court has never answered these fundamental questions about the constitutional uses of guns. It has paid scant attention to the Second Amend- ment, providing little guidance in the gun-control debate. Two frequently cited late-nineteenth-century cases relating to the Second Amendment were more about federalism than about the right to bear arms. *Presser v. Illinois*, decided in 1886, involved a challenge to a state law prohibiting private citizens from organiz- ing their own military units and parades. The Court held that the Second Amendment was a limitation on federal, not state, power, reflecting the prevail- ing view (now discredited) that the Bill of Rights in general applied only to the federal government, not to the states. (A hundred years ago the Court did not apply the First Amendment to the states either.) *Presser* followed *U.S. v. Cruik- shank*, which held that the federal government could not protect people from pri- vate infringement of their rights to assemble and bear arms. *Cruikshank*, decided in 1876, invalidated the federal convictions of participants in the lynching of two black men. This ruling, essentially concerned with limiting federal police power, is virtually irrelevant to Second Amendment debates today, although it has been cited to support the proposition that an oppressed minority has a compelling need (or a natural right) to bear arms in self-defense.

The most significant Supreme Court decision on the Second Amendment was *U.S. v. Miller* (1939), a less-than-definitive holding now cited approvingly by both sides in the gun-control debate. *Miller* involved a prosecution under the 1934 National Firearms Act. Jack Miller and his accomplice had been convicted of transporting an unregistered shotgun of less than regulation length across state lines. In striking down their Second Amendment claim and upholding their con- viction, the Court noted that no evidence had been presented that a shotgun was in fact a militia weapon, providing no factual basis for a Second Amendment claim. This ruling implies that the Second Amendment could protect the right to bear arms suitable for a militia.

Advocates of gun control or prohibition like the *Miller* case because it makes the right to bear arms dependent on at least the possibility of service in a militia. They cite the Court's declaration that the Second Amendment was obviously intended to "assure the continuation and render possible the effectiveness" of state militias; they place less emphasis on the Court's apparent willingness to permit private citizens to possess military weapons. Citing *Miller*, a dealer at a gun show told me that the Second Amendment protects the ownership of only such devices as machine guns, Stingers, and grenade throwers. But advocates of gun ownership don't generally emphasize this awkward implication of *U.S.* v. *Miller* any more than their opponents do: it could lead to prohibitions on handguns. They like the *Miller* decision because it delves into the history of the Second Amendment and stresses that for the framers, the militia "comprised all males physically capable of acting in concert for the common defense."

This view of the militia as an inchoate citizens' army, not a standing body of professionals, is central to the claim that the Second Amendment protects the rights of individual civilians, not simply the right of states to organize and arm militias. And, in fact, fear and loathing of standing armies did underlie the Second Amendment, which was at least partly intended to ensure that states would be able to call up citizens in defense against a tyrannical central government. (Like the Bill of Rights in general, the Second Amendment was partly a response to concerns about federal abuses of power.) James Madison, the author of the Second Amendment, invoked in *The Federalist Papers* the potential force of a citizen militia as a guarantee against a federal military coup.

> Let a regular army, fully equal to the resources of the country, be formed; and let it be entirely at the devotion of the federal government: still it would not be going too far to say that the State governments with the people on their side would be able to repel the danger.... To [the regular army] would be opposed a militia amounting to near half a million of citizens with arms in their hands, officered by men chosen from among themselves, fighting for their common liberties and united and conducted by governments possessing their affection and confidence. It may well be doubted whether a militia thus circumstanced could ever be conquered by such a proportion of regular troops. Those who are best acquainted with the late successful resistance of this country against the British arms will be most inclined to deny the possibility of it. Besides the advantage of being armed, which the Americans possess over the people of almost every other nation, the existence of subordinate governments, to which the people are attached and by which the militia officers are appointed, forms a barrier against the enterprises of ambition, more insurmountable than any which a simple government of any form can admit of.

This passage is enthusiastically cited by advocates of the right to bear arms, because it supports their notion of the militia as the body of people, privately armed; but it's also cited by their opponents, because it suggests that the militia is activated and "conducted" by the states, and it stresses that citizens are "attached" to their local governments. The militia envisioned by Madison is not simply a "collection of unorganized, privately armed citizens," Dennis Henigan, a handgun-control advocate, has argued.

That Madison's reflections on the militia and the Supreme Court's holding in *U.S.* v. *Miller* can be cited with some accuracy by both sides in the debate testifies to the hybrid nature of Second Amendment rights. The Second Amendment presumes (as did the framers) that private citizens will possess private arms; Madison referred offhandedly to "the advantage of being armed, which the Americans possess." But Madison also implied that the right to bear arms is based in the obligation of citizens to band together as a militia to defend the common good, as opposed to the prerogative of citizens to take up arms individually in pursuit of self-interest and happiness.

The tension at the heart of the Second Amendment, which makes it so difficult to construe, is the tension between republicanism and liberal individualism. (To put it very simply, republicanism calls for the subordination of individual interests to the public good; liberalism focuses on protecting individuals against popular conceptions of the good.) A growing body of scholarly literature on the Second Amendment locates the right to bear arms in republican theories of governance. In a 1989 article in the *Yale Law Journal* that helped animate the Second Amendment debate, the University of Texas law professor Sanford Levinson argued that the Second Amendment confers an individual right to bear arms so that, in the republican tradition, armed citizens might rise up against an oppressive state. Wendy Brown, a professor of women's studies at the University of California at Santa Cruz, and David C. Williams, a law professor at Cornell University, have questioned the validity of a republican right to bear arms in a society that lacks the republican virtue of being willing to put communal interests first. Pro-gun activists don't generally acknowledge the challenge posed by republicanism to the individualist culture that many gun owners inhabit. They embrace republican justifications for gun ownership, stressing the use of arms in defending the community, at the same time that they stress the importance of guns in protecting individual autonomy.

Advocates of the right to bear arms often insist that the Second Amendment is rooted in both collective and individual rights of self-defense—against political oppression and crime—without recognizing how those rights conflict. The republican right to resist oppression is the right of the majority, or the people, not the right of a small religious cult in Waco, Texas, or of a few survivalist tax protesters in Idaho. The members of these groups have individual rights against the government, state and federal. (Both the American Civil Liberties Union and the NRA protested the government's actions in Waco and its attack on the survivalist Randy Weaver and his family.) But refuseniks and refugees from society are not republicans. They do not constitute the citizen militia envisioned by the framers, any more than they stand for the American community; indeed, they stand against it—withdrawing from the body politic, asserting their rights to alienation and anomie or membership in exclusionary alternative communities of their own. Republicanism can't logically be invoked in the service of libertarianism. It elevates civic virtue over individualism, consensus over dissent.

Nor can social-contract theory be readily invoked in support of a right to arm yourself in a war against street crime, despite the claims of some gun-ownership advocates. The right or power to engage in punishment or retribution is precisely what is given up when you enter an ordered civil society. The loss of self-help remedies is the price of the social contract. "God hath certainly appointed Government to restrain the partiality and violence of Men," John Locke wrote. A person may always defend his or her life when threatened, but only when there is no chance to appeal to the law. If a man points his sword at me and demands my purse, Locke explained, I may kill him. But if he steals my purse by stealth and then raises a sword to defend it, I may not use force to get it back. "My Life not being in danger, I may have the *benefit of appealing* to the Law, and have Reparation for my 100£ that way."

Locke was drawing a line between self-defense and vigilantism which many gun owners would no doubt respect. Others would point to the inability of the criminal-justice system to avenge crimes and provide reparation to victims, and thus they would assert a right to engage in self-help. Social-contract theory, however, might suggest that if the government is no longer able to provide order, or justice, the remedy is not vigilantism but revolution; the utter failure of law enforcement is a fundamental breach of trust. And, in fact, there are large pockets of disaffected citizens who do not trust the government to protect them or to provide impartial justice, and who might be persuaded to rise up against it, as evidenced by the disorder that followed the 1992 acquittal of police officers who assaulted Rodney King. Was Los Angeles the scene of a riot or of an uprising?

Injustice, and the sense of oppression it spawns, are often matters of perspective—particularly today, when claims of political victimization abound and there is little consensus on the demands of public welfare. We use the term "oppression" promiscuously, to describe any instance of discrimination. In this climate of grievance and hyperbole, many acts of violence are politicized. How do we decide whether an insurrection is just? Don Kates observes that the Second Amendment doesn't exactly confer the right to resist. He says, "It gives you a right to win."

The prospect of armed resistance, however, is probably irrelevant to much public support for gun ownership, which reflects a fear of crime more than a fear or loathing of government. People don't buy guns in order to overthrow or even to thwart the government; in the belief that the police can't protect them, people buy guns to protect themselves and their families. Recognizing this, the NRA appeals to fear of crime, particularly crime against women. ("Choose to refuse to be a victim," NRA ads proclaim, showing a woman and her daughter alone in a desolate parking lot at night.) And it has countered demands for tougher gun controls not with radical individualist appeals for insurrection but with statist appeals for tougher anti-crime laws, notably stringent mandatory-minimum sentences and parole reform. There is considerable precedent for the NRA's appeal to state authority: founded after the Civil War, with the mission of teaching soldiers to shoot straight, in its early years the NRA was closely tied to the military and dependent on government largesse; until recently it drew considerable moral support from the police. Today, however, statist anti-crime campaigns are mainly matters of politics for the NRA and for gun advocates in general; laws mandating tough sentences for the criminal use of firearms defuse demands for firearm controls. Personal liberty—meaning the liberty to own guns and use them against the government if necessary—is these people's passion.

Gun advocates are apt to be extravagantly libertarian when the right to own guns is at stake. At heart many are insurrectionists—at least, they need to feel prepared. Nothing arouses their anger more, I've found, than challenges to the belief that private gun ownership is an essential check on political oppression. . . .

. . . "Using a national epidemic of crime and violence as their justification, media pundits and collectivist politicians are aggressively campaigning to disarm private citizens and strengthen federal law enforcement powers," proclaims a special edition of *The New American,* a magazine on sale at gun shows. After gun control, the editors suggest, the greatest threat to individual liberty is the Clinton plan for providing local police departments with federal assistance. "Is it possible that some of those who are advocating a disarmed populace and a centralized police system have totalitarian designs in mind? It is worth noting that this is exactly what happened in many countries during this century."

This can be dismissed as ravings on the fringe, but it captures in crazed form the hostility toward a powerful central government which inspired the adoption of the Second Amendment right to bear arms 200 years ago and fuels support for it today. Advocates of First Amendment rights, who believe firmly that free speech is both a moral imperative and an instrument of democratic governance, should understand the passion of Second Amendment claims.

They should be sympathetic as well to the more dispassionate constitutional arguments of gun owners. Civil libertarians who believe that the Bill of Rights in general protects individuals have a hard time explaining why the Second Amendment protects only groups. They have a hard time reconciling their opposition to prohibitions of problematic behavior, such as drug abuse, with their support for the prohibition of guns. (Liberals tend to demonize guns and gun owners the way conservatives tend to demonize drugs and pornography and the people who use them.) In asserting that the Second Amendment provides no individual right to bear arms or that the right provided is anachronistic and not worth its cost, civil libertarians place themselves in the awkward position of denying the existence of a constitutional right because they don't value its exercise.

The civil-libertarian principles at issue in the gun debate are made clear by the arguments of First Amendment and Second Amendment advocates, which are strikingly similar—as are the arguments their opponents use. Pornography rapes, some feminists say. Words oppress, according to advocates of censoring hate speech. "Words Kill," declared a Planned Parenthood ad following the abortion-clinic shootings in Brookline, Massachusetts, last year. And all you can say in response is "Words don't kill people; people kill people." To an anti-libertarian, the literature sold at gun shows may seem as dangerous as the guns; at a recent gun show I bought *Incendiaries,* an army manual on unconventional warfare; *Exotic Weapons: An Access Book; Gunrunning for Fun and Profit;* and *Vigilante Handbook,* which tells me how to harass, torture, and assassinate people. Should any of this material be censored? If it were, it would be sold on the black market; and the remedy for bad speech is good speech, First Amendment devotees point out. According to Second Amendment supporters, gun-control laws affect only law-abiding gun owners, and the best defense against armed criminals is armed victims; the remedy for the bad use of guns in violent crime is the good use of guns in self-defense.

Of course, guns do seem a bit more dangerous than books, and apart from a few anti-pornography feminists, most of us would rather be accosted by a man with a video than a man with a gun. But none of our constitutional rights are absolute. Recognizing that the Second Amendment confers an individual right to bear arms would not immunize guns from regulation; it would require that the government establish a necessity, not just a desire, to regulate. The majority of gun owners, Don Kates suggests, would be amenable to gun controls, such as waiting periods and even licensing and training requirements, if they didn't perceive them as preludes to prohibition. The irony of the Second Amendment debate is that acknowledging an individual right to bear arms might facilitate gun control more than denying it ever could.

But it will not facilitate civic engagement or the community that Americans are exhorted to seek. The civil-libertarian defense of Second Amendment rights is not a republican one. It does not derive the individual right to bear arms from republican notions of the militia; instead it relies on traditional liberal views of personal autonomy. It is a communitarian nightmare. If the war against crime has replaced the Cold War in popular culture, a private storehouse of guns has replaced the fallout shelter in the psyche of Americans who feel besieged. Increasingly barricaded, mistrustful of their neighbors, they've sacrificed virtue to fear. ■

The Comparative Context

Since the days of the French Revolution, other nations have looked to the United States for advice and inspiration on constitutions and constitutionalism. The impact of the U.S. Constitution was especially pronounced after World War II; the constitutions of Germany and Japan were strongly influenced by American ideas.

The collapse of communism in the late 1980s and early 1990s provided a similar opportunity. Like their counterparts in earlier eras, the men and women who drafted constitutions for the new regimes of Eastern Europe also sought guidance from the United States. As the law professor A. E. Dick Howard explains, constitution writers in Europe and elsewhere face the challenging task of grafting American ideas about rights, consent of the governed, limited government, and the rule of law onto their own cultures and experiences. Americans, he suggests, can learn from the new European constitutions just as Europeans can learn from us.

Questions

1. What ideas from the U.S. Constitution are most clearly reflected in the new wave of constitution-writing? What ideas are not reflected in the new constitutions?
2. What can Americans learn about constitutions and constitutionalism from the experiences of these other nations?

1.7 How Ideas Travel: Rights at Home and Abroad (1993)

A. E. Dick Howard

Neither time nor place can cabin ideas. In 1987 United States citizens celebrated the two hundredth anniversary of their Constitution, and in 1991 they marked the bicentennial of their Bill of Rights. At just the same time—as if history were a creative choreographer—the peoples of Central and Eastern Europe were proving the resilience of old ideas about freedom, human dignity, and democracy. After living for so many years under oppressive one-party regimes, people in Central and Eastern Europe and the Soviet sphere now find themselves questing for choices long denied them.

New times require new constitutions. Nearly every country, even the most repressive, has a "constitution." We are all too familiar with constitutions, such as the Soviet Union's 1936 Constitution, whose glowing promises of justice and human dignity have little relation to reality. Such documents must be discarded, and authentic constitutionalism planted in their place.

Thus, as the United States reflected on the two-hundred-year odyssey of its Bill of Rights, Russians, Poles, Bulgarians, and others began to write new constitutions. At the core of each of these new documents lies a bill of rights. Indeed, in January 1991 the national assembly of the Czech and Slovak Federal Republic gave priority to the adoption of a new bill of rights; meanwhile debate continued on other constitutional provisions—in particular, those effecting a division of powers between the federal government and the two republics.

Those who draft a bill of rights must understand the history and traditions of the country for which the document is being created. One who sought to write a bill of rights for Hungary, for example, would need to know about the great Golden Bull of 1222 (which is to Hungarian history what Magna Carta is to that of England), the impact of Enlightenment thought on eighteenth-century Hungary, and the reformist thrust of the 1848 revolution. Likewise, a Polish drafter would wish to recall the legacy of Polish Constitutionalism, including the notable Constitution of 3 May 1791—the world's second national constitution (after the Philadelphia Constitution of 1787).

Stating a people's rights is not, however, a parochial exercise. Drafters of bills of rights look not only to their own country's experience but also to that of other countries. Professors and scholars who work with constitutional commissions in Central and Eastern Europe are well read; they know the *Federalist Papers* and the writings of Western theorists such as John Locke and Montesquieu. Drafting commissions invite experts from other countries to pore over drafts and offer comments and advice.

A. E. Dick Howard, "How Ideas Travel: Rights at Home and Abroad," in A. E. Dick Howard, ed., *Constitution Making in Eastern Europe* (Washington, D.C.: Woodrow Wilson Center Press, 1993), pp. 9–10, 14–20. Reprinted with the permission of the author.

Traffic is heavy between the United States and the emerging democracies, as well as between those countries and the capitals of Western Europe. Americans who travel to consult on new constitutions are sometimes dubbed "constitutional Johnny Appleseeds." West European experts are equally in demand. . . .

In the years immediately following World War II, it was possible to speak of the "American century." With much of Europe in ashes, and Asia yet to become a major economic force, the United States enjoyed immense influence. In Japan, the staff of General Douglas MacArthur's headquarters drafted a new constitution in seven days for that defeated country. Similarly, the mark of American ideas on West Germany's postwar constitution is evident.

Even in the period after World War II, however, the influence of American constitutionalism was variable. In Africa, for example, British barristers and scholars were enlisted to work on constitutions for British colonies, such as Ghana, that were becoming independent nations.

The upheavals in Central and Eastern Europe since the winter of 1989 have brought a burst of attention to constitutions and bills of rights. An American who reads the draft of a bill of rights or constitution for one of the region's fledgling democracies will find much that is familiar but also much that is not.

Two hundred years after their drafting, the United States Constitution and the Bill of Rights are widely recognized as furnishing paradigms of the fundamental principles that define constitutional democracy. These principles include:

1. *Consent of the governed.* The first three words of the United States Constitution—"We the People"—embody the principle of consent of the governed. But American constitutionalism has also worked out the modes by which genuinely representative government can exist, including freedom to form political parties, fair apportionment of legislative seats, a liberal franchise, and free and fair elections.

2. *Limited government.* Constitutionalism pays special attention—through devices such as separation of powers and checks and balances—to preventing power from being concentrated in such a way that it becomes a threat to individual liberty.

3. *The open society.* Central to American precepts of individual liberty are the rights to believe what one will, to embrace what religious beliefs one chooses, to engage in free and robust debate, to oppose the orthodoxy of the moment. No part of the Constitution is a more powerful beacon than the First Amendment.

4. *Human dignity and the sanctity of the individual.* It is no accident that the Bill of Rights accords such detailed attention to criminal procedure. A good measure of the respect accorded human rights is how the state treats those charged with or suspected of criminal activity. The sanctity of the individual also connotes aspects of personal privacy and autonomy, those zones of private life into which the state may not intrude at all or only for demonstrable and pressing public needs.

5. *The rule of law.* The principle of due process of law, an idea as old as Magna Carta, requires fairness and impartiality in both criminal and civil proceedings. A corollary of fairness is equality. Constitutionalism's moral fabric is put to special test by discrimination involving race, religion, or similar factors. Liberty and equality may, at times, seem to be in tension with each other, but by and large they go hand in hand.

Bills of rights being drafted in Central and Eastern Europe parallel, in some respects, the principles flowing from the Bill of Rights of the United States Constitution and from American constitutionalism. Every draft bill of rights contains, in one form or another, assurances of free speech, freedom of conscience, and the right to form political parties. No draft fails to include some version of the antidiscrimination principle, which bans discrimination on the basis of nationality, ethnicity, religion, or other enumerated grounds. Procedural protections for those accused of crime are invariably included.

Other provisions of bills of rights being proposed or adopted in Central and Eastern Europe, however, will strike the American observer as less familiar, and in some cases disturbing. There are respects in which the bills of rights in the region go beyond the requirements of American constitutional law. There are other ways in which they fall short.

The Bill of Rights of the United States Constitution declares what government may *not* do; it is what Justice Hugo L. Black once called a list of "thou shalt nots." The document reflects the view that the function of a bill of rights is to limit government's powers. Central and East European drafters have enlarged this meaning of "rights." A legacy of the twentieth-century notion of positive government, an age of entitlements, is bills of rights that declare affirmative rights. Such bills include, of course, the traditional, negative rights, but they also spell out claims upon government, such as the right to an education, the right to a job, or the benefits of care in one's old age.

It may well be that, notwithstanding the language of the United States Bill of Rights, judicial gloss on the Constitution has brought American jurisprudence closer to the idea of affirmative rights than theory might suggest. The United States Supreme Court has rejected the argument that education is a "fundamental" right under the Fourteenth Amendment. Yet one who reads the many cases (especially those in lower courts) regarding school desegregation, education for the children of illegal aliens, and other school cases may well conclude that, in many respects, education is indeed a protected constitutional right. Be that as it may, bills of rights in the newer nations make explicit rights (such as education) that are, at most, only implicit in American constitutional law.

Thus the Charter of Fundamental Rights and Freedoms of the Czech and Slovak Federal Republic, adopted in January 1991, declares that workers "are entitled to fair remuneration for work and to satisfactory working conditions." Other sections decree free medical care, material security in one's old age, maternity benefits, and assistance to assure the needy of "basic living conditions." At the same time, some new bills of rights promise less than they seem to. Free speech will enjoy only qualified protection. Although stating that one may speak freely, the typical draft bill of rights proceeds to list significant exceptions. Drafts commonly state that advocacy of "fascism" or "communism" is excepted from the constitution's protection, or that speech may be forbidden if it conflicts with "public morality" or with the "constitutional order." Such exceptions overshadow the rule, especially when a draft (as always seems the case) does not require some finding of "clear and present danger" or a similar standard to justify a restriction on speech.

For example, Romania's Constitution, adopted in 1991, declares the "freedom to express ideas, opinions, and beliefs" to be "inviolable." But the document then adds that the law "prohibits defamation of the country and the nation; provocation to war or aggression, and to ethnic, racial, class, or religious hatred; incitement to discrimination, territorial separatism, or public violence; and obscene acts, contrary to good morals." What ethnic Hungarian, inclined to complain about conditions in Transylvania, would care to rely on his or her right to speak freely as being "inviolable" in the face of such sweeping and malleable exceptions?

Draft bills of rights, in addition to banning various forms of discrimination, often declare affirmative rights of culture, language, and education. The Czech and Slovak charter, for example, guarantees national and ethnic minorities the right to education in their language, the right to use that language in official settings, and the right to participation (form unspecified) in the settlement of matters concerning those minorities. But left unaddressed in most drafts is the explosive question whether rights of national minorities are simply rights of the individuals who make up those minorities or take on the character of group rights—an issue of utmost gravity wherever, as in so much of Central and Eastern Europe, disparate racial and ethnic groups are involved.

A constitution must, of course, be planted in a country's own soil to take root. One should not expect that a Bulgarian or Pole drafting a constitution or bill of rights will copy the American model, or any other model. Moreover, one should not be surprised that Central and East Europeans will draft documents that, at least in their specific provisions, bear more resemblance to fundamental laws in Western Europe than to American documents.

Several forces pull Central and East European drafters and lawmakers into the European orbit. After decades of an Iron Curtain, the people of the region yearn to rejoin the "family of Europe." Ties of tradition include the strong appeal of French ideas in some intellectual circles and the long-standing custom of legal scholars in many countries to view German scholarship as offering the highest and most rigorous standards.

New bills of rights also reflect the hope of the emerging democracies to be fully accepted as members of the civilized community of nations. Drafters thus study such documents as the Universal Declaration of Human Rights and the European Convention on Human Rights. Lofty aspirations are also coupled with more practical considerations: countries aspiring to membership in such regional arrangements as the European Community want to be seen as having fundamental laws in line with principles accepted in Western Europe.

Increasingly in this century, bills of rights have come to resemble political party platforms that appeal to this or that constituency, though in the poorest countries such rhetoric inevitably confronts the hard realities of poverty and privation. The revolutionaries who drafted Mexico's 1917 Constitution paid special attention to labor and social welfare, decreeing the rights to an eight-hour workday, a minimum wage, and workers' compensation—subjects on which constitutions are commonly silent. That document's Article 123 is considered so important that a street in Mexico City is named for it.

India's 1950 Constitution reflects the ethos of a Ghandian state. Its Directive Principles of State Policy point India toward the goal of a welfare state, the creation of a "casteless and classless society," and the promotion of world peace.

Perhaps the most baroque use of a bill of rights to legislate public policy is found in Brazil's 1988 Constitution. Rather than convene a constituent assembly, Brazil's leaders asked their Congress to draft a new constitution. All 559 members of Congress participated, dividing themselves into eight committees, each with three subcommittees. These twenty-four subcommittees worked without any master plan. The resulting document is unrivaled among constitutions for conferring favors on special-interest groups. There are, for example, thirty-seven sections dealing with just the rights of workers. Some rights, such as one day off in seven, derived from Brazil's 1946 Constitution; others, such as a forty-four–hour work week, had not been legally mandated before the adoption of the 1988 Constitution.

In South Africa, delegates to the drafting table consider[ed] proposals to use the bill of rights to compensate for past inequalities. An African National Congress draft provide[d] for diverting resources from richer to poorer areas "in order to achieve a common floor of rights for the whole country." The judiciary would be "transformed in such a way as to consist of men and women drawn from all sections of South African society." The nation's land, waters, and sky are declared to be the "common heritage" of the people of South Africa, and the state's agencies and organs are admonished to take measures against air and water pollution and other kinds of environmental harm.

The use of a bill of rights as an affirmative tool presents special problems. The traditional rights, such as expression or assembly, tell government what it *cannot* do and may be enforced through injunctions and other familiar judicial remedies. Affirmative rights tell government what it *must* do. Here enforcement is more problematic. Affirmative rights commonly entail legislative implementation or decisions about allocation of resources, tasks for which courts are often ill-suited. Anyone familiar with cases in which American judges have become administrators of school systems, prisons, or other public institutions will understand the skewing effect that decreeing affirmative rights has on public budgets.

The fortunes of Americans and peoples in the new democracies intertwine in many ways. Bills of rights—verbal declarations of fundamental aspirations—are a visible reflection of a shared legacy and common concerns. To flourish, however, constitutionalism requires skillful political leadership, viable political parties, a healthy press and media, an independent bench and bar, a sound economy, and a system of education in which young minds will prosper. A good constitution and bill of rights can foster these things but cannot assure them.

Ultimately, for rights to be respected there must be a mature civic spirit—an attitude in the minds of ordinary citizens. A nation of people who do not understand the basic precepts of free government are unlikely to keep it alive and vibrant. Describing his Bill for the More General Diffusion of Knowledge, Thomas Jefferson called for "rendering the people the safe, as they are the ultimate, guardians of their own liberty."

This lesson is as cogent in Washington or Albany as it is in Moscow or Warsaw. Americans have good cause to celebrate two hundred years of the Bill of Rights. They likewise have every reason to hope for the principles of that document to take root in the lands now free of tyrannical rule.

Neither East nor West can take liberty for granted. Witnessing the making of constitutions in the emerging democracies is an occasion for probing the lessons implicit therein: the nature and meaning of rights, the means by which they are enforced, and the habits of mind that keep them alive. ■

View from the Inside

It is all too easy to view the participants in the constitutional debate as detached philosophers crafting a new system of government in a political vacuum. The political scientist John P. Roche, by contrast, sees the men who met in Philadelphia in 1787 as practical politicians operating within very real political constraints. In Roche's view, much of the elegant political philosophy that emerged from the debate, especially in the *Federalist Papers,* originated as simple matters of political compromise. Roche's treatment of the Framers as politicians is probably overstated, but it offers a welcome perspective on the constitutional debate.

Questions

1. Madison, Roche suggests, was originally in favor of a "unitary central government" but compromised over the course of the convention. What factors created the necessity for such a compromise? What were the essential outlines of the compromise?
2. What features of the Constitution reflect the Framers practical—in contrast to their philosophical—concerns?

1.8 The Founding Fathers: A Reform Caucus in Action (1961)

John P. Roche

Standard treatments of the Convention divide the delegates into "nationalists" and "states'-righters" with various improvised shadings ("moderate nationalists," etc.), but these are *a posteriori* categories which obfuscate more than they clarify. What is striking to one who analyzes the Convention as a case-study in democratic politics is the lack of clear-cut ideological divisions in the Convention. Indeed, I submit that the evidence—Madison's *Notes,* the correspondence of the delegates, and debates on ratification—indicates that this was a remarkably homogeneous body on the ideological level. Yates and Lansing, Clinton's two chaperones for Hamilton, left in disgust on July 10. (Is there anything more tedious than sitting through endless disputes on matters one deems fundamentally misconceived. It takes an iron will to spend a hot summer as an ideological *agent provocateur.*) Luther Martin, Maryland's bibulous narcissist, left on September 4 in a huff when he discovered that others did not share his

John P. Roche, "The Founding Fathers: A Reform Caucus in Action," *American Political Science Review* 55 (1961): pp. 799–816. Reprinted by permission.

self-esteem; others went home for personal reasons. But the hard core of delegates accepted a grinding regimen throughout the attrition of a Philadelphia summer precisely because they shared the Constitutionalist goal.

Basic differences of opinion emerged, of course, but these were not ideological; they were *structural*. If the so-called "states'-rights" group had not accepted the fundamental purposes of the Convention, they could simply have pulled out and by doing so have aborted the whole enterprise. Instead of bolting, they returned day after day to argue and to compromise. An interesting symbol of this basic homogeneity was the initial agreement on secrecy: these professional politicians did not want to become prisoners of publicity; they wanted to retain that freedom of maneuver which is only possible when men are not forced to take public stands in the preliminary stages of negotiation. There was no legal means of binding the tongues of the delegates: at any stage in the game a delegate with basic principled objections to the emerging project could have taken the stump (as Luther Martin did after his exit) and denounced the convention to the skies. Yet Madison did not even inform Thomas Jefferson in Paris of the course of the deliberations and available correspondence indicates that the delegates generally observed the injunction. Secrecy is certainly uncharacteristic of any assembly marked by strong ideological polarization. This was noted at the time: the *New York Daily Advertiser*, August 14, 1787, commented that the " . . . profound secrecy hitherto observed by the Convention [we consider] a happy omen, as it demonstrates that the spirit of party on any great and essential point cannot have arisen to any height."

Commentators on the Constitution who have read *The Federalist* in lieu of reading the actual debates have credited the Fathers with the invention of a sublime concept called "Federalism." Unfortunately *The Federalist* is probative evidence for only one proposition: that Hamilton and Madison were inspired propagandists with a genius for retrospective symmetry. Federalism, as the theory is generally defined, was an improvisation which was later prompted into a political theory. Experts on "Federalism" should take to heart the advice of David Hume, who warned in his *Of the Rise and Progress of the Arts and Sciences* that ". . . there is no subject in which we must proceed with more caution than in [history], lest we assign causes which never existed and reduce what is merely contingent to stable and universal principles." In any event, the final balance in the Constitution between the states and the nation must have come as a great disappointment to Madison, while Hamilton's unitary views are too well known to need elucidation.

It is indeed astonishing how those who have glibly designated James Madison the "father" of Federalism have overlooked the solid body of fact which indicates that he shared Hamilton's quest for a unitary central government. To be specific, they have avoided examining the clear import of the Madison-Virginia Plan, and have disregarded Madison's dogged inch-by-inch retreat from the bastions of centralization. The Virginia Plan envisioned a unitary national government effectively freed from and dominant over the states. The lower house of the national legislature was to be elected directly by the people of the states with membership proportional to population. The upper house was to be selected by the lower and the two chambers would elect the executive and choose the judges. The national government would be thus cut completely loose from the states.

The structure of the general government was freed from state control in a truly radical fashion, but the scope of the authority of the national sovereign as Madison initially formulated it was breathtaking. . . . The national legislature was to be empowered to disallow the acts of state legislatures and the central government was vested in addition to the powers of the nation under the Articles of Confederation, with plenary authority wherever ". . . the separate States are incompetent or in which the harmony of the United States may be interrupted by the exercise of individual legislation." Finally, just to lock the door against state intrusion, the national Congress was to be given the power to use military force on recalcitrant states. This was Madison's "model" of an ideal national government, though it later received little publicity in *The Federalist*.

The interesting thing was the reaction of the Convention to this militant program for a strong autonomous central government. Some delegates were startled, some obviously leery of so comprehensive a project of reform, but nobody set off any fireworks and nobody walked out. Moreover, in the two weeks that followed, the Virginia Plan received substantial endorsement *en principe*; the initial temper of the gathering can be deduced from the approval "without debate or dissent," on May 31, of the Sixth Resolution which granted Congress the authority to disallow state legislation ". . . contravening *in its opinion* the Articles of Union." Indeed, an amendment was included to bar states from contravening national treaties.

The Virginia Plan may therefore be considered, in ideological terms, as the delegates' Utopia, but as the discussions continued and became more specific, many of those present began to have second thoughts. After all, they were not residents of Utopia or guardians in Plato's Republic who could simply impose a philosophical ideal on subordinate strata of the population. They were practical politicians in a democratic society, and no matter what their private dreams might be, they had to take home an acceptable package and defend it—and their own political futures—against predictable attack. On June 14 the breaking point between dream and reality took place. Apparently realizing that under the Virginia Plan, Massachusetts, Virginia and Pennsylvania could virtually dominate the national government—and probably appreciating that to sell this program to "the folks back home" would be impossible—the delegates from the small states dug in their heels and demanded time for a consideration of alternatives. One gets a graphic sense of the inner politics from John Dickinson's reproach to Madison: "You see the consequences of pushing things too far. Some of the members from the small States wish for two branches in the General Legislature and are friends to a good National Government; but we would sooner submit to a foreign power than . . . be deprived of an equality of suffrage in both branches of the Legislature, and thereby be thrown under the domination of the large States."

The bare outline of the *Journal* entry for Tuesday, June 14, is suggestive to anyone with extensive experience in deliberative bodies. "It was moved by Mr. Patterson [*sic*, Paterson's name was one of those consistently misspelled by Madison and everybody else] seconded by Mr. Randolph that the further consideration of the report from the Committee of the whole House [endorsing the Virginia Plan] be postponed til tomorrow, and before the question for postponement was taken. It was moved by Mr. Randolph seconded by Mr. Patterson that the House adjourn." The House adjourned by obvious prearrangement of the two principals:

since the preceding Saturday when Brearley and Paterson of New Jersey had announced their fundamental discontent with the representational features of the
Virginia Plan, the informal pressure had certainly been building up to slow down
the streamroller. Doubtless there were extended arguments at the Indian Queen
between Madison and Paterson, the latter insisting that events were moving
rapidly towards a probably disastrous conclusion, towards a political suicide pact.
Now the process of accommodation was put into action smoothly—and wisely,
given the character and strength of the doubters. Madison had the votes, but this
was one of those situations where the enforcement of mechanical majoritarianism
could easily have destroyed the objectives of the majority: the Constitutionalists
were in quest of a qualitatitve as well as a quantitative consensus. This was hardly
from deference to local Quaker custom; it was a political imperative if they were
to attain ratification.

[I]

According to the standard script, at this point the "states'-rights" group inter-
vened in force behind the New Jersey Plan, which has been characteristically por-
trayed as a reversion to the *status quo* under the Articles of Confederation with
but minor modifications. A careful examination of the evidence indicates that
only in a marginal sense is this an accurate description. It is true that the New Jersey Plan put the states back into the institutional picture, but one could argue that
to do so was a recognition of political reality rather than an affirmation of states'-
rights. A serious case can be made that the advocates of the New Jersey Plan, far
from being ideological addicts of states'-rights, intended to substitute for the Virginia Plan a system which would both retain strong national power and have a
chance of adoption in the states. The leading spokesman for the project asserted
quite clearly that his views were based more on counsels of expediency than on
principle; said Paterson on June 16: "I came here not to speak my own sentiments,
but the sentiments of those who sent me. Our object is not such a Governmt. as
may be best in itself, but such a one as our Constituents have authorized us to prepare, and as they will approve." This is Madison's version; in Yates' transcription,
there is a crucial sentence following the remarks above: "I believe that a little
practical virtue is to be preferred to the finest theoretical principles, which cannot
be carried into effect." In his preliminary speech on June 9, Paterson had stated
". . . to the public mind we must accommodate ourselves," and in his notes for this
and his later effort as well, the emphasis is the same. The *structure* of government
under the Articles should be retained:

2. Because it accords with the Sentiments of the People

   [Proof:] 1. Coms. [Commissions from state legislatures defining the jurisdiction of the
   delegates]
   2. News-papers—Political Barometer. Jersey never would have sent Delegates under the first [Virginia] Plan—

   Not here to sport Opinions of my own. Wt. [What] can be done. A little practicable
   Virtue preferable to Theory.

This was a defense of political acumen, not of states'-rights. In fact, Paterson's notes of his speech can easily be construed as an argument for attaining the substantive objectives of the Virginia Plan by a sound political route, *i.e.,* pouring the new wine in the old bottles. With a shrewd eye, Paterson queried:

> Will the Operation and Force of the [central] Govt. depend upon the mode of Representn.—No—it will depend upon the Quantum of Power lodged in the leg. ex. and judy. Departments—Give [the existing] Congress the same Powers that you intend to give the two Branches, [under the Virginia Plan] and I apprehend they will act with as much Propriety and more Energy . . .

In other words, the advocates of the New Jersey Plan concentrated their fire on what they held to be the *political liabilities* of the Virginia Plan—which were matters of institutional structure—rather than on the proposed scope of national authority. Indeed, the Supremacy Clause of the Constitution first saw the light of day in Paterson's Sixth Resolution; the New Jersey Plan contemplated the use of military force to secure compliance with national law; and finally Paterson made clear his view that under either the Virginia or the New Jersey systems, the general government would ". . . act on individuals and not on states." From the states'-rights viewpoint, this was heresy; the fundament of that doctrine was the proposition that any central government had as its constituents the states, not the people, and could only reach the people through the agency of the state government.

Paterson then reopened the agenda of the Convention, but he did so within a distinctly nationalist framework. Paterson's position was one of favoring a strong central government in principle, but opposing one which in fact *put the big states in the saddle.* (The Virginia Plan, for all its abstract merits, did very well by Virginia.) As evidence for this speculation, there is a curious and intriguing proposal among Paterson's preliminary drafts of the New Jersey Plan:

> Whereas it is necessary in Order to form the People of the U.S. of America in to a Nation, that the States should be consolidated, by which means all the Citizens thereof will become equally intitled to and will equally participate in the same Privileges and Rights . . . it is therefore resolved that all the Lands contained within the Limits of each state individually, and of the U.S. generally be considered as constituting one Body or Mass, and be divided into thirteen or more integral parts.
>
> Resolved, That such Divisions or integral Parts shall be styled Districts.

This makes it sound as though Paterson was prepared to accept a strong unified central government along the lines of the Virginia Plan if the existing states were eliminated. He may have gotten the idea from his New Jersey colleague Judge David Brearley, who on June 9 had commented that the only remedy to the dilemma over representation was ". . . that a map of the U.S. be spread out, that all the existing boundaries be erased, and that a new partition of the whole be made into 13 equal parts." According to Yates, Brearley added at this point, ". . . then a government on the present [Virginia Plan] system will be just."

This proposition was never pushed—it was patently unrealistic—but one can appreciate its purpose: it would have separated the men from the boys in the large-state delegations. How attached would the Virginians have been to their reform principles if Virginia were to disappear as a component geographical unit (the largest) for representational purposes? Up to this point, the Virginians had been in the happy position of supporting high ideals with that inner confidence born of knowledge that the "public interest" they endorsed would nourish their private interest. Worse, they had shown little willingness to compromise. Now the delegates from the small states announced that they were unprepared to be offered up as sacrificial victims to a "national interest" which reflected Virginia's parochial ambition. Caustic Charles Pinckney was not far off when he remarked sardonically that ". . . the whole [conflict] comes to this": "Give N. Jersey an equal vote, and she will dismiss her scruples, and concur in the Natil. system." What he rather unfairly did not add was that the Jersey delegates were not free agents who could adhere to their private convictions; they had to take back, sponsor and risk their reputations on the reforms approved by the Convention—and in New Jersey, not in Virginia.

Paterson spoke on Saturday, and one can surmise that over the weekend there was a good deal of consultation, argument, and caucusing among the delegates. One member at least prepared a full length address: on Monday Alexander Hamilton, previously mute, rose and delivered a six-hour oration. It was a remarkably apolitical speech; the gist of his position was that *both* the Virginia and New Jersey Plans were inadequately centralist, and he detailed a reform program which was reminiscent of the Protectorate under the Cromwellian *Instrument of Government* of 1653. It has been suggested that Hamilton did this in the best political tradition to emphasize the moderate character of the Virginia Plan, to give the cautious delegates something *really* to worry about; but this interpretation seems somehow too clever. Particularly since the sentiments Hamilton expressed happened to be completely consistent with those he privately—and sometimes publicly—expressed throughout his life. He wanted, to take a striking phrase from a letter to George Washington, a "strong well mounted government"; in essence, the Hamilton Plan contemplated an elected life monarch, virtually free of public control, on the Hobbesian ground that only in this fashion could strength and stability be achieved. The other alternatives, he argued, would put policymaking at the mercy of the passions of the mob; only if the sovereign was beyond the reach of selfish influence would it be possible to have government in the interests of the whole community.

From all accounts, this was a masterful and compelling speech, but (aside from furnishing John Lansing and Luther Martin with ammunition for later use against the Constitution) it made little impact. Hamilton was simply transmitting on a different wave-length from the rest of the delegates; the latter adjourned after his great effort, admired his rhetoric, and then returned to business. It was rather as if they had taken a day off to attend the opera. Hamilton, never a particularly patient man or much of a negotiator, stayed for another ten days and then left, in considerable disgust, for New York. Although he came back to Philadelphia sporadically and attended the last two weeks of the Convention, Hamilton played no part in the laborious task of hammering out the Constitution. His day came later when he led the New York Constitutionalists into the savage imbroglio over ratification—an arena in which his unmatched talent for dirty political infighting may well have won the day. For instance, in the New York Ratifying Convention,

Lansing threw back into Hamilton's teeth the sentiments the latter had expressed in his June 18 oration in the Convention. However, having since retreated to the fine defensive positions immortalized in *The Federalist*, the Colonel flatly denied that he had ever been an enemy of the states, or had believed that conflict between states and nation was inexorable! As Madison's authoritative *Notes* did not appear until 1840, and there had been no press coverage, there was no way to verify his assertions, so in the words of the reporter, ". . . a warm personal altercation between [Lansing and Hamilton] engrossed the remainder of the day [June 28, 1788]."

[II]

On Tuesday morning, June 19, the vacation was over. James Madison led off with a long, carefully reasoned speech analyzing the New Jersey Plan which, while intellectually vigorous in its criticisms, was quite conciliatory in mood. "The great difficulty," he observed, "lies in the affair of Representation; and if this could be adjusted, all others would be surmountable." (As events were to demonstrate, this diagnosis was correct.) When he finished, a vote was taken on whether to continue with the Virginia Plan as the nucleus for a new constitution: seven states voted "Yes"; New York, New Jersey, and Delaware voted "No"; and Maryland, whose position often depended on which delegates happened to be on the floor, divided. Paterson, it seems, lost decisively; yet in a fundamental sense he and his allies had achieved their purpose: from that day onward, it could never be forgotten that the state governments loomed ominously in the background and that no verbal incantations could exorcise their power. Moreover, nobody bolted the convention: Paterson and his colleagues took their defeat in stride and set to work to modify the Virginia Plan, particularly with respect to its provisions on representation in the national legislature. Indeed, they won an immediate rhetorical bonus; when Oliver Ellsworth of Connecticut rose to move that the word "national" be expunged from the Third Virginia Resolution ("Resolved that a *national* Government ought to be established consisting of a *supreme* Legislative, Executive and Judiciary"), Randolph agreed and the motion passed unanimously. The process of compromise had begun.

For the next two weeks, the delegates circled around the problem of legislative representation. The Connecticut delegation appears to have evolved a possible compromise quite early in the debates, but the Virginians and particularly Madison (unaware that he would later be acclaimed as the prophet of "federalism") fought obdurately against providing for equal representation of states in the second chamber. There was a good deal of acrimony and at one point Benjamin Franklin—of all people—proposed the institution of a daily prayer; practical politicians in the gathering, however, were mediating more on the merits of a good committee than on the utility of Divine intervention. On July 2, the ice began to break when through a number of fortuitous events—and one that seems deliberate—the majority against equality of representation was converted into a dead tie. The Convention had reached the stage where it was "ripe" for a solution (presumably all the therapeutic speeches had been made), and the South Carolinians proposed a committee. Madison and James Wilson wanted none of it, but with only Pennsylvania dissenting, the body voted to establish a working party on the problem of representation.

The members of this committee, one from each state, were elected by the delegates—and a very interesting committee it was. Despite the fact that the Virginia Plan had held majority support up to that date, neither Madison nor Randolph was selected (Mason was the Virginian) and Baldwin of Georgia, whose shift in position had resulted in the tie, was chosen. From the composition, it was clear that this was not to be a "fighting" committee: the emphasis in membership was on what might be described as "second-level political entrepreneurs." On the basis of the discussions up to that time, only Luther Martin of Maryland could be described as a "bitter-ender." Admittedly, some divination enters into this sort of analysis, but one does get a sense of the mood of the delegates from these choices—including the interesting selection of Benjamin Franklin, despite his age and intellectual wobbliness, over the brilliant and incisive Wilson or the sharp, polemical Gouverneur Morris, to represent Pennsylvania. His passion for conciliation was more valuable at this juncture than Wilson's logical genius, or Morris' acerbic wit.

There is a common rumor that the Framers divided their time between philosophical discussions of government and reading the classics in political theory. Perhaps this is as good a time as any to note that their concerns were highly practical, that they spent little time canvassing abstractions. A number of them had some acquaintance with the history of political theory (probably gained from reading John Adams' monumental compilation A Defense of the Constitutions of Government, the first volume of which appeared in 1786), and it was a poor rhetorician indeed who could not cite Locke, Montesquieu, or Harrington in support of a desired goal. Yet up to this point in the deliberations, no one had expounded a defense of states'-rights or the "separation of powers" on anything resembling a theoretical basis. It should be reiterated that the Madison model had no room either for the states or for the "separation of powers": effectively all governmental power was vested in the national legislature. The merits of Montesquieu did not turn up until The Federalist; and although a perverse argument could be made that Madison's ideal was truly in the tradition of John Locke's Second Treatise of Government, the Locke whom the American rebels treated as an honorary president was a pluralistic defender of vested rights, not of parliamentary supremacy.

It would be tedious to continue a blow-by-blow analysis of the work of the delegates; the critical fight was over representation of the states and once the Connecticut Compromise was adopted on July 17, the Convention was over the hump. Madison, James Wilson, and Gouverneur Morris of New York (who was there representing Pennsylvania!) fought the compromise all the way in a last-ditch effort to get a unitary state with parliamentary supremacy. But their allies deserted them and they demonstrated after their defeat the essentially opportunist character of their objections—using "opportunist" here in a non-pejorative sense, to indicate a willingness to swallow their objections and get on with the business. Moreover, once the compromise had carried (by five states to four, with one state divided), its advocates threw themselves vigorously into the job of strengthening the general government's substantive powers—as might have been predicted, indeed, from Paterson's early statements. It nourishes an increased respect for Madison's devotion to the art of politics, to realize that this dogged fighter could sit down six months later and prepare essays for *The Federalist* in contradiction to his basic convictions about the true course the Convention should have taken. . . .

[III]

Drawing on their vast collective political experience, utilizing every weapon in the politician's arsenal, looking constantly over their shoulders at their constituents, the delegates put together a Constitution. It was a makeshift affair; some sticky issues (for example, the qualification of voters) they ducked entirely; others they mastered with that ancient instrument of political sagacity, studied ambiguity (for example, citizenship), and some they just overlooked. In this last category, I suspect, fell the matter of the power of the federal courts to determine the constitutionality of acts of Congress. When the judicial article was formulated (Article III of the Constitution), deliberations were still in the stage where the legislature was endowed with broad power under the Randolph formulation, authority which by its own terms was scarcely amenable to judicial review. In essence, courts could hardly determine when ". . . the separate States are incompetent or . . . the harmony of the United States may be interrupted"; the National Legislature, as critics pointed out, was free to define its own jurisdiction. Later the definition of legislative authority was changed into the form we know, a series of stipulated powers, *but the delegates never seriously reexamined the jurisdiction of the judiciary under this new limited formulation.* All arguments on the intention of the Framers in this matter are thus deductive and *a posteriori*, though some obviously make more sense than others.

The Framers were busy and distinguished men, anxious to get back to their families, their positions, and their constituents, not members of the French Academy devoting a lifetime to a dictionary. They were trying to do an important job, and do it in such a fashion that their handiwork would be acceptable to very diverse constituencies. No one was rhapsodic about the final document, but it was a beginning, a move in the right direction, and one they had reason to believe the people would endorse. In addition, since they had modified the impossible amendment provisions of the Articles (the requirement of unanimity which could always be frustrated by "Rogues Island") to one demanding approval by only three-quarters of the states, they seemed confident that gaps in the fabric which experience would reveal could be rewoven without undue difficulty. . . . ■

Chapter 2

Federalism

The idea of dividing political power between a central government and its component parts while preserving both elements was one of the great innovations of American political thought. In the eighteenth century, the accepted wisdom was that sovereignty—that is, the ultimate political power in a community—could not be divided. In a confederation, either the states would have to retain sovereignty, authorizing the national government to take on only certain specific tasks with the approval of all the states, or the states would lose their power and identity and be swallowed up into one great whole. There was, according to this line of thought, no middle ground.

Throughout the constitutional debate of the 1780s, the Antifederalists clung to this traditional point of view. The Articles of Confederation, after all, were just that: a confederation of fully sovereign states that came together in a league, much like a modern alliance, for certain limited purposes. The Articles began, in fact, "We the . . . Delegates of the States." The Antifederalists conceded that the Articles needed modification, but they resisted attempts to strengthen the national government too much, fearing that it would become a threat to the sovereignty of the states.

The Federalists' great innovation was the creation of a new conception of federalism. Under this theory, ultimate sovereignty rested in the people; they delegated some of their sovereignty to the national government, some to the states, and retained some for themselves. Within their respective spheres of authority, both the states and the national government were supreme.

The Antifederalists' charge that such a system could not work was dismissed out of hand by the Federalists. Nevertheless, in the more than two hundred years since the ratification of the Constitution, power has definitely shifted from the states to the national government. This shift of power began in the early days of the Republic, when Congress claimed broad powers to regulate commerce and encourage economic expansion. It accelerated in the late 1800s and early 1900s, as the national government expanded its regulation of railroads and other national industries, established a national banking system, and began to enforce the provisions of the Bill of Rights against the states. But the most dramatic expansion of national power came during and after the New Deal of the 1930s, when Washington took on a wide range of new responsibilities in regulating the national economy. After a brief effort to block these programs on constitutional grounds, the Supreme Court reversed itself, upholding New Deal programs across the board. By the 1960s, the Court's decisions led many scholars to conclude that there were no real constitutional limitations on the powers of the national government.

The 1960s and 1970s also saw a dramatic increase in the amount and scope of federal grants to the states. Along with federal money came increased federal influence on the states. Federal highway money, for example, was conditioned on the states' compliance with a national speed limit and a 21-year-old drinking age. In general, the Supreme Court upheld these indirect applications of national power.

By the 1970s and 1980s, however, critics of national power began to score points with their efforts to restrain the role of the national government and return power to the states. Supporters of this "new federalism" urged the national government to give the states money with few or no strings attached; to refrain from "unfunded mandates," which impose costly requirements on the states without reimbursement; and, in general, to scale back the breadth and scope of its regulatory activities. These efforts to shift the long-term balance of power away from Washington took on new momentum after the Republican party gained control of Congress in the 1990s. Moreover, in recent years the Supreme Court has shown a new willingness to police the boundaries of national and state power, and to impose new restraints on the national government.

Throughout the centuries, a major player in the struggle between the national government and the states has been the U.S. Supreme Court. Early on, the Court made a series of critical decisions—the most important of which was *McCulloch v. Maryland* (1819)—establishing itself as the key arbiter between the national government and the states and laying the foundation for a broad expansion of national power. Since at least the 1950s, the Court has been a key actor in applying to the states national standards on civil rights and civil liberties. Given that the Court is and always has been a component part of the national government, is it any surprise that the national government seems to have emerged triumphant from its power struggles with the states?

Chapter Questions

1. What is the meaning of "dual federalism"? How does the theory of dual federalism differ from traditional understandings of the nature of sovereignty?
2. How does federalism in practice differ from federalism in theory? Is there a difference between the national government's theoretical power over the states and the relationship, in practice, between the national government and the states?
3. What are the advantages and disadvantages of a federal system of government?

# Foundations

One of the key differences of opinion between the Federalists and the Antifederalists, as their names imply was over the question of federalism. The Antifederalists, as the political scientist Herbert Storing explains in selection 2.1, objected to the Constitution above all because they feared that it would concentrate power in the national government at the expense of the states. Rather than throw away the Articles of Confederation and starting over with the Constitution, the Antifederalists advocated merely modifying and updating the Articles, leaving sovereignty in the states. The Federalists, by contrast, viewed the weakness of the national government as the principal problem with the Articles of Confederation, and urged that its powers and responsibilities be significantly expanded.

In *The Federalist* Nos. 39 and 45, James Madison (author of the *Federalist Papers* with John Jay and Alexander Hamilton), makes general arguments in favor of the new system of government. In No. 39, he defends the Constitution against charges that it would be anti-Republican and that it would allow the states to be swallowed up by the national government. In No. 45, he again makes the argument that the national government will never threaten the sovereignty or authority of the states. Just beneath the surface, however, Madison's tilt toward a strong national government becomes clear. All prior confederacies have perished because the central government was too weak, he writes in No. 45; moreover, "as far as the sovereignty of the States cannot be reconciled to the happiness of the people," he declares, "Let the former be sacrificed to the latter."

Madison's argument that the "powers delegated by the proposed Constitution to the federal government are few and defined," while "those which are to remain in the State governments are numerous and indefinite" is still formally true. All actions of the national government must be justified with reference to a specific provision of the Constitution granting that power (see the Constitution, Article I, section 8). By contrast, the states possess broadly defined "police" powers—that is, powers to regulate the public health, safety, welfare, and morals.

The powers of the national government may be limited in theory, but in practice the Supreme Court has interpreted the Constitution's grants of power in broad terms. The key case was *McCulloch v. Maryland* (1819), which held that the Constitution gave Congress sweeping powers and broad discretion to choose how to carry out those powers. Although on occasion the Court has deviated from this principle, in general it has followed the logic of *McCulloch* and refused to interfere with congressional attempts to assert national authority.

Thus Madison's argument in *Federalist* No. 45 that "the State governments will have the advantage of the federal government . . . [in] the disposition and faculty of resisting and frustrating the measures of the other" has been disproved by history. Certainly since the Civil War, there has been no successful threat to federal supremacy. In any event, Madison's emphasis in No. 45 on the importance of a strong national government makes one wonder whether the argument was made seriously in the first place.

Although the Antifederalists lost the debate over the Constitution, it would be unfair to dismiss their views as narrow-minded, unsophisticated, or incorrect. As you read the selections in this section, remember that the Antifederalists were not merely "against" the Constitution; like the Federalists, they had strong beliefs and political principles and a coherent way of looking at politics.

Questions

1. How did the Antifederalists define federalism?
2. What did they view as the major threat posed by the new "federalism" of the U.S. Constitution?

3. What are the reasons Madison gives for his argument that the states will be able to resist the encroachments of the national government—just as the members of earlier confederations were able to do so? How does the Court's decision in *McCulloch* affect this argument?
4. Why do you think that threats to the supremacy of the federal government have been unsuccessful?

2.1 What the Antifederalists Were For (1981)

Herbert Storing

Far from straying from the principles of the American Revolution, as some of the Federalists accused them of doing, the Anti-Federalists saw themselves as the true defenders of those principles. "I am fearful," said Patrick Henry, "I have lived long enough to become an old fashioned fellow: Perhaps an invincible attachment to the dearest rights of man, may, in these refined enlightened days, be deemed *old fashioned*: If so, I am contented to be so: I say, the time has been, when every pore of my heart beat for American liberty, and which, I believe, had a counterpart in the breast of every true American." The Anti-Federalists argued, as some historians have argued since, that the Articles of Confederation were the constitutional embodiment of the principles on which the Revolution was based:

> Sir, I venerate the spirit with which every thing was done at the trying time in which the Confederation was formed. America had then a sufficiency of this virtue to resolve to resist perhaps the first nation in the universe, even unto bloodshed. What was her aim? Equal liberty and safety. What ideas had she of this equal liberty? Read them in her Articles of Confederation.

The innovators were impatient to change this "most excellent constitution," which was "sent like a blessing from heaven," for a constitution "essentially differing from the principles of the revolution, and from freedom," and thus destructive of the whole basis of the American community. "Instead of repairing the old and venerable fabrick, which sheltered the United States, from the dreadful and cruel storms of a tyrannical British ministry, they built a stately palace after their own fancies. . . ."

The principal characteristic of that "venerable fabrick" was its federalism: the Articles of Confederation established a league of sovereign and independent states whose representatives met in congress to deal with a limited range of common concerns in a system that relied heavily on voluntary cooperation. Federalism means that the states are primary, that they are equal, and that they possess

---

Herbert Storing, *What The Antifederalists Were For* (Chicago: University of Chicago Press, 1981), pp. 9–14. Reprinted with permission of The University of Chicago Press.

the main weight of political power. The defense of the federal character of the American union was the most prominent article of Anti-Federalist conservative doctrine. While some of the other concerns were intrinsically more fundamental, the question of federalism was central and thus merits fuller discussion here, as it did in that debate.

To begin with an apparently small terminological problem, if the Constitution was opposed because it was anti-federal how did the opponents come to be called Anti-Federalists? They usually denied, in fact, that the name was either apt or just, and seldom used it themselves. They were, they often claimed, the true federalists. Some of them seemed to think that their proper name had been filched, while their backs were turned, as it were, by the pro-Constitution party, which refused to give it back; and versions of this explanation have been repeated by historians. Unquestionably the Federalists saw the advantage of a label that would suggest that those who opposed the Constitution also opposed such a manifestly good thing as federalism. But what has not been sufficiently understood is that the term "federal" had acquired a specific ambiguity that enabled the Federalists not merely to take but to keep the name.

One of the perennial issues under the Articles of Confederation involved the degree to which the general government—or the instrumentality of the federation per se—was to be supported or its capacity to act strengthened. In this context one was "federal" or "anti-federal" according to his willingness or unwillingness to strengthen or support the institutions of the federation. This was James Wilson's meaning when he spoke of the "fœderal disposition and character" of Pennsylvania. It was Patrick Henry's meaning when he said that, in rejecting the Constitution, New Hampshire and Rhode Island "have refused to become federal." It was the meaning of the New York Assembly when in responding coolly to the recommendations of the Annapolis Convention it nevertheless insisted on its "truly federal" disposition. This usage had thoroughly penetrated political discussion in the United States. In the straightforward explanation of Anti-Federalist George Bryan, "The name of Federalists, or Federal men, grew up at New York and in the eastern states, some time before the calling of the Convention, to denominate such as were attached to the general support of the United States, in opposition to those who preferred local and particular advantages. . . ." Later, according to Bryan, "this name was taken possession of by those who were in favor of the new federal government, as they called it, and opposers were called Anti-Federalists." Recognizing the pre-1787 usage, Jackson Turner Main tries, like Bryan, to preserve the spirit of Federalist larceny by suggesting that during the several years before 1787 "the men who wanted a strong national government, who might more properly be called 'nationalists,' began to appropriate the term 'federal' for themselves" and to apply the term "antifederal" to those hostile to the measures of Congress and thus presumably unpatriotic. But there was nothing exceptional or improper in the use of the term "federal" in this way; the shift in meaning was less an "appropriation" than a natural extension of the language, which the Federalists fully exploited.

The point of substance is that the Federalists had a legitimate *claim* to their name and therefore to their name for their opponents. Whether they had a better claim than their opponents cannot be answered on the basis of mere linguistic usage but only by considering the arguments. When, during the years of the Confederation, one was called a "federal man," his attachment to the principles of federalism was not at issue; that was taken for granted, and the point was that he was a man who (given this federal system) favored strengthening the "federal" or general authority. The ambiguity arose because strengthening the federal *authority* could be carried so far as to undermine the federal *principle;* and that was precisely what the Anti-Federalists claimed their opponents were doing. Thus The Impartial Examiner argued that, despite the "sound of names" on which the advocates of the Constitution "build their fame," it is the opponents who act "on the broader scale of true *fœderal principles.*" They desire "a continuance of each distinct sovereignty—and are anxious for such a degree of energy in the general government, as will cement the union in the strongest manner." It was possible (or so the Anti-Federalists believed) to be a federalist in the sense of favoring a strong agency of the federation and, at the same time, to be a federalist in the sense of adhering to the principle of league of independent states. In the name of federalism in the former sense, it was claimed, the proponents of the Constitution had abandoned federalism in the latter (and fundamental) sense.

The Anti-Federalists stood, then, for federalism in opposition to what they called the consolidating tendency and intention of the Constitution—the tendency to establish one complete national government, which would destroy or undermine the states. They feared the implications of language like Washington's reference, in transmitting the Constitution to Congress, to the need for "the consolidation of our Union." They saw ominous intentions in Publius' opinion that "a NATION, without a NATIONAL GOVERNMENT, is, in my view, an awful spectacle." They resented and denied suggestions that "we must forget our local habits and attachments" and "be reduced to one faith and one government." They saw in the new Constitution a government with authority extending "to every case that is of the least importance" and capable of acting (preeminently in the crucial case of taxation) at discretion and independently of any agency but its own. Instead of thus destroying the federal character of the Union, "the leading feature of every amendment" of the Articles of Confederation ought to be, as Yates and Lansing expressed it, "the preservation of the individual states, in their uncontrouled constitutional rights, and . . . in reserving these, a mode might have been devised of granting to the confederacy, the monies arising from a general system of revenue; the power of regulating commerce, and enforcing the observance of foreign treaties, and other necessary matters of less moment."

A few of the Anti-Federalists were not sure, it is true, that consolidation would be so bad, if it were really feasible. James Monroe went so far as to say that "to collect the citizens of America, who have fought and bled together, by whose joint and common efforts they have been raised to the comparatively happy and exalted theatre on which they now stand; to lay aside all those jarring interests and discordant principles, which state legislatures if they do not create, certainly foment and increase, arrange them under one government and make them one people, is an idea not only elevated and sublime, but equally benevolent and humane." And, on the other hand, most of the Federalists agreed or professed to agree that consolidation was undesirable. Fisher Ames, defending the Constitution in Massachusetts, spoke the language of many Federalists when he insisted that "too much provision cannot be made against a consolidation. The state governments represent the wishes, and feelings, and local interests of the people. They are the safeguard and ornament of the Constitution; they will protract the period of our liberties; they will afford a shelter against the abuse of power, and will be the natural avengers of our violated rights." Indeed, expressions of rather strict federal principles were not uncommon on the Federalist side, although they were often perfunctory or shallow.

Perhaps the most conciliatory Federalist defense of federalism, and not accidentally one of the least satisfactory in principle, was contained in a line of argument put forward by James Wilson and some others to the effect that, just as individuals have to give up some of their natural rights to civil government to secure peaceful enjoyment of civil rights, so states must give up some of theirs to federal government in order to secure peaceful enjoyment of federal liberties. But the analogy of civil liberty and federal liberty concedes the basic Anti-Federal contentions, and Wilson did not consistently adhere to it. As each individual has one vote in civil society, for example, so each state ought, on this analogy, to have one vote in federal society. As the preservation of the rights of individuals is the object of civil society, so the preservation of the rights of states (not individuals) ought to be the object of federal society. But these are Anti-Federal conclusions. Thus, when Agrippa assessed the proposed Constitution from the point of view of the interests of Massachusetts, he did so on *principled* ground, the same ground that properly leads any man to consider the civil society of which he is or may become a member, not exclusively but first and last, from the point of view of his interest in his life, liberty, and property. Wilson, on the other hand, argued for the priority of the general interest of the Union over the particular interests of the states. And this position is not defensible—as Wilson's own argument sufficiently demonstrates—on the basis of the federal liberty–civil liberty analogy.

The more characteristic Federalist position was to deny that the choice lay between confederation and consolidation and to contend that in fact the Constitution provided a new form, partly national and partly federal. This was Publius' argument in *The Federalist*, no. 39. It was Madison's argument in the Virginia ratifying convention. And it was the usual argument of James Wilson himself, who emphasized the strictly limited powers of the general government and the essential part to be played in it by the states. The Anti-Federalists objected that all such arguments foundered on the impossibility of dual sovereignty. "It is a solecism in politics for two coordinate sovereignties to exist together. . . ." A mixture may exist for a time, but it will inevitably tend in one direction or the other, subjecting the country in the meantime to "all the horrors of a divided sovereignty." Luther Martin agreed with Madison that the new Constitution presented a novel mixture of federal and national elements; but he found it "just so much federal in appearance as to give its advocates in some measure, an opportunity of passing it as such upon the unsuspecting multitude, before they had time and opportunity to examine it, and yet so predominantly national as to put it in the power of its movers, whenever the machine shall be set agoing, to strike out every part that has the appearance of being federal, and to render it wholly and entirely a national government."

The first words of the preamble sufficiently declare the anti-federal (in the strict sense) character of the Constitution, Patrick Henry thought; and his objection thundered over the Virginia convention sitting in Richmond:

> [W]hat right had they to say, *We the People?* My political curiosity, exclusive of my anxious solicitude for the public welfare, leads me to ask, who authorised them to speak the language of, *We, the People,* instead of *We, the States?* States are the characteristics, and the soul of a confederation. If the States be not the agents of this compact, it must be one great consolidated National Government of the people of all the States.

The clearest minds among the Federalists agreed that states are the soul of a confederacy. That is what is wrong with confederacies: "The fundamental principle of the old Confederation is defective; we must totally eradicate and discard this principle before we can expect an efficient government."

Here lies the main significance of the mode of ratification in the proposed Constitution. The new procedure—ratification by special state conventions rather than by Congress and the state legislatures and provision that the Constitution shall be established on ratification of nine states (as between them), rather than all thirteen states as required under the Articles of Confederation—was not merely illegal; it struck at the heart of the old Confederation. It denied, as Federalists like Hamilton openly admitted, the very basis of legality under the Articles of Confederation. The requirement in the Articles of Confederation for unanimous consent of the states to constitutional changes rested on the assumption that the states are the basic political entities, permanently associated indeed, but associated entirely at the will and in the interest of each of the several states. Even if it were granted that government under the Articles had collapsed (which most Anti-Federalists did not grant), there was no justification for abandoning the principles of state equality and unanimous consent to fundamental constitutional change. As William Paterson had put it in the Philadelphia Convention,

> If we argue the matter on the supposition that no Confederacy at present exists, it cannot be denied that all the States stand on the footing of equal sovereignty. All therefore must concur before any can be bound. . . . If we argue on the fact that a federal compact actually exists, and consult the articles of it we still find an equal Sovereignty to be the basis of it.

Whether in the Articles of Confederation or outside, the essential principle of American union was the equality of the states. As Luther Martin had argued in Philadelphia, "the separation from G. B. placed the 13 States in a state of nature towards each other; [and] they would have remained in that state till this time, but for the confederation. . . ."

The provision for ratifying the Constitution rested, in the main, on the contrary assumption that the American states are not several political wholes, associated together according to their several wills and for the sake of their several interests, but are, and always were from the moment of their separation from the King of England, parts of one whole. Thus constitutional change is the business of the people, not of the state legislatures, though the people act in (or through) their states. As one nation divided into several states, moreover, constitutional change is to be decided, not by unanimous consent of separate and equal entities, but by the major part of a single whole—an extraordinary majority because of the importance of the question. The Federalists contended that the colonies declared their independence not individually but unitedly, and that they had never been independent of one another. And the implication of this view is that the foundation of government in the United States is the interest of the nation and not the interests of the states. "The Union is essential to our being as a nation. The pillars that prop it are crumbling to powder," said Fisher Ames, staggering through a metaphorical forest. "The Union is the vital sap that nourishes the tree." The Articles of Confederation, in this view, were a defective instrument of a preexisting union. The congressional resolution calling for the Philadelphia Convention had described a means—"for the sole and express purpose of revising the Articles of Confederation"—and an end—to "render the federal constitution adequate to the exigencies of Government & the preservation of the Union." If there was any conflict, the means ought to be sacrificed to the end. The duty of the Philadelphia Convention and the members of the ratifying conventions was to take their bearings, not from the defective means, but from the great end, the preservation and well-being of the Union. ■

2.2 *Federalist* No. 39 (1788)

James Madison

Outline

  I. The nature of republican government and whether the Constitution is truly republican in form and substance.

 II. Whether the government of the United States is *federal* or *national* in character, or a combination of the two.

    A. The establishment of the Union.

    B. The establishment of the institutions of the United States government.

    C. The operation of the government.

    D. The scope of the government's powers.

    E. The process of amending the Constitution.

III. Conclusion: the mixed nature of the United States government as partly federal, partly national.

• • •

The first question that offers itself is whether the general form and aspect of the government be strictly republican. It is evident that no other form would be reconcilable with the genius of the people of America; with the fundamental principles of the Revolution; or with that honorable determination which animates every votary of freedom to rest all our political experiments on the capacity of mankind for self-government. If the plan of the convention, therefore, be found to depart from the republican character, its advocates must abandon it as no longer defensible.

What, then, are the distinctive characters of the republican form? Were an answer to this question to be sought, not by recurring to principles but in the application of the term by political writers to the constitutions of different States, no satisfactory one would ever be found. Holland, in which no particle of the supreme authority is derived from the people, has passed almost universally under the denomination of a republic. The same title has been bestowed on Venice, where absolute power over the great body of the people is exercised in the most absolute manner by a small body of hereditary nobles. Poland, which is a mixture of aristocracy and of monarchy in their worst forms, has been dignified with the same appellation. The government of England, which has one republican branch only, combined with an hereditary aristocracy and monarchy, has with equal impropriety been frequently placed on the list of republics. These examples, which are nearly as dissimilar to each other as to a genuine republic, show the extreme inaccuracy with which the term has been used in political disquisitions.

If we resort for a criterion to the different principles on which different forms of government are established, we may define a republic to be, or at least may bestow that name on, a government which derives all its powers directly or indirectly from the great body of the people, and is administered by persons holding their offices during pleasure for a limited period, or during good behavior. It is *essential* to such a government that it be derived from the great body of the society, not from an inconsiderable proportion or a favored class of it; otherwise a handful of tyrannical nobles, exercising their oppressions by a delegation of their powers, might aspire to the rank of republicans and claim for their government the honorable title of republic. It is *sufficient* for such a government that the persons administering it be appointed, either directly or indirectly, by the people; and that they hold their appointments by either of the tenures just specified; otherwise every government in the United States, as well as every other popular government that has been or can be well organized or well executed, would be degraded from the republican character. According to the constitution of every State in the Union, some or other of the officers of government are appointed indirectly only by the people. According to most of them, the chief magistrate himself is so appointed. And according to one, this mode of appointment is extended to one of the coordinate branches of the legislature. According to all the constitutions, also, the tenure of the highest offices is extended to a definite period, and in many instances, both within the legislative and executive departments, to a period of years. According to the provisions of most of the constitutions, again, as well as according to the most respectable and received opinions on the subject, the members of the judiciary department are to retain their offices by the firm tenure of good behavior.

On comparing the Constitution planned by the convention with the standard here fixed, we perceived at once that it is, in the most rigid sense, conformable to it. The House of Representatives, like that of one branch at least of all the State legislatures, is elected immediately by the great body of the people. The Senate, like the present Congress and the Senate of Maryland, derives its appointment indirectly from the people. The President is indirectly derived from the choice of the people, according to the example in most of the States. Even the judges, with all other officers of the Union, will, as in the several States, be the choice, though a remote choice, of the people themselves. The duration of the appointments is equally conformable to the republican standard and to the model of State constitutions. The House of Representatives is periodically elective, as in all the States; and for the period of two years, as in the State of South Carolina. The Senate is elective for the period of six years, which is but one year more than the period of the Senate of Maryland, and but two more than that of the Senates of New York and Virginia. The President is to continue in office for the period of four years; as in New York and Delaware the chief magistrate is elected for three years, and in South Carolina for two years. In the other States the election is annual. In several of the States, however, no explicit provision is made for the impeachment of the chief magistrate. And in Delaware and Virginia he is not impeachable till out of office. The President of the United States is impeachable at any time during his continuance in office. The tenure by which the judges are to hold their places is, as it unquestionably ought to be, that of good behavior. The tenure of the ministerial offices generally will be a subject of legal regulation, conformably to the reason of the case and the example of the State constitutions.

Could any further proof be required of the republican complexion of this system, the most decisive one might be found in its absolute prohibition of titles of nobility, both under the federal and the State governments; and in its express guaranty of the republican form to each of the latter.

"But it was not sufficient," say the adversaries of the proposed Constitution, "for the convention to adhere to the republican form. They ought with equal care to have preserved the *federal* form, which regards the Union as a *Confederacy* of sovereign states; instead of which they have flamed a *national* government, which regards the Union as a *consolidation* of the States." And it is asked by what authority this bold and radical innovation was undertaken? The handle which has been made of this objection requires that it should be examined with some precision.

Without inquiring into the accuracy of the distinction on which the objection is founded, it will be necessary to a just estimate of its force, first, to ascertain the real character of the government in question; secondly, to inquire how far the convention were authorized to propose such a government; and thirdly, how far the duty they owed to their country could supply any defect of regular authority.

First.—In order to ascertain the real character of the government, it may be considered in relation to the foundation on which it is to be established; to the sources from which its ordinary powers are to be drawn; to the operation of those powers; to the extent of them; and to the authority by which future changes in the government are to be introduced.

On examining the first relation, it appears, on one hand, that the Constitution is to be founded on the assent and ratification of the people of America, given by deputies elected for the special purpose; but, on the other, that this assent and ratification is to be given by the people, not as individuals composing one entire nation, but as composing the distinct and independent States to which they respectively belong. It is to be the assent and ratification of the several States, derived from the supreme authority in each State—the authority of the people themselves. The act, therefore, establishing the Constitution will not be a *national* but a *federal* act.

That it will be a federal and not a national act, as these terms are understood by the objectors—the act of the people, as forming so many independent States, not as forming one aggregate nation—is obvious from this single consideration: that it is to result neither from the decision of a *majority* of the people of the Union, nor from that of a *majority* of the States. It must result from the *unanimous* assent of the several States that are parties to it differing no otherwise from their ordinary assent than in its being expressed, not by the legislative authority, but by that of the people themselves. Were the people regarded in this transaction as forming one nation, the will of the majority of the whole people of the United States would bind the minority, in the same manner as the majority in each State must bind the minority; and the will of the majority must be determined either by a comparison of the individual votes, or by considering the will of the majority of the States as evidence of the will of a majority of the people of the United States. Neither of these rules has been adopted. Each State, in ratifying the Constitution, is considered as a sovereign body independent of all others, and only to be bound by its own voluntary act. In this relation, then, the new Constitution will, if established, be a *federal* and not a *national* constitution.

The next relation is to the sources from which the ordinary powers of government are to be derived. The House of Representatives will derive its powers from the people of America; and the people will be represented in the same proportion and on the same principle as they are in the legislature of a particular State. So far the government is *national*, not *federal*. The Senate, on the other hand, will derive its powers from the States as political and coequal societies; and these will be represented on the principle of equality in the Senate, as they now are in the existing Congress. So far the government is *federal*, not *national*. The executive power will be derived from a very compound source. The immediate election of the President is to be made by the States in their political characters. The votes allotted to them are in a compound ratio, which considers them partly as distinct and coequal societies, partly as unequal members of the same society. The eventual election, again, is to be made by that branch of the legislature which consists of the national representatives; but in this particular act they are to be thrown into the form of individual delegations from so many distinct and coequal bodies politic. From this aspect of the government it appears to be of a mixed character, presenting at least as many *federal* as *national* features.

The difference between a federal and national government, as it relates to the *operation of the government*, is by the adversaries of the plan of the convention supposed to consist in this, that in the former the powers operate on the political bodies composing the Confederacy in their political capacities; in the latter, on the individual citizens composing the nation in their individual capacities. On trying the Constitution by this criterion, it fails under the *national* not the *federal* character; though perhaps not so completely as has been understood. In several cases, and particularly in the trial of controversies to which States may be parties, they must be viewed and proceeded against in their collective and political capacities only. But the operation of the government on the people in their individual capacities, in its ordinary and most essential proceedings, will, in the sense of its opponents, on the whole, designate it, in this relation, a *national* government.

But if the government be national with regard to the *operation* of its powers, it changes its aspect again when we contemplate it in relation to the extent of its powers. The idea of a national government involves in it not only an authority over the individual citizens, but an indefinite supremacy over all persons and things, so far as they are objects of lawful government. Among a people consolidated into one nation, this supremacy is completely vested in the national legislature. Among communities united for particular purposes, it is vested partly in the general and partly in the municipal legislatures. In the former case, all local authorities are subordinate to the supreme; and may be controlled, directed, or abolished by it at pleasure. In the latter, the local or municipal authorities form distinct and independent portions of the supremacy, no more subject, within their respective spheres, to the general authority than the general authority is subject to them, within its own sphere. In this relation, then, the proposed government cannot be deemed a *national* one; since its jurisdiction extends to certain enumerated objects only, and leaves to the several States a residuary and inviolable sovereignty over all other objects. It is true that in controversies relating to the boundary between the two jurisdictions, the tribunal which is ultimately to decide is to be established under the general government. But this does not change the principle of the case. The decision is to be impartially made, according to the rules of the Constitution; and all the usual and most effectual precautions are taken to secure this impartiality. Some such tribunal is clearly essential to prevent an appeal to the sword and a dissolution of the compact; and that it ought to be established under the general rather than under the local governments, or, to speak more properly, that it could be safely established under the first alone, is a position not likely to be combated.

If we try the Constitution by its last relation to the authority by which amendments are to be made, we find it neither wholly *national* nor wholly *federal*. Were it wholly national, the supreme and ultimate authority would reside in the *majority* of the people of the Union; and this authority would be competent at all times, like that of a majority of every national society to alter or abolish its established government. Were it wholly federal, on the other hand, the concurrence of each State in the Union would be essential to every alteration that would be binding on all. The mode provided by the plan of the convention is not founded on either of these principles. In requiring more than a majority, and particularly in computing the proportion by *States*, not by *citizens*, it departs from the national and advances towards the *federal* character; in rendering the concurrence of less than the whole number of States sufficient, it loses again the federal and partakes of the *national* character.

The proposed Constitution, therefore, even when tested by the rules laid down by its antagonists, is, in strictness, neither a national nor a federal Constitution, but a composition of both. In its foundation it is federal, not national; in the sources from which the ordinary powers of the government are drawn, it is partly federal and partly national; in the operation of these powers, it is national, not federal; in the extent of them, again, it is federal, not national; and, finally in the authoritative mode of introducing amendments, it is neither wholly federal nor wholly national. ∎

2.3 *Federalist* No. 45 (1788)

James Madison

Outline

  I. Importance of increasing the powers of the national government at the expense of the states.

 II. Historical weakness of central governments in confederacies.

    A. Ancient times.

    B. Feudal times.

III. Advantages of the states in their relations with the national government.

    A. States as constituent and essential parts of the national government.

    B. Relatively small size of the national government.

    C. Few and defined powers of the national government.

    D. Advantages of the states in times of peace.

IV. Conclusion: Constitution as invigorating the powers of the national government more than it adds to them.

• • •

The adversaries to the plan of the convention, instead of considering in the first place what degree of power was absolutely necessary for the purposes of the federal government, have exhausted themselves in a secondary inquiry into the possible consequences of the proposed degree of power to the governments of the particular States. But if the Union, as has been shown, be essential to the security of the people of America against foreign danger; if it be essential to their security against contentions and wars among the different States; if it be essential to guard them against those violent and oppressive factions which embitter the blessings of liberty and against those military establishments which must gradually poison its very fountain; if, in a word, the Union be essential to the happiness of the people of America, is it not preposterous to urge as an objection to a government, without which the objects of the Union cannot be attained, that such a government may derogate from the importance of the governments of the individual States? Was, then, the American Revolution effected, was the American Confederacy formed, was the precious blood of thousands spilt, and the hard-earned substance of millions lavished, not that the people of America should enjoy peace, liberty, and safety, but that the governments of the individual States, that particular municipal establishments, might enjoy a certain extent of power and be arrayed with certain dignities and attributes of sovereignty? We have heard of the impious doctrine in the old world, that the people were made for kings, not kings for the people. Is the same doctrine to be revived in the new, in another shape—that the solid happiness of the people is to be sacrificed to the views of political institutions of a different form? It is too early for politicians to presume on our forgetting that the public good, the real welfare of the great body of the people, is the supreme object to be pursued; and that no form of government whatever has any other value than as it may be fitted for the attainment of this object. Were the plan of the convention adverse to the public happiness, my voice would be, Reject the plan. Were the Union itself inconsistent with the public happiness, it would be, Abolish the Union. In like manner, as far as the sovereignty of the States cannot be reconciled to the happiness of the people, the voice of every good citizen must be, Let the former be sacrificed to the latter. How far the sacrifice is necessary has been shown. How far the unsacrificed residue will be endangered is the question before us.

Several important considerations have been touched in the course of these papers, which discountenance the supposition that the operation of the federal government will by degrees prove fatal to the State governments. The more I revolve the subject, the more fully I am persuaded that the balance is much more likely to be disturbed by the preponderancy of the last than of the first scale.

We have seen, in all the examples of ancient and modern confederacies, the strongest tendency continually betraying itself in the members to despoil the general government of its authorities, with a very ineffectual capacity in the latter to defend itself against the encroachments. Although, in most of these examples, the system has been so dissimilar from that under consideration as greatly to weaken any inference concerning the latter from the fate of the former, yet, as the States will retain under the proposed Constitution a very extensive portion of active sovereignty, the inference ought not to be wholly disregarded. In the [ancient] Achæan league it is probable that the federal head had a degree and species of power which gave it a considerable likeness to the government framed by the convention. The Lycian Confederacy, as far as its principles and form are transmitted, must have borne a still greater analogy to it. Yet history does not inform us that either of them ever degenerated, or tended to degenerate, into one consolidated government. On the contrary, we know that the ruin of one of them proceeded from the incapacity of the federal authority to prevent the dissensions, and finally the disunion, of the subordinate authorities. These cases are the more worthy of our attention as the external causes by which the component parts were pressed together were much more numerous and powerful than in our case; and consequently less powerful ligaments within would be sufficient to bind the members to the head and to each other.

In the feudal system, we have seen a similar propensity exemplified. Notwithstanding the want of proper sympathy in every instance between the local sovereigns and the people, and the sympathy in some instances between the general sovereign and the latter, it usually happened that the local sovereigns prevailed in the rivalship for encroachments. Had no external dangers enforced internal harmony and subordination, and particularly, had the local sovereigns possessed the affections of the people, the great kingdoms in Europe would at this time consist of as many independent princes as there were formerly feudatory barons.

The State governments will have the advantage of the federal government, whether we compare them in respect to the immediate dependence of the one on the other; to the weight of personal influence which each side will possess; to the powers respectively vested in them; to the predilection and probable support of the people; to the disposition and faculty of resisting and frustrating the measures of each other.

The State governments may be regarded as constituent and essential parts of the federal government; whilst the latter is nowise essential to the operation or organization of the former. Without the intervention of the State legislatures, the President of the United States cannot be elected at all. They must in all cases have a great share in his appointment, and will, perhaps, in most cases, of themselves determine it. The Senate will be elected absolutely and exclusively by the State legislatures. Even the House of Representatives, though drawn immediately from the people, will be chosen very much under the influence of that class of men whose influence over the people obtains for themselves an election into the State legislatures. Thus, each of the principal branches of the federal government will owe its existence more or less to the favor of the State governments, and must consequently feel a dependence, which is much more likely to beget a disposition too obsequious than too overbearing towards them. On the other side, the component parts of the State governments will in no instance be indebted for their appointment to the direct agency of the federal government, and very little, if at all, to the local influence of its members.

The number of individuals employed under the Constitution of the United States will be much smaller than the number employed under the particular States. There will consequently be less of personal influence on the side of the former than of the latter. The members of the legislative, executive, and judiciary departments of thirteen and more States, the justices of peace, officers of militia, ministerial officers of justice, with all the county, corporation, and town officers, for three millions and more of people, intermixed and having particular acquaintance with every class and circle of people must exceed, beyond all proportion, both in number and influence, those of every description who will be employed in the administration of the federal system. Compare the members of the three great departments of the thirteen States, excluding from the judiciary department the justices of peace, with the members of the corresponding departments of the single government of the Union; compare the militia officers of three millions of people with the military and marine officers of any establishment which is within the compass of probability, or, I may add, of possibility, and in this view alone, we may pronounce the advantage of the States to be decisive. If the federal government is to have collectors of revenue, the State governments will have theirs also. And as those of the former will be principally on the seacoast, and not very numerous, whilst those of the latter will be spread over the face of the country, and will be very numerous, the advantage in this view also lies on the same side. It is true that the Confederacy is to possess, and may exercise, the power of collecting internal as well as external taxes throughout the States; but it is probable that this power will not be resorted to, except for supplemental purposes of revenue; that an option will then be given to the States to supply their quotas by previous collections of their own; and that the eventual collection, under the immediate authority of the Union, will generally be made by the officers, and according to the rules, appointed by the several States. Indeed it is extremely probable that in other instances, particularly in the organization of the judicial power, the officers of the States will be clothed with the correspondent authority of the Union. Should it happen, however, that separate collectors of internal revenue should be appointed under the federal government, the influence of the whole number would not bear a comparison with that of the multitude of State officers in the opposite scale. Within every district to which a federal collector would be allotted, there would not be less than thirty or forty, or even more, officers of different descriptions, and many of them persons of character and weight whose influence would lie on the side of the State.

The powers delegated by the proposed Constitution to the federal government are few and defined. Those which are to remain in the State governments are numerous and indefinite. The former will be exercised principally on external objects, as war, peace, negotiation, and foreign commerce; with which last the power of taxation will, for the most part, be connected. The powers reserved to the several States will extend to all the objects which, in the ordinary course of affairs, concern the lives, liberties, and properties of the people, and the internal order, improvement, and prosperity of the State.

The operations of the federal government will be most extensive and important in times of war and danger; those of the State governments in times of peace and security. As the former periods will probably bear a small proportion of the latter, the State governments will here enjoy another advantage over the federal government. The more adequate, indeed, the federal powers may be rendered to the national defense, the less frequent will be those scenes of danger which might favor their ascendancy over the governments of the particular States.

If the new Constitution be examined with accuracy and candor, it will be found that the change which it proposes consists much less in the addition of NEW POWERS to the Union than in the invigoration of its ORIGINAL POWERS. The regulation of commerce, it is true, is a new power; but that seems to be an addition which few oppose and from which no apprehensions are entertained. The powers relating to war and peace, armies and fleets, treaties and finance, with the other more considerable powers, are all vested in the existing Congress by the Articles of Confederation. The proposed change does not enlarge these powers; it only substitutes a more effectual mode of administering them. The change relating to taxation may be regarded as the most important; and yet the present Congress have as complete authority to REQUIRE of the States indefinite supplies of money for the common defense and general welfare as the future Congress will have to require them of individual citizens; and the latter will be no more bound than the States themselves have been to pay the quotas respectively taxed on them. Had the States complied punctually with the Articles of Confederation, or could their compliance have been enforced by as peaceable means as may be used with success towards single persons, our past experience is very far from countenancing an opinion that the State governments would have lost their constitutional powers, and have gradually undergone an entire consolidation. To maintain that such an event would have ensued would be to say at once that the existence of the State governments is incompatible with any system whatever that accomplishes the essential purposes of the Union. ■

American Politics Today

No area of American politics has undergone as much change in the past few years as has the relationship between the national government and the states. After decades of talk about the "New Federalism," the combination of a Republican-controlled Congress, a sympathetic Supreme Court, and a president willing to compromise allowed for a significant shift of power from Washington to the state capitals. In this selection, the journalist Garry Wills surveys the realities of American federalism at the turn of the new century.

Questions

1. How has the distribution of power between Washington and the states changed in recent years? What implications do these changes have for the shape of American public policy?
2. How would the Federalists and Antifederalists (see selections 2.1 through 2.3) evaluate the trends in American federalism described in this selection?

2.4 The War Between the States . . . and Washington (1998)

Garry Wills

Some people play favorites with the Bill of Rights. The favorite amendment of gangsters is the fifth (no self-incrimination), of liberals the first (free speech), of drug dealers the fourth (no unauthorized search), of gun fondlers the second (to bear arms). Now, many people have a new favorite, the long-neglected 10th (powers not specifically assigned to Washington are reserved to the states). As recently as 1985, when the Supreme Court reversed one of its rare decisions based on the amendment (*Garcia* canceling *Usery*), the 10th was being called a dead letter. Certainly few people tried to "take the 10th" the way gangsters and fellow travelers "took the fifth."

But now the amendment has many takers. The Supreme Court used it in 1992, 1995 and 1997 and shows an eagerness to extend that run. Bob Dole, in his last year in the Senate, began carrying the words of the amendment around with him for instant recitation. Newt Gingrich's insurgents relied on it in 1994 to preach devolution of power from the Federal to the state level. Even President Clinton gives states the title Louis Brandeis thought up for them, "laboratories of democracy." Gov. Tommy Thompson of Wisconsin thinks it is high time for the amendment to be resurrected. He claims he has been a voice for the 10th crying in the wilderness for many years.

The change is not just a matter of theory. States and localities are manifesting a new energy, almost a frenzy, in starting, altering or killing programs. In education alone, they have pioneered charter schools, vouchers for private schools, the canceling of affirmative action in colleges, the retrenchment of bilingualism, new rules for immigrant children, different approaches to truancy and various approaches to teaching religion in public schools or allowing religious groups to gather on public grounds.

In crime, states have reintroduced capital punishment and passed "three strikes" laws. They have experimented with "truth in sentencing" (no parole), mandatory sentencing, alternative sentencing and victims' compensation.

In politics, they have promoted term limits, tax caps, mandatory spending percentages, public campaign financing, the control of union dues and extensions of the ballot initiative.

On sexual morality, the states have enacted or reversed bills on gay rights, repealed sodomy laws, supported unmarried partners' benefits and proposed or opposed marriage between homosexuals.

On welfare, the states have tried different forms of job training and placement, compulsory work, public employment or compensated private employment and various forms of benefits for mothers on welfare (including child care and health insurance).

On the environment, they have regulated business, formed new protected areas and successfully defied Federal regulations (for example, on the disposal of nuclear waste in *New York v. United States* in 1992).

On health, they have considered regulations on assisted suicide, H.M.O.'s, late-term abortions and insurance affecting AIDS patients.

On guns, they have passed bills to protect concealed weapons or to impose local restrictions. They have defeated Federal restrictions on guns near schools (*Lopez*, 1995) and the attempt to use local sheriffs to implement the Brady Bill (*Printz*, 1997).

On a whole range of such issues, the states have been out ahead of Federal programs, reversing a long-term trend. In the Progressive era, regulation of corporations was sought at the national level. In the Bull Moose movement, and during Woodrow Wilson's first term, intellectuals aspired to policy roles in Washington. With the New Deal, their drift toward the center became a stampede. From that point on, an overlapping series of crises (Depression, world war, cold war) led to central mobilization and control of resources. But now, with the end of this half-century of crisis, people with new ideas and a passion for public policy are turning away from Washington and attacking social issues at the state and local levels.

This shift raises deep questions about the virtues of direct democracy, the merits of federalism and the possibility of isolating states from the national society.

California, as usual, has blundered furthest outward. Ronald Reagan went forth from California to shrink the Federal Government and essentially failed. Howard Jarvis stayed home in California and succeeded. His Proposition 13 capped property taxes and thereby (his critics allege) wrecked the state's public education system. The state's punitive measures against immigrants and their children have been checked by the courts, have backfired against their sponsors (including Gov. Pete Wilson) and have unsettled candidates dependent on Hispanic or Asian voters. Draconian term limits (six years for Assembly members) were supposed to curtail careerism, the power of special interests, cronyism and the lobbyists' sway—but have increased all four.

Peter Schrag, in his sobering new book, "Paradise Lost," describes what occurred at the first great turnovers of office, six years after term limits passed in 1990: "By general agreement, the 1995–'96 term-limits-crunch session of the California Legislature was probably the most mean-spirited and unproductive in memory, a unique combination of instability, bad behavior, political frenzy and legislative paralysis. In the two years between 1995 and 1997, California had five Assembly Speakers, two different Republican Assembly leaders, two Republican Senate leaders and eight special legislative elections, not counting runoffs, among them three recalls."

It is probably unfair to judge any movement by its effect in California. Some local programs have shown initial promise—school vouchers in Ohio, charter schools in Arizona, inventive policing in New York, job training in Michigan, public campaign financing in Maine. Much of the activity has been stimulated or guided by a new generation of Republican governors, whose careers depend on making the programs work. The emphasis on localism is partly a byproduct of the fact that three-quarters of the American people now live under Republican governors.

The foremost champion of local control among the governors is Tommy Thompson, a short, chunky man from Elroy, Wis. (population 1,500), who has a Cagney strut and very modest amounts of modesty. "We started it," he says. "I was the front-runner because I started looking at the Federal laws and figuring how I'd go to Washington and get waivers." Such waivers are special dispensations from Federal regulations. "I'm the only governor who still has waivers in existence, in the area of welfare, from Presidents Reagan, Bush and Clinton. I think I've got 75 outstanding waivers, which changed Federal law in over 200 instances in the area of welfare."

Welfare is not the only policy on which Thompson has been an innovator. In education, he fought truancy with "Learnfare" and set up choice schools, charter schools, "prep tech" and apprenticing and high-school courses for college credit. He talks of a "broad menu" of options for students. He clearly does not think that local government has to mean minimal government.

In fact, his administration (begun in 1986) has been a kind of mini-New Deal for proliferating programs, acronyms and slogans—P.F.R. (Parental and Family Responsibility), S.S.F. (Self-Sufficiency First), W.E.J.T. (Work Experience and Job Training Program), Work First, Work Not Welfare, Children First. Many of these have been folded into his master plan, implemented this year as W2 (short-hand for W.W., or Wisconsin Works). His critics say that some of those plans have come and gone so fast they are impossible to evaluate. But he says they should be judged as steps toward his overall plan, whose parts are still being assembled.

He has a health plan for the poor (Badger Care) that awaits more waivers. ("President Clinton is setting on it now.") His job-training program is similarly stymied by Washington. "There are 163 different kinds of rules and regulations dealing with school-to-work and job-ready money from the Federal Government. It's just plain idiotic."

Thompson has moved further and faster than other governors in taking control of his state's activities on many levels, but he says he cannot be judged until his whole plan is in operation and that will not happen until Washington unties his hands. Naturally, since he thinks he is just beginning to get his schemes in place after 12 years in the Governor's Mansion, he is adamantly opposed to term limits: "If you have people dumb enough to keep running for office, like me, you should let the people decide."

Thompson's central planning can look good if you consider the California alternative. There, the governor's hands are tied, not so much by Washington as by popular initiatives that have made a traffic jam of election ballots. In 1990, the state's ballot pamphlet setting forth the voters' choices ran to 222 pages. At a city election in San Francisco, there were more than 100 items. Voters, apparently, did not notice that in 1988 they passed one measure for public financing of campaigns (Proposition 68) and, simultaneously, another measure (Proposition 73) outlawing it.

Nor is California alone in this sharpening appetite for plebiscites. In 1996, 90 ballot initiatives were up for passage in 20 states. The referendum, too, is becoming more important, as Maine's overthrow of a gay-rights law demonstrated.

The contrast between California's free-for-all and Wisconsin's central planning shows that the cry for localism is not for a single good thing (state government) against an equally monolithic bad thing (the Federal Government). Local government can be improvisational or controlled, experimental or rigid, or anything in between.

Governor Thompson is certainly not a champion of localism if that means cities or counties or the State Legislature can defy his general strategy. He boasts of the 290 items he vetoed in the first budget submitted by the Legislature. He has used the line-item veto more than 1,500 times.

Advocates of direct democracy, like Robert Wiebe, the political historian and theorist, oppose "government by experts," and Thompson sometimes makes fun of Washington "know-it-alls" who could not pass his "Elroy test" (what his little hometown knows is good for it). But Thompson also boasts of his reliance on experts, called in from all quarters to help him with planning. One of those experts, Lawrence Mead, wants to make welfare "the new paternalism," frankly telling people what is good for them. Temperamentally, Thompson is inclined to such hectoring certitude, despite his populist campaign rhetoric.

I recently followed Thompson, who was out to greet some constituents at the state environmental center. With men, he has some of Mario Cuomo's locker-room bluster. ("Don't be a wimp.") With women, he is a palsy chin-chucker. Despite the fact that both his parents were teachers and his wife still is (sixth grade in Elroy), he uses what must pass as "street talk" in rural Wisconsin—"setting" for sitting, "oncommon" for uncommon, "secatary" for secretary.

He presents himself as embattled and with few allies: "I'm the only one still talking devolution." The Republican Congress is "as bad as the President." He feels that he has the spirit of Fighting Bob La Follette, the Wisconsin progressive—except that La Follette went after big business and Thompson is a sworn foe of big government (at least in Washington). If one of Thompson's projects fails, he wants us to believe, it will be because of his encirclement by foes.

To get a "top down" view of the states' new activism, I interviewed President Clinton in April. He had just come in from a Rose Garden announcement of his education program. Clinton, the policy wonk, was eager to talk governmental relations even when aides were trying to move him to the next event. He finds the states'-rights activism a healthy development.

"What the states did in assuming greater responsibilities was mostly positive—in education, in taking advantage of the opportunity Congress gave them to be more active in covering more children under child health programs. What my Administration tried to do was, basically, to emphasize two things—No. 1, states as laboratories of democracy, principally in education, health care and welfare reform; and secondly, actually reduce the aggregate volume of regulations on them in areas where I thought there was too much micromanagement."

Thompson would clearly not see this waiving of authority as sufficient. He would like even less Clinton's caveat that, in giving up some power to the states, the Federal Government was freed to do new things. "We have been more active in some areas than the Federal Government traditionally has been—in education, in wiring of schools and in trying to actually help them hire teachers to lower class size, the way we broke new ground by helping local law enforcement hire new officers." In short, Clinton does not see the states shoving the Federal Government off the scene but interacting with it in new ways.

Clinton is critical of the Supreme Court's tendency to exclude Washington from state-level activity, going beyond what Clinton praises as "basically a pragmatic reallocation of power between the states and the Federal Government over the last 20 years." He is especially upset by the Supreme Court's Brady Bill decision, "the most troubling of all because it said we couldn't even ask the local law-enforcement officials to do a minor ministerial job" of running background checks on gun purchasers.

On the other hand, Clinton takes a surprisingly benign view of state initiatives that express popular feeling rather than court-imposed mandates: "I don't agree with a lot of those votes, but I think they're votes that people have the right to make as long as they don't contravene a Federal statute or the Constitution.

"Usually there is a legitimate concern that these referenda are designed to address. Either representative government is going to have to move quickly into the breach when one of these proposals is on the ballot, so that it is not necessary by election time, or the progressive populists are going to have to put their own counter-proposals on the ballot. I don't think you can stop this movement any time soon when people want to have a more direct say on public issues."

We can see, by counterpointing the remarks of the Governor and the President, that there is little prospect of agreement in detail on the future of states' rights. The President is well disposed toward ballot initiatives, the most direct form of democracy. Governor Thompson is uneasy about uncoordinated proposals that might intrude on his master strategy. Though he once proposed introducing the initiative into the Wisconsin Constitution, that was when he was a young legislator. Now, he says, he is not interested in raising that issue.

Yet as the 10th Amendment fundamentalist, Thompson welcomes the Court's new interest in states' rights—while the President resists any effort to break up the partnership. The place where this disagreement causes a head-on collision is the devolution of power over things like welfare. Thompson thinks Washington has been too slow and niggardly in turning over money. Clinton's liberal critics, by contrast, think he was too quick to untie strings over welfare programs. The President himself considered the Republican bill he sighed too sweeping on some matters, but feels he remedied that by restoring food stamps and child-care provisions.

I asked him if he thinks that state welfare programs, spotty in their success even during a prosperous time, will stand up when economic reverses come. "Absolutely, as long as we keep the fundamental protection for children. We had, in my view, state-by-state settling of reimbursement for welfare families anyway.

"Before I signed the welfare bill, the reimbursement schedule for a family of three on welfare went from a low of $185 in Mississippi and Texas to a high of $660 in Vermont, and most states had welfare payments that were lower in real dollar terms, considerably lower, than they had been in the early 70's, because they had not kept up with inflation. So the Congress, long before I came along, had de facto ceded the monthly payments to the states anyway. Now the states are responsible.

"In the old days, nobody had to take responsibility for the welfare of the family and of the children, or whether there was a work-based program. Everybody could always kick the responsibility around. They could say that 'in our state the Federal Government has all these rules—and, oh, by the way, it's operated by the county.' I think that locating responsibility and fixing it with the states will be more positive than negative."

It is here that Thompson gets heated in his comments on the President. "President Clinton has done everything he possibly can to stymie what we're trying to do in Wisconsin." He has words just as harsh for Donna Shalala of Health and Human Services. "I could get matching grants" for new programs, Thompson complains, but the Government will not turn over the money he feels he needs. On this point Thompson will get no help from the Federal courts. They have repeatedly ruled that states have to observe Federal conditions if they accept Federal money.

Thompson desperately needs Federal money. As he readily admits, Workfare, at least at the outset and for some time to come, is more costly than welfare. To train people for work, to deal with obstacles to work (alcohol, drugs, mental problems), to find jobs, to motivate employers, to offer child care for those going to work, to provide health insurance—all this is not only expensive in itself but also has to be closely monitored. That is why the per-person yearly cost for people on welfare has gone up under Thompson, from $9,000 to $15,000.

Thompson's programs bring back the resented "social worker," who was an irritant under the old paternalism. His Learnfare program, for instance, was meant to dock welfare payments to any family whose child was not attending school. This involved keeping accurate truancy records, comparing them with welfare payments and weighing any alleviating circumstances (illness, transportation problems, children no longer living with their families, etc.). According to Pamela Fendt, a policy analyst at the University of Wisconsin at Milwaukee's Center for Economic Development, Learnfare saved $3 million in welfare payments but cost $14 million.

The expenses of Workfare exert tremendous pressure on the system to remove people from the program, one way or another. That is why Governor Thompson has tried to reach job-placement goals faster than required by Federal rules. One way to remove people from the rolls is simply to declare them ineligible. In Wisconsin, as in other states, many of those declared ineligible were reinstated on appeal. In Wisconsin, as in other states, the numbers going off welfare are not matched with reported jobs and income. Marcus White, associate director for the Interfaith Conference of Greater Milwaukee, says that there has been a quantum leap in the people showing up at Milwaukee shelters and soup kitchens, suggesting that not everyone disappearing from the welfare rolls is getting work.

So far, with the help of a booming economy in Wisconsin, the Governor has kept scrambling ahead of any clear signs of failure. When I suggest that Federal oversight might be justified by less commendable showings in other states, he is dismissive. "They're always saying that, that the states were going to be having a race to the bottom. I told them: 'You're wrong. That may have happened in the 40's and 50's. But right now you've got governors who are so darn competitive. They don't want to read that they're not taking care of the poor, and they're not going to let a governor in an adjoining state get ahead of them. We're very competitive'"

But Gov. Phil Batt of Idaho is not, apparently, feeling any competitive pressures. His state has cut welfare rolls by 77 percent, belying President Clinton's claim that disparities will be less acute under the new system. Idaho, which has the highest incidence of child abuse in the nation, spends $17 per capita for child welfare, as opposed to $99.30 in New York.

Peter Edelman, who resigned from the Department of Health and Human Services to protest Clinton's signing of the 1996 welfare bill, has kept a close eye on subsequent developments in the states. "There are some bright spots," he says. "There are some good states—Maine, Vermont, Rhode Island, Minnesota, Oregon. But there are some very bad states—Idaho, Mississippi, Georgia—and some states, like Pennsylvania, are not doing much. In California, the Governor proposed a bad plan that the Legislature blocked."

Governor Thompson claims that the states are sure to do things better than the Federal Government, since they are closer to the peoples' needs and wants. "The new ideas are coming from the governors, and when you have that clash of ideas, you're going to bring out the best in education or in government."

When I suggest that not all the ideas coming from the states are great ones, he is quick, as ever, to the challenge: "Tell me some that aren't." I name term limits, three-strikes, anti-immigration measures, anti-gay measures. "You're right," he says. "I'll grant you there are some examples. But tell me some things in Wisconsin you don't like."

Thompson believes that the government closest to the people is the best government, which many people take to be a truism of democracy. Alexis de Tocqueville, during his 1831 visit to America, noted that "the Federal Government scarcely ever interferes in any but foreign affairs; and the governments of the states in reality direct society in America." The result, according to Tocqueville, was a "tyranny of the majority," by which local prejudice and conformity received no outside challenge.

It is the same complaint Madison had against the states' autonomy under the Articles of Confederation. The people were, in effect, the judges in their own cause—which always leads to skewed judgments. John Jay, arguing in "The Federalist" for a larger union, said that the people least likely to make wise policy about Native Americans were those in the friction of greatest proximity to them. It is the same lesson we learned, in this century, from the assertions of Southern leaders that they best understood blacks.

Though popular sentiment must be expressed in popular government, it is clear that some kinds of dispute need impartial arbiters. The effort of some states to deny education to the children of illegal immigrants, or legal rights to homosexuals, or organization to unions, shows that popular sentiment can be harsh with unpopular people.

Actually, there is no danger of returning to the Jacksonian days of independent states. Even if you remove the Federal Government from the scene, other national organizations cut across state lines and have to be addressed in a national way.

When I asked Governor Thompson why he did not start his new educational programs in the public schools, he said the teachers' union was too powerful. "If I wanted to hire you from Northwestern to teach in the public schools, I could not give you a contract. The union has to decide what you can teach and where. You might end up teaching music in an out-of-the-way school." Even allowing for hyperbole, teachers' unions are national organizations that can be hard to deal with on the state level.

The best proof of the states' vulnerability to national forces is the flow of outside money and influence into the local arena. When Maine put up its referendum to remove a gay rights law, religious organizations sent in money for ads and teams of "ex-gays" traveled there to support the measure. At an advanced level of communications and transportation, and with the complex organization of religious, ideological and educational enterprises, a return to the independent states of Jackson's time is impossible. To deal with national organizations, whether corporations or unions, philanthropies or crime syndicates, the states are often going to need help from the national Government.

President Clinton ended our interview by noticing how the hard line between domestic and foreign policy is being dissolved. There is a parallel softening of the division between state and national life, not just in government but in every sphere. This does not mean that states are not better at handling some things or at conducting experiments not easily tried on a national scale. There will be, as Clinton says, new kinds of interaction, dialogue and dispute. All that is healthy. But a 10th Amendment fundamentalism that looks back to the muscular states of the Jacksonian era is, by now, an exercise in nostalgia for "good old days" that were not all that good. ■

The Comparative Context

The American model of federalism holds great attraction to many Europeans, who see the American constitutional system as a blueprint for the evolving European Union (EU). But the history of American federalism offers little hope that the road to a federal Europe will be perfectly smooth and direct. The fierce battles over federal and state power in the nineteenth century, and the continued debate over fundamental principles in the twentieth and twenty-first centuries, testify to the difficulty of the task of making "one out of many." In this cautionary article, the editors of the British magazine *The Economist* warn Europe's people and its politicians not to copy the New World's example without first studying its history.

Questions

1. What aspects of the American experience might provide advocates of a "United States of Europe" with a sense of optimism about the future of Europe? What aspects might produce pessimism?
2. What advice does *The Economist* give to advocates of a united Europe? Why?

2.5 If You Sincerely Want to Be a United States . . . (1991)

I magine a hot summer in Paris. By grace of a kindly time-warp, a group of European eminences have assembled for a conference. Charles de Gaulle is their chairman. Among those attending are John Maynard Keynes (who has a continent-wide reputation, though he is still only 29) and Albert Einstein. Bertrand Russell is not there—he is holidaying on Cape Cod—but he barrages the proceedings by fax. Russell is kept abreast of things by young King Juan Carlos of Spain, who, with Keynes, provides the driving force of the conference.

Impossible, except in one of those rosy early-morning dreams. Now remember the men who gathered at Philadelphia in the summer of 1787. George Washington was the chairman. Alexander Hamilton, whose short life never knew a dull moment, was there, as was James Madison, a pragmatic man of principle who would later become president. Together, they directed the conference. Benjamin Franklin was there too, though somewhat in his dotage. Thomas Jefferson (compared with whom Bertrand Russell was a startlingly narrow fellow) was not there, but kept an eye on things from Paris.

It is no offence to Jacques Delors and his friends to say that the people now charged with trying to create a political union in Europe do not inspire such awe. Yet the job of the two intergovernmental conferences the European Community has assembled this year is not different in kind from that which faced America's constitutional convention 204 years ago. Constitution-writing is also in vogue in the Soviet Union, as that country's central government and its 15 surly republics struggle to redefine their relations with each other; though that is a matter of trying to stop a bad union falling apart, not creating a good new one. Might the most mature and successful constitutional settlement in the world have some lessons for these European parvenus?

They Were One, and They Knew It

Start with two great differences between America then and Europe now. The America that declared its independence from Britain in 1776 was, except for its black slaves, an extraordinarily homogeneous society.

Think of those huge distances, and those primitive communications, and wonder at the early Americans' sense of cohesion. Although North and South already showed the difference that had to be bridged by war in 1861–65, Americans shared some essential attributes. A few German and Dutch dissenters apart, their stock was solidly British. Their intellectual heroes (a nod to Montesquieu notwithstanding) were from the British tradition: Hobbes and Locke, Smith and Hume. Their language was English; their law was English law; their God an English God.

Wherever on the coast they settled, they had originally had to win the land by backbreaking struggle (even in the Carolinas, whose plantations were far bigger than New England farms). Three thousand perilous miles from England, they had all learnt the same self-sufficiency. Most of them, or their fathers, had fought Indians.

And those who did not leave for Canada after the break with Britain had a second thing in common: they had all won their independence from an external power, by force of arms. Their successful war of liberation made them feel more clearly "American" than ever before.

Yet that war had been prosecuted by 13 states, not one; and it did not forge anything that, to modern eyes, looks like a nation-state. Indeed, this absence of unity was made explicit by the articles of confederation, which the 13 states signed in 1781. Article 2 said that the states retained their "sovereignty, freedom and independence." They merely (article 3) entered into a "firm league of friendship with each other."

After only six years, the articles of 1781 were deemed unsatisfactory enough to warrant revision. The result—today's constitution—provided a system of government that was federal in form, but with a much stronger central government than had existed before. So, if Europe wants to learn from America, it had better start with a look at the supposed defects of those articles.

In broad terms, critics of the confederation argued that it was unstable, an awkward half-way house between a collection of independent states and a truly single country. Their criticisms concentrated on two things: economics, in particular the internal market of the 13 states; and foreign policy, the ability of the states to fend off foreign dangers.

Take economics first. The monetary and fiscal policy of the America that had just chucked out the British was chaotic. Congress (the body of delegates that had, so far as possible, directed the war against Britain, and whose position was formalised by the articles) could not pay off its creditors. It had no taxing power, and could only issue "requisitions" (in effect, requests for money) to the states. Some paid; some did not. Some states took over the responsibility for the part of the national debt that was owed to their own citizens, and then paid this in securities they issued themselves. There was a shortage of sound money (coin). Some states issued paper money themselves; much of it soon lost its face value. The currency of one state was not normally legal tender in another.

Tariff policy was a particular bugbear. States with small towns and few ports, such as New Jersey and Connecticut, were at the mercy of big states like Pennsylvania and New York, through whose ports America's imports flowed. Tariffs levied by New York would be paid by consumers in (say) Connecticut; but Connecticut's treasury derived no benefit from these tariffs. In short, the internal barriers to trade were big.

Abroad, the 13 states faced a ring of dangers. Britain still held Canada and a string of forts to the west of the United States. If it wished, it could have encircled the 13 states; its troops burnt Washington in 1812. Spain controlled Florida and—worse—it presided over navigation on the Mississippi.

Americans with a sense of where history was taking them (meaning most Americans of the time) well knew that, in Europe, loose confederations were vulnerable to their enemies. Some members of Congress compared that body to the Polish parliament, whose every member had a veto. The comparison hurt: at that time, Poland was being divided three ways by its enemies. The German confederation, or Holy Roman Empire, was notoriously feeble. It was characterised, said Madison, by "the licentiousness of the strong and the oppression of the weak"—a "nerveless" body "agitated with unceasing fermentation in its bowels."

The Americans decided they wanted calmer bowels and a better circulation. In the *Federalist Papers*—the collection of essays written by Hamilton, Madison and John Jay after the convention of 1787—Hamilton was to weave together the economic and political arguments. Trade wars between the states, he suggested, would sooner or later turn into shooting wars. Given the lack of unity of the American states, European powers (with their "pernicious labyrinths of politics and wars") would divide and rule. The destiny to which God had pointed America would vanish in the ensuing strife.

That was putting it a bit high. Many historians today argue that, far from being on the edge of economic collapse, the America of the 1780s was happy and rich. Peter Aranson of Emory University in Georgia says that, although there was little immigration, the new country's population grew as fast in that decade as at almost any time in American history. No sign of hardship there. Trade wars were ending as the states found ways to reduce or remove the tariffs on goods passing through their territory to another state. Had each state's currency been legal tender elsewhere, good money might sooner or later have driven out bad.

The Three Big Things of 1787

For all that, Hamilton and the others who wanted a stronger central government won the day in Philadelphia. The convention's report was adopted by the states, though not without a few close shaves. And America got the constitution it still has. How has it lasted so long? For three main reasons that should interest today's Europeans.

The first was that the constitution created an executive—the president—where none had existed before. The president embodied a response to those external threats. He was to be the commander-in-chief of the armed forces. Although Congress had the power to declare war (and jealously preserves it), the president, with the advice and consent of the Senate, could conclude treaties and appoint ambassadors. He was to be the instrument of a unified foreign policy. This was made explicit by the constitution's first article, which prohibited any of the states from entering into any treaty, alliance or confederation, and from keeping troops, and from engaging in war unless it was invaded or was in imminent danger.

Second, the constitution was a document of limited powers. It gave to the central government (or so went the theory) only those powers specifically allocated to it. The tenth amendment made plain what Hamilton and Madison thought implicit: "The powers not delegated to the United States by the Constitution," it says, "nor prohibited to it by the states, are reserved to the states respectively, or to the people."

Third, the constitution recognised a "judicial power," and established a Supreme Court. The court, among other things, was to have jurisdiction over all cases arising "under the constitution" (and the constitution itself was declared to be "the supreme law of the land"). It also had jurisdiction over disputes between any one of the states and the United States, and between two or more states themselves. Members of the Supreme Court had no date of retirement. In other words, the Supreme Court was to be charged with deciding whether the practice of government conformed with the theory as laid down in the constitution.

How might modern Europeans use the American experience? Those who believe that the European Community is destined to be more than a collection of nation-states—an argument heard since the days of Monnet and Schuman—concentrate on the supposed instability of the original American confederation. Look at the Soviet Union, on the other hand, and you may conclude that that argument cuts the other way. It is the tight union of Stalin and Brezhnev that is unstable; it will survive, if it survives at all, only if it is converted into a much looser confederation.

Western Europe's federalists have a reply. In two respects, they argue, the Community has already learnt the lesson of the American constitution's success. Since the late 1950s the European Court of Justice has arrogated to itself the power to declare acts of member states or of Community institutions to have no effect if they contravene the Treaty of Rome, the EC's founding charter. And the notion of subsidiarity—that decisions in the Community should be taken at the lowest governmental level possible—is a rough-and-ready approximation to the American constitution's commitment to limited powers. Subsidiarity is not, or not yet, a matter of general Community law, but the idea is treated with growing respect.

Moreover, late 20th-century Europeans share the 18th-century American desire to create a single market and remove barriers to internal trade. Here the Americans found it necessary to make the states cede some sovereignty, and to grant the union some powers it had not previously possessed. The states were forbidden to levy their own external tariffs. In the so-called "commerce clause" of the constitution, the federal government was given the exclusive power to "regulate commerce with foreign nations, and among the several states."

In much the same way, Project 1992 is designed to realise the Community's dream of a single market, free of all internal impediments. European federalists would argue that the goal of monetary union is all of a piece with this. If a single trading block has 12 national currencies, the transactions costs of trade will always be higher than if there was but one. Americans at the 1787 convention would have recognised the force of this; the constitution they wrote forbids states to coin their own money. (Still, it was not until 1913 that America established a stable system for guiding national monetary policy.)

But that is not the whole of the American lesson. Those Europeans who doubt whether the American experience of federalism can be applied to Europe will find Americans ready to argue their case for them. One argument of America's own anti-federalists (still around, two centuries later) strikes a particular chord.

America's anti-federalists say the combination of a broad commerce clause and a powerful Supreme Court has been disastrous. It is a simple matter to show that almost anything is a matter of "inter-state commerce." Even if a company does almost all its business within one state, for instance, it may still use the federal postal service. Once interstate commerce has been proved, the central government can easily decide that such commerce is within its regulatory competence. As Mr Aranson has pointed out, as early as 1870 the Supreme Court held that Congress could insist on the inspection of steamships travelling entirely within the waters of one state, if other vessels on those waters carried goods bound for other states.

According to the anti-federalists, the breadth of the commerce clause means that an activist Supreme Court, given an inch, takes a mile. The power of states to regulate their own affairs has been diminished, and the power of the central government has been allowed to increase excessively.

Non-Americans living in America, wrapped in the red tape of federalism (try working out where to get your car exhaust tested each year if you bought the car in Virginia, live in Maryland and work in the District of Columbia), may think the argument over-done; they usually pray for less power for the individual states, not more. But many Americans still worry about excessive centralisation. So do people on the other side of the Atlantic.

Europeans fearful of being turned into "identikit Europeans," in Margaret Thatcher's phrase, therefore have American allies. Such Europeans will note Mr Aranson's warning that America's commerce clause "sustains national cartels that cross state boundaries and empower states, often with federal assistance, to cartelise markets." These Europeans suspect that a Community "social charter" will mean all European states sooner or later being required to have the same laws on health and welfare.

The Right to Opt Out

Europe's anti-federalists can draw further succour from America. The part of a future Europe that most Europeans find it hardest to picture clearly is the idea of Europe acting towards the outside world with a united mind, a single will.

Different Europeans, faced with a challenge abroad, can behave in radically different ways. This is partly because Europe is still far from being the homogeneous society that America was from the start. Europe is still a place of separate nationalisms, to an extent that America never was; those nationalisms have grown milder in the past half-century, but they have not vanished. Although almost all of Europe suffered the same frightful war 50 years ago, the various Europeans have very different memories of it. And this past year they have displayed very different feelings about such things as standing up to Saddam Hussein, a rebuking Mikhail Gorbachev for re-embracing his country's old guard.

This has a direct constitutional implication. Recall how important foreign policy, the threat abroad, was to Madison and Hamilton. They would have considered a union without a single foreign and defence policy to be a nonsense on stilts. So they created a powerful executive, independent of the states, to take control of that policy. Even those Europeans who want a single foreign policy shy away from a European equivalent of the American presidency. Yet without a president, embodying within his person a common will towards the world outside, it is hard to see how Europeans can create what Americans would regard as a federal Europe.

The non-homogeneity, and the hesitation about a European president as powerful as America's, will not necessarily remain as influential as they are today. But one awkward lesson from America is permanent. This is the fact that America did not take its final political shape in 1787; three-quarters of a century later, the founding fathers' structure blew up.

Most non-Americans do not realise how large the civil war of 1861-65 looms in America's collective memory. It killed more than 600,000 people, foreshadowing the efficient slaughter that Europe did not experience until Verdun and the Somme 50 years later. In its last year, when the North's armies under Grant and Sherman marched into the South's heartland, it became unbearably brutal. If you are going to have a constitution linking several states that cherish their sovereignty, it is worth making sure in advance that it does not lead to the kind of war America's constitution led to.

Unfair! yell Northern historians, for whom it is an article of faith that the civil war was fought not over a constitutional principle (the right of states to secede from the union) but over a social injustice (slavery). The Northerners have a case, even though—as Southerners never tire of pointing out—the abolition of slavery was not formally an original aim of the war: the fact is that, without slavery, the Southerners would not have wanted to secede. Since Europe's federalists would argue that nothing divides European countries from each other as passionately as slavery divided North and South, they may feel justified in ignoring the terrible warning of the civil war.

They would be wrong. Nobody knows what explosive arguments the future of Europe will bring. Some countries may see relations with Russia as the right centerpiece for Europe's foreign policy; others may put relations with America in that place; still others will focus on the Arab world to Europe's south. Some Europeans may want far more restrictive immigration policies than others, which could lead to some sharp intra-European border tensions. Country X will favour fewer controls on arms sales abroad than Country Y. Europe's capacity to speak and act as one is still almost entirely theoretical. If Europeans are genuinely interested in learning from the American experience, this lesson should be taken to heart: make it clear in advance that, whatever union is to be forged, states can leave it, unhindered, at will. ■

 # View from the Inside

The Republican losses in the 1998 congressional elections nearly obscured the party's successes in the states, where the party scored victories in both gubernatorial and state-house elections. Among the winners was Governor George Walker Bush of Texas, who was easily reelected to a second term. Bush, the elder son of the former president, campaigned on a theme of "compassionate conservatism," downplaying divisive issues such as abortion and school prayer, and reaching out to minorities, especially Hispanics. Bush's impressive victory instantly catapulted him into the 2000 presidential campaign, with polls showing him clearly ahead of several potential challengers.

In this selection, the reporter Jonathan Walters takes a behind-the-scenes view of Bush's efforts to govern Texas, the nation's second-largest state.

Questions

1. How do Bush's roles, responsibilities, and authority differ from those of the president of the United States? What techniques has Bush used to increase the power and leverage of his office?
2. In what ways has Governor Bush sought to increase his political support beyond the traditional base of the Republican Party? How has Bush managed to maintain the support of his traditional base while seeking to attract new groups of voters?

2.6 The Taming of Texas (1998)

Jonathan Walters

Ask George W. Bush how hard it is to govern Texas, and he's glad to tell you. He swings his arms open wide to denote the vastness of the domain that he can't control. "You don't get everything you want," he says, understating the case considerably. "A dictatorship would be a lot easier."

Jonathan Walters, "The Taming of Texas," *Governing* (July 1998), pp. 18–22. Reprinted with permission of the publisher.

Now, there's nothing unusual about a governor lamenting that he can't get everything he wants—especially in Texas, where the lack of gubernatorial power is written right into the state constitution. What's unusual is what George Bush has done with his situation. He hasn't merely accepted the limitations on his power—he has made them into a political virtue. From tort reform to tax reform, the provisions he has asked for and the provisions he has signed into law have never exactly lined up; on some major initiatives, they have been drastically different.

And yet every time the governor has accepted half a loaf, he has enhanced his reputation. Three and a half years into his first gubernatorial term, he is on the verge of conciliating his way not only to landslide reelection but to the front rank of Republican presidential contention.

Ever since the day he took office, Bush's approach has been based on the simple realities of government in Texas: About all any governor can do is hang on and hope to get the beast moving a few steps in the direction he wants to take it. Bush has not only turned that technique to political advantage—he has actually made steady progress in moving Texas his way, even if it is a half a step at a time.

"From the start," says Hugo Berlanga, a 22-year veteran of the legislature, "Governor Bush truly understood his role as chief executive officer of the State of Texas. He allows the legislature to come up with initiatives and then he works with us accordingly, rather than trying to dictate to the legislature what he wants us to do. He is a good listener and is never set in concrete."

Whether the governor's conciliatory style will hold up over the trials of the next couple of years is the most interesting question these days in Austin. At the moment, Bush is campaigning for a second term on a platform that features one of the most ambitious educational reform proposals to be floated in any state in recent years. It would require every third-, fifth- and eighth-grade pupil to pass statewide tests before advancing to the next grade. If enacted, it will make Texas the nation's foremost experiment in doing away with "social promotion," the pro-forma shuffling of students from one grade to the next, regardless of achievement.

The idea is already getting picked at by critics all over the spectrum. Some think it would be unfair to minorities; some question whether the state should be so deeply involved in promotion requirements; others wonder about the potential cost, because Bush has promised that with the new requirements will also come extensive remedial help for students who don't pass the test on the first try.

What's fairly easy to predict is how the governor will try to sell his program. He will spend large amounts of time and energy negotiating with the legislature over the details; he will impress everyone with his sincerity, patience and personal goodwill; and he will again end up with a half-step toward what was contained in his original proposal—a half-step whose provisions will be dictated in part by the Democratic opposition.

Will it be enough to keep the Bush magic alive in Texas? Will it further his prospects beyond Texas?

Hard to say.

As willing as he is to express his desire for a little autocracy, the fact is that it's compromise that seems to come most naturally to him—especially compromise with the opposition party. Indeed, after a bitter gubernatorial campaign in 1994 against Democratic incumbent Ann Richards, who wasn't shy about attacking Bush personally, Bush came to Austin with anything but revenge on his mind. Before the election, he paid a quiet visit to Lieutenant Governor Bob Bullock, a Democrat who arguably has as much constitutional clout as the governor does. "I went to see him at his house," Bush recalls, "and I just said, 'I don't know if I'm going to win or not, but I think I'm going to win and I'd like to know you.' It was an ice-breaker."

What Bush brought to that meeting was more than political savvy; it was a highly distinctive personal style. A graduate of Yale College and Harvard Law School, Bush is certainly no Texas good old boy, but he's not the transparent Yankee that his father is, either. He has always moved comfortably between the worlds of Old and new Texas—the cow towns and the gated suburbs, the terse ranchers and the Houston millionaires. He is, in other words, a hybrid: a little rumpled at the edges, possessed of a slight drawl, and yet trim and tanned the way a respectable middle-aged Ivy Leaguer is supposed to look. . . .

[Unlike many of his Republican gubernatorial counterparts, however, Bush has not] really been tested under fire. Unlike the class of governors that arrived in the deep recession of the late 1980s and early '90s—Wilson, Michigan's John Engler, Massachusetts' William F. Weld—Bush took over the reins of state government in a season of prosperity that has only gotten more prosperous. As one veteran Austin journalist sums it up: "This is a great time to be governor of Texas."

But that does not mean that governing Texas, even in good times, is easy. As in most Southern states, the constitution written in 1876 reacted to Reconstruction-era excesses by stripping the governor of most traditional executive powers and handing them to the legislature. More than in almost any other state, the 19th-century system remains in place in Texas. Only a handful of agencies are run by direct gubernatorial appointees; the rest are run by commissions or boards whose members stay in office even after the governor who appointed them is gone. Under the state's constitution, the governor can veto legislation, call special legislative sessions and submit a budget, but the budget he submits is treated merely as an advisory message. The legislature's version is the real budget of Texas.

If there is a power center in Austin, it is the lieutenant governor's office. The lieutenant governor presides over the Senate, appoints committees and committee chairs, controls the flow of bills and co-chairs the Legislative Budget Board along with the House majority leader. Governors who don't get along with lieutenant governors in Texas can find themselves pretty well boxed out of the law-making game.

Bush makes no secret of his position in the Austin pecking order. "When the legislature is in town," he says, "the legislature is the powerful body. There's no question about it." In admitting that, he is saying nothing particularly new. And yet his candor and modesty have been music to the ears of the legislature's leaders, and have led them to be magnanimous in return. "The legislative leadership and the governor have worked together very well," says Democratic House Speaker James E. "Pete" Laney. "It's amazing what you can do when you don't care who gets the credit."

Which is why the 1995 Texas legislative session—the governor's first—delivered a good deal of what both Bush and legislators wanted, even if it was built on compromise and led to no national headlines about landmark accomplishment.

In his 1994 campaign, Bush stumped on a four-theme platform that proposed changes in welfare, education, juvenile justice and the state's trial lawyer-friendly civil justice system. After his first legislative session in 1995, the governor signed what were advertised as "reform" bills on all those subjects.

Calling any of this legislation "reform" probably overstated its sweep in every case. And virtually all of what was accomplished had already been done in other places. But taken together, the new laws represented significant achievements for a governor whose main source of power is the power of persuasion. Under the changes in tort law, punitive damages were capped at $750,000 (Bush wanted it to be $500,000, Bullock was pushing $1 million; characteristically, they met in the middle). The education law pushed more control and accountability down to local school districts. The welfare changes included the basics: work requirements and time-limited assistance for the able-bodied. The juvenile justice law added more prison beds and lowered the age at which offenders could be tried as adults.

Some of Bush's critics argued that the governor did little but jump in front of issues that were already moving—tort, education, welfare and juvenile justice bills had been percolating in the legislature since the previous session. But others argued that all this legislation survived in large part thanks to the governor's focus. "There is a lot of pressure, particularly on a governor, to expend political capital on a range of issues," says Republican state Senator Teel Bivins. "The real challenge as an elected official is to limit yourself to a few issues and know more about them than anyone else." In Bivins' view, Bush did that.

Last year, however, the governor learned that one's own partisan troops can sometimes be the toughest to lead. In his 1997 state of the state address, he departed from his previous tactic of hopping aboard existing legislation and unveiled a sweeping plan to overhaul the state's tax system.

Billed as property tax relief, the plan would have eliminated $6 billion in local school property taxes over two years, and replaced $5 billion of the lost revenue by broadening the state's sales tax base and by moving more business taxes to the service sector. (Texas has no state income tax; Bush is on record as opposing one.) In many ways, the proposal simply represented an adjustment to the Texas economy's gradual shift away from capital- and production-intensive businesses to more of a white-collar service base.

But as sensible as the plan might have been from a policy standpoint, politically it was a disaster. The Texas House, controlled by Democrats, did pass a much-altered version of Bush's bill. But with the chairman of the state Republican Party openly criticizing the plan as anti-business tax reform, it was ultimately killed by the Republican Senate. It was a loss that by Washington scorekeeping standards might have been considered akin to President Clinton's bungling of health care reform.

But the state chose not to interpret it that way. In a textbook demonstration of his political style, Bush compromised and cajoled and came out of the fight with something that he wanted: a $1 billion school property tax cut—the largest tax cut in the state's history, as the governor takes pains to point out.

To some sitting on the sidelines during the tax reform fight, the whole drive seemed quixotically naïve. "It was doomed from the start," says one veteran Austin lobbyist. But to others who were in the thick of it, it was a display of guts. "It took a lot of courage to push that measure," says Democratic Representative Steve Wolens. "He took an enormous amount of criticism from his own party, and he stuck with it."

Not that the governor spends a whole lot of time and energy routinely battling his natural constituencies. He is a pro-business conservative who believes that the private sector and the free market should be trusted to carry the freight in maintaining a prosperous and healthy Texas. The tort bills that he signed are regarded by some consumer advocates as business-friendly to a fault; it took a Democratic member of the Texas House to push legislation that would require insurance companies to pass identified savings from tort reform down to individual policy holders.

Bush's stance on the environment is likewise textbook free-market. On the long-running debate in Texas over whether ranching hurts the environment, Bush asks, "Who best to worry about the quality of the land and the quality of the water than people who live off the land? Owning land, owning private property can lead to good environmental policy." His centerpiece environmental initiative to date has been to ask air-polluting industries grandfathered in the state's 1971 clean air law to voluntarily reduce emissions.

And when questioned about the state's continually high poverty rates among school-age children, he responds in a similarly Republican way: "How do we make people more wealthy? You expand the economy. You teach people to read, write and subtract. You reduce the number of babies born out of wedlock."

What Bush is not, though, is rabidly doctrinaire in his conservatism. While he lines up on most issues with the politically powerful Christian Coalition in Texas, the relationship is arm's length. Bush will fight for local control of schools, but he won't stump the state arguing that those schools ought to be teaching creationism. When the Texas State Education Agency, under Bush's guidance, developed a curriculum to teach values in schools, it was launched with all the typical rhetoric about helping youngsters find their moral compass. What it didn't come with was a state mandate requiring that local schools actually adopt it.

In fact, if Bush is doctrinaire about anything, it's that the state should restrain itself from telling localities how to conduct their public business. The job of state government, he says, is to set goals, provide some resources and monitor performance, but otherwise try to stay out of the way. "In Texas," he argues, "the state has been deciding which textbooks to use and there've been big fights over whether a particular textbook is worthwhile or not. My position is that schools should have a range of books from which to choose, and which book a school ultimately decides to use should be a local decision."

It is a devolutionary approach to governing that, not surprisingly, Bush would also like to apply to state and federal relations. He sounds disappointed, even annoyed, at the tendency of the current Republican Congress to impose new legal requirements on states that receive federal money. "Mandates are mandates," he says, "regardless of the philosophical bent of the person doing the mandating." But then he throws in a jab at President Clinton: "It starts at the White House."

Bush is still miffed about the manhandling that Texas took from the U.S. Department of Health and Human Services over its request for a waiver of federal law allowing it to privatize welfare eligibility determination. The request was denied in part because social services advocates feared that private corporations would try to save money by cutting back on the number of people receiving benefits. But another part of the problem was a heavy lobbying effort by labor unions battling to avoid the loss of unionized state jobs. State-federal relations are not likely to improve, Bush charges, "when you play special-interest politics" and "have the AFL-CIO setting waiver policy."

In fact, if the governor has a quarrel going with anyone in Texas right now, it is organized labor. The Texas AFL-CIO has distributed buttons caricaturing Bush as Pinocchio, claiming that the governor reneged on key appointments. They also claim that he has gone out of his way to veto labor-friendly legislation. Last fall, an editorial in the *Austin American-Statesman* lambasted Bush for allowing the feud to hinder the work of the Texas Workforce Commission, a labor-management cooperative dedicated to overseeing the state's employment and training efforts (including its welfare-to-work effort). At the time of the editorial, commissioners had been shuffling on and off the panel, and fewer than half of the 28 regional development boards that the commission was supposed to help organize and oversee were in place.

Bush has other less-than-enthusiastic constituents. Environmental activists regard his laissez-faire approach as naïve at best, pandering at worst. The governor's joint appearance at a press conference earlier this year with Texas Utilities, touting the success of his voluntary emissions effort, had environmentalists shaking their heads. In their opinion, the fact that the utility had cut its 210,000 tons of annual grandfathered air pollution emissions by a paltry 1.4 percent wasn't very newsworthy (Bush counters that overall, the program has been effective).

But Texas is a conservative state, and the opinions of environmentalists and labor unions are not likely to have a huge impact on the governor as he turns his attention to the 76th Texas Legislature next year.

What might have an effect on him is the climate of national politics. If Bush does have real presidential aspirations, then the 76th Legislature will be his big chance to make a mark nationally, as his colleagues in such places as Wisconsin and New Jersey have done. And this leads some to wonder whether he might be tempted to alter his style a bit, take a little more partisan stance, bend a little less when it comes to negotiating on high-profile bills such as his education reform proposal.

For anyone interested in a presidential nomination, the advantages of a shift in that direction are obvious. Whether Bush would feel comfortable doing it, however, is a different question. As he himself might say, compromise isn't the stuff of compelling campaign rhetoric. It's merely the stuff of effective governing. ∎

 Chapter 3

Civil Liberties

The American commitment to individual rights and liberties is one of the distinguishing characteristics of our political system. Even more striking is the fact that we have a written Bill of Rights and that we rely to a great extent on the judicial system to define and defend the rights enumerated there.

Originally the Bill of Rights applied only to the federal government. The First Amendment, for example, states explicitly that *"Congress* shall make no law ... abridging the freedom of speech." An 1833 case, *Barron* v. *Baltimore,* made it clear that the restrictions of the first eight amendments were not intended to interfere with laws passed by the states. Over the course of the twentieth century, however, the Supreme Court has applied the various provisions of the Bill of Rights, one by one, to the states.

The emphasis in American politics on individual rights raises two sorts of problems. The first involves balancing competing rights. The publication of the name of a rape victim, for example, might violate the victim's right to privacy; punishing such publication, on the other hand, might interfere with a newspaper's right to free speech. Such problems can be extremely troubling, but even more serious are problems that pit the interests of an individual against society itself. How far can society go in promoting citizenship and loyalty before its interests are outweighed by the individual's rights to free speech and free exercise of religion? To a great extent, the abortion cases (selections 3.2 and 3.3) fit in this category, as the courts balance society's right to protect unborn life against a woman's right to privacy.

The other readings in this chapter provide essential background for understanding these and other civil liberties issues. Selection 3.1, from John Stuart Mill's *On Liberty,* presents the classic liberal argument for individuality; selection 3.4 discusses the impact of American ideas on the Universal Declaration of Human Rights; and selection 3.5 examines the issue of individual rights in the context of the criminal law.

Chapter Questions

1. What are "civil liberties"? Why are they important in a society that values freedom? Why is freedom of thought and expression particularly important?
2. How are individual rights defined and balanced against the rights of other citizens and against the interests of society at large? What factors work to tip such a balancing process in favor of society? In favor of individual rights?

 # Foundations

One of the greatest advocates of civil liberties was the English philosopher John Stuart Mill. Published in 1859, Mill's *On Liberty* is perhaps the most important statement of the "importance of freedom for the discovery of truth and for the full development of individuality."* Although written in England, Mill's argument found a more receptive audience in the United States; his ideas greatly influenced the U.S. Supreme Court in later years, especially the opinions of Justices Oliver Wendell Holmes, who served on the Court from 1902 to 1932, and Louis Brandeis, who served from 1916 to 1939.

Mill was a utilitarian; he believed that all arguments had to be grounded in practical reason and justified with reference to the social good that would be brought about or the social evils that would be prevented. Therefore, his argument for allowing the individual the maximum freedom to decide how to live stresses the reasons that such freedom ultimately is good for society, even if the opinions expressed are clearly wrong. Note that his argument—unlike American constitutional arguments—is not based on claims of individual rights. Still, Mill's reasoning lies behind American liberal arguments as to the importance of protecting liberty under the Bill of Rights.

Questions

1. How does Mill justify the protection of individuality even when an individual's actions are clearly detrimental to that person's own well-being?
2. What does Mill mean by the "despotism of custom"? How does it operate? What effect does it have? Is Mill's characterization of his society applicable as well to our own? Why or why not?

3.1 On Liberty (1859)

John Stuart Mill

We have now recognised the necessity to the mental well-being of mankind (on which all their other well-being depends) of freedom of opinion, and freedom of the expression of opinion, on four distinct grounds; which we will now briefly recapitulate.

First, if any opinion is compelled to silence, that opinion may, for aught we can certainly know, be true. To deny this is to assume our own infallibility.

Secondly, though the silenced opinion be an error, it may, and very commonly does, contain a portion of truth; and since the general or prevailing opinion on

---

John Stuart Mill, *On Liberty* (London: J. W. Parker and Son, 1859).

*David Spitz, Preface to John Stuart Mill, *On Liberty* (New York: W. W. Norton & Co., 1975), p. vii.

any subject is rarely or never the whole truth, it is only by the collision of adverse opinions that the remainder of the truth has any chance of being supplied.

Thirdly, even if the received opinion be not only true, but the whole truth; unless it is suffered to be, and actually is, vigorously and earnestly contested, it will, by most of those who receive it, be held in the manner of a prejudice, with little comprehension or feeling of its rational grounds. And not only this, but, fourthly, the meaning of the doctrine itself will be in danger of being lost, or enfeebled, and deprived of its vital effect on the character and conduct; the dogma becoming a mere formal profession, inefficacious for good, but cumbering the ground, and preventing the growth of any real and heartfelt conviction from reason or personal experience.

• • •

Such being the reasons which make it imperative that human beings should be free to form opinions, and to express their opinions without reserve; and such the baneful consequences to the intellectual, and through that to the moral nature of man, unless this liberty is either conceded, or asserted in spite of prohibition; let us next examine whether the same reasons do not require that men should be free to act upon their opinions—to carry these out in their lives, without hindrance, either physical or moral, from their fellow-men, so long as it is at their own risk and peril. This last proviso is of course indispensable. No one pretends that actions should be as free as opinions. On the contrary, even opinions lose their immunity when the circumstances in which they are expressed are such as to constitute their expression a positive instigation to some mischievous act. An opinion that corn-dealers are starvers of the poor, or that private property is robbery, ought to be unmolested when simply circulated through the press, but may justly incur punishment when delivered orally to an excited mob assembled before the house of a corn-dealer, or when handed about among the same mob in the form of a placard. Acts, of whatever kind, which, without justifiable cause, do harm to others, may be, and in the more important cases absolutely require to be, controlled by the unfavourable sentiments, and, when needful, by the active interference of mankind. The liberty of the individual must be thus far limited; he must not make himself a nuisance to other people. But if he refrains from molesting others in what concerns them, and merely acts according to his own inclination and judgment in things which concern himself, the same reasons which show that opinion should be free, prove also that he should be allowed, without molestation, to carry his opinions into practice at his own cost. That mankind are not infallible; that their truths, for the most part, are only half-truths; that unity of opinion, unless resulting from the fullest and freest comparison of opposite opinions, is not desirable, and diversity not an evil, but a good, until mankind are much more capable than at present of recognising all sides of the truth, are principles applicable to men's modes of action, not less than to their opinions. As it is useful that while mankind are imperfect there should be different opinions, so it is that there should be different experiments of living; that free scope should be given to varieties of character, short of injury to others; and that the worth of different modes of life should be proved practically, when any one thinks fit to try them. It is desirable, in short, that in things which do not primarily concern others, individuality should assert itself. Where, not the person's own character, but the traditions or customs of other people are the rule of conduct, there is wanting one of the principal ingredients of human happiness, and quite the chief ingredient of individual and social progress.

In maintaining this principle, the greatest difficulty to be encountered does not lie in the appreciation of means towards an acknowledged end, but in the indifference of persons in general to the end itself. If it were felt that the free development of individuality is one of the leading essentials of well-being; that it is not only a coordinate element with all that is designated by the terms civilisation, instruction, education, culture, but is itself a necessary part and condition of all those things; there would be no danger that liberty should be undervalued, and the adjustment of the boundaries between it and social control would present no extraordinary difficulty. But the evil is, that individual spontaneity is hardly recognised by the common modes of thinking as having any intrinsic worth, or deserving any regard on its own account. The majority, being satisfied with the ways of mankind as they now are (for it is they who make them what they are), cannot comprehend why those ways should not be good enough for everybody; and what is more, spontaneity forms no part of the ideal of the majority of moral and social reformers, but is rather looked on with jealousy, as a troublesome and perhaps rebellious obstruction to the general acceptance of what these reformers, in their own judgment, think would be best for mankind. Few persons, out of Germany, even comprehend the meaning of the doctrine which Wilhelm von Humboldt, so eminent both as a *savant* and as a politician, made the text of a treatise—that "the end of man, or that which is prescribed by the eternal or immutable dictates of reason, and not suggested by vague and transient desires, is the highest and most harmonious development of his powers to a complete and consistent whole"; that, therefore, the object "towards which every human being must ceaselessly direct his efforts, and on which especially those who design to influence their fellow-men must ever keep their eyes, is the individuality of power and development"; that for this there are two requisites, "freedom, and variety of situations"; and that from the union of these arise "individual vigour and manifold diversity," which combine themselves in "originality."

Little, however, as people are accustomed to a doctrine like that of von Humboldt, and surprising as it may be to them to find so high a value attached to individuality, the question, one must nevertheless think, can only be one of degree. No one's idea of excellence in conduct is that people should do absolutely nothing but copy one another. No one would assert that people ought not to put into their mode of life, and into the conduct of their concerns, any impress whatever of their own judgment, or of their own individual character. On the other hand, it would be absurd to pretend that people ought to live as if nothing whatever had been known in the world before they came into it; as if experience had as yet done nothing towards showing that one mode of existence, or of conduct, is preferable to another. Nobody denies that people should be so taught and trained in youth as to know and benefit by the ascertained results of human experience. But it is the privilege and proper condition of a human being, arrived at the maturity of his faculties, to use and interpret experience in his own way. It is for him to find out what part of recorded experience is properly applicable to his own circumstances and character. The traditions and customs of other people are, to a certain extent, evidence of what their experience has taught *them;* presumptive evidence, and as such, have a claim to his deference: but, in the first place, their experience may be too narrow; or they may not have interpreted it rightly. Secondly, their interpretation of experience may be correct, but unsuitable to him. Customs are made for customary circumstances and customary characters; and his circumstances or his character may be uncustomary. Thirdly, though the customs be both good as customs, and suitable to him, yet to conform to custom, merely *as* custom, does not educate or develop in him any of the qualities which are the distinctive endowment of a human being. The human faculties of perception, judgment, discriminative feeling, mental activity, and even moral preference, are exercised only in making a choice. He who does anything because it is the custom makes no choice. He gains no practice either in discerning or in desiring what is best. The mental and moral, like the muscular powers, are improved only by being used. The faculties are called into no exercise by doing a thing merely because others do it, no more than by believing a thing only because others believe it. If the grounds of an opinion are not conclusive to the person's own reason, his reason cannot be strengthened, but is likely to be weakened, by his adopting it: and if the inducements to an act are not such as are consentaneous to his own feelings and character (where affection, or the rights of others, are not concerned) it is so much done towards rendering his feelings and character inert and torpid, instead of active and energetic.

He who lets the world, or his own portion of it, choose his plan of life for him, has no need of any other faculty than the ape-like one of imitation. He who chooses his plan for himself, employs all his faculties. He must use observation to see, reasoning and judgment to foresee, activity to gather materials for decision, discrimination to decide, and when he has decided, firmness and self-control to hold to his deliberate decision. And these qualities he requires and exercises exactly in proportion as the part of his conduct which he determines according to his own judgment and feelings is a large one. It is possible that he might be guided in some good path, and kept out of harm's way, without any of these things. But what will be his comparative worth as a human being? It really is of importance, not only what men do, but also what manner of men they are that do it. Among the works of man, which human life is rightly employed in perfecting and beautifying, the first in importance surely is man himself. Supposing it were possible to get houses built, corn grown, battles fought, causes tried, and even churches erected and prayers said, by machinery—by automatons in human form—it would be a considerable loss to exchange for these automatons even the men and women who at present inhabit the more civilised parts of the world, and who assuredly are but starved specimens of what nature can and will produce. Human nature is not a machine to be built after a model, and set to do exactly the work prescribed for it, but a tree, which requires to grow and develop itself on all sides, according to the tendency of the inward forces which make it a living thing.

It will probably be conceded that it is desirable people should exercise their understandings, and that an intelligent following of custom, or even occasionally an intelligent deviation from custom, is better than a blind and simply mechanical adhesion to it. To a certain extent it is admitted that our understanding should be our own: but there is not the same willingness to admit that our desires and impulses should be our own likewise; or that to possess impulses of our own, and of any strength, is anything but a peril and a snare. Yet desires and impulses are as much a part of a perfect human being as beliefs and restraints: and strong impulses are only perilous when not properly balanced; when one set of aims and inclinations is developed into strength, while others, which ought to co-exist with them, remain weak and inactive. It is not because men's desires are strong that they act ill; it is because their consciences are weak. There is no natural connection between strong impulses and a weak conscience. The natural connection is the other way. To say that one person's desires and feelings are stronger and more various than those of another, is merely to say that he has more of the raw material of human nature, and is therefore capable, perhaps of more evil, but certainly of more good. Strong impulses are but another name for energy. Energy may be turned to bad uses; but more good may always be made of an energetic nature, than of an indolent and impassive one. Those who have most natural feeling, are always those whose cultivated feelings may be made the strongest. The same strong susceptibilities which make the personal impulses vivid and powerful, are also the source from whence are generated the most passionate love of virtue, and the sternest self-control. It is through the cultivation of these that society both does its duty and protects its interests: not by rejecting the stuff of which heroes are made, because it knows not how to make them. A person whose desires and impulses are his own—are the expression of his own nature, as it has been developed and modified by his own culture—is said to have a character. One whose desires and impulses are not his own, has no character, no more than a steam-engine has a character. If, in addition to being his own, his impulses are strong, and are under the government of a strong will, he has an energetic character. Whoever thinks that individuality of desires and impulses should not be encouraged to unfold itself, must maintain that society has no need of strong natures—is not the better for containing many persons who have much character—and that a high general average of energy is not desirable.

In some early states of society, these forces might be, and were, too much ahead of the power which society then possessed of disciplining and controlling them. There has been a time when the element of spontaneity and individuality was in excess, and the social principle had a hard struggle with it. The difficulty then was to induce men of strong bodies or minds to pay obedience to any rules which required them to control their impulses. To overcome this difficulty, law and discipline, like the Popes struggling against the Emperors, asserted a power over the whole man, claiming to control all his life in order to control his character—which society had not found any other sufficient means of binding. But society has now fairly got the better of individuality; and the danger which threatens human nature is not the excess, but the deficiency, of personal impulses and preferences. Things are vastly changed since the passions of those who were strong by station or by personal endowment were in a state of habitual rebellion against laws and ordinances, and required to be rigorously chained up to enable the persons within their reach to enjoy any particle of security. In our times, from the highest class of society down to the lowest, every one lives as under the eye of a hostile and dreaded censorship. Not only in what concerns others, but in what concerns only themselves, the individual or the family do not ask themselves—what do I prefer? or, what would suit my character and disposition? or, what would allow the best and highest in me to have fair play, and enable it to grow and thrive? They ask themselves, what is suitable to my position? what is usually done by persons of my station and pecuniary circumstances? or (worse still) what is usually done by persons of a station and circumstances superior to mine? I do not mean that they choose what is customary in preference to what suits their own inclination. It does not occur to them to have any inclination, except for what is customary. Thus the mind itself is bowed to the yoke: even in what people do for pleasure, conformity is the first thing thought of; they like in crowds; they exercise choice only among things commonly done: peculiarity of taste, eccentricity of conduct, are shunned equally with crimes: until by dint of not following their own nature they have no nature to follow: their human capacities are withered and starved: they become incapable of any strong wishes or native pleasures, and are generally without either opinions or feelings of home growth, or properly their own.

• • •

It is not by wearing down into uniformity all that is individual in themselves, but by cultivating it, and calling it forth, within the limits imposed by the rights and interests of others, that human beings become a noble and beautiful object of contemplation; and as the works partake the character of those who do them, by the same process human life also becomes rich, diversified, and animating, furnishing more abundant aliment to high thoughts and elevating feelings, and strengthening the tie which binds every individual to the race, by making the race infinitely better worth belonging to. In proportion to the development of his individuality, each person becomes more valuable to himself, and is therefore capable of being more valuable to others. There is a greater fulness of life about his own existence, and when there is more life in the units there is more in the mass which is composed of them. As much compression as is necessary to prevent the stronger specimens of human nature from encroaching on the rights of others, cannot be dispensed with; but for this there is ample compensation even in the point of view of human development. The means of development which the individual loses by being prevented from gratifying his inclinations to the injury of others, are chiefly obtained at the expense of the development of other people. And even to himself there is a full equivalent in the better development of the social part of his nature, rendered possible by the restraint put upon the selfish part. To be held to rigid rules of justice for the sake of others, develops the feelings and capacities which have the good of others for their object. But to be restrained in things not affecting their good, by their mere displeasure, develops nothing valuable, except such force of character as may unfold itself in resisting the restraint. If acquiesced in, it dulls and blunts the whole nature. To give any fair play to the nature of each, it is essential that different persons should be allowed to lead different lives. In proportion as this latitude has been exercised in any age, has that age been noteworthy to posterity. Even despotism does not produce its worst effects, so long as individuality exists under it; and whatever crushes individuality is despotism, by whatever name it may be called, and whether it professes to be enforcing the will of God or the injunctions of men.

Having said that the individuality is the same thing with development, and that it is only the cultivation of individuality which produces, or can produce, well-developed human beings, I might here close the argument: for what more or better can be said of any condition of human affairs than that it brings human beings themselves nearer to the best things they can be? or what worse can be said of any obstruction to good than that it prevents this? Doubtless, however, these considerations will not suffice to convince those who most need convincing; and it is necessary further to show, that these developed human beings are of some use to the undeveloped—to point out to those who do not desire liberty, and would not avail themselves of it, that they may be in some intelligible manner rewarded for allowing other people to make use of it without hindrance.

In the first place, then, I would suggest that they might possibly learn something from them. It will not be denied by anybody, that originality is a valuable element in human affairs. There is always need of persons not only to discover new truths, and point out when what were once truths are true no longer, but also to commence new practices, and set the example of more enlightened conduct, and better taste and sense in human life. This cannot well be gainsaid by anybody who does not believe that the world has already attained perfection in all its ways and practices. It is true that this benefit is not capable of being rendered by everybody alike: there are but few persons, in comparison with the whole of mankind, whose experiments, if adopted by others, would be likely to be any improvement on established practice. But these few are the salt of the earth; without them, human life would become a stagnant pool. Not only is it they who introduce good things which did not before exist; it is they who keep the life in those which already exist. If there were nothing new to be done, would human intellect cease to be necessary? Would it be a reason why those who do the old things should forget why they are done, and do them like cattle, not like human beings? There is only too great a tendency in the best beliefs and practices to degenerate into the mechanical; and unless there were a succession of persons whose ever-recurring originality prevents the grounds of those beliefs and practices from becoming merely traditional, such dead matter would not resist the smaller shock from anything really alive, and there would be no reason why civilisation should not die out, as in the Byzantine Empire. Persons of genius, it is true, are, and are always likely to be, a small minority; but in order to have them, it is necessary to preserve the soil in which they grow. Genius can only breathe freely in an *atmosphere* of freedom. Persons of genius are, *ex vi termini*, more individual than any other people—less capable, consequently, of fitting themselves, without hurtful compression, into any of the small number of moulds which society provides in order to save its members the trouble of forming their own character. If from timidity they consent to be forced into one of these moulds, and to let all that part of themselves which cannot expand under the pressure remain unexpanded, society will be little the better for their genius. If they are of a strong character, and break their fetters, they become a mark for the society which has not succeeded in reducing them to commonplace, to point out with solemn warning as "wild," "erratic," and the like; much as if one should complain of the Niagara river for not flowing smoothly between its banks like a Dutch canal.

I insist thus emphatically on the importance of genius, and the necessity of allowing it to unfold itself freely both in thought and in practice, being well aware that no one will deny the position in theory, but knowing also that almost every one, in reality, is totally indifferent to it. People think genius a fine thing if it enables a man to write an exciting poem, or paint a picture. But in its true sense, that of originality in thought and action, though no one says that it is not a thing to be admired, nearly all, at heart, think that they can do very well without it. Unhappily this is too natural to be wondered at. Originality is the one thing which unoriginal minds cannot feel the use of. They cannot see what it is to do for them: how should they? If they could see what it would do for them, it would not be originality. The first service which originality has to render them, is that of opening their eyes: which being once fully done, they would have a chance of being themselves original. Meanwhile, recollecting that nothing was ever yet done which some one was not the first to do, and that all good things which exist are the fruits of originality, let them be modest enough to believe that there is something still left for it to accomplish, and assure themselves that they are more in need of originality, the less they are conscious of the want. . . .

The despotism of custom is everywhere the standing hindrance to human advancement, being in unceasing antagonism to that disposition to aim at something better than customary, which is called, according to circumstances, the spirit of liberty, or that of progress or improvement. . . .

[I]t is not easy to see how [Individuality] can stand its ground [against the despotism of custom and other influences that stand against it]. It will do so with increasing difficulty, unless the intelligent part of the public can be made to feel its value—to see that it is good there should be differences, even though not for the better, even though, as it may appear to them, some should be for the worse. If the claims of individuality are ever to be asserted, the time is now, while much is still wanting to complete the enforced assimilation. It is only in the earlier stages that any stand can be successfully made against the encroachment. The demand that all other people shall resemble ourselves grows by what it feeds on. If resistance waits till life is reduced *nearly* to one uniform type, all deviations from that type will come to be considered impious, immoral, even monstrous and contrary to nature. Mankind speedily become unable to conceive diversity, when they have been for some time unaccustomed to see it. ■

 # American Politics Today

Surely the most controversial decision the Supreme Court has made in recent years is that a woman's right to obtain an abortion is protected by the U.S. Constitution. The original decision, handed down in 1973 in *Roe* v. *Wade* (selection 3.2) sparked extraordinary controversy and inflamed an issue that remains divisive and contentious. "Pro-life" groups sprang up to attack the decision; "pro-choice" groups rose to its defense. The battle has raged ever since.

The Court's decision in *Roe* v. *Wade* made essentially four points. First, the right to terminate a pregnancy is included within the constitutional right to privacy. Second, the Fourteenth Amendment (which protects the right to life, liberty, and property) is not applicable to an unborn fetus. Third, a state cannot arbitrarily decide that life begins at conception and thereby block the woman's right to obtain an abortion. Finally, the woman's right of privacy is not absolute; the state's interest in protecting the potential life of the fetus grows as the fetus grows and eventually outweighs the woman's right. In the first trimester of pregnancy, therefore, the state could not interfere at all with her choice; during the second, it could regulate the abortion procedure but not prohibit abortion altogether; in the third, the state could completely ban all abortions.

Antiabortion groups mounted a strong campaign against *Roe*. The appointment of five new justices by Republican presidents Ronald Reagan and George Bush shifted the balance of power on the Supreme Court, and *Roe* seemed increasingly under threat throughout the 1980s. In 1989, in *Webster* v. *Reproductive Health Services*, the Court seemed on the brink of overturning *Roe* altogether, but in 1992 Justice Sandra Day O'Connor led a slim majority in affirming a woman's constitutional right to terminate her pregnancy (*Planned Parenthood of Southeastern Pennsylvania* v. *Casey*, selection 3.3). Although *Casey* upheld the core rulings in *Roe*, it expanded somewhat the government's power to regulate the abortion right.

Questions

1. What is the constitutional basis for the right to privacy elaborated in *Roe* v. *Wade?* What provisions of the Constitution and the Bill of Rights support the idea that the Constitution protects privacy?
2. How does the abortion right proclaimed in *Casey* differ from that announced in *Roe?*

3.2 *Roe* v. *Wade* (1973)

Justice Harry A. Blackmun

M r. Justice Blackmun delivered the opinion of the Court.

This [case] . . . present[s] constitutional challenges to state criminal abortion legislation. . . .

We forthwith acknowledge our awareness of the sensitive and emotional nature of the abortion controversy, of the vigorous opposing views, even among physicians, and of the deep and seemingly absolute convictions that the subject inspires. One's philosophy, one's experiences, one's exposure to the raw edges of human existence, one's religious training, one's attitudes toward life and family and their values, and the moral standards one establishes and seeks to observe, are all likely to influence and to color one's thinking and conclusions about abortion.

---

410 U.S. 113 (1973).

In addition, population growth, pollution, poverty, and racial overtones tend to complicate and not to simplify the problem.

Our task, of course, is to resolve the issue by constitutional measurement, free of emotion and of predilection. We seek earnestly to do this, and, because we do, we have inquired into, and in this opinion place some emphasis upon, medical and medical-legal history and what that history reveals about man's attitudes toward the abortion procedure over the centuries. We bear in mind, too, Mr. Justice Holmes' admonition in his now-vindicated dissent in *Lochner v. New York* (1905):

> [The Constitution] is made for people of fundamentally differing views, and the accident of our finding certain opinions natural and familiar or novel and even shocking ought not to conclude our judgment upon the question whether statutes embodying them conflict with the Constitution of the United States.

• • •

[I]

The Constitution does not explicitly mention any right of privacy. In a line of decisions, however, going back perhaps as far as *Union Pacific R. Co. v. Botsford* (1891), the Court has recognized that a right of personal privacy, or a guarantee of certain areas of zones of privacy, does exist under the Constitution. In varying contexts, the Court or individual Justices have, indeed, found at least the roots of that right in the First Amendment; in the Fourth and Fifth Amendments; in the penumbras of the Bill of Rights; in the Ninth Amendment; or in the concept of liberty guaranteed by the first section of the Fourteenth Amendment. These decisions make it clear that only personal rights that can be deemed "fundamental" or "implicit in the concept of ordered liberty" are included in this guarantee of personal privacy. They also make it clear that the right has some extension to activities relating to marriage, procreation, contraception, family relationships, and child rearing and education.

This right of privacy, whether it be founded in the Fourteenth Amendment's concept of personal liberty and restrictions upon state action, as we feel it is, or, as the District Court determined, in the Ninth Amendment's reservation of rights to the people, is broad enough to encompass a woman's decision whether or not to terminate her pregnancy. The detriment that the State would impose upon the pregnant woman by denying this choice altogether is apparent. Specific and direct harm medically diagnosable even in early pregnancy may be involved. Maternity, or additional offspring, may force upon the woman a distressful life and future. Psychological harm may be imminent. Mental and physical health may be taxed by child care. There is also the distress, for all concerned, associated with the unwanted child, and there is the problem of bringing a child into a family already unable, psychologically and otherwise, to care for it. In other cases, as in this one, the additional difficulties and continuing stigma of unwed motherhood may be involved. All these are factors the woman and her responsible physician necessarily will consider in consultation.

On the basis of elements such as these, appellant and some *amici* argue that the woman's right is absolute and that she is entitled to terminate her pregnancy at whatever time, in whatever way, and for whatever reason she alone chooses. With this we do not agree. Appellant's arguments that Texas either has no valid interest at all in regulating the abortion decision, or no interest strong enough to support any limitation upon the woman's sole determination, are unpersuasive. The Court's decisions recognizing a right of privacy also acknowledge that some state regulation in areas protected by that right is appropriate. As noted above, a State may properly assert important interests in safeguarding health, in maintaining medical standards, and in protecting potential life. At some point in pregnancy, these respective interests become sufficiently compelling to sustain regulation of the factors that govern the abortion decision. The privacy right involved, therefore, cannot be said to be absolute. In fact, it is not clear to us that the claim asserted by some *amici* that one has an unlimited right to do with one's body as one pleases bears a close relationship to the right of privacy previously articulated in the Court's decisions. The Court has refused to recognize an unlimited right of this kind in the past.

We, therefore, conclude that the right of personal privacy includes the abortion decision, but that this right is not unqualified and must be considered against important state interests in regulation.

• • •

Where certain "fundamental rights" are involved, the Court has held that regulation limiting these rights may be justified only by a "compelling state interest," and that legislative enactments must be narrowly drawn to express only the legitimate state interests at stake.

In the recent abortion cases, . . . courts have recognized these principles. Those striking down state laws have generally scrutinized the State's interests in protecting health and potential life, and have concluded that neither interest justified broad limitations on the reasons for which a physician and his pregnant patient might decide that she should have an abortion in the early stages of pregnancy. Courts sustaining state laws have held that the State's determinations to protect health or prenatal life are dominant and constitutionally justifiable.

The . . . [State] argue[s] that the fetus is a "person" within the language and meaning of the Fourteenth Amendment. In support of this, they outline at length and in detail the well-known facts of fetal development. If this suggestion of personhood is established, the appellant's case, of course, collapses, for the fetus' right to life would then be guaranteed specifically by the Amendment. The appellant conceded as much on reargument. On the other hand, the appellee conceded on reargument that no case could be cited that holds that a fetus is a person within the meaning of the Fourteenth Amendment.

The Constitution does not define "person" in so many words. Section 1 of the Fourteenth Amendment contains three references to "person." The first, in defining "citizens," speaks of "persons born or naturalized in the United States." The word also appears both in the Due Process Clause and in the Equal Protection Clause. "Person" is used in other places in the Constitution: in the listing of qualifications for Representatives and Senators, in the Apportionment Clause, in the Migration and Importation provision, in the Emolument Clause, in the Electors provisions, in the provision, outlining qualifications for the office of President, in the Extradition provisions, and in the Fifth, Twelfth, and Twenty-second Amendments, as well as in §§2 and 3 of the Fourteenth Amendment. But in nearly all these instances, the use of the word is such that it has application only postnatally. None indicates, with any assurance, that it has any possible pre-natal application.

All this, together with our observation, that throughout the major portion of the 19th century prevailing legal abortion practices were far freer than they are today, persuades us that the word "person," as used in the Fourteenth Amendment, does not include the unborn. . . .

This conclusion, however, does not of itself fully answer the contentions raised by Texas, and we pass on to other considerations.

B. The pregnant woman cannot be isolated in her privacy. She carries an embryo and, later, a fetus, if one accepts the medical definitions of the developing young in the human uterus. The situation therefore is inherently different from marital intimacy, or bedroom possession of obscene material, or marriage, or procreation, or education. . . . As we have intimated above, it is reasonable and appropriate for a State to decide that at some point in time another interest, that of health of the mother or that of potential human life, becomes significantly involved. The woman's privacy is no longer sole and any right of privacy she possesses must be measured accordingly.

Texas urges that, apart from the Fourteenth Amendment, life begins at conception and is present throughout pregnancy, and that, therefore, the State has a compelling interest in protecting that life from and after conception. We need not resolve the difficult question of when life begins. When those trained in the respective disciplines of medicine, philosophy, and theology are unable to arrive at any consensus, the judiciary, at this point in the development of man's knowledge, is not in a position to speculate as to the answer.

• • •

[II]

In view of all this, we do not agree that, by adopting one theory of life, Texas may override the rights of the pregnant woman that are at stake. We repeat, however, that the State does have an important and legitimate interest in preserving and protecting the health of the pregnant woman, whether she be a resident of the State or a nonresident who seeks medical consultation and treatment there, and that it has still *another* important and legitimate interest in protecting the potentiality of human life. These interests are separate and distinct. Each grows in substantiality as the woman approaches term and, at a point during pregnancy, each becomes "compelling."

With respect to the State's important and legitimate interest in the health of the mother, the "compelling" point, in the light of present medical knowledge, is at approximately the end of the first trimester. This is so because of the now-established medical fact, . . . that until the end of the first trimester mortality in abortion may be less than mortality in normal childbirth. It follows that, from and after this point, a State may regulate the abortion procedure to the extent that the regulation reasonably relates to the preservation and protection of maternal health. Examples of permissible state regulation in this area are requirements as to the qualifications of the person who is to perform the abortion; as to the licensure of that person; as to the facility in which the procedure is to be performed, that is, whether it must be a hospital or may be a clinic or some other place of less-than-hospital status; as to the licensing of the facility; and the like.

This means, on the other hand, that, for the period of pregnancy prior to this "compelling" point, the attending physician, in consultation with his patient, is free to determine, without regulation by the State, that, in his medical judgment, the patient's pregnancy should be terminated. If that decision is reached, the judgment may be effectuated by an abortion free of interference by the State.

With respect to the State's important and legitimate interest in potential life, the "compelling" point is at viability. This is so because the fetus then presumably has the capability of meaningful life outside the mother's womb. State regulation protective of fetal life after viability thus has both logical and biological justifications. If the State is interested in protecting fetal life after viability, it may go so far as to proscribe abortion during that period, except when it is necessary to preserve the life or health of the mother.

Measured against these standards, [Texas] in restricting legal abortions to those "procured or attempted by medical advice for the purpose of saving the life of the mother," sweeps too broadly. The statute makes no distinction between abortions performed early in pregnancy and those performed later, and it limits to a single reason, "saving" the mother's life, the legal justification for the procedure. The statute, therefore, cannot survive the constitutional attack made upon it here.

• • •

3.3 *Planned Parenthood of Southeastern Pennsylvania v. Casey* (1992)

Justice Sandra Day O'Connor

Justice O'Connor, Justice Kennedy, and Justice Souter announced the judgment of the Court. . . .

I

Liberty finds no refuge in a jurisprudence of doubt. Yet 19 years after our holding that the Constitution protects a woman's right to terminate her pregnancy in its early stages, that definition of liberty is still questioned. . . .

At issue in these cases are five provisions of the Pennsylvania Abortion Control Act of 1982. . . . The Act requires that a woman seeking an abortion give her informed consent prior to the abortion procedure, and specifies that she be provided with certain information at least 24 hours before the abortion is performed. For a

505 U.S. 833#(1992).

minor to obtain an abortion, the Act requires the informed consent of one of her parents, but provides for a judicial bypass option if the minor does not wish to or cannot obtain a parent's consent. Another provision of the Act requires that, unless certain exceptions apply, a married woman seeking an abortion must sign a statement indicating that she has notified her husband of her intended abortion. The Act exempts compliance with these three requirements in the event of a medical emergency. . . . In addition to the above provisions regulating the performance of abortions, the Act imposes certain reporting requirements on facilities that provide abortion services.

• • •

After considering the fundamental constitutional questions resolved by *Roe*, principles of institutional integrity, and the rule of *stare decisis* [which states that courts should respect their previous decisions], we are led to conclude this: the essential holding of *Roe v. Wade* should be retained and once again reaffirmed.

It must be stated at the outset and with clarity that *Roe's* essential holding, the holding we reaffirm, has three parts. First is a recognition of the right of the woman to choose to have an abortion before viability and to obtain it without undue interference from the State. Before viability, the State's interests are not strong enough to support a prohibition of abortion or the imposition of a substantial obstacle to the woman's effective right to elect the procedure. Second is a confirmation of the State's power to restrict abortions after fetal viability, if the law contains exceptions for pregnancies which endanger a woman's life or health. And third is the principle that the State has legitimate interests from the outset of the pregnancy in protecting the health of the woman and the life of the fetus that may become a child. These principles do not contradict one another; and we adhere to each.

• • •

. . . In 1973, [this Court] confronted the already-divisive issue of governmental power to limit personal choice to undergo abortion, for which it provided a new resolution based on the due process guaranteed by the Fourteenth Amendment. Whether or not a new social consensus is developing on that issue, its divisiveness is no less today than in 1973, and pressure to overrule the decision, like pressure to retain it, has grown only more intense. A decision to overrule *Roe's* essential holding under the existing circumstances would address error, if error there was, at the cost of both profound and unnecessary damage to the Court's legitimacy, and to the Nation's commitment to the rule of law. It is therefore imperative to adhere to the essence of *Roe's* original decision, and we do so today.

[II]

From what we have said so far it follows that it is a constitutional liberty of the woman to have some freedom to terminate her pregnancy. We conclude that the basic decision in *Roe* was based on a constitutional analysis which we cannot now repudiate. The woman's liberty is not so unlimited, however, that from the outset the State cannot show its concern for the life of the unborn, and at a later point in fetal development the State's interest in life has sufficient force so that the right of the woman to terminate the pregnancy can be restricted. . . .

Roe established a trimester framework to govern abortion regulations. Under this elaborate but rigid construct, almost no regulation at all is permitted during the first trimester of pregnancy; regulations designed to protect the woman's health, but not to further the State's interest in potential life, are permitted during the second trimester; and during the third trimester, when the fetus is viable, prohibitions are permitted provided the life or health of the mother is not at stake. . . .

The trimester framework no doubt was erected to ensure that the woman's right to choose not become so subordinate to the State's interest in promoting fetal life that her choice exists in theory but not in fact. We do not agree, however, that the trimester approach is necessary to accomplish this objective. A framework of this rigidity was unnecessary and in its later interpretation sometimes contradicted the State's permissible exercise of its powers.

Though the woman has a right to choose to terminate or continue her pregnancy before viability, it does not at all follow that the State is prohibited from taking steps to ensure that this choice is thoughtful and informed. Even in the earliest stages of pregnancy, the State may enact rules and regulations designed to encourage her to know that there are philosophic and social arguments of great weight that can be brought to bear in favor of continuing the pregnancy to full term and that there are procedures and institutions to allow adoption of unwanted children as well as a certain degree of state assistance if the mother chooses to raise the child herself. "[T]he Constitution does not forbid a State or city, pursuant to democratic processes, from expressing a preference for normal childbirth." It follows that States are free to enact laws to provide a reasonable framework for a woman to make a decision that has such profound and lasting meaning. This, too, we find consistent with *Roe*'s central premises, and indeed the inevitable consequence of our holding that the State has an interest in protecting the life of the unborn.

We reject the trimester framework, which we do not consider to be part of the essential holding of *Roe*. Measures aimed at ensuring that a woman's choice contemplates the consequences for the fetus do not necessarily interfere with the right recognized in *Roe*, although those measures have been found to be inconsistent with the rigid trimester framework announced in that case. . . . Only where state regulation imposes an undue burden on a woman's ability to make this decision does the power of the State reach into the heart of the liberty protected by the Due Process Clause. . . .

A finding of an undue burden is a shorthand for the conclusion that a state regulation has the purpose or effect of placing a substantial obstacle in the path of a woman seeking an abortion of a nonviable fetus. A statute with this purpose is invalid because the means chosen by the State to further the interest in potential life must be calculated to inform the woman's free choice, not hinder it. And a statute which, while furthering the interest in potential life or some other valid state interest, has the effect of placing a substantial obstacle in the path of a woman's choice cannot be considered a permissible means of serving its legitimate ends. . . .

[Applying its new "undue burden" test, the Court ruled that Pennsylvania could require a doctor to inform a woman seeking an abortion of the nature of the procedure, the health risks of the abortion and of childbirth, and the "probable gestational age of the child"; impose a 24-hour waiting period prior to the actual abortion procedure; require the consent of a parent or of a judge before an abortion could be performed on a young woman under the age of 18; and impose various recordkeeping and reporting requirements on doctors and hospitals. However, the Court ruled that a state requirement that a woman notify her husband prior to obtaining an abortion did constitute an "undue burden" and was therefore unconstitutional.]

Chief Justice Rehnquist, with whom Justice White, Justice Scalia, and Justice Thomas join, concurring in the judgment in part and dissenting in part.

The joint opinion, following its newly-minted variation on *stare decisis*, retains the outer shell of *Roe* v. *Wade* but beats a wholesale retreat from the substance of that case. We believe that *Roe* was wrongly decided, and that it can and should be overruled consistently with our traditional approach to *stare decisis* in constitutional cases. We would . . . uphold the challenged provisions of the Pennsylvania statute in their entirety.

• • •

The joint opinion of Justices O'Connor, Kennedy, and Souter cannot bring itself to say that *Roe* was correct as an original matter, but the authors are of the view that "the immediate question is not the soundness of *Roe*'s resolution of the issue, but the precedential force that must be accorded to its holding." Instead of claiming that *Roe* was correct as a matter of original constitutional interpretation, the opinion therefore contains an elaborate discussion of *stare decisis*. This discussion of the principle of *stare decisis* appears to be almost entirely dicta, because the joint opinion does not apply that principle in dealing with *Roe*. *Roe* decided that a woman had a fundamental right to an abortion. The joint opinion rejects that view. *Roe* decided that abortion regulations were to be subjected to "strict scrutiny" and could be justified only in the light of "compelling state interests." The joint opinion rejects that view. *Roe* analyzed abortion regulation under a rigid trimester framework, a framework which has guided this Court's decisionmaking for 19 years. The joint opinion rejects that framework.

• • •

The joint opinion thus turns to what can only be described as an unconventional—and unconvincing—motion of reliance, a view based on the surmise that the availability of abortion since *Roe* has led to "two decades of economic and social developments" that would be undercut if the error of *Roe* were recognized. The joint opinion's assertion of this fact is undeveloped and totally conclusory. In fact, one can not be sure to what economic and social developments the opinion is referring. Surely it is dubious to suggest that women have reached their "places in society" in reliance upon *Roe*, rather than as a result of their determination to obtain higher education and compete with men in the job market, and of society's increasing recognition of their ability to fill positions that were previously thought to be reserved only for men.

In the end, having failed to put forth any evidence to prove any true reliance, the joint opinion's argument is based solely on generalized assertions about the national psyche, on a belief that the people of this country have grown accustomed to the *Roe* decision over the last 19 years and have "ordered their thinking and living around" it. As an initial matter, one might inquire how the joint opinion can view the "central holding" of *Roe* as so deeply rooted in our constitutional culture, when it so casually uproots and disposes of that same decision's trimester framework. Furthermore, at various points in the past, the same could have been said about this Court's erroneous decisions that the Constitution allowed "separate but equal" treatment of minorities . . . or that "liberty" under the Due Process Clause protected "freedom of contract." The simple fact that a generation or more had grown used to these major decisions did not prevent the Court from correcting its errors in those cases, nor should it prevent us from correctly interpreting the Constitution here.

The sum of the joint opinion's labors in the name of *stare decisis* and "legitimacy" is this: *Roe* v. *Wade* stands as a sort of judicial Potemkin Village, which may be pointed out to passers by as a monument to the importance of adhering to precedent. But behind the facade, an entirely new method of analysis, without any roots in constitutional law, is imported to decide the constitutionality of state laws regulating abortion. Neither *stare decisis* nor "legitimacy" are truly served by such an effort.

We have stated above our belief that the Constitution does not subject state abortion regulations to heightened scrutiny. A woman's interest in having an abortion is a form of liberty protected by the Due Process Clause, but States may regulate abortion procedures in ways rationally related to a legitimate state interest.

[The opinion went on to examine and uphold all of the requirements at issue in the case.] ■

 # The Comparative Context

The idea that human beings have rights, and that governments have a responsibility to protect those rights, is a cornerstone of American constitutionalism. With the creation of the United Nations after World War II, human rights began to emerge as a critical concern of the international community as well. The member states of the United Nations formalized their commitment to human rights in 1948, with the adoption of the Universal Declaration of Human Rights.

The Universal Declaration, of course, was not self-enforcing. Half a century after its adoption, the broad proclamations of the Declaration remain closer to the ideal than the reality of world politics. But the rights proclaimed in the American Declaration of Independence and in the United States Constitution were not self-enforcing either; progress even in the United States was slow and uncertain for much of our history. The United

States did not abolish slavery until 1865, for example, and did not even begin to recognize the equality of women until the 1960s.

In recent years, advocates of an aggressive human rights policy have been heartened by several key international developments, including the prosecutions of war criminals in Bosnia and international efforts to hold the former Chilean dictator Augusto Pinochet accountable for human rights abuses committed by his government.

In this selection, the constitutional scholar Louis Henkin discusses the relationship between the Universal Declaration of Human Rights and the United States Constitution.

Questions

1. In what respects does the Universal Declaration draw on the United States Constitution? In what areas does the Universal Declaration go beyond the Constitution to advance rights not specifically protected under American law?
2. Why did the authors of the Universal Declaration stress the need to make "national rights effective under national laws and through national institutions"? What difficulties face the international community in its efforts to protect human rights and punish abuses in countries that violate the principles of the Universal Declaration?

3.4 The Universal Declaration and the U.S. Constitution (1998)

Louis Henkin

The Universal Declaration of Human Rights has been acclaimed as perhaps the most important international document of the twentieth century. It established human rights as the idea of our times. It is commonly recognized as the birth certificate of the International Human Rights Movement, marking and confirming the new international concern with human rights. It is the authoritative definition and catalog of human rights. It has been the basis for the contemporary international law of human rights—the source of two international human rights covenants and other conventions, and of a customary law of human rights. In what is perhaps its most significant contribution, it has inspired and promoted "constitutionalism" and respect for human rights in national societies around the world.

The Universal Declaration did not invent the idea of human rights, nor did it fill that idea with rights of its own creation. The Declaration adopted an idea hundreds of years old and filled it with particular rights derived from principles of "natural rights," from historic assertions of rights by brave persons and bold peoples, and from bills of rights composed in America and France in the eighteenth

---

Louis Henkin, "The Universal Declaration and the U.S. Constitution," *PS: Political Science and Politics* (September 1998, Vol. XXXI, No. 3), pp. 512–515 (abridged). Reprinted by permission.

century. One notable source for the "catalog" of rights in the Universal Declaration was the Constitution of the United States and its 200 years of interpretive
jurisprudence.

In turn, during the half century since the Declaration was proclaimed, it has
been a rich source for new "rights instruments" and has enriched rights in older
polities. Rights in the United States have not been overt, avowed beneficiaries of
the Declaration, but they have not escaped its subtler influences.

International Human Rights as National Rights

Since 1948 the world has seen the birth of more than 100 new states with new
constitutions, as well as the adoption of new or significantly amended constitutions by older states. Every new constitution, every old constitution that is importantly revised, bears the mark of the Universal Declaration. Almost all
constitutions now have a bill of rights reflecting the spirit and influence of the
Declaration, some of them also its letter. National courts have resorted to the Declaration in the application and interpretation of constitutional rights. The Universal Declaration, having linked in its first preambular clause "the inherent dignity" and "the equal and inalienable rights of all members of the human family,"
helped establish "human dignity" as the touchstone of rights for national constitutional cultures.

The significance of the Universal Declaration for national constitutional cultures reflects the essential character of the international human rights movement
and of the international law of human rights. Human rights are legitimate, recognized claims by every individual upon his or her *national society*, which that society is duty-bound to recognize and to realize, to respect and to ensure. Generally, a
society gives effect to human rights through national institutions and national
laws that prohibit, prevent, and deter violation of human rights and provide domestic remedies for violations that have occurred.

Human rights, then, are national rights, rights of the individual in his or her society, enforced and given effect by national laws. Strictly, there are no "international human rights"; strictly, there is no "international law of human rights." The
purpose of international concern with human rights is to make national rights
effective under national laws and through national institutions. The purpose of
international law relating to human rights and of international human rights institutions is to make national human rights law and institutions effective instruments for securing and ensuring human rights. In an ideal world—if national laws
and institutions were fully effective—there would be no need for international
human rights laws and institutions. In a sense, if international human rights laws
and institutions were wholly successful, they would be self-liquidating, they would
lose their *raison d'etre*.

The national character of human rights is reflected in the Universal Declaration in various ways. Though prepared by an international body under international auspices, the Declaration is "Universal," not "International." (The word
"international" appears only in the clause encouraging resort to international
measures to secure national observance of human rights.) The Declaration, is a
"declaration," not a treaty. As conceived, and by its terms, the Declaration does

not create international legal obligations: it does not even urge states to assume international obligations. Rather, it calls on states to recognize the rights of their inhabitants under their national laws, and to take measures to realize human rights through national institutions within their own societies.

The Universal Declaration and U.S. Constitutional Jurisprudence

The U.S. Constitution, and the constitutional culture it engendered, were a principal conduit for the idea of rights later espoused by the Universal Declaration, and a principal source of many—not all—of the rights recognized in the Declaration. U.S. constitutional jurisprudence inspired the Universal Declaration in spirit, in principle, and in detail. A half century of coexistence may have played the Declaration back a little into U.S. constitutional jurisprudence.

U.S. Constitutional Sources of the Declaration   Since human rights are rights under national law, since the Universal Declaration aimed to set forth individual rights for national systems, it was to be expected that those who drafted the Declaration drew heavily on constitutional bills of rights, principally the Bill of Rights of the U.S. Constitution, and the Declaration of the Rights of Man and of the Citizen which was the progeny of the French Revolution.

In fact, and understandably, those who drafted the Universal Declaration bettered the eighteenth-century instruction. The French Declaration had only a short constitutional life; France had no significant constitutional jurisprudence between 1793 and 1946, when the French Declaration was revived and incorporated by reference in the first post-War constitution of the Fourth Republic. But the French Declaration had lived on in French hagiography and in the culture of France, and traces of the French Declaration are clearly visible in the Universal Declaration.

The influence of the United States Constitution and its jurisprudence on the Universal Declaration is substantial. By the time the Declaration came to be drafted, the U.S. Constitution had been the heart of an established and acclaimed constitutional polity and constitutional culture for more than a hundred and fifty years; by 1948, the U.S. Constitution had had more than 150 years of interpretation and application. . . .

The Universal Declaration, drafted in 1947–48, drew heavily on the modifications and extensions of rights in the United States effected by 150 years of Supreme Court interpretation. The right to property is protected in the Declaration in broad terms (Article 17). The presumption of innocence, not expressed in the U.S. Constitution, is explicit in the Declaration (Article 11). So are the freedoms of movement and residence within the country, and the right to leave and return to one's country (Article 13).

But the Universal Declaration bettered the Supreme Court's instruction as well. The Declaration recognizes rights beyond those the Supreme Court has found in the U.S. Constitution—a right to freedom from torture, not only a prohibition on the use of evidence obtained by torture (or other coercion); a right to be free from any inhuman or degrading treatment; and not only from cruel and unusual punishment for crime, but from inhuman or degrading treatment for any purpose (Article 5).

The Universal Declaration went far beyond the U.S. Constitution and its judicial interpretations in a major respect. Famously, the Universal Declaration called on states to secure an array of "welfare rights," now known as economic and social rights including rights to social security, work and leisure, a standard of living adequate for health and well-being, and education. Such rights are not guaranteed by the U.S. Constitution (though some are recognized by a few state constitutions), but are, at best, legislative entitlements," and subject therefore to budgetary constraints, political whim, and the ebb and flow of compassion and "compassion fatigue."

The Declaration and the Constitution: Reciprocal Influence   The Universal Declaration, proclaimed without dissent in 1948, has not been formally revisited. New states that have come into existence since 1948 have had no way of "adhering" to the Declaration, but all of them have accepted it by reference in numerous resolutions, and some states have done so in other international instruments (such as the Helsinki Final Act) and by reference in national constitutional and other legal instruments. The status in international law of the Declaration (and of some of its particular provisions) continues to be debated, but the Declaration maintains important political and cultural influence, both in international life and in particular states and societies. There have been few formal uses of the Declaration in law, however, and little "jurisprudence" of interpretation of the Declaration to which developments in national jurisprudence—e.g., in that of the United States—might contribute.

The influence of the Declaration on U.S. constitutional jurisprudence, in turn, has not been large or prominent. The Declaration has been cited only five times in the pages of *Supreme Court Reports* and in no instance decisively, and not at all in the past 25 years. Lower federal courts also have invoked the Declaration only infrequently, and not with compelling effect.

It should not be surprising that hard evidence of influence by the Declaration on U.S. constitutional jurisprudence is difficult to find and to demonstrate. The United States had an established rights jurisprudence and was well-set in its constitutional ways when the Declaration was promulgated. In view of the important contribution of the U.S. Constitution to the Declaration, similarities and parallels between them are numerous, but it would not be necessary, and would perhaps be "impolitic," for lawyers and judges to cite the Declaration as authority where there is parallel and equal support in the text of the U.S. Constitution or in established constitutional jurisprudence.

Historically and culturally, moreover, the United States has not been avowedly receptive to external influence, and U.S. constitutional jurisprudence in particular has been notoriously resistant to foreign legal authority. Especially since the end of the Cold War, the United States has again been withdrawing into "self-sufficiency," and the Supreme Court and its constitutional jurisprudence have not escaped that trend. In particular, the commitment to economic and social rights in the Declaration, fostered by the memory of FDR's "freedom from want" and the influence of Eleanor Roosevelt, has dissipated.

But, avowedly or not, U.S. constitutional jurisprudence has not remained impervious to the international rights jurisprudence the Declaration represents. Insofar as the Universal Declaration has reflected a universal ideology and a common morality, its influences, if difficult to prove, ought not be doubted.

I offer a few notable examples. The radical development in the United States of the equal protection of the laws, as epitomized by *Brown* v. *Board of Education* (1954), came while the world was making equality in rights, and nondiscrimination, on grounds of race in particular, a principal norm of international human rights law. Similarly, the United States came to universal suffrage in 1962, when the Supreme Court found it to be required, not by some muffled constitutional commitment to democracy and representative government but by a commitment to equality newly applied to an old problem: If one person is entitled to vote, the Court ruled, all are entitled to vote, and to vote equally (*Wesberry* v. *Sims* 1964; *Reynolds* v. *Sims* 1964). Can it be that the Supreme Court came to those radical results without looking about, outside the United States, without regard to the ideology, and the content, of the Universal Declaration?

The Universal Declaration, moreover, is not only for constitutional consumption. It was also designed to inspire national laws and national legal-political cultures. Was President Lyndon Johnson impervious, was he not responding, to what the Universal Declaration represented, as he led the United States towards the Great Society? Influence is a continuing force, and a process. United States constitutional jurisprudence has developed in quantum leaps and by continuous seepage. Whether knowingly or unconsciously, the Declaration, I am satisfied, and what it represents in the international culture of the past half century, has had its influence on the U.S. Constitution and on the laws of the United States.

One might anticipate further changes to which the Declaration will speak. Some elements in U.S. constitutional jurisprudence are long overdue for change. The notion that U.S. immigration, including alien deportation laws, are not subject to constitutional restraint, sprang full blown from the brow of the Supreme Court more than 100 years ago (*The Chinese Exclusion Case* 1889); was questioned, though reaffirmed, by the Court nearly 50 years ago (*Galvan* v. *Press* 1954); and still begs for change today in the spirit of the Universal Declaration which speaks to the right to return to "one's country," and the right "to seek and to enjoy" asylum. That doctrine was not mandated by anything in the Constitution, and can be changed without formal constitutional amendment. And the doughty "due process clause," which came to the rescue to help reconceive the right to privacy (the "new privacy," as in *Roe* v. *Wade*, 1973), is also available for change.

Similarly, the text of the U.S. Constitution prohibits cruel and unusual punishment for crime, but reinterpretation of the due process clause could bring us closer to the Declaration by banning torture and all other inhuman and degrading treatment in any context. The right to life is the primary right proclaimed by the Universal Declaration; it ought to inform our jurisprudence on capital punishment. And what cannot be, or should not be, done by constitutional interpretation, can be done by federal and state legislation, in the spirit of the Declaration.

In particular, the United States can reinforce its commitment to economic and social rights declared in the Universal Declaration. If we cannot bring ourselves to declare them "rights," we can well legislate them as entitlements. Our ideology, our values, were not frozen in 1791 when the Bill of Rights was adopted, or in 1868 when the 14th Amendment was ratified. The equal protection of the laws came to mean much beyond what was thought in 1868. Universal suffrage came only 35 years ago, without constitutional amendment. By legislation, by civil rights and voting rights acts, we have moved towards our aspirations for the Great Society. It is time for the United States to take the Universal Declaration seriously in other respects, in all respects.

The United States does not have to vote for, or "ratify," the Universal Declaration again. But especially when, in the name of "cultural relativism" and state "sovereignty," the Declaration is under attack by some who fear the human rights idea it represents, the United States should, on every occasion and by every means, reaffirm its identification with the Declaration and its ideology, with its content, its universality, its fundamental commitment to human dignity. ∎

 # View from the Inside

The right to "due process of law" is one of the fundamental protections of the United States Constitution. Due process rights are particularly important in the context of criminal proceedings, where a defendant's property, liberty, or even life may be at stake. Among the constitutional rights guaranteed to criminal defendants are the right to remain silent, the right to an attorney, the right to a trial by jury, and the right to be free from unreasonable searches and seizures.

Also high on the list of due process protections for criminal defendants is the right not to be convicted of a crime except upon proof "beyond a reasonable doubt." This traditional formula, as the attorney Alan Dershowitz argues, serves vitally important values beyond the "search for truth" in any particular case. Dershowitz's discussion of this critical issue draws heavily on his experience as a defense attorney in the 1995 O. J. Simpson murder case.

Questions

1. What, in Dershowitz's view, is the purpose of a criminal trial? Why is it not, in simple terms at least, a "search for truth"?
2. What values are served by the courts' insistence on the "reasonable doubt" standard? What values would be served by lowering the burden of proof in criminal cases? What would be the advantages and disadvantages of abandoning the reasonable doubt standard in criminal cases?

3.5 Is the Criminal Trial a Search for Truth? (1997)

Alan Dershowitz

The term "search for truth" was repeatedly invoked by both sides of the Simpson case. A review of the trial transcript reveals that this phrase was used more than seventy times. The prosecutors claimed that they were searching for truth and that the defense was deliberately obscuring it. Where it was in their interest to have the jury hear evidence that would hurt Simpson—such as the details of arguments between him and his former wife—the prosecutors argued that the search for truth required the *inclusion* of such evidence, despite its marginal relevance. On other occasions, they argued that the search for truth required the *exclusion* of evidence that demonstrated that one of their key witnesses, Los Angeles Police Detective Mark Fuhrman, had not told the truth at the trial. The defense also claimed the mantle of truth and accused the prosecution of placing barriers in its path. And throughout the trial, the pundits observed that neither side was really interested in truth, only in winning. They were right—and wrong.

In observing this controversy, I was reminded of the story of the old rabbi who, after listening to a husband complaining bitterly about his wife, replied, "You are right, my son." Then, after listening to a litany of similar complaints from the wife, he responded, "You are right, my daughter." The rabbi's young student then remarked, "But they can't both be right"—to which the rabbi replied, "You are right, my son." So too, in the context of a criminal case, the prosecution is right when it says it is searching for truth—a certain kind of truth. The defense is also searching for a certain kind of truth. Yet both are often seeking to obscure the truth for which their opponent is searching. In arguing to exclude evidence that Fuhrman had perjured himself when he denied using the "N" word, Marcia Clark said just that:

> This is a search for the truth, but it's a search for the truth of who committed these murders, your Honor. Not who Mark Fuhrman is. That truth will be sought out in another forum. We have to search for this truth now, and I beg the court to keep us on track and to allow the jury to pursue that search for the truth based on evidence that is properly admissible in this case and relevant to that determination.

The truth is that most criminal defendants are, in fact, guilty. Prosecutors, therefore, generally have the *ultimate* truth on their side. But since prosecution witnesses often lie about some facts, defense attorneys frequently have *intermediate* truth on their side. Not surprisingly, both sides emphasize the kind of truth that they have more of. To understand this multilayered process, and the complex role

Alan Dershowitz, *Reasonable Doubts: The Criminal Justice System and the O. J. Simpson Case* (New York: Touchstone Books, 1997), pp. 34–48.

"truth" plays in it, it is important to know the difference between a criminal trial and other more single-minded searches for truth.

What is a criminal trial? And how does it differ from a historical or scientific inquiry? These are among the questions posed in a university-wide course I teach at Harvard, along with Professors Robert Nozick, a philosopher, and Stephen J. Gould, a paleontologist. The course, entitled "Thinking About Thinking," explores how differently scientists, philosophers, historians, lawyers, and theologians think about and search for truth. The goal of the historian and scientist, at least in theory, is the uncovering or discovery of truth. The historian seeks to determine what actually happened in the recent or distant past by interviewing witnesses, examining documents, and piecing together fragmentary records. The paleontologist searches for even more distant truths by analyzing fossils, geological shifts, dust and DNA. Since what's past is prologue, for both the historian and the scientist, efforts are often made to extrapolate from what did occur to what will occur, and generalizations—historical or scientific rules—are proposed and tested.

Although there are ethical limits on historical and scientific inquiry, the ultimate test of a given result in these disciplines is its truth or falsity. Consider the following hypothetical situation. An evil scientist (or historian) beats or bribes some important truth out of a vulnerable source. That truth is then independently tested and confirmed. The evil scientist might be denied his Nobel Prize for ethical reasons, but the truth he discovered is no less the truth because of the improper means he employed to arrive at it. Scientists condemn "scientific fraud" precisely because it risks producing falsity rather than truth. But if a fraudulent experiment happened to produce a truth that could be replicated in a nonfraudulent experiment, that truth would ultimately become accepted.

Put another way, there are no "exclusionary rules" in history or science, as there are in law. Historical and scientific inquiry is supposed to be neutral as to truth that is uncovered. Historians should not favor a truth that is "politically," "patriotically," "sexually," or "religiously" correct. In practice, of course, some historians and scientists may very well skew their research to avoid certain truths—as Trofim Lysenko did in the interests of Stalinism, or as certain racial theorists did in the interests of Hitlerism. But in doing so, they would be acting as policymakers rather than as historians or scientists.

The discovery of historical and scientific truths is not entrusted to a jury of laypeople selected randomly from the population on the basis of their ignorance of the underlying facts. The task of discovering such truths is entrusted largely to trained experts who have studied the subject for years and are intimately familiar with the relevant facts and theories.

Historical and scientific inquiries do not require that fact-finders necessarily be representative of the general population, in race, gender, religion, or anything else—as jurors must be. To be sure, a discipline that discriminates runs the risk of producing falsehood, since truth is not the domain of any particular group. But again, historical and scientific truths may be just as valid if arrived at by segregationists as if by integrationists. In history and science, truth achieved by unfair means is preferred to falsity achieved by fair means.

Nor are historical and scientific truths determined on the basis of adversarial contests in which advocates—with varying skills, resources, and styles—argue for different results. Although the quest for peer approval—tenure, prizes, book contracts, and so on—may become competitive, the historical or scientific method is not premised on the view that the search for truth is best conducted through adversarial conflict.

Finally, all "truths" discovered by science or history are always subject to reconsideration based on new evidence. There are no prohibitions against "double jeopardy." Nor is there any deference to considerations of "finality"; nor are there statutes of limitations. In sum, the historical and scientific inquiry is basically a search for objective truth. Perhaps it is not always an untrammeled search for truth. Perhaps the ends of truth do not justify all ignoble means. But the goal is clear: objective truths as validated by accepted, verifiable, and, if possible, replicable historical and scientific tests.

The criminal trial is quite different in several important respects. Truth, although *one* important goal of the criminal trial, is not its *only* goal. If it were, judges would not instruct jurors to acquit a defendant whom they believe "probably" did it, as they are supposed to do in criminal cases. The requirement is that guilt must be proved "beyond a reasonable doubt." But that is inconsistent with the quest for objective truth, because it explicitly prefers one kind of truth to another. The preferred truth is that the defendant did *not* do it, and we demand that the jurors err on the side of that truth, even in cases where it is probable that he did do it. Justice John Harlan said in the 1970 Supreme Court *Winship* decision that, "I view the requirement of proof beyond a reasonable doubt in a criminal case as bottomed on a fundamental value that it is far worse to convict an innocent man than to let a guilty man go free." As one early-nineteenth-century scholar explained, "The maxim of the law . . . is that it is better that ninety-nine . . . offenders shall escape than that one innocent man be condemned." More typically, the ratio is put at ten to one.

In a criminal trial, we are generally dealing with a decision that must be made under conditions of uncertainty. We will never know with absolute certainty whether Sacco and Vanzetti killed the paymaster and guard at the shoe factory, whether Bruno Hauptmann kidnapped and murdered the Lindbergh baby, or whether Jeffrey MacDonald bludgeoned his wife and children to death. In each of these controversial cases, the legal system was certain enough to convict—and in two of them, to execute. But doubts persist, even decades later.

Those who believe that O. J. Simpson did murder Nicole Brown and Ronald Goldman must acknowledge that they cannot know that "truth" with absolute certainty. They were not there when the crimes occurred or when the evidence was collected and tested. They must rely on the work and word of people they do not know. The jurors in the Simpson case were not asked to vote on whether they believed "he did it." They were asked *whether the prosecution's evidence proved beyond a reasonable doubt that he did it.* Juror number three, a sixty-one-year-old white woman named Anise Aschenbach, indicated that she believed that Simpson was probably guilty "but the law wouldn't allow a guilty verdict." Had the Simpson trial been purely a search for truth, this juror would have been instructed to vote for conviction, since in her view that was more likely the "truth" than that he didn't do it. But she was instructed to arrive at a "false" verdict, namely that although in her view he probably committed the crimes, yet as a matter of law he did not.

This anomaly has led some reformers to propose the adoption of the old Scottish verdict "not proven" instead of the Anglo-American verdict of "not guilty." Even the words "not guilty" do not quite convey the sense of "innocent," although acquitted defendants are always quick to claim that they have been found "innocent." Some commentators have suggested that alternative verdicts—"guilty," "innocent," and "not proven"—be available so that when jurors believe that the defendant did not do it, they can reward him with an affirmative declaration of innocence rather than merely a negative conclusion that his guilt has not been satisfactorily proved.

• • •

If the only goal of the adversary system were to find "the truth" in every case, then it would be relatively simple to achieve. Suspects could be tortured, their families threatened, homes randomly searched, and lie detector tests routinely administered. Indeed, in order to facilitate this search for truth, we could all be subjected to a regimen of random blood and urine tests, and every public building and workplace could be outfitted with surveillance cameras. If these methods—common in totalitarian countries—are objected to on the ground that torture and threats sometimes produce false accusations, that objection could be overcome by requiring that all confessions induced by torture or threats must be independently corroborated. We would still never tolerate such a single-minded search for truth, nor would our constitution, because we believe that the ends—even an end as noble as truth—do not justify every possible means. Our system of justice thus reflects a balance among often inconsistent goals, which include truth, privacy, fairness, finality, and equality.

Even "truth" is a far more complex goal than may appear at first blush. There are different kinds of truth at work in our adversary system. At the most basic level, there is the ultimate truth involved in the particular case: "Did he do it?" Then there is the truth produced by cases over time, which may be in sharp conflict. For example, the lawyer-client privilege—which shields certain confidential communications from being disclosed—may generate more truth over the long run by encouraging clients to be candid with their lawyers. But in any given case, this same privilege may thwart the ultimate truth—as in the rare case where a defendant confides in his lawyer that he did it. The same is true of other privileges, ranging from the privilege against self-incrimination to rape shield laws, which prevent an accused rapist from introducing the prior sexual history of his accuser.

Even in an individual case, there are different types—or layers—of truth. The defendant may have done it—ultimate truth—but the police may have lied in securing the search warrant. Or the police may even have planted evidence against guilty defendants, as New York state troopers were recently convicted of doing, and as some jurors believed the police did in the Simpson case.

The Anglo-American criminal trial employs the adversary system to resolve disputes. This system, under which each side tries to win by all legal and ethical means, may be conducive to truth in the long run, but it does not always produce truth in a given case. Nor is it widely understood or accepted by the public.

One night, during the middle of the Simpson trial, my wife and I were attending a concert at Boston Symphony Hall. When it was over a woman ran down the center aisle. We thought she was headed toward the stage to get a close look at Midori, who was taking bows. But the woman stopped at our row and started shouting at me: "You don't deserve to listen to music. You don't care about justice. All you care about is winning." I responded, "You're half right. When I am representing a criminal defendant, I do care about winning—by all fair, lawful, and ethical means. That's how we try to achieve justice in this country—by each side seeking to win. It's called the adversary system."

I did not try to persuade my critic, since I have had little success persuading even my closest friends of the morality of the Vince Lombardi dictum as it applies to the role of defense counsel in criminal cases: "Winning isn't everything. It's the only thing."

There are several reasons why it is so difficult to explain this attitude to the public. First, hardly anybody ever admits publicly that winning is their goal. Even the most zealous defense lawyers proclaim they are involved in a search for truth. Such posturing is part of the quest for victory, since lawyers who candidly admit they are interested in the truth are more likely to win than lawyers who say they are out to win. Second, although defense attorneys are supposed to want to win— regardless of what they say in public—prosecutors are, at least in theory, supposed to want justice. Indeed, the motto of the U.S. Justice Department is "The Government wins when Justice is done." That is the theory. In practice, however, each side wants to win as badly as the other. Does anyone really doubt that Marcia Clark wanted to win as much as Johnnie Cochran did? She told the jury during her closing argument that she had stopped being a defense attorney and became a prosecutor so that she could have the luxury of looking at herself in the mirror every morning and knowing that she always told juries the truth, and that she would only ask for a conviction where she could prove that the defendant was, in fact, guilty. But notwithstanding these assertions, Clark and other prosecutors put Mark Fuhrman on the stand after having been informed that he was a racist, a liar, and a person capable of planting evidence even before they called him as a trial witness. An assistant district attorney, among others, warned the Simpson prosecutors about Fuhrman. The prosecutors also saw his psychological reports, in which he admitted his racist attitudes and actions. The only thing they didn't know was that Fuhrman—and they—would be caught by the tape-recorded interviews that Fuhrman gave an aspiring screenwriter, Laura Hart McKinny. If the tapes had not surfaced, the prosecutors would have attempted to destroy the credibility of the truthful good Samaritan witnesses who came forward to testify about Fuhrman's racism. Only the tapes stopped them from doing that.

Clark behaved similarly with regard to Detective Philip Vannatter. Any reasonable prosecutor should have been suspicious of Vannatter's testimony that when he went to the O. J. Simpson estate in the hours following the discovery of the double murder, he no more suspected Simpson of the killings than he did

Robert Shapiro. That testimony had all the indicia of a cover story, and yet Clark allowed it to stand uncorrected.

In practice, the adversary system leads both sides to do everything in their power—as long as it is lawful and ethical—to win. Since most defendants are guilty, it follows that the defense will more often be in the position of advocating ultimate falsity than will the prosecution. But since the prosecution always puts on a case—often relying on police testimony—whereas the defense rarely puts on any affirmative case, it follows that the prosecution will more often be in the position of using false testimony in an effort to produce its ultimately true result.

Outrage at Simpson's acquittal is understandable in those who firmly believe that he did it. No one wants to see a guilty murderer go free, or an innocent defendant go to prison. But our system is judged not only by the accuracy of its results, but also by *the fairness of the process*. Indeed, the Supreme Court has said that our system must tolerate the occasional conviction, imprisonment, *and even execution* of a possibly innocent defendant because of considerations of finality, federalism, and deference to the jury. The United States Supreme Court recently recognized that "our judicial system, like the human beings who administer it, is fallible" and that innocent defendants have at times been wrongfully convicted. The Court concluded that some wrongful convictions and even executions of innocent defendants must be tolerated "because of the very disruptive effect that entertaining claims of actual innocence would have on the need for finality in capital cases, and the enormous burden that having to retry cases based on often stale evidence would place on the States."

While reasonable people may, and do, disagree with that conclusion, it surely must follow from our willingness to tolerate some innocents being wrongly executed by our less than perfect system that we must be prepared to tolerate the occasional freeing of defendants who are perceived to be guilty. This is a Rubicon we, as a society, crossed long before the Simpson verdict—although one might not know it from the ferocity of the reaction to that verdict. As I mentioned earlier, the exclusionary rule is based on our willingness to free some guilty defendants in order to serve values often unrelated to truth. It is interesting to contrast the public reaction to the *jury's* acquittal with what would have happened if Simpson had gone free as a result of the *judge's* application of the exclusionary rule.

What would the public reaction have been if the trial judge had ruled that the original search of Simpson's estate had been unconstitutional and all its fruits had to be suppressed? Such a ruling might have wounded the prosecution's case—although perhaps not mortally. It would have excluded from evidence the bloody glove found behind Simpson's house, the socks found in his bedroom, the blood found in the driveway. It might also have tainted the warrants, which were based, at least in part, on the evidence observed during the initial search. These warrants produced a considerable amount of evidence which might also have had to be suppressed. Indeed, had the search of Simpson's estate been declared unconstitutional, virtually everything found in and around the estate might have been subject to exclusion.

That would still have left the other half of the prosecution's case—everything found at the crime scene—since no probable cause or warrant was required for searches and seizures at Nicole Brown's condominium. But the quantity of the prosecution's evidence against Simpson would have been considerably reduced if the evidence seized at the Simpson estate had been suppressed as the fruits of an unconstitutional search.

Had the trial judge suppressed all the Simpson estate evidence, there would have been a massive public outcry against the judge, the exclusionary rule, the Constitution, and the system. This outcry would have increased in intensity if this suppression had led—either directly or indirectly—to the acquittal of the defendant. "Guilty Murderer Is Freed Because of Legal Technicality," the headlines would have shouted. Conservatives would have demanded abolition of the exclusionary rule. But many liberals and civil libertarians who today rail against the jury verdict in the Simpson case would have defended the decision as the price we pay for preserving our constitutional rights.

This is all, of course, in the realm of the hypothetical, since it is unlikely that any judge—certainly any elected judge with higher aspirations—would have had the courage to find the search unconstitutional and thus endanger the prosecution's case. Recently, I had lunch with a former student who was seeking to be appointed to the California Superior Court. I asked her how she would answer the following question if it were put to her by the judicial nominating committee: "Would you have ruled the search unconstitutional if you believed the police were lying about why they went to Simpson's house, climbed the gate, and entered?" Without a moment's hesitation she responded: "No way. No judge would—are you kidding?"

I think my former student overstated the case in saying that *no* judge would have had the guts to find the police were lying in the Simpson case, but I believe that most judges would do what the two trial judges almost certainly did here: assume a variation of the position of the three monkeys, hearing no lies and seeing no lies. And judges speak the lie of pretending to believe witnesses who they must know are not telling the truth. What does it say about our system of justice that so many judges would pretend to believe policemen they know are lying, rather than follow the unpopular law excluding evidence obtained in violation of the Constitution? I am not alone in believing that the judges in the Simpson case could not really have believed what they said they believed. As Scott Turow argued in a perceptive op-ed piece the day after the verdict:

> The detectives' explanation as to why they were at the house is hard to believe. . . . Four police detectives were not needed to carry a message about Nicole Simpson's death. These officers undoubtedly knew what Justice Department statistics indicate: that half of the women murdered in the United States are killed by their husbands or boyfriends. Simple probabilities made Mr. Simpson a suspect. . . . Also, Mark Fuhrman had been called to the Simpson residence years earlier when Mr. Simpson was abusing his wife. . . .

The fact that the district attorney's office put these officers on the witness stand to tell this story and that the [judge] accepted it is scandalous. It is also routine. . . .

Turow then went on to blame the prosecutor and the judges:

> To lambaste only Detectives Fuhrman and Vannatter misses the point. . . . It was the Los Angeles District Attorney's Office that put them on the stand. It was Judge Kennedy-Powell [the judge who presided at the preliminary hearing] who took their testimony at face value rather than stir controversy by suppressing the most damning evidence in the case of the century. And it was Judge Lance Ito who refused to reverse her decision. . . .

Neither the prosecutors nor the judges were searching very hard for the truth of why the detectives went to the Simpson residence. They apparently thought that the disclosure of that truth would make the proving of what they believed was a more important truth—that the defendant was guilty—more difficult. Thus, some people believe that the search for one truth in a criminal case can be served by tolerating other half-truths and even lies. But I believe the prosecution's decision to call Detectives Vannatter and Fuhrman to the witness stand may have been the final nail in a coffin that had been built even earlier by the police. That costly decision was thoughtlessly made by prosecutors who have become so accustomed to police perjury about searches and seizures that they did not even pause to consider its possible impact on this jury. ■

 Chapter 4

Civil Rights

The civil rights movement was one of the central forces in American politics in the second half of the twentieth century. Nearly a hundred years after Lincoln's Emancipation Proclamation freed the slaves, the United States began to address the gross disparities between the promise of racial equality and the reality of racial discrimination.

By the 1940s, the struggle for racial equality moved to the political arena as well. The legal battles continued through the 1940s and led ultimately to the landmark school desegregation case, *Brown* v. *Board of Education,* decided in 1954. *Brown* overturned the Supreme Court's 1896 decision in *Plessy* v. *Ferguson,* which had upheld "separate but equal" facilities as constitutional (selections 4.1 through 4.3).

At the same time, the struggle for racial equality moved to the political arena. The adoption of a civil rights plank in the Democratic party's 1948 platform led thirty-five southern delegates to walk out of the convention, and later 6,000 southerners met in a separate convention to nominate J. Strom Thurmond of South Carolina on the so-called Dixiecrat ticket. Also in 1948, President Harry Truman ordered the desegregation of the U.S. armed forces.

The political branches did not really move forward on civil rights, however, until the 1960s. In 1963, President John F. Kennedy proposed major civil rights legislation, although Congress did not act. Pressure was building, however; a series of events in 1963, including police violence in Birmingham, Alabama, and a major march on Washington, D.C., greatly raised the visibility of the movement. The following year, after Kennedy's assassination, President Lyndon B. Johnson pushed through the most important civil rights legislation since the 1860s, the Civil Rights Act of 1964. A year later Congress added the Voting Rights Act of 1965, which at last secured for minorities a meaningful right to vote.

Recent years have seen controversy and divisiveness in the civil rights area. One major area of controversy is affirmative action, which involves race-conscious and race-specific remedies to problems of past and present discrimination. The theoretical foundations of arguments for and against affirmative action are considered in selection 4.6, which deals with the problem of minority rights in multicultural societies.

The civil rights movement gave rise to a number of similar attempts to secure equality to other victims of legal and societal discrimination. One offshoot was the women's rights movement, which successfully persuaded the Supreme Court to extend the equal protection of the law to women. Although the idea of equality for women has gained widespread acceptance, other areas of controversy have arisen. These include the problem of sexual harassment, which is dealt with in selections 4.4 and 4.5—the former a landmark Supreme Court case and the latter a contemporary look at this complex issue.

Other minority groups continue to struggle for even the basic protections of the law. Gays and lesbians, for example, still face widespread discrimination, and have had difficulty in many cases in advancing and protecting their rights in court. The story of Margarethe Cammermeyer, a decorated army officer who was forced out of the military after she disclosed her sexual orientation (see selection 4.6) is typical.

For women, African Americans, and members of other minority groups, the civil rights movement is an ongoing struggle. This chapter approaches this complex and varied subject from a multitude of different perspectives.

Chapter Questions

1. At the heart of any discussion of civil rights is the meaning of equality. What alternative views on equality are illustrated in the readings in this chapter? How has the meaning of equality changed over the past 200 years?
2. How have legal conceptions of civil rights changed over the past century? Consider *Plessy*, *Brown*, and the affirmative action controversy.
3. Consider the new questions and problems faced by advocates of civil rights in the 1990s, among them the extension of civil rights to previously unprotected groups, including women, and tensions both inside and outside the civil rights movement. How are these tensions related to the goals and purposes of the original civil rights movement?

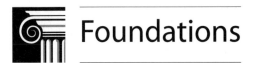 Foundations

Any discussion of civil rights in the modern era must start with *Brown* v. *Board of Education,* the 1954 school desegregation case. The impact of *Brown* on race and politics in the United States has been immense. Although *Brown* itself had little effect on school segregation in the Deep South, it set in motion a process that led to the civil rights movement, the Civil Rights Act of 1964, and a host of federal and state programs designed to eliminate and address the effects of racial discrimination.

Brown reversed *Plessy* v. *Ferguson* (selection 4.1), an 1896 case that upheld the segregation of railroad cars in Louisiana. *Brown* based its rejection of *Plessy* on narrow grounds relating to the dangers of segregation in the educational process. In practice, however, the elimination of segregation in public schools led quickly to judicial determinations that all state-sponsored segregation was unconstitutional.

Chief Justice Earl Warren, who wrote the *Brown* opinion, avoided a direct attack on segregation in general; note specifically how his 1954 argument differs from the 1896 dissent of Justice John Harlan in *Plessy*. Warren's concern was twofold: he sought to ensure that the Court would speak with one voice, and believed that an approach such as Harlan's might alienate one or more members of the Court; and he wanted to avoid giving potential critics of the decision a broad target to aim at. His opinion, though criticized by some as insufficiently high-minded, got the job done.

The decision in *Brown* was accompanied by a parallel decision in *Bolling* v. *Sharpe* (selection 4.3), which dealt with segregation in the District of Columbia. Because the Equal Protection Clause applies to the states and not to the federal government, the Court used the Due Process Clause to strike down segregation in the District.

The first *Brown* decision simply announced that segregated schools were unconstitutional. Implementation of that decision was postponed one year, until 1955, when the Court ordered the federal district courts to implement *Brown* "with all deliberate speed."

Questions

1. Why, in Earl Warren's view, are "separate educational facilities inherently unequal"?
2. Does Justice Harlan's dissent in *Plessy* provide an alternative approach to deciding *Brown*? What are the advantages and disadvantages of this approach?

4.1 *Plessy* v. *Ferguson* (1896)

Justice Henry B. Brown,
dissent by Justice John Marshall Harlan

This case turns upon the constitutionality of an act of the General Assembly of the State of Louisiana, passed in 1890, providing for separate railway carriages for the white and colored races.

• • •

The constitutionality of this act is attacked upon the ground that it conflicts with the Thirteenth Amendment of the Constitution, abolishing slavery, and the Fourteenth Amendment, which prohibits certain restrictive legislation on the part of the States.

1. That it does not conflict with the Thirteenth Amendment, which abolished slavery and involuntary servitude, except as a punishment for crime, is too clear for argument. Slavery implies involuntary servitude—a state of bondage; the ownership of mankind as a chattel, or at least the control of the labor and services of one man for the benefit of another, and the absence of a legal right to the disposal of his own person, property and services. This amendment was said in the *Slaughter-house cases* to have been intended primarily to abolish slavery, as it had been previously known in this country, and that it equally forbade Mexican peonage or the Chinese coolie trade, when they amounted to slavery or involuntary servitude, and that the use of the word "servitude" was intended to prohibit the use of all forms of involuntary slavery, of whatever class or nature. It was

---

163 U.S. 537 (1896).

intimated, however, in that case that this amendment was regarded by the statesmen of that day as insufficient to protect the colored race from certain laws which had been enacted in the Southern States, imposing upon the colored race onerous disabilities and burdens, and curtailing their rights in the pursuit of life, liberty and property to such an extent that their freedom was of little value; and that the Fourteenth Amendment was devised to meet this exigency.

So, too, in the *Civil Rights cases* it was said that the act of a mere individual, the owner of an inn, a public conveyance or place of amusement, refusing accommodations to colored people, cannot be justly regarded as imposing any badge of slavery or servitude upon the applicant, but only as involving an ordinary civil injury, properly cognizable by the laws of the State, and presumably subject to redress by those laws until the contrary appears. "It would be running the slavery argument into the ground," said Mr. Justice Bradley, "to make it apply to every act of discrimination which a person may see fit to make as to the guests he will entertain, or as to the people he will take into his coach or cab or car, or admit to his concert or theatre, or deal with in other matters of intercourse or business."

A statute which implies merely a legal distinction between the white and colored races—a distinction which is founded in the color of the two races, and which must always exist so long as white men are distinguished from the other race by color—has no tendency to destroy the legal equality of the two races, or reestablish a state of involuntary servitude. Indeed, we do not understand that the Thirteenth Amendment is strenuously relied upon by the plaintiff in error in this connection.

2. By the Fourteenth Amendment, all persons born or naturalized in the United States, and subject to the jurisdiction thereof, are made citizens of the United States and of the State wherein they reside; and the States are forbidden from making or enforcing any law which shall abridge the privileges or immunities of citizens of the United States, or shall deprive any person of life, liberty or property without due process of law, or deny to any person within their jurisdiction the equal protection of the laws.

The proper construction of this amendment was first called to the attention of this court in the *Slaughter-house cases,* which involved, however, not a question of race, but one of exclusive privileges. The case did not call for any expression of opinion as to the exact rights it was intended to secure to the colored race, but it was said generally that its main purpose was to establish the citizenship of the negro; to give definitions of citizenship of the United States and of the States, and to protect from the hostile legislation of the States the privileges and immunities of citizens of the United States, as distinguished from those of citizens of the States.

The object of the amendment was undoubtedly to enforce the absolute equality of the two races before the law but in the nature of things it could not have been intended to abolish distinctions based upon color, or to enforce social, as distinguished from political equality, or a commingling of the two races upon terms unsatisfactory to either. Laws permitting, and even requiring, their separation in places where they are liable to be brought into contact do not necessarily imply the inferiority of either race to the other, and have been generally, if not universally, recognized as within the competency of the state legislatures in the exercise of their police power. The most common instance of this is connected with the establishment of separate schools for white and colored children, which has been held to be a valid exercise of the legislative power even by courts of States where the political rights of the colored race have been longest and most earnestly enforced.

• • •

So far, then, as a conflict with the Fourteenth Amendment is concerned, the case reduces itself to the question whether the statute of Louisiana is a reasonable regulation, and with respect to this there must necessarily be a large discretion on the part of the legislature. In determining the question of reasonableness it is at liberty to act with reference to the established usages, customs and traditions of the people, and with a view to the promotion of their comfort, and the preservation of the public peace and good order. Gauged by this standard, we cannot say that a law which authorizes or even requires the separation of the two races in public conveyances is unreasonable, or more obnoxious to the Fourteenth Amendment than the acts of Congress requiring separate schools for colored children in the District of Columbia, the constitutionality of which does not seem to have been questioned, or the corresponding acts of state legislatures.

We consider the underlying fallacy of the plaintiff's argument to consist in the assumption that the enforced separation of the two races stamps the colored race with a badge of inferiority. If this be so, it is not by reason of anything found in the act, but solely because the colored race chooses to put the construction upon it. The argument necessarily assumes that if, as has been more than once the case, and is not unlikely to be so again, the colored race should become the dominant power in the state legislature, and should enact a law in precisely similar terms, it would thereby relegate the white race to an inferior position. We imagine that the white race, at least, would not acquiesce in this assumption. The argument also assumes that social prejudices may be overcome by legislation, and that equal rights cannot be secured to the negro except by an enforced commingling of the two races. We cannot accept this proposition. If the two races are to meet upon terms of social equality, it must be the result of natural affinities, a mutual appreciation of each other's merits and a voluntary consent of individuals. As was said by the Court of Appeals of New York in *People v. Gallagher*, "this end can neither be accomplished nor promoted by laws which conflict with the general sentiment of the community upon whom they are designed to operate. When the government, therefore, has secured to each of its citizens equal rights before the law and equal opportunities for improvement and progress, it has accomplished the end for which it was organized and performed all of the functions respecting social advantages with which it is endowed." Legislation is powerless to eradicate racial instincts or to abolish distinctions based upon physical differences, and the attempt to do so can only result in accentuating the difficulties of the present situation. If the civil and political rights of both races be equal one cannot be inferior to the other civilly or politically. If one race be inferior to the other socially, the Constitution of the United States cannot put them upon the same place.

• • •

Mr. Justice Harlan dissenting.

By the Louisiana statute, the validity of which is here involved, all railway companies (other than street railroad companies) carrying passengers in that State are required to have separate but equal accommodations for white and colored persons, "by providing two or more passenger coaches for each passenger train, *or* by dividing the passenger coaches by a *partition* so as to secure separate accommodations." Under this statute, no colored person is permitted to occupy a seat in a coach assigned to white persons; nor any white person, to occupy a seat in a coach assigned to colored persons. The managers of the railroad are not allowed to exercise any discretion in the premises, but are required to assign each passenger to some coach or compartment set apart for the exclusive use of his race. If a passenger insists upon going into a coach or compartment not set apart for persons of his race, he is subject to be fined, or to be imprisoned in the parish jail. Penalties are prescribed for the refusal or neglect of the officers, directors, conductors and employees of railroad companies to comply with the provisions of the act.

● ● ●

In respect of civil rights, common to all citizens, the Constitution of the United States does not, I think, permit any public authority to know the race of those entitled to be protected in the enjoyment of such rights. Every true man has pride of race, and under appropriate circumstances when the rights of others, his equals before the law, are not to be affected, it is his privilege to express such pride and to take such action based upon it as to him seems proper. But I deny that any legislative body or judicial tribunal may have regard to the race of citizens when the civil rights of those citizens are involved. Indeed, such legislation, as that here in question, is inconsistent not only with that equality of rights which pertains to citizenship, National and State, but with the personal liberty enjoyed by every one within the United States.

● ● ●

The white race deems itself to be the dominant race in this country. And so it is, in prestige, in achievements, in education, in wealth and power. So, I doubt not, it will continue to be for all time, if it remains true to its great heritage and holds fast in the principles of constitutional liberty. But in view of the Constitution, in the eye of the law, there is in this country no superior, dominant, ruling class of citizens. There is no caste here. Our Constitution is color-blind, and neither knows nor tolerates classes among citizens. In respect of civil rights, all citizens are equal before the law. The humblest is the peer of the most powerful. The law regards man as man, and takes no account of his surroundings or of his color when his civil rights as guaranteed by the supreme law of the land are involved. It is, therefore, to be regretted that this high tribunal, the final expositor of the fundamental law of the land, has reached the conclusion that it is competent for a State to regulate the enjoyment by citizens of their civil rights solely upon the basis of race. ■

4.2 *Brown v. Board of Education* (1954)

Chief Justice Earl Warren

M r. Chief Justice Warren delivered the opinion of the Court.

These cases come to us from the States of Kansas, South Carolina, Virginia, and Delaware. They are premised on different facts and different local conditions, but a common legal question justifies their consideration together in this consolidated opinion.

In each of the cases, minors of the Negro race, through their legal representatives, seek the aid of the courts in obtaining admission to the public schools of the community on a nonsegregated basis. In each instance, they had been denied admission to schools attended by white children under laws requiring or permitting segregation according to race. This segregation was alleged to deprive the plaintiffs of the equal protection of the laws under the Fourteenth Amendment. In each of the cases other than the Delaware case, a three-judge federal district court denied relief to the plaintiffs on the so-called "separate but equal" doctrine announced by this Court in *Plessy* v. *Ferguson.* Under that doctrine, equality of treatment is accorded when the races are provided substantially equal facilities, even though these facilities be separate. In the Delaware case, the Supreme Court of Delaware adhered to that doctrine, but ordered that the plaintiffs be admitted to the white schools because of their superiority to the Negro schools.

The plaintiffs contend that segregated public schools are not "equal" and cannot be made "equal," and that hence they are deprived of the equal protection of the laws. Because of the obvious importance of the question presented, the Court took jurisdiction. Argument was heard in the 1952 Term, and reargument was heard this Term on certain questions propounded by the Court.

Reargument was largely devoted to the circumstances surrounding the adoption of the Fourteenth Amendment in 1868. It covered exhaustively consideration of the Amendment in Congress, ratification by the states, then existing practices in racial segregation, and the views of proponents and opponents of the Amendment. This discussion and our own investigation convince us that, although these sources cast some light, it is not enough to resolve the problem with which we are faced. At best, they are inconclusive. The most avid proponents of the post-War Amendments undoubtedly intended them to remove all legal distinctions among "all persons born or naturalized in the United States." Their opponents, just as certainly, were antagonistic to both the letter and the spirit of the Amendments and wished them to have the most limited effect. What others in Congress and the state legislatures had in mind cannot be determined with any degree of certainty.

An additional reason for the inconclusive nature of the Amendment's history, with respect to segregated schools, is the status of public education at that time. In the South, the movement toward free common schools, supported by general

---

347 U.S. 483 (1954).

taxation, had not yet taken hold. Education of white children was largely in the hands of private groups. Education of Negroes was almost nonexistent, and practically all of the race were illiterate. In fact, any education of Negroes was forbidden by law in some states. Today, in contrast, many negroes have achieved outstanding success in the arts and sciences as well as in the business and professional world. It is true that public school education at the time of the Amendment had advanced further in the North, but the effect of the Amendment on Northern States was generally ignored in the congressional debates. Even in the North, the conditions of public education did not approximate those existing today. The curriculum was usually rudimentary; ungraded schools were common in rural areas; the school term was but three months a year in many states; and compulsory school attendance was virtually unknown. As a consequence, it is not surprising that there should be so little in the history of the Fourteenth Amendment relating to its intended effect on public education.

In the first cases in this Court construing the Fourteenth Amendment, decided shortly after its adoption, the Court interpreted it as proscribing all state-imposed discriminations against the Negro race. The doctrine of "separate but equal" did not make its appearance in this Court until 1896 in the case of *Plessy* v. *Ferguson*, involving not education but transportation. American courts have since labored with the doctrine for over half a century. In this Court, there have been six cases involving the "separate but equal" doctrine in the field of public education. In *Cumming* v. *County Board of Education* and *Gong Lum* v. *Rice* the validity of the doctrine itself was not challenged. In more recent cases, all on the graduate school level, inequality was found in that specific benefits enjoyed by white students were denied to Negro students of the same educational qualifications. In none of these cases was it necessary to re-examine the doctrine to grant relief to the Negro plaintiff. And in *Sweatt* v. *Painter*, the Court expressly reserved decision on the question whether *Plessy* v. *Ferguson* should be held inapplicable to public education.

In the instant cases, that question is directly presented. Here, unlike *Sweatt* v. *Painter*, there are findings below that the Negro and white schools involved have been equalized, or are being equalized, with respect to buildings, curricula, qualifications and salaries of teachers, and other "tangible" factors. Our decision, therefore, cannot turn on merely a comparison of these tangible factors in the Negro and white schools involved in each of the cases. We must look instead to the effect of segregation itself on public education.

In approaching this problem, we cannot turn the clock back to 1868 when the Amendment was adopted, or even to 1896 when *Plessy* v. *Ferguson* was written. We must consider public education in the light of its full development and its present place in American life throughout the Nation. Only in this way can it be determined if segregation in public schools deprives these plaintiffs of the equal protection of the laws.

Today, education is perhaps the most important function of state and local governments. Compulsory school attendance laws and the great expenditures for education both demonstrate our recognition of the importance of education to our democratic society. It is required in the performance of our most basic public responsibilities, even service in the armed forces. It is the very foundation of good citizenship. Today it is a principal instrument in awakening the child to cultural values, in preparing him for later professional training, and in helping him to adjust normally to his environment. In these days, it is doubtful that any child may reasonably be expected to succeed in life if he is denied the opportunity of an education. Such an opportunity, where the state has undertaken to provide it, is a right which must be made available to all on equal terms.

We come then to the question presented: Does segregation of children in public schools solely on the basis of race, even though the physical facilities and other "tangible" factors may be equal, deprive the children of the minority group of equal educational opportunities? We believe that it does.

In *Sweatt* v. *Painter*, in finding that a segregated law school for Negroes could not provide them equal educational opportunities, this Court relied in large part on "those qualities which are incapable of objective measurement but which make for greatness in a law school." In *McLaurin* v. *Oklahoma State Regents*, the Court, in requiring that a Negro admitted to a white graduate school be treated like all other students, again resorted to intangible considerations: ". . . his ability to study, to engage in discussions and exchange views with other students, and, in general, to learn his profession." Such considerations apply with added force to children in grade and high schools. To separate them from others of similar age and qualifications solely because of their race generates a feeling of inferiority as to their status in the community that may affect their hearts and minds in a way unlikely ever to be undone. The effect of this separation on their educational opportunities was well stated by a finding in the Kansas case by a court which nevertheless felt compelled to rule against the Negro plaintiffs:

> Segregation of white and colored children in public schools has a detrimental effect upon the colored children. The impact is greater when it has the sanction of the law; for the policy of separating the races is usually interpreted as denoting the inferiority of the negro group. A sense of inferiority affects the motivation of a child to learn. Segregation with the sanction of law, therefore, has a tendency to [retard] the educational and mental development of negro children and to deprive them of some of the benefits they would receive in a racial[ly] integrated school system.

Whatever may have been the extent of psychological knowledge at the time of *Plessy* v. *Ferguson*, this finding is amply supported by modern authority.* Any language in *Plessy* v. *Ferguson* contrary to this finding is rejected.

We conclude that in the field of public education the doctrine of "separate but equal" has no place. Separate educational facilities are inherently unequal. Therefore, we hold that the plaintiffs and others similarly situated for whom the actions

---

*[This footnote, number 11 in the original, has become famous. It is frequently referred to simply as "footnote 11."] K. B. Clark, Effect of Prejudice and Discrimination on Personality Development (Midcentury White House Conference on Children and Youth, 1950); Witmer and Kotinsky, Personality in the Making (1952), c. VI; Deutscher and Chein, The Psychological Effects of Enforced Segregation: A Survey of Social Science Opinion, 26 J. Psychol 259 (1948); Chein, What Are the Psychological Effects of Segregation Under Conditions of Equal Facilities?, 3 Int. J. Opinion and Attitude Res. 229 (1949); Brameld, Educational Costs, in Discrimination and National Welfare (MacIver, ed., 1949), 44–48; Frazier, The Negro in the United States (1949), 674–681. And see generally Myrdal, An American Dilemma (1944).

have been brought are, by reason of the segregation complained of, deprived of the equal protection of the laws guaranteed by the Fourteenth Amendment. This disposition makes unnecessary any discussion whether such segregation also violates the Due Process Clause of the Fourteenth Amendment.

Because these are class actions, because of the wide applicability of this decision, and because of the great variety of local conditions, the formulation of decrees in these cases presents problems of considerable complexity. On reargument, the consideration of appropriate relief was necessarily subordinated to the primary question—the constitutionality of segregation in public education. We have now announced that such segregation is a denial of the equal protection of the laws. In order that we may have the full assistance of the parties in formulating decrees, the cases will be restored to the docket, and the parties are requested to present further argument on Questions 4 and 5 previously propounded by the Court for the reargument this Term. The Attorney General of the United States is again invited to participate. The Attorneys General of the states requiring or permitting segregation in public education will also be permitted to appear as *amici curiae* upon request to do so by September 15, 1954, and submission of briefs by October 1, 1954.

It is so ordered. ■

4.3 *Bolling* v. *Sharpe* (1954)

Chief Justice Earl Warren

Mr. Chief Justice Warren delivered the opinion of the Court.

This case challenges the validity of segregation in the public schools of the District of Columbia. The petitioners, minors of the Negro race, allege that such segregation deprives them of due process of law under the Fifth Amendment. They were refused admission to a public school attended by white children solely because of their race. They sought the aid of the District Court for the District of Columbia in obtaining admission. That court dismissed their complaint. The Court granted a writ of certiorari before judgment in the Court of Appeals because of the importance of the constitutional question presented.

We have this day held that the Equal Protection Clause of the Fourteenth Amendment prohibits the states from maintaining racially segregated public schools. The legal problem in the District of Columbia is somewhat different, however. The Fifth Amendment, which is applicable in the District of Columbia, does not contain an equal protection clause as does the Fourteenth Amendment which applies only to the states. But the concepts of equal protection and due process, both stemming from our American ideal of fairness, are not mutually exclusive. The "equal protection of the laws" is a more explicit safeguard of prohibited unfairness than "due process of law," and, therefore, we do not imply that the two are always interchangeable phrases. But, as this Court has recognized, discrimination may be so unjustifiable as to be violative of due process.

Classifications based solely upon race must be scrutinized with particular care, since they are contrary to our traditions and hence constitutionally suspect. As long ago as 1896, this Court declared the principle "that the Constitution of the United States, in its present form, forbids, so far as civil and political rights are concerned, discrimination by the General Government, or by the States, against any citizen because of his race." And in *Buchanan* v. *Warley*, the Court held that a statute which limited the right of a property owner to convey his property to a person of another race was, as an unreasonable discrimination, a denial of due process of law.

Although the Court has not assumed to define "liberty" with any great precision, that term is not confined to mere freedom from bodily restraint. Liberty under law extends to the full range of conduct which the individual is free to pursue, and it cannot be restricted except for a proper governmental objective. Segregation in public education is not reasonably related to any proper governmental objective, and thus it imposes on Negro children of the District of Columbia a burden that constitutes an arbitrary deprivation of their liberty in violation of the Due Process Clause.

In view of our decision that the Constitution prohibits the states from maintaining racially segregated public schools, it would be unthinkable that the same Constitution would impose a lesser duty on the Federal Government. We hold that racial segregation in the public schools of the District of Columbia is a denial of the due process of law guaranteed by the Fifth Amendment to the Constitution. ■

 # American Politics Today

Only in the 1970s did the Supreme Court begin to enforce the right of women—and men—to be free from sex discrimination. In a series of cases, the Court held that sex discrimination is permissible only if the government can show an "exceedingly persuasive justification" for its actions, and that laws or policies are based on "reasoned analysis rather than through the mechanical application of traditional, often inaccurate, assumptions about the proper roles of men and women." In 1996, for example, the Court ruled that a state-supported military college could not exclude women, even to promote diversity in educational approaches or to preserve a school's "unique method of character development and leadership training."

In recent years, the Court's attention has turned also to the issue of sexual harassment. In a line of cases stretching back to 1986, the justices have ruled that sexual harassment is banned by the Civil Rights Act of 1964, and that the law applies not only to the harassment of women by men but also to the reverse—and that it extends to "same-sex" harassment as well. Although difficult to define and enforce, federal protection against sexual harassment is now firmly rooted in American law.

The two selections in this section both deal with the issue of sexual harassment. Selection 4.4 is a brief excerpt from. *Meritor Savings Bank* v. *Vinson,* the original 1986 case establishing that sexual harassment is prohibited under the Civil Rights Act. Selection 4.5 provides a summary of the Supreme Court's more recent decision in this area, and presents a series of real-life examples that demonstrate the complexities of this area of law.

Questions

1. How does the Court define sexual harassment? What is the difference between "*quid pro quo*" harassment and hostile environment harassment?
2. How does the law seek to balance the individual's right to be free from sexual harassment against the rights of other individuals? Against the interests of schools and employers?

4.4 *Meritor Savings Bank* v. *Vinson* (1986)

Chief Justice William Rehnquist

This case presents important questions concerning claims of workplace "sexual harassment" brought under Title VII of the Civil Rights Act of 1964.

I

In 1974, respondent Mechelle Vinson met Sidney Taylor, a vice-president of what is now petitioner Meritor Savings Bank (bank) and manager of one of its branch offices. When respondent asked whether she might obtain employment at the bank, Taylor gave her an application, which she completed and returned the next day; later that same day, Taylor called her to say that she had been hired. With Taylor as her supervisor, respondent started as a teller-trainee, and thereafter was promoted to teller, head teller, and assistant branch manager. She worked at the same branch for four years, and it is undisputed that her advancement there was based on merit alone. In September, 1978, respondent notified Taylor that she was taking sick leave for an indefinite period. On November 1, 1978, the bank discharged her for excessive use of that leave.

Respondent brought this action against Taylor and the bank, claiming that, during her four years at the bank, she had "constantly been subjected to sexual harassment" by Taylor in violation of Title VII. She sought injunctive relief, compensatory and punitive damages against Taylor and the bank, and attorney's fees. . . .

At . . . trial, the parties presented conflicting testimony about Taylor's behavior during respondent's employment. Respondent testified that, during her probationary period as a teller-trainee, Taylor treated her in a fatherly way and made no sexual advances. Shortly thereafter, however, he invited her out to dinner and, during the course of the meal, suggested that they go to a motel to have sexual relations. At first she refused, but out of what she described as fear of losing her job, she eventually agreed. According to respondent, Taylor thereafter made repeated demands upon her for sexual favors, usually at the branch, both during and after business hours; she estimated that over the next several years she had intercourse with him some 40 or 50 times. In addition, respondent testified that Taylor fondled her in front of other employees, followed her into the women's restroom when she went there alone, exposed himself to her, and even forcibly raped her on several occasions. These activities ceased after 1977, respondent stated, when she started going with a steady boyfriend.

Respondent also testified that Taylor touched and fondled other women employees of the bank, and she attempted to call witnesses to support this charge. . . . Finally, respondent testified that, because she was afraid of Taylor, she never reported his harassment to any of his supervisors and never attempted to use the bank's complaint procedure.

Taylor denied respondent's allegations of sexual activity, testifying that he never fondled her, never made suggestive remarks to her, never engaged in sexual intercourse with her, and never asked her to do so. He contended instead that respondent made her accusations in response to a business-related dispute. The bank also denied respondent's allegations, and asserted that any sexual harassment by Taylor was unknown to the bank and engaged in without its consent or approval.

The District Court denied relief [to Vinson], but did not resolve the conflicting testimony about the existence of a sexual relationship between respondent and Taylor. It found instead that

> [i]f [respondent] and Taylor did engage in an intimate or sexual relationship during the time of [respondent's] employment with [the bank], that relationship was a voluntary one having nothing to do with her continued employment at [the bank] or her advancement or promotions at that institution.

The court ultimately found that respondent "was not the victim of sexual harassment and was not the victim of sexual discrimination" while employed at the bank. . . .

The Court of Appeals for the District of Columbia Circuit reversed. . . . The court stated that a violation of Title VII may be predicated on either of two types of sexual harassment: harassment that involves the conditioning of concrete employment benefits on sexual favors, and harassment that, while not affecting economic benefits, creates a hostile or offensive working environment. The court drew additional support for this position from the Equal Employment Opportunity Commission's Guidelines on Discrimination Because of Sex, which set out these two types of sexual harassment claims. Believing that "Vinson's grievance was clearly of the [hostile environment] type," and that the District Court had not considered whether a violation of this type had occurred, the [Appeals] court [ordered the lower court to reconsider its decision.]

The court further concluded that . . . if the evidence otherwise showed that "Taylor made Vinson's toleration of sexual harassment a condition of her employment," her voluntariness "had no materiality whatsoever." . . .

II

Title VII of the Civil Rights Act of 1964 makes it

> an unlawful employment practice for an employer . . . to discriminate against any individual with respect to his compensation, terms, conditions, or privileges of employment, because of such individual's race, color, religion, sex, or national origin.

The prohibition against discrimination based on sex was added to Title VII at the last minute on the floor of the House of Representatives. The principal argument in opposition to the amendment was that "sex discrimination" was sufficiently different from other types of discrimination that it ought to receive separate legislative treatment. This argument was defeated, the bill quickly passed as amended, and we are left with little legislative history to guide us in interpreting the Act's prohibition against discrimination based on "sex."

[Vinson] argues, and the Court of Appeals held, that unwelcome sexual advances that create an offensive or hostile working environment violate Title VII. Without question, when a supervisor sexually harasses a subordinate because of the subordinate's sex, that supervisor "discriminate[s]" on the basis of sex. [The bank] apparently does not challenge this proposition. It contends instead that, in prohibiting discrimination with respect to "compensation, terms, conditions, or privileges" of employment, Congress was concerned with what petitioner describes as "tangible loss" of "an economic character," not "purely psychological aspects of the workplace environment." In support of this claim [the bank] observes that, in both the legislative history of Title VII and this Court's Title VII decisions, the focus has been on tangible, economic barriers erected by discrimination.

We reject [the bank's] view. First, the language of Title VII is not limited to "economic" or "tangible" discrimination. The phrase "terms, conditions, or privileges of employment" evinces a congressional intent "'to strike at the entire spectrum of disparate treatment of men and women'" in employment. [The bank] has pointed to nothing in the Act to suggest that Congress contemplated the limitation urged here.

Second, in 1980 the [Equal Employment Opportunity Commission] issued Guidelines specifying that "sexual harassment," as there defined, is a form of sex discrimination prohibited by Title VII. . . . The EEOC Guidelines fully support the view that harassment leading to noneconomic injury can violate Title VII.

In defining "sexual harassment," the Guidelines first describe the kinds of workplace conduct that may be actionable under Title VII. These include "[u]nwelcome sexual advances, requests for sexual favors, and other verbal or physical conduct of a sexual nature." Relevant to the charges at issue in this case, the Guidelines provide that such sexual misconduct constitutes prohibited "sexual harassment," whether or not it is directly linked to the grant or denial of an economic *quid pro quo,* where

> such conduct has the purpose or effect of unreasonably interfering with an individual's work performance or creating an intimidating, hostile, or offensive working environment.

In concluding that so-called "hostile environment" (*i.e.,* non *quid pro quo*) harassment violates Title VII, the EEOC drew upon a substantial body of judicial decisions and EEOC precedent holding that Title VII affords employees the right to work in an environment free from discriminatory intimidation, ridicule, and insult. . . .

Since the Guidelines were issued, courts have uniformly held, and we agree, that a plaintiff may establish a violation of Title VII by proving that discrimination based on sex has created a hostile or abusive work environment. As the Court of Appeals for the Eleventh Circuit wrote in *Henson v. Dundee*,

> Sexual harassment which creates a hostile or offensive environment for members of one sex is every bit the arbitrary barrier to sexual equality at the workplace that racial harassment is to racial equality. Surely, a requirement that a man or woman run a guantlet of sexual abuse in return for the privilege of being allowed to work and make a living can be as demeaning and disconcerting as the harshest of racial epithets.

Of course, . . . not all workplace conduct that may be described as "harassment" affects a "term, condition, or privilege" of employment within the meaning of Title VII. [For example, the "mere utterance of an ethnic or racial epithet which engenders offensive feelings in an employee" would not affect the conditions of employment to [a] sufficiently significant degree to violate Title VII). For sexual harassment to be actionable, it must be sufficiently severe or pervasive "to alter the conditions of [the victim's] employment and create an abusive working environment." [Mechelle Vinson's] allegations in this case—which include not only pervasive harassment but also criminal conduct of the most serious nature—are plainly sufficient to state a claim for "hostile environment" sexual harassment. . . .

Accordingly, the judgment of the Court of Appeals reversing the judgment of the District Court is affirmed, and the case is remanded for further proceedings consistent with this opinion. ∎

4.5 Tales From the Front Line of Sexual Harassment (1998)

Margot Slade

Sexual harassment laws have always been notoriously confusing, so there was much cheering when the Supreme Court clarified things by issuing new harassment guidelines last month.

The Court made it clear that employers are always legally responsible for the harassing behavior of supervisors. But it made the world a bit safer for employers by offering them a defense: an effective anti-harassment policy and complaint procedures that employees disregard at their own risk. The Court helped both sides understand what harassment is by explaining in a case involving men that it is the conduct that is at issue—not the sex or sexual desires of the people involved.

In clarifying matters, however, the Court invited new kinds of sexual harassment complaints, from people who turned down sexual advances or felt threatened in the workplace but did not suffer professional harm, and from men and women intimidated by the behavior of people of the same sex.

So there's still plenty of uncertainty for employers and employees alike. In the wake of the Court's new rulings, for example, employers must consider how to make policies comprehensive and what kinds of policies reflect "reasonable care" in preventing and correcting harassment. And even where ineffective policies exist, employees must now consider the consequences of sidestepping them.

Lawyers for both plaintiffs and employers, and the consultants who help companies devise and update their policies, say it will all come down to the white-knuckle moment when a judge or jury decides what is reasonable or not. Here are case studies drawn from the files of consultants and interpreted in light of the Supreme Court's new rulings.

Sexual Hazing

A manufacturing company has a heavily immigrant multiracial work force. At one of its union plants, the integration of women has been recent and difficult. There is a history here of hazing that takes a sexual form. There is a history, too, of management efforts to discipline men for harassing women—the company has a written anti-harassment policy—and of union support for the men.

An African man, a recent arrival to the United States, is hired. Within days, he makes clear that he objects on religious grounds to explicit discussions of sexuality, whether in words, jokes or descriptions of someone's sexual activities. But the more he protests, the more his co-workers—joined occasionally by a department manager—indulge in sexual banter.

Soon, the new employee is ostracized. He spends more time alone reading, sometimes religious materials, which prompts more heckling. The shop steward warns the men to tone it down or risk management discipline. They don't.

The new employee disregards the union's grievance procedure—he does not report management's inaction. He also disregards the chain of command spelled out in the company's complaint process and goes to an executive demanding relief.

Resolution: Management transfers the worker to another plant, explaining that the workplace environment was too poisonous to heal. His co-workers are chastised, and for a while the atmosphere during breaks is less sexually charged.

Comments: Management is lucky, said Peggy Garrity, a Santa Monica, Calif., litigator who represents plaintiffs in discrimination cases. Even though the company had a policy and acted appropriately in the end, "the new employee could have sued and the company would have had little defense," she said.

Supervisors knew what was happening. And given the company's history, and a supervisor's participation in the heckling, the employee's action was not unreasonable. Freada Klein of Klein Associates Inc. in Cambridge, Mass., a consultant on issues of workplace bias, said the company needed to retool its policy "to articulate general principles, not situation-specific rules." And it should institute a training program so everyone understands that crude or sexual behavior is no longer tolerated.

Falling Off the Fast Track

At a profitable, publicly held company, rumors of the chief executive's affairs with women on staff are rampant. This executive has even acted inappropriately at social gatherings toward the wives of the company's directors—uninvited touching, for example. The wives have told their husbands.

In recent months, the executive has become smitten with the business acumen and beauty of a female manager, who is perceived by many colleagues as being on a fast track. She is bold in her thinking and actions, which to many male colleagues makes her a threat. She has enjoyed a string of business successes, but a recent deal went badly awry.

At a company cocktail party, the chief executive continually brushes against her as he talks about his sexual conquests. She resorts to the company's complaint process, which is spelled out in a policy distributed to employees.

During the weeks after the party, the manager is denied a bonus and is removed from a high-visibility task force. She cries retaliation. The executive insists the company was responding to her soured deal. "She wants to be judged on her performance," he tells his directors. "So be it."

Resolution: The woman is leaving the company, which is trying to head off a lawsuit with a negotiated settlement.

Comments: The company, Ms. Klein said, would lose a lawsuit, since "reasonable care" means taking preventive measures. "The directors knew there was a problem" and should have been predisposed to interpret the executive's actions as retaliation.

Paul Salvatore, a partner in the labor and employment law department of Proskauer Rose in New York, agreed, saying, "This c.e.o. was a walking liability." This kind of situation is extremely difficult, he added, because few company policies anticipate that the problem supervisor will be a chief executive. "Who are you going to complain to and about?" he said.

The Reluctant Complainer

A high-level manager visits a client in Scandinavia, where he attends an office function. Returning to the United States, he regales his female colleague with stories of late-night dinners and club hopping, where the entertainers were scantily clad women. He even brings photographs, knowing his female colleague is a world traveler who has visited Scandinavia.

An administrative assistant who works for him and several other executives overhears the conversation. She is scandalized. After a time, the manager offers to show her the photographs. She says no thanks, so he removes them from sight.

There is more. The administrative assistant knows through the grapevine that the manager belongs to an in-house group whose members exchange bawdy jokes via E-mail. One day, the manager inadvertently sends her such a message. He realizes his mistake and apologizes. Later, he asks her to retrieve a budget report from his in-box, but the top item is a soft-porn video.

The administrative assistant tells no one, but avoids working for the manager. She explains to her supervisor that she's not comfortable with him. The supervisor inquires further and she recounts the E-mail and video stories. When asked why she didn't speak up earlier, the administrative assistant says she thought she wouldn't be taken seriously.

Resolution: Following the company's sexual harassment policy, an investigator determines that the E-mail message was indeed inadvertent and that the video had been manufactured by the manager's client. But a memo is sent to all employees saying that the use of E-mail for bawdy jokes is inappropriate and must stop. The manager is sent for training to help him develop better judgment. He is also given a new assistant, so that no one need worry about perceived retaliation or the fairness of the woman's job evaluations.

Comments: "Well handled," Mr. Salvatore said. "That's how it should work." Had the woman sued, he added, the company had a defense: a viable complaint process and her decision not to use it. But Ms. Garrity and Ms. Klein said the woman's situation needs monitoring since other employees might blame her for the manager's censure and the shutdown of the E-mail exchange.

One of the Guys

A woman works as a supervisor at a construction company—a traditionally male environment. She prides herself on being able to deflect the sexual bantering common on the job.

There is a problem with one project and the company brings in a new district manager, expressing confidence that he can salvage it.

The manager arranges to meet the woman at different times to observe the crews, review the books and, he says, learn from her expertise. Soon he's calling her at home suggesting they meet for breakfast. She senses that something's amiss, but she figures she can handle it.

Then she starts getting job-related messages on her home answering machine at all hours of the night. She E-mails responses to the office. One evening she answers the phone and it's him, asking questions he could have posed at the office. Suddenly he says: "I always see you in a hard hat and overalls. What are you wearing now?" She changes the subject and hangs up.

She is panicked. After all, he's a star and she's expendable; the company and the industry have long tolerated sexual bantering and worse, and she has a reputation for being unflappable, which she wants to uphold. So although the company has a written sexual harassment policy and process—admittedly minimal and devoid of training—she doesn't use it.

The woman loses sleep and feels ill much of the time. Meanwhile, the man takes her to lunch, casually brushing against her hand during the meal.

One night, while she is working late, he appears and insists they go out. She says no and tries to leave. He blocks the way, kissing her on the mouth. She pushes him aside and rushes home.

Resolution: Her health deteriorates. She goes on disability leave, never to return, and then sues.

Comments: "This is the cutting edge of rock-and-roll," Mr. Salvatore said. "The company policy may be ineffective, but I don't know that she'd win." Forget her pride and the disparity between her power and his, Ms. Garrity said—she was a supervisor who understood complaint procedures. "She'd have to throw herself on the mercy of the court to explain why not using them was reasonable," she said. This company, she added, "has a good shot at a solid defense." ∎

The Comparative Context

The Western political tradition, writes the political scientist Will Kymlicka in selection 4.6, "has been surprisingly silent" on questions involving the rights of ethnic, racial, linguistic, and cultural minorities. Instead, "political theorists have operated with an idealized model" of politics in which "fellow citizens share a common descent, language, and culture." This theoretical gap has serious practical implications—in particular, in his view, Western political systems are ill-equipped to deal with the increasingly important and divisive issues arising from their diversity.

In this selection, Kymlicka provides a theoretical model for recognizing what he calls "group-differentiated rights"—the idea, that is, that citizens may be entitled to certain rights because of their membership in a particular group. Although it runs counter to much of our political tradition, the idea of group rights, Kymlicka suggests, is legitimate, and ought to be taken seriously.

Questions

1. Why are traditional rights principles insufficient to deal with the problem of minority groups? Why is it necessary to "supplement traditional human rights principles with a theory of minority rights"?
2. What are the implications of Kymlicka's approach for affirmative action? For "English-only" legislation? For minority representation in Congress and in state legislatures?

4.6 Multicultural Citizenship (1995)

Will Kymlicka

1. The Issues

Most countries today are culturally diverse. According to recent estimates, the world's 184 independent states contain over 600 living language groups, and 5,000 ethnic groups. In very few countries can the citizens be said to share the same language, or belong to the same ethnonational group.

Will Kymlicka, *Multicultural Citizenship: A Theory of Minority Rights* (New York: Oxford University Press, 1995), pp. 1–6, 26–28, 30–33. Reprinted by permission of Oxford University Press.

This diversity gives rise to a series of important and potentially divisive questions. Minorities and majorities increasingly clash over such issues as language rights, regional autonomy, political representation, education curriculum, land claims, immigration and naturalization policy, even national symbols, such as the choice of national anthem or public holidays. Finding morally defensible and politically viable answers to these issues is the greatest challenge facing democracies today. In Eastern Europe and the Third World, attempts to create liberal democratic institutions are being undermined by violent nationalist conflicts. In the West, volatile disputes over the rights of immigrants, indigenous peoples, and other cultural minorities are throwing into question many of the assumptions which have governed political life for decades. Since the end of the Cold War, ethnocultural conflicts have become the most common source of political violence in the world, and they show no sign of abating.

... There are no simple answers or magic formulas to resolve all these questions. Some conflicts are intractable, even when the disputants are motivated by a sense of fairness and tolerance, which all too often is lacking. Moreover, every dispute has its own unique history and circumstances that need to be taken into account in devising a fair and workable solution. My aim is to step back and present a more general view of the landscape—to identify some key concepts and principles that need to be taken into account, and so clarify the basic building blocks for a liberal approach to minority rights.

The Western political tradition has been surprisingly silent on these issues. Most organized political communities throughout recorded history have been multiethnic, a testament to the ubiquity of both conquest and long-distance trade in human affairs. Yet most Western political theorists have operated with an idealized model of the polis in which fellow citizens share a common descent, language, and culture. Even when the theorists themselves lived in polyglot empires that governed numerous ethnic and linguistic groups, they have often written as if the culturally homogeneous city-states of Ancient Greece provided the essential or standard model of a political community.

To achieve this ideal of a homogeneous polity, governments throughout history have pursued a variety of policies regarding cultural minorities. Some minorities were physically eliminated, either by mass expulsion (what we now call "ethnic cleansing") or by genocide. Other minorities were coercively assimilated, forced to adopt the language, religion, and customs of the majority. In yet other cases, minorities were treated as resident aliens, subjected to physical segregation and economic discrimination, and denied political rights.

Various efforts have been made historically to protect cultural minorities, and to regulate the potential conflicts between majority and minority cultures. Early in this century, bilateral treaties regulated the treatment of fellow nationals in other countries. For example, Germany agreed to accord certain rights and privileges to ethnic Poles residing within its borders, so long as Poland provided reciprocal rights to ethnic Germans in Poland. This treaty system was extended, and given a more multilateral basis, under the League of Nations.

However, these treaties were inadequate. For one thing, a minority was only ensured protection from discrimination and oppression if there was a "kin state" nearby which took an interest in it. Moreover, the treaties were destabilizing, because where such kin states did exist, they often used treaty provisions as grounds for invading or intervening in weaker countries. Thus Nazi Germany justified its invasion of Poland and Czechoslovakia on the grounds that these countries were violating the treaty rights of ethnic Germans on their soil.

After World War II, it was clear that a different approach to minority rights was needed. Many liberals hoped that the new emphasis on "human rights" would resolve minority conflicts. Rather than protecting vulnerable groups directly, through special rights for the members of designated groups, cultural minorities would be protected indirectly, by guaranteeing basic civil and political rights to all individuals regardless of group membership. Basic human rights such as freedom of speech, association, and conscience, while attributed to individuals, are typically exercised in community with others, and so provide protection for group life. Where these individual rights are firmly protected, liberals assumed, no further rights needed to be attributed to the members of specific ethnic or national minorities:

> the general tendency of the postwar movements for the promotion of human rights has been to subsume the problem of national minorities under the broader problem of ensuring basic individual rights to all human beings, without reference to membership in ethnic groups. The leading assumption has been that members of national minorities do not need, are not entitled to, or cannot be granted rights of a special character. The doctrine of human rights has been put forward as a substitute for the concept of minority rights, with the strong implication that minorities whose members enjoy individual equality of treatment cannot legitimately demand facilities for the maintenance of their ethnic particularism.

Guided by this philosophy, the United Nations deleted all references to the rights of ethnic and national minorities in its Universal Declaration of Human Rights.

The shift from group-specific minority rights to universal human rights was embraced by many liberals, partly because it seemed a natural extension of the way religious minorities were protected. In the sixteenth century, European states were being torn apart by conflict between Catholics and Protestants over which religion should rule the land. These conflicts were finally resolved, not by granting special rights to particular religious minorities, but by separating church and state, and entrenching each's individual freedom of religion. Religious minorities are protected indirectly, by guaranteeing individual freedom of worship, so that people can freely associate with other co-religionists, without fear of state discrimination or disapproval.

Many post-war liberals have thought that religious tolerance based on the separation of church and state provides a model for dealing with ethnocultural differences as well. On this view, ethnic identity, like religion, is something which people should be free to express in their private life, but which is not the concern of the state. The state does not oppose the freedom of people to express their particular cultural attachments, but nor does it nurture such expression—rather, to adapt Nathan Glazer's phrase, it responds with "benign neglect." The members of ethnic and national groups are protected against discrimination and prejudice, and they are free to try to maintain whatever part of their ethnic heritage or identity they wish, consistent with the rights of others. But their efforts are purely private, and it is not the place of public agencies to attach legal identities or disabilities to cultural membership or ethnic identity. This separation of state and ethnicity precludes any legal or governmental recognition of ethnic groups, or any use of ethnic criteria in the distribution of rights, resources, and duties.

Many liberals, particularly on the left, have made an exception in the case of affirmative action for disadvantaged racial groups. But in a sense this is the exception that proves the rule. Affirmative action is generally defended as a temporary measure which is needed to move more rapidly towards a "colour-blind" society. It is intended to remedy years of discrimination, and thereby move us closer to the sort of society that would have existed had we observed the separation of state and ethnicity from the beginning. Thus the UN Convention on Racial Discrimination endorses affirmative action programmes only where they have this temporary and remedial character. Far from abandoning the ideal of the separation of state and ethnicity, affirmative action is one method of trying to achieve that ideal.

Some liberals, particularly on the right, think it is counterproductive to pursue a "colour-blind" society through policies that "count by race." Affirmative action, they argue, exacerbates the very problem it was intended to solve, by making people more conscious of group differences, and more resentful of other groups. This dispute amongst liberals over the need for remedial affirmative action programmes is a familiar one in many liberal democracies.

But what most post-war liberals on both the right and left continue to reject is the idea of *permanent* differentiation in the rights or status of the members of certain groups. In particular, they reject the claim that group-specific rights are needed to accommodate enduring cultural differences, rather than remedy historical discrimination. As we will see in subsequent chapters, post-war liberals around the world have repeatedly opposed the idea that specific ethnic or national groups should be given a permanent political identity or constitutional status.

However, it has become increasingly clear that minority rights cannot be subsumed under the category of human rights. Traditional human rights standards are simply unable to resolve some of the most important and controversial questions relating to cultural minorities: which languages should be recognized in the parliaments, bureaucracies, and courts? Should each ethnic or national group have publicly funded education in its mother tongue? Should internal boundaries (legislative districts, provinces, states) be drawn so that cultural minorities form a majority within a local region? Should governmental powers be devolved from the central level to more local or regional levels controlled by particular minorities, particularly on culturally sensitive issues of immigration, communication, and education? Should political offices be distributed in accordance with a principle of national or ethnic proportionality? Should the traditional homelands of indigenous peoples be reserved for their benefit, and so protected from encroachment by settlers and resource developers? What are the responsibilities of minorities to integrate? What degree of cultural integration can be required of immigrants and refugees before they acquire citizenship?

The problem is not that traditional human rights doctrines give us the wrong answer to these questions. It is rather that they often give no answer at all. The right to free speech does not tell us what an appropriate language policy is; the right to vote does not tell us how political boundaries should be drawn, or how powers should be distributed between levels of government; the right to mobility does not tell us what an appropriate immigration and naturalization policy is. These questions have been left to the usual process of majoritarian decision-making within each state. The result, I will argue, has been to render cultural minorities vulnerable to significant injustice at the hands of the majority, and to exacerbate ethnocultural conflict.

To resolve these questions fairly, we need to supplement traditional human rights principles with a theory of minority rights. The necessity for such a theory has become painfully clear in Eastern Europe and the former Soviet Union. Disputes over local autonomy, the drawing of boundaries, language rights, and naturalization policy have engulfed much of the region in violent conflict. There is little hope that stable peace will be restored, or that basic human rights will be respected, until these minority rights issues are resolved.

It is not surprising, therefore, that minority rights have returned to prominence in international relations. For example, the Conference on Security and Co-operation in Europe (CSCE) adopted a declaration on the Rights of National Minorities in 1991, and established a High Commissioner on National Minorities in 1993. The United Nations has been debating both a Declaration on the Rights of Persons Belonging to National or Ethnic, Religious and Linguistic Minorities (1993), and a Draft Universal Declaration on Indigenous Rights (1988). The Council of Europe adopted a declaration on minority language rights in 1992 (the European Charter for Regional or Minority Languages). Other examples could be given.

However, these declarations remain controversial. Some were adopted hastily, to help prevent the escalation of conflict in Eastern Europe. As a result, they are quite vague, and often seem motivated more by the need to appease belligerent minorities than by any clear sense of what justice requires. Both the underlying justification for these rights, and their limits, remain unclear.

I believe it is legitimate, and indeed unavoidable, to supplement traditional human rights with minority rights. A comprehensive theory of justice in a multicultural state will include both universal rights, assigned to individuals regardless of group membership, and certain group-differentiated rights or "special status" for minority cultures.

Recognizing minority rights has obvious dangers. The language of minority rights has been used and abused not only by the Nazis, but also by apologists for racial segregation and apartheid. It has also been used by intolerant and belligerent nationalists and fundamentalists throughout the world to justify the domination of people outside their group, and the suppression of dissenters within the group. A liberal theory of minority rights, therefore, must explain how minority rights coexist with human rights, and how minority rights are limited by principles of individual liberty, democracy, and social justice.

● ● ●

2. Three Forms of Group-Differentiated Rights

Virtually all liberal democracies are either multinational or polyethnic, or both. The "challenge of multiculturalism" is to accommodate these national and ethnic differences in a stable and morally defensible way. In this section, I will discuss some of the most important ways in which democracies have responded to the demands of national minorities and ethnic groups.

In all liberal democracies, one of the major mechanisms for accommodating cultural differences is the protection of the civil and political rights of individuals. It is impossible to overstate the importance of freedom of association, religion, speech, mobility, and political organization for protecting group difference. These rights enable individuals to form and maintain the various groups and associations which constitute civil society, to adapt these groups to changing circumstances, and to promote their views and interests to the wider population. The protection afforded by these common rights of citizenship is sufficient for many of the legitimate forms of diversity in society.

Various critics of liberalism—including some Marxists, communitarians, and feminists—have argued that the liberal focus on individual rights reflects an atomistic, materialistic, instrumental, or conflictual view of human relationships. I believe that this criticism is profoundly mistaken, and that individual rights can be and typically are used to sustain a wide range of social relationships. Indeed, the most basic liberal right—freedom of conscience—is primarily valuable for the protection it gives to intrinsically social (and non-instrumental) activities.

However, it is increasingly accepted in many countries that some forms of cultural difference can only be accommodated through special legal or constitutional measures, above and beyond the common rights of citizenship. Some forms of group difference can only be accommodated if their members have certain group-specific rights—what Iris Young calls "differentiated citizenship."

For example, a recent government publication in Canada noted that:

> In the Canadian experience, it has not been enough to protect only universal individual rights. Here, the Constitution and ordinary laws also protect other rights accorded to individuals as members of certain communities. This accommodation of both types of rights makes our constitution unique and reflects the Canadian value of equality that accommodates difference. The fact that community rights exist alongside individual rights goes to the very heart of what Canada is all about.

It is quite misleading to say that Canada is unique in combining universal individual rights and group-specific "community rights." Such a combination exists in many other federal systems in Europe, Asia, and Africa. As I noted earlier, even the constitution of the United States, which is often seen as a paradigm of individualism, allows for various group-specific rights, including the special status of American Indians and Puerto Ricans.

It is these special group-specific measures for accommodating national and ethnic differences that I will focus on. There are at least three forms of group-specific rights: (1) self-government rights; (2) polyethnic rights; and (3) special representation rights. I will say a few words about each. . . .

1. Self-government Rights   In most multination states, the component nations are inclined to demand some form of political autonomy or territorial jurisdiction, so as to ensure the full and free development of their cultures and the best interests of their people. At the extreme, nations may wish to secede, if they think their self-determination is impossible within the larger state.

The right of national groups to self-determination is given (limited) recognition in international law. According to the United Nations' Charter, "all peoples have the right to self-determination." However, the UN has not defined "peoples," and it has generally applied the principle of self-determination only to overseas colonies, not internal national minorities, even when the latter were subject to the same sort of colonization and conquest as the former. This limitation on self-determination to overseas colonies (known as the "salt-water thesis") is widely seen as arbitrary, and many national minorities insist that they too are "peoples" or "nations," and, as such, have the right of self-determination. They demand certain powers of self-government which they say were not relinquished by their (often involuntary) incorporation into a larger state.

One mechanism for recognizing claims to self-government is federalism, which divides powers between the central government and regional subunits (provinces/states/cantons). Where national minorities are regionally concentrated, the boundaries of federal subunits can be drawn so that the national minority forms a majority in one of the subunits. Under these circumstances, federalism can provide extensive self-government for a national minority, guaranteeing its ability to make decisions in certain areas without being outvoted by the larger society.

For example, under the federal division of powers in Canada, the province of Quebec (which is 80 per cent francophone) has extensive jurisdiction over issues that are crucial to the survival of the French culture, including control over education, language, culture, as well as significant input into immigration policy. The other nine provinces also have these powers, but the major impetus behind the existing division of powers, and indeed behind the entire federal system, is the need to accommodate the Québécois. At the time of Confederation, most English Canadian leaders were in favour of a unitary state, like Britain, and agreed to a federal system primarily to accommodate French Canadians. . . .

2. Polyethnic Rights   As I noted earlier, immigrant groups in the last thirty years have successfully challenged the "Anglo-conformity" model which assumed that they should abandon all aspects of their ethnic heritage and assimilate to existing cultural norms and customs. At first, this challenge simply took the form of demanding the right freely to express their particularity without fear of prejudice or discrimination in the mainstream society. It was the demand, as Walzer put it, that "politics be separated from nationality—as it was already separated from religion."

But the demands of ethnic groups have expanded in important directions. It became clear that positive steps were required to root out discrimination and prejudice, particularly against visible minorities. For this reason, anti-racism policies are considered part of the "multiculturalism" policy in Canada and Australia, as are changes to the education curriculum to recognize the history and contribution of minorities. However, these policies are primarily directed at ensuring the effective exercise of the common rights of citizenship, and so do not really qualify as group-differentiated citizenship rights.

Some ethnic groups and religious minorities have also demanded various forms of public funding of their cultural practices. This includes the funding of ethnic associations, magazines, and festivals. Given that most liberal states provide funding to the arts and museums, so as to preserve the richness and diversity of our cultural resources, funding for ethnic studies and ethnic associations can be seen as falling under this heading. Indeed, some people defend this funding simply as a way of ensuring that ethnic groups are not discriminated against in state funding of art and culture. Some people believe that public funding agencies have traditionally been biased in favour of European-derived forms of cultural expression, and programmes targeted at ethnic groups remedy this bias. A related demand . . . is for the provision of immigrant language education in schools.

Perhaps the most controversial demand of ethnic groups is for exemptions from laws and regulations that disadvantage them, given their religious practices. For example, Jews and Muslims in Britain have sought exemption from Sunday closing or animal slaughtering legislation; Sikh men in Canada have sought exemption from motorcycle helmet laws and from the official dress-codes of police forces, so that they can wear their turban; Orthodox Jews in the United States have sought the right to wear the yarmulka during military service; and Muslim girls in France have sought exemption from school dress-codes so that they can wear the *chador*.

These group-specific measures—which I call "polyethnic rights"—are intended to help ethnic groups and religious minorities express their cultural particularity and pride without it hampering their success in the economic and political institutions of the dominant society. Like self-government rights, these polyethnic rights are not seen as temporary, because the cultural differences they protect are not something we seek to eliminate. But, . . . unlike self-government rights, polyethnic rights are usually intended to promote integration into the larger society, not self-government.

3. Special Representation Rights   While the traditional concern of national minorities and ethnic groups has been with either self-government or polyethnic rights, there has been increasing interest by these groups, as well as other non-ethnic social groups, in the idea of special representation rights.

Throughout the Western democracies, there is increasing concern that the political process is "unrepresentative," in the sense that it fails to reflect the diversity of the population. Legislatures in most of these countries are dominated by middle-class, able-bodied, white men. A more representative process, it is said, would include members of ethnic and racial minorities, women, the poor, the disabled, etc. The under-representation of historically disadvantaged groups is a general phenomenon. In the United States and Canada, women, racial minorities, and indigenous peoples all have under one-third of the seats they would have based on their demographic weight. People with disabilities and the economically disadvantaged are also significantly underrepresented.

One way to reform the process is to make political parties more inclusive, by reducing the barriers which inhibit women, ethnic minorities, or the poor from becoming party candidates or party leaders; another way is to adopt some form of proportional representation, which has historically been associated with greater inclusiveness of candidates.

However, there is increasing interest in the idea that a certain number of seats in the legislature should be reserved for the members of disadvantaged or marginalized groups. During the debate in Canada over the Charlottetown Accord, for example, a number of recommendations were made for the guaranteed representation of women, ethnic minorities, official language minorities, and Aboriginals.

Group representation rights are often defended as a response to some systemic disadvantage or barrier in the political process which makes it impossible for the group's views and interests to be effectively represented. In so far as these rights are seen as a response to oppression or systemic disadvantage, they are most plausibly seen as a temporary measure on the way to a society where the need for special representation no longer exists—a form of political "affirmative action." Society should seek to remove the oppression and disadvantage, thereby eliminating the need for these rights.

However, the issue of special representation rights for groups is complicated, because special representation is sometimes defended, not on grounds of oppression, but as a corollary of self-government. A minority's right to self-government would be severely weakened if some external body could unilaterally revise or revoke its powers, without consulting the minority or securing its consent. Hence it would seem to be a corollary of self-government that the national minority be guaranteed representation on any body which can interpret or modify its powers of self-government (e.g. the Supreme Court). Since the claims of self-government are seen as inherent and permanent, so too are the guarantees of representation which flow from it (unlike guarantees grounded on oppression).

This is just a brief sketch of three mechanisms used to accommodate cultural differences. . . . Virtually every modern democracy employs one or more of these mechanisms. Obviously, these three kinds of rights can overlap, in the sense that some groups can claim more than one kind of right. For example, indigenous groups may demand both special representation in the central government, in virtue of their disadvantaged position, and various powers of self-government, in virtue of their status as a "people" or "nation." But these rights need not go together. An oppressed group, like the disabled, may seek special representation, but have no basis for claiming either self-government or polyethnic rights. Conversely, an economically successful immigrant group may seek polyethnic rights, but have no basis for claiming either special representation or self-government, etc. ■

 # View from the Inside

Few issues have caused as much controversy in recent years as the question of gay rights. For many Americans, the focal point of the gay rights question was the issue of gays in the military. When Bill Clinton became president in 1993, he moved quickly to end the military's ban on gay soldiers. Opposition to the idea was so fierce, however, that Clinton settled on a policy of "don't ask, don't tell"—a system in which soldiers

could still be jailed or discharged simply because they were gay, but in which military officials did not go out of their way to ask about or investigate matters of sexual orientation. This policy has drawn fire from all sides, but it has been upheld by the courts, and it
remains the law of the land. ·

One of the most celebrated cases involving gays in the military involved Col. Margarethe Cammermeyer, who before her discharge in 1992 was the chief nurse of the
Washington State National Guard and in position to compete for the position of Chief
Nurse of the Army. Then, during a routine security clearance interview, she disclosed
that she was a lesbian. Cammermeyer's words set in motion a chain of events that would
end her military career but that would, in the end, help force the issue of gays in the military to the top of the national agenda.

In this brief excerpt from her autobiography, Cammermeyer describes her rapid descent from a decorated hero to a military pariah.

Questions

1. What arguments are used to justify the ban on gays in the military? How are
   those arguments influenced by the particular circumstances of Cammermeyer's
   case?
2. In what ways is discrimination against gays similar to discrimination against
   African Americans, women, or other minority groups? In what ways is discrimination against gays different? What are the implications of these similarities
   and differences for the question of gays in the military?

4.7 Serving in Silence (1994)

Margarethe Cammermeyer

On April 28, 1989, I started to work at half-past six, as I did every morning,
expecting the day to be like any other. Friday was clinic, when I met with
patients one after another, reviewed the progress of their treatment strategies, monitored their medications, and listened to their concerns. Immediately
after the last appointment, I was expected at my realtor's office to sign an offer on
a new home, just south of Seattle, with a view of Puget Sound. And wedged in between—almost unnoticeable in the crush of other demands—I had a meeting
with Agent Brent Troutman of the Defense Investigative Service, as part of my
military work. I remember clearly the agent's requesting a face-to-face interview
with me and how difficult it had been to find time in my schedule.

As I parked my car and entered the hospital, I decided it would be best to meet
with Agent Troutman in my office, away from the distractions of the clinic. I
didn't feel apprehension. After all, this was my turf. He had courteously promised
it would take no more than forty-five minutes of my time and would be a routine

---

interview. And that's what I expected it to be. From my protected position— colonel and Chief Nurse of the Washington State National Guard—from naïveté, and perhaps from denial, I wasn't apprehensive about answering questions concerning my application for a top-secret clearance.

But something made me schedule it on the busiest day of my week. Something kept me from thinking about the kinds of questions the agent might ask and what my answers would be.

With classes, weekend duty in the National Guard, and research on my doctorate, this was the earliest time I had been able to squeeze him into my schedule. Fortunately, a graduate student training with me was available to cover my brief absence. The student could handle my patients during that time—and I'd be close at hand should anything come up she needed me for—so I'd agreed to meet with him at eleven o'clock.

While demanding and busy, my life now was filled with average-sized joys and disappointments. It had a rhythm I liked. The trajectory of change through which I had been propelled so rapidly after my divorce in 1980 had slowed. I called my own shots and counted my own blessings, which were many. And most important, my life was filled with the needs and accomplishments of my four sons.

I believed the turmoil in my life was over.

At forty-seven, I had just a few more goals to achieve before a graceful military retirement. I had wanted to be national Chief Nurse and a general since I first joined the Army in 1961. Now I had the background, the military experience, and the professional education (particularly since my doctorate was almost completed) to compete for that position. I had already taken the Basic and Advanced Officers' courses, the Command and General Staff course, and the Chemical Casualty Care Course, but I had not been to the War College. To position myself for my next promotion, I needed to take courses there, which required I upgrade my military clearance to top secret. And to do that I had to meet with Agent Troutman.

After a morning of examining and evaluating patients, I greeted Brent Troutman. We chatted pleasantly as we walked to my office. Ironically, it was in the basement in a remote part of the building. Built below ground level, it had only one little window up near the ceiling. As the interview dragged on, the forty-five minutes stretching to hours, the room began to feel like a prison cell. Before it was over, I felt that I had spent the day in a dungeon undergoing an interrogation as part of a spy drama.

Agent Troutman spread out papers on the desk and began asking the questions on his list, which I answered without hesitation. Midway through these routine inquiries, he read from his form a question that concerned homosexuality. Curiously, I don't remember the exact wording, though the question would change my life.

I took a breath; a little moment passed. Up to a few years before, I wouldn't have been hesitant. I would have affirmed my heterosexuality and the interview would have proceeded without a hitch. But I had changed, had painfully and slowly come to terms with my identity.

I really had no idea that day in 1989 what the consequences of my honesty could possibly be. This was before the media focus on gays in the military. I wasn't familiar with the few lawsuits challenging the policy. Personally, I'd never known anyone who had been investigated or discharged because of his or her sexual orientation. In fact, I didn't know what the regulations actually said. I assumed commanders had discretion in handling these matters. I believed the Constitution I had sworn to defend as a soldier permitted those, like myself, with unblemished records to serve regardless of the color of their skin, their ethnic background, their religion, or their sexual orientation.

As the question hung in the air, I had no choice about what my answer would be. This was a top-secret clearance—I was asking to be deemed worthy of trust and to prove I couldn't be blackmailed by anyone. Of course, I'd tell the truth. Even though it was a truth I'd given a name to less than a year before. Even though the small clutch in my throat told me this might change everything.

I said, "I am a lesbian."

The routine interview turned into an interrogation. Agent Troutman stayed until 4:00 P.M. He then came back an hour later with a statement he had written for me to sign. They weren't my words, but he wanted me to sign my name to them as though they were. He'd condensed a five-hour interview into a short page. There were phrases I'd never used, comments I'd never made. I crossed them out and signed only what was left.

As I was investigated and discharged, this statement served as the basis of my prosecution. My four words had begun an ordeal. At the time, hurrying out of my dungeon-like office to get to my last patients of the day, I tried to shake off the feeling that the military I loved would now become my adversary.

I finished at the clinic, and I got to the real-estate office in time. I wasn't late. But that's all I remember. The world was spinning. I felt numb.

The next years would be a journey both lonely and exposing. I have been interviewed, quoted, avoided, and sought after. There were times I felt helpless, times I want to hide. I waited with anguish for the mail, hoping for, yet dreading, the letter from the military that would tell me what was going to happen next. Would the Army accept me or discharge me? Would I be court-martialed or retired? Would the regulation banning gays be changed or would I be drummed out in shame? Waiting, walking to the mailbox, hoping this day's delivery would have news of what the military would do.

I have been luckier than many others who have suffered discrimination in the armed forces. My investigation, while filled with intimidation and unsubstantiated innuendos, was not the witch-hunt others have endured. I wasn't arrested or put in prison, as has happened too often. I wasn't beaten up or killed—the tragic fate of Allen Schindler and others who were not protected by the government they served and loved. I didn't lose my civilian job. A strong family surrounded me. My brothers and my father have never wavered in their support. My sons and daughters-in-laws have lovingly, tenaciously stood by me with good-natured irritation at all the fuss. But still, my military career has been taken from me. Despite the mollifying words of the officer who headed my military hearing, "You are a great American," I was discharged.

I'm not angry at the military—it gave me the honor and opportunity to serve my country for twenty-six years. And though no longer in uniform, I still serve. My mission now is to dispel people's stereotypes of gays and lesbians. The chains of prejudice are made of ignorance and fear.

So I've folded my uniform and put it away. I avoid the flag (although even now, if alone, I sometimes salute it, because it's not the flag but the government that's a fraud). At ceremonies, I rise with everyone and begin the pledge of allegiance, but catch my breath in the middle, stop. I cannot say the last line because it is not true.

During my years in uniform, I served according to the motto: duty, honor, and integrity. Those ideals defined the military for me. Several times in this ordeal, soon after my first meeting with Agent Troutman and through the years of investigations that followed, I was asked by other officials if I wasn't just "stressed" or confused when I said I was a lesbian. They offered me opportunities to recant, to return to silence, and all would be forgotten. There is no choice. I'd rather sacrifice my uniform than my integrity.

But I never really thought that would be the way it would play out. No, as naïve as it sounds, I didn't think that in America I would have to choose between being honest and serving my country. Not in the hours with Agent Troutman in April 1989, not in the two and a half years of investigations and hearings, not in the numerous meetings—explaining my position, my record, my commendations for service—did I believe it would come down to losing my military career because of prejudice and hate. Not until my last day in uniform. The day of my discharge.

I had always dreamed that I would retire with full military honors, in a parade with a band playing and tears flowing. But the tears on the day of my discharge were not expressions of pride and honor. I put on my uniform and medals for the last time, arrived on the post to turn in my field gear, keys, and identification card. I would no longer drive up to the gate, present my badge to the entry guard, receive and return a smart salute, with permission to pass onto the post. It was over. It really had come to that.

The servicemen and -women under my command gave me their final salute. Our military demeanor was broken by hugs, and smiles, and tears. There were people from the media, attorneys who were carrying my case forward, well-wishers from the National Guard. Everyone was warm and generous. I felt shame, but I didn't let anyone know that by the way I presented myself. I had not convinced the military to let me stay and serve, had not persevered to change a regulation: I felt the shame of failure. Honesty brought wholeness to my life and shattered it.

At the end of the goodbyes, with the press conference over and the attorneys and TV crews packing to go, a pickup truck drove up. A man in slacks and a sport shirt and a woman in a jogging suit jumped out. The woman paced in the parking lot, yelling to be heard above the quiet conversations around me. She pointed to the man, stuck out her chin, and screamed at me, "My husband spent forty years in the Air Force, forty years of his life to protect our country from people like you."

Everyone stopped talking. I said quietly, "No, that's not what he was protecting us from."

She cut me off, yelling, "I feel like vomiting."

I started to walk toward her. My attorney put her hand on my arm, saying, "Don't, Grethe."

"At least," I explained to my lawyer, "if she has someplace to throw the darts they won't be thrown at so many others."

Something drew me to her. Here I was in my uniform, my unit behind me. Soldiers don't retreat. I could confront her.

She waved her fists in the air. "You're tearing down the American family, you're tearing down the America that I love, that I would give my life for."

I was next to her. My voice was calm, an automatic response to someone out of control. "I almost gave mine for it . . ."

She spat the words in my face: "I wish you had." Someone behind me gasped.

I stood as tall as I could, without anger or surprise or fear.

I had learned to steel myself against hatred during my divorce. Suddenly, as I looked into this woman's furious eyes, the memory of those times hit me. Nine years before, after my weekly visits with my sons, my ex-husband, Harvey, would line up the boys and make them join him in jeering at me. They would chant: "Dyke, queer." These little men, ages four to eleven, yelling, their faces twisted in pain and confusion. I would drive away speechless, cowed, crying. The words weren't true for me then. I believed it was only an expression of Harvey's anger, but even so, I couldn't defend myself. I went away. Rebuilt my life. Did my work, won awards, was obedient, missed my sons, avoided controversy, found my life partner, forgot to be apprehensive about hate.

Until the day of my discharge. ■

Chapter 5

Political Culture and Public Opinion

Political culture and public opinion are closely interrelated. Both refer to the beliefs, values, and ideas held by the people of a nation. But there is a key difference: political culture involves beliefs, values, and ideas that are deeply held and widely shared, whereas public opinion focuses on the people's views on a wide range of issues and controversies. Thus public opinion may change from moment to moment, while a nation's political culture may remain remarkably stable over time—even over many generations.

In modern times, public opinion is weighed and measured on an ongoing basis, primarily through the use of public opinion polls. Many such polls (like the one reported on in selection 5.2) are conducted by news organizations; others are carried out by academic researchers, commercial polling firms, and political organizations and campaigns. Polls can be manipulated or mismanaged, of course, but on the whole they provide an accurate snapshot of Americans' views on a variety of subjects.

By contrast, American political culture is notoriously difficult to measure. Pronouncements on the subject are likely to be filled with assumptions and overgeneralizations, and often neglect minority viewpoints and subcultures. Used judiciously, however, political culture is an important concept that can provide keen insights into the nature of American society and politics.

Because we are immersed in our own political culture, Americans may have difficulty even seeing that we have an identifiable and common set of beliefs about government and politics. Perhaps the best way to understand American political culture, therefore, is to see ourselves through the eyes of people from other cultures.

The most noteworthy foreign observer of American politics in our history was Alexis de Tocqueville (see selection 5.1). Tocqueville visited the United States in the 1830s, and, like many other observers of the American scene, was struck by the American commitment to equality, liberty, participation in politics, and religion. To this day, visitors to the United States often remark on the informal, easy manner in which Americans relate to one another, on our deep-seated religiosity, and—at least until recently—on our passion for politics. We are, in a word, a *democratic* society—not only in politics but in our attitudes toward public and private life. Our underlying belief in democracy and all it connotes forms an essential part of the American polity.

This chapter examines several different aspects of political culture and public opinion in the United States. In addition to a brief excerpt from Tocqueville, the chapter also presents a survey of the current state of public opinion on "values" issues (selection 5.2); a discussion of the long-running argument as to whether American political culture is fundamentally different from that of other nations (selection 5.3); and a look into the troubling question of whether public opinion polls encourage public officials to follow public opinion rather than lead it. Throughout, the common theme is to explore the underlying beliefs and values upon which the American political system rests.

Chapter Questions

1. What attitudes and assumptions about politics are distinctly "American"—that is, seem to be widely held by most Americans, no matter what their background or political affiliation? How do these attitudes and assumptions differ from those of other nations?
2. How have American political culture and Americans' political beliefs changed since Tocqueville visited 150 years ago? Since the 1960s? Since the early 1990s? Are these changes permanent and fundamental, or fleeting and insignificant?

 # Foundations

Alexis de Tocqueville, a French nobleman, traveled to the United States in 1831 to study and report back to the French government on the American prison system. As a result of his nine-month trip, he produced not only a report on the prison system but also *Democracy in America,* which, published in 1835, was immediately hailed as a masterpiece of political and social commentary. It remains one of the most important books ever written about American political life. (Tocqueville, incidentally, was accompanied on his trip by his friend Gustave de Beaumont, who also wrote a book on America. It was a novel about a slave woman in Baltimore, titled *Marie,* or *Slavery in the United States.*)

Although he wrote more than 150 years ago, Tocqueville's keen observations of life in the United States offer insights into American political culture that are still valid. The following excerpt highlights the nature of American democracy and the centrality of equality to Americans' understanding of politics.

Questions

1. To what extent is American politics today still based on the idea of equality? Consider not only questions of legal or political equality but also social equality.
2. What examples from modern life support Tocqueville's views on the nature of American democracy? What examples contradict his analysis?

5.1 Democracy in America (1835)

Alexis de Tocqueville

Social Condition of the Anglo-Americans

A social condition is commonly the result of circumstances, sometimes of laws, oftener still of these two causes united; but wherever it exists, it may justly be considered as the source of almost all the laws, the usages, and the ideas, which regulate the conduct of nations: whatever it does not produce, it modifies.

It is, therefore, necessary, if we would become acquainted with the legislation and the manners of a nation, to begin by the study of its social condition.

The Striking Characteristic of the Social Condition of the Anglo-Americans Is Its Essential Democracy

Many important observations suggest themselves upon the social condition of the Anglo-Americans; but there is one which takes precedence of all the rest. The social condition of the Americans is eminently democratic; this was its character at the foundation of the colonies, and is still more strongly marked at the present day.

[Great] equality existed among the emigrants who settled on the shores of New England. The germ of aristocracy was never planted in that part of the Union. The only influence which obtained there was that of intellect; the people were used to reverence certain names as the emblems of knowledge and virtue. Some of their fellow-citizens acquired a power over the rest which might truly have been called aristocratic, if it had been capable of invariable transmission from father to son.

This was the state of things to the east of the Hudson: to the southwest of that river, and in the direction of the Floridas, the case was different. In most of the states situated to the southwest of the Hudson some great English proprietors had settled, who had imported with them aristocratic principles and the English law of descent. I have explained the reasons why it was impossible ever to establish a powerful aristocracy in America; these reasons existed with less force to the southwest of the Hudson. In the south, one man, aided by slaves, could cultivate a great extent of country: it was therefore common to see rich landed proprietors. But their influence was not altogether aristocratic as that term is understood in Europe, since they possessed no privileges; and the cultivation of their estates being carried on by slaves, they had no tenants depending on them, and consequently no patronage. Still, the great proprietors south of the Hudson constituted a superior class, having ideas and tastes of its own, and forming the center of political action. This kind of aristocracy sympathized with the body of the people, whose passions and interests it easily embraced; but it was too weak and too short-lived to excite either love or hatred for itself. This was the class which headed the insurrection in the south, and furnished the best leaders of the American revolution.

At the period of which we are now speaking, society was shaken to its center: the people, in whose name the struggle had taken place, conceived the desire of exercising the authority which it had acquired; its democratic tendencies were awakened; and having thrown off the yoke of the mother-country, it aspired to independence of every kind. The influence of individuals gradually ceased to be felt, and custom and law united together to produce the same result.

But the law of descent was the last step to equality. I am surprised that ancient and modern jurists have not attributed to this law a greater influence on human affairs. It is true that these laws belong to civil affairs: but they ought nevertheless to be placed at the head of all political institutions; for, while political laws are only the symbol of a nation's condition, they exercise an incredible influence upon its social state. They have, moreover, a sure and uniform manner of operating upon society, affecting, as it were, generations yet unborn.

Through their means man acquires a kind of preternatural power over the future lot of his fellow-creatures. When the legislator has once regulated the law of inheritance, he may rest from his labor. The machine once put in motion will go on for ages, and advance, as if self-guided, toward a given point. When framed in a particular manner, this law unites, draws together, and vests property and power in a few hands: its tendency is clearly aristocratic. On opposite principles its action is still more rapid; it divides, distributes, and disperses both property and power. Alarmed by the rapidity of its progress, those who despair of arresting its motion endeavor to obstruct by difficulties and impediments; they vainly seek to counteract its effect by contrary efforts: but it gradually reduces or destroys every obstacle, until by its incessant activity the bulwarks of the influence of wealth are ground down to the fine and shifting sand which is the basis of democracy. When the law of inheritance permits, still more when it decrees, the equal division of a father's property among all his children, its effects are of two kinds: it is important to distinguish them from each other, although they tend to the same end.

In virtue of the law of partible inheritance, the death of every proprietor brings about a kind of revolution in property: not only do his possessions change hands, but their very nature is altered; since they are parcelled into shares, which become smaller and smaller at each division. This is the direct, and, as it were, the physical effect of the law. It follows, then, that in countries where equality of inheritance is established by law, property, and especially landed property, must have a tendency to perpetual diminution. The effects, however, of such legislation would only be perceptible after a lapse of time, if the law was abandoned to its own working; for supposing a family to consist of two children (and in a country peopled as France is, the average number is not above three), these children, sharing among them the fortune of both parents, would not be poorer than their father or mother.

But the law of equal division exercises its influence not merely upon the property itself, but it affects the minds of the heirs, and brings their passions into play. These indirect consequences tend powerfully to the destruction of large fortunes, and especially of large domains.

Among the nations whose law of descent is founded upon the right of primogeniture, landed estates often pass from generation to generation without undergoing division. The consequence of which is, that family feeling is to a certain degree incorporated with the estate. The family represents the estate, the estate the family; whose name, together with its origin, its glory, its power, and its virtues, is thus perpetuated in an imperishable memorial of the past, and a sure pledge of the future.

When the equal partition of property is established by law, the intimate connection is destroyed between family feeling and the preservation of the paternal estate; the property ceases to represent the family; for, as it must inevitably be divided after one or two generations, it has evidently a constant tendency to diminish, and must in the end be completely dispersed. The sons of the great landed proprietor, if they are few in number, or if fortune befriend them, may indeed entertain the hope of being as wealthy as their father, but not that of possessing the same property as he did; their riches must necessarily be composed of elements different from his.

Now, from the moment when you divest the land-owner of that interest in the preservation of his estate which he derives from association, from tradition, and from family pride, you may be certain that sooner or later he will dispose of it; for there is a strong pecuniary interest in favor of selling, as floating capital produces higher interest than real property, and is more readily available to gratify the passions of the moment.

Great landed estates which have once been divided, never come together again; for the small proprietor draws from his land a better revenue in proportion, than the large owner does from his; and of course he sells it at a higher rate. The calculations of gain, therefore, which decided the rich man to sell his domain, will still more powerfully influence him against buying small estates to unite them into a large one.

What is called family pride is often founded upon an illusion of self-love. A man wishes to perpetuate and immortalize himself, as it were, in his great-grandchildren. Where the *esprit de famille* ceases to act, individual selfishness comes into play. When the idea of family becomes vague, indeterminate, and uncertain, a man thinks of his present convenience; he provides for the establishment of the succeeding generation, and no more.

Either a man gives up the idea of perpetuating his family, or at any rate he seeks to accomplish it by other means than that of a landed estate.

Thus not only does the law of partible inheritance render it difficult for families to preserve their ancestral domains entire, but it deprives them of the inclination to attempt it, and compels them in some measure to cooperate with the law in their own extinction.

The law of equal distribution proceeds by two methods: by acting upon things, it acts upon persons; by influencing persons, it affects things. By these means the law succeeds in striking at the root of landed property, and dispersing rapidly both families and fortunes.

Most certainly it is not for us, Frenchmen of the nineteenth century, who daily behold the political and social changes which the law of partition is bringing to pass, to question its influence. It is perpetually conspicuous in our country, overthrowing the walls of our dwellings and removing the landmarks of our fields. But although it has produced great effects in France, much still remains for it to do. Our recollections, opinions, and habits, present powerful obstacles to its progress.

In the United States it has nearly completed its work of destruction, and there we can best study its results. The English laws concerning the transmission of property were abolished in almost all the states at the time of the revolution. The law of entail was so modified as not to interrupt the free circulation of property. The first having passed away, estates began to be parcelled out; and the change became more and more rapid with the progress of time. At this moment, after a lapse of little more than sixty years, the aspect of society is totally altered; the families of the great landed proprietors are almost all commingled with the general mass. In the state of New York, which formerly contained many of these, there are but two who still keep their heads above the stream; and they must shortly disappear. The sons of these opulent citizens have become merchants, lawyers, or physicians. Most of them have lapsed into obscurity. The last trace of hereditary ranks and distinctions is destroyed—the law of partition has reduced all to one level.

I do not mean that there is any deficiency of wealthy individuals in the United States; I know of no country, indeed, where the love of money has taken stronger hold on the affections of men, and where a profounder contempt is expressed for the theory of the permanent equality of property. But wealth circulates with inconceivable rapidity, and experience shows that it is rare to find two succeeding generations in the full enjoyment of it.

This picture, which may perhaps be thought overcharged, still gives a very imperfect idea of what is taking place in the new states of the west and southwest. At the end of the last century a few bold adventurers began to penetrate into the valleys of the Mississippi, and the mass of the population very soon began to move in that direction: communities unheard of till then were seen to emerge from their wilds: states, whose names were not in existence a few years before, claimed their place in the American Union; and in the western settlements we may behold democracy arrived at its utmost extreme. In these states, founded off hand, and as it were by chance, the inhabitants are but of yesterday. Scarcely known to one another, the nearest neighbors are ignorant of each other's history. In this part of the American continent, therefore, the population has not experienced the influence of great names and great wealth, nor even that of the natural aristocracy of knowledge and virtue. None are there to wield that respectable power which men willingly grant to the remembrance of a life spent in doing good before their eyes. The new states of the west are already inhabited; but society has no existence among them.

It is not only the fortunes of men which are equal in America; even their acquirements partake in some degree of the same uniformity. I do not believe there is a country in the world where, in proportion to the population, there are so few uninstructed, and at the same time so few learned individuals. Primary instruction is within the reach of everybody; superior instruction is scarcely to be obtained by any. This is not surprising; it is in fact the necessary consequence of what we have advanced above. Almost all the Americans are in easy circumstances, and can therefore obtain the first elements of human knowledge.

In America there are comparatively few who are rich enough to live without a profession. Every profession requires an apprenticeship, which limits the time of instruction to the early years of life. At fifteen they enter upon their calling, and thus their education ends at the age when ours begins. Whatever is done afterward, is with a view to some special and lucrative object; a science is taken up as a matter of business, and the only branch of it which is attended to is such as admits of an immediate practical application.

In America most of the rich men were formerly poor: most of those who now enjoy leisure were absorbed in business during their youth; the consequence of which is, that when they might have had a taste for study they had no time for it, and when the time is at their disposal they have no longer the inclination.

There is no class, then, in America in which the taste for intellectual pleasures is transmitted with hereditary fortune and leisure, and by which the labors of the intellect are held in honor. Accordingly there is an equal want of the desire and the power of application to these objects.

A middling standard is fixed in America for human knowledge. All approach as near to it as they can; some as they rise, others as they descend. Of course, an immense multitude of persons are to be found who entertain the same number of ideas on religion, history, science, political economy, legislation, and government. The gifts of intellect proceed directly from God, and man cannot prevent their unequal distribution. But in consequence of the state of things which we have here represented, it happens, that although the capacities of men are widely different, as the Creator has doubtless intended they should be, they are submitted to the same method of treatment.

In America the aristocratic element has always been feeble from its birth; and if at the present day it is not actually destroyed, it is at any rate so completely disabled that we can scarcely assign to it any degree of influence in the course of affairs.

The democratic principle, on the contrary, has gained so much strength by time, by events, and by legislation, as to have become not only predominant but all-powerful. There is no family or corporate authority, and it is rare to find even the influence of individual character enjoy any durability.

America, then, exhibits in her social state a most extraordinary phenomenon. Men are there seen on a greater equality in point of fortune and intellect, or in other words, more equal in their strength, than in any other country of the world, or, in any age of which history has preserved the remembrance.

Political Consequences of the Social Condition of the Anglo-Americans

The political consequences of such a social condition as this are easily deductible.

It is impossible to believe that equality will not everywhere find its way into the political world as it does everywhere else. To conceive of men remaining for ever unequal upon one single point, yet equal on all others, is impossible; they must come in the end to be equal upon all.

Now I know of only two methods of establishing equality in the political world: every citizen must be put in possession of his rights, or rights must be granted to no one. For nations which have arrived at the same stage of social existence as the Anglo-Americans, it is therefore very difficult to discover a medium between the sovereignty of all and the absolute power of one man: and it would be vain to deny that the social condition which I have been describing is equally liable to each of these consequences.

There is, in fact, a manly and lawful passion for equality, which excites men to wish all to be powerful and honored. This passion tends to elevate the humble to the rank of the great; but there exists also in the human heart a depraved taste for equality, which impels the weak to attempt to lower the powerful to their own level, and reduces men to prefer equality in slavery to inequality with freedom. Not that those nations whose social condition is democratic naturally despise liberty; on the contrary, they have an instinctive love of it. But liberty is not the chief and constant object of their desire; equality is their idol: they make rapid and sudden efforts to obtain liberty, and if they miss their aim, resign themselves to their disappointment; but nothing can satisfy them except equality, and rather than lose it they resolve to perish.

On the other hand, in a state where the citizens are nearly on an equality, it becomes difficult for them to preserve their independence against the aggressions of power. No one among them being strong enough to engage singly in the struggle with advantage, nothing but a general combination can protect their liberty: and such a union is not always to be found.

From the same social position, then, nations may derive one or the other of two great political results; these results are extremely different from each other, but they may both proceed from the same cause.

The Anglo-Americans, are the first who, having been exposed to this formidable alternative, have been happy enough to escape the dominion of absolute power. They have been allowed by their circumstances, their origin, their intelligence, and especially by their moral feeling, to establish and maintain the sovereignty of the people.

• • •

Political Associations in the United States

In no country in the world has the principle of association been more successfully used, or more unsparingly applied to a multitude of different objects, than in America. Beside the permanent associations which are established by law under the names of townships, cities, and counties, a vast number of others are formed and maintained by the agency of private individuals.

The citizen of the United States is taught from his earliest infancy to rely upon his own exertions, in order to resist the evils and the difficulties of life; he looks upon the social authority with an eye of mistrust and anxiety, and he only claims its assistance when he is quite unable to shift without it. This habit may even be traced in the schools of the rising generation, where the children in their games are wont to submit to rules which they have themselves established, and to punish misdemeanors which they have themselves defined. The same spirit pervades every act of social life. If a stoppage occurs in a thoroughfare, and the circulation of the public is hindered, the neighbors immediately constitute a deliberative body; and this extemporaneous assembly gives rise to an executive power, which remedies the inconvenience, before anybody has thought of recurring to an authority superior to that of the persons immediately concerned. If the public pleasures are concerned, an association is formed to provide for the splendor and the regularity of the entertainment. Societies are formed to resist enemies which are exclusively of a moral nature, and to diminish the vice of intemperance: in the United States associations are established to promote public order, commerce, industry, morality, and religion; for there is no end which the human will, seconded by the collective exertions of individuals, despairs of attaining.

I shall hereafter have occasion to show the effects of association upon the course of society, and I must confine myself for the present to the political world. When once the right of association is recognized, the citizens may employ it in several different ways.

An association consists simply in the public assent which a number of individuals give to certain doctrines; and in the engagement which they contract to promote the spread of those doctrines by their exertions. The right of associating with these views is very analogous to the liberty of unlicensed writing; but societies thus formed possess more authority than the press. When an opinion is represented by a society, it necessarily assumes a more exact and explicit form. It numbers its partisans, and compromises their welfare in its cause; they, on the other hand, become acquainted with each other, and their zeal is increased by their number. An association unites the efforts of minds which have a tendency to diverge, in one single channel, and urges them vigorously toward one single end which it points out.

The second degree in the right of association is the power of meeting. When an association is allowed to establish centers of action at certain important points in the country, its activity is increased, and its influence extended. Men have the opportunity of seeing each other; means of execution are more readily combined; and opinions are maintained with a degree of warmth and energy which written language cannot approach. . . .

Why Democratic Nations Show a More Ardent and Enduring Love of Equality Than of Liberty

The first and most intense passion which is engendered by the equality of conditions is, I need hardly say, the love of that same equality. My readers will therefore not be surprised that I speak of it before all others.

Everybody has remarked, that in our time, and especially in France, this passion for equality is every day gaining ground in the human heart. It has been said a hundred times that our contemporaries are far more ardently and tenaciously attached to equality than to freedom; but, as I do not find that the causes of the fact have been sufficiently analyzed, I shall endeavor to point them out.

It is possible to imagine an extreme point at which freedom and equality would meet and be confounded together. Let us suppose that all the members of the community take a part in the government, and that each one of them has an equal right to take a part in it. As none is different from his fellows, none can exercise a tyrannical power: men will be perfectly free, because they will all be entirely equal; and they will all be perfectly equal, because they will be entirely free. To this ideal state democratic nations tend. Such is the completest form that equality can assume upon earth; but there are a thousand others which, without being equally perfect, are not less cherished by those nations.

The principle of equality may be established in civil society, without prevailing in the political world. Equal rights may exist of indulging in the same pleasures, of entering the same professions, of frequenting the same places—in a word, of living in the same manner and seeking wealth by the same means, although all men do not take an equal share in the government.

A kind of equality may even be established in the political world, though there should be no political freedom there. A man may be the equal of all his country-men save one, who is the master of all without distinction, and who selects equally from among them all the agents of his power.

Several other combinations might be easily imagined, by which very great equality would be united to institutions more or less free, or even to institutions wholly without freedom.

Although men cannot become absolutely equal unless they be entirely free, and consequently equality, pushed to its furthest extent, may be confounded with free-dom, yet there is good reason for distinguishing the one from the other. The taste which men have for liberty, and that which they feel for equality, are, in fact, two different things; and I am not afraid to add, that, among democratic nations, they are two unequal things.

Upon close inspection, it will be seen that there is in every age some peculiar and preponderating fact with which all others are connected; this fact almost al-ways gives birth to some pregnant idea or some ruling passion, which attracts to it-self, and bears away in its course, all the feelings and opinions of the time: it is like a great stream, toward which each of the surrounding rivulets seem to flow.

Freedom has appeared in the world at different times and under various forms; it has not been exclusively bound to any social condition, and it is not confined to democracies. Freedom cannot, therefore, form the distinguishing characteristic of democratic ages. The peculiar and preponderating fact which marks those ages as its own is the equality of conditions; the ruling passion of men in those periods is the love of this equality. Ask not what singular charm the men of democratic ages find in being equal, or what special reasons they may have for clinging so tena-ciously to equality rather than to the other advantages which society holds out to them: equality is the distinguishing characteristic of the age they live in; that, of itself, is enough to explain that they prefer it to all the rest.

But independently of this reason there are several others, which will at all times habitually lead men to prefer equality to freedom.

If a people could ever succeed in destroying, or even in diminishing, the equal-ity which prevails in its own body, this could only be accomplished by long and laborious efforts. Its social condition must be modified, its laws abolished, its opin-ions superseded, its habits changed, its manners corrupted. But political liberty is more easily lost; to neglect to hold it fast, is to allow it to escape.

Men therefore not only cling to equality because it is dear to them; they also adhere to it because they think it will last for ever.

That political freedom may compromise in its excesses the tranquillity, the property, the lives of individuals, is obvious to the narrowest and most unthinking minds. But, on the contrary, none but attentive and clear-sighted men perceive the perils with which equality threatens us, and they commonly avoid pointing them out. They know that the calamities they apprehend are remote, and flatter themselves that they will only fall upon future generations, for which the present generation takes but little thought. The evils which freedom sometimes brings with it are immediate; they are apparent to all, and all are more or less affected by them. The evils which extreme equality may produce are slowly disclosed; they creep gradually into the social frame; they are only seen at intervals, and at the moment at which they become most violent, habit already causes them to be no longer felt.

The advantages which freedom brings are only shown by length of time; and it is always easy to mistake the cause in which they originate. The advantages of equality are instantaneous, and they may constantly be traced from their source.

Political liberty bestows exalted pleasures, from time to time, upon a certain number of citizens. Equality every day confers a number of small enjoyments on every man. The charms of equality are every instant felt, and are within the reach of all: the noblest hearts are not insensible to them, and the most vulgar souls exult in them. The passion which equality engenders must therefore be at once strong and general. Men cannot enjoy political liberty unless it has been purchased by some sacrifices, and they never obtain it without great exertions. But the pleasures of equality are self-proffered: each of the petty incidents of life seems to occasion them, and in order to taste them nothing is required but to live.

Democratic nations are at all times fond of equality, but there are certain epochs at which the passion they entertain for it swells to the height of fury. This occurs at the moment when the old social system, long menaced, completes its own destruction after a last intestine struggle, and when the barriers of rank are at length thrown down. At such times men pounce upon equality as their booty, and they cling to it as to some precious treasure which they fear to lose. The passion for equality penetrates on every side into men's hearts, expands there, and fills them entirely. Tell them not that by this blind surrender of themselves to an exclusive passion, they risk their dearest interests: they are deaf. Show them not freedom escaping from their grasp, while they are looking another way: they are blind—or rather, they can discern but one sole object to be desired in the universe.

What I have said is applicable to all democratic nations: what I am about to say concerns the French alone. Among most modern nations, and especially among all those of the continent of Europe, the taste and the idea of freedom only began to exist and to extend itself at the time when social conditions were tending to equality, and as a consequence of that very equality. Absolute kings were the most efficient levellers of ranks among their subjects. Among these nations equality preceded freedom: equality was therefore a fact of some standing, when freedom was still a novelty: the one had already created customs, opinions, and laws belonging to it, when the other, alone and for the first time, came into actual existence. Thus the latter was still only an affair of opinion and of taste, while the former had already crept into the habits of the people, possessed itself of their manners, and given a particular turn to the smallest actions in their lives. Can it be wondered that the men of our own time prefer the one to the other?

I think that democratic communities have a natural taste for freedom: left to themselves, they will seek it, cherish it, and view any privation of it with regret. But for equality, their passion is ardent, insatiable, incessant, invincible: they call for equality in freedom; if they cannot obtain that, they still call for equality in slavery. They will endure poverty, servitude, barbarism—but they will not endure aristocracy.

This is true at all times, and especially true in our own. All men and all powers seeking to cope with this irresistible passion, will be overthrown and destroyed by it. In our age, freedom cannot be established without it, and despotism itself cannot reign without its support. ∎

 # American Politics Today

Politics in the modern era hardly seems to support the idea that Americans are united in a common political culture. Instead, politics today seems to emphasize a wide range of conflicts over fundamental values. Some Americans have even proclaimed the existence of a "culture war," starkly dividing the nation as never before.

The culture conflicts of the present day, write the *Washington Post* reporters David S. Broder and Richard Morin, can be traced to the struggles of the 1960s. Moreover, Americans do not line up neatly on one side or the other of the cultural battlefield. Instead, as the public's reaction to the Bill Clinton–Monica Lewinsky affair suggests, many Americans are deeply torn between the two sides.

Questions

1. What values were challenged by the cultural "revolution" of the 1960s? What values struggled to emerge in their place? How were these conflicting values reflected in the contentious politics surrounding the Clinton impeachment controversy?
2. Do modern controversies over values threaten to undermine the existence of a distinctive and unified American political culture? Or should these conflicts be seen as taking place under the broad umbrella of American political culture?

5.2 A Question of Values (1999)

David S. Broder and Richard Morin

The sharply divided public reaction to the impeachment of President Clinton has provided a dramatic showcase of a struggle for American values that goes back to the 1960s and remains unresolved today.

David S. Broder and Richard Morin, "A Question of Values," *Washington Post*, January 11, 1999, pp. 6–7, Weekly Edition. Copyright © 1999, The Washington Post. Reprinted with permission.

As an emblematic figure from that troubled decade, polls and analysts say, Clinton confronts his fellow citizens with choices between deeply held moral standards and an abhorrence of judging others' behavior, a conflict the baby boomers have stirred all their adult lives.

This survey about values by The Washington Post, the Henry J. Kaiser Family Foundation and Harvard University follows on reports emphasizing the growing tolerance Americans now display for groups such as homosexuals that have suffered discrimination and toward practices ranging from interracial marriage to premarital sex that once might have been condemned. That tolerance also extends to free expression of controversial views.

But few issues are more revealing than Clinton's impeachment when it comes to highlighting how values have changed over the past 30 years. Almost without exception, experts interviewed said the public verdict in his case is far different than it would have been in the late '60s because the values environment has changed.

That conflict over the social order is notably less violent than it was in 1968, when the assassinations of Martin Luther King Jr. and Robert F. Kennedy, anti-Vietnam War demonstrations, urban riots, and violent clashes between police and protesters at the Democratic National Convention scarred the nation's consciousness. But 1998, with a bitter, year-long battle in the courts and Congress climaxing in the first presidential impeachment in 130 years, has left deep divisions across social, political and generational lines.

They begin, according to the Post/Kaiser/Harvard survey, with a near-even split between those (50 percent) who think a president "has a greater responsibility than leaders of other organizations to set the moral tone for the country" and those (48 percent) who say, "As long as he does a good job running the country, a president's personal life is not important."

Reflecting the partisanship engendered by the long investigation of Clinton's relationship with Monica S. Lewinsky, most Republicans demand a moral example and most Democrats reject it.

But sociologists and other students of American life interviewed in late December said the divisions go much deeper and have their roots in long-standing controversy generated not just by Clinton but by his baby boom generation.

While most Americans want Clinton to finish his term, and prefer censure as an alternative, few believe he is a good role model. Seven in 10 Americans—including a majority of baby boomers—said in the survey that Clinton does not have high personal moral or ethical standards. Six in 10—again including a majority of baby boomers—also said his standards are no better or worse than "most people of his generation."

The public sees a nation that lacks agreed-upon ethical guidelines for itself. More than six out of 10 said the country "was greatly divided when it comes to the most important values," rather than being in agreement. Ironically, on this one question there was unity. Republicans and Democrats, men and women, young and old all said they see a society split on moral and ethical issues.

With some exceptions, the experts tend to agree. Some describe it as a battle of extremes—the Puritanism of the Religious Right vs. the permissiveness of the aging children of the '60s. Others see the acceptance of Clinton's actions as proof that Americans are utterly cynical about their political leaders, mute spectators at a television drama they despise but cannot escape.

Some say it is a symptom of national ambivalence, of individuals longing for moral values but resistant to imposing their standards on others. And the more hopeful say the preference for censuring the president—rather than absolving him or removing him—is a healthy effort at synthesizing those opposing tendencies.

A few optimists say the upshot of all the discussion will be a standard for future presidents that is both more demanding and more realistic.

Few of the scholars are comfortable with the status quo, however.

"No analysis can absolve the people themselves of responsibility for the quandary we appear to be in," says Don Eberly, director of the Civil Society Project in Harrisburg, Pa. "Nonjudgmentalism, the trump card of moral debate, seems to have gained strength among the people, especially in the sexual realm, and this clearly does not bode well for America."

Over the last 30 years, polling shows the proportion of people saying they think their fellow citizens generally are as honest and moral as they used to be has fallen significantly. In a 1952 survey, as many answered yes as said no. In 1965, there were three yeses for every four noes. But this year there were almost three noes (71 percent) for every yes (26 percent).

In the same period, trust in government also has declined radically. In 1968, 61 percent said they trusted the government in Washington to do the right thing most or all the time; in 1998, only 33 percent felt that way.

Pollster Dan Yankelovich writes that "the transformation in values from the mid-'60s to the late-'70s confronts us with one of the sharpest discontinuities in our cultural history." In that period's "radical extension of individualism . . . from the political domain to personal lifestyles," he notes, the concepts of duty, social conformity, respectability and sexual morality were devalued, in favor of expressiveness and pleasure seeking.

This was a time in which Bill Clinton, moving through his twenties at Georgetown, Oxford and Yale, rejected military service, experimented with marijuana. But in general, according to his biographer, Washington Post reporter David Maraniss, Clinton followed "a moderate course during an increasingly immoderate period." The stamp of that period remained on Clinton, in at least two areas: the evasiveness that characterized his dealings with the "threat" of military service and the permissiveness he allowed in his sexual life.

In judging Clinton's morals to be typical of his generation—only 7 percent thought them better; 27 percent, worse—most of those surveyed made it clear they disapproved of them.

Yankelovich argues that in the 1990s, "a shift is now occurring toward a perception of the self as a moral actor with obligations and concerns as well as rights . . . we are beginning to measure a shift back toward absolute as distinct from relative values." That theme of individual responsibility is one Clinton has emphasized in his speeches, if not always in his actions.

From this perspective, the divided public verdict on the Clinton case represents not just a legal argument about the standards for impeachment and removal of a president, or a partisan battle between Republicans and Democrats, but also an unresolved debate about fundamental values.

At the extremes, the conflict amounts almost to the "culture war" some trace directly back to the 1960s. Randy Tate of the Christian Coalition and William J. Bennett, former Education secretary, have accused Clinton of subverting standards of honesty and decency so blatantly that he cannot be allowed to remain in office. Harvard professor Alan Dershowitz and many Democrats in the House have accused Clinton's opponents—notably independent counsel Kenneth W. Starr—of practicing "sexual McCarthyism," trampling civil liberties and invading people's privacy.

Alan Wolfe, a Boston University sociologist, argued in his book, "One Nation, After All," that the "culture war" is confined to political elites, and that most individuals struggle to balance their yearning for clear standards against their discomfort with passing judgment on others.

Wolfe said in an interview that he sees exactly that happening in the Clinton case—"even though people are torn, they are looking to find a way to negotiate through these competing impulses." Wolfe says he thought last January, when Lewinsky first became a household name, that "people would forgive adultery but lying in public would not pass. But people realized that the lying and the adultery were part of the same thing. I don't agree, but I recognize the wisdom in making that connection."

Others see the conflict in starker—and more worrisome—terms. David Blankenhorn, president of the Institute of American Values in New York, says the reaction to Clinton demonstrates that "many middle-class Americans obey an 11th Commandment: Thou shalt not judge. They view morality as a private matter. What I find troublesome is that . . . apart from treason, there is nothing worse than a democratic leader engaging in ongoing public lying. And yet, a substantial number of Americans have accepted this. . . . Remove ethics, and it makes this a society where politics trumps everything else."

Several observers traced this back to the 1960s. Christopher Gates, president of the Denver-based National Civic League, says that pollster George Gallup Jr. "says the '60s and '70s were the time when our country fell apart and the bonds began to dissolve. You had a war between the generations, a war between the genders, you had Vietnam, break-ins, resignations, pardons. You had a huge dissolution of trust. And we have gone from a time when we presumed good intentions on the part of our leaders to the presumption of bad intentions."

Blankenhorn suggests that as a result of that legacy, "Clinton is in many ways the beneficiary of people's very low expectations of politicians and government."

But Georgia Sorenson, director of the center for political leadership and participation of the University of Maryland, points out that "participation has been deteriorating since the '60s, and it makes it hard for any person to lead now, no matter how committed."

Michael Sandel, director of the Harvard Institute for Policy Studies, says the consequences go further. "We've witnessed a politics of scandal, sensation and spectacle that has turned the president into another figure in the celebrity culture," he says. "The majesty and dignity of the presidency have been stripped away, but paradoxically that hasn't destroyed the popularity of this president. "As citizens, we have become just spectators, even voyeurs. . . . We've told the pollsters we want the whole issue to be over, and yet we can't bring ourselves to change the channel. . . . It reflects a cynicism beyond mistrust. It reflects a view that government really doesn't matter, except as it provides occasional spectacular entertainment. It is not good news for democracy."

The Post/Kaiser/Harvard survey attempted to test Sandel's thesis by asking how many respondents had contacted their members of Congress about the impeachment issue. About one out of nine—11 percent—claimed to have done so. Among the vast majority who did not, the main reasons were that they didn't think it would make a difference (53 percent) or the issue wasn't important enough for them to get involved (21 percent).

But other experts interviewed are not nearly so concerned about public indifference or a decline in trust or an erosion of values. And there was some support for their views in the survey. About half those interviewed (48 percent) said they thought their representative in Congress had paid at least "a fair amount of attention" to opinions in their district, while only a third (35 percent) thought their elected officials largely ignored their constituents.

Charles Quigley, executive director of the Center for Civic Education in Calabasas, Calif., says, "What the Clinton thing says to me is that the majority are making subtle, sophisticated distinctions. They condemn what he did, but they want proportionality in punishment. They're questioning not only Clinton's values but those of the people who have gone after him."

Michael Josephson, president of the Josephson Institute of Ethics in Marina del Ray, Calif., and David Mathews, president of the Charles F. Kettering Foundation in Dayton, Ohio, say the partisanship of the House impeachment proceedings sent a worrisome signal to people. "Everyone thinks it is [political] positioning," Josephson says. "Otherwise, why would Republicans and Democrats come out so differently?"

"But," Mathews adds, "they have deep feelings about accountability and taking responsibility, not just by the president but by everyone. And when they see it disappearing, it scares them."

That may be true, but Wolfe and Eberly say politicians are not seen as the ones to lead a values revival. "When government becomes involved in moral matters, Americans are no longer sure they can trust it," Wolfe wrote in "One Nation, After All."

Eberly says: "The people just don't see the answer to our moral condition coming predominantly from lawmakers. . . . Americans tend to be generous toward sinners and hard on hypocrites, and the working assumption of many Americans is that most politicians fall into the latter category. While the American people strongly disapproved of Clinton's behavior, they grew steadily more unwilling to approve of action against him as it became clear that Congress would serve as judge and jury."

When asked what will be important to them in the presidential election of 2000, more of those surveyed in the Post/Kaiser/Harvard poll said the candidates' stands on issues than the combined total for those naming personal morals and ethics and broad principles and values.

On the other hand, looking to the future, a majority of Americans—55 percent—said in the survey they fear this society will become too accepting of behaviors that are bad for people, while 38 percent said their greatest worry was that the country would become too intolerant of actions that pose no such threat.

The survey indicates the divisions that have marked the past 30 years are likely to continue into the next generation.

Although more young people between 18 and 34 say they are more pessimistic about the threat of moral decline than their parents and grandparents, they are also more conflicted over values. They, more than their elders, express the greatest tolerance toward divorce, adultery and casual drug use. While many young Americans say that values are important to their politics, young adults are the least likely to agree that a president has a special obligation to "set an example with his personal life." ■

 # The Comparative Context

The idea that American political culture differs fundamentally from the political cultures of Europe and elsewhere in the world has long been central to discussions of American politics. As we have seen, this so-called American exceptionalism thesis was first put forward by Tocqueville (see selection 5.1) in the 1830s. Later, it reemerged as part of the effort to explain why the United States—unlike virtually every other industrialized society—failed to develop a viable socialist or communist movement. In this essay, the political scientist Seymour Martin Lipset examines the history of the American exceptionalism thesis and explains how America's distinctive political culture helps illuminate the peculiar nature of American liberalism and conservatism.

Questions

1. Why, according to advocates of the American exceptionalism thesis, did the United States develop a political culture different and distinct from those of Europe? What role did the American Revolution play in the development of this unique political culture?
2. How do American conceptions of liberalism and conservatism differ from their European counterparts? How does the American exceptionalism thesis help explain these differences?

5.3 American Exceptionalism: A Double-Edged Sword (1997)

Seymour Martin Lipset

B orn out of revolution, the United States is a country organized around an ideology which includes a set of dogmas about the nature of a good society. Americanism, as different people have pointed out, is an "ism" or ideology in the same way that communism or fascism or liberalism are isms. As G. K. Chesterton put it: "America is the only nation in the world that is founded on a creed. That creed is set forth with dogmatic and even theological lucidity in the Declaration of Independence. . . ." As noted in the Introduction, the nation's ideology can be described in five words: liberty, egalitarianism, individualism, populism, and laissez-faire. The revolutionary ideology which became the American Creed is liberalism in its eighteenth- and nineteenth-century meanings, as distinct from conservative Toryism, statist communitarianism, mercantilism, and *noblesse oblige* dominant in monarchical, state-church-formed cultures.

Other countries' senses of themselves are derived from a common history. Winston Churchill once gave vivid evidence to the difference between a national identity rooted in history and one defined by ideology in objecting to a proposal in 1940 to outlaw the anti-war Communist Party. In a speech in the House of Commons, Churchill said that as far as he knew, the Communist Party was composed of Englishmen and he did not fear an Englishman. In Europe, nationality is related to community, and thus one cannot become un-English or un-Swedish. Being an American, however, is an ideological commitment. It is not a matter of birth. Those who reject American values are un-American.

The American Revolution sharply weakened the *noblesse oblige*, hierarchically rooted, organic community values which had been linked to Tory sentiments, and enormously strengthened the individualistic, egalitarian, and anti-statist ones which had been present in the settler and religious background of the colonies. These values were evident in the twentieth-century fact that, as H. G. Wells pointed out close to ninety years ago, the United States not only has lacked a viable socialist party, but also has never developed a British or European-type Conservative or Tory party. Rather, America has been dominated by pure bourgeois, middle-class individualistic values. As Wells put it: "Essentially America is a middle-class [which has] become a community and so its essential problems are the problems of a modern individualistic society, stark and clear." He enunciated a theory of America as a liberal society, in the classic anti-statist meaning of the term:

> It is not difficult to show for example, that the two great political parties in America represent only one English party, the middle-class Liberal party. . . . There are no Tories . . .

and no Labor Party. . . . [T]he new world [was left] to the Whigs and Nonconformists and to those less constructive, less logical, more popular and liberating thinkers who became Radicals in England, and Jeffersonians and then Democrats in America. All Americans are, from the English point of view, Liberals of one sort or another. . . .

The liberalism of the eighteenth century was essentially the rebellion . . . against the monarchical and aristocratic state—against hereditary privilege, against restrictions on bargains. Its spirit was essentially anarchistic—the antithesis of Socialism. It was anti-State.

Comparative Perspectives

In dealing with national characteristics it is important to recognize that comparative evaluations are never absolutes, that they always are made in terms of more or less. The statement that the United States is an egalitarian society obviously does not imply that all Americans are equal in any way that can be defined. This proposition usually means (regardless of which aspect is under consideration—social relations, status, mobility, etc.) that the United States is more egalitarian than Europe.

Comparative judgments affect all generalizations about societies. This is such an obvious, commonsensical truism that is seems almost foolish to enunciate it. I only do so because statements about America or other countries are frequently challenged on the ground that they are not absolutely true. Generalizations may invert when the unit of comparison changes. For example, Canada looks different when compared to the United States than when contrasted with Britain. Figuratively, on a scale of 0 to 100, with the United States close to 0 on a given trait and Britain at 100, Canada would fall around 30. Thus, when Canada is evaluated by reference to the United States, it appears as more elitist, law-abiding, and statist, but when considering the variations between Canada and Britain, Canada looks more anti-statist, violent, and egalitarian.

The notion of "American exceptionalism" became widely applied in the context of efforts to account for the weakness of working-class radicalism in the United States. The major question subsumed in the concept became why the United States is the only industrialized country which does not have a significant socialist movement or Labor party. That riddle has bedeviled socialist theorists since the late nineteenth century. Friedrich Engels tried to answer it in the last decade of his life. The German socialist and sociologist Werner Sombart dealt with it in a major book published in his native language in 1906, *Why Is There No Socialism in the United States?* As we have seen, H. G. Wells, then a Fabian, also addressed the issue that year in *The Future in America.* Both Lenin and Trotsky were deeply concerned because the logic of Marxism, the proposition expressed by Marx in *Das Kapital* that "the more developed country shows the less developed the image of their future," implied to Marxists prior to the Russian Revolution that the United States would be the first socialist country.

Since some object to an attempt to explain a negative, a vacancy, the query may of course be reversed to ask why has America been the most classically liberal polity in the world from its founding to the present? Although the United States remains the wealthiest large industrialized nation, it devotes less of its income to welfare and the state is less involved in the economy than is true for other developed countries. It not only does not have a viable, class-conscious, radical political movement, but its trade unions, which have long been weaker than those of almost all other industrialized countries, have been steadily declining since the mid-1950s. . . .

An emphasis on American uniqueness raises the obvious question of the nature of the differences. There is a large literature dating back to at least the eighteenth century which attempts to specify the special character of the United States politically and socially. One of the most interesting, often overlooked, is Edmund Burke's speech to the House of Commons proposing reconciliation with the colonies, in which he sought to explain to his fellow members what the revolutionary Americans were like. He noted that they were different culturally, that they were not simply transplanted Englishmen. He particularly stressed the unique character of American religion. J. Hector St. John Crèvecoeur, in his book *Letters from an American Farmer*, written in the late eighteenth century, explicitly raised the question, "What is an American?" He emphasized that Americans behaved differently in their social relations, were much more egalitarian than other nationalities, that their "dictionary" was "short in words of dignity, and names of honor," that is, in terms through which the lower strata expressed their subservience to the higher. Tocqueville, who observed egalitarianism in a similar fashion, also stressed individualism, as distinct from the emphasis on "group ties" which marked Europe.

These commentaries have been followed by a myriad—thousands upon thousands—of books and articles by foreign travelers. The overwhelming majority are by educated Europeans. Such writings are fruitful because they are comparative; those who wrote them emphasized cross-national variations in behavior and institutions. Tocqueville's *Democracy*, of course, is the best known. As we have seen, he noted that he never wrote anything about the United States without thinking of France. As he put it, in speaking of his need to contrast the same institutions and behavior in both countries, "without comparisons to make, the mind doesn't know how to proceed." Harriet Martineau, an English contemporary, also wrote a first-rate comparative book on America. Friedrich Engels and Max Weber were among the contributors to the literature. There is a fairly systematic and similar logic in many of these discussions.

Beyond the analysis of variations between the United States and Europe, various other comparisons have been fruitful. In previous writings, I have suggested that one of the best ways to specify and distinguish American traits is by contrast with Canada. There is a considerable comparative North American literature, written almost entirely by Canadians. They have a great advantage over Americans since, while very few of the latter study their northern neighbor, it is impossible to be a literate Canadian without knowing almost as much, if not more, as most Americans about the United States. Almost every Canadian work on a given subject (the city, religion, the family, trade unions, etc.) contains a great deal about the United States. Many Canadians seek to explain their own country by dealing with differences or similarities south of the border. Specifying and analyzing variations among the predominantly English-speaking countries—Australia, Canada, Great Britain, New Zealand, and the United States—is also useful precisely because the differences among them generally are smaller than between each and non-Anglophonic societies. I have tried to analyze these variations in *The First New Nation*. The logic of studying societies which have major aspects in common was also followed by Louis Hartz in treating the overseas settler societies—United States, Canada, Latin America, Australia, and South Africa—as units for comparison. Fruitful comparisons have been made between Latin America and Anglophonic North America, which shed light on each.

Some Latin Americans have argued that there are major common elements in the Americas which show up in comparisons with Europe. Fernando Cardoso, a distinguished sociologist and now president of Brazil, once told me that he and his friends (who were activists in the underground left in the early 1960s) consciously decided not to found a socialist party as the military dictatorship was breaking down. They formed a populist party because, as they read the evidence, class-conscious socialism does not appeal in the Americas. With the exceptions of Chile and Canada (to a limited extent), major New World left parties from Argentina to the United States have been populist. Cardoso suggested that consciousness of social class is less salient throughout most of the Americas than in postfeudal Europe. However, I do not want to take on the issue of how exceptional the Americas are; dealing with the United States is more than enough.

Liberalism, Conservatism, and Americanism

The United States is viewed by many as the great conservative society, but it may also be seen as the most classically liberal polity in the developed world. To understand the exceptional nature of American politics, it is necessary to recognize, with H. G. Wells, that conservatism, as defined outside of the United States, is particularly weak in this country. Conservatism in Europe and Canada, derived from the historic alliance of church and government, is associated with the emergence of the welfare state. The two names most identified with it are Bismarck and Disraeli. Both were leaders of the conservatives (Tories) in their countries. They represented the rural and aristocratic elements, sectors which disdained capitalism, disliked the bourgeoisie, and rejected materialistic values. Their politics reflected the values of *noblesse oblige*, the obligation of the leaders of society and the economy to protect the less fortunate.

The semantic confusion about liberalism in America arises because both early and latter-day Americans never adopted the term to describe the unique American polity. The reason is simple. The American system of government existed long before the word "liberal" emerged in Napoleonic Spain and was subsequently accepted as referring to a particular party in mid-nineteenth-century England, as distinct from the Tory or Conservative Party. What Europeans have called "liberalism," Americans refer to as "conservatism": a deeply anti-statist doctrine emphasizing the virtues of laissez-faire. Ronald Reagan and Milton Friedman, the two current names most frequently linked with this ideology, define conservatism in America. And as Friedrich Hayek, its most important European exponent noted, it includes the rejection of aristocracy, social class hierarchy, and an established state church. As recently as the April and June 1987 issues of the British magazine *Encounter*, two leading trans-Atlantic conservative intellectuals, Max Beloff (Lord Beloff) and Irving Kristol, debated the use of titles. Kristol argued that

Britain "is soured by a set of very thin, but tenacious, aristocratic pretensions . . . [which] foreclose opportunities and repress a spirit of equality that has yet to find its full expression. . . ." This situation fuels many of the frustrations that make "British life . . . so cheerful, so abounding in *ressentiment*." Like Tocqueville, he holds up "social equality" as making "other inequalities tolerable in modern democracy." Beloff, a Tory, contended that what threatens conservatism in Britain "is not its remaining links with the aristocratic tradition, but its alleged in-difference to some of the abuses of capitalism. It is not the Dukes who lose us votes, but the 'malefactors of great wealth. . . .'" He wondered "why Mr. Kristol believes himself to be a 'conservative,'" since he is "as incapable as most Ameri-cans of being a conservative in any profound sense." Lord Beloff concluded that "Conservatism must have a 'Tory' element or it is only the old 'Manchester School,'" i.e., liberal.

Canada's most distinguished conservative intellectual, George Grant, empha-sized in his *Lament for a Nation* that "Americans who call themselves 'Conser-vatives' have the right to that title only in a particular sense. In fact, they are old-fashioned liberals. . . . Their concentration on freedom from governmental in-terference has more to do with nineteenth century liberalism than with tradi-tional conservatism, which asserts the right of the community to restrain freedom in the name of the common good." Grant bemoaned the fact that American conservatism, with its stress on the virtues of competition and links to business ideology, focuses on the rights of individuals and ignores communal rights and obligations. He noted that there has been no place in the American political phi-losophy "for the organic conservatism that predates the age of progress. Indeed, the United States is the only society on earth that has no traditions from before the age of progress." The recent efforts, led by Amitai Etzioni, to create a "com-munitarian" movement are an attempt to transport Toryism to America. British and German Tories have recognized the link and have shown considerable inter-est in Etzioni's ideas.

Still, it must be recognized that American politics have changed. The 1930s produced a qualitative difference. As Richard Hofstadter wrote, this period brought a "social democratic tinge" to the United States for the first time in its history. The Great Depression produced a strong emphasis on planning, on the welfare state, on the role of the government as a major regulatory actor. An earlier upswing in statist sentiment occurred immediately prior to World War I, as evi-denced by the significant support for the largely Republican Progressive move-ment led by Robert LaFollette and Theodore Roosevelt and the increasing strength (up to a high of 6% of the national vote in 1912) for the Socialist Party. They failed to change the political system. Grant McConnell explains the failure of the Progressive movement as stemming from "the pervasive and latent ambigu-ity in the movement" about confronting American anti-statist values. "Power as it exists was antagonistic to democracy, but how was it to be curbed without the erection of superior power?"

Prior to the 1930s, the American trade union movement was also in its major-ity anti-statist. The American Federation of Labor (AFL) was syndicalist, believed in more union, not more state power, and was anti-socialist. Its predominant leader for forty years, Samuel Gompers, once said when asked about his politics, that he guessed he was three quarters of an anarchist. And he was right. Europeans and others who perceived the Gompers-led AFL as a conservative organization because it opposed the socialists were wrong. The AFL was an extremely militant organization, which engaged in violence and had a high strike rate. It was not conservative, but rather a militant anti-statist group. The United States also had a revolutionary trade union movement, the Industrial Workers of the World (IWW). The IWW, like the AFL, was not socialist. It was explicitly anarchist, or rather, anarcho-syndicalist. The revived American radical movement of the 1960s, the so-called New Left, was also not socialist. While not doctrinally anarchist, it was much closer to anarchism and the IWW in its ideology and organizational structure than to the Socialists or Communists.

The New Deal, which owed much to the Progressive movement, was not socialist either. Franklin Roosevelt clearly wanted to maintain a capitalist economy. In running for president in 1932, he criticized Herbert Hoover and the Republicans for deficit financing and expanding the economic role of the government, which they had done in order to deal with the Depression. But his New Deal, also rising out of the need to confront the massive economic downsizing, drastically increased the statist strain in American politics, while furthering public support for trade unions. The new labor movement which arose concomitantly, the Committee for (later Congress of) Industrial Organization (CIO), unlike the American Federation of Labor (AFL), was virtually social democratic in its orientation. In fact, socialists and communists played important roles in the movement. The CIO was much more politically active than the older Federation and helped to press the Democrats to the left. The Depression led to a kind of moderate "Europeanization" of American politics, as well as of its labor organizations. Class factors became more important in differentiating party support. The conservatives, increasingly concentrated among the Republicans, remained anti-statist and laissez-faire, but many of them grew willing to accommodate an activist role for the state.

This pattern, however, gradually inverted after World War II as a result of long-term prosperity. The United States, like other parts of the developed world, experienced what some have called an economic miracle. The period from 1945 to the 1980s was characterized by considerable growth (mainly before the mid-1970s), an absence of major economic downswings, higher rates of social mobility both on a mass level and into the elites, and a tremendous expansion of higher educational systems—from a few million to 11 or 12 million going to colleges and universities—which fostered that mobility. America did particularly well economically, leading Europe and Japan by a considerable margin in terms of new job creation. A consequence of these developments was a refurbishing of the classical liberal ideology, that is, American conservatism. The class tensions produced by the Depression lessened, reflected in the decline of the labor movement and lower correlations between class position and voting choices. And the members of the small (by comparative standards) American labor movement are today significantly less favorable to government action than European unionists. Fewer than half of American union members are in favor of the government providing a decent standard of living for the unemployed, as compared with 69 percent of West German, 72 percent of British, and 73 percent of Italian unionists. Even before Ronald Reagan entered the White House in 1981, the United States had a lower rate of taxation, a less developed welfare state, and many fewer government-owned industries than other industrialized nations. ∎

View from the Inside

Public opinion polls are not simply neutral devices used to measure American public opinion. They have become tools of the trade for politicians and presidents, especially in recent years. Pollsters play a key role in helping candidates to shape their campaigns and in helping political leaders govern.

The use of pollsters by presidents and other politicians has become the source of some controversy. Critics point out that the overuse of public opinion polls tends to turn leaders into followers and also encourages politicians to tell the public only what they want to hear—a practice that can lead to erratic public policy, a dangerous short-term point of view, and a loss of critically needed perspective. Paradoxically, critics suggest, politicians who rely too much on public opinion polls may end up losing touch with the people; they would be better off relying instead on their own political instincts and leadership abilities.

In selection 5.4, political commentator Michael Barone recounts the history of pollsters in the White House and assesses the appropriate role of the presidential pollster in modern American government.

Questions

1. Would you advise an incoming president to hire a full-time White House pollster? What advantages would such an adviser bring to the president? What dangers might he or she present? In answering, consider especially the experiences of the Clinton presidency.

2. Consider the role of the political pollster in American governance in the light of the arguments concerning democracy presented by James Madison in *Federalist* No. 10 (selection 1.1). Do public opinion polls increase the possibility that majority factions will exert an overpowering influence at the national level?

5.4 The Power of the Presidents' Pollsters (1988)

Michael Barone

As the president-elect was preparing to enter office, he received some advice from his pollster. Patrick Caddell told Jimmy Carter that, although the president was about to undertake new responsibilities, he should con-

---

Michael Barone, "The Power of the Presidents' Pollsters," *Public Opinion* 11 (September/October 1988), pp. 2–4, 57. Reprinted from *Public Opinion,* formerly a Washington-based magazine of politics, business, and culture.

tinue "campaigning." He should use fireside chats and town hall meetings, he should eschew the accoutrements of high office and shun the luxuries of the rich. The advice evidently was heeded. In his first act after taking the oath, Carter stepped out of the presidential limousine and walked down Pennsylvania Avenue to the White House. Within weeks he appeared on television before a fire, wearing a sweater and talking unpretentiously to the American people.

Over the next four years, the advice changed, and the president did not always follow it. But Patrick Caddell, seldom seen in Washington in the Carter years without his White House pass dangling from his breast pocket, achieved a level of influence greater than that of any pollster before or since.

It was a precedent not entirely congenial to the polling profession. Political pollsters, after all, earn their fees by helping politicians win elections; Caddell's client saw a big lead wind up as a narrow victory in 1976 and was soundly defeated in 1980. An argument can be made—and I would make it—that Carter did entirely too much "campaigning" in his four years in office and not enough governing, that he spent too much time emphasizing the outsider themes that had worked for him as an unknown challenger and not enough time establishing himself as an insider who knew how to lead.

Even so, the Carter-Caddell experience did not result in the banishment of pollsters from the White House. Ronald Reagan's pollster, Dr. Richard Wirthlin, has been conducting frequent surveys during the Reagan years (paid for by the national Republican party, as Caddell's were by the national Democratic party, even when Carter had a primary opponent). Wirthlin has been less influential than Caddell, but his work has made an imprint on the Reagan presidency. This year Robert Teeter for George Bush and Irwin "Tubby" Harrison for Michael Dukakis are wearing the "pollsters general" mantle. Pollsters are with us in presidential politics and presidential governing, and they are likely to remain so. All this raises interesting questions: How did they get there? How should they be used now that they're there?

Humble Beginnings

The answer is that pollsters got to the White House even before Dr. George Gallup published his first public opinion survey in October 1935. That was a month after the murder of Huey Long, and so Gallup was not able to give us any results on one of the tantalizing might-have-beens of political history: how much damage would Long have done as a third-party candidate against Franklin Roosevelt in 1936? But Roosevelt himself had already received a report on that, at dinner in June 1935 with James Farley, Joseph Kennedy, and Will Hays, the 1920s Republican national chairman and 1930s movie czar—how one would like to have been a fly on that wall!—plus a statistician named Emil Hurja. Hurja presented results from a poll that showed "the president weaker that [sic] at any time since his inauguration" and "showed that [Roosevelt] would carry without difficulty all of the western states with the possible exception of Colorado, including Wisconsin and Minnesota, of course. It showed that in the eastern states he had lost some ground, which, of course, does not worry us because that condition can be corrected in due course." From the results—I have not been able to track down any written version—Farley predicted that Roosevelt would be elected by a five-million-vote plurality, and that Long would win three to four million votes and run uniformly throughout the country. Translated into percentage terms, this comes to something like a 51–39 percent Roosevelt lead over the Republicans, with 10 percent for Long, a drop from Roosevelt's 57–40 percent win over Herbert Hoover in 1932; it would have cost him Massachusetts, New Jersey, and Ohio, and have made New York and Michigan unsure.

Hurja's poll may have done something to inspire Roosevelt's shift to the left in May and June 1935, even though it seems that move started three weeks before, after NRA was declared unconstitutional May 27. Roosevelt had other reasons to believe that Long was a threat. The most sophisticated of the day's polls, Elmo Roper's quarterly surveys that began appearing in *Fortune* in July 1935, had made it clear that most voters were wary of the economic redistributionist politics of some New Dealers and were hostile to the militant new CIO unions. But while this was true of the traditional base each party had held since the Civil War—the Republican northern farmlands and the Democratic Deep South—these policies were popular among the electoral groups that were not firmly attached to either party—the Jews of New York City and the German- and Scandinavian-American Progressives of Wisconsin, Minnesota, and the old Northwest. Roosevelt seems to have understood this without polls, for this was the coalition he had been thinking about assembling since the 1920s. But polls helped convince liberal Republicans to appeal to the swing groups.

Wendell Willkie was surely aware of the *Fortune* polls, since *Fortune* managing editor Russell Davenport was his campaign organizer. Willkie made a point of saying blunt and supposedly impolitic things, which any reader of the *Fortune* polls would have known were widely popular. As Davenport himself wrote in the April 1940 issue, "The fascinating characteristic of Mr. Willkie's position is that most people will agree with it."

The always well-organized and professionally advised Thomas E. Dewey also consulted polls closely. He studied the national polls and even polls in supposedly one-party states such as Florida. "Through Ben Duffey of the New York advertising agency Batten, Barton, Durstine and Osborne," writes Dewey's definitive biographer Richard Norton Smith, "daily telephone conversations were arranged with pollster Archibald Crossley. Both Gallup and Roper offered to make known their findings to Duffey in advance of publication. Gallup did have one question. Why, he asked Duffey, did the Republican campaign want to spend money on polling? The results, after all, were a 'foregone conclusion.'"

So both candidates in 1948 may have appreciated the limits of polling better than the pollsters. Dewey because he didn't seem to trust them (Gallup's last poll was taken October 15–25 and showed Truman with a gain that would certainly prompt any of today's pollsters to stay in the field), Truman because he, like most other Democrats of the times, paid little attention to polls.

Polls Taking Root

Gallup and other pollsters for years had suggested that polls predicted election results, rather than make the more modest but more accurate claim (accurate probably even in 1948) that they showed opinion at a particular time; and by comparing their final polls to election results, calculated to even tenths of a percentage, they suggested that polls have a greater precision than they can ever realistically claim. Pollsters paid for these sins after 1948, when their final surveys all showed Dewey well ahead.

In the 1952 campaign neither side (even the Eisenhower campaign with its advertising agents) seems to have relied much on pollsters or paid much attention to them. Eisenhower himself overrode the professionals and insisted on campaigning in the South, where he believed correctly that he could carry several states. Among Taft conservatives it had become dogma that there was a huge reservoir of conservative votes among nonvoters—a dogma that surely would not have been supported by polls. Adlai Stevenson's backers quickly developed a distaste for "selling a candidate like soap" and for the survey research associated with such efforts. Most published polls during the campaign showed the race closer than in 1948, with the result that the final 56–44 percent Eisenhower margin came as a great surprise.

When in 1960 the pollster finally became a fixture of a major presidential campaign, the scene was not some high-tech office but a "pink-and-white children's bedroom on the second floor" of one of the Kennedy Hyannis Port houses. It

> had been cleared that evening as a data-analysis section, the beds removed, the baby chairs thrust to the side, a long table set up with mounds of voting statistics; there public opinion analyst Lou Harris was codifying reports received from the communications center downstairs and from the four teletypewriters of the wire agencies installed in the adjacent bedroom.

Back before the networks established reliable voter analysis models—their projections seesawed from a Kennedy landslide to a Nixon landslide on election night—Harris was doing most of this not very useful work himself, for except perhaps in Chicago the votes had already been cast. Harris, however, had done other work in the campaign, sampling opinion nationally, testing responses to issues, looking at poll results in a particular state. This was important in a campaign that was always tightly contested and in which at least the Kennedys (if not the television networks) were aware that past patterns would not obtain. Reactions to new issues and—even more important—the ties of ancestral religion would make all the difference.

The Kennedys' reliance on Lou Harris in the 1960 campaign was the first of several instances in which the Democrats, once so scornful of poll takers, seem to have used them at least as assiduously as the usually better-heeled Republicans. In 1964 Lyndon Johnson was endlessly fascinated with the polls that showed him so popular, and he hired Oliver Quayle as his pollster (Harris having gone out of the candidate polling business in 1963); Barry Goldwater, painfully aware that his was a losing cause, was more interested in being faithful to his principles and his followers than in following any advice that might be suggested by the polls. In 1968 Richard Nixon clearly ran a more organized and deliberate campaign than Hubert Humphrey, whose campaign consultant Joseph Napolitan was typing out his fall campaign plan as Humphrey was being nominated in Chicago in the last week of August. Yet neither campaign, in my view, fully appreciated the insights that sophisticated polling could have provided in that confusing and turbulent year.

Humphrey, for example, was clearly out of sync with opinion when he champi-oned, a month after Martin Luther King was murdered, "the politics of joy." Nixon, who saw Humphrey's support rise while his remained stagnant around the 43 percent level, was not much better.

The Players in Presidential Polling

Around this time the pollsters who have dominated presidential polling in most of the years since had begun to emerge. Robert Teeter, of Detroit's Market Opinion Research, is a quiet, calm, thoughtful, ideologically tolerant Republican from the ancestral Republican territory of outstate Michigan, who has played some role in every Republican presidential campaign since 1968. He was the lead pollster in Gerald Ford's very nearly successful attempt to overcome a 62–29 deficit in 1976—a campaign that sounded the themes of national pride and accomplish-ment that proved so resonant for Ronald Reagan in the 1980s—and he was the lead pollster for George Bush in 1980 and 1988. The other major Republican poll-ster has been Richard Wirthlin, a Mormon academic from Utah who bridled at supporting Barry Goldwater in 1964 but who has been Ronald Reagan's pollster since 1970. Wirthlin has calmly provided the president with figures and recom-mended strategies that, over the years, have sometimes pleased and sometimes en-raged Reagan's ideological supporters.

On the Democratic side the dominant figure from 1972 until sometime in 1984 was Patrick Caddell. Only twenty-two years old in 1972, a Harvard undergraduate from a career military family in the redneck city of Jacksonville, Florida, he man-aged to attach himself to George McGovern's longshot campaign. Caddell's great contribution there was the idea, common in academia, of alienation: it was he who counseled McGovern to appeal to supporters of George Wallace on the grounds that they all wanted a change and a removal of the people in power in Washington.

Caddell's problem was that he became a kind of johnny-one-note. A similar alienation theme worked well for Jimmy Carter, as he campaigned in the wake of Watergate in 1975 and 1976 as a candidate who was not from Washington, was not a lawyer, who carried his own suitbag, and who would never lie to you. As late as July 1979, Caddell wrote Carter a memorandum describing a national "malaise" and helped to put together the domestic summit in which Carter ludicrously sum-moned government officials and national notables up to his mountaintop—as if he were not in charge of the government himself.

Caddell's and Carter's strategy was still to run against Washington and against government—an approach that became unsustainable when Carter was in Wash-ington and headed the government. In contrast, Ronald Reagan once in office used his 1940s movie experience—the best popular culture since Dickens—and identified himself and his political cause with the heart of the country and the concerns that most citizens have at heart.

Caddell's approach was adolescent, always complaining about the grownups in power. Reagan's approach was adult, celebrating the success of those who have worked hard over the years and inviting the next generation to join them. For a moment in the 1970s, when Americans' confidence in their government and their country was low, Caddell's adolescent approach struck a chord. But over the longer haul, as the success of our own country and the weaknesses of our adversaries became harder to hide, Reagan's adult approach summed up the national mood better.

What Polls Can't Do

Do pollsters manipulate politicians who will manipulate voters in turn? These have been the fears of intellectuals ever since the polling profession was born. Actually, the fears go back further. Politicians have always been eager to understand public opinion in any way they can, if only by sampling the opinion of their neighbors and relatives as every American family does at the Thanksgiving dinner table. The fear is that the pollster, being in possession of information so much more reliable and so much more capable of producing political results than anyone else, can become a kind of Svengali.

The history I have recounted does not, I think, substantiate such fears. A Caddell can influence one candidate's campaign, but that influence is still limited in time and place. Politicians are increasingly sophisticated about using pollsters, having learned with the public to understand the limitations of the polling instrument and having observed that following slavishly the implications of any poll at one moment does not guarantee a favorable result in the long run. The ultimate limit is that voters want officeholders who not only campaign effectively but who also govern effectively. And the instincts, the policies, the strategies that produce effective governance are no more discoverable by pollsters than they are by anyone else.

Polling is a tool, not magic; and political pollsters at their best are inspired mechanics, like the guys who without saying an articulate word in English, can get your old Ford Mustang or your old musty refrigerator working again. They are not—certainly they are not yet—our masters. ■

 Chapter 6

Interest Groups

Interest groups play a vital role in American politics. Along with political parties, they are the most important way that Americans organize to express their views and make their demands on government. Interest groups play key roles in the electoral arena and in government policymaking. They are active in all three branches of the federal government and in the states.

Interest groups are by no means free of controversy. Government responsiveness to interest groups, if carried too far, can lead to the triumph of special interests at the expense of the public interest. Group involvement in support of particular candidates can be a legitimate way for citizens to advance their interests, but such activity can all too easily cross the line into influence peddling and vote buying.

Above all, the controversy over interest groups rests on a critical debate in modern political science: whether the clash of group interests, if fought on a level playing field where all groups are represented fairly and equitably, will inevitably or even generally result in the victory of the public interest. Those who believe that the public interest is, in effect, the sum of the private interests advocate a large number of effective interest groups. Those on the other side look for ways to limit the power and influence of interest groups in order to allow the public interest to emerge.

This chapter examines the roles played by interest groups in American politics, with particular attention to the dramatic changes in interest group activity over recent decades. It also probes a deeper question: What role should interest groups play in American politics, and should their role be expanded or diminished in order to serve the public interest?

Chapter Questions

1. Is a system of interest group politics consistent with the idea of democracy? Reread Madison's *Federalist* No. 10 and *Federalist* No. 51 (selections 1.1 and 1.4) as you consider your answer.
2. Why are interest groups important in the American political system? What roles do they play? How have the roles of interest groups changed in the past several decades?

⬛ Foundations

What exactly is an interest group? What is a public interest group, and what distinguishes it from a special interest group? Before examining interest groups in any detail, it is essential to have an accurate understanding of the meaning of these terms and the nature of interest group politics.

The following selection presents a classic explanation and description of interest group politics. Central to the political scientist E. E. Schattschneider's understanding of interest groups are their size and their narrow focus. Interest groups, by definition, are small and specialized. As such, they can be distinguished from political parties, which, to be effective, must be both large and broad-based. A political system that encourages the formation of interest groups, and responds to their arguments, demands, and pressures, will of necessity differ from one in which citizens express their views and make their demands felt primarily through the political parties.

Since Schattschneider's book was published in the early 1960s, American politics has, if anything, become even more focused around interest groups. The role of parties as effective mechanisms for transmitting the demands of citizens to their elected representatives has correspondingly diminished.

Schattschneider's analysis, though more than a generation old, remains an excellent introduction to the theoretical underpinnings of interest group politics.

Questions

1. What characteristics distinguish a special interest group from a public interest group? Is this distinction meaningful, in Schattschneider's view?
2. What would one expect to be the logical result of a political system in which small interest groups dominate? What are the implications of such a system for the role of political parties? for the structure of government institutions? for the nature of public policy?

6.1 The Scope and Bias of the Pressure System (1960)

E. E. Schattschneider

Pressure groups have played a remarkable role in American politics, but they have played an even more remarkable role in American political theory. Considering the political condition of the country in the first third of the

---

twentieth century, it was probably inevitable that the discussion of special-interest pressure groups should lead to development of "group" theories of politics in which an attempt is made to explain everything in terms of group activity, i.e., an attempt to formulate a universal group theory. Since one of the best ways to test an idea is to ride it into the ground, political theory has unquestionably been improved by the heroic attempt to create a political universe revolving about the group. Now that we have a number of drastic statements of the group theory of politics pushed to a great extreme, we ought to be able to see what the limitations of the idea are. . . .

We might begin to break the problem into its component parts by exploring the distinction between public and private interests. If we can validate this distinction, we shall have established one of the boundaries of the subject.

As a matter of fact, the distinction between *public* and *private* interests is a thoroughly respectable one; it is one of the oldest known to political theory. In the literature of the subject, the public interest refers to general or common interests shared by all or by substantially all members of the community. Presumably no community exists unless there is some kind of community of interests, just as there is no nation without some notion of national interests. If it is really impossible to distinguish between private and public interests, the group theorists have produced a revolution in political thought so great that it is impossible to foresee its consequences. For this reason the distinction ought to be explored with great care.

At a time when nationalism is described as one of the most dynamic forces in the world, it should not be difficult to understand that national interests actually do exist. It is necessary only to consider the proportion of the American budget devoted to national defense to realize that the common interest in national survival is a great one. Measured in dollars this interest is one of the biggest things in the world. Moreover, it is difficult to describe this interest as special. The diet on which the American leviathan feeds is something more than a jungle of disparate special interests. In the literature of democratic theory the body of common agreement found in the community is known as the "consensus," without which it is believed that no democratic system can survive.

The reality of the common interest is suggested by demonstrated capacity of the community to survive. There must be something that holds people together.

In contrast with the common interests are the special interests. The implication of this term is that these are interests shared by only a few people or a fraction of the community; they *exclude* others and may be *adverse* to them. A special interest is exclusive in about the same way as private property is exclusive. In a complex society it is not surprising that there are some interests that are shared by all or substantially all members of the community and some interests that are not shared so widely. The distinction is useful precisely because conflicting claims are made by people about the nature of their interests in controversial matters.

Perfect agreement within the community is not always possible, but an interest may be said to have become public when it is shared so widely as to be substantially universal. Thus, the difference between 99 percent agreement and perfect agreement is not so great that it becomes necessary to argue that all interests are special, that the interests of the 99 percent are as special as the interests of the

1 percent. For example, the law is probably doing an adequate job of defining the public interest in domestic tranquility despite the fact that there is nearly always one dissenter at every hanging. That is, the law defines the public interest in spite of the fact that there may be some outlaws.

Since one function of theory is to explain reality, it is reasonable to add that it is a good deal easier to explain what is going on in politics by making a distinction between public and private interests than it is to attempt to explain *everything* in terms of special interests. The attempt to prove that all interests are special forces us into circumlocutions such as those involved in the argument that people have special interests in the common good. The argument can be made, but it seems a long way around to avoid a useful distinction.

What is to be said about the argument that the distinction between public and special interests is "subjective" and is therefore "unscientific"?

All discussions of interests, special as well as general, refers to the motives, desires, and intentions of people. In this sense the whole discussion of interests is subjective. We have made progress in the study of politics because people have observed some kind of relation between the political behavior of people and certain wholly impersonal data concerning their ownership of property, income, economic status, professions, and the like. All that we know about interests, private as well as public, is based on inferences of this sort. Whether the distinction in any given case is valid depends on the evidence and on the kinds of inferences drawn from the evidence.

The only meaningful way we can speak of the interests of an association like the National Association of Manufacturers is to draw inferences from the fact that the membership is a select group to which only manufacturers may belong and to try to relate that datum to what the association does. The implications, logic, and deductions are persuasive only if they furnish reasonable explanations of the facts. That is all that any theory about interests can do. It has seemed persuasive to students of politics to suppose that manufacturers do not join an association to which only manufacturers may belong merely to promote philanthropic or cultural or religious interests, for example. The basis of selection of the membership creates an inference about the organization's concerns. The conclusions drawn from this datum seem to fit what we know about the policies promoted by the association; i.e., the policies seem to reflect the exclusive interests of manufacturers. The method is not foolproof, but it works better than many other kinds of analysis and is useful precisely because special-interest groups often tend to rationalize their special interests as public interests.

Is it possible to distinguish between the "interests" of the members of the National Association of Manufacturers and the members of the American League to Abolish Capital Punishment? The facts in the two cases are not identical. First, *the members of the A.L.A.C.P. obviously do not expect to be hanged.* The membership of the A.L.A.C.P. is not restricted to persons under indictment for murder or in jeopardy of the extreme penalty. *Anybody* can join A.L.A.C.P. Its members oppose capital punishment, although they are not personally likely to benefit by the policy they advocate. The inference is therefore that the interest of the A.L.A.C.P. is not adverse, exclusive, or special. It is not like the interest of the Petroleum Institute in depletion allowances. . . .

... The question here is not whether the distinction can be made but whether or not it is worth making. Organization has been described as "merely a stage or degree of interaction" in the development of a group.

The proposition is a good one, but what conclusions do we draw from it? We do not dispose of the matter by calling the distinction between organized and unorganized groups a "mere" difference of degree because some of the greatest differences in the world are differences of degree. As far as special-interest politics is concerned the implication to be avoided is that a few workmen who habitually stop at a corner saloon for a glass of beer are essentially the same as the United States Army because the difference between them is merely one of degree. At this point we have distinction that makes a difference. The distinction between organized and unorganized groups is worth making because it ought to alert us against an analysis which begins as a general group theory of politics but ends with a defense of pressure politics as inherent, universal, permanent, and inevitable. This kind of confusion comes from the loosening of categories involved in the universalization of group concepts.

Since the beginning of intellectual history, scholars have sought to make progress in their work by distinguishing between things that are unlike and by dividing their subject matter into categories to examine them more intelligently. It is something of a novelty, therefore, when group theorists reverse this process by discussing their subject in terms so universal that they wipe out all categories, because this is the dimension in which it is least possible to understand anything.

If we are able, therefore, to distinguish between public and private interests and between organized and unorganized groups we have marked out the major boundaries of the subject; *we have given the subject shape and scope.* We are now in a position to attempt to define the area we want to explore. Having cut the pie into four pieces, we can now appropriate the piece we want and leave the rest to someone else. For a multitude of reasons *the most likely field of study is that of the organized, special-interest groups.* The advantage of concentrating on organized groups is that they are known, identifiable, and recognizable. The advantage of concentrating on special-interest groups is that they have one important characteristic in common; they are all exclusive. This piece of the pie (the organized special-interest groups) we shall call the *pressure system.* The pressure system has boundaries we can define; we can fix its scope and make an attempt to estimate its bias.

It may be assumed at the outset that all organized special-interest groups have some kind of impact on politics. A sample survey of organizations made by the Trade Associations Division of the United States Department of Commerce in 1942 concluded that "From 70 to 100 percent (of these associations) are planning activities in the field of government relations, trade promotion, trade practices, public relations, annual conventions, cooperation with other organizations, and information services."

The subject of our analysis can be reduced to manageable proportions and brought under control if we restrict ourselves to the groups whose interests in politics are sufficient to have led them to unite in formal organizations having memberships, bylaws, and officers. A further advantage of this kind of definition is, we may assume, that the organized special-interest groups are the most self-conscious, best developed, most intense and active groups. Whatever claims can be made for a group theory of politics ought to be sustained by the evidence concerning these groups, if the claims have any validity at all.

The organized groups listed in the various directories (such as *National Associations of the United States*, published at intervals by the United States Department of Commerce) and specialty yearbooks, registers, etc. and the *Lobby Index*, published by the United States House of Representatives, probably include the bulk of the organizations in the pressure system. All compilations are incomplete, but these are extensive enough to provide us with some basis for estimating the scope of the system.

By the time a group has developed the kind of interest that leads it to organize, it may be assumed that it has also developed some kind of political bias because *organization is itself a mobilization of bias in preparation for action*. Since these groups can be identified and since they have memberships (i.e., they include and exclude people), it is possible to think of the *scope* of the system.

When lists of these organizations are examined, the fact that strikes the student most forcibly is that *the system is very small*. The range of organized, identifiable, known groups is amazingly narrow; there is nothing remotely universal about it. There is a tendency on the part of the publishers of directories of associations to place an undue emphasis on business organizations, an emphasis that is almost inevitable because the business community is by a wide margin the most highly organized segment of society. Publishers doubtless tend also to reflect public demand for information. Nevertheless, the dominance of business groups in the pressure system is so marked that it probably cannot be explained away as an accident of the publishing industry.

The business character of the pressure system is shown by almost every list available. *National Associations of the United States* lists 1,860 business associations out of a total of 4,000 in the volume, though it refers without listing (p. VII) to 16,000 organizations of businessmen. One cannot be certain what the total content of the unknown associational universe may be, but, taken with the evidence found in other compilations, it is obvious that business is remarkably well represented. Some evidence of the over-all scope of the system is to be seen in the estimate that 15,000 national trade associations have a gross membership of about one million business firms. The data are incomplete, but even if we do not have a detailed map this is the shore dimly seen.

Much more directly related to pressure politics is the *Lobby Index, 1946–1949* (an index of organizations and individuals registering or filing quarterly reports under the Federal Lobbying Act), published as a report of the House Select Committee on Lobbying Activities. In this compilation, 825 out of a total of 1,247 entries (exclusive of individuals and Indian tribes) represented business. A selected list of the most important of the groups listed in the *Index* (the groups spending the largest sums of money on lobbying) published in the *Congressional Quarterly Log* shows 149 business organizations in a total of 265 listed.

The business or upper-class bias of the pressure system shows up everywhere. Businessmen are four or five times as likely to write to their congressmen as manual laborers are. College graduates are far more apt to write to their congressmen than people in the lowest educational category are.

The limited scope of the business pressure system is indicated by all available statistics. Among business organizations, the National Association of Manufacturers (with about 20,000 corporate members) and the Chamber of Commerce of the United States (about as large as the N.A.M.) are giants. Usually business associations are much smaller. Of 421 trade associations in the metal-products industry listed in *National Associations of the United States,* 153 have a membership of less than 20. The median membership was somewhere between 24 and 50. Approximately the same scale of memberships is to be found in the lumber, furniture, and paper industries where 37.3 percent of the associations listed had a membership of less than 20 and the median membership was in the 25 to 50 range.

The statistics in these cases are representative of nearly all other classifications of industry.

Data drawn from other sources support this thesis. Broadly, the pressure system has an upper-class bias. There is overwhelming evidence that participation in voluntary organizations is related to upper social and economic status; the rate of participation is much higher in the upper strata than it is elsewhere. The general proposition is well stated by Lazarsfeld:

> People on the lower SES levels are less likely to belong to any organizations than the people on high SES (Social and Economic Status) levels. (On an A and B level, we find 72 percent of these respondents who belong to one or more organizations. The proportion of respondents who are members of formal organizations decreases steadily as SES level descends until, on the D level only 35 percent of the respondents belong to any associations.)

The bias of the system is shown by the fact that *even nonbusiness organizations reflect an upper-class tendency.*

Lazarsfeld's generalization seems to apply equally well to urban and rural populations. The obverse side of the coin is that large areas of the population appear to be wholly outside the system of private organization. A study made by Ira Reid of a Philadelphia area showed that in a sample of 963 persons, 85 percent belonged to no civic or charitable organization and 74 percent belonged to no occupational, business, or professional associations, while another Philadelphia study of 1,154 women showed that 55 percent belonged to no associations of any kind.

A *Fortune* farm poll taken some years ago found that 70.5 percent of farmers belonged to no agricultural organizations. A similar conclusion was reached by two Gallup polls showing that perhaps no more than one third of the farmers of the country belonged to farm organizations, while another *Fortune* poll showed that 86.8 percent of the low-income farmers belonged to no farm organizations. All available data support the generalization that the farmers who do not participate in rural organizations are largely the poorer ones.

A substantial amount of research done by other rural sociologists points to the same conclusion. Mangus and Cottam say, on the basis of a study of 556 heads of Ohio farm families and their wives:

The present study indicates that comparatively few of those who ranked low on the scale of living took any active part in community organizations as members, attendants, contributors, or leaders. On the other hand, those families that ranked high on the scale of living comprised the vast majority of the highly active participants in formal group activities. . . . Fully two-thirds of those in the lower class as defined in this study were nonparticipants as compared with only one-tenth of those in the upper class and one-fourth of those in the middle class. . . . When families were classified by the general level-of-living index, 16 times as large a proportion of those in the upper classes as of those in the lower class were active participants. . . .

Along the same line Richardson and Bauder observe, "Socio-economic status was directly related to participation." In still another study it was found that "a highly significant relationship existed between income and formal participation." It was found that persons with more than four years of college education held twenty times as many memberships (per one hundred persons) as did those with less than a fourth-grade education and were forty times as likely to hold office in nonchurch organizations, while persons with an income over $5,000 hold ninety-four times as many offices as persons with incomes less than $250.

D. E. Lindstrom found that 72 percent of farm laborers belonged to no organizations whatever.

There is a great wealth of data supporting the proposition that participation in private associations exhibits a class bias.

The class bias of associational activity gives meaning to the limited scope of the pressure system, because *scope and bias are aspects of the same tendency.* The data raise a serious question about the validity of the proposition that special-interest groups are a universal form of political organization reflecting *all* interests. As a matter of fact, to suppose that everyone participates in pressure-group activity and that all interests get themselves organized in the pressure system is to destroy the meaning of this form of politics. The pressure system makes sense only as the political instrument of a segment of the community. It gets results by being selective and biased; *if everybody got into the act, the unique advantages of this form of organization would be destroyed, for it is possible that if all interests could be mobilized the result would be a stalemate.*

Special-interest organizations are most easily formed when they deal with small numbers of individuals who are acutely aware of their exclusive interests. To describe the conditions of pressure-group organization in this way is, however, to say that it is primarily a business phenomenon. Aside from a few very large organizations (the churches, organized labor, farm organizations, and veterans' organizations) the residue is a small segment of the population. *Pressure politics is essentially the politics of small groups.*

The vice of the groupist theory is that it conceals the most significant aspects of the system. The flaw in the pluralist heaven is that the heavenly chorus sings with a strong upper-class accent. Probably about 90 percent of the people cannot get into the pressure system.

The notion that the pressure system is automatically representative of the whole community is a myth fostered by the universalizing tendency of modern group theories. *Pressure politics is a selective process* ill designed to serve diffuse interests. The system is skewed, loaded, and unbalanced in favor of a fraction of a minority.

On the other hand, pressure tactics are not remarkably successful in mobilizing general interests. When pressure-group organizations attempt to represent the interests of large numbers of people, they are usually able to reach only a small segment of their constituencies. Only a chemical trace of the fifteen million Negroes in the United States belong to the National Association for the Advancement of Colored People. Only one five hundredths of 1 percent of American women belong to the League of Women Voters, only one sixteen hundredths of 1 percent of the consumers belong to the National Consumers' League, and only 6 percent of American automobile drivers belong to the American Automobile Association, while about 15 percent of the veterans belong to the American Legion.

The competing claims of pressure groups and political parties for the loyalty of the American public revolve about the difference between the results likely to be achieved by small-scale and large-scale political organization. Inevitably, the outcome of pressure politics and party politics will be vastly different. ■

 # American Politics Today

One of the most significant changes in the role of interest groups in American politics in recent decades has come in the area of campaign funding. The Federal Election Campaign Act of 1974 put strict limits on the amount of money that individuals could contribute to federal campaigns, but it also opened up new opportunities for political action committees (or PACs) to become involved in campaign finance. Although the campaign act put limits on PAC contributions, these have proven easy to evade or circumvent. PACs are also free to spend money independently on behalf of causes and candidates, as long as they do not coordinate or consult with a candidate or campaign.

The role of PACs in funding political campaigns has raised serious questions. Since most PACs are connected with business organizations, critics of the system worry that candidates and officeholders have become too beholden to corporate interests. Others are concerned that ideological PACs on both the left and the right have contributed to the polarization of American politics.

In this selection, the political scientist Paul S. Herrnson examines the role of interest group and political action committees in American campaign politics.

Questions

1. In what ways might PACs be considered as an asset to democracy? In what ways might they be regarded as a detriment to democracy?
2. Does Herrnson's description of the role of PACs in modern campaigns support or undermine E. E. Schattschneider's argument (selection 6.1) on the "scope and bias" of the interest group system?

6.2 Interest Groups, PACs, and Campaigns (1998)

Paul S. Herrnson

E lections are the most important connection between citizens and those who represent them in public office. Through elections citizens have the opportunity to express their approval or dissatisfaction with the job performance of individual officeholders or the government in general. Elections also provide the general public with the opportunity to have some input into the direction of public policy. Individual citizens, however, are not the only ones who use the electoral connection to express their views about politics. Businesses, labor unions, professional associations, and a variety of other groups—some of which are at best only loosely organized—also use elections to influence public policy. This chapter presents an overview of the activities of interest groups in federal elections.

From Pulpits to PACs

The potential for significant election-oriented interest group activity exists anywhere that a group can be found or organized. Churches, boardrooms, union halls, condominium association meeting rooms, and even the World Wide Web provide venues in which political organizing commonly occurs. The groups that assemble in these places often provide endorsements, volunteers, financial support, and other campaign assistance to candidates for the House, the Senate, the presidency, and state and local offices.

For most of the twentieth century, interest groups made three kinds of contributions to the election process. One had to do with the recruitment of candidates. Labor unions, civic clubs, and some other groups encouraged potential candidates to run for office and participated in their nomination campaigns. Interest group activity in this aspect of elections was important but was often secondary to that of political parties, which have traditionally played a more central role in candidate recruitment.

Another contribution that interest groups made to the election process was organizational. Labor unions, ethnic clubs, and business concerns provided campaign volunteers, sponsored rallies, endorsed candidates, and helped the candidates disseminate their messages. One of the groups' most important contributions to the campaign was to deliver the votes of their members on election day. Groups that had a large concentrated base strongly identified with and committed to the group's political causes were highly influential in elections. Some groups,

Paul S. Herrnson, "Interest Groups, PACs, and Campaigns," in Paul S. Herrnson, Ronald G. Shaiko, and Clyde Wilcox, *The Interest Group Connection: Electioneering, Lobbying, and Policymaking in Washington* (Chatham, NJ: Chatham House Publishers, Inc., 1998), pp. 37–51. Reprinted by permission of the publisher.

particularly unions, had enough members and political clout to enable a candidate to secure a party nomination and win the general election.

The final contribution that interest groups made was financial. Corporations, trade associations, unions, and other groups historically have helped finance election campaigns. For much of U.S. political history, many groups have made contributions directly from their own treasuries or organized fund-raising committees and events.

Interest groups continue to participate in these aspects of federal elections, but they have adapted their activities to meet the opportunities and constraints that exist in the current legal, technological, and political environment. The modern political action committee (PAC), for example, emerged during the 1970s as a specialized form of organization that contributes money and other campaign support directly to federal candidates. A PAC can be most easily understood as the election arm of an interest group. In most cases, a business, union, trade association, or some other "parent" group is responsible for establishing a PAC. Yet, for most "ideological" or "nonconnected" PACs, the PAC is the organization itself.

The Federal Election Campaign Act of 1974 (FECA), its amendments, and Federal Election Commission (FEC) rulings are primarily responsible for the rise of PACs as a major force in federal elections. The law prohibits corporations, unions, trade associations, and most other groups from making campaign contributions to federal candidates, but it allows these organizations to set up PACs to collect donations from individuals and distribute them as campaign contributions to federal candidates. PACs are allowed to accept contributions of up to $5,000 per year from an individual or another PAC. In order to qualify as a PAC an organization must raise money from at least fifty donors and spend it on five or more federal candidates.

The FECA allows PACs to contribute a maximum of $5,000 per congressional candidate during each phase of the election cycle (primary, general election, and runoff). A PAC can also contribute up to $5,000 to a candidate for a presidential nomination and give another $5,000 to any presidential candidate in the general election who opts not to receive federal funds. Nevertheless, the rules governing presidential campaign finance deemphasize the roles of PACs in presidential elections. The public funding provisions for nomination contests provide matching funds for individual but not PAC contributions, thereby encouraging candidates to pursue individual rather than PAC contributions. The public funding provisions for the general election ban presidential candidates who accept federal funds from taking contributions from any sources, including PACs. The fact that every major-party candidate for the presidency between 1976 and 1996 has accepted public funding has encouraged most PACs to focus their efforts on congressional rather than presidential elections.[1]

There are other important aspects of federal elections in which some PACs, as well as corporations, unions, and other groups, participate. One is concerned with the financing of party committees and their campaign activities. PACs are al-

---

[1]Candidate-sponsored PACs are the exception to the rule. These committees are frequently used to pay for some of the preliminary activities that politicians conduct before declaring their candidacies for the nomination.

lowed to contribute up to $15,000 per year to the federal accounts of national party committees. The parties can redistribute these funds as campaign contributions and expenditures made in direct coordination with federal campaigns or, as the result of a recent Supreme Court ruling, as independent expenditures made without the knowledge or consent of individual candidates.[2] PACs, individuals, and other organized groups can also make unlimited contributions to the soft money or nonfederal accounts that national parties use to help finance their internal operations, party-building activities, voter mobilization efforts, and generic campaign advertisements.[3]

A second activity is concerned with coordinating the campaign efforts of individuals. Many PAC directors, industry executives, and leaders of other groups work to coordinate the contributions of their colleagues and other big givers. They do this through sponsoring fund-raising events and serving on candidates' fund-raising committees. In some cases, these groups engage in a controversial practice called "bundling," in which a PAC or individual group leader collects contribution checks from individuals and delivers them under one cover to a candidate. Bundling is a highly effective form of contributing because it enables a group to steer more money to a candidate than it can otherwise legally contribute, and it allows both individual givers and groups to gain recognition for their contributions.

Individuals, PACs, and parties can also make unlimited independent expenditures to advocate the election or defeat of a federal candidate as long as those expenditures are not coordinated with the candidate's campaign. Corporations, unions, and other groups are prohibited from spending money from their treasuries or operating accounts expressly to advocate voting for or against a particular candidate. Nevertheless a loophole in the law enables them to conduct "issue advocacy" campaigns in which they disseminate information designed to harm or help a candidate (or promote an issue) that does not directly tell people to vote for or against that candidate. Many groups, such as the AFL-CIO, have recently sought to take advantage of this loophole by carrying out issue advocacy campaigns designed to advance a candidate's standing with voters or detract from an opponent's level of support. Finally, these groups can also make unlimited expenditures to communicate with their members.

Pathways to Capitol Hill

Candidate Recruitment   Candidate recruitment and selection is an activity that has traditionally been carried out by local party organizations. During the late nineteenth and early twentieth centuries, local party bosses handpicked candidates for Congress and other offices. Organized interests did not have a formal role in candidate selection, but business owners, union leaders, and other local elites were sometimes part of the machine. They were often consulted because their support could be instrumental in winning elections.

---

[2]See *Colorado Republican Federal Campaign Committee* v. *Federal Election Commission*, U.S. 64 U.S.L. 4663 (1996).

[3]Soft money is raised and spent largely outside the federal law and is subject to limits imposed by state laws.

The introduction of modern primaries and caucuses opened the candidate selection process to a broader array of individuals and groups. By depriving the bosses of the ability to handpick their party's nominees, the new process created opportunities for a greater variety of individuals to compete for nominations. The process also increased the influence that ordinary citizens and organized groups could have on the nomination process. Individuals and groups began to play a larger role in shaping the pool of potential candidates and waging campaigns for the nomination.

Some contemporary interest groups work to encourage politicians who are sympathetic to their causes to run for Congress. Among them are EMILY's List, which recruits pro-choice Democratic women, and the Clean Water Action Vote Environment PAC, which recruits environmentalist candidates of both parties. These groups promise campaign contributions and other forms of support to those who ultimately decide to run for Congress. A few labor and professional association PACs, such as the AFL-CIO's Committee on Political Education (COPE) and the American Medical Association's AMPAC, take polls to encourage politicians who support their group's positions to run. Before the 1996 election, the National Federation of Independent Business PAC went so far as to host a campaign training school for prospective candidates who supported the group's pro-business agenda. PAC activities can be important in helping an individual decide to run for Congress, but interest groups are less influential in candidate recruitment than are parties. Moreover, both groups and parties pale in influence when compared to a potential candidate's family and friends.

Campaign Activities   PACs play an important role in the financing of congressional elections. Over 4,500 PACs were registered with the FEC during the 1996 election cycle, and roughly 3,000 of these PACs actually contributed nearly $204 million to primary and general election candidates for the House and the Senate. The biggest spenders were corporate PACs, which contributed roughly $78.2 million. These were followed by trade association PACs, which contributed $60.2 million; labor PACs, which contributed $48 million; and ideological PACs, which contributed another $24 million. PACs sponsored by corporations without stock and cooperatives contributed another $2.1 million and $4.4 million, respectively. The scales of PAC-giving are clearly tipped in favor of business over labor interests.

Moreover, PAC contributions are fairly concentrated among a relatively small number of groups. Fewer than 450 PACs, or approximately 10 percent of all registered committees, distributed roughly $165.6 million in contributions, or 76 percent of the total distributed in the 1996 elections. Just 180 PACs (4 percent of all PACs), accounted for nearly $124.6 million in contributions (57 percent of the total). Few elements of American society are represented in the top 4 percent of PACs, and most are not represented in the top 10 percent. Many groups, such as the poor and homeless, have no representation in the PAC community. Although PAC goals and strategies vary, and PAC contributions may offset each other under some circumstances, figures on PAC formation and PAC spending serve to dispel pluralist notions that all interests are equally represented in the PAC community and have a comparable impact on the financing of congressional elections.

The distribution of PAC contributions to congressional candidates further demonstrates that there are other systematic biases to interest group activity in elections. PACs contributed $140.4 million in major-party contested House elections in 1996.[4] The lion's share of this money—nearly 75 percent—went to incumbents. Contestants for open seats received 12 percent, and challengers received a mere 13 percent. The patterns for Senate elections were similar. Of the nearly $43.7 million that PACs spent in contested Senate elections, just 46 percent went to incumbents, slightly over 12 percent went to challengers, and 42 percent went to open-seat candidates.

The incumbent orientation of most PAC activity largely reflects the contributions of business-oriented committees, including most corporate and trade association PACs. Most of these committees focus on narrow issues that could affect their profits or those of their members. These PACs make contributions to ensure that their lobbyists have access to important policymakers. Backing likely winners is one of their first decision rules. This results in most of their money going to incumbents, who enjoy reelection rates of over 90 percent in the House and roughly 75 percent in the Senate. A second rule is to back individuals who have the potential to influence legislation that is of importance to the PAC and its parent organizations. Access-oriented PACs give a great deal of their money to party leaders and the chairs, ranking members, and members of committees and subcommittees that legislate in areas of concern to their sponsors.

A second group of PACs is more concerned with influencing the composition of Congress than seeking economic gain or maintaining access to the legislature's current membership. Nonconnected PACs, often referred to as ideological committees, make contributions to candidates who share their views on one or more often highly charged issues. Ideological PACs contribute a greater portion of their funds to congressional challengers and open-seat contestants than do most other committees. Most ideological PACs seek to back candidates in competitive contests, but some give contributions to ideologically sympathetic candidates who are long-shots in order to encourage their political careers. Ideological PACs make more independent expenditures than any other group, accounting for nearly half of those made in 1994.

The last group of PACs consciously pursues both goals. PACs that follow "mixed" strategies, which include most labor union and some trade association committees, contribute to powerful incumbents to maintain access to important policymakers. They also contribute to challengers and open-seat candidates in hotly contested races in order to help elect candidates who share their views. As a group, PACs that use mixed strategies make substantially more independent expenditures than corporate PACs and substantially fewer than nonconnected committees.

Some PACs also provide candidates with assistance in a variety of aspects of campaigning, including fund-raising, strategic, and grassroots support. EMILY's List is credited with helping to steer millions of dollars worth of individual contributions to pro-choice Democratic women. The Wish List plays a similar role for

---

[4]These figures are for general election candidates in typical races only. They exclude candidates involved in uncontested races, in runoff elections, or contests won by independents.

pro-choice Republican women. The Business Industry-Political Action Committee (BI-PAC) and COPE are examples of "lead PACs" that seek to influence the contribution decisions of other pro-business and labor PACs.

The National Committee for an Effective Congress (NCEC) is unusual in that it gives candidates technical and strategic assistance in lieu of cash. It provides Democratic candidates with geodemographic targeting data that help them identify pockets of likely supporters and persuadable voters. It then helps the candidates formulate campaign strategies designed to maximize their numbers of voters. The PAC plays a role in elections that is similar to that of the parties' congressional campaign committees.

Many ideological PACs, unions, religious organizations, and civic groups provide candidates with valuable endorsements and the volunteers needed to stamp envelopes, distribute campaign literature door-to-door, and mobilize voters on election day. Some also finance television, radio, and print advertisements criticizing congressional incumbents for their roll-call votes and failure to take action on issues that are of importance to their members. The AFL-CIO, which has traditionally been an important source of support for Democratic candidates, announced it would spend $35 million and target seventy-five vulnerable congressional districts, many occupied by GOP House freshmen, to help the Democrats in their unsuccessful attempt to regain control of Congress in 1996. In addition to contributing money directly to the Democratic candidates through its PAC, the union aired television and radio commercials and organized its members at the grassroots. "The Coalition," a group of thirty-one business organizations headed by the U.S. Chamber of Commerce, sought to counter the AFL-CIO's effort but fell short of matching the union's campaign expenditures and voter mobilization activities.

Churches have historically been the locus of much of the political activity of African Americans. The voter registration and mobilization efforts of black churches have usually helped Democratic candidates. In the early 1980s, church-based organizations, such as the Christian Coalition, began to play an important role in mobilizing grassroots support for conservative Republicans. Before the 1996 election, the group announced plans to distribute 67 million voter guides.

Some candidates find interest group assistance to be extremely helpful. A few who are involved in very close elections may even consider it to have been critical to their success. As a group, PACs are the second-largest source of campaign money in congressional elections, surpassed only by individuals. During the 1996 elections, PAC funds accounted for just 30 percent of the money collected by House and 15 percent of the money collected by Senate general election candidates. Congressional candidates and their campaign aides consider PACs and other interest groups to be a major source of assistance in fund raising.

Congressional campaigners also consider interest groups helpful in other aspects of campaigning requiring technical expertise, in-depth research, political connections, and grassroots efforts. During the 1994 congressional elections, a number of interest groups, such as the National Association of Home Builders, Chamber of Commerce, National Federation of Independent Business, and the Christian Coalition, helped finance the research and advertising that went into the House Republicans' Contract with America and the nationalized election campaign that accompanied it. These groups and others representing various interests and causes across the political spectrum were even more active in the campaigns of Democrats and Republicans in 1996. Nevertheless, most candidates appraise the assistance they receive from interest groups to be somewhat less important than what they receive from party committees.

The Road to the White House

Potential candidates for the presidency rarely need encouragement to run for office. The formal process by which one secures a major-party nomination lasts roughly a year, but aspirants for the White House spend years laying the groundwork for their campaigns. Interest groups often play important roles in this process by inviting candidates to address their members and donating funds to the PACs, tax-exempt organizations, and non-profit foundations that the candidates use to finance these preliminary presidential forays.

As noted earlier, the FECA makes individual contributions more valuable than PAC contributions in presidential elections. PACs rarely account for more than 2 percent of the money raised by major-party candidates during the primary season. But the law does not inhibit other organized group activity in campaign funding and other aspects of presidential elections. Interest groups influence the financing of presidential nomination campaigns by organizing fund-raising events, sharing their mailing lists, and coordinating the contributions of their members. Barred from contributing directly to candidates during the general election, groups assist candidates indirectly by contributing funds to their political party. A significant portion of these funds are contributed in soft money.

Corporations, trade associations, unions, ideological groups, and individuals representing these and other organizations contributed roughly $262 million in soft money to Democratic and Republican Party committees during the 1996 election cycle. The Democratic National Committee (DNC) raised $101.9 million and other Democratic committees raised an additional $20.9 million, while their GOP counterparts raised $111 million and $27.2 million.[5] Corporations, such as Archer Daniels Midland (ADM), and labor unions, such as the United Steelworkers, are among the top soft money contributors. ADM and its chairman, Dwayne Andreas, contributed in excess of $1 million to Republican Party committees and Bush's prenomination campaign committee in 1992, $977,000 of which was contributed as soft money. For safe measure, ADM and Andreas also contributed $90,000 to the DNC and an additional $50,000 to the Democratic Congressional Campaign Committee during the closing days of the general election campaign. Reflecting organized labor's staunch support for Democrats, the Steelworkers contributed $398,876 in soft money to the Democratic Party in 1992 and nothing to the GOP. It is virtually impossible to pinpoint exactly where all these funds were spent, but significant portions went to voter registration and mobilization drives and party-building activities designed to influence the outcome of the presidential election.

---

[5]The figures have been adjusted to account for transfers among party committees.

Interest groups also campaign for presidential candidates using many of the same activities they use in congressional elections. They use independent expenditures on television, radio, newspaper, and direct-mail advertisements to advance the election of one candidate over another. In 1992 they spent $3.2 million to advocate the election or defeat of George Bush, Bill Clinton, and Ross Perot. The biggest beneficiary was Bush; PACs made over $2 million in independent expenditures on his behalf and less than $35,000 against him.

Interest groups carry out issue advocacy campaigns to support a candidate's efforts without expressly promoting the candidate's election or the opponent's defeat. Groups also use internal communications to influence their members' voting decisions and turnout, and to recruit campaign volunteers. Finally, interest group money plays an important role in financing the major parties' conventions. The host committees for the 1996 Democratic and Republican conventions raised $13.6 million and $12.4 million, respectively, from corporations, unions, trade associations, and individuals who represented these and other interests.

At the Crossroads

The 1992 presidential and 1994 congressional elections led to a significant reversal of the pattern of divided government. Most of the interest group activity in congressional elections that occurred prior to 1994 was conditioned by the Democrats' control over Congress. The Democrats had held a majority of House seats for an uninterrupted forty years between 1954 and 1994, and they controlled the Senate for most of this period. Not surprisingly congressional Democrats were the primary beneficiaries of most interest group activity before the Republican takeover.

The 1994 elections ushered in a new era on Capitol Hill. Republican control of both the House and the Senate created a new set of realities for interest groups, particularly PACs. How have PACs responded to these realities? Have most continued to support Democrats, or have they switched their primary loyalties to the GOP? The patterns for the House are particularly striking. The Republican takeover had a profound impact on the partisan distribution of early PAC money. The contributions that corporate and trade association PACs made during the 1996 election cycle are almost the opposite of those given during the 1994 election. In 1994 corporate and trade association PACs gave roughly 58 percent of their House contributions to Democrats; in 1996 they gave two-thirds to the Republicans. These PACs' support for the GOP's pro-business agenda and desire to gain access to newly installed Republican committee and subcommittee chairs are principally responsible for the dramatic switch. Their concern with maintaining access to powerful members is an important factor in explaining both the PACs' switch to the Republicans and their continued contributions to incumbent Democrats. Democratic control of the White House also probably discouraged some PACs from abandoning the Democrats in favor of the GOP.

Ideological PACs were also influenced by the Republican takeover. They were able to galvanize their members, collecting and spending substantial sums. Their early contributions suggest that conservative PACs mobilized their members in order to help the GOP maintain control of the House. These PACs contributed over three times more money to House Republicans in 1996 than they did in 1994, while liberal PAC contributions to Democrats fell slightly.

Even some labor PACs, which have traditionally been among the staunchest supporters of Democratic candidates, changed their giving patterns in response to the Republicans' winning control of the House. Labor PAC contributions to Republican incumbents increased from 3 percent in 1994 to 7 percent in 1996 as these groups attempted to secure access to the newly empowered Republican majority. The Seafarer's Union, for example, gave only $51,100, or 10 percent of its House contributions, to fourteen House Republicans in the entire 1994 election, but gave $73,000, or 29 percent of its funds, to twenty-nine GOP House members during the first session of the 104th Congress—a full year before the 1996 election.

It is more difficult to assess the impact of the Republican takeover of the Senate on PAC activities because different Senate seats are up for election every two years and the idiosyncrasies of the states and candidates involved can have a major impact on campaign finance patterns. Nevertheless, the evidence suggests that many PACs, especially corporate committees, adjusted their early giving in Senate races in response to the GOP takeover of the upper chamber. Corporate PACs gave 59 percent of their Senate contributions to Republicans and 42 percent to Democrats in 1994. In 1996 these numbers changed dramatically when corporate committees gave 81 percent of their money to Republicans and 19 percent to Democrats. Trade association PACs also responded to the GOP's 1994 success. These groups had distributed 44 percent of their Senate contributions to Democrats and 57 percent to Republicans in 1994, but gave nearly three-quarters of their Senate contributions to GOP candidates in 1996.

The partisan distribution of ideological and labor PAC money was also affected by the Republicans winning control of the Senate. Republicans collected 44 percent of the ideological PAC money distributed to Senate candidates in 1994. The mobilization of conservative PAC dollars enabled GOP candidates to gather two-thirds of the PAC money ideological PACs distributed in 1996. Republican Senate candidates made only small inroads into the labor community. In 1994 Republicans received only 3 percent of all labor contributions to Senate candidates. In 1996 GOP candidates collected 5 percent of these funds.

While the patterns of early PAC activity in congressional elections have changed, it would be wrong to state that PACs have deserted the Democratic Party. Instead, the giving patterns suggest that some PACs, including many representing corporations and trade associations, have responded cautiously to the new order on Capitol Hill. They are more supportive of Republican incumbents because the GOP has become the majority party in both chambers, but most PACs continue to give substantial amounts to powerful incumbents on both sides of the aisle. Candice Nelson's analysis of early PAC contributions to House committee leaders and House Commerce Committee members supports this thesis, demonstrating that PAC funds to the recently installed Republican committee chairmen have increased significantly, but Democratic committee leaders continue to hold their own in PAC fund raising.

. . . [T]he figures presented in tables [6.1] and [6.2] suggest that the flow of early PAC dollars was informed by a sense of caution and a set of strategic

Table 6.1 ■ The Distribution of PAC Contributions in the 1994 and 1996 House Elections

	Corporate		Trade association		Labor		Nonconnected	
	1994	1996	1994	1996	1994	1996	1994	1996
Democrats								
Incumbents								
Competitive contests	35%	11%	33%	12%	44%	22%	36%	12%
Uncompetitive contests	19	16	18	16	26	27	13	11
Challengers								
Competitive contests	—	1	1	4	5	25	2	13
Uncompetitive contests	—	—	1	—	7	6	2	2
Open seats								
Competitive contests	2	1	5	3	11	10	8	4
Uncompetitive contests	1	1	1	2	4	3	3	1
Republicans								
Incumbents								
Competitive contests	4	25	4	24	—	3	3	24
Uncompetitive contests	26	36	23	29	3	4	12	15
Challengers								
Competitive contests	6	2	6	3	—	—	10	7
Uncompetitive contests	—	—	—	1	—	—	1	1
Open seats								
Competitive contests	4	5	5	5	—	—	6	8
Uncompetitive contests	3	2	3	2	—	—	3	2
Total (in thousands)	$38,213	$46,118	$34,411	$40,054	$30,110	$35,781	$10,520	$13,718

Notes: The figures include only PAC contributions to general election candidates in two-party contested races. Candidates involved in uncontested races, runoff elections, or contests won by independents are excluded.

"—" indicates that PACs spent less than 0.5 percent of their funds in these races. Some numbers do not add to 100 percent because of rounding.

N for 1994 = 776; *N* for 1996 = 812.

Source: Compiled from Federal Election Commission data.

Table 6.2 ■ The Distribution of PAC Contributions in the 1994 and 1996 Senate Elections

	Corporate		Trade association		Labor		Nonconnected	
	1994	1996	1994	1996	1994	1996	1994	1996
Democrats								
Incumbents								
Competitive contests	30%	6%	31%	8%	47%	19%	34%	11%
Uncompetitive contests	4	2	4	2	5	4	4	2
Challengers								
Competitive contests	—	1	1	3	13	15	2	5
Uncompetitive contests	2	—	1	—	8	2	2	—
Open seats	6	10	7	15	23	52	14	15
Republicans								
Incumbents								
Competitive contests	7	32	9	28	1	2	6	22
Uncompetitive contests	19	13	19	10	1	2	14	8
Challengers								
Competitive contests	9	9	7	7	—	—	10	8
Uncompetitive contests	—	—	—	—	—	1	—	—
Open seats	24	27	21	26	1	1	14	26
Total (in thousands)	$17,864	$16,547	$10,362	$10,982	$6,611	$6,316	$5,170	$6,292

Notes: The figures include only PAC contributions to general election candidates in two-party contested races.

"—" indicates that PACs spent less than 0.5 percent of their funds in these races.

Some numbers do not add to 100 percent because of rounding.

N for 1994 = 68; *N* for 1996 = 68.

Source: Compiled from Federal Election Commission data.

considerations that emphasized supporting incumbents. PAC giving in 1995 and 1996 reflected the uncertainty surrounding the question of which party would control Congress following the 1996 elections and a strategic principle shared (then and now) by most corporate, trade association, and other business-oriented PACs that emphasizes maintaining access to powerful congressional leaders of both parties.

Unlike congressional elections, most of the interest group activity that took place in recent presidential contests occurred while a Republican was in the White House or was favored to capture it. In 1992, Democratic candidate Bill Clinton won the presidency, vanquishing incumbent Republican George Bush. Assessing the impact that a reversal of fortunes has on interest group activity in presidential elections is more difficult than it is for the House and the Senate because presidential candidates rely mainly on money collected from individual citizens and the federal government to finance their campaigns. PAC dollars do not play a big role in their campaigns.

Interest group money does, however, make its way into presidential election campaigns. . . . [B]oth President Clinton and GOP nominee Bob Dole were able to help their respective parties raise substantial sums of soft money from corporations, unions, trade associations, and individuals who represent particular groups. These funds, and the independent expenditures, internal communications, and issue advocacy campaigns that these groups undertake, played an important role in the 1996 presidential election. ■

The Comparative Context

Like other interest groups, foreign nations have a great stake in political decision making in Washington. Not surprisingly, therefore, foreign governments spend large sums of money to lobby American officials and to influence American public opinion in favor of policies they support.

Many foreign governments run such lobbying efforts, but few have come under as much scrutiny as that of Japan. Although the "Japanese Lobby" is extensive and influential and in many ways unique, argue the political scientists Ronald J. Hrebenar and Clive S. Thomas in this selection, the efforts of the Japanese government are not out of proportion to the stakes involved. Moreover, they suggest, criticism of the Japanese lobby may be based more on deep-seated prejudice than on the facts.

Questions

1. Why does the Japanese government direct much of its energy toward influencing the American public, as well as the American government? What methods does Japan use to influence American public opinion?

2. How do the activities of the Japanese lobby differ from those of other governments who seek to influence American policy and public opinion? How are they similar?

6.3 The Japanese Lobby in Washington

Ronald J. Hrebenar and Clive S. Thomas

When Michael Crichton's novel *Rising Sun* was released as a motion picture in the summer of 1993, there was considerable reaction from Japanese Americans, native Japanese, Asian Americans, and even non-Japanese Americans. On the *New York Times* op-ed page Roger M. Pang wrote:

> The Asians are the villains. . . . Mr. Crichton's larger purpose is to present a dark vision of Japan's economic ambitions. . . . [T]he book portrays the Japanese as hard-edged exploiters of an increasingly vulnerable America.

Pang's comments echo the concerns of many Japanese regarding the stereotypes many Americans hold about contemporary Japan, concerns that extend to cultural misunderstandings, economic difficulties, and political confusions. The Japanese government and many individual Japanese are also convinced that many Americans simply do not understand enough about Japanese culture to appreciate differences in behavior in the two societies. They are also convinced that many Americans, including some of the nation's top political and business leaders, blame Japan for the inability of the United States to compete in recent years and for American political problems in various parts of the world. A *New York Times-*CBS News-Tokyo Broadcasting poll of July 6, 1993, supported these conclusions. Covering Japanese and American attitudes toward each other, the poll found that nearly two-thirds of Japanese polled described their country's relations with the United States as "unfriendly." This was the highest such negative Japanese response ever recorded in these polls.

For all of the above reasons, Japanese organizations have spent billions of dollars in recent years to influence American attitudes toward Japan, Japanese culture, Japanese politics, and Japanese business and its practices. In his 1990 book, *Agents of Influence*, Pat Choate dubbed these efforts "the Japan Lobby."

• • •

From Ronald J. Hrebenar and Clive S. Thomas, "The Japanese Lobby in Washington: How Different Is It?" in Allan J. Cigler and Burdett A. Loomis, eds., *Interest Group Politics,* 4th ed. (Washington: CQ Press, 1995), pp. 349–367. Reprinted by permission of Congressional Quarterly.

The Three Parts of the Japan Lobby

Although few organizations are pure examples of a particular type of lobby, one can divide them into three major subcategories: cultural, economic, and political. The Japan lobby comprises all three of these strains.

Japan's Cultural Lobby

Japan's cultural lobby centers on several large organizations headquartered in New York City. These include the Japan Foundation, the Japan society, and the United States-Japan Foundation. Two of these organizations—the foundations—essentially operate as funding sources for many other, largely American organizations that affect American attitudes toward Japan. . . .

The Japan Foundation   The Japan Foundation—or *Kokusai Koryu Kikin*—is perhaps the best known of the Japanese cultural organizations in the United States. Founded as a special body of the Ministry of Foreign Affairs in October 1972, its aim is to deepen other nations' understanding of Japan, to promote better mutual understanding among nations, and to encourage friendship and goodwill. Funded by the Japanese government and the Japanese private sector, its program budget had grown to ¥15.74 billion by 1992. That same year it had a staff of 199 and fifteen overseas offices. New programs had been instituted, such as the Japanese Language Institute (July 1989), the ASEAN Cultural Center (1990), and the Center for Global Partnership (CGP, April 1991). The Japan Foundation had become the core organization of Japan's international cultural-exchange activities.

To accomplish its goals, the Japan Foundation promotes Japanese studies abroad by providing grants to organizations and offering financial assistance to researchers. It also supports Japanese-language education overseas (including salary assistance for full-time Japanese language instructors), student study tours, Japanese speech contests, the translation and publishing of Japanese materials, and the broadcasting of Japanese language educational television programs. All together, the Japan Foundation in 1992–1993 granted more than $2.9 million to 35 individuals and 236 institutions in the United States. . . .

Japan-United States Friendship Commission   Perhaps the most unusual of the Japanese cultural organizations is the Japan-United States Friendship Commission (JUSFC), an independent agency of the U.S. government "dedicated to promoting mutual understanding and cooperation between the United States and Japan." It administers grant programs in support of Japanese studies in the United States, policy oriented research, public affairs and education, American studies in Japan, and the arts. The JUSFC was established by Congress in 1975 to administer a trust fund formed from part of the Japanese government's repayment for U.S. facilities built in Okinawa and later returned to Japan and for postwar American assistance to Japan. Annual income from the fund amounts to about $34 million. JUSFC is administered by a commission of U.S. officials including members of the Senate and House, representatives from the Department of State and the Department of Education, and the chairs of the national endowments for the arts and for the humanities.

A major part of JUSFC's budget goes into training the next generation of American Japanese scholars. To further this goal, programs have been started to provide for graduate student fellowships, graduate school faculty and curriculum development, library support, faculty research, language training, and general programs of public education. In general, the Commission seeks to fund very focused, collaborative research projects. Recent research has been funded through the Social Science Research Council and the University of California-Berkeley.

The Japan Society   The Japan Society uses grants from various foundations and from Japanese and American corporations to expand American understanding of Japan. Founded in 1907, the Society is the oldest Japanese cultural advocate in the United States. With a full-time staff of sixty, eight thousand individual members, and four thousand corporate members, it is also the largest. Cyrus Vance, the Society's 1992 chairman, noted in the organization's 1990–1991 report:

> As an organization devoted to enlightened and mutually enriching relations between the United States and Japan, the Japan Society had its work cut out for it this past year. . . . I sense real urgency about the danger of the negative trend characterizing mutual attitudes. We seem to be drifting rather mindlessly toward thinking of each other in adversarial terms. . . . This kind of challenge brings out the best in the Japan Society, its members and supporters.

The heart of the Japan Society's effort to promote mutual understanding is the U.S.-Japan Program which, with a staff of ten and three major orientations—corporate, public policy, and outreach/education, provides forums for discussion of the political, economic, business, and social issues that affect the two countries, as well as educational programs that promote cross-cultural understanding. . . .

The Japanese Economic Lobby

The Japanese economic lobby is composed of several types of professional organizations that fit together nicely to represent Japanese business interests. One part generates a tidal wave of general economic data and specific subsector analyses; another provides think-tank advocacy for Japanese economic policies; and others represent specific industries through trade associations.

The Japan Economic Institute of America   Located in Washington, D.C., the Japan Economic Institute of America (JEIA)—the reconstituted and legitimized successor of the previously discussed U.S.-Japan Trade Council—is the primary source in the United States for economic and business data on Japan. JEIA is a unit of the Japanese Ministry of Foreign Affairs, which largely funds its operations. Those operations include hosting a series of seminars on Japan, with an emphasis on business and trade issues. However, its major contribution to the understanding of Japan lies in its three publications: the *Japan Economics Report* (weekly); the *Japan-U.S. Business Report* (monthly); and the *Japan Economic Survey* (monthly). JEIA also issues periodic reports on Japan. In recent years, these have covered Japanese fiscal policy, budgetary process, defense, trade competition, education, banking, foreign affairs, industrial policy, labor, political reform, U.S.-Japan trade relations, health policy, and the status of women. For those seeking detailed and current information on Japan, these publications are among the best in the world. The current president of JEIA is Arthur Alexander. With a doctorate in economics from Johns Hopkins University, Alexander came from The Rand Corporation to head JEIA's staff of seven.

Other Organizations and Operations in the Economic Arena   C. Fred Bergsten is the head of a powerhouse that has had a profound effect on U.S.-Japanese economic relationships. Located in Washington, D.C., the Institute for International Economics (IIE) derives part of its research funding from Japanese sources. The organization is cited frequently in the *New York Times* and the *Washington Post*. Whenever a story is published on U.S. trade problems or Japanese economics, C. Fred Bergsten of the IIE seems to appear "to put the issue into proper perspective." Bergsten is also a favorite expert source of Hobart Rowen, the chief economics writer of the *Washington Post* and nationally syndicated columnist.

Information has always been the primary objective of Japanese organizations— inside and outside Japan—and Japan has developed a formidable information gathering network. The Japanese are voracious accumulators and consumers of information of all kinds: political, social, and economic. Much of the money the Japan lobby spends in the United States is allocated for the collection and interpretation of such information. The Japanese government, in particular, through its fifteen consulates in the United States, is a major collector of all types of hard data and opinion. Complementing the consular operations of the Ministry of Foreign Affairs is the JETRO program of the Ministry of International Trade and Industry (MITI). The JETRO program not only promotes Japanese business, but also conducts so-called soft-side propaganda campaigns that use the provision of information as their vehicle.

Akio Morita, the head of Sony Corporation, founded a group of 160 Japanese companies with major investments in the United States. Originally named the Council for Better Investment in the United States, the group was renamed the Council for Better Corporate Citizenship in 1989. Now led by the powerful Japanese business association Keidanren, the Council's goal is to defeat adverse policies in the United States on both the state and federal levels.

Japan's Political Lobby

Choate faults the Japan lobby for its recruitment of high-level American governmental officials to work for Japanese interests. The list of prominent Americans who have lobbied or consulted for Japan in recent years is indeed impressive:

◆ William Colby, director of central intelligence in the Reagan administration
◆ Richard Allen, President Reagan's National Security Adviser
◆ Frank Fahrenkopf, former chair of the Republican National Committee
◆ Robert Strauss, former chair of the Democratic National Committee
◆ Stanton Anderson, former deputy assistant secretary of state
◆ Stuart Eizenstat, former White House domestic policy chief
◆ Henry Kissinger, former secretary of state
◆ Ron Brown, former chair of the Democratic National Committee and President Clinton's secretary of commerce

The above is only a small sample of the prominent Americans who work for Japanese interests. As Holstein comments, the longer list reads "like a who's who of Washington's toughest, savviest political operators." Brother International Corporation has used Hogan & Hartson to represent its interests; Fujisawa USA hired Hill and Knowlton. Toyota Motor Sales USA has its own lobbyist, Mary Khim. Toyota's major rival, Nissan, pulled a major coup in 1991 when it engaged Tim MacCarthy, the lobbyist for the Motor Vehicle Manufacturing Association of the United States, to direct Nissan North America's governmental and industry affairs. Pointing to the fact that Nissan has the largest automobile manufacturing plant in the United States, MacCarthy argues that "We're a good American company.

Because of the importance of trade issues in the U.S.-Japan relationship, the Office of the U.S. Trade Representative has become a training ground for Japanese lobbyists. Several years of service in the federal government produce the experience and connections required to secure a lucrative position with a Japanese corporation or an American law firm representing Japanese interests. As U.S. Trade Representative in 1977–1979, Robert Strauss met frequently with Japanese governmental and corporate leaders. In 1990, he and his company arranged the merger of Matsushita Electric Corporation and MCA, the Hollywood media giant. Strauss is described as a lawyer-lobbyist "who can do everything." . . .

In 1993, Japanese interests hired more than 125 American law firms, economic consultants, and public relations firms. As a case in point, Howard Baker, former U.S. senator and White House chief of staff under Ronald Reagan, wrote a very favorable article for the Spring 1992 issue of the prestigious journal, *Foreign Affairs*. The article analyzed U.S.-Japanese economic relations and recommended closer economic and political links between the two nations. It never mentioned that Howard Baker had been and continued to be a lobbyist and lawyer for Japanese corporations. Baker's law firm had helped negotiate the Matsushita takeover of the Hollywood media powerhouse MCA in 1990; for its work in the transaction Baker's firm earned more than $1.6 million. When William Hyland, the editor of *Foreign Affairs*, was asked if he had known about Baker's relationship with Japan before the article was accepted for publication, he responded: "I had no idea that Baker was a lobbyist when the article was submitted. If I had known, I would have had to think twice [about publishing it]." Hyland noted that Baker's first draft had been too mild in its treatment of Japan; it was revised to make the analysis more critical.

One of Tokyo's problems is trouble may occur at so many points in the policy-making process. Expert help to deal with these potential trouble points often is very specialized. Take, for example, two of the major lobbying firms representing foreign interests in Washington, D.C.: Black, Manafort, Stone & Kelly and Neill & Co. The *forte* of Black, Manafort had been its long-term relationship with the Republican White House. However, Black, Manafort has had almost no access with the Democratic Congress. Neill & Co. has had great congressional access, but, until Bill Clinton's election in 1992, had little executive branch access.

The Japan lobby has been particularly effective in dealing with Congress and especially congressional staff. This tactic began in a serious manner in the early 1980s. In 1984, a major Japanese research institute published a study of the significance of congressional staff in the policymaking process. The study received a great deal of informed attention in Japan and was republished in summary forms in influential Japanese media sources. The Japanese Embassy in Washington now assigns four officials to become experts on congressional staff members, and the Japan lobby in general spends a great deal of money wining and dining congressional staff in parties with the ambassador and many smaller lunches. Key staffers are offered expense-paid fact-finding trips to Japan. Noting that many other nations have picked up this tactic from the Japanese, Choate argues that much of the opposition to ethics reform legislation comes from congressional staff members who worry about not being eligible for jobs with foreign lobbies after their government service is finished.

In Good Company

Media reporting of the huge expenditures of the Japan lobby make it appear as though only the Japanese are spending big money to influence American public policy. There is much evidence, however, to indicate that the Japanese are not the only big spenders in the foreign lobbying game. The Kuwaiti government in 1990–1991 reportedly spent millions of dollars on lobbying and public relations to secure American support for the Gulf War. The substantial Kuwaiti account was only a small part of the billings of Hill and Knowlton's Washington, D.C. office— an estimated $38 million in 1990. The same year, Hong Kong trading companies paid R. Marc Nuttle, the former executive director of the Republican National Congressional Campaign Committee, $200,000 to lobby on the renewal of China's favored trading status.

Even the poorest, least developed nations have spent millions of dollars lobbying Washington. Kenya and Zaire pay $1 million a year to secure the lobbying services of Black, Manafort. Liberia pays about half that amount to Neill & Co. Solo lobbyist Bruce Cameron charges Third World nations such as Mozambique and Guatemala a minimum of $100,000 a year for lobbying services.

Among developed nations, Japan's reported expenditures, although high, are not wholly incommensurate with their economic relationship with the United States. The Canadian lobby spent about $22.7 million in 1992, compared to $60 million for Japan, $13 million for Germany, $12.8 million for France, and $11 million for Mexico. Estimates of the lobbying expenditures of various nations vary depending on what is counted and how. One source suggests that in 1989 the Japanese were spending $45 million a year on public relations, $140 million on corporate philanthropy, and $30 million on academic research grants. Like all estimates of lobbying expenditures heard and repeated in Washington these numbers are largely fiction, but they give some idea of the relative effort of various nations. Choate estimates the annual expenditures of the Japan lobby at $400 million, a figure he contrasts with the $402 million reported to have been paid by all foreign interests to their U.S. registered lobbyists in 1987.

Mitchell's study of direct foreign investments and political action committees (PACs) found that in proportion to their economic stake in America the Swiss and Canadians were politically overrepresented in the United States compared to the Japanese. The companies in which the Japanese have invested were found to have a much smaller share of foreign money than was the case with Canadian and Swiss companies in this country. When ownership was combined with PAC spending for 1987–1988, British companies emerged as the largest foreign participants in American politics; Japanese companies ranked sixth. With regard to their representation by lobbyists in Washington, Mitchell found that Japanese companies were not disproportionately engaged; indeed, they were outweighed by the British and Canadians. Only when parent firms were included did the Japanese firms hire more Washington representatives than any other nation.

It is interesting that the Japan lobby makes less frequent use of PACs than do other foreign interests seeking influence in the United States. Federal law prohibits foreign-owned firms from making political contributions in U.S. elections, but a Federal Election Commission ruling cleared the way for U.S. subsidiaries of foreign corporations to set up PACs provided the PAC officers and contributors were U.S. citizens. In 1986, ninety-two such PACs were identified in a *National Journal* article; three years later, the total was 118 PACs, which collectively contributed $2.8 million to federal candidates in the 1987–1988 election cycle, about 5 percent of all corporate PAC contributions during that cycle. Of the ten largest foreign-owned corporate PACs contributing to congressional candidates during the 1987–1988 election cycle, not one was Japanese. The top-ranked foreign-owned PACs were formed by corporations owned by British, Dutch, Swiss, Canadian, Saudi, Hong Kong, German, and Kuwaiti interests. Of the aforementioned 118 PACs run by corporations owned by foreign interests, only twelve had Japanese ties. Mitchell reports that the dozen Japanese PACs gave $370,000 to federal candidates in 1987–1988.

Robert Morse, executive vice-president of the Economic Strategy Institute, a Washington think tank formed the Japan critic Clyde Prestowitz, argues that if PACs owned by foreign interests were restricted in reform legislation, it would not reduce the influence of the Japan lobby very much:

> The Japanese prefer indirection: They don't like head-on types of things. The Japanese prefer to increase their political influence by hiring well connected lobbyists and by, increasingly, making donations to U.S. foundations, educational and charitable institutions.

• • •

The reaction to Choate's *Agents of Influence* was strong indeed. The Japanese and their well-paid representatives took offense to being singled-out as "an evil force" when many other nations were behaving similarly. Hiroshi Hirabashi, the economic minister at the Japanese Embassy in Washington complained: "Why are they pointing mainly at the Japanese and not the British, not the Dutch, not the Canadians, not the Koreans?" Many Americans used Choate's arguments to reaffirm their belief that America was "losing the war on a variety of fronts" to the Japanese, who were not playing the game fairly.

Two basic themes seem to account for most of the American emotion on the question: long-term American bias against Japan and the refusal of many

Americans to attribute the recent economic difficulties of the United States to their own actions. After all, it is easier to blame someone else for one's difficulties after a long run of tremendous successes, and the Japanese make perfect targets, especially now that the Soviet threat has receded. The Japan lobby has become a symbol of 150 years of distrust and misunderstanding between Japan and the United States.

In fact, however, Japan's lobbying efforts appear to be commensurate to the stakes it holds in its relations with the United States. Meanwhile, the Japan lobby has shifted its emphasis away from the use of expensive lobbyists toward the utilization of American organizations and Japanese subsidiaries to get its message to American political leaders.

The fact that Japan's lobbying efforts are commensurate with its stake in the United States does not mean foreign lobbying in this country is not a problem. Although he was perhaps unfair in singling out Japan, Choate has shown clearly how foreign interests can buy access to our nation's policy makers and opinion leaders. Japan is not the only nation that has come to understand Jessie Unruh's classic observation that "money is the mother's milk of politics." Many nations appear to understand that there appear to be few in Washington whose services cannot be rented if not purchased. ■

 # View from the Inside

A few decades ago, interest group activity in Washington was dominated by what the journalist Hedrick Smith called "old-breed lobbying"—an insider's game that thrives on the "clubbiness of the old-boy network" and that "turns on the camaraderie of personal friendships" of Washington power-brokers. In recent years, however, "old-breed lobbying" has given way to "new-breed lobbying"—an approach that combines techniques borrowed from mass marketing and public relations, and that takes advantage of new technologies, including the fax machine, email, and the Internet.[1]

In this selection, the *The New York Times* reporter Alison Mitchell examines the new style of lobbying in the nation's capital.

Questions

1. What are the advantages and disadvantages of new-breed as opposed to old-breed lobbying from the interest groups' point of view?
2. Is "new-breed" lobbying an improvement over "old-breed" lobbying from the point of view of American democracy?

---

[1]Hedrick Smith, *The Power Game: How Washington Really Works* (New York: Random House, 1988).

6.4 A New Form of Lobbying Puts Public Face on Private Interest (1998)

Alison Mitchell

From the nondescript headquarters of his Houston construction firm, Leo E. Linbeck Jr., a lanky, bow-tied executive with a drawl, is masterminding a crusade to overturn the nation's tax system.

Once, someone like him might have hired some of Washington's "Gucci Gulch" lobbyists to prowl the well-trod marble corridors outside Congress's tax committees. But Mr. Linbeck, with Texas-style audacity, wants to engineer a populist uprising to replace the income tax code with a national sales tax. And so with $15 million from some initial investors and mass fund-raising, he has run a media advertising campaign and employed an army of consultants, pollsters, political strategists, marketers, academics and yes, even a few lobbyists, to energize the citizenry.

"Imagine what it would be like if you were in Congress and you got a thousand phone calls a week and letters and E-mails and faxes," Mr. Linbeck said. "Not people from all over the country, but your constituents, people whose names you recognize, the people who were at the polls with you, who live down the street."

Mr. Linbeck and his fellow investors in Americans for Fair Taxation are unusual in the scale of their ambition. But their methods have become commonplace as lobbying has undergone a revolution over the past decade.

Rarely now does a well-connected Washington lobbyist work alone. Instead, the lobbyist has become just one of many players running national campaigns designed to create a "grass-roots" ground swell in support, or more often in opposition, to legislation before Congress.

In their million-dollar costs and in their reliance on television, polling and grass-roots constituency building, these efforts most resemble Presidential campaigns. And they are now so pervasive and sophisticated that it has become difficult to distinguish between a lobbying effort, an issue advocacy campaign and a citizens movement.

Some of these efforts are genuinely grass-roots movements. But others are deceptions in which a special interest pays to create the appearance of a popular ground swell. The growth of these techniques has spread the wealth of the influence industry beyond the lawyer-lobbyists to a new class of political professionals who often play overlapping roles as advisers to Presidential and Congressional candidates, corporate tacticians and media pundits.

In a world where the distinctions and conflicts between their multiple roles seem to matter less and less and can even be a business advantage, strategists who are ideological enemies in politics put their differences aside to work together on large-scale corporate campaigns.

Alison Mitchell, "A New Form of Lobbying Puts Public Face on Private Interest," *The New York Times,* September 30, 1998, pp. A1, A14. Copyright © 1998 by The New York Times. Reprinted by permission.

The trend is the outgrowth of several developments in technology and politics. E-mail, computer databases, talk radio and 24-hour cable television all make it easier to organize and send a political message across the country at warp speed.

At the same time, power in Washington has been dispersed so that new ways are needed to influence more legislators. The media-age politician is far more likely to be moved by polls, television ads and mass constituent contacts than by party discipline, a committee chairman or a Washington wise man. And the Republicans in Congress know that they came to power with the help of several groups with grass-roots memberships: the National Federation of Independent Business, the National Rifle Association, the Christian Coalition.

"There's a couple of evolutions happening simultaneously," said Keith Appell, of Creative Response Concepts, a Republican public relations firm. "There's Republican sensitivity to grass-roots and certain lobbying methods you didn't have before and the explosion of media in the communications age."

Public policy experts debate whether the new methods of lobbying have made it more democratic by taking it out of the back rooms of the Capitol or whether they have simply made it harder for interests without money to compete in the public arena.

"It's part of a trend in Washington where rational debate on issues gets buried in big-budget sound bites," said Edward L. Yingling, the chief lobbyist for the American Bankers Association.

Mr. Linbeck said of his way of moving Congress: "It's not as orderly. It's not as predictable. It's not as controlled as some might want it to be. But I think those are positive attributes."

The convergence of lobbying and politics is evident in how Mr. Linbeck has gone about his crusade. He estimated that the effort would take several years and ultimately cost an extraordinary $90 million, a sum possible only if hundreds of thousands of Americans join his cause. Right now, tax reform is only a glimmer far on the horizon of Congress.

Some of the initial money spent by Mr. Linbeck's group went to hire prominent academics and research organizations to work on the 23 percent national sales tax. But to speed the organizing and make the sales tax proposal as politically appealing as possible, Americans for Fair Taxation also turned to national experts in politics, using Denis Calabrese, a Houston Republican consultant and onetime aide to Representative Dick Armey of Texas, as his chief strategist. With Mr. Calabrese's help, Americans for Fair Taxation has hired an all-star cast from both parties to propel the sales tax. . . .

"Clients and industries have come to appreciate there are no solo pilots in this town," said Jack Quinn, who returned to the law firm of Arnold & Porter after resigning as White House counsel. "Now you send armies, ships, tanks, aircraft, infantry, Democrats and Republicans, grass-roots specialists, people with special relationships."

In many cases, much about these campaigns remains undisclosed, from the cost to the proponents. Many consultants who were willing to explain their techniques would not identify their clients.

In 1995 the new Republican-led Congress approved major changes in how Congress does business. It imposed a ban on gifts and passed tough new disclosure

requirements for lobbyists. But the legislation did not include reporting requirements for "grass-roots" lobbying such as telephone and letter-writing campaigns,
even if the campaigns were generated by hired lobbyists and organizers. An earlier
effort to pass a disclosure law that would have required reporting on such lobbying
faltered in the Democratic-led Congress in 1994 when Representative Newt Gingrich, then the House Republican whip, branded the measure an "anti-religious"
attempt to chill growing grass-roots conservative movements.

Numerous movements on the political scene have genuine grass-roots memberships, from the Christian Coalition to the Sierra Club. But creating citizens'
movements, or the semblance of citizens' movements, on demand has also become
big business.

Public relations firms and boutique shops advertise such arcane-sounding spe-
cialities as: "development of third-party allies" or "grass-roots recruitment and mobilization" or "grass-tops lobbying." The goal of these campaigns is to persuade
ordinary voters to serve as the front-line advocates for the paying clients.

"In terms of the concept, you move beyond candidate advertising and beyond
party organizations and form your own free-standing operation around an issue,"
said Brian A. Lunde, a former executive director of the Democratic National
Committee who specializes in this kind of organizing. "The day of the P.A.C.
check and the steak dinner and the golf dinner is over."

Practitioners said a grass-roots effort can cost from $40,000 for a small-scale at-
tempt to sway the vote of just one or two crucial members of a subcommittee to
many millions of dollars to sway a majority.

Three years ago, Campaigns & Elections magazine, a trade journal, conducted a
painstaking survey and concluded that "grass-roots lobbying," apart from more traditional lobbying, had become an $800 million industry in 1993 and 1994.

And advertising adds to the cost.

"The inside game of lobbying is in decline," said Mike Murphy, who was a
media consultant in 1996 to the Republican Presidential candidates Lamar
Alexander and Bob Dole. "The outside game of consumer messaging, of marshal-
ing public opinion, is advancing and increasing, and savvy companies have
figured out that the best experts to hire to do this kind of work are political
consultants."

The Evolution: Reaching the Masses Is Easier Than Ever

Two decades ago, corporations rarely used any of these techniques. Grass-roots
mobilizations were the province of environmentalists, the civil rights movement
or opponents of the war in Vietnam. Television advertising on legislation would
have been considered an extravagant waste of money.

But in the early 1980's, campaign strategists looking for business during years
without major elections and corporations looking for a better way to argue their
case found common ground.

Mr. Sewell, who made the transition from Democratic politics, recalled that his
first experience with issue campaigning came when the AT&T Corporation, in
the wake of divestiture, hired the political public relations firm where he then
worked.

"They didn't know what they were asking for," he said. "They thought they needed something like what was in a political campaign. We didn't know quite what to make of it, but we started developing programs whereby we understood that just like a member of Congress has a constituency, a corporation has a constituency. Our job was to go and identify that constituency and mobilize that constituency to advocate a point of view."

Since then such campaigns have become prevalent.

The Internet, E-mail, talk radio and computerized fax machines have made it far easier to organize national constituencies and instruct them on when to deluge Congress with letters and telephone calls.

At the same time, the Congressional gift ban cut down on opportunities for traditional lobbyists to wine and dine lawmakers.

And as party discipline has waned, members of Congress have also proved ever more responsive to television advertising or contacts from home, or the ups and downs of instantly sampled public opinion.

"You have entrepreneurial politicians not disciplined by the party but by their own images," Mr. Murphy said. "The mainspring in this is that public opinion counts."

Or at least the element of public opinion that is marshaled by the paid organizers and image makers. "There may be a lot of people who agree with your position but they will never get involved," Mr. Sewell said. "It's our job to find the people who would agree with the position and get them involved."

Television Advertising: Small Screen Helps Make a Big Statement

Often these days, it is television advertising that frames the terms of discussion for the Congress.

Five years ago, when the Health Insurance Association of America used its $17 million "Harry and Louise" commercials to help defeat President Clinton's plan for universal health insurance, the effort was pioneering.

"It was a big gamble in that nobody had done this kind of thing on that scale before," said Ben Goddard, a partner in the Malibu-based Goddard-Claussen firm that made the commercials.

Now Mr. Goddard's firm has its own Washington office. And media advertising on a legislative issue recently passed another milestone: the estimated $40 million radio and television advertising campaign that the five largest tobacco companies used this spring to defeat anti-tobacco legislation was the most expensive and sustained issue advocacy campaign ever undertaken on legislation, according to the Annenberg Public Policy Center of the University of Pennsylvania.

Such advertising campaigns are usually accompanied by mobilizations designed to make average citizens the advocates for the paying clients. Sometimes the advertisements help lobbyists find those sympathizers by running 800-numbers.

Some of these efforts amount to easily spotted carpet-bombing of Congress with form letters and patch-through telephone calls.

Senator John McCain, the Arizona Republican who sponsored the anti-tobacco bill, was swamped with form letters opposing it sent by members of the National Smokers Alliance, which receives financing from the Philip Morris

Companies Inc., the Brown & Williamson Tobacco Corporation and the Lorillard Tobacco Company.

Senator Tom Harkin, Democrat of Iowa, also received letters opposing his position on tobacco, but from one part of his state.

"I couldn't figure out why I would get all these letters from one area," Mr. Harkin said. "It turns out they work for a Kraft food plant owned by R. J. Reynolds. But there was no disclosure of that."

Many of the creators of grass-roots lobbying campaigns for business say that, at their best, the campaigns mobilize real people with a sincere interest in the cause: sometimes company employees, shareholders, retirees, or vendors and sometimes individuals carefully selected through sophisticated demographic research.

Take the campaign waged this year by the nation's credit unions to preserve their expanded memberships in the face of a Supreme Court ruling that Federal regulators had overstepped when they allowed employee groups too small to form their own credit union to join others.

To pass their legislation over the opposition from the banks, the credit unions hired a large Washington cast of lobbyists, strategists and public relations specialists to mount an issue campaign that would take advantage of the fact that credit unions have loyal customers who favor them over banks. One person familiar with the campaign said it cost about $12 million over two years. The strategists deployed every weapon in the lobbying arsenal, from television commercials to talk radio to letter-writing campaigns to 800-numbers in credit unions that customers could use to call Congress. The campaign culminated in a rally of 7,000 supporters on the West Lawn of the Capitol.

Buddy Gill, a former Democratic campaign coordinator who was the credit unions' strategist, said, "Members of Congress had a classic dilemma. They want the support of their local banks and their campaign contributions, but they also want the votes of over 100,000 credit union people."

The credit unions raised money, too. Some credit union members paid $25 to $100 apiece to hold special fund-raisers for certain lawmakers.

The American Bankers Association had its own in-house specialists in "grass-roots" lobbying, but decided that it would not run the same kind of campaign as the credit unions. "We knew from our polling and focus groups and others this was not a battle we would be able to win in terms of grass-roots volume," said Mr. Yingling, the chief lobbyist for the association. "We had to win it in terms of the quality of the debate." But in the last two weeks before the Senate was to vote, the banks did turn to an 800-number to generate thousands of telegrams to Congress.

After this summer's loss, Mr. Yingling said his group was re-examining its budget for future grass-roots efforts. "This is just going to continue to escalate," he said.

What Does It Mean? Private Interests, Not People, Call the Shots

These changes in lobbying are taking place at the same time that party politics is metamorphosing in the television age, with fund-raisers replacing block captains and the public increasingly cut off from either party. And some say these lobbying efforts are the politics of the future. "It's like the election industry back in the

70's," Mr. Lunde said. "This is the same thing. It's the next generation of political campaign in the country."

Practitioners differed over whether the new practices were reinvigorating participation or squelching it.

Mr. Linbeck of Texas said that his sales tax movement gives citizens a chance to dictate an agenda to Congress instead of acting like vassals.

"I think we have a form of contemporary feudalism," he said. "Now how do you reverse that in a relatively benign way? A loud demonstration to the electorate that they do not have to be a supplicant with respect to a very important issue for them. And if they are interested in this and run with it to the extent that the polling, focus groups and test markets suggest they will, it will be a leverage point for creating a different view of government by the average person."

Critics argue that so much money is being poured into these efforts that their true purpose is to drown out competing viewpoints. "The whole effort of these campaigns is to prevent a second opinion from occurring," said David Cohen, a co-director of the Advocacy Institute, which teaches citizens groups how to make their cases.

Senator Carl Levin, a Michigan Democrat who was one of the leaders of the fight for lobbying disclosure, said that the problem with some of the techniques was that they could create a distorted picture when firms are paid to generate a certain number of telephone calls or telegrams.

"Suddenly a member of Congress is getting 50 phone calls on something," Mr. Levin said. "That's a lot of phone calls. What the member doesn't know is that 950 other people were contacted and said, 'No way.'"

The Grass Tops: Advice From Sources Lawmakers Will Heed

Because mass mobilizations have become so prevalent, a number of firms have become experts in a technique known as "grass-tops" lobbying, aimed at mobilizing an elite as opposed to the masses.

The goal is to figure out to whom a member of Congress cannot say no: his chief donor, his campaign manager, a political mentor. The lobbyist then tries to persuade that person to take his client's side. If the method works, the member of Congress may never know that a person contacting him had been revved up by a lobbyist.

To pull off this feat, Washington lobbying and public relations firms keep databases of organizers across the country, most of them with backgrounds in politics. Richard Pinsky, of West Palm Beach, Fla., who managed Mr. Dole's Florida primary campaign in 1996, is one of them.

Last year, with Florida a swing delegation in a House fight over trade, the Dewey Square Group, a public relations firm, relied on Mr. Pinsky to find prominent citizens to lobby certain House members to support giving President Clinton "fast-track" trade negotiating authority.

In one case, Mr. Pinsky said, he asked Bob Martinez, Florida's former Republican governor, who has an international trade practice, to contact Representative

Jim Davis, a Democratic freshman. "It wasn't necessarily that a former Republican governor would have influence on a Democratic Congressman," Mr. Pinsky said, "as that the Governor lived in his district."

Mr. Davis, who did come to support the President, said that he had independently sought to talk to the former governor. And he said it did not matter if Mr. Pinsky had also contacted Mr. Martinez because, "I knew he had a business interest in promoting trade. I took it into account."

But he added that if someone without an obvious interest contacted him on an issue because of the involvement of a Washington lobbying firm, he would want to know about the role of the intermediaries. ∎

 Chapter 7

The Media

A free and unbridled press is one of the safeguards of American liberty. The United States, as Supreme Court Justice William Brennan wrote in 1964, has maintained a "profound national commitment to the principle that debate on public issues should be uninhibited, robust, and wide-open." The press plays a critical role in promoting democracy by exposing official mismanagement and corruption, providing data on which citizens can make key decisions, and generally providing the people with a window on the activities of their government and the government with feedback on the opinions and viewpoints of the people.

The role of the media in the United States today, however, is not so simple. The media not only reports the news; it also decides what is and what is not news. It not only reports on public opinion; it also plays a vital role in shaping public opinion. In theory, the media may be free and unencumbered, but journalists live and work in a complex environment: their employers are themselves large corporations, which depend on other larger corporations for necessary advertising revenue; they have their own agendas to pursue, both professionally and, some would say, ideologically; they must both entertain and inform, especially on television; they are easily manipulated and used by government officials and candidates; they must cope with short deadlines and often with limited information; and they must continually try to fight off boredom, bias, and a pack mentality.

All of this is complicated by television, which has become the dominant medium in the United States. More Americans get their news on television than in any other form. Campaigns are waged and the country is governed through media performances, sound bites, and photo opportunities. Understanding television and knowing how to use it can get a candidate elected and help him or her govern; consider, for example, John F. Kennedy and Ronald Reagan. Failing to project the right media image can ruin both a candidate and a president, as an endless trail of defeated politicians could easily testify.

This chapter focuses on three key themes. Selection 7.1 examines the constitutional commitment to freedom of the press through the prism of *New York Times* v. *United States,* a 1971 Supreme Court decision that refused to allow government censorship of the media, even when national security was arguably at stake. Selections 7.2 and 7.3 investigate how the news media decide which stories to cover, and how to cover them, the first selection by looking at the Monica Lewinsky affair, the second by examining how the media cover foreign news. Finally, selection 7.4 provides an insight into the uneasy relationship between the White House press corps and the president's press secretary, who must maintain credibility with the media even while "spinning" the news to the advantage of the president.

Chapter Questions

1. What roles do the media play in American politics? How do these roles conflict with one another or with the economic, personal, or professional interests of journalists or with the interests of the corporations for which most of them work?
2. What influences the media's decisions on what news to report and how to report it? To what extent do the media control the agenda in American politics? To what extent are the media manipulated by politicians and government officials?

 # Foundations

The media's critical role in the American political system is grounded in the First Amendment to the United States Constitution, which protects both freedom of speech and freedom of the press. The American commitment to a free press can be traced back as far as 1735, when the printer John Peter Zenger was acquitted by a New York jury, even though he admitted to violating the law by publishing criticisms of the colonial government. It was not until the twentieth century, however, that the Supreme Court translated that commitment into legally enforceable doctrine.

The media are not at liberty to publish or broadcast anything they want, of course. Newspapers can still be sued for libel, which involves the publication of false statements damaging to the reputation of an individual or organization, although the rules laid down by the Supreme Court make it difficult for public officials and public figures to win such suits. The broadcast media are more heavily regulated, with television and radio stations subjected to licensing requirements and to rules prohibiting or limiting certain kinds of speech, including sexually explicit materials. In general, however, the American press remains remarkably free from governmental control or interference.

One of the Supreme Court's landmark decisions on press freedom was the 1971 case of *New York Times Co.* v. *United States.* The case arose when the *Times* began to publish the so-called Pentagon Papers, a series of secret documents concerning the Vietnam War. Citing national security considerations, the Nixon administration immediately went to court, asking a federal judge for an injunction (or order) forcing the newspaper to cease publication of the papers. The judge agreed, at least until the issue could be resolved by the courts. Meanwhile, several other newspapers—including the Washington Post—began publishing the papers and joined the lawsuit. Within a matter of weeks, the matter was argued before the Supreme Court, which threw out the lower court order by a vote of six to three, clearing the way for publication.

There was no majority opinion in the case. Instead, eight justices submitted separate opinions. The opinion of Justice Hugo Black, which was joined by Justice William O. Douglas, is a passionate and eloquent statement by one of the First Amendment's strongest supporters. Black's opinion underscores the importance of a free press in any democratic society.

Questions

1. What was the purpose of the First Amendment, according to Black? Why is a free press, in his view, essential to the creation and maintenance of a free society?
2. Why does Black reject the Nixon administration's argument that the injunctions in this case were justified by considerations of national security?

7.1 *New York Times* v. *United States* (1971)

Justice Hugo C. Black

I adhere to the view that the Government's case against the Washington Post should have been dismissed and that the injunction against the New York Times should have been vacated without oral argument when the cases were first presented to this Court. I believe that every moment's continuance of the injunctions against these newspapers amounts to a flagrant, indefensible, and continuing violation of the First Amendment. . . . In my view it is unfortunate that some of my Brethren are apparently willing to hold that the publication of news may sometimes be enjoined. Such a holding would make a shambles of the First Amendment.

Our Government was launched in 1789 with the adoption of the Constitution. The Bill of Rights, including the First Amendment, followed in 1791. Now, for the first time in the 182 years since the founding of the Republic, the federal courts are asked to hold that the First Amendment does not mean what it says, but rather means that the Government can halt the publication of current news of vital importance to the people of this country.

In seeking injunctions against these newspapers and in its presentation to the Court, the Executive Branch seems to have forgotten the essential purpose and history of the First Amendment. When the Constitution was adopted, many people strongly opposed it because the document contained no Bill of Rights to safeguard certain basic freedoms. They especially feared that the new powers granted to a central government might be interpreted to permit the government to curtail freedom of religion, press, assembly, and speech. In response to an overwhelming public clamor, James Madison offered a series of amendments to satisfy citizens

---

New York Times Co. v. *United States*, 403 U.S. 713 (1971).

that these great liberties would remain safe and beyond the power of government to abridge. Madison proposed what later became the First Amendment in three parts, two of which are set out below, and one of which proclaimed: "The people shall not be deprived or abridged of their right to speak, to write, or to publish their sentiments; and the freedom of the press, as one of the great bulwarks of liberty, shall be inviolable." The amendments were offered to curtail and restrict the general powers granted to the Executive, Legislative, and Judicial Branches two years before in the original Constitution. The Bill of Rights changed the original Constitution into a new charter under which no branch of government could abridge the people's freedoms of press, speech, religion, and assembly. . . . Madison and the other Framers of the First Amendment, able men that they were, wrote in language they earnestly believed could never be misunderstood: "Congress shall make no law . . . abridging the freedom . . . of the press. . . ." Both the history and language of the First Amendment support the view that the press must be left free to publish news, whatever the source, without censorship, injunctions, or prior restraints.

In the First Amendment the Founding Fathers gave the free press the protection it must have to fulfill its essential role in our democracy. The press was to serve the governed, not the governors. The Government's power to censor the press was abolished so that the press would remain forever free to censure the Government. The press was protected so that it could bare the secrets of government and inform the people. Only a free and unrestrained press can effectively expose deception in government. And paramount among the responsibilities of a free press is the duty to prevent any part of the government from deceiving the people and sending them off to distant lands to die of foreign fevers and foreign shot and shell. In my view, far from deserving condemnation for their courageous reporting, the New York Times, the Washington Post, and other newspapers should be commended for serving the purpose that the Founding Fathers saw so clearly. In revealing the workings of government that led to the Vietnam war, the newspapers nobly did precisely that which the Founders hoped and trusted they would do.

The Government's case here is based on premises entirely different from those that guided the Framers of the First Amendment. The Solicitor General [on behalf of the U.S. government] has carefully and emphatically stated:

> Now, Mr. Justice [BLACK], your construction of . . . [the First Amendment] is well known, and I certainly respect it. You say that no law means no law, and that should be obvious. I can only say, Mr. Justice, that to me it is equally obvious that "no law" does not mean "no law," and I would seek to persuade the Court that is true. . . . [T]here are other parts of the Constitution that grant powers and responsibilities to the Executive, and . . . the First Amendment was not intended to make it impossible for the Executive to function or to protect the security of the United States.

And the Government argues in its brief that in spite of the First Amendment, "[t]he authority of the Executive Department to protect the nation against publication of information whose disclosure would endanger the national security stems from two interrelated sources: the constitutional power of the President over the conduct of foreign affairs and his authority as Commander-in-Chief."

In other words, we are asked to hold that despite the First Amendment's emphatic command, the Executive Branch, the Congress, and the Judiciary can make laws enjoining publication of current news and abridging freedom of the press in the name of "national security." The Government does not even attempt to rely on any act of Congress. Instead it makes the bold and dangerously far-reaching contention that the courts should take it upon themselves to "make" a law abridging freedom of the press in the name of equity, presidential power and national security, even when the representatives of the people in Congress have adhered to the command of the First Amendment and refused to make such a law. To find that the President has "inherent power" to halt the publication of news by resort to the courts would wipe out the First Amendment and destroy the fundamental liberty and security of the very people the Government hopes to make "secure." No one can read the history of the adoption of the First Amendment without being convinced beyond any doubt that it was injunctions like those sought here that Madison and his collaborators intended to outlaw in this Nation for all time.

The word "security" is a broad, vague generality whose contours should not be invoked to abrogate the fundamental law embodied in the First Amendment. The guarding of military and diplomatic secrets at the expense of informed representative government provides no real security for our Republic. The Framers of the First Amendment, fully aware of both the need to defend a new nation and the abuses of the English and Colonial governments, sought to give this new society strength and security by providing that freedom of speech, press, religion, and assembly should not be abridged. This thought was eloquently expressed in 1937 by Mr. Chief Justice Hughes—great man and great Chief Justice that he was—when the Court held a man could not be punished for attending a meeting run by Communists.

> The greater the importance of safeguarding the community from incitements to the overthrow of our institutions by force and violence, the more imperative is the need to preserve inviolate the constitutional rights of free speech, free press and free assembly in order to maintain the opportunity for free political discussion, to the end that government may be responsive to the will of the people and that changes, if desired, may be obtained by peaceful means. Therein lies the security of the Republic, the very foundation of constitutional government. ∎

American Politics Today

The Bill Clinton–Monica Lewinsky story obsessed the American media for more than a year. But the presidential sex scandal was more than just a major news story; as John Cassidy argues, it also became a major business. The media's economic interest in reporting the story underscores the fact that the American media is dominated by for-profit corporations and provides a revealing look into the realities of the media marketplace.

Questions

1. How were the media's decisions on covering the Lewinsky scandal influenced by economic considerations, according to Cassidy?
2. What are the implications of Cassidy's argument for understanding and assessing the role of the media in present-day American politics? If he is right, is the media's role in a democratic society (as discussed, for example, by Justice Black in selection 7.1) strengthened or weakened?

7.2 Monicanomics (1998)

John Cassidy

E arlier this year, the big media companies launched a new product that they were enormously excited about—the Monica Lewinsky story—only to run into a lack of enthusiasm from customers. In survey after survey, people said that they were tired of hearing about the White House intern. Instead of tapering off, however, the production and the consumption of Monica-related stories continued to increase, and at an exponential rate. By last week, when Ken Starr, the Independent Counsel, presented his report to Congress, the newspapers and television networks often appeared to be producing nothing else, and the cable news channels—CNN, MSNBC and Fox—which *were* producing almost nothing else, were receiving splendid ratings.

Can this paradox be explained? To an economist, it suggests that the scandal's endurance as a major media story, despite the distaste it arouses in so many people, is merely an example of how the laws of supply and demand function (or malfunction) in the modern age. Granted, most students don't learn this brand of economics in Econ. 101, but among professional economists it is a rapidly expanding field of research. In the emerging paradigm, which is based on increasing returns to scale, network effects, and information contagion, all sorts of strange things can happen. Supply curves can slope down instead of up, demand curves can slope up instead of down, and phenomena like the Lewinsky scandal can take on a self-reinforcing dynamic of their own.

Start with the supply curve. Like many knowledge businesses, the Monica enterprise originated as a startup. Linda Tripp, frustrated with her career as a civil servant, decided to moonlight as a freelance writer, exploiting information supplied by her "friend" Monica. When Starr and Michael Isikoff, the *Newsweek* reporter, got involved, the elements for a lucrative business were rapidly put in place: a product with guaranteed appeal to consumers (a sex scandal involving the President), a cheap and eager workforce (Starr's investigators, who were being financed by the taxpayers), and a ready distribution channel (the media). Once the

---

John Cassidy, "Monicanomics 101," *The New Yorker* (September 21, 1998), pp. 73–77. Reprinted by permission of The New Yorker.

Lewinsky business was up and running, it entered a period of explosive growth, such as is experienced by many new businesses if they are lucky.

To understand why this happened, it is necessary to review a few fundamental economic concepts. In elementary textbooks, industries face "diminishing returns to scale," which means that their unit costs of production rise as their output increases, and consequently their supply curves slope upward. As output increases, prices rise. However, the news business (as is true of most other information-based industries) doesn't work this way: it operates in an environment of "increasing returns to scale." Once the big money has been spent on establishing a production-and-distribution system, extra programming can be produced and reproduced at little cost, so prices tend to fall as output increases. The only additional inputs a broadcaster needs in order to manufacture more news are an attractive face to read the stories, some film footage to illustrate them, and an assortment of pundits to discuss them. (The pundits cost nothing; they usually appear free, in order to build their brand recognition, which can be exploited in other media, such as newspaper columns, books, and speaking engagements.) In extreme cases, additional output may be so cheap to produce that firms can literally give it away. (This is what Netscape is doing with its Internet browser, for example.)

Companies like General Electric (the parent of NBC), Walt Disney (which owns ABC), and Time Warner (which owns CNN) have now recognized the possibilities generated by the presence of increasing returns. A few years ago, NBC produced three hours of news a day for one channel; these days, it produces twenty-seven hours of news a day for three channels—NBC, CNBC, and MSNBC. [When] Starr's report reached Capitol Hill, MSNBC, which NBC co-owns with Microsoft, began its Lewinsky coverage at 9 A.M., and continued it, practically uninterrupted, through the day, culminating with two hours of its regular program, "White House in Crisis," at 10 P.M. G.E.'s scandal output wasn't confined to MSNBC. On Wednesday evening, viewers could select MSNBC, CNBC, or NBC for their Monica fix. This may seem like overkill, but there are sound economic reasons, on the demand side of the market as well as on the supply side, for the broadcasters' behavior.

The big media companies face an acute dilemma: in this information-sodden era, when consumers are presented with a plethora of options for entertainment and diversion, how do you persuade them to sample your goods? The Hollywood film studios have provided one answer: concentrate your resources on a few major releases each year. If one of these "event movies" takes off, it pays for the rest of the production slate, and much more besides. Silicon Valley has come up with another possible solution: create a seductive "killer app," such as Adobe Illustrator or Netscape Navigator, which certain consumers will consider essential to their work or leisure. The news producers have reached the same conclusion as the film studios, many of which are owned by the same parent companies, and the result is "event journalism"—gripping human narratives, usually involving celebrities, that go on for months. Stories like these don't come along often, but when one does— the Gulf War, the murder trial of O. J. Simpson, the life and death of Princess Diana, the Monica Lewinsky scandal—the news factories ratchet up their marketing and production schedules accordingly.

Whatever its faults, event journalism undoubtedly succeeds economically. Between the third quarter of 1997 and the second quarter of 1998, MSNBC's ratings practically doubled. President Clinton's August 17th statement from the White House about the Lewinsky scandal brought CNN its highest viewing figure since the verdict in the O.J. trial and enabled Fox News Channel to record its highest viewing figures ever. Why does this happen? Most journalists are convinced that the explanation is gross hypocrisy—that people tell pollsters they are uninterested in the President's sex life and then log on to the Drudge Report and savor the latest details about Miss Lewinsky's cigar tricks. This may be partly true, but there is another, more convincing explanation—one that relies on the peculiar economics of networks.

Networks come in two varieties: physical networks, such as the national power grid and the Internet, and virtual networks, such as the communities of film-goers and television viewers. The basic idea underlying network economics remains the same in both varieties, and it is clearly expressed in a forthcoming book, entitled "Information Rules," by two Berkeley professors, Carl Shapiro and Hal Varian: "Other things being equal, it's better to be connected to a bigger network than a smaller one." With computers and telephones, the benefits of bigness are obvious: the more people who are on your network, the more people you can communicate with. (Mathematically speaking, the total benefits are proportional to the square of the number of people on the network, so a network with twenty people attached is four times as useful as a network with ten people attached.) In a virtual network, the benefits are pretty much the same: if all the workers in an office went to see "Saving Private Ryan" last weekend, they all have something to talk about on their lunch break. Anybody who hasn't seen the film pays a social price for not going to the theatre.

"Conversation, which links people through meme transmission, is fundamental to why we buy, and why we want to buy what others are buying," Winslow Farrell writes in his new book, "How Hits Happen: Forecasting Predictability in a Chaotic Marketplace." He also writes, "At some point, we cease to be autonomous purchasing individuals and join the crowd." According to Farrell, a former NASA rocket scientist who is now a partner at Coopers & Lybrand, the key to successful management in the information business is to recognize which products have the potential to create these network effects—economists call them "network externalities"—and promote them as aggressively as possible. This is what Twentieth Century Fox and Paramount did with "Titanic," it is what CNN did with the Gulf War, and it is what MSNBC is trying to do with the Lewinsky story.

Once a news story generates network effects, it enjoys a "positive feedback" process, in which the fact that some people are already talking about it persuades others to show an interest. In due course, a story may "lock in," and rival events will be starved of public attention. People who have invested enough time to learn the minute details of a journalistic "event"—Where was the bloody glove found? What did Kato hear thumping outside his wall? What happened to the golf bag?—are understandably reluctant to move on to another one, where they will have to start over. Consequently, it takes something dramatic to bring the previous event story to an end, or, in the language of television news, "closure": in the O.J. case, that something was the verdict; with Princess Diana, it was her funeral.

The Princess dominated Britain's popular newspapers for more than fifteen years. During that period, Fleet Street editors regularly vowed to back off from their intrusive coverage, but the economic logic of event journalism proved too strong to resist.

The new economics also provides a framework in which it is possible to explain—in part, at least—the strange behavior of Ken Starr. The Independent Counsel has been variously described by his opponents as an arch-conservative, a religious fanatic, and a bumbling incompetent. A better analogy is a Malaysian real-estate developer in the early nineteen-nineties or a factory manager in the former Soviet Union. The key point is that Starr, unlike most American businessmen, faces a "soft-budget constraint": he can spend as much money as he wants, enter whatever market segment he wishes, and carry on in this manner indefinitely. Given this setup, it is not surprising that the Whitewater investigation has steadily expanded, venturing into unprofitable markets, such as Vincent Foster's death, Filegate, and Travelgate. A normal C.E.O., having spent his shareholders' capital and failed to produce a marketable product, would have been fired, but Starr was never a normal businessman.

The fault doesn't lie with him; it lies with a statute that provides no incentive for special prosecutors to act in the interests of the people who employ them. There is now an entire branch of economics dealing with the "principal-agent problem," which arises whenever somebody is hired to do a job that cannot be perfectly monitored. In the private sector, a number of ways have evolved to address this conundrum. They include paying workers generous wages, which encourages them not to shirk; granting employees stock options, which aligns their interests with those of the shareholders; introducing contigency fees, which does the same thing; and encouraging hostile takeovers, which allows incompetent managers to be replaced. Unfortunately, it is not clear how to apply these techniques to the public sector, where market forces are largely absent. Paying special prosecutors success fees would be controversial, and so would allowing other lawyers to petition the Justice Department for Starr's job. When the Independent Counsel Act expires next year, Congress is likely to fall back on more politically acceptable options, such as providing Starr's successors with narrower contracts.

As for Bill Clinton, he is by training a lawyer, not an economist, and his recent behavior suggests that he hasn't learned much about the commercial logic underlying the Lewinsky coverage. If his aim was to put the scandal behind him, he needed to provide a dramatic finale—one that would shift the information dynamics in his favor. His failure to do this in his August 17th speech allowed the media pundits to interpret the speech as just another installment in a long-running saga, and his insistence that "even Presidents have private lives" didn't make any lasting impression. From an economic perspective, there is no distinction between public and private. Ever since F.D.R.'s fireside radio chats, media executives have recognized the President as a "killer app"—someone who can be relied upon to cut through the clutter and seize people's attention. In subsequent years, as information has become all but ubiquitous, and the competitive pressures facing the media have continually increased, the zone of privacy surrounding the Oval Office incumbent has shrunk commensurately.

Clinton was aware of this situation when he took up with Monica Lewinsky, and his affair with her presents a powerful challenge to economic theories that explain people's actions in terms of self-interested cost-benefit analysis. (In most economic models, individuals are seen as automatons who maximize "utility functions" by obeying a set of mathematical "first order conditions.") The putative costs of the President's trysts may appear to outweigh any conceivable pleasure he obtained from them, but some economists might argue otherwise. One possibility is that Clinton is a person who enjoys taking gambles just for the sake of doing so, even though he knows he is likely to lose. Economists refer to such people as "risk lovers," compared with the majority of the population, who are "risk averse." Many risk lovers play the horses or frequent casinos, but there is no evidence that the President has speculated in areas outside his romantic life. Another explanation consistent with optimizing behavior is that Clinton discounts the future costs of his actions at a furious rate, and so even potentially disastrous outcomes don't deter him from doing what he wants, precisely because they are in the future. (This is the reasoning that some economists use to explain deadly addictions, like cigarette smoking, as voluntary acts.) A third possibility is that the President underestimated the likelihood of being caught, in which case his cost-benefit sums were biased.

On the other hand, casual sex of the Clinton variety may fall into a vexing category that economists have come to call "non-market transactions." Even the Chicago School, which believes that economics can explain practically everything, has struggled with promiscuity. Richard Posner and Tomas Philipson attempted to explain the persistence of unsafe sex among gay men as a result of rational decision-making, but they weren't very successful. A colleague of theirs at Chicago, the Nobel laureate Gary Becker, tried to construct a broader economic theory of love, but he focussed on the psychological and practical benefits provided by children and families, and not on the momentary pleasures of the flesh enjoyed by the President and his intern. It may be that in Bill Clinton's peculiar case there are limits to the scope of economic analysis. Some things, perhaps, cannot be reduced to a set of mathematical equations. ∎

 # The Comparative Context

News from around the globe may be vitally important, but media coverage of foreign policy issues and of events overseas lags far behind coverage of domestic news stories. In this selection, James F. Hoge, Jr., the editor of *Foreign Affairs* magazine, examines why the American media fail to provide full coverage of foreign news, and whether this lack of coverage matters. Ultimately, he suggests, the media is uninterested in foreign news because the public is uninterested. The public's lack of interest, however, may stem from the media's failure to make foreign news interesting, relevant, and accessible.

Questions

1. Why has foreign news coverage declined in the American media in recent years?
2. How could the American media improve foreign news coverage, according to Hoge? What factors help explain why the media are unwilling or unable to expand foreign news coverage?

7.3 Foreign News: Who Gives a Damn? (1997)

James F. Hoge, Jr.

If the death and funeral of Princess Diana were the appropriate indicator, there is no dearth of foreign news in American media. TV anchors and correspondents were called back from vacation and dispatched to London and Paris. Newspapers added special sections, and piled on heart-tugging headlines. Newsmagazines devoted half or more of their pages to Di. The Internet overflowed with sorrowful chat and conspiratorial speculation.

But the story of Diana, of course, was not foreign news. Rather it was a compelling human-interest tale of the tangled life, shocking death, and ceremonial funeral of the best-known celebrity in the world that happened to take place abroad. On Friday, September 5, the day before the Westminster pageantry, another figure of global renown, Mother Teresa, died at age eighty-seven. Prominent, if far more subdued, coverage recounted the work of the missionary nun who won a Nobel Peace Prize. After the over-the-top coverage of Princess Diana, network anchors found their presence required in Calcutta for Mother Teresa's state funeral a week later, even though it appeared on American television just after midnight.

The everyday stuff of foreign news is more prosaic. It consists of political and economic events that raise policy issues and force governments and people to choose. Except for the collapse of the Soviet Union in 1989–90, the coverage of such international news in American media has steadily declined since the late seventies, when the cold war lost its sense of imminent danger.

The shrinkage was neatly symbolized this summer during Hong Kong's transition from British to Chinese rule. The three major networks sent their anchors half-way around the world for the historic ceremony, and all three filed advance stories in the preceding days. The turnover itself found CBS and ABC anchors Dan Rather and Peter Jennings reporting live from mid-morning to early afternoon of July 1. But NBC, under contract to cover the Wimbledon tennis tournament, cut for *only three minutes* to Tom Brokaw in Hong Kong. For more than

James F. Hoge, Jr., "Foreign News: Who Gives a Damn?" Reprinted from *Columbia Journalism Review* (November-December 1997), pp. 48–52. © 1997 by Columbia Journalism Review.

that, NBC viewers had to wait until the evening news—unless they switched channels to another network or perhaps to MSNBC, the Microsoft-NBC cable news network that carried live, a full-length coverage of the ceremony to a very limited audience.

NBC spokespeople argued lamely that the Hong Kong transition was ceremonial and fully anticipated. It lacked breaking news significance unless something went wrong. And were something to go awry, NBC had the resources in place for sustained live coverage. (More to the point, the Wimbledon contract was a tight one.)

Competitor Roone Arledge, chairman of ABC News, saw things differently. "It was an opportunity to show our viewers the spectacle of the end of the British empire, a truly historic moment that people are entitled to see and interested in seeing." The viewing public agreed, providing ABC and CBS 4.8 and 4.4 ratings respectively while the tennis netted 2.2 for NBC.

In an earlier era before there was cable and fragmented audiences, all three networks would have used their technology and talent to the maximum in covering the Hong Kong story. Times change and there is nothing that says news decisions shouldn't too. "A lot of the foreign news coverage ten years ago was deadly dull," observed the broadcast trade magazine editor Andrew Tyndall in an interview with the *Columbia Journalism Review* last spring. However one assesses the differing news judgments concerning the Hong Kong transition, it is further evidence of declining media interest in foreign affairs.

The Size of the Decline

A survey by the news agency executive Claude Moisy for the Joan Shorenstein Center showed a drop in time devoted to foreign news on network TV from 45 percent in the 1970s to 13.5 percent by 1995. And TV networks increasingly employ stringers or make deals with foreign providers to gather the news more cheaply. Foreign news is even scarcer on radio. Increasingly, commercial stations broadcast syndicated news services, which are cut-and-paste assemblages of wire service and newspaper accounts, few of them about foreign events. In Washington, D.C., nineteen radio stations rely on one or the other of two news-packaging operations for minimal headline services. "For the average station, news is a dying area," says John Matthews, news director for radio station WMAL in Washington.

In newspapers, foreign news dropped from 10.2 percent of the [total news coverage] in 1971 to 6 percent by 1982, according to a National Advertising Bureau study. Other surveys indicate further decline in the years since.

A California State University journalism professor, Michael Emery, in 1989 found only 2.6 percent of the non-advertising space in ten leading American newspapers devoted to news from abroad.

As for the newsweeklies, Hall's Magazine Editorial Reports found that from 1985 to 1995 the space devoted to international news declined from 24 percent to 14 percent in *Time*, from 22 percent to 12 percent in *Newsweek*, and 20 percent to 14 percent in *U.S. News and World Report*. Editors struck the same explanatory chord when interviewed by *The New York Times*. "Week in and week out, international news has been a bit less urgent" (Walter Isaacson, managing editor,

Time). "There is a diminution of coverage, simply because the issues are less relevant" (Mortimer Zuckerman, editor in chief, *U.S. News*). Maynard Parker, editor of *Newsweek*, says that featuring a foreign subject on the cover results in a 25 percent drop in newsstand sales. Zuckerman concurs: "The poorest-selling covers of the year are always those on international news."

A post–cold war provincialism is not exclusive to the U.S. The International Institute of Communications in London found in a recent study that the much-touted globalization of news is more myth than reality in most parts of the world. West European television stations and quality newspapers remain, as they have historically been, more internationally minded than U.S. media. But even they pay scant attention to developments in Asia and Latin America.

Paradoxically, the number of reporters overseas for all U.S. media is up. A survey by the *Newspaper Research Journal* identified 820 full-time U.S. foreign correspondents in the early '90s versus 429 in the mid-'70s. Some of the increase, of course, is explained by the fast growth of business and economic publications and news services, such as Reuters, Bloomberg, Dow Jones. The Associated Press has also expanded its corps of overseas correspondents.

When Knight-Ridder announced in July that it was shifting direction of eight overseas bureaus from the newspaper chain's four large metros to a single foreign desk in Washington, some observers saw yet another diminishment in resources devoted to foreign coverage. At the large Knight-Ridder papers, editors and correspondents expressed concern that the move was a money-saving, dumbing-down initiative. Speaking anonymously, Knight-Ridder staffers told a *New York Times* reporter that they feared the reorganization meant more time would be spent "covering breaking news with short, quick articles and less time developing more in-depth articles about trends overseas." Indeed, few lengthy, expensive trend stories were being picked up by Knight-Ridder's thirty-five newspapers except for the four metros, *The Philadelphia Inquirer*, *The Detroit Free Press*, *The Miami Herald*, and *The San Jose Mercury News*.

Knight-Ridder executives argue that consolidating the direction of the foreign bureaus is meant to get more, not less, foreign news into the chain's newspapers. And while there are undoubtedly some efficiencies, the move would appear not to be about saving money. No bureaus are being closed, no correspondents recalled. In fact, two extra editors are being hired for the Washington-based foreign desk. Gary Blonston, Knight-Ridder Washington bureau chief, says that internal studies showed that there is public interest in foreign news—if it is made interesting and relevant.

What Knight-Ridder had was a communications problem. Too few editors except those at the four big newspapers knew what the foreign correspondents were doing. And too few correspondents knew what the editors wanted. Now, Blonston says, "the foreign service will file on the major stories of the day because that is our job and it maintains sources. But the emphasis will remain on enterprise and explanatory journalism," with special attention to such post–cold war topics as economic relations, environmental protection, the social and economic status of women, and "the next soft subject that helps explain the human condition."

Though there still will be some lengthy articles as the material warrants, most stories will come in at about 1,000 words for daily use and 1,500 words for Sunday editions. Correspondents will be rotated every three years with openings available to "the cream of the crop" among reporters within and outside Knight-Ridder.

The Reasons Why

A world less threatening to America is less newsy, as the newsweekly editors put it. Or in the more colloquial words of television veteran Reuven Frank, sunshine is a weather report, a raging storm is news. The assumption is that lagging public interest explains the shrinkage in media attention. But opinion surveys over the past decade, coupled with the experiential evidence of editors and producers, show that isn't necessarily so.

News consumers do register less interest in traditional state-to-state affairs and in regional or ethnic conflicts that seem to lack wider significance. For example, a survey in 1995 by the Washington-based Center for The People & The Press found that a low of 8 percent of the American public paid "very close" attention to events in Bosnia except for a brief spurt to 23 percent in 1993. The war in Chechnya never hit more than 10 percent. The picture improves somewhat when the issues are international extensions of domestic concerns such as control of crime, drug trafficking, and pollution or advances in health care. But international economic news, even when directly connected to American jobs and trade, rates low attention from the general public.

To the general public, much of foreign news seems confusing and without sufficient significance to justify working it out. Dennis Ryerson, editor of *The Des Moines Register*, says of the low-level conflicts around the globe, "You need a scorecard just to keep up. So we're confused and not directly affected, and besides we have other issues to worry about closer to home."

The shifting news agenda, then, is another reason cited for less public interest. Security is inherently more interesting than economics, now the focus of much U.S. policy overseas. The ascendancy of television as the medium of communication for the general public is yet another contributing factor. TV's emphasis on dramatic images and short narratives and the intense battle for audiences amid proliferating choices of outlets all work against foreign news. Crises do get covered but without context by correspondents who are "parachuted" in to report the inflammation. The veteran NBC and ABC foreign correspondent Garrick Utley wrote in the March/April issue of *Foreign Affairs* of a five-day period in 1978 when from his London base he was dispatched to cover "South Moluccans seizing hostages in the Netherlands, the Israeli incursion to the Litani River in southern Lebanon, and the kidnapping of Prime Minister Aldo Moro in Rome."

Andie Tucher reported in this magazine that Tom Brokaw led his March 13 broadcast from New York with the dramatic evacuation of several hundred Americans during the "meltdown" of Albania, a country "whose name had first been breathed on the weeknight newscast just the previous evening."

CNN's world affairs correspondent Ralph Beigleiter thinks the last decade has seen a marked increase in consumer-driven journalism in both print and broadcast. Late sports scores, better weather forecasts, health and life-style tips, these are what are promoted. He sees the trend intensifying as interactive media increase the consumer's capacity to choose. "I cannot grab you by the lapels and say,

'You may not know where Bosnia is, but here is why you ought to know,'" Beigleiter observed at a Freedom Forum Media Studies Center discussion in February. "That is the problem with the Web. You can find what you want to know on it, but you miss the seeding of stories on subjects about which you may not know anything."

Media proprietors may be more the problem than changes in news or technology or public attention. Seymour Topping, former managing editor of *The New York Times*, says, "The great threat today to intelligent coverage of foreign news is not so much a lack of interest as it is a concentration of ownership that is profit-driven and a lack of inclination to meet responsibilities, except that of the bottom line."

Today's large, public media companies are more profit-obsessed than some of the private proprietors of old. They are also confronting more intense competition for volatile consumer attention. Even if media companies were moved by traditional journalistic responsibilities, pressure would be on editors and producers to make their news "products" what the marketers in the business call "user friendly."

Topping himself recognizes that shorter attention spans and other changes in the consumer market cannot be ignored, and if the newspaper "is not being read, there is a great problem." So there is a movement toward news summaries, particularly for much of the daily flow of international events.

Editors are also looking for local implications that would increase the relevance of foreign news for their audiences. Several recent Pulitzer Prize entries stressed the effects of overseas developments on local economies and the involvement of local people in distant humanitarian efforts. *The Houston Chronicle*, for example, published a riveting account of the poor treatment of ill children in Romania as experienced by a visiting Houston medical group.

Local tie-ins are also used by major papers like the *Los Angeles Times*, the *Chicago Tribune*, and *The Wall Street Journal*. A *Journal* story by James L. Sterba struck commentators John Maxwell Hamilton and George A. Krimsky writing in the *Gannett Center Journal* as the "quintessential" example. Sterba reported how people in India manufacture manhole covers for people in Phoenix, Arizona; Newport News, Virginia; and other U.S. cities.

Editors are pushing correspondents to write compellingly about the lives of people overseas, serious human-interest stories in place of "process" accounts that document the step-by-step evolution of an issue like the movement for a common European currency. More attention is being paid to the public agenda of international concerns—the management of crime, drug, health and environmental challenges. Michael Getler, editor of the *International Herald Tribune* and former foreign editor of *The Washington Post*, says his former paper looks to young reporters, rotated rather than permanently assigned to overseas posts, as best equipped to handle the new agenda and subjects involving science and technology and economies.

Does It Matter?

There is no consensus on whether the decline in public attention and media coverage of foreign affairs is cause for alarm. Some, including the notable political thinker Samuel Huntington of Harvard, are hardly overwrought. Writing in the

September issue of *Foreign Affairs*, Huntington finds it understandable that in a time of relative security Americans would delegate, within prescribed boundaries of "no surprises," the day-to-day oversight of foreign affairs to professionals. Meanwhile, businessmen and others with a direct need to know have plenty of elite and niche sources of information, both print and electronic. Publications and news services devoted to international business and economics have proliferated.

Even if one accepts that the country's international relations with remain in the hands of a small, informed establishment with the tactic consent of a relatively indifferent public, some informed observers raise a flag of warning. Claude Moisy writes in his Shorenstein study that "there will always be circumstances in which the public at large will be stirred to make itself heard on an international issue out of a perception, right or wrong, that the very 'raison d'être' of the nation is at stake. In these cases the public will not necessarily react on the basis of knowledge, but more likely on the basis of emotions aroused by mass media. But because of the exceptional extent of public involvement, these rare cases have the potential of becoming turning points in the life of the country. That is why the amount and quality of international news carried by these changing mass media, or the lack thereof, remain relevant to the conduct of the foreign policy of the United States."

When Topping, now administrator of the Pulitzer Prizes and a professor at the Columbia University Graduate School of Journalism, was the *Time*'s foreign editor, he insisted upon stationing correspondents in areas that were not getting a lot of attention. He believed there was an obligation "to keep on covering foreign news, even if it is not great consumer stuff . . . While the public may at this particular time not be showing a great deal of interest in foreign affairs, the reporting of the media still has an impact on the power structure."

And to Moisy's point, the cycle will turn and the reasons for public concern and involvement will reappear. Responsible media will have attempted to keep the public prepared. Ultimately in a democracy, that is the rationale for sustaining media coverage of international affairs. By that standard, much of the press gets a mixed report card at best. Elites in business, the professions, and government have ample news and information sources. It is the general public that is being shortchanged by media that have yet to exhibit the combination of effort and talent to make news of the wider world interesting and relevant. ∎

 # View from the Inside

The president's press secretary plays a critical role. On a day-to-day basis, he or she is the president's main link to the White House press corps and, through them, to the American people. The press secretary's main job is to "spin" actual or potential news stories in order to make the president look good.

The press secretary's relationship with the White House press corps is by nature delicate. To earn the reporters' trust, the secretary must be honest. But to present the president's best face to the public, he or she must bob and weave around the truth, or at least wink at it.

Mike McCurry, who served as President Clinton's press secretary from 1995 to 1998, was the acknowledged grand master of this delicate balancing act. In this excerpt from *Spin Cycle*—subtitled *How the White House and the Media Manipulate the News*—the reporter Howard Kurtz describes McCurry's methods.

Questions

1. How did Mike McCurry manage to maintain the confidence of the White House press corps while at the same time "spinning" news stories in a positive way?
2. Are White House efforts at "spin control" legitimate in a democratic society, or do they undermine the American political system? Do such efforts compromise the media's role as a bulwark against the government? When does the White House cross the line between acceptable "spin" and unacceptable deception?

7.4 The Master of Spin (1998)

Howard Kurtz

One thing about Mike McCurry, he knew how to play the game. He understood the ebb and flow of the fungible commodity called news. A trim, blue-eyed man with thinning blond hair, a pink complexion, and an often bemused expression, McCurry was a spinmeister extraordinaire, deflecting questions with practiced ease, sugar-coating the ugly messes into which the Clintonites seemed repeatedly to stumble. He would mislead reporters on occasion, or try to pass them off to one of the damage-control lawyers who infested the public payroll. He would yell at offending correspondents, denounce their stories as inaccurate, denigrate them to their colleagues and their bosses. He would work the clock to keep damaging stories off the evening news, with its huge national audience. Yet with his considerable charm and quick wit, McCurry somehow managed to maintain friendly relations with most of the reporters who worked the White House beat. He would go to dinner with reporters, share a beer, give them a wink and a nod as he faithfully delivered the administration's line. He was walking the tightrope, struggling to maintain credibility with both the press and the president, to serve as an honest broker between the antagonists.

Each day, it seemed, McCurry faced a moral dilemma. He stood squarely at the intersection of news and propaganda, in the white-hot glare of the media spotlight, the buffer between self-serving administration officials and a cynical pack of reporters. The three principles of his job, he believed, were telling the truth, giv-

---

ing people a window on the White House, and protecting the president, but the last imperative often made the first two difficult. If the corporate spokesman for Exxon or General Motors stretched the truth on occasion, well, that was seen as part of the job. McCurry himself had once been a corporate flack, trumpeting the virtues of the National Pork Producers Council. But now he worked for the head hog, and more was expected of the presidential press secretary, whose every syllable was transcribed by news agencies. He was the public face of the administration. His credibility, not just the president's, was on the line.

As the campaign fundraising scandal exploded, McCurry found himself facing the question that had dogged every presidential press secretary since the Nixon administration: whether it is possible to tell the truth, or something approximating the truth, in a highly polarized and constantly shifting political atmosphere. McCurry dearly prized his personal reputation for candor. He developed a series of rules and rationalizations to persuade himself that while he sometimes tiptoed up to the line separating flackery from falsehood, he never crossed it.

Yet McCurry was more than just the White House publicist. In a news-saturated age the press secretary was a celebrity in his own right, laying down the rhetorical law on dozens of issues, saying things the president wanted said but could not, for reasons of propriety, say himself. McCurry's predecessors had gone on to write books, join university faculties, or, like Dee Dee Myers, host their own television shows and give speeches for $15,000 a pop. But all this came at a considerable price: the gut-wrenching pressure, the seven-day weeks, the hostile questions day after day.

• • •

When McCurry took over in 1995, he quickly established that he knew what was going on. He attended any meeting he thought was worth his time. He got answers from the president when necessary. He was a year and a half into his job before he found himself misleading the press.

The messy situation bubbled to the surface on a campaign trip to Orlando in the summer of 1996. It was two weeks after the tabloid revelations about Dick Morris and his $200-an-hour call girl had upstaged the president on the final day of the Democratic convention. When the story broke, Morris called McCurry on the president's campaign train, which was chugging toward Chicago, and started to describe what had happened. "Stop, Dick," McCurry said. He warned Morris not to tell him the sordid details so he could plead ignorance with the press. A don't ask/don't tell policy was often the safest course for a spokesman.

Now White House officials wanted to put the banished political consultant and his sexual antics behind them. But the tabloid frenzy had not yet run its course. *The National Enquirer* and its sister publication, *The Star*, were back with new, equally bizarre allegations about Morris: he had a secret mistress in Texas and had fathered a six-year-old girl—a "love child," in the overheated parlance of the tabs. The story was a disaster for a campaign trying to run on a platform of school uniforms and family values. The question, McCurry knew, was whether the mainstream press had had its fill of Dick Morris, or whether the story would spread from the supermarket rags to the media elite. After all, this was no ordinary hired gun; Clinton had been friends with Morris since the consultant first helped him win the Arkansas governorship in 1978.

At the briefing that Friday afternoon, reporters asked McCurry if the president knew of the *Enquirer* and *Star* reports. McCurry was cagey. He said Clinton was aware of the articles but that "he has no knowledge of whether it is true or not."

That didn't satisfy CBS's Rita Braver. What, she demanded, was Clinton's reaction to the stories? "He said, 'Is it true?' And we said, 'We don't know,'" McCurry recalled. Trying to shut down this line of questioning, he used a tactic that had worked well for the Clinton camp during the '92 campaign. He chided Braver for basing her question on mere "tabloids," as if such behavior were beneath her. When John Harris of *The Washington Post* called later and pressed him about the chronology, McCurry lectured him, too, about descending into the tabloid gutter.

The strategy was quite premeditated. "I was trying to blow the thing off and get back to the news the president was trying to make," McCurry said later.

But one reporter wouldn't let the matter drop. Matthew Cooper of *Newsweek* called McCurry the next day and got him to acknowledge that Clinton had known of Morris's out-of-wedlock daughter all along, that he had been given the news the previous year by Erskine Bowles.

How, then, could McCurry have stuck to his story of presidential ignorance? His explanation was as convoluted as Clinton's shifting stories about the draft. It was all a misunderstanding, McCurry claimed. He said the president's "Is it true?" response was not about Dick Morris's mistress or the child. Instead, he said, Clinton was questioning the *Enquirer*'s report that Morris was still dating the Texas woman, and had entertained her a month earlier in the $440-a-night Jefferson Hotel suite where he had also frolicked with prostitute Sherry Rowlands. In true spokesman fashion, McCurry said he saw no conflict between Clinton's employment of Morris and his "very strong concern about child support."

Still, the press secretary's ploy paid off. Unable to confirm that Clinton knew of the relationship and uneasy about chasing the tabloids, none of the networks reported on Morris's triple life. Nor did *The New York Times* or the *L.A. Times* or *USA Today*. *The Washington Post* mentioned the mistress in a single paragraph deep in a campaign story. Now that reporters knew the president had knowingly employed a political strategist who had fathered an illegitimate child—well, it was old news. The press had moved on. McCurry and his boss had dodged another bullet.

One of McCurry's pet projects in the wake of the election was to convince Clinton to court the media, to turn his fabled charm on the small band of men and women who chewed up and spit out his words for the American public. Clinton had little use for the fourth estate—he had not forgotten the way its members tormented him over the scandals of his first term, from Gennifer Flowers to Paula Jones to Whitewater, Travelgate, and Filegate—and he was stubbornly resisting McCurry's peacemaking initiatives. Why should he, the president of the United States, the man in charge of America's nuclear arsenal, have to romance journalists whose job was to cover him? And why did a small pack have to trail him whenever he went to a bookstore or a restaurant, even when he was out jogging? McCurry patiently explained that this was the "body watch," part of their job description; he might be shot, or just stumble and fall, or stop to answer questions.

"That's their game, not mine," Clinton replied. "They don't have to follow me when I jog. I'm not going to make news or talk about nuclear war."

It was a discussion they had had many times. Here was one of the great retail politicians of the modern age, a man who had to shake every hand in the room, who would spend ten minutes arguing with a recalcitrant voter while his staff anxiously beckoned him to the next event, and yet he had little patience for reporters with megaphones that could reach millions. They were, in his view, largely nitpickers, naysayers, political handicappers with little interest in the substance of governing. They thrived on building themselves up by knocking him down.

Dick Morris, who knew Clinton as well as anyone, concluded after the campaign that the president hated the press. "He is contemptuous of reporters," Morris said. "He feels they're a sleazy group of people who lie a lot, who pursue their own agendas, who have a pack mentality. He feels they are a necessary evil."

What really infuriated the president, and Hillary, was the way the press kept changing the parameters of scandal. First the two of them would be accused of improperly benefiting from an Arkansas land deal. When that didn't pan out, the focus would shift to another land development, or a fraudulent loan, or missing billing records, or, when all else failed, the supposed cover-up. But the press never told anyone they had been cleared of the original charges. The reporters just kept morphing the Whitewater saga into some new configuration. They seemed to have a bottomless appetite for the most trivial semblance of an allegation.

The president's aides believed that Clinton was surprisingly naive about the press. He thought that if you were nice to reporters, they would be nice to you. George Stephanopoulos had often been struck by Clinton's feeling of betrayal when some journalist whom he had been courting wrote a tough piece. The president didn't understand that it was nothing personal, just part of the game. White House staffers were surprised that he hadn't become more inured to this sort of rough-and-tumble during his twelve years as governor.

If you would spend a fraction of your persuasive skills winning them over, McCurry argued, there would be a big payoff. But Clinton, angry about various slights, his resolve buttressed by thick layers of scar tissue, would not play. These journalists were wedded to "the old notion that all politicians are hopelessly corrupt and incompetent," he said. Screw the press.

And yet on a Friday afternoon in the waning days of 1996, McCurry finally got his way as the president sat down in the small dining room off the Oval Office with three high-profile pundits: *Newsweek*'s Jonathan Alter, Gerald Seib of *The Wall Street Journal*, and Jacob Weisberg of *Slate*, Microsoft's online magazine. McCurry had selected them as a provocative group of progressive writers who would be receptive to Clinton's view of the world. "Alter bites my ass sometimes, but at least he understands what we're trying to do," Clinton once told an aide. The session was declared off-the-record, so Clinton could relax.

The president gave them The Treatment. He showed them around the Oval Office, the small adjacent study, where he had a bunch of ties laid out, and his private dining room. He told Alter that he had liked one of his recent columns. Weisberg gave him a *Slate* cap, and Clinton put it on and posed for a picture. They chatted about China policy and other issues over cider and cookies. When Alter asked about campaign finance reform, Clinton noted that Weisberg had just written "a great story" on the subject and proceeded to critique it. The atmosphere seemed far less stilted than during the four times that Alter had formally interviewed Clinton.

Perhaps it was mere coincidence, but after the off-the-record meeting, Alter hailed the president in *Newsweek* as "the salesman with the best understanding of women" and "the creator of a new kind of values politics. . . . Clinton's first important insight—confirmed by his constant reading of polls—is that Americans are not nearly as divided as we sometimes think. . . .

"We mostly missed a big story sitting right under our noses, one of the great acts of political theft in recent memory. In 1996, Bill Clinton—that's right, BILL CLINTON—grabbed family values for the Democrats, and he's not about to give them back."

Seib cast his *Wall Street Journal* column as an exercise in mind reading. "If you're President Clinton, here's how you might see things this holiday season. . . . What is to be your legacy? Perhaps it lies in being the Baby Boomer who saves entitlement programs for the Baby Boomers as they head toward retirement. . . . Maybe you try some small confidence-building measures before attempting any big fix." Readers never suspected that the columnists had gotten their information from a certain inside source.

But McCurry was interested in more than just a couple of favorable columns. He wanted Clinton to see journalists in what he called a "defanged mode," not peppering him with prosecutorial questions. McCurry's fantasy was that POTUS, as White House aides called the president of the United States, could have sessions like this with Howell Raines, the editorial page editor of *The New York Times*, and Leonard Downie, executive editor of *The Washington Post*, who would see, in an easygoing atmosphere, that Clinton was a thoughtful guy.

The biggest complaint among White House reporters was how remote they felt from the man they were supposed to be covering. McCurry agreed that this was a problem. When the campaign was over he arranged a get-acquainted session between Clinton and seven of the new correspondents who would be covering him in the second term. They gathered in the Map Room, whose wall is adorned by the 1945 military map that hung there when FDR left the White House for the last time. Clinton, nursing a sore throat, slouched on the couch sipping tea. He told the reporters, who munched cookies on the chairs around him, that they would have to do most of the talking. Then, of course, he held forth for an hour and ten minutes.

Clinton was surprisingly candid, and the chat ranged from whether he and his wife would adopt a child—they had decided against it—to his view of Steve Stockman, the far-right Texan congressman. "He's crazy," Clinton said.

That session was also off-the-record. Soon afterward, the seven reporters got together and compared the notes they had hastily scribbled after the meeting. Karen Tumulty of *Time* magazine wanted to use an anecdote about Madeleine Albright. Peter Baker of *The Washington Post* wanted to cite a comment Clinton had made about his old pal James Carville. McCurry finally cut a deal in which seven items could be used without attributing them to Clinton. The reporters could say "the president has told friends . . ." or "the president is known to believe . . ."

Reporters didn't like the off-the-record rule, since they had to beg for each usable crumb. But McCurry felt it was best that Clinton be able to sound off without weighing each word. He had not forgotten the infamous "funk" episode of 1995, when the president, in jeans and cowboy boots, had a forty-five minute chat with reporters aboard Air Force One about the mood of the country. The conversation was going fine until Clinton declared that he wanted to "get people out of their funk."

The pack quickly pounced. Clinton was widely ridiculed for his assessment of the national disposition, which was likened to Jimmy Carter's disastrous "malaise" speech in 1979.

"See, this is what happens," Clinton told his staff. "You try to let people understand what you are thinking and what your motivations are, and it just becomes a game of gotcha."

Senior White House officials chastised McCurry for putting the president in such a vulnerable position, and he considered it his greatest blunder as press secretary. But he didn't want to shut off all informal communication. Six months later, when Clinton was returning from a trip to Israel on Air Force One, McCurry tried again, this time decreeing that the conversation was on something called "psych background," meaning that reporters could pretend to tap into the president's brain without attributing any comments to the Big Guy. Clinton rambled for three hours about the Middle East, the Bible, the college basketball playoffs, violence on television, even the peach cobbler aboard the flight, all without saying anything inflammatory. But the exercise was so transparent that it came off as silly. John Harris of *The Washington Post* attributed the remarks to "a talkative and opinionated fellow" on the plane who was "intimately familiar with the thinking of Clinton."

Still, the president seemed to be growing more comfortable with the give-and-take. Flying back from Little Rock on the day after the election, he fell into a freewheeling conversation with print reporters on the plane. But nothing was ever simple in dealing with the press. The television and radio correspondents quickly complained to McCurry that the session did them no good because they had no usable videotape or sound. McCurry pondered the situation for a moment.

"Come up to the front of the plane," he said. "We'll re-create the moment. You can ask the same questions." In a remarkable bit of staging, the cameramen gathered around the president while the reporters asked the same questions that had been asked moments before, eliciting the same answers. Then one reporter slipped in an extra question and McCurry got mad.

McCurry could give as good as he got, and when he didn't want to answer a question, he could stonewall with the best of them. Deborah Orin found this out the hard way.

The feisty *New York Post* reporter with the jet-black hair and tabloid-tough manner had known McCurry for fifteen years and liked him, most of the time. But she couldn't stand the way he dealt with her from the podium. If he didn't want to address a sensitive question, he would deflect it, duck it, dismiss it. He would needle the person who asked it. What he wouldn't do was provide a straight answer.

It was "an attempt to marginalize reporters who asked embarrassing questions," Orin said later. She took the briefings seriously. Orin was naturally combative, but it was more than that. The daily encounter was a chance to hold the

White House accountable, one of the few public opportunities to challenge the official line.

Many of the veterans considered the briefings stupefyingly dull, a colossal waste of time. CBS's Rita Braver skipped them whenever possible. Brit Hume, the long-time ABC correspondent, would stand up and and leave if the droning went on too long. At other times Hume would sit in his booth at the back of the pressroom and listen with one ear to the closed-circuit monitor. If he heard something that annoyed him, he would come loping up to the front and interrogate McCurry, just to show him that the reporters were still awake. But with McCurry slinging so much bull from the podium, it hardly seemed worth the bother. If he uttered any newsworthy syllables, the reporters could read the transcript on their computer screens within minutes.

Orin worked for a conservative newspaper that delighted in Clinton sex scandals, and in the summer of 1996, the scandal of the moment involved Gary Aldrich's book, *Unlimited Access*. A former FBI agent assigned to the White House, Aldrich had written a screed that depicted the Clintonites as sloppy, rude, drug-addled Deadheads. The first headlines, gleefully trumpeted by the *New York Post* (which serialized the book), had Clinton sneaking out under a blanket in the back seat of a car for late-night trysts at the downtown Marriott. It was, as it turned out, a fourth-hand rumor that no one could corroborate.

The White House assumed a full War Room footing in an effort to discredit the book. George Stephanopoulos called every reporter he knew, arguing that the book was tabloid trash, riddled with errors and beneath the dignity of any serious news organization. Stephanopoulos and Mark Fabiani, the White House lawyer in charge of scandal management, went to the ABC bureau a few blocks from the White House and urged producers there to bump Aldrich from a scheduled Sunday appearance on *This Week with David Brinkley*. Leon Panetta called Bob Murphy, ABC's vice president for news, with the same message.

McCurry, traveling with the president in Lyons, France, pulled aside Robin Sproul, ABC's Washington bureau chief, and launched into a red-faced tirade. He was really hot. There would be consequences if ABC put Aldrich on the air, he said. The network's requests to talk to the president would be dropped, including Clinton's planned interview with Barbara Walters that fall, McCurry warned. White House officials might be reluctant to appear on ABC programs. When the Brinkley show put Aldrich on anyway—along with Stephanopoulos—McCurry said that ABC had "damaged" the president. "We'll remember that," he said. Stephanopoulos even made the ludicrous claim that Bob Dole's campaign was involved, since Craig Shirley, a conservative publicist who had once done volunteer work for the Dole camp, was helping to promote the book.

Though the administration's counterattack didn't scare ABC, it did help to turn the rest of the establishment media against the Aldrich book. After the book's numerous errors and rumors were exposed by the Brinkley show, *Newsweek*, and other news organizations, *Larry King Live* and *Dateline NBC* both dropped planned interviews with Aldrich. And while *Unlimited Access* went on to become a best-seller—ballyhooed as The Book the Clinton White House Doesn't Want You to Read—the assault had sent an important signal. The Clintonites were willing to use intimidation tactics to quash an unfavorable story. If journalists found them too heavy-handed, well, that was a price they had to pay to neutralize the book. McCurry later apologized to Robin Sproul, but he had clearly shown his willingness to use the brass knuckles.

Still, Orin believed that there was legitimate material in Aldrich's book, incidents that the ex-FBI man would be in a position to know. He had written that Craig Livingstone, a mid-level White House aide who later resigned for improperly obtaining FBI files on Republicans, had once issued a memo chastising White House staffers for writing bad checks. What about that? Either there was a memo or there wasn't. Orin soon pressed McCurry at the gaggle, but he deflected the question. A few days later she tried again to ask about "some of the charges made by Gary Aldrich."

"Still trying to resurrect him, huh?" McCurry shot back.

Orin pressed on: Was there a Craig Livingstone memo on bad checks? True or not?

"I am not going to check, because most of what he writes in that book has already been proven to be without merit," McCurry said.

"If it's not true, why don't you want to check it?"

"I don't think it's worth my time to check."

A CBS producer, Mark Knoller, piped up. "But Deborah's question is legitimate, isn't it, Mike?"

The book, McCurry told Orin, was "filled with lies. And your newspaper, as I recall, reprinted large portions of it."

"And it printed your denials, Mike. But the question is a question about a memo. Did or didn't he issue such a memo?"

"I do not know."

"Will you check?"

"No."

Why not?

"Because I don't want to," McCurry said. Then he threw down the gauntlet: "Does any other news organization want to pose the question?"

It was a tense moment. McCurry was suddenly the playground bully, challenging the rest of the gang to stand up for Deborah Orin. There was an uncomfortable silence. "Okay, hearing none, any other questions?" McCurry said. Another reporter asked about a Pentagon initiative, and the briefing moved on.

Orin felt humiliated. Her whole body was shaking. Afterward, several reporters approached her and apologized for their behavior. "They felt as if their balls had been cut off while my limb was cut off," Orin said later. "The press corps was totally emasculated."

One reporter told her, "I didn't want to use up any chits for your story." Orin was stunned. The dirty little secret of covering the White House, she felt, was there wasn't much that McCurry and his colleagues would do to help you. Oh, you might get an early leak on some budget proposal or presidential appointment, but by and large everyone, whether in favor or not, was fed the same thin gruel. And most of the reporters would not stick their necks out and risk losing what little access they had. They had become too passive. McCurry, she realized, was winning the war. ■

 Chapter 8

Parties and Elections

Elections are a critical part of any democratic political system. They provide the clearest and most important opportunity for citizens to participate in self-government. They help ensure that the government respects the will of the people, at least in a general way, and, by providing a mechanism to demonstrate "the consent of the governed," help to make government legitimate.

In the modern world, elections are typically fought not just by candidates but by political parties. Political parties help organize political life, making it easier for voters to make choices and to effect results, and making it easier for public officials to organize governing majorities. In the United States, parties also provide a bridge between the legislative and executive branches by providing natural allies for the president in both Houses of Congress.

Parties and elections, however, raise profound questions about the nature and efficacy of democratic politics. American parties, in particular, have been notoriously weak; members of the same political party may have little in common with one another, and (as Bill Clinton learned in 1993 and 1994) even one-party control of both branches of government is no guarantee of success in policy making. Moreover, American elections are strongly influenced by special interest groups, most importantly through the campaign finance system, and by the media, which both influences the process and which, in turn, is easily manipulated by candidates and public officials.

The various selections in this chapter explore a variety of themes. Selection 8.1 presents a classic critique of American political parties as weak and ineffectual. Selections 8.2 and 8.3 attempt to make sense of the ups and downs of electoral politics in the 1990s. Selection 8.4 examines the American two-party system in comparison with the multiparty systems common elsewhere in the world, and selection 8.5 presents a look at the lighter side of the chaotic process by which we choose our presidents.

Chapter Questions

1. How have American parties and elections changed over the past several decades? Consider the impact of television; political action committees (see selection 8.2); and changes in the relative strengths and issue positions of the two major parties.
2. What are the implications for American politics of the rise of third-party and nonparty candidates? Of the increasingly ideological nature of the debate be-

tween the two parties? Of the increasing cynicism and nonparticipation of the American voters?

 # Foundations

Fifty years ago, a group of political scientists representing the committee on political parties of the American Political Science Association (APSA) issued a report on the weaknesses and inadequacies of the American party system. In their report, the APSA committee argued that the nation's political parties needed to be both "responsible and effective"—in other words, they needed to be "accountable to the public" while "able to cope with the great national problems of modern government."

The APSA committee's critique remains valid today. Although the American party system has changed greatly in the past half century, American parties remain relatively weak, and, except in rare circumstances, are unable to propose a coherent program to the American people and, if elected, carry that program into law. To matters worse, the modern American electorate seems to prefer divided government, with one party in control of Congress and the other in control of the White House. Thus even if the two parties were each able to operate responsibly and effectively, they would probably have difficulty doing so together.

Questions

1. What does the Committee mean by a "responsible and effective" party system? In what ways are modern American parties more responsible and/or effective than their counterparts in 1950? In what ways are they less responsible and/or effective?

2. Would American government be improved or harmed by the emergence of a party system in line with the APSA's recommendations? Why?

8.1 Towards a More Responsible Two Party System (1950)

APSA Committee on Political Parties

Americans are reasonably well agreed about the purposes served by the two major parties as long as the matter is discussed in generalities. When specific questions are raised, however, agreement is much more limited. We

"Towards a More Responsible Two-Party System" (Report of the APSA Committee on Political Parties), *American Political Science Review* 44 (1950), pp. 17–24.

cannot assume, therefore, a commonly shared view about the essential characteristics of the party system. But we can and must state our own view.

In brief, our view is this: *The party system that is needed must be democratic, responsible and effective*—a system that is accountable to the public, respects and expresses differences of opinion, and is able to cope with the great problems of modern government. Some of the implications warrant special statement, which is the purpose of this section.

I. A Stronger Two-party System

1. *The Need for an Effective Party System.* In an era beset with problems of unprecedented magnitude at home and abroad, it is dangerous to drift without a party system that helps the nation to set a general course of policy for the government as a whole. In a two-party system, when both parties are weakened or confused by internal divisions or ineffective organization it is the nation that suffers. When the parties are unable to reach and pursue responsible decisions, difficulties accumulate and cynicism about all democratic institutions grows.

An effective party system requires, first, that the parties are able to bring forth programs to which they commit themselves and, second, that the parties possess sufficient internal cohesion to carry out these programs. In such a system, the party program becomes the work program of the party, so recognized by the party leaders in and out of the government, by the party body as a whole, and by the public. This condition is unattainable unless party institutions have been created through which agreement can be reached about the general position of the party.

Clearly *such a degree of unity within the parties cannot be brought about without party procedures that give a large body of people an opportunity to share in the development of the party program.* One great function of the party system is to bring about the widest possible consent in relation to defined political goals, which provides the majority party with the essential means of building public support for the policies of the government. Democratic procedures in the internal affairs of the parties are best suited to the development of agreement within each party.

2. *The Need for an Effective Opposition Party.* The argument for a stronger party system cannot be divorced from measures designed to make the parties more fully accountable to the public. *The fundamental requirement of such accountability is a two-party system in which the opposition party acts as the critic of the party in power, developing, defining and presenting the policy alternatives which are necessary for a true choice in reaching public decisions.*

Beyond that, the case for the American two-party system need not be restated here. The two-party system is so strongly rooted in the political traditions of this country and public preference for it is so well established that consideration of other possibilities seems entirely academic. When we speak of the parties without further qualification, we mean throughout our report the two major parties. The inference is not that we consider third or minor parties undesirable or ineffectual within their limited orbit. Rather, we feel that the minor parties in the longer run have failed to leave a lasting imprint upon both the two-party system and the basic processes of American government.

In spite of the fact that the two-party system is part of the American political tradition, it cannot be said that the role of the opposition party is well understood. This is unfortunate because democratic government is greatly influenced by the character of the opposition party. The measures proposed elsewhere in our report to help the party in power to clarify its policies are equally applicable to the opposition.

The opposition most conducive to responsible government is an organized party opposition, produced by the organic operation of the two-party system. When there are two parties identifiable by the kinds of action they propose, the voters have an actual choice. On the other hand, the sort of opposition presented by a coalition that cuts across party lines, as a regular thing, tends to deprive the public of a meaningful alternative. When such coalitions are formed after the elections are over, the public usually finds it difficult to understand the new situation and to reconcile it with the purpose of the ballot. Moreover, on that basis it is next to impossible to hold either party responsible for its political record. This is a serious source of public discontent.

II. Better Integrated Parties

1. *The Need for a Party System with Greater Resistance to Pressure.* As a consciously defined and consistently followed line of action keeps individuals from losing themselves in irresponsible ventures, so a program-conscious party develops greater resistance against the inroads of pressure groups.

The value of special-interest groups in a diversified society made up of countless groupings and specializations should be obvious. But organized interest groups cannot do the job of the parties. Indeed, it is only when a working formula of the public interest in its *general* character is made manifest by the parties in terms of coherent programs that the claims of interest groups can be adjusted on the basis of political responsibility. Such adjustment, once again, calls for the party's ability to honor its word.

There is little to suggest that the phenomenal growth of interest organizations in recent decades has come to its end. Organization along such lines is a characteristic feature of our civilization. To some extent these interest groups have replaced or absorbed into themselves older local institutions in that they make it possible for the government and substantial segments of the nation to maintain contact with each other. It must be obvious, however, that *the whole development makes necessary a reinforced party system that can cope with the multiplied organized pressures*. The alternative would be a scheme perhaps best described as government by pressure groups intent upon using the parties to deflect political attention from themselves.

By themselves, the interest groups cannot attempt to define public policy democratically. Coherent public policies do not emerge as the mathematical result of the claims of all of the pressure groups. The integration of the interest groups into the political system is a function of the parties. Any tendency in the direction of a strengthened party system encourages the interest groups to align themselves with one or the other of the major parties. Such a tendency is already at work. One of the noteworthy features of contemporary American politics is the fact that not a few interest groups have found it impossible to remain neutral toward both parties. To illustrate, the entry of organized labor upon the political scene has in turn impelled antagonistic special interests to coalesce in closer political alignments.

In one respect the growth of the modern interest groups is exerting a direct effect upon the internal distribution of power within the parties. They counteract and offset local interests; they are a nationalizing influence. Indeed, the proliferation of interest groups has been one of the factors in the rise of national issues because these groups tend to organize and define their objectives on a national scale.

Parties whose political commitments count are of particular significance to interest organizations with large membership such as exist among industrial workers and farmers, but to a lesser extent also among businessmen. Unlike the great majority of pressure groups, these organizations through their membership—and in proportion to their voting strength—are able to play a measurable role in elections. Interest groups of this kind are the equivalent of organizations of voters. For reasons of mutual interest, the relationship between them and the parties tends to become explicit and continuing.

A stronger party system is less likely to give cause for the deterioration and confusion of purposes which sometimes passes for compromise but is really an unjustifiable surrender to narrow interests. *Compromise among interests is compatible with the aims of a free society only when the terms of reference reflect an openly acknowledged concept of the public interest.* There is every reason to insist that the parties be held accountable to the public for the compromises they accept.

2. The Need for a Party System with Sufficient Party Loyalty. It is here not suggested, of course, that the parties should disagree about everything. Parties do not, and need not, take a position on all questions that allow for controversy. The proper function of the parties is to develop and define policy alternatives on matters likely to be of interest to the whole country, on issues related to the responsibility of the parties for the conduct of either the government or the opposition.

Needed clarification of party policy in itself *will not cause the parties to differ more fundamentally or more sharply than they have in the past.* The contrary is much more likely to be the case. The clarification of party policy may be expected to produce a more reasonable discussion of public affairs, more closely related to the political performance of the parties in their actions rather than their words. *Nor is it to be assumed that increasing concern with their programs will cause the parties to erect between themselves an ideological wall.* There is no real ideological division in the American electorate, and hence programs of action presented by responsible parties for the voter's support could hardly be expected to reflect or strive toward such division.

It is true at the same time that ultimately any political party must establish some conditions for membership and place some obligations on its representatives in government. Without so defining its identity the party is in danger of ceasing to be a party. To make party policy effective the *parties have the right and the duty to announce the terms to govern participation in the common enterprise.* This basic proposition is rarely denied, nor are precedents lacking. But there are practical difficulties in the way of applying restraints upon those who disregard the stated terms.

It is obvious that an effective party cannot be based merely or primarily on the expulsion of the disloyal. To impose discipline in any voluntary association is possible only as a last resort and only when a wide consensus is present within the association. Discipline and consensus are simply the front and rear sides of the same coin. *The emphasis in all consideration of party discipline must be*, therefore, *on positive measures to create a strong and general agreement on policies*. Thereafter, the problem of discipline is secondary and marginal.

When the membership of the party has become well aware of party policy and stands behind it, assumptions about teamwork within the party are likely to pervade the whole organization. Ultimately it is the electorate itself which will determine how firmly it wants the lines of party allegiance to be drawn. Yet even a small shift of emphasis toward party cohesion is likely to produce changes not only in the structure of the parties but also in the degree to which members identify themselves with their party.

Party unity is always a relative matter. It may be fostered, but the whole weight of tradition in American politics is against very rigid party discipline. As a general rule, the parties have a basis for expecting adherence to the party program when their position is reasonably explicit. Thus it is evident that the disciplinary difficulties of the parties do not result primarily from a reluctance to impose restraints but from the neglect of positive measures to give meaning to party programs.

As for party cohesion in Congress, the parties have done little to build up the kind of unity within the congressional party that is now so widely desired. Traditionally congressional candidates are treated as if they were the orphans of the political system, with no truly adequate party mechanism available for the conduct of their campaigns. Enjoying remarkably little national or local party support, congressional candidates have mostly been left to cope with the political hazards of their occupation on their own account. *A basis for party cohesion in Congress will be established as soon as the parties interest themselves sufficiently in their congressional candidates to set up strong and active campaign organizations in the constituencies.* Discipline is less a matter of what the parties do *to* their congressional candidates than what the parties do *for* them.

III. More Responsible Parties

1. *The Need for Parties Responsible to the Public. Party responsibility means the responsibility of both parties to the general public, as enforced in elections.*

Responsibility of the party in power centers on the conduct of the government, usually in terms of policies. The party in power has a responsibility, broadly defined, for the general management of the government, for its manner of getting results, for the results achieved, for the consequences of inaction as well as action, for the intended and unintended outcome of its conduct of public affairs, for all that it plans to do, for all that it might have foreseen, for the leadership it provides, for the acts of all of its agents, and for what it says as well as for what it does.

Party responsibility includes the responsibility of the opposition party, also broadly defined, for the conduct of its opposition, for the management of public discussion, for the development of alternative policies and programs, for the bipartisan policies which it supports, for its failures and successes in developing the issues of public policy, and for its leadership of public opinion. The opposition is as responsible for its record in Congress as is the party in power. It is important that the opposition party be effective but it is equally important that it be responsible, for an irresponsible opposition is dangerous to the whole political system.

Party responsibility to the public, enforced in elections, implies that there be more than one party, for the public can hold a party responsible only if it has a choice. Again, unless the parties identify themselves with programs, the public is unable to make an intelligent choice between them. The public can understand the general management of the government only in terms of policies. When the parties lack the capacity to define their actions in terms of policies, they turn irresponsible because the electoral choice between the parties becomes devoid of meaning.

As a means of achieving responsibility, the clarification of party policy also tends to keep public debate on a more realistic level, restraining the inclination of party spokesmen to make unsubstantiated statements and charges. When party policy is made clear, the result to be expected is a more reasonable and profitable discussion, tied more closely to the record of party action. When there is no clear basis for rating party performance, when party policies cannot be defined in terms of a concrete program, party debate tears itself loose from the facts. Then wild fictions are used to excite the imagination of the public.

2. *The Need for Parties Responsible to Their Members. Party responsibility includes also the responsibility of party leaders to the party membership, as enforced in primaries, caucuses and conventions.* To this end the internal processes of the parties must be democratic, the party members must have an opportunity to participate in intraparty business, and the leaders must be accountable to the party. Responsibility demands that the parties concern themselves with the development of good relations between the leaders and the members. Only thus can the parties act as intermediaries between the government and the people. Strengthening the parties involves, therefore, the improvement of the internal democratic processes by which the leaders of the party are kept in contact with the members.

The external and the internal kinds of party responsibility need not conflict. Responsibility of party leaders to party members promotes the clarification of party policy when it means that the leaders find it necessary to explain the policy to the membership. Certainly the lack of unity within the membership cannot be overcome by the fiat of an irresponsible party leadership. A democratic internal procedure can be used not merely to test the strength of the various factions within a party but also to resolve the conflicts. The motives for enlarging the areas of agreement within the parties are persuasive because unity is the condition of success.

Intraparty conflict will be minimized if it is generally recognized that national, state and local party leaders have a common responsibility to the party membership. Intraparty conflict is invited and exaggerated by dogmas that assign to local party leaders an exclusive right to appeal to the party membership in their area.

Occasions may arise in which the parties will find it necessary to apply sanctions against a state or local party organization, especially when that organization is in open rebellion against policies established for the whole party. There are a variety of ways in which recognition may be withdrawn. It is possible to refuse to seat delegates to the National convention; to drop from the National Committee members representing the dissident state organization; to deny legislative committee assignments to members of Congress sponsored by the disloyal organization; and to appeal directly to the party membership in the state or locality, perhaps even promoting a rival organization. The power to take strong measures is there.

It would be unfortunate, however, if the problem of party unity were thought of as primarily a matter of punishment. Nothing prevents the parties from explaining themselves to their own members. The party members have power to insist that local and state party organizations and leaders cooperate with the party as a whole; all the members need is a better opportunity to find out what party politics is about. The need for sanctions is relatively small when state and local organizations are not treated as the restricted preserve of their immediate leaders. National party leaders ought to have access to party members everywhere as a normal and regular procedure because they share with local party leaders responsibility to the same party membership. It would always be proper for the national party leaders to discuss all party matters with the membership of any state or local party organization. Considering their great prestige, wise and able national party leaders will need very little more than this opportunity.

The political developments of our time place a heavy emphasis on national issues as the basis of party programs. As a result, the party membership is coming to look to the national party leaders for a larger role in intraparty affairs. There is some evidence of growing general agreement within the membership of each party, strong enough to form a basis of party unity, provided the parties maintain close contact with their own supporters.

In particular, *national party leaders have a legitimate interest in the nomination of congressional candidates*, though normally they try hard to avoid the appearance of any intervention. Depending on the circumstances, this interest can be expressed quite sufficiently by seeking a chance to discuss the nomination with the party membership in the congressional district. On the other hand, it should not be assumed that state and local party leaders usually have an interest in congressional nominations antagonistic to the interest of the national leaders in maintaining the general party policy. As a matter of fact, congressional nominations are not considered great prizes by the local party organization as generally as one might think. It is neglect of congressional nominations and elections more than any other factor that weakens party unity in Congress. It should be added, however, that what is said here about intraparty relations with respect to congressional nominations applies also to other party nominations. ■

 # American Politics Today

American electoral politics in the 1990s was marked by dramatic reversals of fortune. In 1992, the Democratic Party won back the White House after a twelve-year lapse; in 1994, the Republican Party recaptured the House and Senate, controlling both houses of Congress for the first time in forty years. The Republican "revolution" of 1994 was short-lived, however. In 1996, President Bill Clinton surprised the pundits by winning a second term, and in 1998 his party bucked the historical trend against a sixth-year president and actually gained seats in the House of Representative.

Making sense out of this topsy-turvy series of events is the goal of the two selections in this section. In the first, the reporter John B. Judis examines the 1998 election returns and concludes the Democrats' surprise showing was the result of the resurgence of the "Mighty Middle"—the centrist voters who hold the balance of power between the two parties. In the second, the commentator Christopher Caldwell argues that the Republican Party has been "captured" by its conservative (and largely Southern) wing, and has thus lost touch with those same moderates. Only by reaching back to the center, he argues, can the Grand Old Party return to dominance.

Questions

1. Who are the voters who comprise the "mighty middle" in American politics? What issues matter most to them? Why did they turn toward the Republicans in the 1994 congressional elections but toward the Democrats in the 1996 presidential race? Why did the Republicans lose ground in 1998?
2. What can the Republican Party do to restore its image with centrist voters? What forces—both inside and outside the party—make this task difficult?

8.2 The Mighty Middle (1998)

John B. Judis

There have been two exceptional elections over the past decade—in 1992 and 1994—that appeared to promise dramatic change. But the other elections have affirmed an equilibrium between the two parties and between the extremes of liberalism and conservatism. They have not mandated inaction—although that has sometimes been the unfortunate result—but rather a cautious, incremental program of reform focused on education, health care, and the environment. They have affirmed Americans' support for Social Security, Medicare, and environmental and consumer regulation, as well as opposition to radicalism of the left or right—whether in the form of a government-run health care system or the privatization of Social Security. And they have signaled the public's discomfort with the social agenda of the religious right.

And so it was with 1998. The Democrats did much better than expected precisely because the public identified them with a cautious, liberal centrism. Those Republicans who did particularly well, such as Texas Governor George W. Bush or Wisconsin Governor Tommy Thompson, were also identified with this kind of political approach. The real losers in the election were right-wing Republicans. In open seats and closely contested races, Democrats were able to defeat Republicans

John B. Judis, "The Mighty Middle," *The New Republic* (November 23, 1998), pp. 23–25. Reprinted by permission of The New Republic, © 1998, The New Republic, Inc.

who championed the right's program of banning abortion, privatizing Social Security, and abolishing federal aid to education. In the 1998 elections, being identified as a "right-wing extremist" became more dangerous to a politician's future than being identified as a "liberal."

In the gubernatorial races, and many of the Senate contests, the public judged candidates by their commitment to using government resources to improve education. Democrats won governor's races in South Carolina, Alabama, Iowa, and California because they advocated vigorous state aid to, and regulation of, education, while their Republican opponents either ignored the issue or opposed new state initiatives. South Carolina gubernatorial candidate Jim Hodges and Alabama candidate Don Siegelman, following the example of outgoing Georgia Governor Zell Miller, called for a state lottery to boost spending on education. In Iowa, Democrat Tom Vilsack advocated spending state money on education, while his Republican opponent, Jim Ross Lightfoot, made a tax cut his first priority. In California, Democrat Gray Davis focused his campaign on creating higher standards for education, while his Republican opponent, Dan Lungren, ran a "back to the future" law-and-order campaign.

Democratic defenses of Social Security also proved pivotal. Much of the Democratic appeal was based on the somewhat spurious issue of the budget surplus. Democrats argued that, by resisting tax cuts, they were "saving" Social Security. Republicans might have argued that, by speeding economic growth, tax cuts would raise Social Security revenues, but having worshiped so many years at the altar of the balanced budget, they were unable to counter these Democratic attacks. Meanwhile, some Republican candidates went looking for trouble by advocating the privatization of Social Security. In Arkansas, Democratic Senate candidate Blanche Lambert Lincoln lambasted Republican Fay Boozman for wanting to replace a mandatory public insurance system with one that allowed private investment accounts. In Mississippi's fourth congressional district, which extends southward from Jackson, Democrat Ronnie Shows ran television ads attacking Republican Delbert Hosemann's plan for private investment. Shows's ads warned that senior citizens' savings could be jeopardized by stock-market volatility and charged that Hosemann was fronting for the securities industry.

In many Northern races, and even in a few Southern ones, Democrats benefited by tying their opponents to the religious right. Republican Fob James in Alabama (a Christian Coalition favorite who once threatened to call in the National Guard to defend the right of a local judge to display the Ten Commandments in his courtroom), Boozman in Arkansas (a proponent of Christian home schooling), Iowa's Lightfoot, Maryland gubernatorial candidate Ellen Sauerbrey, Washington Senate candidate Linda Smith, and Kansas Congressman Vince Snowbarger were all hurt by their identification with the religious right. And then there was California Senate candidate Matt Fong, who had, at one point, staked himself to a healthy lead over incumbent Democrat Barbara Boxer by painting himself as a moderate. On October 25, *The San Francisco Examiner* revealed that, during his primary campaign against a conservative opponent, Fong had donated $50,000 to the Traditional Values Coalition, a virulently anti-gay, anti-abortion lobby run by the Reverend Louis Sheldon, who describes himself as a "lobbyist for the Lord." Soon after Fong's contribution, Sheldon had thrown his support behind him in the primary. Fong spent the last ten days of the campaign trying unsuccessfully to reconcile his claims of moderation—and his endorsement by the gay Log Cabin Republicans—with his financial support for Sheldon.

The Democrats' success will doubtless spark a new round in the debate between party liberals and "New Democrats." But the lessons of the election don't entirely fit the arguments of either faction.

The party's success clearly demonstrates that Democrats cannot uniformly adopt the kind of inflexible liberal stands activists championed during the 1970s and 1980s. While a steep recession might alter public opinion, many Americans remain suspicious of ambitious government programs and of spending that singles out Democratic constituencies. Take Northern California's Contra Costa County as an example. While Representative George Miller could champion the Democrats' old-time religion in blue-collar Richmond, Ellen Tauscher, who represents the neighboring high-tech suburbs of Walnut Creek and Livermore, could not. Fortunately, Democrats have become quite pragmatic on such matters: John Dalrymple, the head of the Contra Costa County Central Labor Council, disagrees with Tauscher's support for NAFTA and for giving the president fast-track trade negotiating authority. But, he says, "The reality is that she is the best Democrat who could be elected from the district."

Indeed, Democrats succeeded in many key contests because the primary voters nominated centrists instead of more traditional liberals. If militant consumer advocate Mark Green and not Representative Charles Schumer had faced New York Senator Al D'Amato, the Republicans probably would have retained the seat. If Harvey Gantt and not John Edwards had run against North Carolina incumbent Republican Lauch Faircloth the election would have focused on affirmative action and urban aid—issues unfavorable to Democratic success—rather than on HMOs and education. The proof for this proposition comes from the closely contested Lexington, Kentucky, district that Democrat Scott Baesler represented before he ran for Senate this year. There, Democrats nominated the most liberal candidate in the primary. He lost.

In some Southern and Southwestern districts, where Protestant fundamentalists and Pentecostals predominate, Democrats went so far as to nominate candidates who shared a conservative social agenda. Charles Stenholm in Texas, Marjorie McKeithen in Louisiana, Ronnie Shows in Mississippi, and Ken Lucas in Kentucky are pro-life Democrats. They are also more fiscally conservative than many Northern Democrats and more inclined to distance themselves from the Clinton administration. But they were still considerably to the left of their far-out Republican opponents. For instance, Stenholm's opponent, Rudy Izzard, whom he defeated after a difficult campaign, wanted to abolish the income tax and withdraw the United States from the United Nations.

Yet, while the 1998 election showed that many Democrats have to move to the center, it defined a center that was still firmly rooted in the legacy of the New Deal, Medicare, and the regulatory reforms of the 1970s. It was, in other words, a *liberal* centrism. Democrats did not win by advocating the partial privatization of Social Security—which the Democratic Leadership Council currently favors—but by defending the current system. If the Democrats were to embrace Republican and securities-industry plans for privatization, they would abandon a major source of their support. Similarly, Democrats also didn't win support by advocating private-school vouchers; quite the contrary, they won by promising to strengthen public education. Tauscher is a perfect example. While she backed some Republican tax cuts and voted for an impeachment inquiry, she rejected Social Security privatization and private-school vouchers.

The election did show that Democrats can appeal to the white, suburban upper-middle class in Contra Costa County, Boulder, Portland, Seattle, and the Research Triangle of Raleigh-Durham-Chapel Hill. But the Democrats would be foolish to target future political appeals exclusively, or even primarily, to this group of voters. After all, this year the Democrats would have fared just as poorly as they did in 1994 were it not for an unusually high voter turnout among the two most famously traditional liberal constituencies: blacks and union families. In Maryland's gubernatorial contest, for instance, black turnout increased from twelve percent of the vote in 1994 to 19 percent in 1998. Black voters provided the margin of victory for Parris Glendening over Sauerbrey. According to national exit polls, union households went from 14 percent of the electorate in 1994 to 23 percent in 1998—a huge jump that was the result of an AFL-CIO get-out-the-vote program. Hispanics were also very important to Democratic successes: Gray Davis won an estimated 75 percent of California's Hispanic vote. Democrats can ignore these constituencies only at their peril.

As for the Republicans, their failure will spur an even more vigorous internal debate. The election's victims were, primarily, those most closely identified with the right—not only Alabama's James and North Carolina's Faircloth but also former Representative Robert Dornan, who lost a rematch with Loretta Sanchez in California, and Assemblyman Tom Bordonaro (also in California), who lost a rematch with Lois Capps. And most of those Republicans who won open seats or upset incumbents ran centrist campaigns. In Sacramento, millionaire businessman Doug Ose, who favors abortion rights, defeated Barbara Alby, a candidate of the Christian right, in a bitterly contested primary—and then went on to capture the seat currently held by retiring Democrat Vic Fazio. Alby would have surely lost.

In Illinois, Republican gubernatorial candidate George Ryan championed abortion rights, gun control, and the environment against his socially conservative Democratic opponent. (Senate victor Peter Fitzgerald is a right-winger, but his triumph was due to the defects of his opponent, Democratic incumbent Carol Moseley-Braun.) George W. Bush ran as a "compassionate conservative" and champion of education reform in Texas. While backed by the religious right, he conspicuously opposed its attempts to force all Texas Republicans to adhere to its agenda. Bush and other successful Republicans also refused to allow the Democrats to monopolize the black and Hispanic vote.

If the Republicans heed this lesson, they will nominate someone like Bush in 2000 without forcing him to embrace a platform written by Pat Buchanan, the Christian Coalition, or Gary Bauer's Family Research Council. A Republican nominee in 2000 will have to distance himself as far from the Christian Coalition as Bill Clinton distanced himself from the Reverend Jesse Jackson's Rainbow Coalition in 1992. If the Republicans ignore the lesson of this election and nominate someone like former Vice President Dan Quayle or Missouri Senator John Ashcroft, or if they demand a kind of conservative doctrinal loyalty oath from Bush or another governor, they could cede control of the White House for the next decade. Almost any Democrat who is considering running for president could defeat a candidate identified with the Republican right.

In the meantime, the Republicans will have to figure out what to do with their majority in Congress. In 1994, the national party developed a platform, the Contract with America, that was designed to appeal to the voters who had backed Ross Perot in 1992. This year, the Republicans had no substantive agenda. They rested their hopes primarily on the scandal swirling around Bill Clinton and, in the campaign's last week, mounted a targeted advertising campaign designed to make the election in key districts a referendum on Clinton's personal behavior. This effort backfired, energizing Democratic voters nationally and dramatizing the Republican Congress's failures. Democrats won exactly those close races in South and North Carolina, Louisiana, Alabama, and Mississippi, where the Republicans had tried to make Monica Lewinsky the issue.

The Republicans have emerged from this campaign in an unenviable position. The nominal winners, they lack a mandate to govern. They also lack a program with which they might acquire a mandate. By contrast, the Democrats have to be inspired by these results. If they read them correctly—if they don't see in them a justification for either a further lurch rightward on Social Security or for the revival of old-style liberalism—and if they accommodate old and new Democrats in the same party, then they could be on the way to reclaiming the majority they lost to Ronald Reagan two decades ago. ∎

8.3 The Southern Captivity of the GOP (1998)

Christopher Caldwell

Stolen Bases

Since the 1960s Republican gains at the national level have been built on two trends. One is regional—the capture of more and more southern seats. The other is sociological—the tendency of suburbanites to vote Republican. The party's 1994 majority came thanks to a gain of nineteen seats in the South. In 1996 Republicans picked up another six seats in the Old Confederacy. But that only makes their repudiation in the rest of the country the more dramatic. The party has been all but obliterated in its historical bastion of New England, where it now holds just four of twenty-three congressional seats. The Democrats, in fact, dominate virtually the entire Northeast. The Republicans lost seats in 1996 all over the upper Midwest—Michigan, Wisconsin (two seats), Iowa, and Ohio (two seats). Fatally, they lost seats in all the states on the West Coast. Their justifiable optimism about the South aside, in 1996 it became clear that the Democratic Party was acquiring regional strongholds of equal or greater strength.

As Walter Dean Burnham, a political scientist at the University of Texas, has noted, the 1996 elections almost diametrically oppose those of 1896. Anyone who is today middle-aged or older was born in a country with a solidly Democratic South and a predominantly Republican Midwest and Northeast, and probably will die in a country in which the Republicans hold the Old Confederacy and the Democrats dominate from the Great Lakes to the Atlantic. In effect, the two parties have spent the twentieth century swapping regional power bases.

Since it is the southern and mountain states—the Republican base—that are adding voters, congressional seats, and electoral votes, this constituency-trading was supposed to be all gravy for the Republicans. It isn't. The bad news for the party in 1996 was not so much regional as sociological. In the suburbs—home to 40 percent of voters, by conservative estimates—Clinton ran even with Bob Dole. Clinton won among eighteen- to twenty-nine-year-olds in 1996 and 1992, reversing Reagan and Bush victories among that cohort in 1984 and 1988, and he also won among Catholics, who had voted Republican in the three previous elections. (In Congress the Republicans won the Catholic vote for the first time ever in 1994; one election later they were routed, by 53 to 45 percent.)

And the Republicans lost heavily among Hispanics, America's fastest-growing voting bloc, who added 1.5 million voters from 1992 to 1996, and will probably add as many again by the next presidential election. This alarming result confounded an earlier Republican optimism. Democrats who had arrogantly assumed that standard-issue minority politics would easily pull Hispanics into the party fold were proved wrong throughout the 1980s. Hispanic voters turned out to be disproportionately entrepreneurial and disproportionately receptive to Republican family-values rhetoric, and gave the party roughly a third of their votes in the three presidential elections from 1980 to 1988. Leaving aside Puerto Ricans and Dominicans in New York, who *do* fit the Democrats' minority paradigm, the Republicans were doing better with the Hispanic vote than might be expected.

But the Republicans in the 104th Congress tried to shore up their Texas and California right wings with hostile rhetoric on immigration. They passed legislation that sought to deprive not just illegal but also legal immigrants of federal benefits. (Newt Gingrich and other Republicans backpedaled in 1997, reversing some of the measures, but the damage was done.) And California's Proposition 187, supported by Republican Governor Pete Wilson and aimed at denying benefits to illegal immigrants, brought angry Hispanics to the polls in unprecedented numbers. Clinton took 72 percent of the Hispanic vote nationwide, including 81 percent in Arizona and 75 percent in California; he took 78 percent of Hispanics under thirty. He nearly split the Hispanic vote even in Florida, where 97 percent of the Cuban population voted for Reagan in 1984.

The hardening loyalty of Hispanics is a catastrophe for the Republicans' presidential prospects. According to census projections, by 2025 the country's two most populous states, California and Texas, will be 43 and 38 percent Hispanic respectively. And earlier in the decade California was hemorrhaging Republicans anyway, owing to what could be called the Fuhrman effect: a large secondary migration of older, middle-class whites who appear to have lost patience with the multiracial, multicultural society already in evidence in the state, and have moved to Idaho, Nevada, Arizona, and other more solidly Republican states of the intermountain West.

These in- and out-migrations, coupled with the growth of lifestyle liberalism and federal Democrats' careful nurturing of West Coast interests, could make California close to unwinnable for Republicans. That would put the White House, too, out of reach for a long time. The only Democrat ever to win California and lose the presidency, after all, was Winfield Hancock—who was defeated by James Garfield in 1880, when the state had six electoral votes.

The Finkelstein Box

These sociological and geographic shifts are part of a broad change in party allegiance. No one has been more astute in outlining its nature than the Republican consultant Arthur Finkelstein, who set the pattern for Republican triumphs in the 1980s by running aggressive, ideological campaigns that went after Democratic candidates for their uncommonsensical "liberalism"—a word that was repeated almost hypnotically in the ads and speeches he wrote. Of late Finkelstein has been criticized by some of his candidates outside the Northeast, largely for having the temerity to suggest that this message must be broadened now that liberals are drubbing Republicans on a range of new issues. These are issues on which the party has historically been silent—education, the environment, and health care, for example. The absence of a Republican voice on them helps to explain why the party has scraped up only about 40 percent of the vote for two presidential elections running.

Finkelstein uses a simple graphic device to show his Republican candidates, geographically, just how differentiated the country is. Put a pen point on Washington, D.C., and draw your way across a map of the continental United States, edging up between Iowa and Nebraska, running through the Dakotas and Montana, dropping down through Washington and Oregon and along the western border of Nevada into California, and then heading back east, with the tips of Texas and Florida south of the line. The box that results leaves you with two different political countries. (See map.) The Finkelstein Box refutes a long-standing axiom among political consultants: that as people prosper and grow more educated and cosmopolitan, they become more likely to be Republicans. In states that have their largest population centers outside the box, no Republican senatorial candidate got a majority in the last election. Inside the box no Democrat got a majority except Mary Landrieu, of Louisiana (and that barely). Although most Republican governors outside the box are pro-choice, almost every single Republican governor inside the box is pro-life.

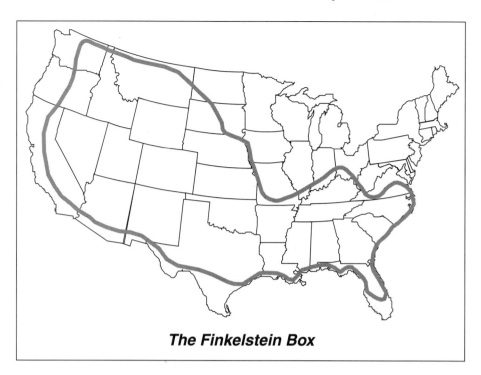

The Finkelstein Box

The Republican Party is increasingly a party of the South and the mountains. The southernness of its congressional leaders—Speaker Newt Gingrich, of Georgia; House Majority Leader Dick Armey and House Majority Whip Tom DeLay, of Texas; Senate Majority Leader Trent Lott, of Mississippi; Senate Majority Whip Don Nickles, of Oklahoma—only heightens the identification. There is a big problem with having a southern, as opposed to a midwestern or a California, base. Southern interests diverge from those of the rest of the country, and the southern presence in the Republican Party has passed a "tipping point," at which it began to alienate voters from other regions.

As southern control over the Republican agenda grows, the party alienates even conservative voters in other regions. The prevalence of right-to-work laws in southern states may be depriving Republicans of the socially conservative midwestern trade unionists whom they managed to split in the Reagan years, and sending Reagan Democrats back to their ancestral party in the process. Anti-government sentiment makes little sense in New England, where government, as even those who hate it will concede, is neither remote nor unresponsive.

The most profound clash between the South and everyone else, of course, is a cultural one. It arises from the southern tradition of putting values—particularly Christian values—at the center of politics. This is not the same as saying that the Republican Party is "too far right"; Americans consistently tell pollsters that they are conservative on values issues. It is, rather, that the Republicans have narrowly defined "values" as the folkways of one regional subculture, and have urged their imposition on the rest of the country. Again, the nonsoutherners who object to this style of politics may be just as conservative as those who practice it. But they are put off to see that "traditional" values are now defined by the majority party as the values of the U-Haul-renting denizens of two-year-old churches and three-year-old shopping malls.

• • •

The Hillary Cluster

There is an ideological component to Clinton's success and the Republicans' failure. The end of the Cold War, the increasing significance of information technology, and the growth of identity politics have caused a social revolution since the badly misunderstood 1980s. It's difficult to tell exactly what is going on, but in today's politics such subjects for discussion as Communist imperialism and welfare queens have been replaced by gay rights, women in the workplace, environmentalism, and smoking. On those issues the country has moved leftward. In 1984 the Republicans held a convention that was at times cheerily anti-homosexual, and triumphed at the polls. In 1992 the party was punished for a Houston convention at which Pat Buchanan made his ostensibly less controversial remarks about culture war. Reagan's Interior Secretary James Watt once teasingly drew a distinction between "liberals" and "Americans" while discussing water use, and pushed a plan to allow oil drilling on national wildlife refuges. By 1997 the New Jersey Republican Party was begging its leaders to improve the party's image by joining the Sierra Club.

This is in part a story of how successful parties create their own monsters. Just as Roosevelt's and Truman's labor legislation helped Irish and Polish and Italian members of the working class move to the suburbs (where they became Republicans), Reaganomics helped to create a mass upper-middle class, a national culture of childless yuppies who want gay rights, bike trails, and smoke-free restaurants. One top Republican consultant estimates that 35 to 40 percent of the electorate now votes on a cluster of issues created by "New Class" professionals—abortion rights, women's rights, the environment, health care, and education. He calls it the "Hillary cluster." The political theorist Jean Bethke Elshtain calls it, more revealingly, "real politics."

And with this new landscape of issues Republicans aren't even on the map. Because of the Reagan victory, the Democrats went through the period of globalization and the end of communism amid self-doubt and soul-searching. The experience left them a supple party that quickly became familiar with the Hillary cluster. Bill Clinton's ideology here is necessarily an inchoate one, and in his heart of hearts he may be to the left of where the country is. But he is the first President to understand that the Hillary cluster is not on one side or the other of a partisan fault line (and that is his greatest contribution to American politics). The American people are not "for" or "against" gay rights. They overwhelmingly say they favor equal rights for gays—but then draw the line at gays in the military. They're for AIDS-research funding—but think gays are pushing their agenda too fast. Americans aren't "for" or "against" environmentalism. They believe that global warming is going on—but waffle on whether major steps should be taken to block it. They have shown a tolerance for paying more taxes to protect the environment, but few list it as their No. 1 concern when asked by pollsters.

Such jagged political fault lines make Americans' ideology look ambiguous by old definitions. In fact, the Boston University sociologist Alan Wolfe doubts whether the old polarity of "conservatives" and "liberals" is any longer meaningful, at least on the increasingly important cultural issues. The big question is whether this blending of conservatives and liberals is happening at the party level—whether President Clinton has effected a wholesale change in his party. Ed Goeas and other Republican pollsters say there's no indication that Clinton is enticing people back to the Democrats. The best evidence, however, from 1996 exit polls is that the Democrats are no longer a liberal party—or at least they are far less liberal than the Republicans are conservative. Whereas 58 percent of Republicans identify themselves as conservative, only a third of Democrats identify themselves as liberal.

To the Republicans, it doesn't much matter. They've missed all of this, and continue to campaign against the Democrats they wish they were contesting: against Jimmy Carter and his economy, against George McGovern and his foreign policy, against Jesse Jackson and his urban policy. They treat the past two presidential elections—the worst back-to-back disasters that either party has suffered since Roosevelt clobbered Herbert Hoover and Alf Landon in 1932 and 1936—as aberrations, much as certain Democrats throughout the eighties insisted that the only "typical" elections since Truman were in 1960 and 1976. According to Jim Chapin, for decades a New York Democratic activist and now the senior policy adviser to the city's public advocate, "Republicans remind me of us in the late seventies and early eighties. They say, 'If you lay our policies out without telling people whose policies they are, they approve of them.' So what! Voters are merely making judgments based on the credibility of the party as an institution. And they're right. In 1980 I knew if people understood what many liberal Democrats *really* wanted, our vote would go down."

People are finding out that the Republicans don't want anything at all, other than to re-elect enough of their members to keep enjoying the fruits of a congressional majority. Lacking a voice on the new 1990s issues, the Republicans are retreating to the issues on which they used to have a voice. In this they resemble those "boomerang kids" who after their first career reversal return home in their late twenties to live with their parents. Republicans are going home to Ronald Reagan but are finding that theirs is no longer the only house on the block promoting the most popular part of his agenda—free-market economics. They're finding that there's nothing to do around the house except dress up their old ideas in the clothes of Clintonite insincerity. Where is the broad argument of a "natural majority" here?

There is none. The Republicans *are* too conservative: their deference to their southern base is persuading much of the country that their vision is a sour and crabbed one. But they're too liberal, too, as their all-out retreat from shrinking the government indicates. At the same time, the Republicans have passed none of the reforms that ingratiated the party with the "radical middle." The Republicans' biggest problem is not their ideology but their lack of one. Stigmatized as rightists, behaving like leftists, and ultimately standing for nothing, they're in the worst of all possible worlds. ■

 # The Comparative Context

The two-party system is a characteristic feature of the American polity. Most of the other democracies in the world, by contrast, have *multiparty* systems, in which one or more major parties are joined by several (and in some cases many) smaller ones.

The historical persistence of the American two-party system is due, in part at least, to the rules of the electoral game. Most American elections reward only the candidate with the most votes—other candidates, no matter how many votes they receive, win nothing. Such "single-member plurality" (or SMP) rules apply in both presidential elections and congressional elections. In the 1992 presidential election, for example, H. Ross Perot won 19 percent of the popular vote, but because he did not finish first in any state, he received no electoral votes. Third-party candidates have historically fared poorly in congressional elections as well; at present, there is only one member of Congress who is not a Democrat or Republican.

The SMP system has distinct advantages for a political system. Perhaps most importantly, single-member plurality rules require candidates to reach out to a large bloc of voters, and encourage compromise and cooperation. But, as the political scientist Douglas J. Amy argues in this selection, the SMP system also raises serious concerns. As an alternative, Amy suggests that the United States consider a proportional representation (or PR) system, which is used by most other democracies in the world today. In a PR system, the number of legislative seats won by a particular party would be roughly proportional to the number of votes it receives—whether or not it attains a plurality in any particular district.

Questions

1. What are the disadvantages of the single-member plurality system, according to Amy? How, in his view, would a PR system address the problems with the SMP system?
2. What arguments would you make in opposition to Amy's proposal? What are the advantages of the SMP system as used in the United States? What problems might arise if we adopted a PR system?
3. How would a PR system change the relationships between members of Congress and party leaders? Between the White House and Congress? Between members of Congress and their constituents?

8.4 Breaking the Two-Party Monopoly

Douglas J. Amy

The Problem of Only Two Parties

For the sake of argument assume that the Democrats and Republicans were to develop into parties offering detailed and distinctly different policy options to the voters. Would this eliminate the problems surrounding our two-party system? The answer is no—because having only two parties from which to choose is itself limiting and problematic. It unreasonably restricts the political options available to the electorate. Many combinations of positions can be taken on the pressing issues of the day, but in our party system they are automatically reduced to two. A simple example illustrates the extent of the problem. Assume that we face only five political issues in an election—say, defense, education, welfare, farm policy, and health policy—and that we can choose to increase or decrease expenditures in each area. Even this simplified situation presents thirty-two combinations of positions that could be offered by parties. In a two-party system, one party might advocate increasing defense spending and cutting the others, and the other party might advocate the opposite. But where does that leave all the voters who desire any of the other combinations? They are left with no choice they can enthusiastically endorse and with the task of deciding which is the lesser of two evils. And that is the basic problem with a two-party system—it simply cannot offer anything approaching a reasonable variety of positions on the issues.

Again, the inherent limitations of choice in our party system become even more obvious when compared with European party systems—systems that offer not only a larger number of parties but also a wider variety of parties with distinct ideologies and policy programs. Voters there have the option of moderate parties in the middle, as well as a socialist party on the far left or a conservative party on the right, or even a Green party that claims to be neither left nor right. In these multiparty systems, voters have a much better chance of finding parties and candidates with policy positions close to their own.

Supporters of the two-party system sometimes suggest that limiting the public to two choices may in fact be an advantage—that reducing our options conveniently minimizes the complexity and difficulty of election choices. The assumption is that any more than two options would strain the intellectual capacity of most voters. But this logic is hardly accepted in others areas of American life. American consumers would be outraged if they were offered only two choices of houses or cars to meet their different needs. As political consumers we should hardly be less infuriated with the same overly restricted electoral choices.

One-Party Systems

Having only two options in the election booth is bad enough, but our choices are often even more restricted than that. In many areas of the country we do not even have a two-party system; we have a one-party system. In cities, counties, and states in which one party has a reliable majority of the voters, that dominant party is usually the only viable option. Indeed, for most of this century, one-party systems have been the rule in most areas of the United States. Until the 1950s the South had a one-party system dominated by the Democrats, while several northern states were often controlled by Republicans. Similar situations remain in many parts of the country today. Recent years have seen some increase in party competition in some states, but one part of the state often is dominated by the Democrats and another by the Republicans.

In this sense, our current party system often closely resembles a corporate oligopoly in which the two dominant companies divide up their territories and agree not to compete with each other in them. Indeed, Mayhew and others present evidence that Republicans and Democrats sometimes collude in exactly this way, with legislators agreeing on gerrymandering schemes that ensure safe districts for the representatives of each party. So it is misleading to call ours a competitive two-party system; often it is more accurately described as a pair of one-party monopolies. The big loser in this situation is the same one that suffers in a one-company territory—the public. Such arrangements severely curtail the choices of American voters and ultimately undermine their power to control the political system. Americans have long been aware of the evils of economic monopolies and oligopolies, but we have been slow to awaken to the dangers of the same arrangements in our party system.

The Electoral Connection

If our two-party system is so frustrating, why does it persist? Why haven't we developed a multiparty system that offers a set of genuine political choices? The first reason is the power of tradition. Most Americans are socialized in our party system and learn to view our political universe in those limited terms. We come to think of having only two parties as natural. The media contribute to this view by giving little coverage to any minor-party candidates who do happen to run, making it more difficult for these challengers to get their messages out and to build larger bases of public support. Equally important, the two parties have also devised numerous election procedures that discourage minor parties. Many states, for example, still require excessively large numbers of voter signatures on petitions before minor parties can even get access to the ballot.

But the electoral rule that is by far the biggest obstacle to the emergence of viable minor parties in the United States is plurality voting. Plurality rules tend to foster two-party systems by systematically discriminating against minor parties and making it extremely difficult for them to achieve any electoral success. In the 1950s the French political scientist Maurice Duverger described the supportive relationship between plurality rules and two-party systems, and it remains one of the most extensively examined propositions in political science. Duverger noted that plurality voting rules tend to work against minor parties in two ways. First is what Duverger called the *mechanical effect* of these rules: The tendency of the plurality system to give the largest party more seats than it deserves and to give smaller parties fewer seats than they deserve. Such underrepresentation is often a problem for the second party, but it can prove disastrous for third or fourth parties.

As a rule, the smaller the party, the larger the proportion of seats out of which it is cheated. For example, in the 1987 British elections for Parliament, the Conservative party won 42.3 percent of the vote and received 57.7 percent of the seats. The second-place Labor party was actually slightly overrepresented as well, winning 30.8 percent of the vote and 35.5 percent of the seats. But the third party, the Alliance of Social Democrats and Liberals, suffered the brunt of the underrepresentation. It received a respectable 22.8 percent of the vote, but was given a minuscule 3.4 percent of the seats in Parliament. Similar fates have befallen third-party efforts in New Zealand's plurality elections. The Social Credit party received 16.1 percent of the vote in 1978, but won only one seat (1.1%) in the ninety-two-seat national parliament. In 1981 its portion of the vote increased to 20.7 percent, but the party only managed to receive two seats (2.2%).

Underrepresentation is typical of the fate of minor parties under plurality rules. And it is quite possible to imagine worse situations, in which minor parties receive a substantial portion of the votes, only to get no seats at all. For example, in 1989 British elections to the European parliament, the British Green party received 15 percent of the vote, but because of plurality election rules received no seats. Similarly, in 1984 the New Zealand party received 12 percent of the vote in that country and no seats. The only way for minor parties to enjoy any kind of consistent electoral success in plurality systems is by being concentrated in local or regional enclaves, where they can sometimes muster a plurality of the votes. This is the case with the small Welsh and Scottish parties in Great Britain; regional popularity allows them to send several members to Parliament. In the United States some third parties have been concentrated in particular states. In the 1930s the Progressive party in Wisconsin was able to elect a governor and many state legislators; during that same period the Farmer-Labor party in Minnesota captured the governorship for three successive terms. Without such regional sanctuaries, however, it is difficult, if not impossible, for minor-party candidates to win office, making it more likely that these parties will be short-lived in single-member plurality systems.

The tendency of the mechanical effect of plurality systems to discourage minor parties is compounded by what Duverger called the *psychological effect* of those rules. Potential supporters will hesitate to vote for a minor-party candidate if they believe that candidate has little chance of winning a plurality or majority of the vote. They fear wasting their votes on a minor-party candidate. It is much more rational for voters to support a candidate who stands a chance of winning—usually one from the two major parties. Thus even though minor parties and their candidates might enjoy some support among the electorate, supporters will often realize that the only realistic choice is to vote for a major-party candidate. This was the case, for instance, for those who supported the Independent John Anderson in the 1980 presidential elections. Opinion polls indicated that up to 24 percent of voters supported Anderson, but only 7 percent cast ballots for him on election day. Similarly a University of Michigan national survey indicated that of those voters who rated Anderson the highest among the three candidates, only 39 percent actually voted for him. In contrast, Ronald Reagan and Jimmy Carter received 95 percent of the votes of people who rated them the highest. Studies done in other countries support the conclusion that voters often will abandon a preferred minor-party candidate to reluctantly cast a vote for a major-party candidate with a better chance of being elected.

Thus plurality rules subject minor parties to a kind of double penalty: They first ensure that these parties will be severely underrepresented in the legislature, which discourages voters from voting for these candidates in the first place. But the plight of minor parties under plurality rules is actually even worse. Minor-party voters also can be contributing to the election of the very candidate they oppose the most. Imagine, for instance, being a voter faced with a choice of a liberal Democrat, a moderate Republican, and a Libertarian. A far-right conservative may be tempted to support the Libertarian candidate, if only as a protest vote, but doing so only takes that vote away from the moderate Republican and thus boosts the chances of the conservative's least preferable candidate, the Democrat. Or take a real example of this dilemma: the 1980 U.S. Senate race in New York. That year three candidates ran—Alphonse D'Amato (Republican party), Elizabeth Holtzman (Democratic party), and Jacob Javits (Liberal party). Eleven percent of the voters opted for Javits, which took votes away from the other liberal candidate, Holtzman. She lost to D'Amato by one percentage point—45 percent to 44 percent—largely because probable supporters defected to Javits. Polls indicated that most of Javits's votes would have gone to Holtzman in a two-way race between she and D'Amato. But in a plurality system those votes for the Liberal party candidate simply ensured that the most conservative candidate won. Thus an additional punishment often is meted out to those who dare vote for minor-party candidates in the United States—the election of the candidate they most detest.

Plurality election rules undermine minor parties primarily by discouraging voters from supporting their candidates. However, scaring voters away can have several secondary effects that further handicap these parties. For example, because minor parties lack a realistic chance of getting candidates elected under current rules, they usually have trouble recruiting experienced and talented politicians. Such politicians are inevitably attracted to the two mainstream parties where the career opportunities are dramatically better. Also minor parties usually have difficulty attracting financial contributors, who are understandably hesitant to invest money in quixotic campaigns. Thus minor parties are caught in a vicious circle: Plurality rules discourage voter support, which makes potential candidates and contributors reluctant to join up, which further erodes the ability of these parties to conduct effective campaigns and to attract voters, and so on. These effects can quickly seal the fate of a minor party.

Clearly, then, our SMP election rules are much of why ours is one of the few countries that continues to lack viable and ongoing minor parties. These parties have not failed to thrive in the United States because Americans are all political centrists who always prefer our two middle-of-the-road parties. The long history of third-party efforts in the United States—including the Populists, Socialists, Progressives, American Independents, and others—clearly indicates that millions of

Americans have frequently been interested in a wider range of political options. But plurality election rules usually squelch such options by putting the minor parties at such a disadvantage that most have found it impossible to survive. By discriminating against minor parties, our plurality rules provide artificial and unfair support for the two major parties. They discourage competition and help to maintain a political oligarchy. Instead of creating an open electoral market in which all parties compete freely for the support of voters, plurality rules put minority parties at a huge competitive disadvantage and virtually ensure the continued dominance of the two major parties.

The Predicament for Nonmainstream Groups

The current U.S. election system also severely limits the organizational options of groups outside the political mainstream. Under SMP rules, political groups on the far left or far right inevitably face a difficult dilemma: they can try to work within the major parties (which will generally tend to ignore them) or they can try to start their own party (which will most likely be doomed). Neither option is particularly attractive or effective. For example, consider the position of those who see themselves to the left of the Democratic party: militant labor unionists, left liberals, democratic socialists, radical environmentalists, feminists, civil rights activists, and others. They often face just this sort of difficult, no-win choice. They can try to work within the Democratic party, but this often turns out to be fruitless. The party generally refuses to adopt genuine leftist political positions out of fear that they might alienate the centrist base. It has also been able to take the support of leftist groups for granted, even without giving them any substantial concessions. Leftists' political impotence within the Democratic party often leads these groups to consider splitting off and starting their own party. But leftist groups intensely disagree on and debate such moves. Many leftists, well aware of the electoral obstacles that exist for minor parties, believe that such efforts are a waste of time and money. In addition, such third-party efforts are often criticized as divisive. For example, NOW's efforts to establish a new women's party created friction with some black political activists who feared that the effort would undercut support for Jesse Jackson, who has chosen to work within the Democratic party.

Forces on the far right have faced similar political predicaments. Some try to fashion a niche within the Republican party, with mixed success. Others strike out on their own and create new parties, including the Right-to-Life party and the U.S. Taxpayers party. But with a few exceptions these parties are quixotic efforts that have failed to elect candidates to office. The main point, of course, is that the frustrating political position of these nonmainstream groups is entirely a creation of the peculiar rules of single-member plurality elections. And the only real way to escape this dilemma is to escape the SMP system itself.

The Need for PR and a Multiparty System

Americans have suffered under our two-party system for so long that we tend to view its problems and limitations as unfortunate but inevitable. In reality, of course, many of these problems are inevitable only under single-member plurality voting rules. The adoption of proportional representation in the United States would go a long way toward addressing many of these shortcomings. PR would allow for the development of a multiparty system with a variety of genuine political alternatives. Minor parties would no longer be unfairly penalized, and they would be able to elect representatives in numbers that reflect their political strength in the electorate. In short, PR would be an antitrust law for the party system. It would discourage party monopolies and oligopolies and allow for free competition among parties. It would create a level playing field on which all parties could vie fairly for public support.

A more hospitable political environment for minor parties under PR would probably result in the expansion of the party system in the United States. Voter support for minor parties would increase as voters realize that voting for minor-party candidates no longer means wasting their votes. Talented politicians would be more attracted to these parties. They could run for office on those tickets without fearing that they are throwing their careers away. Donations to these parties would probably increase as the contributors realize that these investments could actually produce some electoral dividends.

It is important to recognize that the adoption of PR in the United States would not *force* us to have a multiparty system; it simply would *allow* such a system to develop, if it reflected the wishes of the American voter. As political scientists often observe, many factors other than electoral systems help determine the number of parties in a political system—such as the number and depth of political cleavages in a society. Thus if American voters choose to support only the two major parties, PR would produce a two-party system, as has happened in Austria. In this sense, PR does not mandate any particular kind of party system; it simply does not inhibit the development of a multiparty system the way plurality rules do. With proportional representation what the public wants in a party system, it gets.

This principle was evident in the experiments with PR in U.S. cities. The effect of PR on party systems varied from city to city, depending on local political conditions and public preferences. In some cities that adopted PR, such as Cincinnati, essentially two parties still contested local elections, though PR produced a much more accurate representation of those parties in the city council. In cities with more heterogeneous political populations, like New York, a vigorous multiparty system emerged. Before the adoption of proportional representation, New York City was dominated by the Democratic machine, which elected virtually the entire city council. The onset of PR broke the political monopoly of the Democrats, and what was a one-party system became a multiparty system. The PR city council in 1947 reflected the wide variety of political persuasions among the New York city electorate and consisted of twelve Democrats, five Republicans, two Liberals, two Communists, and two American Laborites.

If we were to move toward a multiparty system today, what new parties would be likely to develop in the United States? A coalition of leftists might break from the Democratic party—perhaps something like the recently formed 21st Century party or the New party. A far right party—perhaps resembling a Moral Majority party—could split off from the Republican party. On the right, the Libertarian party probably would see some growth in membership as electing its candidates became more realistic. Another possibility is an independent, nonideological centrist party—perhaps along the lines of the group that supported Ross Perot's presidential candidacy in 1992. In areas with concentrations of racial minorities, we could see the emergence of an African-American party or a Latino party. PR could also spur growth in the several Green parties that have already sprouted in the United States. Other parties are possible—the variety limited only by the wishes of American voters.

Is it likely that the two major parties would fracture into smaller parties and disappear entirely? Probably not. One reason for their persistence is the presence and importance of presidential elections in our political system. Unlike parliamentary systems, the chief executive in our presidential system is elected separately by a plurality vote. The winning presidential candidate must garner a majority or substantial plurality of the vote, and this requirement encourages large political parties like the Democrats and Republicans. These broad-based parties are best equipped to muster the wide voter support required. In fact, the presidential election may be much of why two-party dominance has been stronger in the United States than in other plurality countries, like Great Britain and Canada, which have parliamentary systems. In any case, the most likely scenario for the United States would be for the Democratic and Republican parties to remain in some form, with a number of minor parties emerging.

• • •

PR: Giving Voters a Real Choice

Voting is one of our most fundamental acts of political choice. But a crucial difference exists between simply having a choice and having a real or a meaningful choice. For any choice to be real, we must have some control over the options we are given. Otherwise our choice may be only a fraud or an illusion. If we were told that we were free to choose between being hit in the face and kicked in the stomach, we would probably protest that this is hardly freedom and really no choice at all. Many Americans find themselves in just that situation with our two-party system. Plurality rules artificially limit our choices to two similar parties, and for many voters this does not seem like a real choice at all. In contrast, proportional representation elections would ensure that voters have as wide a variety of distinct political choices as they desire. The adoption of PR in the United States would finally allow the American voter—not our plurality election rules—to decide which political parties and political views deserve to be represented in our legislatures. Putting this power of choice back in the hands of the American voters would help make our election system much more fair and democratic. ■

 # View from the Inside

American political campaigns have always comprised a mixture of the serious and the absurd. In an effort to investigate the comical side of the campaign trail, the reporter Michael Lewis trailed the various and sundry Republican candidates for president during the early days of the 1996 race. Although they are entertaining, Lewis' reports from the front lines also raise serious questions about the way Americans choose their elected leaders.

Questions

1. What are the strengths and weaknesses of the way party candidates for president are selected in the United States? Does the marathon-like course of primaries and caucuses give Americans a true sense of what each candidate would bring to the White House? Does the current system adequately reflect the views of a wide cross-section of the voting public?
2. Does the current campaign system add to voter cynicism and alienation? How might the system be improved or reformed?

8.5 Trail Fever

Michael Lewis

January 18 [1996]

Time and *Newsweek* are here in Iowa, gearing up to put Steve Forbes on their covers. David Broder is here from the Washington *Post*. Gene Randall is here from CNN, not so much to ask as to *perform* a few questions on the TV screen beside Forbes. Sam Donaldson is here, looking more like another candidate than a reporter as he is driven from Forbes event to Forbes event in the back of a dark blue Cadillac. And everywhere he goes Forbes is greeted by friendly crowds too large to count. The reporters from AP and Reuters do what they always do in these difficult situations when a candidate draws serious crowds. Each makes a rough guess of the number of people in the room. They then average these totals to create a fact for posterity.

If you had asked me who of all the rich men I had ever met was least likely to go courting the American voter, I would have given you Steve Forbes's name first. I have rarely encountered anyone so perfectly unhappy shaking hands and making small talk, so thoroughly uncomfortable in his skin. The sheer unease of his manners and conversation is a match for the most constipated English aristocrat. The reason is that he was raised in the manner of a constipated English aristocrat. The heir to the heir to the *Forbes* magazine fortune, he spent his boyhood on a horse farm in New Jersey. He attended Princeton in the late 1960s and, at the height of the antiestablishment sentiment, founded a magazine called *Business Today*. Somehow privilege and temperament conspired to make him a misfit.

And yet under the unwatchful gaze of the cameras something is happening. His deep unease is being transformed into a dignified reticence. His reluctance to take any kind of conversational risk is being interpreted as a calculated display of

---

political prudence. The television cameras flatten the landscape they seek to depict and, in the case of Forbes, make the strange seem simply ordinary. The cameras create the illusion that a candidate is being watched when in fact he is being hidden.

The most striking thing about the Forbes campaign is its repetitiveness. Spend a few hours stumping with Forbes in Iowa or New Hampshire and you've heard just about every word he will ever speak. Each of his speeches is not merely a reasonable approximation of the last but a near-perfect replica. All the other candidates have their favorite lines but try, with varying degrees of success, to find different ways to make the same points. With Forbes nothing is left to chance; it's the same every time, right down to the gestures and the taut grin he uses to punctuate his lines. He sets his wristwatch down on the podium together with his left hand and a single sheet of paper—though he never actually looks at his notes. Instead his eyes sweep across the crowd, left to right, with the same rhythmic efficiency as the carriage of a typewriter. I time his eye movements. Each sweep is almost exactly the same length, about eight seconds.

Offstage he is much the same as on. If he is unable to repeat himself he ducks. Shoulder to shoulder with journalists in his campaign van, bouncing over potholes at sixty miles an hour, he responds to questions not only in the same words but in the same *tone* as in his stump speech. "Why do you think the other candidates ganged up on you in Iowa?" I ask him. "They represent the politics of the past versus a vibrant vision of the future," he replies, automatically. Carving through the New Hampshire state assembly cafeteria en route to deliver his speech, he stops to converse with three ladies. It turns out that one of them has worked with the AFL-CIO. "Why aren't you going to keep the minimum wage?" she asks, a bit aggressively. "I worked closely with [former AFL-CIO president] Lane Kirkland at Radio Free Europe," says Forbes, apropos of nothing, and then bolts before the cameras have time to record the exchange.

I watch Forbes deliver the same speech half a dozen times before I get close enough to find evidence to support my hunch—or perhaps my hope—that a perfectly strict routine is not as straightforward as it appears. At the Chubb Life Insurance Company in Concord, New Hampshire, I find myself standing immediately behind him, waiting for his inner jukebox to produce the same tunes. I assumed that he read from the same written text but to my amazement see that he actually uses loose notes, as if he had just thought up his speech in the car on the way over. The notes are not even crisp and neatly typed, but a mess of slashes, signs, and keywords. They are the work not of a drone but of a man who is forever trying new things on for size, or at least thinks he is. The top few inches looks like this:

+ FRUSTRATE
XXXXXXX
+ GTR
− XXXXX
+ GROWTH
XXXX——

What the hell is *that* all about? I wonder but am interrupted by a second surprise: the microphone goes on the blink. There's a little crackle on the line that interferes with Forbes's speech. He looks up and spontaneously says, "That's Bob Dole." The room breaks up, and even Forbes himself can't quite believe it—he's made a joke. In the context of his performance that one little line is the equivalent of the invention of the microchip. An awkward smile of true, unexpected delight breaks sloppily across his face. A few years back there was a television commercial for the Special Olympics that concluded with a retarded boy bursting through the tape at the finish line and breaking into a joyous, heart-tugging smile. Forbes now wears exactly the same expression. He has a Special Olympics smile.

Suddenly I realize what I am watching: a man attempting to disprove what he is with what he says. Forbes is spending $35 million to ensure that every voter in Iowa and New Hampshire will hear the same commercial attacking Bob Dole something like forty times before Election Day. Its gist is that Dole is a dried-up old Washington hack while Forbes is a vital business giant who understands invention and entrepreneurship. Forbes is consumed by his faith that if you lower people's taxes you unleash their passions and inspire them to take all manner of risks. The flat tax is his Heloise, his Laura, his Dark Lady. And yet there he sits, astride a half-billion trust-fund dollars, unwilling to risk even a conversation or to stray from a single word in his memorized text. If I hadn't just watched Phil Gramm spending $20 million to persuade people that he alone knows the value of the dollar, I might have been shocked. But now I understand that running seriously for president requires a man not to look too closely at himself.

• • •

The debate lasts ninety minutes, and while it is no doubt tedious to anyone who hasn't followed the eight remaining candidates, it is the highest entertainment for those few of us who have. It's like watching a B movie: everyone remains perfectly inside his narrow character. Bouncing up and down like a Puerto Rican shortstop, Lamar lashes into Dole while at the same time decrying negative advertising. Forbes lashes into Lamar about his personal finances, prompting Lamar to lash back. Buchanan lashes into "Mr. Greenspan and Mr. Rubin," thus creating job opportunities for anti-anti-Semites. Morry lashes into the English language. All manner of strange linguistic events occur in the interstices of Morry's synapses: "practicality" becomes "pracality," "frustrated" becomes "flustrated," "Strom Thurmond" becomes "Strong Thermal." It is its own kind of poetry, an improvement on the clichés of life and politics. In the space of five minutes the man is capable of referring to himself as a "country pumpkin," or claiming that he bought his wife a "Norman Mailer dress." (It turns out to be a Nicole Miller dress.) But Morry's poetry has no place in politics.

The debate produces one memorable moment, when Dole waves a few snapshots and tries to make a joke of Steve Forbes's endless advertising aimed at him. "They didn't even use a good picture of me," Dole says, "so Steve, I brought some pictures. So if you are going to use negative ads—"

"Senator, no pretty picture can get around what you've done on taxes," replies Forbes.

"Yeah, yeah. I know your problem," says Dole. "You've got a lot of money. You're trying to buy this election."

The joke's gone sour because Dole's gone sour. There is an awkward moment when Dole fumbles the snapshots with his left hand to Bob Dornan on his right, who passes them on to Forbes, who doesn't even bother to look at them. The biggest winner is B-1 Bob Dornan, who now somehow produces a foot-high blowup of himself holding his grandchild. The timing is so perfect that it looks planned, but it is a stroke of pure luck—Dornan had no idea Dole was going to turn up with snapshots. Like all the luck in this campaign, it isn't Dole's. You know you have hit bottom when you are successfully parodied by Bob Dornan.

Other than that, Dole simply mutters disconnected phrases in response to the attacks on him from all sides. He treats the debate as he treats the press and the voters—as an undignified distraction from his lifelong quest for the White House. "It's an abomination," a Dole aide later tells me, "that Bob Dole has to share a platform with Morry Taylor." But it's worse than that: Dole has arrived at the point where he needs Morry to defend him. "Senator Dole," Morry says, exhibiting his typical unwillingness to join in with any mob, "he's been a champion, a good old warhorse for the Republican Party. He's taken all the blows they whack at him tonight." Good old Morry.

• • •

February 16–18 [1996]

By the time I catch up to the Dole campaign it has lost interest in disseminating the Dole family photo album. I ask five different Dole aides the identity of the baby held by Dole. It seems an innocent enough query—after all, this was the picture Dole had selected for publication. I get no answer. The basic pose of the Dole campaign is, the less anyone finds out about its candidate the better. You can spot the Dole office in the row of glass boxes on the ground floor of the Manchester Holiday Inn: it's the one with newspaper taped up on the glass to prevent people from looking in. Dole himself remains largely out of sight. He makes two or three very brief, formal appearances each day and is otherwise unavailable for interviews.

Dole's speeches add nothing to the general blank picture. The act is always the same. The announcer shouts the names of all the state politicians who have endorsed Dole; they race out onto the stage one at a time like ballplayers before a game. Dole waits in the background until the crowd reaches a low fever pitch. When he comes out he stands at the podium with his left foot and left side jutted forward, though he is right-handed, and his crippled right hand resting on the podium. Almost always he starts in with something self-deprecating: "That's a lot better than the speech is going to be," something like that. It is the clearest remark Dole will ever utter. The few words he speaks worth hearing are words he didn't intend to speak. Gaffes. A gaffe, the journalist Michael Kinsley has said, is when a politician tells the truth. "We didn't plan it this way," Dole gaffes one morning, inside a New Hampshire factory. "I didn't realize jobs and trade and what makes America work would become important in the last few days."

A dozen times I listen to his talk, pen poised idly over paper. Nothing. Not a thought, not an image, not a quote. It takes me a while to figure out why this is, but then it strikes me: Bob Dole isn't running for president. The *concept* of Bob Dole is running. The man himself has subcontracted out all the dirty work to people who make their careers managing reality for politicians. That is why he is referring to himself in the third person. He isn't there, at least not in any meaningful sense. Every Dole speech leaves me feeling that a man like this runs for the presidency not because he thinks he should be president. He thinks no one else should be president, so it might as well be him.

Everything that I or any other citizen will discover about Bob Dole is discovered by accident. I stalk him through the snow at the world dogsledding championship and watch him meet and greet the pooches. A schoolgirl approaches him as he's about to leave and, after nabbing a photo, asks him if he's had fun. "You learn a lot out here campaigning," Dole says, motioning to a sled of twenty dogs. "They're all nice dogs, too. Not like the Congress." He thinks no one is listening. He said it just for the fun of it. I catch him in a back room before a speech to a Rotary Club. He thinks no one is looking. He checks out his reflection in the mirror furtively—his hair is sprayed and dyed—and then whips out of his pocket a tiny canister and squirts two quick blasts of breath spray into his mouth. A few years ago in an interview with *60 Minutes* he broke down in sobs while explaining that one of the consequences of his war wound is a reluctance to look at himself squarely in the mirror, which just goes to show that insistently not looking in the mirror is itself a form of vanity.

Still, I'll bet Dole is the guy in the race that people most want to like but can't quite figure out how to do it. Much as I loathe his approach to getting elected, I, too, want to like him. Every night after a day with Dole I return home and recall a pair of mental pictures that the day has badly blemished. The first is the one of Dole recuperating from his war wounds as described by the author Richard Ben Cramer: hanging from a pole by his bad right arm and trying to straighten it out until he was sweating and crying from the pain.

The second is a windy afternoon in June 1994 in a graveyard on the French coast, a few days after Dole says he realized he had to run for president one last time. I had traveled to Normandy on Clinton's plane to witness the D-Day celebrations, but about halfway through, the rawness of the thing killed any interest I had in trying to whip off some copy about it, and so I stopped being a journalist and just started watching. Just before Clinton addressed the veterans of the invasion, I found myself walking alone through the rows of white crosses until I reached a place where there was no one else but a pair of old soldiers. They seemed ancient, though, of course, they could not have been much older than Bob Dole. They were trembling and leaning on each other as they looked down on a cross, and at first I thought it was just from the strains of age. Then I saw the name and place on the cross: Stenson (I'll say) from Mississippi. The dates on the cross explained that the boy had died at the age of nineteen on the first day of the invasion. The old men wore name tags, too: Stenson from Mississippi. Two of three brothers had survived that day. They were crying without tears.

That's Dole, I would like to believe. He has the emotions, or at least you can sense them lurking inside him, but he has no idea how to give them proper expression. He is crying without tears. ∎

 Chapter 9

The Congress

Over the long term of American history, it is fair to conclude that Congress has lost political power to the executive branch. Since the New Deal, Congress has been forced to delegate more and more power to the federal bureaucracy, which has the expertise and resources to deal with the increasingly complex and diverse roles of the federal government. Since America's rise to power in international affairs after World War II, Congress has also lost power to what some observers have called the "imperial presidency."

Congress nevertheless remains the focal point of the American national government. Its power in domestic affairs remains paramount, and in recent years it has struggled to regain some of its lost power in foreign policy as well. No president can afford to ignore or slight Congress, especially its leadership, and no agency can afford to ignore or slight a congressional committee or subcommittee with jurisdiction over its affairs. Interest groups direct the lion's share of their energies toward Congress, and the media often take their cues from Congress as to what issues are worth considering. The federal courts, whatever else they do, must focus their energies in large part on interpreting congressional statutes. Presidents may propose, as the saying goes, but Congress disposes; and Congress retains the power to investigate wrongdoing in the executive branch, has final budgetary and taxing authority, has the power to confirm executive and judicial appointments, and, as Bill Clinton learned, has the power of impeachment as well.

Three themes dominate the diverse readings in this chapter. The first, and oldest, is the ongoing struggle for power between the legislative and executive branches. The separation of powers as conceived in 1787 did not resolve the division of authority between the two branches: the Framers deliberately created a system in which the two "political branches" would continually joust with each other for power (see Chapter 1).

Second, this chapter examines a critically important trend within the legislative branch: the resurgence of the power of the congressional leadership in recent years. The leadership's reassertion of power, combined with divided party control of Congress and the White House, has given rise to what the political scientist Barbara Sinclair calls "the new legislative process" (see selection 9.3), in which the old, textbook forms of lawmaking have given way to new, top-down approaches. Some have argued (see selection 9.4) that the power of the congressional leadership should be even stronger, making the American system of government more like the parliamentary systems typical around the globe.

Finally, at the heart of this chapter is a question about the nature of representative government in the United States. Although the Framers clearly wanted congressmen to "refine and filter" the public's views (see *Federalist* No. 10, selection 1.1), members of Congress have always considered themselves "local men, locally minded, whose business began and ended with the interests of their constituency."* This tension between the local interest and the national interest, and between the will of their constituents and their own view of the public interest, remains a problem for members of Congress even today. The Federalists' thoughts on these matters are presented in selections 9.1 and 9.2, and the problem of representation as it relates to women in Congress is explored in selection 9.5.

Chapter Questions

1. Review the Federalists' conception of the separation of powers (selections 1.2 through 1.4). In what ways does the operation of the modern Congress underscore the Framers' belief that "ambition must be made to counteract ambition"? What evidence is there in the readings in this chapter to suggest that Congress plays an active role in the administrative process and that the president plays an active role in the legislative process? The readings in Chapter 10 (The Presidency) may cast light on these questions as well.
2. In what ways has the congressional leadership become stronger in recent years? What are the implications of this trend?
3. What roles do members of Congress play? How do these roles conflict with one another? How do members of Congress seek to balance their own goals, their constituents' interests, and the public or national interest?

 Foundations

The Federalists' view of representation was twofold. Representatives were expected not only to represent their constituents' interests but also to "refine and enlarge the public views, by passing them through the medium of a chosen body of citizens, whose wisdom may best discern the true interest of their country and whose patriotism and love of justice will be least likely to sacrifice it to temporary or partial considerations" (*Federalist* No. 10; see selection 1.1). Congress was expected to be a deliberative body that would think about and consider public questions and resolve them in the public interest. Thus, the Framers made the connection between congressmen and their constituents close but not too close: elections were to be held every two years, not every year, despite the popular eighteenth-century slogan that "when annual election ends, tyranny begins." Senators were to be elected every six years, and by the state legislatures, not by the people directly.

---

*Bernard Bailyn, *The Ideological Origins of the American Revolution* (Cambridge: Belknap Press of Harvard University Press, 1967), p. 162.

The Framers' views on representation and on Congress's role as the primary decision-making body, at least in matters of domestic policy, form the background for this chapter. *Federalist* No. 55, written by James Madison, defends the small size of the original Congress (only sixty-five members) as a way of securing "the benefits of free consultation and discussion." Moreover, the Framers thought, a small House would encourage representatives to think of the national interest instead of the local interest when they voted on public questions. On the other hand, as *Federalist* No. 57 points out, the Framers believed the members of Congress would still be close to their constituents and would still faithfully represent their interests in the federal capital.

Questions

1. What does Madison mean when he writes, "Had every Athenian citizen been a Socrates, every Athenian assembly would still have been a mob"?
2. How might a member of Congress seek to balance his or her role as the representative of a local district with the sometimes conflicting role of acting in the interest of the entire nation?

9.1 *Federalist* No. 55 (1788)

James Madison

Outline

I. Critics' objections to the relatively small size of the House of Representatives (sixty-five members).

II. Madison's response.

    A. General remarks on the problem of size of legislatures.

    B. Specific remarks on the U.S. House of Representatives.

        1. Size of House will increase as population increases.

        2. Size of House is not dangerous to the public liberty.

The number of which the House of Representatives is to consist forms another and a very interesting point of view under which this branch of the federal legislature may be contemplated. Scarce any article, indeed, in the whole Constitution seems to be rendered more worthy of attention by the weight of character and the apparent force of argument with which it has been assailed. The charges exhibited against it are, first, that so small a number of representatives will be an unsafe depositary of the public interests; second, that they will not possess a proper knowledge of the local circumstances of their numerous constituents; third, that they will be taken from that class of citizens which will sympathize least with the feelings of the mass of the people and be most likely to aim at a permanent elevation of the few on the depression of the many; fourth, that defective as the number will be in the first instance, it will be more and more disproportionate, by the increase of the people and the obstacles which will prevent a correspondent increase of the representatives.

In general it may be remarked on this subject that no political problem is less susceptible of a precise solution than that which relates to the number most convenient for a representative legislature; nor is there any point on which the policy of the several States is more at variance, whether we compare their legislative assemblies directly with each other, or consider the proportions which they respectively bear to the number of their constituents. Passing over the difference between the smallest and largest States, as Delaware, whose most numerous branch consists of twenty-one representatives, and Massachusetts, where it amounts to between three and four hundred, a very considerable difference is observable among States nearly equal in population. The number of representatives in Pennsylvania is not more than one fifth of that in the State last mentioned. New York, whose population is to that of South Carolina as six to five, has little more than one third of the number of representatives. As great a disparity prevails between the States of Georgia and Delaware or Rhode Island. In Pennsylvania, the representatives do not bear a greater proportion to their constituents than of one for every four or five thousand. In Rhode Island, they bear a proportion of at least one for every thousand. And according to the constitution of Georgia, the proportion may be carried to one to every ten electors; and must unavoidably far exceed the proportion in any of the other states.

Another general remark to be made is that the ratio between the representatives and the people ought not to be the same where the latter are very numerous as where they are very few. Were the representatives in Virginia to be regulated by the standard in Rhode Island, they would, at this time, amount to between four and five hundred; and twenty or thirty years hence, to a thousand. On the other hand, the ratio of Pennsylvania, if applied to the State of Delaware, would reduce the representative assembly of the latter to seven or eight members. Nothing can be more fallacious than to found our political calculations on arithmetical principles. Sixty or seventy men may be more properly trusted with a given degree of power than six or seven. But it does not follow that six or seven hundred would be proportionably a better depositary. And if we carry on the supposition to six or seven thousand, the whole reasoning ought to be reversed. The truth is that in all cases a certain number at least seems to be necessary to secure the benefits of free consultation and discussion, and to guard against too easy a combination for improper purposes; as, on the other hand, the number ought at most to be kept within a certain limit, in order to avoid the confusion and intemperance of a multitude. In all very numerous assemblies, of whatever characters composed, passion never fails to wrest the scepter from reason. Had every Athenian citizen been a Socrates, every Athenian assembly would still have been a mob.

It is necessary also to recollect here the observations which were applied to the case of biennial elections. For the same reason that the limited powers of the Congress, and the control of the State legislatures, justify less frequent election than the public safety might otherwise require, the members of the Congress need be less numerous than if they possessed the whole power of legislation, and were under no other than the ordinary restraints of other legislative bodies.

With these general ideas in our minds, let us weigh the objections which have been stated against the number of members proposed for the House of Representatives. It is said, in the first place, that so small a number cannot be safely trusted with so much power.

The number of which this branch of the legislature is to consist, at the outset of the government, will be sixty-five. Within three years a census is to be taken, when the number may be augmented to one for every thirty thousand inhabitants; and within every successive period of ten years the census is to be renewed, and augmentations may continue to be made under the above limitations. It will not be thought an extravagant conjecture that the first census will, at the rate of one for every thirty thousand, raise the number of representatives to at least one hundred. Estimating the Negroes in the proportion of three fifths, it can scarcely be doubted that the population of the United States will by that time, if it does not already, amount to three millions. At the expiration of twenty-five years, according to the computed rate of increase, the number of representatives will amount to two hundred; and of fifty years, to four hundred. This is a number which, I presume will put an end to all fears arising from the smallness of the body. I take for granted here what I shall, in answering the fourth objection, hereafter show, that the number of representatives will be augmented from time to time in the manner provided by the Constitution. On a contrary supposition, I should admit the objection to have very great weight indeed.

The true question to be decided, then, is whether the smallness of the number, as a temporary regulation, be dangerous to the public liberty? Whether sixty-five members for a few years, and a hundred or two hundred for a few more, be a safe depositary for a limited and well-guarded power of legislating for the United States? I must own that I could not give a negative answer to this question, without first obliterating every impression which I have received with regard to the present genius of the people of America, the spirit which actuates the State legislatures, and the principles which are incorporated with the political character of every class of citizens. I am unable to conceive that the people of America, in their present temper, or under any circumstances which can speedily happen, will choose, and every second year repeat the choice of, sixty-five or a hundred men who would be disposed to form and pursue a scheme of tyranny or treachery. I am unable to conceive that the State legislatures, which must feel so many motives to watch and which possess so many means of counteracting the federal legislature, would fail either to detect or to defeat a conspiracy of the latter against the liberties of their common constituents. I am equally unable to conceive that there are at this time, or can be in any short time, in the United States, any sixty-five or a hundred men capable of recommending themselves to the choice of the people at large, who would either desire or dare, within the short space of two years, to betray the solemn trust committed to them. What change of circumstances time, and a fuller population of our country may produce requires a prophetic spirit to declare, which makes no part of my pretensions. But judging from the circumstances now before us, and from the probable state of them within a moderate period of time, I must pronounce that the liberties of America cannot be unsafe in the number of hands proposed by the federal Constitution. . . .

As there is a degree of depravity in mankind which requires a certain degree of circumspection and distrust, so there are other qualities in human nature which justify a certain portion of esteem and confidence. Republican government presupposes the existence of these qualities in a higher degree than any other form. Were the pictures which have been drawn by the political jealousy of some among us faithful likenesses of the human character, the inference would be that there is not sufficient virtue among men for self-government; and that nothing less than the chains of despotism can restrain them from destroying and devouring one another. ■

9.2　*Federalist* No. 57 (1788)

James Madison

Outline

I. Madison's responses to the charge that the members of the House of Representatives will not have sympathy with the common people.

  A. Members of the House will be elected by the people.

  B. Every citizen of the appropriate age will be eligible for election to the House.

  C. For several reasons, the representatives will remain loyal to their constituents.

    1. In general, representatives will be men of high character.

    2. They will show gratitude and affection for those who elected them.

    3. They will be attached to representative government out of pride and vanity.

    4. They will be subject to frequent elections.

    5. Their constituents will insist they subject themselves to every law they make.

The *third* charge against the House of Representatives is that it will be taken from that class of citizens which will have least sympathy with the mass of the people, and be most likely to aim at an ambitious sacrifice of the many to the aggrandizement of the few.

Of all the objections which have been framed against the federal Constitution, this is perhaps the most extraordinary. Whilst the objection itself is leveled against a pretended oligarchy, the principle of it strikes at the very root of republican government.

The aim of every political constitution is, or ought to be, first to obtain for rulers men who possess most wisdom to discern, and most virtue to pursue, the common good of the society; and in the next place, to take the most effectual precautions for keeping them virtuous whilst they continue to hold their public trust. The elective mode of obtaining rulers is the characteristic policy of republican government. The means relied on in this form of government for preventing their degeneracy are numerous and various. The most effectual one is such a limitation of the term of appointments as will maintain a proper responsibility to the people.

Let me now ask what circumstance there is in the constitution of the House of Representatives that violates the principles of republican government, or favors the elevation of the few on the ruins of the many? Let me ask whether every circumstance is not, on the contrary, strictly conformable to these principles, and scrupulously impartial to the rights and pretensions of every class and description of citizens?

Who are to be the electors of the federal representatives? Not the rich, more than the poor; not the learned, more than the ignorant; not the haughty heirs of distinguished names, more than the humble sons of obscure and unpropitious fortune. The electors are to be the great body of the people of the United States. They are to be the same who exercise the right in every State of electing the corresponding branch of the legislature of the State.

Who are to be the objects of popular choice? Every citizen whose merit may recommend him to the esteem and confidence of his country. No qualification of wealth, of birth, of religious faith, or of civil profession is permitted to fetter the judgment or disappoint the inclination of the people.

If we consider the situation of the men on whom the free suffrages of their fellow-citizens may confer the representative trust, we shall find it involving every security which can be devised or desired for their fidelity to their constituents.

In the first place, as they will have been distinguished by the preference of their fellow citizens, we are to presume that in general they will be somewhat distinguished also by those qualities which entitle them to it, and which promise a sincere and scrupulous regard to the nature of their engagements.

In the second place, they will enter into the public service under circumstances which cannot fail to produce a temporary affection at least to their constituents. There is in every breast a sensibility to marks of honor, of favor, of esteem, and of confidence, which, apart from all considerations of interests, is some pledge for grateful and benevolent returns. Ingratitude is a common topic of declamation against human nature; and it must be confessed that instances of it are but too frequent and flagrant, both in public and in private life. But the universal and extreme indignation which it inspires is itself a proof of the energy and prevalence of the contrary sentiment.

In the third place, those ties which bind the representative to his constituents are strengthened by motives of a more selfish nature. His pride and vanity attach him to a form of government which favors his pretensions and gives him a share in its honors and distinctions. Whatever hopes or projects might be entertained by a few aspiring characters, it must generally happen that a great proportion of the men deriving their advancement from their influence with the people would have more to hope from a preservation of the favor than from innovations in the government subversive of the authority of the people.

All these securities, however, would be found very insufficient without the restraint of frequent elections. Hence, in the fourth place, the House of Representatives is so constituted as to support in the members an habitual recollection of their dependence on the people. Before the sentiments impressed on their minds by the mode of their elevation can be effaced by the exercise of power, they will be compelled to anticipate the moment when their power is to cease, when their exercise of it is to be reviewed, and when they must descend to the level from which they were raised; there forever to remain unless a faithful discharge of their trust shall have established their title to a renewal of it.

I will add, as a fifth circumstance in the situation of the House of Representatives, restraining them from oppressive measures, that they can make no law which will not have its full operation on themselves and their friends, as well as on the great mass of the society. This has always been deemed one of the strongest bonds by which human policy can connect the rulers and the people together. It creates between them that communion of interests and sympathy of sentiments of which few governments have furnished examples; but without which every government degenerates into tyranny. If it be asked, what is to restrain the House of Representatives from making legal discriminations in favor of themselves and a particular class of society? I answer: the genius of the whole system; the nature of just and constitutional laws; and, above all, the vigilant and manly spirit which actuates the people of America—a spirit which nourishes freedom, and in return is nourished by it.

If this spirit shall ever be so far debased as to tolerate a law not obligatory on the legislature, as well as on the people, the people will be prepared to tolerate anything but liberty.

Such will be the relation between the House of Representatives and their constituents. Duty, gratitude, interest, ambition itself, are the cords by which they will be bound to fidelity and sympathy with the great mass of the people. It is possible that these may all be insufficient to control the caprice and wickedness of men. But are they not all that government will admit, and that human prudence can devise? Are they not the genuine and the characteristic means by which republican government provides for the liberty and happiness of the people? . . . ■

 # American Politics Today

Most American government students must learn the basics of how a bill becomes a law in the United States Congress. First, the bill must be introduced in both the House and Senate. Then the bill is referred to the relevant committee in each house, which holds hearings and makes whatever changes it deems necessary. Then the bill is sent back to the full House and Senate, which conduct floor debates and consider formal amendments. If the bill clears both houses, it may be sent to a conference committee to work out minor differences, before being sent back to the House and Senate for final approval. Finally, the bill is sent to the president for signature or veto.

For better or worse, as the political scientist Barbara Sinclair explains, this traditional model is rarely followed in the modern Congress. Bills are frequently sent to more than one committee; multiple bills are often combined into large, "omnibus" legislation covering a wide range of subjects; and bills are often rewritten at every stage in the process after informal negotiations among congressional leaders and between Congress and the White House. This "new legislative process," as Sinclair describes it, is partly a consequence of divided government (in which Congress and the White House are controlled by different political parties). The new legislative process was also made possible by the strengthening of the congressional leadership in the 1980s and 1990s and, in turn, has helped to make the leadership even more powerful.

Questions

1. What are some of the characteristics of the "new legislative process," according to Sinclair? How does the new legislative process differ from the traditional legislative process?
2. What are the implications of the new legislative process for the role of individual legislators? For committee and subcommittee government? For the relationship between Congress and the White House? For representative government in the United States?
3. How do the House and Senate differ in terms of the "new legislative process"? What accounts for these differences between the two houses of Congress?

9.3 Party Leaders and the New Legislative Process (1997)

Barbara Sinclair

As 1995 drew to a close, President Bill Clinton, Speaker of the House Newt Gingrich, and Senate Majority Leader Bob Dole sat face-to-face attempting to negotiate a comprehensive budget agreement, a task that entailed making a host of major changes in policy. That this mode of policy making did not strike Americans as particularly out of the ordinary indicates just how much the legislative process has changed in recent years. Although it received less media attention, the legislative process on the budget bill in the months before the summit talks was also far from what would have been considered normal only a few years ago. In both chambers a large number of committees had a hand in drafting the legislation, and the resulting bill was an enormous omnibus measure. In the House, floor procedure was tailored especially to the specific problems this bill raised, and in both chambers majority party leaders were intensely involved throughout the process.

As this example suggests, the how-a-bill-becomes-a-law diagram that is a staple of American government textbooks in reality describes the legislative process on fewer and fewer of the major measures Congress considers. Rather than being sent to one committee in each chamber, a measure may be considered by several

---

Barbara Sinclair, "Party Leaders and the New Legislative Process," in Lawrence C. Dodd and Bruce I. Oppenheimer, eds., *Congress Reconsidered*, Sixth Edition, (Washington, DC: CQ Press, 1997), pp. 229, 232, 234–236, 240–244. Reprinted by permission of the Congressional Quarterly.

committees, and some measures bypass committees altogether. In addition, after a bill has been reported, but before it reaches the floor, substantive changes are often worked out via informal processes. Omnibus measures of great scope are a regular part of the legislative scene, and formal executive-congressional summits to work out deals on legislation are no longer considered extraordinary. On the House floor, most major legislation is considered under complex and usually restrictive rules, often tailored to deal with problems specific to that bill. In the Senate, bills are regularly subject to large numbers of not necessarily germane floor amendments, and filibuster threats are an everyday fact of life, affecting all aspects of the legislative process and making cloture votes a routine part of the process.

• • •

Omnibus Legislation, the Budget Process, and Summits

Omnibus legislation—bills with great substantive scope often involving, directly or indirectly, many committees—is now a regular part of the congressional agenda. Such measures increased as a proportion of the congressional agenda of major legislation from zero in the 91st Congress (1969–1970) to 8 percent in the 94th (1975–1976)—all budget resolutions—to 20 percent in the 97th (1981–1982) and 100th (1987–1988). In the Congresses of the 1990s, omnibus measures made up about 11 percent of major measures.

Some omnibus measures are the result of the 1974 budget act. The act requires an annual budget resolution and, in the 1980s and 1990s, the budget resolution often called for a reconciliation bill. Beyond that, the decision to package legislation into an omnibus measure is discretionary, and it is principally the majority party leadership that decides. Measures may be packaged into an omnibus bill for several reasons: to pass unpalatable but necessary legislation; to force the president to accept legislative provisions that, were they sent to him in freestanding form, he would veto; or to raise the visibility of popular legislation and garner partisan credit. During the Reagan and Bush administrations, for example, House Democratic leaders packaged legislation on issues such as trade and drugs into high-profile omnibus measures to compete with the White House for media attention and public credit and to protect favored provisions from a veto. During the 103d Congress, congressional leaders did not need to pressure President Clinton into signing their legislation, but the usefulness of omnibus measures for enacting tough bills or for raising the visibility of popular measures led to their continued use. A number of modest provisions were packaged into a big anticrime bill, and omnibus budget measures were used to pass Clinton's economic program.

• • •

New Processes and Procedures as Leadership Tools in the House

Traditionally, the legislative process would begin with the referral of a bill to a single committee, which would be largely responsible for its fate. In 1995 the Republicans' bill to abolish the Commerce Department was referred to eleven House committees. Although the number of committees was unusual, the fact that more than one committee was involved was not. In the contemporary House about one bill in five is referred to more than one committee. Major legislation is even more likely to be sent to several committees; between 1987 and 1995, about a third was.

Multiple referral of legislation was not possible before 1975, when the House passed a rule providing for it. The new rule came about for two reasons: the House's inability to realign outdated committee jurisdictions and reform-minded members' desire to increase opportunities for broad participation in the legislative process. The rule was amended in 1977 to give the Speaker the power to set deadlines for committees to report legislation. As revised in 1995, the rule directs the Speaker to designate a lead committee with the most responsibility for the legislation; once that committee has reported, the other committees are required to report under fairly strict deadlines.

For the Speaker, the frequency with which major legislation is multiply referred presents opportunities, but also problems. One problem is that when legislation is referred to several committees, the number of people who must come to agreement is multiplied, complicating and slowing down the legislative process. Often, multiple referral forces the Speaker to be the jurisdictional and substantive mediator, a role that brings with it influence as well as headaches. On contentious legislation, the leaders of the several committees involved may not be able to work out their differences without help. If the party leaders have to get involved, they gain influence over the substance of the legislation. Furthermore, when several committees work on the same piece of legislation, the committee process is more open to influence by party leaders; no one committee can consider such a bill its private business. Multiple referral also gives the Speaker the opportunity to set time limits for the reporting out of legislation. During the first one hundred days of the 104th Congress, when the new Republican majority was attempting to bring all the items in the Contract with America to the floor, that power gave added weight to Speaker Gingrich's stringent informal deadlines.

Although legislation is routinely considered by more than one committee, sometimes bills bypass committee consideration altogether. Skipping committee review was a rare occurrence before the 1980s; for example, in 1969 and 1970 and in 1975 and 1976, committees were bypassed on only 2 percent of the major legislation. By the late 1980s, however, almost 20 percent of major measures were never considered by a committee in the House. The frequency dropped to 6 percent in the 103d Congress; it then rose to 11 percent in 1995, but, as we shall see, that relatively low rate is somewhat misleading.

• • •

This method of passing legislation is a radical change from the way things used to be done. In the prereform House, autonomous committees crafted legislation behind closed doors and usually passed it unchanged on the floor with little help from the party leadership. As a matter of fact, party leadership intrusion into the legislative process on matters of substance was considered illegitimate. As House members became less willing to defer to committees and more willing to question committee bills on the floor, as multiple referral destroyed committees' monopoly over legislation in their area of jurisdiction, and as the political climate became harsher and the political stakes higher, committees became less capable of crafting legislation that could pass the chamber without help. In responding to their members' demands for assistance, majority party leaders were drawn more deeply into the substantive aspects of the legislative process and, in effect, changed how the process works. Now party leaders often involve themselves well before legislation is reported from committee.

Moreover, party leaders frequently take a role in working out substantive adjustments to legislation *after* it has been reported from committee. In the prereform 91st Congress, no major legislation was subject to such postcommittee adjustments; in the 94th, 4 percent was—all budget resolutions. In the early 1980s, the frequency jumped to almost one major measure in four and, in the late 1980s and early 1990s, averaged a little more than one in three. In 1995 almost half of major measures underwent some sort of postcommittee adjustment.

• • •

The Triumph of Individualism and the New Legislative Process in the Senate

The contemporary legislative process in the Senate is shaped by senators' rampant individualism and their leaders' attempts to do their jobs within that context. Senators now routinely exploit the enormous prerogatives Senate rules give the individual to further their own agendas.

In an institutional setting where every member is able—and often willing—to impede the legislative process, leaders must accommodate individual members to legislate successfully. The increase in postcommittee adjustments to legislation in the Senate reflects this accommodation. Rare in the 1970s even on major legislation—only 2 percent of major measures underwent postcommittee adjustments in the 91st and 94th Congresses—the frequency jumped to about 20 percent in the 1980s and then to more than 33 percent in the early 1990s. In 1995 more than 60 percent of major legislation was subject to postcommittee adjustments. Although the negotiations that produce these modifications are sometimes undertaken by committee leaders or other interested senators, the party leaders often become involved.

Senate individualism is most evident on the floor. Senators can use their power to offer as many amendments as they choose to almost any bill, not only to further their policy preferences but also to bring up issues leaders might like to keep off the floor, to make political points, and to force their political opponents in the chamber to cast tough votes. Senators regularly use their amending prerogatives for all these purposes. Because, in most cases, amendments need not be germane, Barbara Boxer, D-Calif., was able to force onto the floor the issue of holding open hearings on the sexual harassment charges against Bob Packwood, R-Ore., even though Majority Leader Dole wanted to keep it off. Boxer offered it as an amendment to a defense authorization bill. For years, Jesse Helms, R-N.C., has been bringing up and forcing votes on amendments on hot button issues such as abortion, pornography, homosexuality, and school prayer. He often does not expect to win, but to provide ammunition for the electoral opponents of senators who disagree with him.

• • •

Given senators' willingness to exploit their right of extended debate, the majority leader, in scheduling legislation and often in crafting it, has little choice but to be responsive to small groups of members or even to individuals. On legislation of secondary importance, before a recess, or late in the session, one senator's objection will suffice to keep a bill off the floor. When a great deal of legislation is awaiting floor consideration, the majority leader cannot afford the time for a filibuster, so even an ambiguous threat to filibuster serves as a veto. This reality has become semi-institutionalized in the practice of holds. Any senator can inform the leader that he or she wishes to place a hold on a measure—a bill, a presidential nomination, or a treaty. Leaders assert that use of this device only guarantees that the senator will be informed before the measure is scheduled for floor consideration; however, if the hold represents a veiled threat to filibuster the measure and if other matters are more pressing, it often constitutes a de facto veto.

The mere threat to filibuster is often sufficient to extract concessions from the supporters of a measure. A number of the Contract with America items that sped through the House were held up in the Senate until their supporters made significant compromises—for example, a bill to impose a moratorium on all new regulations was transformed, under a filibuster threat, into a measure giving Congress forty-five days to review new regulations. In the 103d Congress a number of Clinton's priorities also ran into troubles in the Senate, not because they lacked the support of a majority but because the sixty votes to cut off debate could not be amassed. Supporters had to make concessions on national service legislation and the voter registration bill (motor voter), for example, to overcome a filibuster or a filibuster threat.

Sometimes a large minority defeats outright legislation supported by a majority. Clinton's stimulus package succumbed to this fate in 1993. Senate Majority Leader George Mitchell, D-Maine, attempted to invoke cloture a number of times, but, even though majorities supported cutting off debate, he was not able to put together the necessary sixty votes. In 1995 Senate Democrats forced Majority Leader Dole to abandon his own bill overhauling federal regulatory procedures; he mustered a majority on several cloture votes but fell short of the sixty needed. In the 103d Congress, of nineteen major measures that failed to become law, twelve were killed by the Senate alone; eight of those ran into filibuster-related problems.

The majority leader's leverage depends not on procedural powers, of which he has few, but on his central position in the chamber; on really difficult and contentious issues, he has a better chance than anyone else in the chamber of negotiating a deal that can get the necessary votes. Consequently his leverage is dependent on senators wanting legislation, but if a substantial minority prefers no legislation to a deal, he has little recourse.

New Legislative Processes: An Assessment

By the end of the first hundred days of the 104th Congress, the House had voted on every measure in the Contract with America, as Republicans had promised, and had passed all but the term limits constitutional amendment, which required a two-thirds vote. In the Senate only five measures—some parts of the preface and of two of the ten planks of the contract—had reached the floor, and only four, mostly relatively uncontroversial measures, had passed. By the end of 1995 just five contract items had become law.

The contract items fared differently in the House and Senate in part because the distribution of preferences differed in the two chambers: moderates made up a larger proportion of the Senate Republican membership than of the House Republican membership, and Senate Republicans had not endorsed the contract. Even more important, however, are the differences in chamber rules and in the tools leaders have available. In the House many of the modifications and innovations in the legislative process allow the party leadership to tailor the process to the problems a particular measure raises and use them to get the measure passed. In the Senate changes in the legislative process have created more problems than opportunities for the majority party leadership.

A brief examination of the legislative process on welfare reform, one of the major contract items, illustrates the differences. In the House three committees—Ways and Means, Education and Economic Opportunity, and Agriculture—reported their provisions by early March. Under strict instructions from the party leadership, Republican committee chairs had pushed the measures through their committees with limited debate and on largely party line votes. The leadership then combined the provisions from the three committees, making alterations where they seemed advisable. The bill was brought to the floor under a tight rule barring votes on several amendments that would have split Republicans. Pro-life Republicans, who feared that provisions cutting off benefits to teenage unwed mothers would encourage abortions, were denied a chance to offer amendments deleting such provisions. The rule was narrowly approved, and the bill passed on a 234–199 party line vote.

The Senate Finance Committee did not report a bill until May 26. Problems within the majority party quickly became apparent: Republicans from the South and Southwest, who represent fast-growing states that offer relatively low welfare benefits, objected to funding formulas based on past welfare expenditures; some conservative senators decried the dropping of House provisions barring unwed teenage mothers from receiving welfare; and Republican moderates believed the legislation did not provide enough money for child care and would allow states to cut their own welfare spending too much.

Because of the saliency and hot-button character of the issue, no one, including most Democrats, wanted to vote against a welfare reform bill, and, had the Republican leadership been able to force an up-or-down vote, the committee bill might well have passed. But because Dole had no way of protecting the legislation from a filibuster or a barrage of amendments on the floor, he had to deal. He, along with Finance Committee Chairman Packwood, took on the task of rewriting the bill. In early August, after several months of negotiations, Dole unveiled a revised bill aimed at satisfying the various factions. The new proposal was a modified version of the Finance Committee bill and incorporated in revised form three other pieces of legislation—the food stamps overhaul from the Agriculture Committee and the child care and job training bills approved by the Labor and Human Resources Committee. Adding these provisions provided a greater scope for compromise.

Floor debate began August 7, and it soon became evident that problems still existed and the bill would not pass before the scheduled recess. Republicans blamed the Democrats, charging that they intended to offer fifty amendments. In fact, the GOP was still split. On September 6, after the recess, Dole brought the bill back to the floor, but he still lacked a secure winning coalition and continued to make changes to placate various groups of Republicans. He began talking with Democrats and moderate Republicans, and on September 15 a compromise was reached; among other provisions, it added substantial funds for child care. On September 19 Dole offered for himself and the minority leader the Dole-Daschle amendment, which incorporated the compromise, and it passed, 87–12, with mostly hardline conservative Republicans opposed. Acceptance of the amendment moderated the Senate welfare bill, which was already more moderate than the House bill. The Senate passed the bill as amended 87 to 12, with only one Republican voting in opposition.

In the House, then, the new legislative process has on balance provided the majority party leadership with effective tools for facilitating the passage of legislation. Backed by a reasonably cohesive majority party, House leaders can engineer passage of legislation quickly and in a form consonant with the preferences of the members of the majority party. In the Senate, as in the House, the party leadership has become more central to the legislative process, but, unlike the Speaker, the Senate majority leader has gained few new tools for dealing with a more unruly membership. The need to accommodate most senators and to build supermajority coalitions to pass legislation in the Senate almost always means the process is slower and often results in more broadly based (or weakening) compromises. Sometimes, it results in no legislation at all. In the contemporary Congress, the legislative process in the two chambers is more distinct in form and in results than ever before. ■

The Comparative Context

In sharp contrast to the United States, most modern democracies operate under *parliamentary* systems of government. In a parliamentary system, the legislative and executive branches are fused, not separated, and the leader of the legislative branch (usually known as the prime minister) also functions as chief executive. Moreover, in such systems the two branches are typically controlled by a single political party, or coalition of parties, and party leaders can expect, and enforce, loyalty from their troops.

The American system of government, of course, is different in all respects. Congress and the White House are independent by constitutional design and, in modern times, are often controlled by different political parties. Congressional leaders, though stronger than they were twenty-five years ago, still cannot compel or count on the unswerving loyalty of their rank-and-file members.

Throughout American history, many political leaders and political scientists have argued that the American system is inferior to the parliamentary system and that the United States should move, more or less radically, in the parliamentary direction. In particular, these would-be reformers argue, a parliamentary system allows the government to act more efficiently and facilitates majority rule. In this essay, the political scientist Leon D. Epstein explains the differences between the two systems of government and analyzes the validity of the reformist arguments. In the end, he suggests, the American system is deeply grounded in American political culture and is thus highly resistant to change.

Questions

1. What are the key differences between the American system of government and most parliamentary systems? What are the advantages and disadvantages of each system?
2. What aspects of American political culture reinforce Americans' commitment to the current system and create resistance to proposals that would make the American system more like most parliamentary systems?

9.4 Changing Perceptions of the British System (1994)

Leon D. Epstein

Since the development of their academic discipline over a century ago, American political scientists have treated British parliamentary democracy as a benchmark in evaluating the American system. For almost half of that century, it is distressing for me to realize, I have tried to contribute to that comparative enterprise. Now I hope only to refurbish previously stated views by taking into account recent political experience and selected scholarly interpretations of that experience. My perspective combines respect for the British political system with a disbelief in the suitability of its parliamentary institutions for the United States. As a corollary, I treat the separation of executive and legislative powers as workable, if not ideal. It is so central in the American system that its drastic transformation, as distinct from marginal changes in its practice, is inconceivable in circumstances short of a catastrophic breakdown of the system itself. These views are hardly unusual. They are at odds only with a scholarly minority that has long advocated American adaptations of British parliamentary government.

Although I should like to think that my views are the product of research and scholarly contemplation, they surely owe something to the place and time of my political education. Wisconsin, where I lived and studied even before World War II, was not an Anglophile stronghold, and I encountered none of the admirers of the British system who reputedly populated academic institutions elsewhere. More importantly, my earliest and presumably formative political engagement was in the 1930s, when the American system appeared successfully responsive to New Deal policies. Later, I learned to appreciate British democracy first by observing it

---

Leon D. Epstein, "Changing Perceptions of the British System," *Political Science Quarterly* 109 (Special Issue, 1994), pp. 483–497. Reprinted with the permission of The Academy of Political Science.

during World War II and then by academically pursuing the subject. But even as I sought to become a British politics specialist, I retained research and teaching interests in American politics. No doubt, the Americanist mark will be recognizable in this article's first two sections on the nature and recent operation of the British political system, and especially plain in the third and concluding section on proposed solutions to American institutional problems.

The Nature of the Model

"British parliamentary democracy" and "British political system" are terms that distinguish a particular version of fused executive and legislative authority from the several other versions of parliamentary government in the universe of democratic nations. "Westminster model" is similarly useful. To be sure, the model resembles other versions of parliamentary government in that any fusion of executive and legislative authority stands in broad contrast to the American separation of powers. But fusion alone is not what principally inspires admiration among American political scientists. It is Britain's strong and stable government by the leadership of a single cohesive party holding a majority of seats in a virtually omnipotent parliamentary body. Peace-time deviations from this pattern have been brief and exceptional in Britain, while the pattern itself has been uncharacteristic of most other European parliamentary democracies. I refer not to checks in some of those nations through effective second chambers and judicial review; the importance of their absence in Britain will be noted later. Here, I am thinking of the typical continental multipartism that makes coalition governments normal practice. Such governments often endure from one election to the next, as do the German but not the Italian. Nevertheless, they usually lack the prized virtue of the British model: one party's full responsibility for governmental policy. Responsibility, in this sense, is what first prompted American admiration of British parliamentary government. The admiration has been sustained, indeed strengthened, as party majorities in the House of Commons became more durable than in Walter Bagehot's day, now ordinarily ensuring a government's tenure between general elections and thus making a government more directly responsible to the electorate.

Britain's majority-party government is as readily associated with single-member, simple-plurality (first-past-the-post) elections as continental European multiparty parliaments are with proportional representation. Neither kind of election, to be sure, guarantees the results with which it is associated; but no one doubts that Britain's first-past-the-post arrangement has returned a majority parliamentary party much more often than would the well known alternative arrangements. Only in one of the fourteen general elections between 1945 and 1992 did it fail to do so. Yet, in none of those fourteen elections did the majority party poll even half of the total national vote for its parliamentary candidates, and in several elections its share was either a little below or a little above two-fifths. Accordingly, first-past-the-post election, or something like it, looks like an essential element of British majority-party government. Perhaps for some Americans observing the British system, first-past-the-post election commands little attention, because unlike many other British institutional practices, it is also an American method. Despite interesting variations, American partisan legislative elections are most often decided by simple pluralities in single-member districts. On this score, transplanting the Westminster model to the United States requires no change. The situation is very different for other significant institutional practices associated with that model.

Start with the organizational roles of political parties. British parliamentary party cohesion is undoubtedly salient for Americans frustrated by notoriously less unified congressional parties. The cohesion is not absolutely uniform; occasionally, dissidents do vote against their party positions, and more exceptionally, revolts are substantial enough to force the leadership of a governing majority party to retreat from a policy position either before or after a parliamentary defeat. After a single such defeat, a government does not really have to resign as long as its majority support is renewed in a specifically labeled vote of confidence as well as in subsequent policy votes. The renewal of support occurs because parliamentary cohesion remains the norm, for the majority party and also for its principal opposition, even though rebellions are more frequent and more serious in certain periods than in others. In this respect, British party behavior so nearly resembles that in other parliamentary regimes that one looks to governmental structure to explain the contrast to American practice. Although members of the U.S. Congress most often find it useful to vote with their parties, their incentives to do so regularly or almost uniformly are modest relative to those of parliamentary members whose support is necessary for their party leaders to retain executive offices and for members themselves to avoid the risk of an untimely election campaign.

The structure of parliamentary government in Britain and elsewhere is associated not only with party cohesion in legislative matters but also with a greater party electoral role than American parties possess. British MPs, much more clearly than members of the U.S. Congress, are elected as supporters of their leaders. They are expected to be loyal partisans both by ordinary voters and, more critically, by the organized party members who choose the candidates to bear major-party labels in general elections. Candidate selection in Britain, however, is not highly centralized as it is in many continental European parties. Each British constituency party customarily selects its parliamentary candidate, subject only to national party rules, assistance, and occasional influence; but the procedure is as likely as a more centralized arrangement to produce reliable partisan candidates. Selection is the business of engaged activists in an organized dues-paying branch of the national party, and such activists tend to prefer a candidate who shares their strongly partisan commitment. The process, therefore, is radically different from the American direct primary in which a large portion of the electorate, with only tenuous party identification, bestows the party label.

Britain's more devotedly partisan selectors expect their candidate, if successfully elected with their considerable help, to support their cause and their national leader. The expectation is so customarily fulfilled that constituency parties seldom need to take measures against their sitting MPs. They may even tolerate occasional dissidents, especially those who are most remote from the opposition party and unthreatening to their own party's hold on office. Nevertheless, constituency parties have the power to deny reselection, and Labour in the 1980s made it easier to exercise that power. Conservative MPs also know that deselection is an ultimate sanction of their local party organization. It need not be much used in order for an MP to bear it in mind.

The greater role of the British party than of the American involves a kind of organization absent in the United States. A regularized dues-paying membership, though suffering currently diminished numbers, gives a degree of democratic legitimacy to candidate selection that we seldom attribute to America's more loosely bounded party organizations, for whose nominations we substitute direct primaries. Moreover, British parties are national as the American are not. Members, through constituency units, belong to a national party and not to any equivalent of American state parties.

In addition to the kind of parties I have described, other institutional elements distinguish British parliamentary government from the American system in ways that are also fundamental in understanding the assumed advantages of strong and responsible government. Power is truly centralized in the party commanding the House of Commons as well as the cabinet, because that fusion of legislative and executive branches is subject to virtually none of the effective checks of a kind that exist in many parliamentary regimes, as well as in the United States. With a unitary rather than a federal system and without a codified higher law constitution, a Commons majority produces legislation that is not subject to invalidation by judicial review in anything like the manner practiced by U.S. courts and in several other democratic nations. Insofar as individual rights are nonetheless protected, it is not by a judiciary's treatment of parliamentary enactments as violations of a Bill of Rights.

Nor is a second legislative chamber able to do more than delay for a limited time the will of a determined government backed by a majority in the Commons. The same can be said for the capacity of the opposition within the Commons to check that majority. This is not to say that opposition criticism in the Commons, or even in the House of Lords, is always of no effect. It has been known to cause a government to become less determined, especially in response to pressures in its own party ranks, and thus to compromise or abandon what turn out to be unpopular policies. But checks of this kind, real enough politically, are not formal institutional veto points.

All of this is familiar, I realize, but worth mentioning in order to emphasize that the British system is notably farther removed from the American than are other parliamentary systems—for example, the German and even the Canadian and Australian whose adaptations of the Westminster model add institutional checks absent in Britain itself. America's traditional cultural attachments to Britain must explain why its democratic system, so drastically different from that of the United States, serves as a model for American academic reformers.

• • •

A Model for the United States?

In speaking of Americans who look with favor on British parliamentary government, as Britons do not with respect to the American separation of executive and legislative powers, I have in mind only limited numbers, mainly in the academic community. We have every reason to assume that an overwhelming majority of Americans in and out of active politics prefer the system to which they are accustomed. That system prevails in each of the fifty states as in the national government, and it has so prevailed since the early days of the Republic when states began separately to elect governors and legislatures if they had not done so previously. No new state has fused executive and legislative authorities in the parliamentary pattern. Such fusion, though possibly subject to challenge in Congress when a state sought admission, would almost surely meet the vague standard of "a Republican Form of Government" guaranteed to each state by Section 4 of Article IV of the U.S. Constitution. The absence of even a single state's experiment with parliamentary government is strong evidence of American dedication to the separation of legislative and executive powers. For a political scientist, it is nonetheless regrettable that no state has tried parliamentary government and thus served as an experimental laboratory as have states in other respects. I know of no advocates of that experimentation. Nor is it discussed as a foreseeable result of an otherwise unfortunate Canadian break-up that would lead one or more provinces to become American states while persisting in their fusion of executive and legislative powers.

● ● ●

Interest . . . is persistently greater in the kind of reform that tries to achieve British-style party government without changing the Constitution. The principal suggestion is to strengthen American political parties mainly by efforts within parties themselves but also with the help of legislation newly favorable to party organizations. Under the rubric of responsible-party government, the advocacy has a hundred-year history and many distinguished academic supporters. Its most famous statement was published in 1950 as a report from a committee of the American Political Science Association.* Then, or on other occasions, proponents of responsible party government wanted to strengthen each of the two potential majority parties by promoting active programmatic memberships, midterm national conventions, closer links between presidential and congressional candidates, cohesive congressional caucuses reflecting national party policies, organizational membership influence in (if not control of) nominations, closed instead of open primaries if there are to be any primaries at all, freedom from burdensome state regulations, public funding of party campaigns, and higher legal limits on private funding of party campaign activities. Fulfilling the entire wish list might come close to establishing indirectly, almost by stealth, the equivalent of British parliamentary party government. So much seems as unrealistic as the straightforward constitutional changes. Both encounter the American political culture's resistance to majoritarian democracy of the British kind. ■

View from the Inside

Although women still make up only a tiny minority of the members of the United States Congress, their numbers, and influence, have been steadily growing. The biggest in-

---

*See selection 6.1.

crease came after the 1992 elections, which added twenty-eight new women members of Congress.

The "Year of the Woman," as 1992 became known, emboldened the women of Congress to push for new legislation guaranteeing every American the right to take an unpaid leave of absence from his or her job to care for a sick child or other family member. The struggle for the Family Leave bill, though ultimately successful, was not easy and provided many lessons for new and experienced members alike.

One of the new members of the Senate in 1993 was Patty Murray (D.-Wash.), who had both personal and political reasons to support the Family Leave bill. Here is her story.

Questions

1. What forces combined to convince Congress to pass the Family and Medical Leave Act? What does this episode suggest, if anything, about the nature and importance of diversity in the United States Congress?
2. According to the author of this selection, have women achieved equality with men in Capitol Hill? Why or why not?

9.5 Women on the Hill (1997)

Clara Bingham

In the Senate chamber on February 2, 1993, Patty Murray rose to make the second speech of her Senate career. Standing only five feet tall behind her shiny mahogany desk, Murray, the youngest woman ever elected to the Senate, looked more like a Senate page than a senator. She had been assigned to desk No. 62, a 174-year-old relic on the far left aisle, three rows above the Senate well. Sixteen years earlier, Murray had been a secretary who took shorthand, typed a hundred words a minute, and had no choice but to quit her job when she became pregnant. Few of the men in the Senate chamber—twenty of whom were millionaires—knew what it was like to get their boss coffee and take dictation for a living.

Murray told her colleagues that she had been twenty-six years old, newly married and working as an executive secretary in Seattle, when she became pregnant with Randy, her first child. Patty and Rob Murray didn't have a nest egg to fall back on, and they needed both salaries. "A family-leave policy would have enabled me to devote my attention to the changes in my family," Murray said. "It would also have given me a very important message about our country: That our families are as important as our jobs." Murray told the Senate that her boss had asked her to quit her job.

The family- and medical-leave bill had been handed to Patty Murray on a silver platter. Unlike Pat Schroeder and Marge Roukema, Murray had done virtually no legislative spadework on the bill. But Murray was a veteran of family-leave battles in the Washington state senate. For what better law could Murray cast her first vote than family leave?

After the speech, Murray sat down, flushed and relieved. To her surprise, other senators came to her desk to congratulate her. One senator told her that he had never before heard anybody talk like that in the Senate chamber. Compared with the usual male senator, who delivered speeches in booming, stentorian tones, Murray had spoken with simplicity and from the heart. She used the word "care" eleven times.

California's Dianne Feinstein, one of the four newly elected Democratic women senators, spoke next. Like Murray, Feinstein had also experienced job discrimination because of her pregnancy. "Thirty-five years ago, when I was pregnant with my daughter, Katherine, there was no maternity leave," said Feinstein. "I left my job to have my child."

These speeches, and their subsequent approval ratings, substantiated Murray's belief that women could reform Congress by simplifying the elevated diction used on the floor: Constituents could feel more connected to a government that spoke to them. "I think women talk in language and in terms that people understand more clearly," Murray said later. "If you listen to the men, they debate economic theory. The economic theory is important, but what really makes people understand what's in a bill is when you talk about what it really means to you." For the rest of the 103rd Congress, Murray would continue to take to the Senate floor with personal anecdotes about her life, her family, and her friends. Her staff would label the senator's style "Patty-speak."

Murray's speech on the Senate floor became the denouement of her four-year struggle on the issue of family and medical leave. In 1989, as a freshman state senator, Murray had a good friend whose sixteen-year-old son was dying of leukemia. At the time, Washington State's law required employers to give their workers six weeks of parental leave to care for a newborn child, but there was no protection if an employee's child fell seriously ill. Murray's friend asked her boss for time off so that she could take care of her son, who only had a few months to live. When her employer told her that they wouldn't guarantee her a job when she returned, she quit. As a result, she lost her health insurance and watched the medical bills pile up. "It was awful," recalled Murray, her eyes brimming with tears. "You shouldn't be forced to choose. It was so *wrong*."

When a family-leave bill was introduced in the Washington state senate that extended parental leave from six to twelve weeks, Murray attached an amendment including medical leave. Powerful business lobbies and the Democratic leadership begged her to drop the amendment. Murray refused to retreat. "The members of the Senate and the House then didn't have a sense of the issue," Murray recalled. "A lot of them were older men whose children were grown up, or who had wives at home to take care of their kids for them." At the time, Murray was the only senator who was a mother with young children. None of her colleagues wanted to be on record voting against a law that allowed parents with terminally ill children to take time off from work without losing their jobs. After

Murray gave an impassioned floor speech, her amendment passed. "Man, I was impressed," a lobbyist told the *Seattle Times*. "She wants to change the world, and she makes you believe there's a good chance she can do it."

When Murray arrived in Washington, D.C., she made a point of setting an example as an enlightened, caring employer. Murray acted on her philosophy that "if you care about your employees as people with lives separate from here [the office] and allow them to have that, they can do a better job." She instituted a strong family-leave policy—ten weeks of paid leave. Then she hired a thirty-three-year-old woman who was seven months pregnant with her first child.

Pam Norick had been born and raised in Seattle, and she had a master's degree in foreign relations and five years of Hill experience. Norick was smart, hardworking, and committed; Murray described her as a "dynamo." When Murray interviewed Norick for the job of Murray's national security adviser, she asked Norick how she planned to do both—be a Senate staffer who would be on call around the clock seven days a week, and be a mother. Norick knew that she would need a flexible work schedule, but before she could bring it up herself, Murray did. To make Norick's life easier, Murray suggested that she could work at home on Fridays. Norick gratefully accepted Murray's offer and became an employee whom Murray mentioned in speeches and interviews as proof of her mandate.

But hiring Norick did not come without its risks. A year later, a senior female staffer without children of her own complained to Murray that she didn't like Norick's special arrangement and thought Norick should be fired if she didn't change it. The complaint incensed Murray. She called a meeting of the entire staff and defended Norick in an inspiring speech. Murray explained that each employee had different responsibilities outside of the office and that everyone's needs were being treated equally. She emphasized that the office had to work as a team and support one another.

• • •

In the House, on February 3, the congresswomen dominated the family-leave debate. They rose one after another to make their first official statements of the congressional session. Marjorie Margolies-Mezvinsky was joined by Leslie Byrne and Jolene Unsoeld, Pat Schroeder and Patsy Mink, Connie Morella and Barbara-Rose Collins, Eva Clayton and Nancy Pelosi. Thirty-seven out of the fifty-four women on the Hill spoke to the merits of H.R. 1, not only as legislators but as working mothers—mothers with sixty-seven children, all told. Their speaking styles were personal and powerful. Patricia Ireland, president of the National Organization for Women, applauded them, noting that their performances were emblematic of the difference women were making on the Hill: "Women bring a different set of priorities," she said.

That day, the U.S. House of Representatives passed the Family and Medical Leave Act by a vote of 265 to 163. The next day, despite Republican filibuster threats, the bill passed in the Senate 71 to 27. All but six of the forty-eight congresswomen and one of the six women senators voted in favor of the bill. A gender gap persisted: 87 percent of all women members of the House voted for the bill, versus 59 percent of all congressmen. All the Democratic congresswomen and half of the Republican congresswomen voted for the legislation. Only 20 percent of Republican men in the House supported the bill.

For the few Republican congresswomen who voted against the family-leave bill, like Representative Deborah Pryce, of Columbus, Ohio, fiscal responsibility prevailed over gender solidarity. Pryce supported family leave in principle; she was a working mother of a two-year-old girl. But she was a fiscal conservative. On the campaign trail, she had called for a balanced budget, more jobs, and less government regulation. Her opponent, Democrat Richard Cordray, in an irony typical of conservative Republican women, was the "women's-issues" candidate.

Her Republican roots went back to Warren, Ohio, where Pryce's father owned a chain of drugstores. Pryce, the oldest of five children, "literally grew up in a small business." Like Patty Murray, Pryce was a pure product of Main Street, with one crucial difference. Patty Murray's father had always been an employee; Deborah Pryce's father had owned the drugstore. As a Republican, and true to her background, Pryce sympathized with business owners. With a vote pending on the Family and Medical Leave Act, she balked at forcing the "heavy hand of government" on businesses. She favored giving companies tax incentives for offering family leave to their employees. Pryce thought the bill would cause the loss of jobs and provoke employers to think twice before hiring women of childbearing age.

By the time the family-leave bill was signed into law, it became clear that Deborah Pryce's first allegiance would be to the Republican party, often leaving women's issues aside when they conflicted with the Republican party position. Pryce alienated Democratic and moderate Republican congresswomen when she spoke out forcefully on the floor against the bill. "Even if you have to vote no," Schroeder would later complain, "why give the speech?" Pryce refused to join the women's caucus, allying herself instead with the Conservative Opportunity Society, a Republican group. Never one to "just hang out with the girls," Pryce soon began to feel unwelcome in the Capitol building's plush, peach-colored Lindy Boggs congressional women's reading room, which, since the 1992 elections, had acquired the atmosphere of an elegant women's club room.

By contrast, the passage of the Family and Medical Leave Act was a personal triumph for Patty Murray. It affirmed her choice to be a working mother. Sometimes the job would have to give. Sometimes her family would have to give. Murray tried to find the middle ground.

Voting in the Senate takes place at night so often that being a senator could almost qualify as a night job. In the middle of the week, Murray's family would drive up to the Hill to eat dinner with Patty at restaurants in Union Station, a three-block walk from her office. By day, Murray tried to make herself as accessible to her family as possible, giving them the phone number for her direct line. During staff meetings, Murray made a practice of giving her family's telephone calls top priority. On Fridays, when the Senate was out of session, Murray asked her staff not to schedule any appointments so that she could work from home, communicating with the office via the telephone and e-mail from her laptop computer.

Murray even gave her children priority over the White House. In the fall of 1994, White House staffers were stunned when Murray arrived thirty minutes late for a high-level health care reform meeting with Hillary Rodham Clinton and a group of senators. No one aside from the president himself is late to White House meetings, especially not for the reason Murray gave: a parent-teacher conference at her son Randy's school. In the beginning of Randy's junior year, Murray had already rescheduled the conference twice. She refused to let Randy down a third time. Murray was surprised when she discovered that the reason for her tardiness had not been greeted as merely routine. "I thought it was perfectly normal," Murray said afterward.

But it was often hard to be normal and a U.S. senator at the same time. Murray longed to spend even an hour with people who were just her friends and nothing more. She remembered returning to Seattle and running into friends whom she hadn't seen in a long time. Gratefully relaxing into a conversation that she hoped would include old, familiar topics such as kids and schools, Murray was brought up short when one of her old friends said to her, "I'm so glad I ran into you! My husband wants money for this project—can you help him?"

Murray tried to maintain a semblance of normalcy in her household. She shunned the active cocktail and dinner-reception circuit that occupied the evenings of most senators and members of Congress. She turned down all breakfast invitations, except for those sponsored by the Washington State congressional delegation. On Saturdays, she drove her daughter Sara to soccer games, rotating "Orange Mom" duty—the mother who brings the plate of orange sections—with the other parents. When Sara needed to bring brownies to school for a bake sale, Patty would find herself, after a twelve-hour day on the Senate floor, breaking out the Duncan Hines in her kitchen.

In spite of Murray's efforts, her children were devastated by the move to the capital. Separating from their schools, their friends, and their extended family made them homesick. Three months after the family had moved to Arlington, Randy took the family car in a fit of rebellion and tried to drive back to Seattle. But his escape was foiled by the Washington Beltway. Randy drove around and around D.C. in circles, unable to find the right exit heading west.

Murray missed Sara's fourteenth birthday party because of late votes, but she vowed to be there for Sara's fifteenth—a promise that required asking favors of the Senate majority leader. Murray told George Mitchell that Sara's birthday constituted an "emergency" situation and asked if there was any way that he could see to it that the Senate could close up shop at a decent hour or predict for her when the votes would be. Mitchell could not oblige. As the clock ticked closer to cake time, the endless quorum calls looked as though they would stretch far into the night. Murray decided to take the risk and drive home, hoping against hope that she would not miss a vote. She was lucky that night. There were no votes.

When it came to public exposure, Murray protected her family like a nervous mother hen. Reporters' requests for interviews with Patty's husband Rob, or Sara and Randy, were automatically denied. The Murrays' house remained "sacrosanct," as Murray's press secretary put it, off limits to both the press and Murray's staff. As a result, Patty often had to inconvenience herself. One afternoon, she needed to give an interview to the CBS Seattle affiliate, but she had already gone home and had promised to pick Sara up from school. Unwilling to break her promise to Sara, and equally unwilling to allow the television crew to come to her house, Murray decided to do the interview in a park near Sara's public school.

On February 5, 1993, a sunny, cool morning, 150 Washington pro-family activists gathered at the White House. Patty Murray and Pat Schroeder were among them. They sat in eight rows of white folding chairs on the Rose Garden's soggy bright-green grass. Leafless cherry tree branches framed the stage where President Clinton stood poised to sign the Family and Medical Leave Act.

In the sixteen days since the inauguration, the administration had been transformed. Six out of Clinton's twenty-one cabinet members would be women, and 37 percent of his first five hundred political appointees were women, the highest number in history. In George Bush's Washington, two women served in the cabinet. Bill Clinton's White House already seemed a friendlier place. And yet, for all the excitement, President Clinton and Vice President Gore stood flanked by the same old faces: Senators Ted Kennedy, Chris Dodd, and George Mitchell and Representatives Bill Ford, Bill Clay, Pat Williams, and Tom Foley. These were the men who had made the Family and Medical Leave Act law—the congressional leadership and the chairmen of the committees and subcommittees that had the power and official jurisdiction over H.R. 1 and S. 5.

"I am proud that the first bill I sign as president truly puts people first," Clinton said, echoing his campaign theme. "It took eight years and two vetoes to make this legislation the law of the land."

And yet, in the second row, Pat Schroeder had been seated behind Hillary Clinton, Tipper Gore, and Marian Wright Edelman. Schroeder was not alone in feeling that she should have been on the stage with the men. But White House protocol dictated who was on stage; committee chairmen and the leadership had to be there. Bill Clinton needed those men standing behind him. They were the ones who he hoped would help him fulfill his ambitious legislative agenda in the 103rd Congress.

The signing of the bill was a victory for Schroeder, but her seat in the second row signified defeat. Although neither a committee chairman nor in the top ranks of the congressional leadership, Schroeder was, for all intents and purposes, the bill's godmother. She remembered how difficult it had been to convince some of the powerful congressmen on the stage to take an interest in her bill back in the eighties, when family leave was unpopular. Now, in the early months of 1993, family leave had virtually no enemies. The men with power had finally embraced the bill: in the macho, high-noon language of lawmaking, these men had won "bragging rights" to it. Schroeder had been outgunned. "When a bill becomes a big deal," she concluded, "boys grab it." The Year of the Woman had proved itself to be exactly that—one election year. It would take many more before women would be able to break the strictures of seniority. ■

Chapter 10

The Presidency

At first glance, the American presidency is the most powerful office in the world. To the president's vast formal powers are added extraordinary informal powers: to lead Congress, to cope with emergency situations, to take charge of world affairs. The president's constitutional authority, broad and expansive, is supplemented by huge delegations of power from Congress and by the power that comes from the prestige of the office itself.

Yet for all his powers, the president is boxed in by limitations of every kind. He must share his constitutional authority with Congress, with which he must continually negotiate and bargain, and with the federal courts, which he can influence only uncertainly and, usually, only in the long run. His own cabinet officials often have their own political bases and their own agendas, and even his personal staff may become ambitious and unreliable. He must spend much of his first term preparing for reelection, and all of his second term, if he has one, with the knowledge that the Constitution forbids him from running again.

In the 1990s, the American president faces restraints from abroad as well. Major U.S. allies—Great Britain, France, Germany, Japan—wield extraordinary economic muscle, and although they look to Washington for guidance, they need not follow where the president leads. U.S. relations with Russia have improved dramatically since the end of the Cold War, but the United States still faces difficult challenges across the globe—all of which must be faced most directly by the president.

The scandals and investigations that dogged President Bill Clinton throughout his presidency—leading to his impeachment by the House of Representatives in 1998—underscore even more forcefully the precarious nature of presidential power in the modern era. The Supreme Court's ruling in 1997 that the president could be sued while in office for alleged acts that occurred before he took office may force future presidents to deal with a barrage of lawsuits from opposition-inspired litigants. Both the traditional media and the new media are now focused more than ever on exposing presidential misconduct, of whatever variety. And the growing tradition of divided party control of Congress and the White House means that the president can no longer count on the support of the legislative branch.

The readings in this chapter share a common theme: they present the paradox of a president whose immense resources are not always sufficient to perform the tasks expected of him by the American people and by the rest of the world. Whether in foreign or domestic affairs, whether dealing with Congress or the president of Russia, the president always seems to be stretching and straining at the limits of his power.

Chapter Questions

1. What are the sources of the president's formal authority? his informal authority?
2. Consider Richard Neustadt's argument (in selection 10.3) that a president's real power comes from his ability to bargain and persuade effectively. What examples of bargaining and persuading can be found in this chapter? Consider the president's foreign affairs power, his dealings with Congress, and his relationship with his own staff, for starters.
3. The presidency, some suggest, is an eighteenth-century office forced to function in a twentieth-century world. How has the presidency adjusted to the extraordinary political, social, and technological changes of the past 200 years? Has this adaptation been successful?

 Foundations

The Framers of the Constitution recognized the importance of a unitary executive. Legislative bodies could deliberate and plan policy in the long run, perhaps, but only a unitary executive could act with the speed, decisiveness, and, when appropriate, secretiveness necessary for effective leadership. These qualities were especially important, the Framers believed, in matters of foreign and military policy.

Americans are so used to a strong presidency that it is easy to forget how much opposition there was in the beginning to such an office. The opponents of the Constitution feared that the presidency would quickly be transformed into an oppressive monarchy (the Articles of Confederation, remember, had no federal executive). They feared the Constitution's broad grants of legislative power to the president (especially the veto power and the power to make treaties), the commander-in-chief clause, and the president's power to appoint the federal judiciary.

Alexander Hamilton's strong defense of presidential power in the *Federalist* No. 70 is a clear indication that the Framers favored both efficiency and liberty and indeed believed that one was impossible without the other. It follows *Federalist* No. 68, in which Hamilton defends the mode of appointment of the president; he suggests that the indirect scheme the Framers designed would ensure to a "moral certainty" that "the office of President will seldom fall to the lot of any man who is not in an eminent degree endowed with the requisite qualifications."

Yet the Antifederalists' fears were not wholly unfounded. Maintaining the balance between a presidency strong enough to do what is required yet constrained enough to be controlled by the people remains a difficult, and daunting, task. The president's only hope of governing under such circumstances, as the political scientist Richard Neustadt suggests (selection 10.3), is to rely not only on his formal powers, but also on his informal powers—especially his power to bargain with and persuade his friends, his opponents, and the American people.

Questions

1. Why is a unitary executive necessary, according to Hamilton? What characteristics does a single individual possess that a body of individuals—Congress, for example—lacks?
2. Have Hamilton's arguments become stronger or weaker over the past 200 years? Has the modern presidency borne out his views or those of his opponents?
3. What advantages does a president have in the bargaining process, according to Richard Neustadt? Does he have any significant advantages or disadvantages in dealing with Congress? with the bureaucracy? with the American people?

10.1 *Federalist* No. 68 (1788)

Alexander Hamilton

Outline

I. Explanation of the means chosen for the appointment of the President of the United States.

   A. The mode of appointment selected—involving the creation of the Electoral College—

      1. Involves the people at large.

      2. Leaves the ultimate choice to those most capable of judging wisely between candidates.

      3. Avoids "tumult and disorder."

      4. Guards against corruption.

      5. Maintains the independence of the chief executive.

   B. Process results in a "moral certainty" that those selected will be qualified.

The mode of appointment of the Chief Magistrate of the United States is almost the only part of the system, of any consequence, which has escaped without severe censure or which has received the slightest mark of approbation from its opponents. The most plausible of these, who has appeared in print, has even deigned to admit that the election of the President is pretty well guarded. [Hamilton refers to the *Letters of a Federal Farmer*, written by an Antifederalist critic of the Constitution.] I venture somewhat further, and hesitate not to affirm that if the manner of it be not perfect, it is at least excellent. It unites in an eminent degree all the advantages the union of which was to be desired.

It was desirable that the sense of the people should operate in the choice of the person to whom so important a trust was to be confided. This end will be answered by committing the right of making it, not to any pre-established body, but to men chosen by the people for the special purpose, and at the particular conjuncture.

It was equally desirable that the immediate election should be made by men most capable of analyzing the qualities adapted to the station and acting under circumstances favorable to deliberation, and to a judicious combination of all the reasons and inducements which were proper to govern their choice. A small number of persons, selected by their fellow-citizens from the general mass, will be most likely to possess the information and discernment requisite to so complicated an investigation.

It was also peculiarly desirable to afford as little opportunity as possible to tumult and disorder. This evil was not least to be dreaded in the election of a magistrate who was to have so important an agency in the administration of the government as the President of the United States. But the precautions which have been so happily concerted in the system under consideration promise an effectual security against this mischief. The choice of *several* to form an intermediate body of electors will be much less apt to convulse the community with any extraordinary or violent movements than the choice of *one* who was himself to be the final object of the public wishes. And as the electors, chosen in each State, are to assemble and vote in the State in which they are chosen, this detached and divided situation will expose them much less to heats and ferments, which might be communicated from them to the people, than if they were all to be convened at one time, in one place.

Nothing was more to be desired than that every practicable obstacle should be opposed to cabal, intrigue, and corruption. These most deadly adversaries of republican government might naturally have been expected to make their approaches from more than one quarter, but chiefly from the desire in foreign powers to gain an improper ascendant in our councils. How could they better gratify this than by raising a creature of their own to the chief magistracy of the Union? But the convention have guarded against all danger of this sort with the most provident and judicious attention. They have not made the appointment of the President to depend on any preexisting bodies of men who might be tampered with beforehand to prostitute their votes; but they have referred it in the first instance to an immediate act of the people of America, to be exerted in the choice of persons for the temporary and sole purpose of making the appointment. And they have excluded from eligibility to this trust all those who from situation might be suspected of too great devotion to the President in office. No senator, representative, or other person holding a place of trust or profit under the United States can be of the number of the electors. Thus without corrupting the body of the people, the immediate agents in the election will at least enter upon the task free from any sinister bias. Their transient existence and their detached situation, already taken notice of, afford a satisfactory prospect of their continuing so, to the conclusion of it. The business of corruption, when it is to embrace so considerable a number of men, requires time as well as means. Nor would it be found easy suddenly to embark them, dispersed as they would be over thirteen States, in any combinations founded upon motives which, though they could not properly be denominated corrupt, might yet be of a nature to mislead them from their duty.

Another and less important desideratum was that the executive should be independent for his continuance in office on all but the people themselves. He might otherwise be tempted to sacrifice his duty to his complaisance for those whose favor was necessary to the duration of his official consequence. This advantage will also be secured, by making his re-election to depend on a special body of representatives, deputed by the society for the single purpose of making the important choice.

All these advantages will be happily combined in the plan devised by the convention; which is, that the people of each State shall choose a number of persons as electors, equal to the number of senators and representatives of such State in the national government who shall assemble within the State, and vote for some fit person as President. Their votes, thus given, are to be transmitted to the seat of the national government, and the person who may happen to have a majority of the whole number of votes will be the President. But as a majority of the votes might not always happen to center on one man, and as it might be unsafe to permit less than a majority to be conclusive it is provided that, in such a contingency, the House of Representatives shall elect out of the candidates who shall have the five highest number of votes the man who in their opinion may be best qualified for the office.

This process of election affords a moral certainty that the office of President will seldom fall to the lot of any man who is not in an eminent degree endowed with the requisite qualifications. Talents for low intrigue, and the little arts of popularity, may alone suffice to elevate a man to the first honors in a single State; but it will require other talents, and a different kind of merit, to establish him in the esteem and confidence of the whole Union, or of so considerable a portion of it as would be necessary to make him a successful candidate for the distinguished office of President of the United States. It will not be too strong to say that there will be a constant probability of seeing the station filled by characters pre-eminent for ability and virtue. And this will be thought no inconsiderable recommendation of the Constitution by those who are able to estimate the share which the executive in every government must necessarily have in its good or ill administration. Though we cannot acquiesce in the political heresy of the poet who says:

> For forms of government let fools contest—
> That which is best administered is best,—

yet we may safely pronounce that the true test of a good government is its aptitude and tendency to produce a good administration. . . . ■

10.2 *Federalist* No. 70 (1788)

Alexander Hamilton

Outline

I. The importance and components of strength and energy in the executive branch.

    A. A strong and energetic executive branch requires unity, duration in office, adequate resources, and sufficient powers.

II. Defense of a unitary (one-person) executive rather than a council.

    A. Importance of limiting dissention and disagreement with the executive branch.

    B. Importance of being able to fix responsibility within the executive branch.

There is an idea, which is not without its advocates, that a vigorous executive is inconsistent with the genius of republican government. The enlightened well-wishers to this species of government must at least hope that the supposition is destitute of foundation; since they can never admit its truth, without at the same time admitting the condemnation of their own principles. Energy in the executive is a leading character in the definition of good government. It is essential to the protection of the community against foreign attacks; it is not less essential to the steady administration of the laws; to the protection of property against those irregular and high-handed combinations which sometimes interrupt the ordinary course of justice; to the security of liberty against the enterprises and assaults of ambition, of faction, and of anarchy. Every man the least conversant in Roman history knows how often that republic was obliged to take refuge in the absolute power of a single man, under the formidable title of dictator, as well against the intrigues of ambitious individuals who aspired to the tyranny, and the seditions of whole classes of the community whose conduct threatened the existence of all government, as against the invasions of external enemies who menaced the conquest and destruction of Rome.

There can be no need, however, to multiply arguments or examples on this head. A feeble executive implies a feeble execution of the government. A feeble execution is but another phrase for a bad execution; and a government ill executed, whatever it may be in theory, must be, in practice, a bad government.

Taking it for granted, therefore, that all men of sense will agree in the necessity of an energetic executive, it will only remain to inquire, what are the ingredients which constitute this energy? How far can they be combined with those other ingredients which constitute safety in the republican sense? And how far does this combination characterize the plan which has been reported by the convention?

The ingredients which constitute energy in the executive are unity; duration; an adequate provision for its support; and competent powers.

The ingredients which constitute safety in the republican sense are a due dependence on the people and a due responsibility.

Those politicians and statesmen who have been the most celebrated for the soundness of their principles and for the justness of their views have declared in favor of a single executive and a numerous legislature. They have, with great propriety, considered energy as the most necessary qualification of the former, and have regarded this as most applicable to power in a single hand; while they have, with equal propriety, considered the latter as best adapted to deliberation and wisdom, and best calculated to conciliate the confidence of the people and to secure their privileges and interests.

That unity is conducive to energy will not be disputed. Decision, activity, secrecy, and dispatch will generally characterize the proceedings of one man in a much more eminent degree than the proceedings of any greater number; and in proportion as the number is increased, these qualities will be diminished.

• • •

Whenever two or more persons are engaged in any common enterprise or pursuit, there is always danger of difference of opinion. If it be a public trust or office in which they are clothed with equal dignity and authority, there is peculiar danger of personal emulation and even animosity. From either, and especially from all these causes, the most bitter dissensions are apt to spring. Whenever these happen, they lessen the respectability, weaken the authority, and distract the plans and operations of those whom they divide. If they should unfortunately assail the supreme executive magistracy of a country, consisting of a plurality of persons, they might impede or frustrate the most important measures of the government in the most critical emergencies of the state. And what is still worse, they might split the community into the most violent and irreconcilable factions, adhering differently to the different individuals who composed the magistracy.

Men often oppose a thing merely because they have had no agency in planning it, or because it may have been planned by those whom they dislike. But if they have been consulted, and have happened to disapprove, opposition then becomes, in their estimation, an indispensable duty of self-love. They seem to think themselves bound in honor, and by all the motives of personal infallibility, to defeat the success of what has been resolved upon contrary to their sentiments. Men of upright, benevolent tempers have too many opportunities of remarking, with horror, to what desperate lengths this disposition is sometimes carried, and how often the great interests of society are sacrificed to the vanity, to the conceit, and to the obstinacy of individuals, who have credit enough to make their passions and their caprices interesting to mankind. Perhaps the question now before the public may, in its consequences, afford melancholy proofs of the effects of this despicable frailty, or rather detestable vice, in the human character.

Upon the principles of a free government, inconveniences from the source just mentioned must necessarily be submitted to in the formation of the legislature; but it is unnecessary, and therefore unwise, to introduce them into the constitution of the executive. It is here too that they may be most pernicious. In the legislature, promptitude of decision is oftener an evil than a benefit. The differences of opinion, and the jarring of parties in that department of the government, though they may sometimes obstruct salutary plans, yet often promote deliberation and circumspection, and serve to check excesses in the majority. When a resolution too is once taken, the opposition must be at an end. That resolution is a law, and resistance to it punishable. But no favorable circumstances palliate or atone for the disadvantages of dissension in the executive department. Here they are pure and unmixed. There is no point at which they cease to operate. They serve to embarrass and weaken the execution of the plan or measure to which they relate, from the first step to the final conclusion of it. They constantly counteract those qualities in the executive which are the most necessary ingredients in its composition—vigor and expedition, and this without any counterbalancing good. In the conduct of war, in which the energy of the executive is the bulwark of the national security, everything would be to be apprehended from its plurality. . . .

But one of the weightiest objections to a plurality in the executive, and which lies as much against the last as the first plan is that it tends to conceal faults and destroy responsibility. Responsibility is of two kinds—to censure and to punishment. The first is the more important of the two, especially in an elective office. Men in public trust will much oftener act in such a manner as to render them unworthy of being any longer trusted, than in such a manner as to make them obnoxious to legal punishment. But the multiplication of the executive adds to the difficulty of detection in either case. It often becomes impossible, amidst mutual accusations, to determine on whom the blame or the punishment of a pernicious measure, or series of pernicious measures, ought really to fall. It is shifted from one to another with so much dexterity, and under such plausible appearances, that the public opinion is left in suspense about the real author. The circumstances which may have led to any national miscarriage or misfortune are sometimes so complicated that where there are a number of actors who may have had different degrees and kinds of agency, though we may clearly see upon the whole that there has been mismanagement, yet it may be impracticable to pronounce to whose account the evil which may have been incurred is truly chargeable. . . . ■

10.3 Presidential Power (1960)

Richard Neustadt

The separateness of institutions and the sharing of authority prescribe the terms on which a President persuades. When one man shares authority with another, but does not gain or lose his job upon the other's whim, his willingness to act upon the urging of the other turns on whether he conceives the action right for him. The essence of a President's persuasive task is to convince such men that what the White House wants of them is what they ought to do for their sake and on their authority.

Persuasive power, thus defined, amounts to more than charm or reasoned argument. These have their uses for a President, but these are not the whole of his resources. For the men he would induce to do what he wants done on their own responsibility will need or fear some acts by him on his responsibility. If they share his authority, he has some share in theirs. Presidential "powers" may be inconclusive when a President commands, but always remain relevant as he persuades. The status and authority inherent in his office reinforce his logic and his charm.

Status adds something to persuasiveness; authority adds still more. When Truman urged wage changes on his Secretary of Commerce while the latter was administering the steel mills, he and Secretary Sawyer were not just two men rea-

From Richard Neustadt, *Presidential Power: The Politics of Leadership from FDR to Carter.* Copyright © 1986 by Allyn & Bacon. Reprinted by permission. (New York: Wiley, 1960), pp. 34–36.

soning with one another. Had they been so, Sawyer probably would never have agreed to act. Truman's status gave him special claims to Sawyer's loyalty, or at least attention. In Walter Bagehot's charming phrase "no man can *argue* on his knees." Although there is no kneeling in this country, few men—and exceedingly few Cabinet officers—are immune to the impulse to say "yes" to the President of the United States. It grows harder to say "no" when they are seated in his oval office at the White House, or in his study on the second floor, where almost tangibly he partakes of the aura of his physical surroundings. In Sawyer's case, moreover, the President possessed formal authority to intervene in many matters of concern to the Secretary of Commerce. These matters ranged from jurisdictional disputes among the defense agencies to legislation pending before Congress and, ultimately, to the tenure of the Secretary, himself. There is nothing in the record to suggest that Truman voiced specific threats when they negotiated over wage increases. But given his *formal* powers and their relevance to Sawyer's other interests, it is safe to assume that Truman's very advocacy of wage action conveyed an implicit threat.

A President's authority and status give him great advantages in dealing with the men he would persuade. Each "power" is a vantage point for him in the degree that other men have use for his authority. From the veto to appointments, from publicity to budgeting, and so down a long list, the White House now controls the most encompassing array of vantage points in the American political system. With hardly an exception, the men who share in governing this country are aware that at some time, in some degree, the doing of *their* jobs, the furthering of *their* ambitions, may depend upon the President of the United States. Their need for presidential action, or their fear of it, is bound to be recurrent if not actually continuous. Their need or fear is his advantage.

A President's advantages are greater than mere listing of his "powers" might suggest. The men with whom he deals must deal with him until the last day of his term. Because they have continuing relationships with him, his future, while it lasts, supports his present influence. Even though there is no need or fear of him today, what he could do tomorrow may supply today's advantage. Continuing relationships may convert any "power," any aspect of his status, into vantage points in almost any case. When he induces other men to do what he wants done, a President can trade on their dependence now *and* later.

The President's advantages are checked by the advantages of others. Continuing relationships will pull in both directions. These are relationships of mutual dependence. A President depends upon the men he would persuade; he has to reckon with his need or fear of them. They too will possess status, or authority, or both, else they would be of little use to him. Their vantage points confront his own; their power tempers his.

Persuasion is a two-way street. Sawyer, it will be recalled, did not respond at once to Truman's plan for wage increases at the steel mills. On the contrary, the Secretary hesitated and delayed and only acquiesced when he was satisfied that publicly he would not bear the onus of decision. Sawyer had some points of vantage all his own from which to resist presidential pressure. If he had to reckon with coercive implications in the President's "situations of strength," so had Truman to be mindful of the implications underlying Sawyer's place as a department head, as steel administrator, and as a Cabinet spokesman for business. Loyalty is reciprocal. Having taken on a dirty job in the steel crisis, Sawyer had strong claims to loyal support. Besides, he had authority to do some things that the White House could ill afford. Emulating Wilson, he might have resigned in a huff (the removal power also works two ways). Or emulating Ellis Arnall, he might have declined to sign necessary orders. Or, he might have let it be known publicly that he deplored what he was told to do and protested its doing. By following any of these courses Sawyer almost surely would have strengthened the position of management, weakened the position of the White House, and embittered the union. But the whole purpose of a wage increase was to enhance White House persuasiveness in urging settlement upon union and companies alike. Although Sawyer's status and authority did not giver him the power to prevent an increase outright, they gave him capability to undermine its purpose. If his authority over wage rates had been vested by a statute, not by revocable presidential order, his power of prevention might have been complete. So Harold Ickes demonstrated in the famous case of helium sales to Germany before the Second World War.

The power to persuade is the power to bargain. Status and authority yield bargaining advantages. But in a government of "separated institutions sharing powers," they yield them to all sides. With the array of vantage points at his disposal, a President may be far more persuasive than his logic or his charm could make him. But outcomes are not guaranteed by his advantages. ■

 # American Politics Today

The American presidency, as the political scientists Thomas E. Cronin and Michael Genovese suggest, is a study in paradox. Americans want their presidents to be powerful, but not too powerful; "presidential" in stature, yet close to the common people; independent-minded yet responsive to public opinion. Appreciating and explaining these paradoxes, they argue, is the key to understanding the American presidency.

Questions

1. How can the paradoxes of the American presidency be explained with reference to American political culture? The constitutional system of checks and balances? Our historical experiences?
2. What circumstances increase a president's ability to persuade or bargain with others successfully? How does public opinion—often expressed through presidential approval ratings—affect a president's informal powers?

10.4 Presidential Paradoxes (1997)

Thomas E. Cronin and Michael Genovese

Our expectations of, and demands on, the president are frequently so contradictory as to invite two-faced behavior by our presidents. Presidential powers are often not as great as many of us believe, and the president gets unjustly condemned as ineffective. Or a president will overreach or resort to unfair play while trying to live up to our demands.

The Constitution is of little help. The founders purposely left the presidency imprecisely defined. This was due in part to their fears of both the monarchy and the masses, and in part to their hopes that future presidents would create a more powerful office than the framers were able to do at the time. They knew that at times the president would have to move swiftly and effectively, yet they went to considerable lengths to avoid enumerating specific powers and duties in order to calm the then widespread fear of monarchy. After all, the nation had just fought a war against executive tyranny. Thus the paradox of the invention of the presidency: To get the presidency approved in 1787 and 1788, the framers had to leave several silences and ambiguities for fear of portraying the office as an overly centralized leadership institution. Yet when we need central leadership we turn to the president and read into Article II of the Constitution various prerogatives or inherent powers that allow the president to perform as an effective national leader.

Today the informal and symbolic powers of the presidency account for as much as the formal, stated ones. Presidential powers expand and contract in response to varying situational and technological changes. The powers of the presidency are thus interpreted so differently that they sometimes seem to be those of different offices. In some ways the modern presidency has virtually unlimited authority for almost anything its occupant chooses to do with it. In other ways, a president seems hopelessly ensnarled in a web of checks and balances. . . .

The following are some of the paradoxes of the presidency. Some are cases of confused expectations. Some are cases of wanting one kind of presidential behavior at one time, and another kind later. Still others stem from the contradiction inherent in the concept of democratic leadership, which on the surface at least, appears to set up "democratic" and "leadership" as warring concepts. Whatever the source, each has implications for presidential performance and for how Americans judge presidential success and failure. . . .

Paradox #1. Americans demand powerful, popular presidential leadership that solves the nation's problems. Yet we are inherently suspicious of strong centralized leadership and especially the abuse of power and therefore we place significant limits on the president's powers.

We admire power but fear it. We love to unload responsibilities on our leaders, yet we intensely dislike being bossed around. We expect impressive leadership from presidents, and we simultaneously impose constitutional, cultural, and political restrictions on them. These restrictions often prevent presidents from living up to our expectations.

Our ambivalence toward executive power is hardly new. The founders knew the new republic needed more leadership, yet they feared the development of a popular leadership institution that might incite the people and yield factious or demagogic government. Thus, the early conception of the American president was of an informed, virtuous statesman whose detached judgment and competence would enable him to work well with Congress and other leaders in making and implementing national public policy. This early presidency, as envisaged by the founders, did not encourage a popularly elected leader who would seek to directly shape and respond to the public's views. On the contrary, popular leadership grounded in the will of the people was "a synonym for demagoguery which, combined with the possibility of majority tyranny, was regarded as the peculiar vice to which democracies were susceptible." The founders' goal was to provide some distance between the public and national leaders, especially the president, that distance to be used to refine the popular view, to allow for leadership and statesmanship rather than to do what the people wanted done. To be sure, the people should be represented through Congress, yet they were not to be embodied in the executive. The president was to exercise wisdom, not responsiveness; judgment, not followership.

But the presidency of 1787 is not the presidency of today. Today it is a larger office, structurally similar to the original design but politically more powerful and more closely connected to popular passions. With the evolution of the nation has come an alternative conception of the presidency—the president is, in essence, the only truly national voice and representative of the American people. New arrangements for nominating and electing presidents have reinforced this conception, as has access to the magic of television. Today's president is seen as an agent of the people who should provide popular leadership. . . .

Presidents are supposed to follow the laws and respect the constitutional procedures that were designed to restrict their power, yet still they must be powerful and effective when action is needed. For example, we approve of presidential military initiatives and covert operations when they work out well, but we criticize presidents and insist they work more closely with Congress when the initiatives fail. We recognize the need for secrecy in certain government actions, but we resent being deceived and left in the dark—again, especially when things go wrong, as in Reagan's Iranian arms sale diversions to the Contras. . . .

In short, we expect presidents, as the most visible representatives of big government and as popular leaders, to solve the entire scope of our problems by mustering all the powers and strengths that office now appears to confer, and then some. We are, however, unwilling to allow presidents to infringe on our rights in any significant way. In a self-help, individualistic, do-it-yourself society (which we still like to think we are), we remain ambivalent about the role of centralized presidential popular leadership because, as a people, we are somewhat ambivalent about the ends of government. We need government, but we resist its powers when we can, and we dislike admitting our growing dependence on it. It is also true that while we want strong leadership, if such leadership comes in the wrong form, we diminish our enthusiasm for it. This results in a dramatic roller coaster ride of strong support for the heroic presidency model followed by equally strong condemnations of presidential power.

Paradox #2. We yearn for the democratic "common person" and also for the uncommon, charismatic, heroic, visionary performance.

We want our presidents to be like us, but better than us. We like to think America is the land where the common sense of the common person reigns. Nourished on a diet of Frank Capra's "common-man-as-hero" movies, and the literary celebration of the average citizen by authors such as Emerson, Whitman, and Thoreau, we prize the common touch. The plain-speaking Harry Truman, the up-from-the-log-cabin "man or woman of the people," is enticing. Few of us, however, settle for anything but the best; we want presidents to succeed and we hunger for brilliant, uncommon, and semiregal performances from presidents.

Thus, while we fought a revolution to depose royalty, part of us yearns for the majesty and symbolism of a royal family.

> From the beginning, American presidential style has had to lean simultaneously in two different directions; the character in the White House should behave with becoming democratic modesty. . . . But he must also express—in word, deed, bearing, personality . . . the greatness of the idea and the people he represents.

King *and* commoner, we yearn for and demand both. The human heart, we are told, secretly and ceaselessly reinvents royalty and quests for the heroic. At the same time, we are told the hero is the individual the democratic nation must guard itself against. . . .

We are often torn between demanding dynamic, charismatic leadership from our presidents and wanting presidents to heed our views. The preeminently successful presidents radiated courage and hope and stirred the hearts and minds of Americans with an almost demagogic ability to simplify and convince. "We need leaders of inspired idealism," said Theodore Roosevelt, "leaders to whom are granted great visions, who dream greatly and strive to make their dreams come true, who can kindle the people with the fire from their own burning souls."

Do we pay a price when we get, permit, or encourage heroic popular leadership in the White House? Does it diminish the vitality of nongovernmental America? Does it possibly dissipate citizen and civic participation and responsibility? We haven't studied these effects carefully enough to know. We do know, however, that those heroic, larger-than-life presidents sometimes have inadvertently weakened the office for their successors. The grand performances of Jefferson, Jackson, Lincoln, Wilson, and FDR made it difficult for their successors to lead. The stretching of the powers and the strenuous performance often invited backlash. It was as if the presidency had roamed too far from the normal and acceptable. Invariably, a leveling of their successors seemed to take place.

There is another related problem with the notion of heroic presidential leadership. Most of the time those who wait around for heroic leaders in the White House are disappointed. This is because most of the time presidents do not provide galvanizing, brilliant policy leadership. In practice, the people make policy more often than presidents do; solutions percolate up rather than being imposed from the top down. Indeed, on many of the more important issues the people generally have to wait for presidents to catch up. In the overall scheme of the untidy policymaking process the public often is out in front, as they were in the move to get out of Vietnam, as they were in civil rights and in demanding better and more sustained arms control negotiations. Thus the old question of who leads whom needs to be addressed. Presidents, much of the time, are shrewd followers; they are not allowed to be heroic, pace-setting, or in-advance-of-their-times leaders.

Paradox #3. We want a decent, just, caring, and compassionate president, yet we admire a cunning, guileful, and, on occasions that warrant it, even a ruthless, manipulative president. . . .

We appear to demand a double-faced personality. We demand the sinister as well as the sincere, the cunning as well as the compassionate, President Mean and President Nice, the president as Clint Eastwood and the president as Mr. Rogers—tough and hard enough to stand up to Khrushchev and North Korea, to Saddam Hussein and the Ayatollah, or to press the nuclear button, yet compassionate enough to care for the ill fed, ill clad and ill housed. In this case, the public seems to want a kindhearted s.o.b. or a clean wheeler-dealer, hard roles to cast and an even harder role to perform over eight years.

Former President Nixon, in writing about leaders he worked with, said a modern-day leader has to employ a variety of unattractive qualities on occasion in order to be effective, or at least to appear effective. Nixon may have carried these practices too far when he was in office, but his retirement writings are instructive nonetheless:

> In evaluating a leader, the key question about his behavioral traits is not whether they are attractive or unattractive, but whether they are useful. Guile, vanity, dissembling—in other circumstances these might be unattractive habits, but to the leader they can be essential. He needs guile in order to hold together the shifting coalitions of often bitterly opposed interest groups that governing requires. He needs a certain measure of vanity in order to create the right kind of public impression. He sometimes has to dissemble in order to prevail on crucial issues.

Nixon should know. Despite other failings, he was often an effective foreign affairs president.

We want decency and compassion at home, but demand toughness and guile when presidents have to deal with our adversaries. We want presidents to be fierce or compassionate, nice or mean, sensitive or ruthless depending on what we want done, on the situation, and, to some extent, on the role models of the recent past. But woe to a president who is too much or too little possessed of these characteristics!

Americans severely criticize would-be leaders who are viewed as soft or afraid to make decisions, use power, or fire anyone. Jimmy Carter, Gerald Ford, and Bill Clinton, among others, were faulted for indecision, timidity, or failure to be pragmatic. Journalists said they merely didn't know how to play "hardball," or were unwilling to display it. . . .

Abraham Lincoln said that few things are wholly good or wholly evil. Most public policies or ideological choices are an indivisible compound of the two. Thus, our best judgment of the balance between them is continually demanded.

The best of presidents are balanced individuals; they are sure of themselves, not dogmatic; they are self-confident, yet always willing to learn from their mistakes.

Paradox #4. We admire the "above politics" nonpartisan or bipartisan approach, yet the presidency is perhaps the most political office in the American system, a system in which we need a creative entrepreneurial master politician.

The public yearns for a statesman in the White House, for a George Washington or a second "era of good feelings"—anything that might prevent partisanship or politics as usual in the White House. Former French President Charles de Gaulle once said, "I'm neither of the left nor of the right nor of the center, but above." In fact, however, the job of president demands that the officeholder be a gifted political broker, ever attentive to changing political moods and coalitions.

Many of our early presidents unambiguously condemned parties while blatantly reaching out for party support when they needed to get their programs through Congress. "It is one of the paradoxes of the office," wrote historian Robert J. Morgan, "that a President must seek to balance his position as chief of his party with an equal need for support of his policies from all quarters of the nation regardless of partisan lines. He owes his office to the efforts of the party which put him there and, yet, once in power, his success as a leader rests in no little measure upon his securing a broad base of popular approval."

Franklin Roosevelt illustrates this well. Appearing so remarkably nonpartisan while addressing the nation, he was in practice one of the craftiest manipulators and political-coalition builders to occupy the White House. He could punish friends and reward enemies when needed, or vice versa. He did not always succeed—for example when he tried to "pack the Court" in 1937 and to purge some Democratic members of Congress in 1938.

Presidents are often expected to be above politics in some respects while being highly political in others. Presidents are never supposed to act with their eyes on the next election, yet their power position demands they must. They are neither supposed to favor any particular group or party nor wheel and deal and twist too many arms. That's politics and that's bad! Instead, a president is supposed to be "president of all the people," above politics. A president is also asked to lead a party, to help fellow party members get elected or reelected, to deal firmly with party barons, interest group chieftains, and congressional political brokers. His ability to gain legislative victories depends on his skills at party leadership and on the size of his party's congressional membership. Jimmy Carter once lamented that "It's very difficult for someone to serve in this office and meet the difficult issues in a proper and courageous way and still maintain a combination of interest-group approval that will provide a clear majority at election time." . . .

This clashing expectation will endure. A standard diagnosis of what's gone wrong in an administration will be that the presidency has become too politicized. But it will be futile to try to take the president out of politics. A more useful approach is to realize that certain presidents try too hard to hold themselves above politics, or at least to give that appearance, rather than engage in it deeply, openly, and creatively. A democratic president has to act politically regarding controversial issues if any semblance of government by consent is to be achieved.

Paradox #5. We want a president who can unify us, yet the job requires taking firm stands, making unpopular or controversial decisions that necessarily upset and divide us.

Closely related to paradox #4, paradox #5 holds that we ask the president to be a national unifier and a *harmonizer* while at the same time the job requires priority setting and *advocacy* leadership. The tasks are near opposites.

It is widely held that presidents must pull us together. Presidents must build coalitions and seek consensus. Presidents must not be too far ahead of their times if they are to be successful.

> He must see what he sees with the eyes of the multitude upon whose shoulders he stands. To get anywhere he must win understanding; to win it, the policy he pursues must never be so remote from the view about him that he cannot get that understanding. At bottom, his real power is in the popular support he can rally. . . .

Our nation is one of the few in the world that calls on its chief executive to serve as it symbolic, ceremonial head of state *and* as its political head of government. Elsewhere, these tasks are spread around. In some nations there is a monarch and a prime minister; in others there are three visible national leaders— a head of state, a premier, and a powerful party chief.

In the absence of an alternative office or institution, we demand that our president act as a unifying force in our lives. Perhaps it all began with George Washington, who so artfully performed this function. At least for a while he truly was above politics, a unique symbol of our new nation. He was a healer, a unifier, and an extraordinary man for several seasons. Today we ask no less of our presidents than that they should do as Washington did, and more.

We have designed a presidential job description, however, that often forces our contemporary presidents to act as national dividers. Presidents must necessarily divide when they act as the leaders of their political parties, when they set priorities to the advantage of certain goals and groups at the expense of others, when they forge and lead political coalitions, when they move out ahead of public opinion and assume the role of national educators, when they choose one set of advisers over another. A president, as a creative executive leader, cannot help but offend certain interests. When Franklin Roosevelt was running for a second term, some garment workers unfolded a great sign that said, "We love him for the enemies he has made." Such is the fate of a president on an everyday basis; if presidents choose to use power they will lose the goodwill of those who preferred inaction.

The opposite is, of course, also true. Presidents obsessed with striving to protect their power and popularity by choosing to act can run into difficulties as well. Presidents may avoid divisive conflict in favor of short-run, low-risk policymaking. Such a president may seem effective but may in reality undermine the confidence of the American people and the credibility of the presidency in the long run. . . .

Paradox #6. We expect our presidents to provide bold, visionary, innovative, *programmatic* leadership and at the same time to *pragmatically* respond to the will of public opinion majorities; that is to say, we expect presidents to lead and to follow, to exercise "democratic leadership."

We want both pragmatic and programmatic leadership. We want principled leadership and flexible, adaptable leaders. *Lead us,* but also *listen to us.*

Most people can be led only where they want to go. "Authentic leadership, wrote James MacGregor Burns, "is a collective process." It emerges from a sensitivity or appreciation of the motives and goals of both followers and leaders. The test of leadership, according to Burns, "is the realization of intended, real change that meets people's enduring needs." Thus a key function of leadership is "to engage followers, not merely to activate them, to commingle needs and aspirations and goals in a common enterprise, and in the process to make better citizens of both leaders and followers.

We want our presidents to offer leadership, to be architects of the future and to offer visions, plans, and goals. At the same time we want them to stay in close touch with the sentiments of the people. We want a certain amount of innovation, but we resist being led too far in any one direction. . . .

We want idealism *and* realism, optimism *and* levelheadedness. Be inspirational, we tell the president, but also be realistic—don't promise more than you can deliver. We ask our presidents to stir our blood, giving us a sense of glory about ourselves, but also to appeal to our reason. Too much inspiration will invariably lead to dashed hopes, disillusionment, and cynicism. The best leaders often suffer from one of their chief virtues—an instinctive tendency to raise aspirations, to summon us to transcend personal interests and subordinate ourselves to dreaming dreams of a bolder, more majestic national community.

Most Americans want to be inspired. We savor the upbeat rhetoric and promises of a brighter tomorrow. We genuinely want to hear about New Nationalism, New Deals, New Frontiers, Great Societies, New American Revolutions, and New Covenants; we want our fears to be assuaged during a "fireside chat" or a "conversation with the President"; we want to be told "the torch has been passed to a new generation of Americans . . . and the glow from that fire can truly light the world." We want something to believe. We want fearless leaders to tell us that the "only fear we have to fear is fear itself," that "we are Number One," that a recession has "bottomed out," or that "America is back standing tall again." To understate the state of the nation is to seem unpresidential.

These promises, while they make electoral and psychological sense, often backfire. As candidates promise too much and build expectations too high, the public is disappointed when reality fails to match promise. This may compel presidents to break their promises, as Bush did when he broke his "Read my lips, no new taxes!" pledge.

Presidents who do not raise hopes are criticized for letting events shape their presidency rather than making things happen. A president who eschewed inspiration of any kind would be rejected as un-American. For people everywhere America has been the land of promise, of possibilities, of dreams. No president can stand in the way of this truth, regardless of the current dissatisfaction about the size of big government in Washington and its incapacity to deliver the services it promises. . . .

"We call them stiff-necked and inflexible when they won't revise a position, fuzzy and opportunistic when they do. . . . We urge them, once nominated, to move to the center, the mainstream . . . and then bash them for fakery and cynicism when they so move." Should it be considered so intolerable for presidents to admit they have changed, grown, seen something differently, yielded to the arguments or evidence or even pleas of others? George Bush suffered immeasurably when he did an about face on his vivid pledge not to raise taxes. And Bill Clinton was not forgiven for abandoning his middle-class tax cut pledge.

Paradox #7. Americans want powerful, self-confident presidential leadership. Yet we are inherently suspicious of leaders who are arrogant, infallible, and above criticism.

We unquestionably cherish our three branches of government with their checks and balances and theories of dispersed and separated powers. We want our presidents to be successful and to share their power with their cabinets, Congress, and other "responsible" national leaders. In theory, we oppose the concentration of power, we dislike secrecy, and we resent depending on any one person to provide all of our leadership.

But Americans also yearn for dynamic, aggressive presidents—even if they do cut some corners. We celebrate the gutsy presidents who make a practice of manipulating and pushing Congress. We perceive the great presidents to be those who stretched their legal authority and dominated the other branches of government. It is still Jefferson, Jackson, Lincoln, and the Roosevelts who get top billing. Whatever may have been the framers' intentions for the three branches, most experts now agree that most of the time, especially in crises, our system works best when the presidency is strong and when we have a self-confident, assertive president.

There is, of course, a fine line between confidence and arrogance, between firmness and inflexibility. We want presidents who are not afraid to exert their will, but at what point does this become antidemocratic, even authoritarian?

We want presidents to consult widely and use the advice of cabinet members and other top advisers. We like the idea of collegial leadership and shared responsibility. But do we want presidents to sacrifice their own ideas and priorities to those of their cabinet officers? No. We elect the president, not the advisers. While we want presidents to be open minded, we also admire the occasional "profile in courage" type of decision. One of the most fondly remembered Lincoln stories underscores this point. President Lincoln supposedly took a vote at a cabinet meeting and it went entirely against him. He announced it this way: "Seven nays and one aye, the ayes have it." But most of the time, Abraham Lincoln followed the leadership of Congress, his advisers, and the general public. . . .

Leaders, of course, must believe in themselves, but they cannot afford to discredit the ideas, plans, counsel, or criticism of others. Leaders who encourage thoughtful dissent in their organizations are, according to several studies, likely to produce better organizational decision-making. Effective presidents encourage and reward criticism without retaliating against the critics. Hitler eliminated his critics. Ahab ignored his. In *Antigone*, Sophocles' King Creon listened almost entirely to himself, which proved fatal. His son, Haemon, chided him in vain, saying, "Let not your first thought be your only thought. Think if there cannot be some other way. Surely, to think you own the only wisdom and yours the only word, the only will, betrays a shallow spirit, an empty heart."

But Creon dismisses his son's advice, saying, "Indeed, am I to take lessons at my time of life from a fellow of his age?" He ignores everyone else as well until it is too late.

We are all a little like Creon. A fine line separates self-confidence from pig-headed pride, boldness from recklessness, mindless adherence to the course from reevaluation and redirection. The challenge is how to blend the competing impulses and combine them effectively in particular situations.

Paradox #8. What it takes to become president may not be what is needed to govern the nation.

To win a presidential election takes ambition, money, luck, and masterful public relations strategies. It requires the formation of an electoral coalition. To govern a democracy requires much more. It requires the formation of a *governing* coalition, and the ability to compromise and bargain.

"People who win primaries may become good presidents—but 'it ain't necessarily so'" wrote columnist David Broder. "Organizing well is important in governing just as it is in winning primaries. But the Nixon years should teach us that good advance men do not necessarily make trustworthy White House aides. Establishing a government is a little more complicated than having the motorcade run on time."

Ambition (in heavy doses) and stiff-necked determination are essential for a presidential candidate, yet too much of either can be dangerous. A candidate must be bold and energetic, but in excess these characteristics can produce a cold, frenetic candidate. To win the presidency obviously requires a single-mindedness, yet our presidents must also have a sense of proportion, be well-rounded, have a sense of humor, be able to take a joke, and have hobbies and interests outside the realm of politics.

To win the presidency many of our candidates (Lincoln, Kennedy, and Clinton come to mind) had to pose as being more progressive or even populist than they actually felt; to be effective in the job they are compelled to appear more cautious and conservative than they often want to be. One of Carter's political strategists said, "Jimmy campaigned liberal, but governed conservative." And as Bill Clinton pointed out toward the end of his first year in office, "We've all become Eisenhower Republicans."

Another aspect of campaigning for the White House is the ambiguous position candidates take on issues in order to increase their appeal to the large bulk of centrist and independent voters. The following is a typical view replete with paradox: "I want my presidential candidate to have clear-cut policies, to be as clear and precise as possible on his positions, not hazy and ambiguous—to run a campaign that educates people and persuades them to adopt the candidate's positions. But I also want my candidate to win—I realize they have to be ambiguous to build the winning coalitions." . . .

Thus, what it takes to become president may differ from what it takes to *be* president. To become president takes a determined, and even a driven, person, a master fund-raiser, a person who is glib, dynamic, charming on television, and hazy on the issues. But once president, the person must be well rounded, careful in reasoning, clear and specific in communications, and not excessively ambitious. It may well be that our existing primary-convention system adds up to an effective obstacle course for testing would-be presidents. But with the experiences of the past generation in mind we have some reason for asking whether our system of electing presidents is not at odds with what is required to end up with a president who is competent, fair-minded, and emotionally healthy.

Paradox #9. The presidency is sometimes too strong, yet other times too weak.

Presidents are granted wide latitude in dealing with events abroad. At times, presidents can act unilaterally, without the express consent of Congress. While the constitutional grounds for such action may be dubious, the climate of expectations allows presidents to act decisively abroad. This being the case, the public comes to think the president can do the same at home. But this is usually not the case. A clashing expectation is built into the presidency when strength in some areas is matched with weakness in other areas.

It often seems that our presidency is *always too strong* and *always too weak*. Always too powerful given our worst fears of tyranny and our ideals of a "government by the people." Always too strong, as well, because it now possesses the capacity to wage nuclear war (a capacity that doesn't permit much in the way of checks and balances and deliberative, participatory government). But always too weak when we remember nuclear proliferation, the rising national debt, the budget deficit, lingering discrimination, poverty, and the clutch of other fundamental problems yet to be solved.

The presidency is always too strong when we dislike the incumbent. Its limitations are bemoaned, however, when we believe the incumbent is striving valiantly to serve the public interest as we define it. The Johnson presidency vividly captured this paradox: many who believed he was too strong in Vietnam also believed he was too weak to wage his War on Poverty. Others believed just the opposite.

Like everyone else, presidents have their good days and their bad days, their creative leadership periods and their periods of isolation, their times of imperiousness and of ineptitude. On their good days we want the presidency to be stronger. On their bad days we want all the checks and balances that can be mustered. The dilemma of the presidency today is that we can't have it both ways. Since President Washington took office we have vastly multiplied the requirements for presidential leadership and made them increasingly difficult to fulfill. Students of the presidency usually conclude that more power, not less, will be needed if presidents are to get the job done. There are now just too many constraints on governmental action—when presidents are at their best.

But if the presidency is to be given more power, should it not also be subject to more controls? Perhaps so. But what controls will curb the power of a president who abuses the public trust and at the same time not undermine the capacity of a fair-minded president to serve the public interest? ■

The Comparative Context

Every political system in the world has some form of executive leadership, explains the political scientist Richard Rose. The American system, which features an independent executive branch, is atypical; the top executive in most modern democracies is the prime minister, who also serves as the head of the legislative branch. Some nations—such as France—have both a president and a prime minister.

In this selection, Rose examines the political systems of the United States, Great Britain, and France in an effort to understand whether these differences in the structure of government make a real difference in the way power is exercised in practice.

Questions

1. What are the main characteristics of a presidential system? Of a prime-ministerial system? Of a hybrid system, such as that of France? What are the implications of these different characteristics for the nature of executive power?
2. How might Richard Neustadt's argument about presidential power (see selection 10.3) be modified if he were writing about executive leadership in Great Britain or France?
3. Do the British and French systems provide lessons for how the American system might be improved?

10.5 Presidents and Prime Ministers (1988)

Richard Rose

The need to give direction to government is universal and persisting. Every country, from Egypt of the pharoahs to contemporary democracies, must maintain political institutions that enable a small group of politicians to make authoritative decisions that are binding on the whole of society. Within every system, one office is of first importance, whether it is called president, prime minister, führer, or dux.

There are diverse ways of organizing the direction of government, not only between democracies and authoritarian regimes, but also among democracies. Switzerland stands at one extreme, with collective direction provided by a federal council whose president rotates from year to year. At the other extreme are countries that claim to centralize authority, under a British-style parliamentary system or in an American or French presidential system, in which one person is directly elected to the supreme office of state.

To what extent are the differences in the formal attributes of office a reflection of substantive differences in how authority is exercised? To what extent do the imperatives of office—the need for electoral support, dependence upon civil servants for advice, and vulnerability to events—impose common responses in practice? Comparing the different methods of giving direction to government in the United States (presidential), Great Britain (prime ministerial and Cabinet), and France (presidential and prime ministerial) can help us understand whether other countries do it—that is, choose a national leader—in a way that is better.

To make comparisons requires concepts that can identify the common elements in different offices. Three concepts organize the comparisons I make: the career

Richard Rose, "Presidents and Prime Ministers," *Society* (March/April 1988), pp. 61–67. Reprinted by permission of Transaction Publishers.

that leads to the top; the institutions and powers of government; and the scope for variation within a country, whether arising from events or personalities.

Career Leading to the Top

By definition, a president or prime minister is unrepresentative by being the occupant of a unique office. The diversity of outlooks and skills that can be attributed to white, university-educated males is inadequate to predict how people with the same social characteristics—a Carter or an Eisenhower; a Wilson or a Heath—will perform in office. Nor is it helpful to consider the recruitment of national leaders deductively, as a management consultant or personnel officer would, first identifying the skills required for the job and then evaluating candidates on the basis of a priori requirements. National leaders are not recruited by examination; they are self-selected, individuals whose driving ambitions, personal attributes, and, not least, good fortune, combine to win the highest public office.

To understand what leaders can do in office we need to compare the skills acquired in getting to the top with the skills required once there. The tasks that a president or prime minister must undertake are few but central: sustaining popular support through responsiveness to the electorate, and being effective in government. Success in office encourages electoral popularity, and electoral popularity is an asset in wielding influence within government.

The previous careers of presidents and prime ministers are significant, insofar as experience affects what they do in office—and what they do well. A politician who had spent many years concentrating upon campaigning to win popularity may continue to cultivate popularity in office. By contrast, a politician experienced in dealing with the problems of government from within may be better at dealing effectively with international and domestic problems.

Two relevant criteria for comparing the careers of national leaders are: previous experience of government, and previous experience of party and mass electoral politics. American presidents are outstanding in their experience of campaigning for mass support, whereas French presidents are outstanding for their prior knowledge of government from the inside. British prime ministers usually combine experience in both fields.

Thirteen of the fourteen Americans who . . . [were] nominated for president of the United States by the Democratic or Republican parties . . . [between 1945 and 1984] had prior experience in running for major office, whether at the congressional, gubernatorial or presidential level. Campaigning for office makes a politician conscious of his or her need for popular approval. It also cultivates skill in dealing with the mass media. No American will be elected president who has not learned how to campaign across the continent, effectively and incessantly. Since selection as a presidential candidate is dependent upon winning primaries, a president must run twice: first to win the party nomination and then to win the White House. The effort required is shown by the fact that in 1985, three years before the presidential election, one Republican hopeful campaigned in twenty-four states, and a Democratic hopeful in thirty. Immediately after the 1986 congressional elections ended, the media started featuring stories about the 1988 campaign.

Campaigning is different from governing. Forcing ambitious politicians to concentrate upon crossing and recrossing America reduces the time available for learning about problems in Washington and the rest of the world. The typical postwar president has had no experience working within the executive branch. The way in which the federal government deals with foreign policy, or with problems of the economy is known, if at all, from the vantage point of a spectator. A president is likely to have had relatively brief experience in Congress. As John F. Kennedy's career illustrates, Congress is not treated as a means of preparing to govern; it is a launching pad for a presidential campaign. The last three presidential elections have been won by individuals who could boast of having no experience in Washington. Jimmy Carter and Ronald Reagan were state governors, experienced at a job that gives no experience in foreign affairs or economic management.

A president who is experienced in campaigning can be expected to continue cultivating the media and seeking a high standing in the opinion polls. Ronald Reagan illustrates this approach. A president may even use campaigning as a substitute for coming to grips with government. Jimmy Carter abandoned Washington for the campaign trail when confronted with mid-term difficulties in 1978. But public relations expertise is only half the job; looking presidential is not the same as acting like a president.

A British prime minister, by contrast, enters office after decades in the House of Commons and years as a Cabinet minister. The average postwar prime minister had spent thirty-two years in Parliament before entering 10 Downing Street. Of that period, thirteen years had been spent as a Cabinet minister. Moreover, the prime minister has normally held the important policy posts of foreign secretary, chancellor of the exchequer or both. The average prime minister has spent eight years in ministerial office, learning to handle foreign and/or economic problems. By contrast with the United States, no prime minister has had postwar experience in state or local government, and by contrast with France, none has been a civil servant since World War II.

The campaign experience of a British prime minister is very much affected by the centrality that politicians give Parliament. A politician seeks to make a mark in debate there. Even in an era of mass media, the elitist doctrine holds that success in the House of Commons produces positive evaluation by journalists and invitations to appear on television, where a politician can establish an image with the national electorate. Whereas an American presidential hopeful has a bottom-up strategy, concentrating upon winning votes in early primaries in Iowa and New Hampshire as a means of securing media attention, a British politician has a top-down approach, starting to campaign in Parliament.

Party is the surrogate for public opinion among British politicians, and with good reason. Success in the Commons is evaluated by a politician's party colleagues. Election to the party leadership is also determined by party colleagues. To become prime minister a politician does not need to win an election; he or she only needs to be elected party leader when the party has a parliamentary majority. Jim Callaghan and Sir Alec Douglas-Home each entered Downing Street this way and lost office in the first general election fought as prime minister.

The lesser importance of the mass electorate to British party leaders is illustrated by the fact that the average popularity rating of a prime minister is usually less than that of an American president. The monthly Gallup poll rating often shows the prime minister approved by less than half the electorate and trailing behind one or more leaders of the opposition.

In the Fifth French Republic, presidents and prime ministers have differed from American presidents, being very experienced in government, and relatively inexperienced in campaigning with the mass electorate. Only one president, François Mitterrand, has followed the British practice of making a political career based on Parliament. Since he was on the opposition side for the first two decades of the Fifth Republic, his experience of the problems of office was like that of a British opposition member of Parliament, and different from that of a minister. Giscard d'Estaing began as a high-flying civil servant and Charles de Gaulle, like Dwight Eisenhower, was schooled in bureaucratic infighting as a career soldier.

When nine different French prime ministers are examined, the significance of a civil service background becomes clear. Every prime minister except for Pierre Mauroy has been a civil servant first. It has been exceptional for a French prime minister to spend decades in Parliament before attaining that office. An Englishman would be surprised that a Raymond Barre or a Couve de Murville had not sat there before becoming prime minister. An American would be even more surprised by the experience that French leaders have had in the ministries as high civil servants, and particularly in dealing with foreign and economic affairs.

The traditional style of French campaigning is plebiscitary. One feature of this is that campaigning need not be incessant. Louis Napoleon is said to have compared elections with baptism; something it is necessary to do—but to do only once. The seven-year fixed term of the French president, about double the statutory life of many national leaders, is in the tradition of infrequent consultation with the electorate.

The French tradition of leadership is also ambivalent; a plebiscite is, after all, a mass mobilization. The weakness of parties, most notably on the Right, which has provided three of the four presidents of the Fifth Republic, encourages a personalistic style of campaigning. The use of the two-ballot method for the popular election of a president further encourages candidates to compete against each other as individuals, just as candidates for the presidential nomination compete against fellow-partisans in a primary. The persistence of divisions between Left and Right ensures any candidate successful in entering the second ballot a substantial bloc of votes, with or without a party endorsement.

On the two central criteria of political leadership, the relationship with the mass electorate, and knowledge of government, there are cross-national contrasts in the typical career. A British or French leader is likely to know far more about government than an American president, but an American politician is likely to be far more experienced in campaigning to win popular approval and elections.

Less for the President to Govern

Journalistic and historical accounts of government often focus on the person and office of the national leader. The American president is deemed to be very powerful because of the immense military force that he can command by comparison to a national leader in Great Britain or France. The power to drop a hydrogen bomb is frequently cited as a measure of the awesome power of an American president; but it is misleading, for no president has ever dropped a hydrogen bomb, and no president has used atomic weapons in more than forty years. Therefore, we must ask: What does an American president (and his European counterparts) do when not dropping a hydrogen bomb?

In an era of big government, a national leader is more a chief than an executive, for no individual can superintend, let alone carry out, the manifold tasks of government. A national leader does not need to make major choices about what government ought to do; he inherits a set of institutions that are committed—by law, by organization, by the professionalism of public employees, and by the expectations of voters—to appropriate a large amount of the country's resources in order to produce the program outputs of big government.

Whereas political leadership is readily personalized, government is intrinsically impersonal. It consists of collective actions by organizations that operate according to impersonal laws. Even when providing benefits to individuals, such as education, health care, or pensions, the scale of a ministry or a large regional or local government is such as to make the institution appear impersonal.

Contemporary Western political systems are first of all governed by the rule of law rather than personal will. When government did few things and actions could be derived from prerogative powers, such as a declaration of war, there was more scope for the initiative of leaders. Today, the characteristic activities of government, accounting for most public expenditure and personnel, are statutory entitlements to benefits of the welfare state. They cannot be overturned by wish or will. . . . Instead of the leader dominating government, government determines much that is done in the leader's name.

In a very real sense, the so-called power of a national leader depends upon actions that his government takes, whether or not this is desired by the leader. Instead of comparing the constitutional powers of leaders, we should compare the resources that are mobilized by the government for which a national leader is nominally responsible. The conventional measure of the size of government is public expenditure as a proportion of the gross national product. By this criterion, French or British government is more powerful than American government. Organization for Economic Cooperation and Development (OECD) statistics show that in 1984 French public expenditure accounted for 49 percent of the national product, British for 45 percent, and American for 37 percent. When attention is directed at central government, as distinct from all levels of government, the contrast is further emphasized. British and French central government collect almost two-fifths of the national product in tax revenue, whereas the American federal government collects only one-fifth.

When a national leader leads, others are meant to follow. The legitimacy of authority means that public employees should do what elected officials direct. In an era of big government, there are far more public employees at hand than in an era when the glory of the state was symbolized by a small number of people clustering around a royal court. Statistics of public employment again show British and French government as much more powerful than American government. Public employment in France accounts for 33 percent of all persons who work, more than Britain, with 31 percent. In the United States, public employment is much less, 18 percent.

The capacity of a national leader to direct public employees is much affected by whether or not such officials are actually employed by central government. France is most centralized, having three times as many public employees working in ministries as in regional or local government. If public enterprises are also reckoned as part of central government, France is even more centralized. In the United States and Great Britain, by contrast, the actual delivery of public services such as education and health is usually shipped out to lower tiers of a federal government, or to a complex of local and functional authorities. Delivering the everyday service of government is deemed beneath the dignity of national leaders in Great Britain. In the United States, central government is deemed too remote to be trusted with such programs as education or police powers.

When size of government is the measure, an American president appears weaker than a French or British leader. By international standards, the United States has a not so big government, for its claim on the national product and the national labor force is below the OECD average. Ronald Reagan is an extreme example of a president who is "antigovernment," but he is not the only example. In the past two decades, the United States has not lagged behind Europe in developing and expanding welfare state institutions that make government big. It has chosen to follow a different route, diverging from the European model of a mixed economy welfare state. Today, the president has very few large-scale program responsibilities, albeit they remain significant: defense and diplomacy, social security, and funding the federal deficit.

By contrast, even an "antigovernment" prime minister such as Margaret Thatcher . . . [found] herself presiding over a government that . . . [claimed] more than two-fifths of the national product in public expenditure. Ministers must answer, collectively and individually in the House of Commons, for all that is done under the authority of an Act of Parliament. In France, the division between president and prime minister makes it easier for the president of the republic to avoid direct entanglement in low status issues of service delivery, but the centralization of government accessarily involves the prime minister and his colleagues.

When attention is turned to the politics of government as distinct from public policies, all leaders have one thing in common, they are engaged in political management, balancing the interplay of forces within government, major economic interests, and public opinion generally. It is no derogation of a national leader's position to say that it has an important symbolic dimension, imposing a unifying and persuasive theme upon what government does. The theme may be relatively clear-cut, as in much of Margaret Thatcher's rhetoric. Or it may be vague and symbolic, as in much of the rhetoric of Charles de Gaulle. The comparative success of Ronald Reagan, an expert in manipulating vague symbols, as against Jimmy Carter, whose technocratic biases were far stronger than his presentational skills, is a reminder of the importance of a national political leader being able to communicate successfully to the nation.

In the United States and France, the president is both head of government and head of state. The latter role makes him president of all the people, just as the former role limits his representative character to governing in the name of a majority (but normally, less than 60 percent) of the voters. A British prime minister does not have the symbolic obligation to represent the country as a whole: the queen does that.

The institutions of government affect how political management is undertaken. The separate election of the president and the legislature in the United States and France create a situation of nominal independence, and bargaining from separate electoral bases. By contrast, the British prime minister is chosen by virtue of being leader of the largest party in the House of Commons. Management of Parliament is thus made much easier by the fact that the British prime minister can normally be assured of a majority of votes there.

An American president has a far more difficult task in managing government than do British and French counterparts. Congress really does determine whether bills become laws, by contrast to the executive domination of law and decree-making in Europe. Congressional powers of appropriation provide a basis for a roving scrutiny of what the executive branch does. There is hardly any bureau that is free from congressional scrutiny, and in many congressional influence may be as strong as presidential influence. By contrast, a French president has significant decree powers and most of the budget can be promulgated. A British prime minister can also invoke the Official Secrets Act and the doctrine of collective responsibility to insulate the effective (that is, the executive) side of government from the representative (that is, Parliament).

Party politics and electoral outcomes, which cannot be prescribed in a democratic constitution, affect the extent to which political management must be invested in persuasion. If management is defined as making an organization serve one's purpose, then Harry Truman gave the classic definition of management as persuasion: "I sit here all day trying to persuade people to do the things they ought to have sense enough to do without my persuading them. That's all the powers of the President amount to." Because both Democratic and Republican parties are loose coalitions, any president will have to invest much effort in persuading fellow partisans, rather than whipping them into line. Given different electoral bases, congressmen may vote their district, rather than their party label. When president and Congress are of opposite parties, then strong party ties weaken the president.

In Great Britain, party competition and election outcomes are expected to produce an absolute majority in the House of Commons for a single party. Given that the prime minister, as party leader, stands and falls with members of Parliament in votes in Parliament and at a general election, a high degree of party discipline is attainable. Given that the Conservative and Labor parties are themselves coalitions of differing factions and tendencies, party management is no easy task. But it is far easier than interparty management, a necessary condition of coalition government, including Continental European governments.

The Fifth Republic demonstrates that important constitutional features are contingent upon election outcomes. Inherent in the constitution of the Fifth Republic is a certain ambiguity about the relationship between president and prime minister. Each president has desired to make his office preeminent. The first three presidents had no difficulty in doing that, for they could rely upon the support of a majority of members of the National Assembly. Cooperation could not be co-erced, but it could be relied upon to keep the prime minister subordinate. . . .

Whether the criterion is government's size or the authority of the national leader vis-à-vis other politicians, the conclusion is the same: the political leaders of Great Britain and France can exercise more power than the president of the United States. The American presidency is a relatively weak office. America's population, economy, and military are not good measures of the power of the White House. Imagine what one would say if American institutions were trans-planted, more or less wholesale, to some small European democracy. We would not think that such a country had a strong leader.

While differing notably in the separate election of a French president as against a parliamentary election of a British prime minister, both offices centralize author-ity within a state that is itself a major institution of society.

As long as a French president has a majority in the National Assembly, then this office can have most influence within government, for ministers are unam-biguously subordinate to the president. The linkage of a British prime minister's position with a parliamentary majority means that as long as a single party has a majority, a British politician is protected against the risks of cohabitation à la française or à la americaine.

Variation within Nations

An office sets parameters within which politicians can act, but the more or less formal stipulation of the rules and resources of an office cannot determine exactly what is done. Within these limits, the individual performance of a president or prime minister can be important. Events too are significant; everyday crises tend to frustrate any attempt to plan ahead, and major crises—a war or domestic disas-ter—can shift the parameters, reducing a politician's scope for action (for exam-ple, Watergate) or expanding it (for example, the mass mobilization that Churchill could lead after Dunkirk).

In the abstract language of social science, we can say that the actions of a na-tional leader reflect the interaction of the powers of office, of events, and of per-sonality. But in concrete situations, there is always an inclination to emphasize one or another of these terms. For purposes of exposition, I treat the significance of events and personality separately: each is but one variable in a multivariate outcome.

Social scientists and constitutional lawyers are inherently generalizers, whereas critical events are unique. For example, a study of the British prime ministership that ignored what could be done in wartime would omit an example of powers temporarily stretched to new limits. Similarly, a study of Winston Churchill's ca-pacities must recognize that his personality prevented him from achieving the na-tion's highest office—until the debacle of 1940 thrust office upon him.

In the postwar era, the American presidency has been especially prone to shock events. Unpredictable and nonrecurring events of importance include the out-break of the Korean War in 1950, the assassination of President Kennedy in 1963, American involvement in the Vietnam War in the late 1960s, and the Watergate scandal, which led to President Nixon's resignation in 1974. . . .

The creation of the Fifth French Republic followed after events in Vietnam and in Algeria that undermined the authority and legitimacy of the government of the Fourth Republic. The events of May 1968 had a far greater impact in Paris than in any other European country. Whereas in 1958 events helped to create a republic with a president given substantial powers, in 1968 events were intended to reduce the authority of the state.

Great Britain has had relatively uneventful postwar government. Many causes of momentary excitement, such as the 1963 Profumo scandal that embarrassed Harold Macmillan, were trivial. The 1956 Suez war, which forced the resignation of Anthony Eden, did not lead to subsequent changes in the practice of the prime ministership, even though it was arguably a gross abuse of power vis-à-vis Cabinet colleagues and Parliament. The 1982 Falklands war called forth a mood of self-congratulation rather than a cry for institutional reform. The electoral boost it gave the prime minister was significant, but not eventful for the office. . . .

While personal factors are often extraneous to government, each individual incumbent has some scope for choice. Within a set of constraints imposed by office and events, a politician can choose what kind of a leader he or she would like to be. Such choices have political consequences. "Do what you can" is a prudential rule that is often overlooked in discussing what a president or prime minister does. The winnowing process by which one individual reaches the highest political office not only allows for variety, but sometimes invites it, for a challenger for office may win votes by being different from an incumbent.

A president has a multiplicity of roles and a multiplicity of obligations. Many— as commander in chief of the armed forces, delivering a State of the Union message to Congress, and presenting a budget—are requirements of the office; but the capacity to do well in particular roles varies with the individual. For example, Lyndon Johnson was a superb manager of congressional relations, but had little or no feel for foreign affairs. By contrast, John F. Kennedy was interested in foreign affairs and defense and initially had little interest in domestic problems. Ronald Reagan . . . [was] good at talking to people, whereas Jimmy Carter and Richard Nixon preferred to deal with problems on paper. Dwight D. Eisenhower brought to the office a national reputation as a hero that he protected by making unclear public statements. By contrast, Gerald Ford's public relations skills, while acceptable in a congressman, were inadequate to the demands of the contemporary presidency.

In Great Britain, Margaret Thatcher . . . [was] atypical in her desire to govern, as well as preside over government. She . . . [applied] her energy and intelligence to problems of government—and to telling her colleagues what to do about them. The fact that she [wanted] . . . to be *the* decision-maker for British government [excited] . . . resentment among civil servants and Cabinet colleagues. This [was] . . . not only a reaction to her forceful personality, but also an expression of surprise: other prime ministers did not want to be the chief decision-maker in government. In the case of an aging Winston Churchill from 1951–55, this could be explained on grounds of ill health. In the case of Anthony Eden, it could be explained by an ignorance of domestic politics.

The interesting prime ministers are those who chose not to be interventionists across a range of government activities. Both Harold Macmillan and Clement

Attlee brought to Downing Street great experience of British government. But Attlee was ready to be simply a chairman of a Cabinet in which other ministers were capable and decisive. Macmillan chose to intervene very selectively on issues that he thought important and to leave others to get on with most matters. . . .

In France, the role of a president varies with personality. De Gaulle approached the presidency with a distinctive concept of the state as well as of politics. By contrast, Mitterand [drew] . . . upon his experience of many decades of being a parliamentarian and a republican. Pompidou was distinctive in playing two roles, first prime minister under de Gaulle, and subsequently president.

Differences between French prime ministers may in part reflect contrasting relationships with a president. As a member of a party different from the president, Chirac . . . [had] partisan and personal incentives to be more assertive than does a prime minister of the same party. Premiers who enter office via the Assembly or local politics, like Chaban-Delmas and Mauroy, are likely to have different priorities than a premier who was first a technocrat, such as Raymond Barre.

Fluctuations in Leaders

The fluctuating effect upon leaders of multiple influences is shown by the monthly ratings of the popularity of presidents and prime ministers. If formal powers of office were all, then the popularity rating of each incumbent should be much the same. This is not the case. If the personal characteristics of a politician were all-important, then differences would occur between leaders, but each leader would receive a consistent rating during his or her term of office. In fact, the popularity of a national leader tends to go up and down during a term of office. Since personality is held constant, these fluctuations cannot be explained as a function of personal qualities. Since there is no consistent decline in popularity, the movement cannot be explained as a consequence of impossible expectations causing the public to turn against whoever initially wins its votes.

The most reasonable explanation of these fluctuations in popularity is that they are caused by events. They may be shock events, such as the threat of military action, or scandal in the leader's office. Alternatively, changes may reflect the accumulation of seemingly small events, most notably those that are reflected in the state of the economy, such as growth, unemployment, and inflation rates. A politician may not be responsible for such trends, but he or she expects to lose popularity when things appear to be going badly and to regain popularity when things are going well.

Through the decades, cyclical fluctuations can reflect an underlying long-term secular trend. In Europe a major secular trend is the declining national importance of international affairs. In the United States events in Iran or Central America remain of as much (or more) significance than events within the United States. In a multipolar world a president is involved in and more vulnerable to events in many places. By contrast, leaders of France and Great Britain have an influence limited to a continental scale, in a world in which international relations has become intercontinental. This shift is not necessarily a loss for heads of government in the European Community. In a world summit meeting, only one nation, the United States, has been first. Japan may seek to exercise political influence matching its growing economic power. The smaller scale of the European Community nations with narrower economic interests create conditions for frequent contact and useful meetings in the European arena which may bring them marginal advantages in world summit meetings too.

If the power of a national leader is measured, as Robert A. Dahl suggests in *Who Governs?*, by the capacity that such an individual has to influence events in the desired direction, then all national leaders are subject to seeing their power eroded as each nation becomes more dependent upon the joint product of the open international economy. This is as true of debtor nations such as the United States has become, as of nations with a positive trade balance. It is true of economies with a record of persisting growth, such as Germany, and of slow growth economies such as Great Britain.

A powerful national leader is very desirable only if one believes that the *Führerprinzip* is the most important principle in politics. The constitutions and politics of Western industrial nations reject this assumption. Each political system is full of constraints upon arbitrary rule, and sometimes of checks and balances that are obstacles to prompt, clear-cut decisions.

The balance between effective leadership and responsiveness varies among the United States, Great Britain, and France. A portion of that variation is organic, being prescribed in a national constitution. This is most evident in a comparison of the United States and Great Britain, but constitutions are variables, as the history of postwar France demonstrates. Many of the most important determinants of what a national leader does are a reflection of changing political circumstances, of trends, and shock events, and of the aspirations and shortcomings of the individual in office. ■

 # View from the Inside

Independent Council Kenneth Starr's detailed report on President Bill Clinton's liaison with Monica Lewinsky was filled with explicit and, some complained, sensationalist details. But it also provided a rare minute-by-minute glimpse into the life of the president of the United States. As the authors of this selection write, the Clinton-Lewinsky relationship unfolded "in moments stolen between the bill-signings, the state dinners and meetings with Government officials and foreign dignitaries." Here are excerpts from the *New York Times'* reconstruction of life inside the White House.

Questions

1. Consider all the events described in this selection that *did not* involve Monica Lewinsky. How do these various presidential activities illustrate the multiple roles played by the president in the American political system?
2. How would you describe the atmosphere in the Clinton White House during this critical period of the president's first term? Assuming this account is

accurate, what factors helped facilitate Clinton's affair with Lewinsky? What factors made the affair difficult to continue and to conceal?

10.6 Public Acts, Private Moments (1998)

Robert D. McFadden, John Kifner, and N. R. Kleinfield

Nov. 15, 1995

It was not a routine Wednesday for Mr. Clinton because a budget impasse with Congress had shut down the Federal Government, and 800,000 Federal workers were staying home for a second day, including over 80 percent of the White House staff.

The President had no public events scheduled, and he did not leave the White House. But he had meetings with aides, as well as with three Senators and a group of farmers. He had an appropriations bill and several proclamations to sign and an interview with a television network.

And there were major foreign problems on his mind. In Dayton, Ohio, negotiations to end the Bosnian war were at a critical stage. The President was grappling with another problem: whether to go through with a long-planned trip to Tokyo the coming weekend for a pan-Asian economic conference.

For days, his aides had debated the pros and cons of the trip, which was intended to ease rising tensions over economic issues. Foreign policy advisers argued he should go and not risk new tensions with Japan, or appear to be held hostage by Congressional Republicans over the budget. But domestic advisers had warned him of Congressional mischief in his absence.

Mr. Clinton early in the day decided to send Vice President Al Gore instead. His announcement would say he could not be away from Washington at such a delicate time. But sensitive to Japanese feelings, he delayed the public announcement until evening—morning in Tokyo—so he could first inform Prime Minister Tomiichi Murayama personally in a telephone call.

Dealing with the budget, Mr. Clinton spoke to Treasury Secretary Robert E. Rubin, who averted a national default by borrowing $61 billion from two civil service retirement funds to cover interest payments on the national debt and other bills, including Social Security payments.

In an interview with the CBS anchor Dan Rather, Mr. Clinton struck a defiant note against the Republicans, saying he would not give in to their "huge cuts in Medicare, Medicaid, education, the environment."

Mr. Clinton signed three proclamations, for National Family Week, National Farm-City Week and National Great American Smokeout Day, which was the next day.

The Family Week proclamation cited a "shared commitment to the importance of family life," in which Americans "first learn important lessons about responsibility." He called for greater efforts to prevent substance abuse, domestic violence and teen-age pregnancy.

The White House was unusually quiet throughout the day because the Federal shutdown had furloughed all but essential employees. As a result, the White House staff of 430 had shrunk to 90. Moreover, some were White House interns, who could continue working because they were not paid. Many, including Ms. Lewinsky, who ordinarily worked in the Old Executive Office Building, near the White House, took on a wide range of added duties that brought them into the White House.

Ms. Lewinsky, who had begun her internship in July 1995, testified before the grand jury that, after about a month, she began making eye contact with the President at White House functions, and both began what she characterized as "intense flirting."

At departure ceremonies and other events, she recalled, she shook Mr. Clinton's hand and introduced herself. Later, when she ran into the President in the White House West Wing, she introduced herself again and, she testified, he responded that he already knew who she was.

While Ms. Lewinsky's regular job was to work on correspondence in the office of the Chief of Staff, Leon E. Panetta, in the Old Executive Office Building, she was assigned during the one-week Federal shutdown to answer phones and run errands in Mr. Panetta's office in the West Wing.

On this day, as on other days during the Federal shutdown, Mr. Clinton went frequently to Mr. Panetta's office, and sometimes talked with Ms. Lewinsky.

At 1:30 P.M., according to the White House logs, Ms. Lewinsky entered the White House. The logs do not show the time of her departure that afternoon, and the Starr report does not say whether Ms. Lewinsky and Mr. Clinton encountered each other in the early afternoon.

At about 3:15 P.M., Mr. Clinton met with the Senate minority leader, Tom Daschle, Democrat of South Dakota, and Senators Byron L. Dorgan and Kent Conrad, both Democrats of North Dakota, and six Dakota farmers. The President told them he would fight steep cuts in farm subsidies that were being advanced by Republicans.

At 5:07 P.M., according to logs cited by the Starr report, Ms. Lewinsky re-entered the White House and resumed work; her departure from the White House was logged at 12:18 A.M. During virtually the same time frame—5:01 P.M. to 12:35 A.M., Mr. Clinton was in the Oval Office or in Mr. Panetta's office, the report said.

That evening, the report said, the President and Ms. Lewinsky "made eye contact" when he went to Mr. Panetta's office, and again later at an informal birthday party for Jennifer Palmieri, a special assistant to Mr. Panetta. At one point, they were alone in the office and, according to the report, "in the course of flirting with him, she raised her jacket in the back and showed him the straps of her thong underwear."

Sometime before 8 P.M., when the White House spokesman announced that the President had canceled his trip to Japan, Mr. Clinton spent 20 minutes on the phone with Prime Minister Murayama in Tokyo.

At about 8 P.M., as Ms. Lewinsky walked to a restroom, she passed the office of a Presidential adviser, George Stephanopoulos, the Starr report said. "The

President was inside alone, and he beckoned her to enter," it went on. "She told him that she had a crush on him. He laughed, then asked if she would like to see his private office."

He led her through a connecting door into the President's private dining room and toward his private study off the Oval Office. Ms. Lewinsky testified: "We talked briefly and sort of acknowledged that there had been a chemistry that was there before and that we were both attracted to each other, and then he asked me if he could kiss me."

In the windowless hallway adjacent to the study, they kissed, the report said, and before returning to her desk she gave the President her name and telephone number.

That evening, Mr. Clinton signed a $36.9 billion appropriations bill to provide money for the Department of Transportation and related agencies for the fiscal year that had begun on Oct. 1. The sum was only $1.4 billion less than the Clinton Administration had sought from Congress, and the White House expressed hearty satisfaction with the outcome of the bipartisan bill.

The Starr report quoted Ms. Lewinsky as saying she was alone in Mr. Panetta's office at about 10 P.M. when the President walked in. He invited her to rendezvous again in Mr. Stephanopoulos's office in a few minutes and she agreed, the report said.

They again returned to the private study and "this time the lights in the study were off," the report said. After a kiss, it said, a sexual encounter ensued. Because the study had uncovered windows, it took place, as did others later, in the windowless hallway adjacent to the study, the report said.

During the encounter, the telephone rang; the President answered it in the study, and while the sexual encounter continued there, he talked with a person Ms. Lewinsky took to be a member of Congress, the report said.

White House records show Mr. Clinton talked to Democratic Representatives Jim Chapman Jr. of Texas from 9:25 P.M. to 9:30 P.M., and John Tanner of Tennessee from 9:31 P.M. to 9:35 P.M., but no mention of a call after 10 P.M. was made. Before and after the sexual episode, the report said, Ms. Lewinsky and Mr. Clinton talked.

"At one point during the conversation," the report said, "the President tugged on the pink intern pass hanging from her neck and said that it might be a problem. Ms. Lewinsky thought that he was talking about access—interns were not supposed to be in the West Wing without an escort—and, in addition, that he might have discerned some 'impropriety' in a sexual relationship with a White House intern."

The duration of the conversation was unclear from the report, which noted only that Ms. Lewinsky left the White House after midnight, and the President was logged out of the Oval Office a short time later.

Nov. 17, 1995

The biggest Government shutdown in history was in its fourth day as the sharply diminished White House staff tried to cope with the heavy flow of Presidential pronouncements, correspondence, meetings, interviews and other activities.

Trying to get the Federal behemoth moving again, Mr. Clinton, as his first task of the morning, sent Congress a stopgap financing bill to get 800,000 Federal employees back to work, but he gave no ground in the budget impasse, warning that he would veto the Republicans' latest spending plan.

Mr. Panetta shuttled about Capitol Hill, seeking a deal, but the Republicans, led by House Speaker Newt Gingrich, refused to compromise on their plans for huge budget cuts, tax cuts and a balanced budget in seven years.

Gathering all the support he could muster, the President met at the White House with a delegation from the Leadership Council of Aging Organizations, representing 41 consumer, research and trade groups. They urged him to veto any bill that would cut money for older Americans.

Mr. Clinton also had a 15-minute Oval Office meeting with Alaska's Democratic Governor, Tony Knowles, who tried without success to persuade the President that oil drilling would have no long-term ill effects in an Arctic wildlife refuge in his state.

The President also acted on several foreign-affairs matters. He rebuked Congress over a Republican-sponsored bill to bar spending to deploy troops to Bosnia, saying it could torpedo the peace talks in Ohio. In a lengthy telephone call, he talked with President Nelson Mandela of South Africa about a multilateral response to Nigeria's hanging of nine human rights advocates, including Ken Saro-Wiwa, the writer.

And in an Oval Office interview with Japanese journalists, Mr. Clinton said he would reschedule his state visit to Japan but was vague about the timing. "I will come as soon as I can," he said. "This is very, very important to me. I hope the Japanese people will understand this is no expression of disrespect by me, either to the Government or the people of Japan."

He also said the United States' military commitment to Japan (47,000 troops) and the Asia-Pacific rim (100,000 troops) would not be diminished, despite calls for reductions in the wake of the rape of a Japanese girl in Okinawa, in which three American servicemen had been accused.

On this Friday night, two days after what Ms. Lewinsky said had been their first sexual encounter, both Mr. Clinton and Ms. Lewinsky worked late. White House logs show she checked out at 8:56 P.M. but returned at 9:38 P.M. for a little over an hour, according to Mr. Starr's report. She was still working in Mr. Panetta's West Wing office.

The report said that at 9:45 P.M., Mr. Clinton stepped into Mr. Panetta's office for one minute, then returned to the Oval Office. Because they were working late, Betty Currie, the President's personal secretary, and other staff members had sent out for pizza.

"I went down to let them know that the pizza was there, and it was at that point when I walked into Mrs. Currie's office that the President was standing there with some other people discussing something," Ms. Lewinsky testified. "And they all came back to the office, and Mr.—I think it was Mr. Toiv—somebody accidentally knocked pizza on my jacket, so I went to go use the restroom to wash it off, and as I was coming out of the restroom, the President was standing in Mrs. Currie's doorway and said, 'You can come out this way.'" Barry Toiv was Mr. Panetta's chief aide.

Ms. Lewinsky and the President went back to the private study off the Oval Office, and there they kissed, she testified. After a few minutes, she said, she told him she had to return to her desk, but Mr. Clinton suggested that she bring him some pizza.

A few minutes later, the report said, she returned with the pizza and told Mrs. Currie, who was now back in her office, that Mr. Clinton had asked for the pizza. Mrs. Currie opened the door for her and said, "Sir, the girl's here with the pizza."

"He told me to come in," Ms. Lewinsky testified. "Mrs. Currie went back to her office and then we went into the back study area again." A sexual encounter similar to the first ensued in the windowless hallway, Ms. Lewinsky related. . . .

Feb. 28, 1996

There were big doings for Chelsea in the works. Yesterday, she had turned 17. To mark the moment, Mr. and Mrs. Clinton had given a dinner for her and 10 of her friends at the Bombay Club, just a block's walk from the White House . There was chocolate cheesecake and a rendition of "Happy Birthday" by the pianist, with the whole restaurant singing along. While the President and the First Lady took the Presidential limousine back, Chelsea insisted on riding in the van with her giggling friends. But that was just the prelude. The Clintons were leaving for New York tomorrow to take their daughter to see some Broadway plays, something she was very much looking forward to.

Before they could set out, though, the President spent a workaday Friday attending to drug policy and cigarette sales and Midwestern winter storms. His major announcement was to certify Mexico as a full ally in the war against illegal drugs, though only after the Mexican Government agreed to commitments demanded by American law enforcement agencies. For the second year, Mr. Clinton did not certify Colombia.

There was other international and domestic news for him to ponder. The Federal Bureau of Investigation was frustrated that the Saudis were not doing more to investigate a truck bombing that had killed 19 American airmen. The Democratic Party, in one more development in the protracted campaign finance drama, said it would be returning $1.5 million more in contributions that it now felt may have been illegal or improper.

Shortly before 11 A.M., President Clinton appeared in the Roosevelt Room and spoke about an initiative to toughen the rules on cigarette sales to children. Among the new rules was a requirement that anyone under 21 who bought a tobacco product was to show a photo ID so that store clerks no longer had to guess the age of customers.

On the legislative front, Mr. Clinton signed into law H. J. Res. 36, which released money for international population assistance programs. He gave out a statement celebrating the third anniversary of the "Brady Act," which provided for a waiting period before someone could buy a handgun, calling the law "one of the most effective public safety measures ever."

In the course of the day, the President announced plans for several appointments, including his nomination of Joel I. Klein as assistant attorney general in the antitrust division of the Department of Justice.

He declared a major disaster in South Dakota, which had been pummeled by a severe winter storm in November, and ordered Federal aid to supplement state and local recovery efforts.

He also freed $250 million for a program to teach Americans about the harmful psychological and physical effects of sex before marriage. The program was to stress that abstinence from extramarital sex was the expected standard of the country.

It had been almost 11 months since the President had had physical contact with Ms. Lewinsky. Her expulsion to the Pentagon had succeeded in separating them. The only times she encountered him were at group events. She had seen him at a reception for the Saxophone Club, a political organization, and went with her family to one of the tapings of the President's weekly radio addresses. She got into the President's 50th birthday party at Radio City Music Hall in Manhattan, as well as a cocktail party for major donors to the Democratic Party. She testified that she saw him at a fund-raiser for Senate Democrats. Noticing that he was wearing a necktie she had given him, she approached him at the event and told him, "Hey, Handsome, I like your tie." She testified that he called her later that night.

"I was insecure about the relationship at times and thought that he would come to forget me easily," the Starr report said Ms. Lewinsky testified. "Usually when I'd see him, it would kind of prompt him to call me. So I made an effort. I would go early and stand in the front so I could see him."

The report said the two continued to talk with some regularity by phone, especially in the months after she began her job at the Pentagon. During the fall '96 campaign, the report said, the President occasionally called while on the road without Mrs. Clinton. At least seven of those conversations, the report said, were sexually explicit. But Ms. Lewinsky complained that she had not seen him privately and, according to her testimony, he told her, "Every day can't be sunshine."

On Feb. 14, 1997, Ms. Lewinsky placed a Valentine's Day ad in The Washington Post intended as a love message to the President. It was addressed to "Handsome."

At 6:29 P.M. on this Friday, Mr. Clinton went to the Roosevelt Room and taped his weekly radio address to the nation. Among those who attended the taping was Ms. Lewinsky. According to her testimony, Mr. Clinton had extended an invitation to her through Mrs. Currie.

In the address, which was broadcast the next morning, Mr. Clinton spoke of the need to prevent drugs from ruining children's lives. "First, we must fight drugs before they reach our borders and keep them out of America," he said, and he explained his decision that day to enlist Mexico in the battle.

At the session, Ms. Lewinsky had her picture taken with the President. She was nervous, the report said she testified, for she had not been alone with him since her days working at the White House. She wore a navy blue dress that she had bought at the Gap.

According to the report, Mr. Clinton told her to see Mrs. Currie after the photo was taken, since he had something to give her. Mr. Clinton, Ms. Lewinsky and Mrs. Currie together went into the back office. Stephen Goodin, an aide to the President, had told Mr. Clinton and Mrs. Currie that he did not want him alone with Ms. Lewinsky, which was why Mrs. Currie chaperoned them, the report said.

Mrs. Currie, however, said, "I'll be right back," and went on to the back dining room where, she testified, she waited for 15 to 20 minutes while the President and Ms. Lewinsky were alone in the study. As belated Christmas presents, Mr. Clinton gave Ms. Lewinsky a hat pin and an edition of Walt Whitman's "Leaves of Grass." He told her he had seen her Valentine's Day message.

In the hallway near a bathroom, Ms. Lewinsky testified, she engaged in a sexual encounter with Mr. Clinton. He heard something and they retreated into the bathroom, but no one disturbed them. According to White House logs cited in the report, Ms. Lewinsky left the White House at 7:07 P.M. ∎

Chapter 11

The Bureaucracy

Bureaucracy is a pervasive and inescapable fact of modern existence. Every large organization in society—not just the government—is managed by a bureaucratic system: tasks are divided among particular experts, and decisions are made and administered according to general rules and regulations. No one who has attended a university, worked for a large corporation, served in the military, or dealt with the government is unfamiliar with the nature of bureaucracies.

Bureaucracies, as the sociologist Max Weber observed, are a necessary feature of modern life. When social organizations are small—as in a small business or a small academic department—decisions can be made and programs carried out by a few individuals using informal procedures and with a minimum of red tape and paperwork. As these organizations grow, it becomes increasingly necessary to delegate authority, develop methods of tracking and assessment, and create general rules instead of deciding matters on a case-by-case basis. Suddenly a bureaucracy has arisen.

In the political realm, bureaucracies serve another purpose. Beginning with the Pendleton Act of 1883, civil service reformers sought to insulate routine governmental decisions from the vagaries of partisan politics—to ensure, in other words, that decisions were made on the basis of merit instead of on the basis of party affiliation. The Pendleton Act greatly reduced the number of presidential appointments in such departments as the Customs Service and the Post Office, putting in place an early version of the merit system. As the federal government's responsibilities grew, the need to keep politics out of such functions as tax collection, administration of social security and welfare, and similar programs became even greater.

The bureaucratization of government therefore serves important purposes: increasing efficiency, promoting fairness, ensuring accountability. Yet at the same time, it creates problems of its own. Bureaucracies have a tendency to grow, to become rigid, to become answerable only to themselves, and to create barriers between citizens and the government. These bureaucratic "pathologies" are well known; they are the subject of frequent editorials and commentaries. Politicians can always count on stories about bureaucratic inefficiency and callousness to strike a chord with the voting public.

As you read the selections in this chapter, keep in mind that the alternative to bureaucratic government in the modern world is not some sort of utopian system in which all decisions are fair, all programs efficient, all children above average. Limiting the power of bureaucracies means increasing the power of other institutions: Congress, the presidency, private businesses, or the courts. Reducing the power of the bureaucracy may also create a government that is less fair or less accountable.

Also keep in mind that bureaucrats—like baseball umpires—are most noticeable when they make mistakes. Americans tend to take for granted the extraordinary number of government programs that work well: the letters delivered correctly and on time, the meat inspected properly, the airplanes that land safely. Criticism and evaluation of the bureaucracy must be kept in a reasonable perspective.

Chapter Questions

1. What role does the bureaucracy play in any large social system? What functions does the bureaucracy perform? What are its most significant characteristics?
2. What is the relationship between the bureaucracy and the other political institutions in the United States? What are the alternatives to bureaucratic power? What are the advantages and disadvantages of these other forms of power?

 # Foundations

Any discussion about bureaucracy—in the United States or anywhere else—must begin with Max Weber, who is best known for his work laying the intellectual foundation for the study of modern sociology. Weber wrote extensively on modern social and political organization; his works include the unfinished *Wirtschaft und Gesellschaft [Economy and Society]* (1922) and the influential *The Protestant Ethic and the Spirit of Capitalism* (1904–1905).

Weber was born in Thuringia, in what is now eastern Germany, in 1864; he died in 1920. Although his observations on bureaucracy draw on historical and contemporary European examples, they were heavily informed by his experiences in the United States. While traveling in the New World, Weber was struck by the role of bureaucracy in a democratic society. The problem, as he saw it, was that a modern democracy required bureaucratic structures of all kinds in the administration of government and even in the conduct of professional party politics. Handing over the reins to a class of unelected "experts," however, threatened to undermine the very basis of democracy itself. In particular, Weber stressed two problems: the unaccountability of unelected civil servants and the bureaucratic tendency toward inflexibility in the application of rules.

In this brief selection, Weber describes the essential nature of bureaucracy.

Questions

1. What are the characteristics of the bureaucratic form of governmental power? What are bureaucracy's strong points? weak points?

2. Why are rules so important in a bureaucracy? What are the advantages and disadvantages of making decisions on the basis of general rules, rather than on a case-by-case basis?

11.1 Bureaucracy (1922)

Max Weber

I: Characteristics of Bureaucracy

Modern officialdom functions in the following specific manner:

I. There is the principle of fixed and official jurisdictional areas, which are generally ordered by rules, that is, by laws or administrative regulations.

1. The regular activities required for the purposes of the bureaucratically governed structure are distributed in a fixed way as official duties.

2. The authority to give the commands required for the discharge of these duties is distributed in a stable way and is strictly delimited by rules concerning the coercive means, physical, sacerdotal, or otherwise, which may be placed at the disposal of officials.

3. Methodical provision is made for the regular and continuous fulfillment of these duties and for the execution of the corresponding rights; only persons who have the generally regulated qualifications to serve are employed.

In public and lawful government these three elements constitute "bureaucratic authority." In private economic domination, they constitute bureaucratic "management." Bureaucracy, thus understood, is fully developed in political and ecclesiastical communities only in the modern state, and, in the private economy, only in the most advanced institutions of capitalism. Permanent and public office authority, with fixed jurisdiction, is not the historical rule but rather the exception. This is so even in large political structures such as those of the ancient Orient, the Germanic and Mongolian empires of conquest, or of many feudal structures of state. In all these cases, the ruler executes the most important measures through personal trustees, table-companions, or court-servants. Their commissions and authority are not precisely delimited and are temporarily called into being for each case.

II. The principles of office hierarchy and of levels of graded authority mean a firmly ordered system of super- and subordination in which there is a supervision of the lower offices by the higher ones. Such a system offers the governed the possibility of appealing the decision of a lower office to its higher authority, in a definitely regulated manner. With the full development of the bureaucratic type, the office hierarchy is monocratically organized. The principle of hierarchical office authority is found in all bureaucratic structures: in state and ecclesiastical structures as well as in large party organizations and private enterprises. It does not matter for the character of bureaucracy whether its authority is called "private" or "public."

When the principle of jurisdictional "competency" is fully carried through, hierarchical subordination—at least in public office—does not mean that the "higher" authority is simply authorized to take over the business of the "lower." Indeed, the opposite is the rule. Once established and having fulfilled its task, an office tends to continue in existence and be held by another incumbent.

III. The management of the modern office is based upon written documents ("the files"), which are preserved in their original or draught form. There is, therefore, a staff of subaltern officials and scribes of all sorts. The body of officials actively engaged in a "public" office, along with the respective apparatus of material implements and the files, make up a "bureau." In private enterprise, "the bureau" is often called "the office."

In principle, the modern organization of the civil service separates the bureau from the private domicile of the official, and, in general, bureaucracy segregates official activity as something distinct from the sphere of private life. Public monies and equipment are divorced from the private property of the official. This condition is everywhere the product of a long development. Nowadays, it is found in public as well as in private enterprises; in the latter, the principle extends even to the leading entrepreneur. In principle, the executive office is separated from the household, business from private correspondence, and business assets from private fortunes. The more consistently the modern type of business management has been carried through the more are these separations the case. The beginnings of this process are to be found as early as the Middle Ages.

It is the peculiarity of the modern entrepreneur that he conducts himself as the "first official" of his enterprise, in the very same way in which the ruler of a specifically modern bureaucratic state spoke of himself as "the first servant" of the state. The idea that the bureau activities of the state are intrinsically different in character from the management of private economic offices is a continental European notion and, by way of contrast, is totally foreign to the American way.

IV. Office management, at least all specialized office management—and such management is distinctly modern—usually presupposes thorough and expert training. This increasingly holds for the modern executive and employee of private enterprises, in the same manner as it holds for the state official.

V. When the office is fully developed, official activity demands the full working capacity of the official, irrespective of the fact that his obligatory time in the bureau may be firmly delimited. In the normal case, this is only the product of a long development, in the public as well as in the private office. Formerly, in all cases, the normal state of affairs was reversed: official business was discharged as a secondary activity.

VI. The management of the office follows general rules, which are more or less stable, more or less exhaustive, and which can be learned. Knowledge of these rules represents a special technical learning which the officials possess. It involves jurisprudence, or administrative or business management.

The reduction of modern office management to rules is deeply embedded in its very nature. The theory of modern public administration, for instance, assumes that the authority to order certain matters by decree—which has been legally granted to public authorities—does not entitle the bureau to regulate the matter by commands given for each case, but only to regulate the matter abstractly. This stands in extreme contrast to the regulation of all relationships through individual privileges and bestowals of favor, which is absolutely dominant in patrimonialism, at least in so far as such relationships are not fixed by sacred tradition. . . .

Technical Advantages of Bureaucratic Organization

The decisive reason for the advance of bureaucratic organization has always been its purely technical superiority over any other form of organization. The fully developed bureaucratic mechanism compares with other organizations exactly as does the machine with the nonmechanical modes of production.

Precision, speed, unambiguity, knowledge of the files, continuity, discretion, unity, strict subordination, reduction of friction and of material and personal costs—these are raised to the optimum point in the strictly bureaucratic administration, and especially in its monocratic form. As compared with all collegiate, honorific, and avocational forms of administration, trained bureaucracy is superior on all these points. And as far as complicated tasks are concerned, paid bureaucratic work is not only more precise but, in the last analysis, it is often cheaper than even formally unremunerated honorific service.

Honorific arrangements make administrative work an avocation and, for this reason alone, honorific service normally functions more slowly; being less bound to schemata and being more formless. Hence it is less precise and less unified than bureaucratic work because it is less dependent upon superiors and because the establishment and exploitation of the apparatus of subordinate officials and filing services are almost unavoidably less economical. Honorific service is less continuous than bureaucratic and frequently quite expensive. This is especially the case if one thinks not only of the money costs to the public treasury—costs which bureaucratic administration, in comparison with administration by notables, usually substantially increases—but also of the frequent economic losses of the governed caused by delays and lack of precision. The possibility of administration by notables normally and permanently exists only where official management can be satisfactorily discharged as an avocation. With the qualitative increase of tasks the administration has to face, administration by notables reaches its limits—today, even in England. Work organized by collegiate bodies causes friction and delay and requires compromises between colliding interests and views. The administration, therefore, runs less precisely and is more independent of superiors; hence, it is less unified and slower. All advances of the Prussian administrative organization have been and will in the future be advances of the bureaucratic, and especially of the monocratic, principle.

Today, it is primarily the capitalist market economy which demands that the official business of the administration be discharged precisely, unambiguously, continuously, and with as much speed as possible. Normally, the very large, modern capitalist enterprises are themselves unequalled models of strict bureaucratic organization. Business management throughout rests on increasing precision, steadiness, and, above all, the speed of operations. This, in turn, is determined by the peculiar nature of the modern means of communication, including, among other things, the news service of the press. The extraordinary increase in the speed by which public announcements, as well as economic and political facts, are transmitted exerts a steady and sharp pressure in the direction of speeding up the tempo of administrative reaction towards various situations. The optimum of such reaction time is normally attained only by a strictly bureaucratic organization.

Bureaucratization offers above all the optimum possibility for carrying through the principle of specializing administrative functions according to purely objective considerations. Individual performances are allocated to functionaries who have specialized training and who by constant practice learn more and more. The "objective" discharge of business primarily means a discharge of business according to *calculable rules* and "without regard for persons."

"Without regard for persons" is also the watchword of the "market" and, in general, of all pursuits of naked economic interests. A consistent execution of bureaucratic domination means the leveling of status "honor." Hence, if the principle of the free-market is not at the same time restricted, it means the universal domination of the class situation." That this consequence of bureaucratic domination has not set in everywhere, parallel to the extent of bureaucratization, is due to the differences among possible principles by which polities may meet their demands.

The second element mentioned, "calculable rules," also is of paramount importance for modern bureaucracy. The peculiarity of modern culture, and specifically of its technical and economic basis, demands this very "calculability" of results. . . . [The] specific nature [of bureaucracy], which is welcomed by capitalism, develops the more perfectly the more the bureaucracy is "dehumanized," the more completely it succeeds in eliminating from official business love, hatred, and all purely personal, irrational, and emotional elements which escape calculation. This is the specific nature of bureaucracy and it is appraised as its special virtue.

The more complicated and specialized modern culture becomes, the more its external supporting apparatus demands the personally detached and strictly "objective" *expert*, in lieu of the master of older social structures, who was moved by personal sympathy and favor, by grace and gratitude. Bureaucracy offers the attitudes demanded by the external apparatus of modern culture in the most favorable combination. As a rule, only bureaucracy has established the foundation for the administration of a rational law conceptually systematized on the basis of such enactments as the latter Roman imperial period first created with a high degree of technical perfection. During the Middle Ages, this law was received along with the bureaucratization of legal administration, that is to say, with the displacement of the old trial procedure which was bound to tradition or to irrational presuppositions, by the rationally trained and specialized expert. ■

 # American Politics Today

Critics of the American bureaucracy frequently attack the public sector as wasteful, inefficient, and unaccountable to the public. Such criticisms, however, are frequently nothing more than cheap shots, for they ignore the very great differences between the public and private sectors. A fair appraisal of the public bureaucracy must begin with a clear view of what we expect from the public sector and of the constraints under which it must operate.

The government, as James Q. Wilson points out in the following selection, does indeed compare badly to the private sector when viewed in terms of economic efficiency. The problem, he suggests, is that government is constrained in ways that the private sector is not. And those constraints, he concludes, come from the people themselves. It is the people—expressing themselves individually, by way of interest groups, or through the legislature—who impose the constraints under which the bureaucracy must operate.

Central to Wilson's argument is his attempt to broaden the concept of efficiency to include more than economic efficiency. If we measure governmental action by the simple standard of economic efficiency—that is, the cost per unit output—government compares badly to the private sector. Once we recognize that a true measure of bureaucratic efficiency must take into account "*all* of the valued outputs"—including honesty, accountability, and responsiveness to particular constituents—the equation becomes more complicated, and perhaps more favorable to the government.

Wilson's argument is no whitewash for the government bureaucracy. Even allowing for all of this, as he points out, government agencies may still be inefficient. Recognizing the multifaceted and complex constraints on government officials will, in any event, provide a reasonable and realistic way to evaluate the bureaucracy.

Questions

1. Wilson suggests that government officials operate under very different constraints from their counterparts in the private sector. What are these differences, and what is their effect? Put another way, why does Wilson assert that "the government can't say 'yes'"?
2. What values other than economic efficiency do we demand of government? Why is the avoidance of arbitrariness so important?

11.2 Bureaucracy: What Government Agencies Do and Why They Do It (1989)

James Q. Wilson

On the morning of May 22, 1986, Donald Trump, the New York real estate developer, called one of his executives, Anthony Gliedman, into his office. They discussed the inability of the City of New York, despite six years of effort and the expenditure of nearly $13 million, to rebuild the ice-skating

---

rink in Central Park. On May 28 Trump offered to take over the rink reconstruction, promising to do the job in less than six months. A week later Mayor Edward Koch accepted the offer and shortly thereafter the city appropriated $3 million on the understanding that Trump would have to pay for any cost overruns out of his own pocket. On October 28, the renovation was complete, over a month ahead of schedule and about $750,000 under budget. Two weeks later, skaters were using it.

For many readers it is obvious that private enterprise is more efficient than are public bureaucracies, and so they would file this story away as simply another illustration of what everyone already knows. But for other readers it is not so obvious what this story means; to them, business is greedy and unless watched like a hawk will fob off shoddy or overpriced goods on the American public, as when it sells the government $435 hammers and $3,000 coffeepots. Trump may have done a good job in this instance, but perhaps there is something about skating rinks or New York City government that gave him a comparative advantage; in any event, no larger lessons should be drawn from it.

Some lessons can be drawn, however, if one looks closely at the incentives and constraints facing Trump and the Department of Parks and Recreation. It becomes apparent that there is not one "bureaucracy problem" but several, and the solution to each in some degree is incompatible with the solution to every other. First there is the problem of accountability—getting agencies to serve agreed-upon goals. Second there is the problem of equity—treating all citizens fairly, which usually means treating them alike on the basis of clear rules known in advance. Third there is the problem of responsiveness—reacting reasonably to the special needs and circumstances of particular people. Fourth there is the problem of efficiency—obtaining the greatest output for a given level of resources. Finally there is the problem of fiscal integrity—assuring that public funds are spent prudently for public purposes. Donald Trump and Mayor Koch were situated differently with respect to most of these matters.

Accountability   The Mayor wanted the old skating rink refurbished, but he also wanted to minimize the cost of the fuel needed to operate the rink (the first effort to rebuild it occurred right after the Arab oil embargo and the attendant increase in energy prices). Trying to achieve both goals led city hall to select a new refrigeration system that as it turned out would not work properly. Trump came on the scene when only one goal dominated: get the rink rebuilt. He felt free to select the most reliable refrigeration system without worrying too much about energy costs.

Equity   The Parks and Recreation Department was required by law to give every contractor an equal chance to do the job. This meant it had to put every part of the job out to bid and to accept the lowest without much regard to the reputation or prior performance of the lowest bidder. Moreover, state law forbade city agencies from hiring a general contractor and letting him select the subcontractors; in fact, the law forbade the city from even discussing the project in advance with a general contractor who might later bid on it—that would have been collusion. Trump, by contrast, was free to locate the rink builder with the best reputation and give him the job.

Fiscal Integrity To reduce the chance of corruption or sweetheart deals the law required Parks and Recreation to furnish complete, detailed plans to every contractor bidding on the job; any changes after that would require renegotiating the contract. No such law constrained Trump; he was free to give incomplete plans to his chosen contractor, hold him accountable for building a satisfactory rink, but allow him to work out the details as he went along.

Efficiency When the Parks and Recreation spent over six years and $13 million and still could not reopen the rink, there was public criticism but no city official lost money. When Trump accepted a contract to do it, any cost overruns or delays would have come out of his pocket and any savings could have gone into his pocket (in this case, Trump agreed not to take a profit on the job).

Gliedman summarized the differences neatly: "The problem with government is that government can't say, 'yes' . . . there is nobody in government that can do that. There are fifteen or twenty people who have to agree. Government has to be slower. It has to safeguard the process."

Inefficiency

The government can't say "yes." In other words, the government is constrained. Where do the constraints come from? From us.

Herbert Kaufman has explained red tape as being of our own making: "Every restraint and requirement originates in somebody's demand for it." Applied to the Central Park skating rink Kaufman's insight reminds us that civil-service reformers demanded that no city official benefit personally from building a project; that contractors demanded that all be given an equal chance to bid on every job; and that fiscal watchdogs demanded that all contract specifications be as detailed as possible. For each demand a procedure was established; viewed from the outside, those procedures are called red tape. To enforce each procedure a manager was appointed; those managers are called bureaucrats. No organized group demanded that all skating rinks be rebuilt as quickly as possible, no procedure existed to enforce that demand, and no manager was appointed to enforce it. The political process can more easily enforce compliance with constraints than the attainment of goals.

When we denounce bureaucracy for being inefficient we are saying something that is half true. Efficiency is a ratio of valued resources used to valued outputs produced. The smaller that ratio the more efficient the production. If the valued output is a rebuilt skating rink, then whatever process uses the fewest dollars or the least time to produce a satisfactory rink is the most efficient process. By this test Trump was more efficient than the Parks and Recreation Department.

But that is too narrow a view of the matter. The economic definition of efficiency (efficiency in the small, so to speak) assumes that there is only one valued output, the new rink. But government has many valued outputs, including a reputation for integrity, the confidence of the people, and the support of important interest groups. When we complain about skating rinks not being built on time we speak as if all we cared about were skating rinks. But when we complain that contracts were awarded without competitive bidding or in a way that allowed bureaucrats to line their pockets we acknowledge that we care about many things besides skating rinks; we care about the contextual goals—the constraints—that we want government to observe. A government that is slow to build rinks but is honest and accountable in its actions and properly responsive to worthy constituencies may be a very efficient government, *if* we measure efficiency in the large by taking into account *all* of the valued outputs.

Calling a government agency efficient when it is slow, cumbersome, and costly may seem perverse. But that is only because we lack any objective way for deciding how much money or time should be devoted to maintaining honest behavior, producing a fair allocation of benefits, and generating popular support as well as to achieving the main goal of the project. If we could measure these things, and if we agreed as to their value, then we would be in a position to judge the true efficiency of a government agency and decide when it is taking too much time or spending too much money achieving all that we expect of it. But we cannot measure these things nor do we agree about their relative importance, and so government always will appear to be inefficient compared to organizations that have fewer goals.

Put simply, the only way to decide whether an agency is truly inefficient is to decide which of the constraints affecting its action ought to be ignored or discounted. In fact that is what most debates about agency behavior are all about. In fighting crime are the police handcuffed? In educating children are teachers tied down by rules? In launching a space shuttle are we too concerned with safety? In building a dam do we worry excessively about endangered species? In running the Postal Service is it important to have many post offices close to where people live? In the case of the skating rink, was the requirement of competitive bidding for each contract on the basis of detailed specifications a reasonable one? Probably not. But if it were abandoned, the gain (the swifter completion of the rink) would have to be balanced against the costs (complaints from contractors who might lose business and the chance of collusion and corruption in some future projects).

Even allowing for all of these constraints, government agencies may still be inefficient. Indeed, given the fact that bureaucrats cannot (for the most part) benefit monetarily from their agencies' achievements, it would be surprising if they were not inefficient. Efficiency, in the large or the small, doesn't pay.

But some critics of government believe that inefficiency is obvious and vast. Many people remember the 1984 claim of the Grace Commission (officially, the President's Private Sector Survey on Cost Control) that it had identified over $400 billion in savings that could be made if only the federal government were managed properly. Though the commission did not say so, many people inferred that careless bureaucrats were wasting that amount of money. But hardly anybody remembers the study issued jointly by the General Accounting Office and the Congressional Budget Office in February 1984, one month after the Grace Commission report. The GAO and CBO reviewed those Grace recommendations that accounted for about 90 percent of the projected savings, and after eliminating double-counting and recommendations for which no savings could be estimated, and other problems, concluded that the true savings would be less than one-third the claimed amount.

Of course, $100 billion is still a lot of money. But wait. It turns out that about 60 percent of this would require not management improvements but policy changes: for example, taxing welfare benefits, ending certain direct loan programs, adopting new rules to restrict Medicare benefits, restricting eligibility for retirement among federal civilian workers and military personnel, and selling the power produced by government-owned hydroelectric plants at the full market price.

That still leaves roughly $40 billion in management savings. But most of this would require either a new congressional policy (for example, hiring more Internal Revenue Service agents to collect delinquent taxes), some unspecified increase in "worker productivity," or buying more services from private suppliers. Setting aside the desirable goal of increasing productivity (for which no procedures were identified), it turns out that almost all of the projected savings would require Congress to alter the goals and constraints of public agencies. If there is a lot of waste (and it is not clear why the failure to tax welfare benefits or to hire more IRS agents should be called waste), it is congressionally directed waste.

Military procurement, of course, is the biggest source of stories about waste, fraud, and mismanagement. There cannot be a reader of this book who has not heard about the navy paying $435 for a hammer or the air force paying $3,000 for a coffeepot, and nobody, I suspect, believes Defense Department estimates of the cost of a new airplane or missile. If ever one needed evidence that bureaucracy is inefficient, the Pentagon supplies it.

Well, yes. But what kind of inefficiency? And why does it occur? To answer these questions one must approach the problem just as we approached the problem of fixing up a skating rink in New York City: We want to understand why the bureaucrats, all of whom are rational and most of whom want to go [sic] a good job, behave as they do.

To begin, let us forget about $435 hammers. They never existed. A member of Congress who did not understand (or did not want to understand) government accounting rules created a public stir. The $3,000 coffeepot existed, but it is not clear that it was overpriced. But that does not mean there are no problems; in fact, the real problems are far more costly and intractable than inflated price tags on hammers and coffeemakers. They include sticking too long with new weapons of dubious value, taking forever to acquire even good weapons, and not inducing contractors to increase their efficiency. What follows is not a complete explanation of military procurement problems; it is only an analysis of the contribution bureaucratic systems make to those problems.

When the military buys a new weapons system—a bomber, submarine, or tank—it sets in motion a procurement bureaucracy comprised of two key actors, the military program manager and the civilian contract officer, who must cope with the contractor, the Pentagon hierarchy, and Congress. To understand how they behave we must understand how their tasks get defined, what incentives they have, and what constraints they face.

Tasks The person nominally in charge of buying a major new weapon is the program manager, typically an army or air force colonel or a navy captain. Officially, his job is to design and oversee the acquisition strategy by establishing specifications and schedules and identifying problems and tradeoffs. Unofficially, his task is somewhat different. For one thing he does not have the authority to make many important decisions; those are referred upward to his military superiors, to Defense Department civilians, and to Congress. For another, the program he oversees must constantly be sold and resold to the people who control the resources (mostly, the key congressional committees). And finally, he is surrounded by inspectors and auditors looking for any evidence of waste, fraud, or abuse and by the advocates of all manner of special interests (contractors' representatives, proponents of small and minority business utilization, and so on). As the Packard Commission observed, the program manager, "far from being the manager of the program . . . is merely one of the participants who can influence it."

Under these circumstances the actual task of the program manager tends to be defined as selling the program and staying out of trouble. Harvard Business School professor J. Ronald Fox, who has devoted much of his life to studying and participating in weapons procurement, found that a program manager must spend 30 to 50 percent of his time defending his program inside DOD and to Congress. It is entirely rational for him to do this, for a study by the General Accounting Office showed that weapons programs with effective advocates survived (including some that should have been terminated) and systems without such advocates were more likely to be ended (even some that should have been completed). Just as with the New York City skating rink, in the Pentagon there is no one who can say "yes" and make it stick. The only way to keep winning the support of the countless people who must say "yes" over and over again is to forge ahead at full speed, spending money at a rate high enough to prevent it from being taken away. . . .

Incentives In theory, military program managers are supposed to win promotions if they have done a good job supervising weapons procurement. In fact, promotions to the rank of general or admiral usually have been made on the basis of their reputation as combat officers and experience as military leaders. According to Fox, being a program manager is often not a useful ticket to get punched if you want to rise to the highest ranks. In 1985, for example, 94 percent of the lieutenant colonels who had commanded a battalion were promoted by the army to the rank of colonel; the promotion rate for lieutenant colonels without that experience was only half as great. The armed services now claim that they do promote procurement officers at a reasonable rate, but Fox, as well as many officers, remain skeptical. The perceived message is clear: Traditional military specialties are a surer route to the top than experience as a program manager. . . .

Civilian contract officers do have a distinct career path, but as yet not one that produces in them much sense of professional pride or organizational mission. Of the more than twenty thousand civilian contract administrators less than half have a college degree and the great majority are in the lower civil-service grades (GS-5 to GS-12). Even the most senior contract officers rarely earn (in 1988) more than $50,000 a year, less than half or even one-third of what their industry counterparts earn. Moreover, all are aware that they work in offices where the top posts usually are held by military officers; in civil-service jargon, the "head room" available for promotions is quite limited. . . .

The best evidence of the weakness of civilian incentives is the high turnover rate. Fox quotes a former commander of the military acquisition program as saying that "good people are leaving in droves" because "there is much less psychic income today" that would make up for the relatively low monetary income. The Packard Commission surveyed civilian procurement personnel and found that over half would leave their jobs if offered comparable jobs elsewhere in the federal government or in private industry.

In short, the incentives facing procurement officials do not reward people for maximizing efficiency. Military officers are rewarded for keeping programs alive and are encouraged to move on to other assignments; civilian personnel have weak inducements to apply a complex array of inconsistent constraints to contract administration.

Constraints   These constraints are not designed to produce efficiency but to reduce costs, avoid waste, fraud, and abuse, achieve a variety of social goals, and maintain the productive capacity of key contractors.

Reducing costs is not the same thing as increasing efficiency. If too little money is spent, the rate of production may be inefficient and the managerial flexibility necessary to cope with unforeseen circumstances may be absent. Congress typically appropriates money one year at a time. If Congress wishes to cut its spending or if DOD is ordered to slash its budget requests, the easiest thing to do is to reduced the number of aircraft, ships, or missiles being purchased in a given year without reducing the total amount purchased. This stretch-out has the effect of increasing the cost of each individual weapon as manufacturers forgo the economies that come from large-scale production. As Fox observes (but as many critics fail to understand), the typical weapons program in any given year is not overfunded, it is *under*funded. Recognizing that, the Packard Commission called for adopting a two-year budget cycle.

Reducing costs and eliminating fraud are not the same as increasing efficiency. There no doubt are excessive costs and there may be fraud in military procurement, but eliminating them makes procurement more efficient only if the costs of eliminating the waste and fraud exceed the savings thereby realized. To my knowledge no one has systematically compared the cost of all the inspectors, rules, and auditors with the savings they have achieved to see if all the checking and reviewing is worth it. Some anecdotal evidence suggests that the checking does not always pay for itself. In one case the army was required to spend $5,400 to obtain fully competitive bids for spare parts that cost $11,000. In exchange for the $5,400 and the 160 days it took to get the bids, the army saved $100. In short, there is an optimal level of "waste" in any organization, public or private: It is that level below which further savings are worth less than the cost of producing them.

The weapons procurement system must serve a number of "social" goals mandated by Congress. It must support small business, provide opportunities for minority-owned businesses, buy American-made products whenever possible, rehabilitate prisoners, provide employment for the handicapped, protect the environment, and maintain "prevailing" wage rates. One could lower the cost of procurement by eliminating some or all of the social goals the process is obliged to honor; that would produce increases in efficiency, narrowly defined. But what interest group is ready to sacrifice its most cherished goal in the name of efficiency? And if none will volunteer, how does one create a congressional majority to compel the sacrifice?

Weapons procurement also is designed to maintain the productive capacity of the major weapons builders. There is no true market in the manufacture of missiles, military aircraft, and naval vessels because typically there is only one buyer (the government) and no alternative uses for the production lines established to supply this buyer. Northrop, Lockheed, Grumman, McDonnell Douglas, the Bath Iron Works, Martin Marietta—these firms and others like them would not exist, or would exist in very different form, if they did not have a continuous flow of military contracts. As a result, each new weapons system becomes a do-or-die proposition for the executives of these firms. Even if the Pentagon cared nothing about their economic well-being it would have to care about the productive capacity that they represent, for if it were ever lost or much diminished the armed services would have nowhere else to turn when the need arose for a new airplane or ship. And if by chance the Pentagon did not care, Congress would; no member believes he or she was elected to preside over the demise of a major employer.

This constraint produces what some scholars have called the "follow-on imperative": the need to give a new contract to each major supplier as work on an old contract winds down. If one understands this it is not necessary to imagine some sinister "military-industrial complex" conspiring to keep new weapons flowing. The armed services want them because they believe, rightly, that their task is to defend the nation against real though hard to define threats; the contractors want them because they believe, rightly, that the nation cannot afford to dismantle its productive capacity; Congress wants them because its members believe, rightly, that they are elected to maintain the prosperity of their states and districts.

When these beliefs encounter the reality of limited resources and the need to make budget choices, almost everyone has an incentive to overstate the benefits and understate the costs of a new weapons system. To do otherwise—to give a cautious estimate of what the weapon will achieve and a candid view of what it will cost—is to invite rejection. And none of the key actors in the process believe they can afford rejection.

The Bottom Line   The incentives and constraints that confront the military procurement bureaucracy push its members to overstate benefits, understate costs, make frequent and detailed changes in specifications, and enforce a bewildering array of rules designed to minimize criticism and stay out of trouble. There are hardly any incentives pushing officials to leave details to manufacturers or delegate authority to strong program managers whose career prospects will depend on their ability to produce good weapons at a reasonable cost.

In view of all this, what is surprising is that the system works as well as it does. In fact, it works better than most people suppose. The Rand Corporation has been studying military procurement for over thirty years. A summary of its findings suggests some encouraging news, most of it ignored amidst the headlines about hammers and coffeepots. There has been steady improvement in the performance of the system. Between the early 1960s and the mid-1980s, cost overruns, schedule slippages, and performance shortfalls have all decreased. Cost overruns of military programs on the average are now no greater than they are for the civil programs of the government such as highway and water projects and public buildings. Moreover, there is evidence that for all its faults the American system seems to work as well or better than that in many European nations.

Improvements can be made but they do not require bright new ideas, more regulations, or the reshuffling of boxes on the organizational chart. The necessary ideas exist in abundance, the top-down reorganizations have been tried without much effect, and the system is drowning in regulations. What is needed are changes in the incentives facing the key members. ■

 # The Comparative Context

Although the American civil service shares many attributes in common with all other bureaucracies, there are nonetheless certain unique features of public administration in the United States. Those differences include matters of structure and function and extend to the way the bureaucracy is viewed by political scientists. Like the bureaucracy it studies, the field of American public administration itself is unique.

The following brief statement of the differences between American and European public administration highlights both the governmental and academic sides of the question. Some of these differences relate to the American constitutional structure; others stem from historical differences between the United States and Europe; still others are a result of differences in political culture.

Questions

1. Of the ten items discussed in this selection, which seem most fundamental? Which seem least consequential?
2. How do the differences noted by the authors of this selection relate to differences in political culture between the United States and other countries (see selections 5.3 and 13.3 as you consider your answer).

11.3 The Distinctive Nature of American Public Administration (1983)

Gerald E. Caiden, Richard A. Lovard, Thomas J. Pavlak, Lynn F. Sipe, and Molly M. Wong

The scope of American public administration is distinct in at least ten ways. First, in contrast to the European tradition, it excludes public law. Public administration is not seen as the exercise of public law. Law is seen as part

Gerald E. Caiden, et al., *American Public Administration: A Bibliographical Guide to the Literature* (New York: Garland Publishing, Inc., 1983), pp. 4–8.

of the judiciary and the judicial system, and under the American doctrine of the separation of powers it is identified with the judicial branch of government, not the executive branch. Until recently, whenever the two overlapped, public administration gave way to the superior claims of the legal profession. Now, with public and administrative law becoming increasingly important to the practice of government, public administration is reaching out into judicial dimensions which the legal profession has been reluctant to explore. Nonetheless, public administration falls far short of the strong legal inclusion found in other countries where public law and public administration are indistinguishable.

Second, in contrast to the British tradition, it has excluded, until relatively recently, considerations of the ends of government and the uses of public office. Public administration has not been seen as the exercise of power. Public power has been seen as part of the study of political science and in the dichotomy that was propounded by Wilson and Goodnow the study of politics and uses made of public office were separated from the study of administration. Whenever the two overlapped, public administration yielded in this case to political science. With the acceptance of the administrative state and the emergence of Big Government, the processes of government can no longer be separated from the purposes to which they are put. Public administration has come now to include the objectives as well as the practices of public management. It has also been reaching out into policy and public interest dimensions which political scientists have been reluctant to explore. Nonetheless, there is still much diffidence, if not downright reluctance, to go beyond the dimensions of the management of public organizations. American public administration falls far short of the strong political inclusion found in other countries where public affairs have never distinguished between policy and administration and where the ends of government have never been separated from the means. Only recently in American public administration has it been realized that the two are (and probably always have been) fused and only recently have strong ideological differences emerged over the role of the administrative state in modern society.

Third, the generalist approach to the administration of public affairs has not been embraced in the United States to the extent that it has been elsewhere. The generalist tradition of the British administrative culture and the stress placed on intellectuality among European bureaucratic elites have provided an inclusive administrative profession to which other public management specialists have been subordinate. In contrast, the early emergence of strong professions in this country before the acceptance of a managerial profession (let alone the notion of a superior administrative cadre in the public bureaucracy) has fragmented the public sector into many rival concerns, few of which have accepted the superior imposition of a generalist administrative elite. Consequently, American public administration has been more of a residual than an inclusive entity. The armed forces and the management of defense have always been excluded, so too have the police and the management of justice, fire fighters, social workers, and teachers as well as members of the traditional professions (law, medicine, religion, higher education) employed in the public sector. These independent professions have jealously guarded their territory against intrusions from a generalist profession of public administrator. Since they were on the scene first, public administration has been reluctant to confront them and has tried to devise an amicable modus vivendi for peaceful coexistence. From a strictly logical point of view, the historical and political boundaries drawn between them make little sense. Compared with other countries, American public administration is less inclusory of public sector activities.

Fourth, the business community has been powerful in the United States and its influence over the public sector has probably been stronger than elsewhere. Many activities directly provided by the public bureaucracy in other countries are provided in the United States by the private sector or the significant third sector betwixt business and government, either directly or under contract with public authorities. Although part of the administrative state, they are not considered part of public administration; that is, scholars and practitioners have been reluctant to include them in their domains. On the one hand, this voluntary abstention has left significant gaps in the study of public administration which are now being filled hesitantly and inadequately. On the other hand, the blurred boundaries among the public, private, and third sectors have also opened up opportunities for the study of their interface which have been seized possibly to a greater extent than elsewhere. The same is probably true of intergovernmental administrative arrangements because of the blurred boundaries and jurisdictions among federal, state, regional, local, and community agencies in the United States.

Public administration in this country, fifth, is pragmatic, not ideological. The major concern has been to discover what works best in the public interest, construed in purely American terms in the light of prevailing conditions; rationalizations, justifications, and theoretical underpinnings have come afterwards. Yet this practical emphasis in American public administration should not be allowed to obscure its strong political roots in liberal democracy and the dominance of political principles over administrative practice and convenience. Democratic liberal values are paramount in American public management theory and practice. They are the lifeblood of the public bureaucracy. They are the unwritten premise on which the administrative state is expected to conduct itself. Since this is so well understood, American public administration has not felt the need to articulate its norms as much as other countries where the conduct of the state is subject to strong ideological differences and continuous political bargaining and shifting compromises.

Sixth, there really is no American public administration. It is a theoretical construct. Like Weber's ideal bureaucracy, it exists nowhere. It is a hybrid of common ideas and practices which have been abstracted from what exists. It is not a complete picture of reality, nor is it a photograph of specific circumstances. The United States is too diverse. Administrative arrangements and practices differ from one place to another, sometimes quite remarkably. In dealing with public administration as it really is, one experiences continual culture shock because experience contrasts so much with expectation. There are no common frames of reference; every office seems to be a law to itself, choosing within limits those practices which best suit itself. It is this variety that confuses and forces a level of abstraction that nowhere conforms exactly with reality. As a result, much in the study of public management is what should be rather than what is, and most is analytical not descriptive.

Next, because of constant change in public administration, history has little contemporary meaning. Historical analysis has little relevance to the present. In any case, administrators are so caught up with the present that they have little time for the past and little interest in having the past reconstructed for them. In brief, there is relatively little administrative history and, as the expense of holding archives for purely historical interest is rarely justifiable, the possibility of reconstructing the past diminishes with every passing year. The task is so daunting that there are few volunteers and precious little market. As a result, there is little historical continuity and many things are continually being rediscovered because often the left hand does not know what the right is doing (or has done). Anyway, Americans are not too proud of their administrative past nor of uncovering administrative skeletons that should remain buried. What is done is done. Only the present counts and making the future better counts even more. Public administration in this country looks forward not back.

Eighth, few figures dominate public administration in the United States. Other countries can point to their administrative heroes, those few individuals who dominated the public bureaucracy in their day or revamped it in their own image which lasted for an appreciable period after them. Not so here. Americans do not indulge in much historical veneration, least of all public administrators. One of the few exceptions is Robert Moses who dominated New York government for decades, but his legacy has almost vanished and his reputation has not lasted. The same applies for the scholastic domain where no figure has emerged comparable in status to a Max Weber or a Maynard Keynes. Leonard White exercised some authority for a period as did Dwight Waldo, but the only Nobel Prize recipient has been Herbert Simon, much of whose pathfinding work was done in public administration, but since the 1950's he has not been associated with the field. If there have been no giants, there have been many persons of commendable stature who between them have made the development of the field a cooperative venture.

Ninth, the absence of an intellectual colossus, lateness in arriving on the American scene, and the tendency to fragmentation, have all caused public administration to fight for its place in the sun. It is frequently overshadowed by such more powerful disciplines as law, political science, and business administration which primarily serve other constituencies. These rivals claim that public administration does not exist or that if it does, it is a minor part of something else (usually themselves), that to be anything more than a minor or subdiscipline, it will have to demonstrate more than it has a proper intellectual or theoretical base, a clear and unquestionable core, well-defined boundaries, and a logically consistent whole. In brief, it should have a distinct and commonly accepted paradigm in order to be accepted as a fully fledged member of the academic community. Outside the United States, public administration does not suffer such intellectual indignity nor react with such an intellectual inferiority complex. In this nation, public administration is continually forced to reaffirm itself, to justify its existence and to protect itself from takeover bids. It is continually searching for its soul, for its *raison d'être*, for its paradigm, for its identity. Periodically, it goes through its "identity crisis" and rediscovers itself. Nowhere else does public administration go through such soul-searching or experience such self-doubts.

Finally, nowhere else is public administration so misunderstood. The environment of public administration is decidedly unfriendly to it. Traditional American values exhort all that public administration is not and cannot be. In a country which once believed that "least government is best government," government management represents, rightly or wrongly, Big Government, bureaucracy, restrictions, taxation, dependency, authority, interference, parasitism, waste, spoils. Admittedly American bureaucracy has its shortcomings and failings, but no matter how well it performs—and to its credit it performs in the main most admirably—it never performs well enough. In mass media, it is rarely given the benefit of the doubt. Its motives are suspect; its actions are detrimental; its results are poor. It is almost axiomatic that business is better, that private enterprise is superior, that private organizations are more economic, efficient, and effective, and that the public sector is none of these things. No matter how satisfied and uncomplaining its clients, public administration cannot shake off its adverse images and stereotypes. It has to spend, perhaps justifiably, much effort not only proving that it does and should exist, but that its performance is good and constantly improving. ■

 # View from the Inside

Harvard economist Robert Reich left the halls of academia in 1993 to begin a term as secretary of labor in the first Clinton administration. Reich's diary of his two-year stint in Washington nicely illustrates the difficulties faced by a newcomer to Washington who is forced to find his way—both literally and figuratively—through the labyrinths of the government bureaucracy.

11.4 Locked in the Cabinet (1997)

Robert B. Reich

March 2 [1993] Washington

This afternoon, I mount a small revolution at the Labor Department. The result is chaos.

Background: My cavernous office is becoming one of those hermetically sealed, germ-free bubbles they place around children born with immune deficiencies. Whatever gets through to me is carefully sanitized. Telephone calls are pre-screened, letters are filtered, memos are reviewed. Those that don't get through are diverted elsewhere. Only Tom, Kitty, and my secretary walk into the office whenever they want. All others seeking access must first be scheduled, and have a sufficient reason to take my precious germ-free time.

I'm scheduled to the teeth. Here, for example, is today's timetable:

> 6:45 A.M.—Leave apartment
> 7:10 A.M.—Arrive office
> 7:15 A.M.—Breakfast with MB from the *Post*
> 8:00 A.M.—Conference call with Rubin
> 8:30 A.M.—Daily meeting with senior staff
> 9:15 A.M.—Depart for Washington Hilton
> 9:40 A.M.—Speech to National Association of Private Industry Councils
> 10:15 A.M.—Meet with Joe Dear (OSHA enforcement)
> 11:15 A.M.—Meet with Darla Letourneau (DOL budget)
> 12:00   —Lunch with JG from National League of Cities
> 1:00 P.M.—CNN interview (taped)
> 1:30 P.M.—Congressional leadership panel
> 2:15 P.M.—Congressman Ford
> 3:00 P.M.—NEC budget meeting at White House
> 4:00 P.M.—Welfare meeting at White House
> 5:00 P.M.—National Public Radio interview (taped)
> 5:45 P.M.—Conference call with mayors
> 6:15 P.M.—Telephone time
> 7:00 P.M.—Meet with Maria Echeveste (Wage and Hour)
> 8:00 P.M.—Kitty and Tom daily briefing
> 8:30 P.M.—National Alliance of Business reception
> 9:00 P.M.—Return to apartment

I remain in the bubble even when I'm outside the building—ushered from place to place by someone who stays in contact with the front office by cellular phone. I stay in the bubble after business hours. If I dine out, I'm driven to the destination and escorted to the front door. After dinner, I'm escorted back to the car, driven to my apartment, and escorted from the car, into the apartment building, into the elevator, and to my apartment door.

No one gives me a bath, tastes my food, or wipes my bottom—at least not yet. But in all other respects I feel like a goddamn two-year-old. Tom and Kitty insist it has to be this way. Otherwise I'd be deluged with calls, letters, meetings, other demands on my time, coming from all directions. People would force themselves on me, harass me, maybe even threaten me. The bubble protects me.

Tom and Kitty have hired three people to handle my daily schedule (respond to invitations, cull the ones that seem most promising, and squeeze all the current obligations into the time available), one person to ready my briefing book each evening so I can prepare for the next day's schedule, and two people to "advance" me by making sure I get where I'm supposed to be and depart on time. All of them now join Tom and Kitty as guardians of the bubble.

"How do you decide what I do and what gets through to me?" I ask Kitty.

"We have you do and see what you'd choose if you had time to examine all the options yourself—sifting through all the phone calls, letters, memos, and meeting invitations," she says simply.

"But how can you possibly *know* what I'd choose for myself?"

"Don't worry," Kitty says patiently. "We know."

They have no way of knowing. We've worked together only a few weeks. Clare and I have lived together for a quarter century and even she wouldn't know.

I trust Tom and Kitty. They share my values. I hired them because I sensed this, and everything they've done since then has confirmed it. But it's not a matter of trust.

The *real* criterion Tom and Kitty use (whether or not they know it or admit it) is their own experienced view of what a secretary of labor with my values and aspirations *should* choose to see and hear. They transmit to me through the bubble only those letters, phone calls, memoranda, people, meetings, and events which they believe *someone like me* ought to have. But if I see and hear only what "someone like me" should see and hear, no original or out-of-the-ordinary thought will ever permeate the bubble. I'll never be surprised or shocked. I'll never be forced to rethink or reevaluate anything. I'll just lumber along, blissfully ignorant of what I *really* need to see and hear—which are things that don't merely confirm my preconceptions about the world.

I make a list of what I want them to transmit through the bubble henceforth:

1. The angriest, meanest ass-kicking letters we get from the public every week.

2. Complaints from department employees about anything.

3. Bad news about fuck-ups, large and small.

4. Ideas, ideas, ideas: from department employees, from outside academics and researchers, from average citizens. Anything that even resembles a good idea about what we should do better or differently. Don't screen out the wacky ones.

5. Anything from the President or members of Congress.

6. A random sample of calls or letters from real people outside Washington, outside government—people who aren't lawyers, investment bankers, politicians, or business consultants; people who aren't professionals; people without college degrees.

7. "Town meetings" with department employees here at headquarters and in the regions. "Town meetings" in working-class and poor areas of the country. "Town meetings" in community colleges, with adult students.

8. Calls and letters from business executives, including those who hate my guts. Set up meetings with some of them.

9. Lunch meetings with small groups of department employees, randomly chosen from all ranks.

10. Meetings with conservative Republicans in Congress.

I send the memo to Tom and Kitty. Then, still feeling rebellious and with nothing on my schedule for the next hour (the NEC meeting scheduled for 3:00 was canceled) I simply walk out of the bubble. I sneak out of my big office by the back entrance and start down the corridor.

I take the elevator to floors I've never visited. I wander to places in the department I've never been. I have spontaneous conversations with employees I'd never otherwise see. *Free at last.*

Kitty discovers I'm missing. It's as if the warden had discovered an escape from the state pen. The alarm is sounded: Secretary loose! Secretary escapes from bubble! Find the Secretary! Security guards are dispatched.

By now I've wandered to the farthest reaches of the building, to corridors never before walked by anyone ranking higher than GS-12. I visit the mailroom, the printshop, the basement workshop.

The hour is almost up. Time to head back. But which way? I'm at the northernmost outpost of the building, in bureaucratic Siberia. I try to retrace my steps but keep coming back to the same point in the wilderness.

I'm lost.

In the end, of course a security guard finds me and takes me back to the bubble. Kitty isn't pleased. "You shouldn't do that," she says sternly. "We were worried."

"It was good for me." I'm defiant.

"We need to know where you *are*." She sounds like the mother of a young juvenile delinquent.

"Next time give me a beeper, and I'll call home to see if you need me."

"You *must* have someone with you. It's not safe."

"This is the Labor Department, not Bosnia."

"You might get lost."

"That's *ridiculous*. How in hell could someone get *lost* in this building?"

She knows she has me. "You'd be surprised." She smiles knowingly and heads back to her office.

• • •

April 15 [1994] Washington

Joe Dear, the assistant secretary for OSHA, whose thankless job is to manage the crossfire between business and labor on the passionate issue of workplace safety, relates the following story.

Last October, Robert Julian, a fifty-three-year-old employee at Bridgestone's tire plant in Oklahoma City, died when his head was crushed in an assembly machine that was supposed to have been shut off before he tried to reset it. In January, another employee's arm was severely mangled and broken in the same factory when he tried to unjam another machine that also was supposed to have been shut off. A month ago, a third employee was bashed on the head and badly burned by dye that was supposed to have been secured. And that's just the last seven months. Bridgestone's Oklahoma City factory has had a long history of gruesome deaths and injuries. The company's other plants have similar problems. Last week, a worker's head was caught in an assembly machine in its Morrison, Tennessee, factory. Co-workers pulled him out, but not before his face was badly mangled.

OSHA investigators have tried to coax Bridgestone into taking a simple precaution to make sure machines are turned off before employees reset or unjam or clean them—the same precaution that every factory in America is supposed to take. It's a lock that cuts the power off, which costs only about six dollars per machine to buy and install. But Bridgestone's executives won't budge. Joe thinks it's because they don't want to give employees the power to shut down the assembly line. The Rubber Workers local might use it for potential bargaining leverage in upcoming contract negotiations.

"We're proposing a seven-and-a-half-million-dollar fine, the maximum," Joe says in a monotone. I can tell he doesn't relish this fight. Bridgestone is a big company, the second-largest tire maker in the world. It'll drag the case through the courts for years unless we eventually settle for a fraction of that. And when we do settle, OSHA will come under heavy criticism for knuckling under. Worse, the final settlement may not be enough to get Bridgestone to mend its ways: The company may figure it's cheaper to pay up and continue risking employees' lives and limbs. It won't be the first time a company has made that kind of calculation.

I'm indignant. "We've *got* to stop this. Maybe they could get away with this kind of thing under the Republicans, but I'll be damned if we're going to let them do this on *our* watch." I can feel righteousness coursing through my veins.

Joe looks skeptical. "We can't go any higher with a fine. We might be able to go to court in Oklahoma City and get an emergency order forcing them to comply there. It's dicey."

"But workers are getting killed and maimed. Why not use all our ammunition?" I'm putting on my holster. "Let's also mobilize *public opinion*."

"Public opinion?" Joe's skepticism deepens.

I explain my theory: "Big companies like Bridgestone spend millions on advertising to boost their public image. If we get this story on television we'll embarrass the hell out of them and strike fear in the hearts of every other corporation that's screwing its workers." I strike the table with my index finger, trying to imitate Lloyd Bentsen (on a subject distinctly unlikely to bestir Bentsen's index finger).

Joe hadn't planned on my fury. He doesn't know how to manage it.

"I want to go out there," I say, simply. "I'll deliver the legal papers in *person*. We'll fly out Sunday night and do it Monday morning. We'll alert the media so they can be on hand. Afterward we'll hold a press conference, maybe with some of the injured workers, even the widows of workers who were killed."

"Widows?" Joe is incredulous. This is no longer a legal matter. It's become an issue of morality and public relations. He warms to the idea. "I'm sure Mrs. Julian will help us."

"Joe," I ask, "is this situation at Bridgestone as outrageous as it seems?"

"Yeah. It's bad, chief."

"Will the employees be with us on this?"

"No question. You'll be a hero."

"Okay, then. We go to Oklahoma City."

I imagine myself galloping into town on a large white stallion, a sheriff's badge pinned to my vest. Few feelings in public office are more exhilarating than self-righteous indignation—or as dangerous.

April 18 Oklahoma City

Late last night, we met in the federal building in downtown Oklahoma City to plan the final details of today's sting operation. With me are Joe Dear, Tom Williamson, who is the department's top lawyer, two security agents, and a press aide. We talk in whispers, although there's no apparent need. The building is nearly empty.

We plan the route that our two vans will follow to the company headquarters, the precise time of departure, when we'll alert the press so that they can set up cameras outside the gate and film us as we enter, when we'll alert the company president so that he has enough time to direct company officials to receive us but not enough to unleash his lawyers and publicists, what I tell the executives inside, and the time and place of the press conference afterward. Mrs. Julian has agreed to appear. The head of the Rubber Workers local is informed. He's thrilled we're here, and guarantees strong support from the workers.

Early this morning I place a call to Bridgestone's president at his home, near the company's Nashville headquarters. The company is Japanese-owned, and its president of North American operations is Matatoshi Ono. Mr. Ono's command of English is not all it might be.

"Hello, this is the Secretary of Labor. Is this the president of Bridgestone Tire and Rubber?"

"Yes. My name Ono."

"I'm sorry to trouble you at home, Mr. Ono, but this is a very important matter and I wanted to be sure to reach you."

"Home? Okay."

"Mr. Ono, the United States government is imposing a heavy fine on your company for failing to protect the safety of its workers, and is filing legal papers today to force the company to use a simple safety device."

"Wha'?"

I repeat the sentence.

"Okay. Okay."

"Do you understand me, Mr. Ono?"

"Understand? Okay."

"Would you like me to arrange for an interpreter?"

"Interpreter? Wha' interpreter? No. Okay."

"Mr. Ono, I'm visiting the Oklahoma City plant later this morning to deliver the legal papers in person. Please make sure your people receive me."

"Ready? Okay."

"Do you have any questions, Mr. Ono?"

"Question? No. Okay."

The morning is misty. Joe Dear, Tom Williamson, and I, along with two security agents, ride in silence across the flat countryside. I'm nervous. What if they don't let us through the gate?

A half-dozen TV cameras are waiting at the gate to record the spectacle. The guard allows us through. We park.

"We've hit the beach, captain," says Joe.

"Walk slowly and keep your ammo dry," I say.

We walk across the lot to the plant entrance. I imagine the scene on the evening news: barely visible through the mist, the silhouettes of America's runty but courageous Secretary of Labor leading his small battalion of gallant men to their fates, as they take on Industrial Evil.

Once we're inside, a nervous receptionist asks us to follow her. We walk down a narrow corridor and into a linoleum-floored room with a Formica table in the center, encircled by several chrome-and-plastic chairs. She says that two gentlemen will be with us shortly, then rushes off. *Is this an ambush?*

Two grim-faced men enter the room and ask us to sit. One is a top executive from company headquarters. The other is the plant manager.

I introduce myself and the others, trying to prevent my voice from betraying my nervousness. "We have come here to present you with court papers alleging that this plant presents an imminent hazard to the safety of its employees," I tell them gravely. Joe removes a half-inch-thick pile of legal papers from his briefcase and places them in the center of the Formica table. The two men stare at the pile, expressionless.

I continue, more forcefully. "We have urged you to correct these hazards in the past, but they have not been corrected. We have no choice but to seek an emergency order which will require you to equip employees on the assembly line with simple devices to turn off the power when they have to clean or unjam the machines. We're also imposing a seven-and-a-half-million-dollar fine."

I look intently at the two men. They stare back. They say nothing.

What *now?* We haven't rehearsed this part. Is this *it?* Are we *done?* At a minimum, I had expected them to try to defend themselves. This would have given me the chance to express outrage. I would berate them for failing to buy six-dollar locks that could have saved lives and limbs. They might have yelled back about government interference in the free market. At this point I'd coolly explain that the government exists to protect American workers from precisely the kind of callous, contemptuous bottom-line indifference to human life and suffering which they and their company represent. Having verbally vanquished them, I would then rise from my chair and, dripping with disdain, abruptly leave the room, followed by my stalwart team.

But neither of them utters a word. I look to Joe for guidance. Joe returns my gaze. Finally, I stand. The two men stand. Joe and the security agents stand. I extend my hand to one of the men. "Good-bye," is all I can think of saying. "Goodbye," is all he says. I shake hands with the other. "Good-bye." "Good-bye."

We march back out of the building and across the parking lot. The camera crews are still lingering outside the gate. I try to look determined, like someone who has just summoned the full force of the United States government.

A half hour later, the press has gathered for a news conference at a downtown hotel to hear of the great battle we have engaged. Mrs. Robert Julian, the widow, stands beside me on a raised platform, a frail woman in her late fifties. Around us are several of the employees who have been injured or maimed in the plant, and gathered around them are thirty or so members of the Rubber Workers local.

I'm at the microphone, explaining why I have come in person to Oklahoma City, describing the mayhem that the company has caused and what actions the department will take. I crank up to full throttle, doing a weak imitation of William Jennings Bryan: "We will *not* allow workers to risk death and dismemberment simply because a company refuses to buy a *six-dollar* piece of safety equipment. American workers are *not* going to be sacrificed on the altar of profits. We're *not* going to allow a competitive race to the bottom when it comes to the lives and limbs of American workers."

The workers around me applaud. Mrs. Julian's eyes fill with tears. There are a few questions from reporters.

Then, having cleaned up Oklahoma City, I ride off into the sunset on the next commercial flight back to Washington. I feel triumphant.

April 19 Washington

The triumph is short-lived.

Soon after I left Oklahoma, Bridgestone's vice president for public affairs held a news conference to rebut the Labor Department's allegations. He claimed the company's own procedures for servicing machinery were fully adequate. They don't need the Labor Department in Washington to tell them how to run their business, he says. The recent deaths and injuries were simply unfortunate accidents.

Then he delivers the bombshell: Bridgestone is closing its Oklahoma City tire factory, effective immediately. All 1,100 workers are out of jobs. He blames the federal government. Bridgestone is unable to comply with federal safety standards, he says.

Today's *Daily Oklahoman* uses my expedition as an illustration of the worst sort of meddling from Washington. In a bitter editorial, it accuses me of grandstanding for political purposes. Its front-page story quotes angry tire workers—now unemployed—saying I should never have come. One asserts that safety was never a problem at the plant: Assembly machines have to be kept running in order to be serviced properly. Checkmate.

Joe Dear and Tom Glynn are at my round table.

"It's not going quite as well as we might have wished," I say, hoping a touch of irony will lighten the mood. They don't smile.

Joe shakes his head. "I can't believe they closed the factory on us."

"So much for public opinion," says Tom. "If it's a choice between a dangerous job and no job, the dangerous job wins."

Kitty enters the room nervously, holding a wire story. "The federal judge in Oklahoma City just refused our request for an emergency order. Bridgestone announced it's reopening the factory *tomorrow*. But it won't reopen if we appeal the ruling."

"They're got us by the short hairs," says Joe.

Tom Glynn asks Joe if he'd considered, before embarking on the expedition, that the *Daily Oklahoman* was rabidly right-wing and that the district judge out there had been a Republican state senator before being appointed to the bench by George Bush. The answer is self-evident. Joe is silent. "It might be a good idea to check out these kinds of things before we do anything like this again," says Tom slowly. He's livid. He hates sloppiness. Tom's approach to public management centers on careful planning. Every option, every alternative, every possible outcome, should be considered in advance. The Oklahoma expedition was a case study in impetuousness.

"It's *my* fault, Tom," I say glumly. "It was my idea."

Self-righteousness blinded me to the pitfalls—not just the politics and ideology of the newspaper and the judge, but the larger political reality. Companies like Bridgestone have access to the best lawyers and public-relations people anywhere. They know how to play hardball when they need to. And they understand how to use to their advantage the deepest fear that haunts blue-collar America today: the fear of losing a decent job.

All I'd considered was the moral superiority of our position, and the thrill of mounting my white horse and galloping into town with guns blazing. I didn't figure that my stallion was old and limped and that the other side was equipped with surface-to-air missiles. It didn't occur to me that public opinion might turn so easily against us.

The meeting breaks up. Joe Dear lingers after Tom and Kitty have left. "Sorry, chief."

"Don't worry about it, Joe."

"Bastards."

"We won't give up," I say. "Even if we can't get the emergency order, we'll pursue the fine. It's big enough to make Bridgestone stop and think."

But I'm haunted by the idea that the company's green-eyeshade executives and lawyers have concluded that it's still cheaper to pay the fine than to give workers the power to stop the machinery when necessary in order to fix it. ∎

Chapter 12

The Judiciary

Some forty years ago, the constitutional scholar Robert G. McCloskey surveyed the history of the Supreme Court of the United States and concluded, "Surely the record teaches that no useful purpose is served when the judges seek the hottest political cauldrons of the moment and dive into the middle of them." Instead, "The Court's greatest successes have been achieved when it has operated near the margins of rather than in the center of political controversy, when it has nudged and gently tugged the nation, instead of trying to rule it."* Writing after the Court's 1954 school desegregation decision but before the controversies over reapportionment of state legislatures, abortion, busing, and school prayer, McCloskey feared for the Court's future if it did not learn the lessons of its past.

The Court, of course, did not follow McCloskey's advice. Over the past four decades, the Supreme Court has become an increasingly important force in American politics and the subject of intense, and at times bitter, political controversy. In the 1960s and 1970s, the Court's most controversial decisions involved questions of civil rights and civil liberties. Although such cases remain prominent on the Court's agenda, in recent years the justices have also turned their attention to other controversial issues, including those arising from the separation of powers, federalism, and economic rights.

All of this judicial activity has created a highly charged political debate over the proper role of the courts in American society. Presidents Reagan and Bush endeavored to reshape the Court along more conservative lines; several of their nominees provoked considerable controversy, and the nomination of Judge Robert Bork was defeated by the Senate. When his turn came, President Bill Clinton tried to push the Court back in the opposite direction. Each new nomination, and each controversial Court decision, has set off a new round of debate.

This chapter surveys the many aspects of the judiciary's role in American politics and society. Related material on questions of civil rights and civil liberties can be found in Chapters 3 and 4.

---

*Robert McCloskey, *The American Supreme Court* (Chicago: University of Chicago Press, 1960), p. 229.

Chapter Questions

1. What are the advantages and disadvantages of leaving political decisions to the courts instead of to the political branches of the federal government or to the states? What qualities do the courts have that make such activism attractive? Unattractive, or even dangerous?
2. What is the relationship between the federal judiciary and the other branches of the federal government? In what ways do the three branches of government work together to make policy? In what ways is the relationship competitive or adversarial?

 # Foundations

The Supreme Court's power to review acts of Congress and decide whether they are unconstitutional is perhaps the most extraordinary power possessed by any court in the world; the decision of five of nine justices can nullify the expressed will of the people's representatives in Congress. Moreover, the Court can strike down laws passed by state or local officials based on a conflict with federal law. Although Supreme Court decisions striking down major acts of Congress have been relatively infrequent, the Court has acted often to nullify unconstitutional measures passed by the states.

Despite the enormity of the Court's power of judicial review, as it is known, this power was not explicitly granted to the Court by the Constitution. The lack of specific language in the Constitution on this point—probably because the delegates could not agree as to whether the state or the federal courts should have the last word—made it necessary for the Supreme Court to claim and defend its power of judicial review later. The justices who were most influential in this struggle were Chief Justice John Marshall and his ally, Justice Joseph Story.

The following two selections trace the highlights of this struggle. The first is Alexander Hamilton's classic defense of judicial review in the *Federalist Papers* No. 78. The second is Marshall's 1803 decision in *Marbury v. Madison,* in which the Supreme Court first claimed the power of judicial review.

Questions

1. Hamilton begins his argument with a defense of the Constitution's provision for life appointment of justices of the Supreme Court. How does this argument relate to his and John Marshall's defense of judicial review?
2. Considering the other readings in this chapter, how reasonable is Hamilton's observation that the courts possess "neither FORCE nor WILL but merely judgment"?

3. Consider the validity of this statement by Justice Oliver Wendell Holmes: "I do not think the United States would come to an end if we lost our power to declare an Act of Congress void. I do think the Union would be imperiled if we could not make that declaration as to the laws of the several States."*

12.1 *Federalist* No. 78 (1788)

Alexander Hamilton

Outline

I. Mode of appointment of federal judges.

II. Necessity of lifetime appointments for federal judges.

A. The judiciary is the least dangerous and the weakest branch; life tenure is essential to preserving its independence from the other branches.

B. Life tenure is particularly important in a system with a limited Constitution, which cannot be preserved in practice except if judges have the authority to strike down laws that are inconsistent with the Constitution (a power known as judicial review).

1. Defense of judicial review.

   i. Congress merely acts as the agent of the people; the Constitution sets out the terms of agency and must take precedence over acts of Congress.

   ii. The Constitution is a fundamental law; it belongs to the judges to give it meaning and to enforce it in preference to any legislative act.

   iii. The Courts cannot substitute their own judgment for that of the legislature; they must exercise judgment, not will.

   iv. Judges must be independent (and thus hold life tenure) in order to play this role without legislative interference.

2. An independent judiciary also protects against legislative acts which do not violate the Constitution but do interfere with private rights.

3. There are a few individuals in society who combine the necessary skill and integrity to be federal judges; life tenure may be necessary to encourage such people to leave the private practice of law for the federal bench.

---

*Oliver Wendell Holmes, "Law and the Court," address delivered February 15, 1913, in *Collected Legal Papers* (New York: Peter Smith, 1952), pp. 295–296.

We proceed now to an examination of the judiciary department of the proposed government.

In unfolding the defects of the existing Confederation, the utility and necessity of a federal judicature have been clearly pointed out. It is the less necessary to recapitulate the considerations there urged, as the propriety of the institution in the abstract is not disputed; the only questions which have been raised being relative to the manner of constituting it, and to its extent. To these points, therefore, our observations shall be confined.

The manner of constituting it seems to embrace these several objects: 1st. The mode of appointing the judges. 2d. The tenure by which they are to hold their places. . . .

First. As to the mode of appointing the judges; this is the same with that of appointing the officers of the Union in general. . . .

Second. As to the tenure by which the judges are to hold their places; this chiefly concerns their duration in office; the provisions for their support; the precautions for their responsibility.

According to the plan of the convention, all judges who may be appointed by the United States are to hold their offices DURING GOOD BEHAVIOR; which is conformable to the most approved of the State constitutions and among the rest, to that of this State. Its propriety having been drawn into question by the adversaries of that plan, is no light symptom of the rage for objection, which disorders their imaginations and judgments. The standard of good behavior for the continuance in office of the judicial magistracy, is certainly one of the most valuable of the modern improvements in the practice of government. In a monarchy it is an excellent barrier to the despotism of the prince; in a republic it is a no less excellent barrier to the encroachments and oppressions of the representative body. And it is the best expedient which can be devised in any government, to secure a steady, upright, and impartial administration of the laws.

Whoever attentively considers the different departments of power must perceive, that, in a government in which they are separated from each other, the judiciary, from the nature of its functions, will always be the least dangerous to the political rights of the Constitution; because it will be least in a capacity to annoy or injure them. The Executive not only dispenses the honors, but holds the sword of the community. The legislature not only commands the purse, but prescribes the rules by which the duties and rights of every citizen are to be regulated. The judiciary, on the contrary, has no influence over either the sword or the purse; no direction either of the strength or of the wealth of the society; and can take no active resolution whatever. It may truly be said to have neither FORCE nor WILL, but merely judgment; and must ultimately depend upon the aid of the executive arm even for the efficacy of its judgments.

This simple view of the matter suggests several important consequences. It proves incontestably, that the judiciary is beyond comparison the weakest of the three departments of power; that it can never attack with success either of the other two; and that all possible care is requisite to enable it to defend itself against their attacks. It equally proves, that though individual oppression may now and then proceed from the courts of justice, the general liberty of the people can never be endangered from that quarter; I mean so long as the judiciary remains truly distinct from both the legislature and the Executive. For I agree, that "there is no liberty, if the power of judging be not separated from the legislative and executive powers." And it proves, in the last place, that as liberty can have nothing to fear from the judiciary alone, but would have every thing to fear from its union with either of the other departments; that as all the effects of such a union must ensue from a dependence of the former on the latter, notwithstanding a nominal and apparent separation; that as, from the natural feebleness of the judiciary, it is in continual jeopardy of being overpowered, awed, or influenced by its coordinate branches; and that as nothing can contribute so much to its firmness and independence as permanency in office, this quality may therefore be justly regarded as an indispensable ingredient in its constitution, and, in a great measure, as the citadel of the public justice and the public security.

The complete independence of the courts of justice is peculiarly essential in a limited Constitution. By a limited Constitution, I understand one which contains certain specified exceptions to the legislative authority; such, for instance, as that it shall pass no bills of attainder, no *ex-post-facto* laws, and the like. Limitations of this kind can be preserved in practice no other way than through the medium of courts of justice, whose duty it must be to declare all acts contrary to the manifest tenor of the Constitution void. Without this, all the reservations of particular rights or privileges would amount to nothing.

Some perplexity respecting the rights of the courts to pronounce legislative acts void, because contrary to the Constitution, has arisen from an imagination that the doctrine would imply a superiority of the judiciary to the legislative power. It is urged that the authority which can declare the acts of another void, must necessarily be superior to the one whose acts may be declared void. As this doctrine is of great importance in all the American constitutions, a brief discussion of the ground on which it rests cannot be unacceptable.

There is no position which depends on clearer principles, than that every act of a delegated authority, contrary to the tenor of the commission under which it is exercised, is void. No legislative act, therefore, contrary to the Constitution, can be valid. To deny this, would be to affirm, that the deputy is greater than his principal; that the servant is above his master; that the representatives of the people are superior to the people themselves; that men acting by virtue of powers, may do not only what their powers do not authorize, but what they forbid.

If it be said that the legislative body are themselves the constitutional judges of their own powers, and that the construction they put upon them is conclusive upon the other departments, it may be answered, that this cannot be the natural presumption, where it is not to be collected from any particular provisions in the Constitution. It is not otherwise to be supposed, that the Constitution could intend to enable the representatives of the people to substitute their WILL to that of their constituents. It is far more rational to suppose, that the courts were designed to be an intermediate body between the people and the legislature, in order, among other things, to keep the latter within the limits assigned to their authority. The interpretation of the laws is the proper and peculiar province of the courts. A constitution is, in fact, and must be regarded by the judges, as a fundamental law. It therefore belongs to them to ascertain its meaning, as well as the meaning of any particular act proceeding from the legislative body. If there should happen to be an irreconcilable variance between the two, that which has the superior obligation and validity ought, of course, to be preferred; or, in other words, the Constitution ought to be preferred to the statute, the intention of the people to the intention of their agents.

Nor does this conclusion by any means suppose a superiority of the judicial to the legislative power. It only supposes that the power of the people is superior to both; and that where the will of the legislature, declared in its statutes, stands in opposition to that of the people, declared in the Constitution, the judges ought to be governed by the latter rather than the former. They ought to regulate their decisions by the fundamental laws, rather than by those which are not fundamental.

This exercise of judicial discretion, in determining between two contradictory laws, is exemplified in a familiar instance. It not uncommonly happens, that there are two statutes existing at one time, clashing in whole or in part with each other, and neither of them containing any repealing clause or expression. In such a case, it is the province of the courts to liquidate and fix their meaning and operation. So far as they can, by any fair construction, be reconciled to each other, reason and law conspire to dictate that this should be done; where this is impracticable, it becomes a matter of necessity to give effect to one, in exclusion of the other. The rule which has obtained in the courts for determining their relative validity is, that the last in order of time shall be preferred to the first. But this is a mere rule of construction, not derived from any positive law, but from the nature and reason of the thing. It is a rule not enjoined upon the courts by legislative provision, but adopted by themselves, as consonant to truth and propriety, for the direction of their conduct as interpreters of the law. They thought it reasonable, that between the interfering acts of an EQUAL authority, that which was the last indication of its will should have the preference.

But in regard to the interfering acts of a superior and subordinate authority, of an original and derivative power, the nature and reason of the thing indicate the converse of that rule as proper to be followed. They teach us that the prior act of a superior ought to be preferred to the subsequent act of an inferior and subordinate authority; and that accordingly, whenever a particular statute contravenes the Constitution, it will be the duty of the judicial tribunals to adhere to the latter and disregard the former.

It can be of no weight to say that the courts, on the pretense of a repugnancy, may substitute their own pleasure to the constitutional intentions of the legislature. This might as well happen in the case of two contradictory statutes; or it might as well happen in every adjudication upon any single statute. The courts must declare the sense of the law; and if they should be disposed to exercise WILL instead of JUDGMENT, the consequence would equally be the substitution of their pleasure to that of the legislative body. The observation, if it prove any thing, would prove that there ought to be no judges distinct from that body.

If, then, the courts of justice are to be considered as the bulwarks of a limited Constitution against legislative encroachments, this consideration will afford a strong argument for the permanent tenure of judicial offices, since nothing will contribute so much as this to that independent spirit in the judges which must be essential to the faithful performance of so arduous a duty.

This independence of the judges is equally requisite to guard the Constitution and the rights of individuals from the effects of those ill humors, which the arts of designing men, or the influence of particular conjunctures, sometimes disseminate among the people themselves, and which, though they speedily give place to better information, and more deliberate reflection, have a tendency, in the meantime, to occasion dangerous innovations in the government, and serious oppressions of the minor party in the community. Though I trust the friends of the proposed Constitution will never concur with its enemies, in questioning that fundamental principle of republican government, which admits the right of the people to alter or abolish the established Constitution, whenever they find it inconsistent with their happiness, yet it is not to be inferred from this principle, that the representatives of the people, whenever a momentary inclination happens to lay hold of a majority of their constituents, incompatible with the provisions in the existing Constitution, would, on that account, be justifiable in a violation of those provisions; or that the courts would be under a greater obligation to connive at infractions in this shape, than when they had proceeded wholly from the cabals of the representative body. Until the people have, by some solemn and authoritative act, annulled or changed the established form, it is binding upon themselves collectively, as well as individually; and no presumption, or even knowledge, of their sentiments, can warrant their representatives in a departure from it, prior to such an act. But it is easy to see, that it would require an uncommon portion of fortitude in the judges to do their duty as faithful guardians of the Constitution, where legislative invasions of it had been instigated by the major voice of the community.

But it is not with a view to infractions of the Constitution only, that the independence of the judges may be an essential safeguard against the effects of occasional ill humors in the society. These sometimes extend no farther than to the injury of the private rights of particular classes of citizens, by unjust and partial laws. Here also the firmness of the judicial magistracy is of vast importance in mitigating the severity and confining the operation of such laws. It not only serves to moderate the immediate mischiefs of those which may have been passed, but it operates as a check upon the legislative body in passing them; who, perceiving that obstacles to the success of iniquitous intention are to be expected from the scruples of the courts, are in a manner compelled, by the very motives of the injustice they meditate, to qualify their attempts. This is a circumstance calculated to have more influence upon the character of our governments, than but few may be aware of. The benefits of the integrity and moderation of the judiciary have already been felt in more States than one; and though they may have displeased those whose sinister expectations they may have disappointed, they must have commanded the esteem and applause of all the virtuous and disinterested. Considerate men, of every description, ought to prize whatever will tend to beget or fortify that temper in the courts: as no man can be sure that he may not be to-morrow the victim of a spirit of injustice, by which he may be a gainer to-day. And every man must now feel, that the inevitable tendency of such a spirit is to sap the foundations of public and private confidence, and to introduce in its stead universal distrust and distress.

That inflexible and uniform adherence to the rights of the Constitution, and of individuals, which we perceive to be indispensable in the courts of justice, can certainly not be expected from judges who hold their offices by a temporary commission. Periodical appointments, however regulated, or by whomsoever made, would, in some way or other, be fatal to their necessary independence. If the power of making them was committed either to the Executive or legislature, there would be danger of an improper complaisance to the branch which possessed it; if to both, there would be an unwillingness to hazard the displeasure of either; if to the people, or the persons chosen by them for the special purpose, there would be too great a disposition to consult popularity, to justify a reliance that nothing would be consulted but the Constitution and the laws.

There is yet a further and a weightier reason for the permanency of the judicial offices, which is deducible from the nature of the qualifications they require. It has been frequently remarked, with great propriety, that a voluminous code of laws is one of the inconveniences necessarily connected with the advantages of a free government. To avoid an arbitrary discretion in the courts, it is indispensable that they should be bound down by strict rules and precedents, which serve to define and point out their duty in every particular case that comes before them; and it will readily be conceived from the variety of controversies which grow out of the folly and wickedness of mankind, that the records of those precedents must unavoidably swell to a very considerable bulk, and must demand long and laborious study to acquire a competent knowledge of them. Hence it is, that there can be but few men in the society who will have sufficient skill in the laws to qualify them for the stations of judges. And making the proper deductions for the ordinary depravity of human nature, the number must be still smaller of those who unite the requisite integrity with the requisite knowledge. These considerations apprise us, that the government can have no great option between fit character; and that a temporary duration in office, which would naturally discourage such characters from quitting a lucrative line of practice to accept a seat on the bench, would have a tendency to throw the administration of justice into hands less able, and less well qualified, to conduct it with utility and dignity. In the present circumstances of this country, and in those in which it is likely to be for a long time to come, the disadvantages on this score would be greater than they may at first sight appear; but it must be confessed, that they are far inferior to those which present themselves under the other aspects of the subject.

Upon the whole, there can be no room to doubt that the convention acted wisely in copying from the models of those constitutions which have established GOOD BEHAVIOR as the tenure of their judicial offices, in point of duration; and that so far from being blamable on this account, their plan would have been inexcusably defective, if it had wanted this important feature of good government. The experience of Great Britain affords an illustrious comment on the excellence of the institution. ■

12.2 *Marbury v. Madison* (1803)

John Marshall

[In 1801, at the very end of his presidential term, John Adams made a number of last-minute judicial appointments, hoping to install members of his own Federalist party in key positions before the Republican president, Thomas Jefferson, took over. One of these

5 U.S. (1 Cranch) 137 (1803).

appointments was given to William Marbury, who was appointed to be a justice of the peace of the District of Columbia. In the confusion of the last few days of Adams's term, however, Marbury's commission was never delivered to him. When President Jefferson came into the White House, he held up Marbury's commission. Marbury sued in the Supreme Court, asking the Court to order the new secretary of state, James Madison, to deliver the commission to him.

The legal and political aspects of the case are extremely complex. Chief Justice Marshall, a staunch Federalist, did not want to condone Jefferson's actions, but he also did not want to risk ordering the administration to deliver the commission; he would be a laughing stock if Jefferson and Madison simply ignored him. He solved this dilemma by writing a strong opinion condemning Jefferson's acts as illegal but refusing to issue a compliance order. To do so, Marshall concluded, would be unconstitutional.

In one stroke, Marshall embarrassed Jefferson, protected his own position, and claimed for the first time the power to review acts of Congress as unconstitutional. The part of the argument making the last point follows.]

· · ·

The question, whether an act, repugnant to the constitution, can become the law of the land, is a question deeply interesting to the United States; but, happily, not of an intricacy proportioned to its interest. It seems only necessary to recognize certain principles, supposed to have been long and well established, to decide it.

That the people have an original right to establish, for their future government, such principles as, in their opinion, shall most conduce to their own happiness, is the basis on which the whole American fabric has been erected. The exercise of this original right is a very great exertion; nor can it, nor ought it, to be frequently repeated. The principles, therefore, so established, are deemed fundamental. And as the authority from which they proceed, is supreme, and can seldom act, they are designed to be permanent.

This original and supreme will organizes the government, and assigns, to different departments, their respective powers. It may either stop here; or establish certain limits not to be transcended by those departments.

The government of the United States is of the latter description. The powers of the legislature are defined, and limited; and that those limits may not be mistaken, or forgotten, the constitution is written. To what purpose are powers limited, and to what purpose is that limitation committed to writing, if these limits may, at any time, be passed by those intended to be restrained? The distinction, between a government with limited and unlimited powers, is abolished, if those limits do not confine the persons on whom they are imposed, and if acts prohibited and acts allowed, are of equal obligation. It is a proposition too plain to be contested, that the constitution controls any legislative act repugnant to it; or, that the legislature may alter the constitution by an ordinary act.

Between these alternatives there is no middle ground. The constitution is either a superior, paramount law, unchangeable by ordinary means, or it is on a level with ordinary legislative acts, and, like other acts, is alterable when the legislature shall please to alter it.

If the former part of the alternative be true, then a legislative act contrary to the constitution is not law: if the latter part be true, then written constitutions are absurd attempts, on the part of the people, to limit a power, in its own nature illimitable.

Certainly all those who have framed written constitutions contemplate them as forming the fundamental and paramount law of the nation, and consequently the theory of every such government must be, that an act of the legislature, repugnant to the constitution, is void.

This theory is essentially attached to a written constitution, and is, consequently to be considered, by this court, as one of the fundamental principles of our society. It is not therefore to be lost sight of in the future consideration of this subject.

If an act of the legislature, repugnant to the constitution, is void, does it, notwithstanding its invalidity, bind the courts, and oblige them to give it effect? Or, in other words, though it be not law, does it constitute a rule as operative as if it was a law? This would be to overthrow in fact what was established in theory; and would seem, at first view, an absurdity too gross to be insisted on. It shall, however, receive a more attentive consideration.

It is emphatically the province and duty of the judicial department to say what the law is. Those who apply the rule to particular cases, must of necessity expound and interpret that rule. If two laws conflict with each other, the courts must decide on the operation of each.

So if a law be in opposition to the constitution; if both the law and the constitution apply to a particular case, so that the court must either decide that case conformably to the law, disregarding the constitution; or conformably to the constitution, disregarding the law; the court must determine which of these conflicting rules governs the case. This is of the very essence of judicial duty.

If, then, the courts are to regard the constitution; and the constitution is superior to any ordinary act of the legislature; the constitution, and not such ordinary act, must govern the case to which they both apply.

Those then who controvert the principle that the constitution is to be considered, in court, as a paramount law, are reduced to the necessity of maintaining that courts must close their eyes on the constitution, and see only the law.

This doctrine would subvert the very foundation of all written constitutions. It would declare that an act which, according to the principles and theory of our government, is entirely void; is yet, in practice, completely obligatory. It would declare, that if the legislature shall do what is expressly forbidden, such act, notwithstanding the express prohibition, is in reality effectual. It would be giving to the legislature a practical and real omnipotence, with the same breath which professes to restrict their powers within narrow limits. It is prescribing limits, and declaring that those limits may be passed at pleasure.

That it thus reduces to nothing what we have deemed the greatest improvement on political institutions—a written constitution—would of itself be sufficient, in America, where written constitutions have been viewed with so much reverence, for rejecting the construction. But the peculiar expressions of the constitution of the United States furnish additional arguments in favour of its rejection.

The judicial power of the United States is extended to all cases arising under the constitution.

Could it be the intention of those who gave this power, to say that, in using it, the constitution should not be looked into? That a case arising under the constitution should be decided without examining the instrument under which it arises?

This is too extravagant to be maintained.

In some cases, then, the constitution must be looked into by the judges. And if they can open it at all, what part of it are they forbidden to read, or to obey?

There are many other parts of the constitution which serve to illustrate this subject. It is declared that "no tax or duty shall be laid on articles exported from any state." Suppose a duty on the export of cotton, of tobacco, or of flour; and a suit instituted to recover it. Ought judgment to be rendered in such a case? ought the judges to close their eyes on the constitution, and only see the law?

The constitution declares that "no bill of attainder or *ex post facto* law shall be passed."

If, however, such a bill should be passed and a person should be prosecuted under it; must the court condemn to death those victims whom the constitution endeavors to preserve?

"No person," says the constitution, "shall be convicted of treason unless on the testimony of two witnesses to the same overt act, or on confession in open court."

Here the language of the constitution is addressed especially to the courts. It prescribes, directly for them, a rule of evidence not to be departed from. If the legislature should change that rule, and declare one witness, or a confession out of court, sufficient for conviction, must the constitutional principle yield to the legislative act?

From these, and many other selections which might be made, it is apparent, that the framers of the constitution contemplated that instrument, as a rule for the government of *courts*, as well as of the legislature.

Why otherwise does it direct the judges to take an oath to support it? This oath certainly applies, in an especial manner, to their conduct in their official character. How immoral to impose it on them, if they were to be used as the instruments, and the knowing instruments, for violating what they swear to support!

The oath of office, too, imposed by the legislature, is completely demonstrative of the legislative opinion on this subject. It is in these words: "I do solemnly swear that I will administer justice without respect to persons, and do equal right to the poor and to the rich; and that I will faithfully and impartially discharge all the duties incumbent on me as according to the best of my abilities and understanding, agreeably to *the constitution*, and laws of the United States."

Why does a judge swear to discharge his duties agreeably to the constitution of the United States, if that constitution forms no rule for his government? If it is closed upon him, and cannot be inspected by him?

If such be the real state of things, this is worse than solemn mockery. To prescribe, or to take this oath, becomes equally a crime.

It is also not entirely unworthy of observation that in declaring what shall be the *supreme* law of the land, the *constitution* itself is first mentioned; and not the laws of the United States generally, but those only which shall be made in *pursuance* of the constitution, have that rank.

Thus, the particular phraseology of the constitution of the United States confirms and strengthens the principle, supposed to be essential to all written constitutions, that a law repugnant to the constitution is void; and that *courts*, as well as other departments, are bound by that instrument. . . . ■

 # American Politics Today

For nearly a generation, conservatives have hoped and liberals have feared that the Supreme Court would turn away from the liberalism and activism of the 1950s and 1960s, when the Court was led by Chief Justice Earl Warren. This long-awaited "counterrevolution" did not occur under Warren's successor, Warren Burger, who presided over a Court that made landmark liberal decisions on abortion, the death penalty, affirmative action, and freedom of speech and religion. With the ascension of Chief Justice William H. Rehnquist in 1986, however, it seemed that the long era of judicial liberalism was finally over.

Presidents Ronald Reagan and George Bush essentially reshaped the Court in the 1980s, appointing five new justices—a clear majority of the Court—along with the new chief justice. As the legal scholar Kathleen M. Sullivan explains, however, the Rehnquist Court, "while it has undoubtedly turned rightward, has never turned as starkly rightward as predicted" by both popular and academic critics. Sullivan calls the gap between the Court's expected and actual conservative tendencies "ideological shortfall," and, in this selection, she explains the factors that created it.

Questions

1. In what ways has the Rehnquist Court disappointed conservative critics of the Warren and Burger Courts? How does Sullivan explain the Court's unexpected behavior?
2. What does the Court's behavior suggest about the relationship between the justices and the larger political process of which they are a part?

12.3 The Jurisprudence of the Rehnquist Court (1998)

Kathleen M. Sullivan

I. Introduction

Popular discourse about the Supreme Court often seeks to characterize its direction in political terms. Yet the Rehnquist Court, while it has undoubtedly turned

Kathleen M. Sullivan, "The Jurisprudence of the Rehnquist Court," *Nova Law Review* 22 (Spring 1998), pp. 743–761. Reprinted by permission of the Nova Law Review and the author.

rightward, has never turned as starkly rightward as predicted in such accounts, even though Presidents Reagan and Bush between them filled five seats on the current Court. To be sure, President Clinton—with two appointments of his own in the last five years—has had the chance to counterbalance the Reagan-Bush nominations. But both before and after Clinton's appointments, it was evident that Justices who were expected to be "conservative" sometimes voted for "liberal" or "moderate" results.

Why might this be so? One explanation might be that court-packing is simply harder than it looks, and a president's ability to predict the judicial orientation of his nominees is inherently prone to error. President Eisenhower is famously said to have labeled as "mistakes" his appointments of Chief Justice Earl Warren and Justice William J. Brennan, Jr. Likewise, President Nixon's appointment of Justice Harry A. Blackmun hardly produced, as expected, a conservative "Minnesota Twin" to Chief Justice Warren Burger. And those who predicted that Justice David Souter's appointment would be a "home run" for conservative causes later lamented that it had been something less than a bunt.

But three other explanations seem more powerful than presidential miscalculation alone. This essay seeks to explore those explanations. First, the institutional structure of the Court may constrain or systematically moderate ideological tendencies. Second, a Justice's jurisprudential commitments may limit his or her expression of ideological orientation. Finally, the very concept of conservative judicial ideology is quite complex, and thus an apparently "liberal" result sometimes represents simply the dominance of one strand of conservatism over others. These institutional, jurisprudential, and ideological factors might help explain the surprising moderation of Justices predicted to be conservative.

II. The Phenomenon of Ideological Shortfall

Without doubt, the Rehnquist Court has taken positions consistent with conservative politics in a variety of constitutional areas since 1980. The Court has narrowed pregnant women's rights against state regulation of abortion and rejected the claim that consensual homosexual sex is protected by the same conception of liberty that had earlier protected access to abortion and contraception. The Court has likewise declined to extend such liberty rights to physician-assisted suicide. The Court has been increasingly willing to invalidate race-based affirmative action programs, even when implemented by the federal government. In an analogous line of cases, the Court has struck down several state attempts to create majority-minority electoral districts. The Court has made it more difficult for challengers to prove that a school district is continuing to violate the requirements of *Brown v. Board of Education.* For the first time in sixty years, the Court has sought to restrain federal power in relation to the power of the states by striking down a congressional assertion of power under the Commerce Clause. Similarly, the Court has struck down congressional efforts to "commandeer" state legislative or executive action. Perhaps nowhere has the Court's conservative trend been more apparent than in the area of criminal justice. Hence, it is difficult to dispute that Presidents Reagan and Bush had considerable success in moving the Court to the political right.

The Court, however, has also issued a number of decisions disappointing conservative advocates. For instance, the Court did not, as many had predicted, overrule *Roe v. Wade*. Nor did it eliminate Establishment Clause restrictions on school prayer. The Court declined to allow the states or Congress to criminalize flag burning. And, notwithstanding other harbingers of an antifederalist revival, the Court forbade state voters from imposing term limits on their federal legislators—albeit narrowly and over a bitter dissent. Some recent decisions extending the Equal Protection Clause drew a cacophony of conservative opposition—for example, a decision barring the exclusion of women from an all-male public academy and a decision barring a state from precluding all claims of discrimination based on homosexual orientation. The Court granted free access to state appeals courts for indigent parents attempting to retain rights of relationship to their children, thus reviving a long-dormant strand of fundamental rights analysis in equal protection law. Finally, the Rehnquist Court has consistently interpreted the Free Speech Clause to forbid government prescriptions of orthodoxy, protecting groups as divergent as leftist flag burners and white supremacist cross burners.

Even in decisions reaching conservative results, the Court has articulated doctrines that stop short of their apparent logical conclusion. For example, in the affirmative action cases, the Court has stopped short of establishing outright color blindness as a constitutional norm, intimating that race-based affirmative action might be upheld on somewhat weaker justifications than would be required of policies discriminating against racial minorities. In cases imposing federalism-based limits on congressional power, the Court has barred congressional acts requiring states to enact or enforce specified policies but allowed similar results to be accomplished by imposing regulatory conditions on federal funding that states find irresistible as a practical matter. And, in free speech challenges, the Court has sometimes split the difference between the speech claim and the government. For example, the Court has struck down a hate speech law while upholding a hate crime penalty enhancement statute, upheld some but not all regulations of anti-abortion protestors, and permitted public airport terminals to ban the solicitation of funds but not the sale or distribution of literature. Such decisions give greater latitude to speakers than might have been expected given the Court's starting assumptions. . . .

III. Institutional Structure

Two features of the Court's institutional situation in relation to the other branches suggest reasons why conservative Justices might vote moderate or liberal. The first and most distinctive institutional feature of the Supreme Court is its relative insulation from political pressures. Politics may play an inevitable role in the nomination and confirmation process, but constitutional guarantees of lifetime tenure and protection from salary cuts afford the Justices considerable opportunity to change their minds. Thus, a Justice's opinions, over time, may cease to bear much resemblance to his or her political profile at the time of nomination and appointment.

Assuming that Justices sometimes diverge from their predicted political profile while in office, is there any structural reason to suppose that the shift will be in a "liberal" rather than a "conservative" direction? To be sure, there are counterexamples. President Kennedy's only appointee, Justice Byron White, arguably grew more conservative during his long tenure on the bench, except for his nearly parliamentary willingness to defer to the (usually Democratic) Congress. But, it is at least plausible to suppose that insulation from political majorities typically creates a structural incentive to articulate and protect the interests of political minorities, if only through repeat exposure to such claims and a desire to distinguish the work of the judiciary from that of the political branches. This tendency will often, though not always, appear politically "liberal."

A second and independent institutional explanation arises from the Justices' concern to protect the Supreme Court's credibility. . . . Conservative Justices might favor results that appear liberal in the short run in order to diffuse any suspicion that they are caving in to political pressure from their conservative sponsors and their allies. One way of doing this is to abide by stare decisis and entrench earlier liberal decisions even if they would not be reached again as an initial matter.

The pivotal joint opinion of Justices Sandra Day O'Connor, Anthony Kennedy, and David Souter in *Planned Parenthood v. Casey,* for example, declined to overrule *Roe v. Wade* in part on the ground that the Court ought not overturn settled law in the face of vehement public controversy over abortion, lest it appear to be doing politics rather than law. Likewise, the Court's recent decisions invalidating most affirmative action programs, but holding out the possibility that some such programs might be justified by remedial or distributive concerns expressed in earlier cases, might be read as seeking to avoid a perception that the Court interprets the Constitution in light of the latest public opinion polls. . . .

IV. Constitutional Jurisprudence

A second explanation of why conservative Justices might vote moderate or liberal is that they have a jurisprudential orientation that moderates or constrains any ideological tendencies they might have. Justices' jurisprudential tendencies tend to follow one of two general approaches to fashioning legal directives. One approach employs bright-line rules, while the other utilizes flexible standards. Rules, generally speaking, bind a legal decision-maker in a fairly determinate manner by capturing underlying principles or policies in ways that then operate independently. What gives a rule its force is that judges will follow it in fairly rote fashion even where a particularized application of the background principle might arguably yield a different result. Standards, on the other hand, allow judges to apply the background principle more directly to a fact situation.

To take a simple example; suppose you wished to ensure safe driving on a highway. You might set a rule: "drive no faster than fifty-five miles per hour." Alternatively, you might set a standard of reasonableness: "drive safely for the highway conditions."

What are the comparative advantages of each approach? Rules constrain the discretion of the decision-maker who applies them and typically require the determination of only very limited issues of fact. For example, under the fifty-five miles per hour rule, a police officer only needs to determine at what speed the car was traveling. The fifty-five miles per hour rule also prevents two police officers from treating identical situations differently, whereas under the "reasonableness" standard, one drive might be ticketed while the other drives away free. Thus, the advantages of rules include certainty, predictability, formal fairness, clear notice to those they govern, and economy in the process of decision-making.

Standards, by contrast, require consideration of more facts. Under the "drive safely for the conditions" standard, for example, a police officer must take into account the time of day, the weather, the volume of traffic, and so forth. Standards thus give more discretion to the decision-maker in deciding particular cases. Though less predictable and more time-consuming to apply than rules, those who favor standards would say that they are more substantively fair and accurate than rules in capturing the relevant policy concern. For example, while the fifty-five miles per hour rule might prohibit a driver from reaching a safe sixty miles per hour on an empty straightaway under sunny skies but permit a driver to travel a treacherous fifty miles per hour on a rain-slicked curve at rush hour, the "drive safely" standard might correct such anomalous outcomes. Advocates of standards also approve their flexibility and capacity to evolve in their application over time with changing mores or circumstances.

Constitutional doctrines, like traffic rules, may be expressed in the form of either rules or standards. Approaches that use categorical, formal, bright-line tests are rule-like. For example, consider holdings that obscenity is unprotected speech, or that the legislature may not wield executive power, or vice versa. Almost as rule-like in practice are tests that use strong presumptions to decide cases once a threshold classification has been made. When the Court employs strict scrutiny—such as to review infringements of fundamental rights, content based suppression of speech, or suspect classifications—it is nearly impossible for the government to prove the law constitutional. Conversely, when the Court employs rationality review—for example, to review challenges to socioeconomic legislation—the Court typically defers to the judgments of the other branches so that it is difficult, if not nearly impossible, for the challenger to win. This two-tiered system of scrutiny limits judicial discretion because once the Court has sorted a challenged law into the appropriate tier, it is confined to the resulting decisional rule, as are the lower courts in deciding analogous cases.

By contrast, constitutional tests that employ balancing, intermediate scrutiny, or functional analysis operate as standards. Consider the Court's express use of intermediate scrutiny to evaluate laws that classify individuals based on gender, as well as facially neutral laws with a disproportionate adverse effect on interstate commerce, and facially neutral laws with a substantial adverse impact on speech or expressive conduct. Intermediate scrutiny, like standard-based reasoning generally, asks how strong the government's interest is in relation to the constitutional policy at stake. Functional analyses of separation of powers challenges provide another example of standard-like reasoning. Whereas formal approaches would condemn any trespass by one branch into another's powers, a functional approach invalidates only those trespasses that go too far. These overtly balancing modes of analysis gives judges considerably greater discretion than the stark extremes of strict or rational review.

The Court deviates from rules to standards, if more informally, whenever it weakens the presumption traditionally embodied in strict scrutiny or rationality review. For example, applying "strict but not fatal" review to race-based affirmative action invites governments employing such measures to try to justify them in Court. Conversely, applying aggressive rationality review to invalidate laws found to reflect irrational animus—for example, the prohibition on gay rights claims struck down in *Romer v. Evans*—invites claimants to challenge measures ranging beyond traditionally suspect classifications. Either way, the two-tier approach collapses into de facto balancing.

A preference for constitutional standards over constitutional rules will tend to register as political moderation because, generally speaking, rules are more effective than standards at effecting sharp and lasting changes in constitutional interpretation. Standards allow the Court to decide cases narrowly: for example, this waiting period is not on its face an undue burden, this wholesale preclusion of gay antidiscrimination claims is unjustified, this particular district was drawn with excessive attention to racial demographics. The use of standards tends to moderate sharp swings between ideological poles; standards allow future courts more discretion to distinguish prior cases and decide cases in fact-specific fashion, and thus to afford more solace and spin opportunities to the losers.

Of the five Justices Presidents Reagan and Bush appointed to the Court, only two (Justices Antonin Scalia and Clarence Thomas) turned out to favor rules; the other three (Justices O'Connor, Kennedy, and Souter) have tended to favor standards. The latter group's preference for standards in deciding constitutional cases furnishes one explanation for unexpectedly moderate or liberal decisions.

To take a few examples, consider first the issue of race-based affirmative action. Four Justices, including Justices Scalia and Thomas, would favor a rule that the Constitution should be color blind, and that no race-conscious measures should ever be permissible, whether aimed at subordinating or benefiting racial minorities. On the other hand, four Justices would apparently defer to many race-conscious measures designed to benefit minorities while still striking down race-conscious measures that are designed to disadvantage minorities, believing that they can perceive the difference between a no trespassing sign and a welcome mat. Between these two camps stands Justice O'Connor—the key swing vote on this issue—who would permit some limited race-conscious measures where they are shown to be closely tied to remedying past discrimination, relatively broadly defined. Justice Kennedy's opinion for the Court in *Miller v. Johnson* does something similar in asking whether race is the "predominant" factor in how electoral district boundaries are drawn, rather than in precluding racial considerations altogether. By saying that race-conscious measures are sometimes, if rarely, permissible, such standards and race-based distinguishing plans give governments the latitude to defend some affirmative action plans and lower courts the wiggle room to uphold them.

To take another example, consider the First Amendment's bar on establishment of religion. As many as four Justices at any given time, led by Justice Scalia, have argued for a narrow rule that only sectarian preferences and outright coercion of faith ought to count as forbidden establishment. Justice O'Connor, however, has led a slim majority of the Court to maintain a broader and more flexible standard, holding that the Establishment Clause also forbids any government action that a reasonable observer would interpret as government "endorsement" of religion. This standard is highly fact-intensive and susceptible to shifting outcomes. For example, a publicly sponsored Christmas creche might be permissible if surrounded by reindeer and a talking wishing well in a shopping district, but not if standing alone on a courthouse staircase. This standard permits courts to invalidate more public religious expression than they would under Justice Scalia's rule.

As a further example, consider the limits of free speech in public spaces other than the traditional public forum of streets and parks. In a 1992 decision involving Hare Krishna devotees seeking to leaflet and solicit in the New York airport terminals, four Justices, led by Chief Justice William Rehnquist, would have established a bright-line rule: airports are not traditional public forums for speech akin to streets and parks, and the First Amendment therefore permits unlimited regulation of speech there, so long as it is viewpoint-neutral. Justices O'Connor and Kennedy, however, steered the Court to a split result: leafleting must be permitted in the airports though soliciting need not. They did so by embracing, in slightly different terms, a standard that focused on whether the particular speech was reasonably compatible with the functioning of the public space. A compatibility inquiry gives more flexibility to the courts to enforce free speech rights than does a rigid hierarchy of types of public places.

As a final example, compare two approaches the Rehnquist Court has taken to separation of powers issues. In *Morrison v. Olson*, the Court took a highly flexible balancing approach in upholding the independent counsel statute by a vote of 8–1. The majority opinion by Chief Justice Rehnquist reasoned that granting authority to prosecute high-level Executive officers to appointees whom the President does not select and may not remove at will does not trench too far upon the Executive power, even if prosecution is inherently executive in nature. A scathing dissent by Justice Scalia objected to this brand of prudentialism in structural matters, arguing that the issue should be the nature and not the degree of the infringement. By contrast, last Term, in *Printz v. United States*, the Court invalidated, by a vote of 5–4, a federal requirement that local law enforcement officers perform background checks on handgun purchasers to ensure their conformity to federal standards. The Court reasoned that structural principles of federalism forbade any conscription of state or local officers in administering federal law, however trivial the burden or desirable the end. Writing this time for the majority, Justice Scalia flatly stated that any "'balancing' analysis is inappropriate," and that "no comparative assessment of the various interests" could overcome the affront to state sovereignty embodied in such a law. Plainly, the *Morrison* standard afforded the government more leeway for structural innovation than the *Printz* rule, and against the political backdrop at the time, appeared unexpectedly politically moderate.

The embrace of standards over rules thus leads conservative Justices to reach results that, in a period when the Court is moving rightward, appear more moderate or liberal than would a rule fashioned from a similar ideological starting point. This observation gives rise to an antecedent question: Why do some Justices favor rules and others favor standards? Why any particular Justice is drawn to either disposition is perhaps ultimately a psychological, biographical, or even aesthetic question. But to the extent the choice is conscious and articulate, it is likely to follow from different conceptions of the judicial role. Like the institutional considerations discussed above in Part II, the choice of rules or standards might be understood as a strategy for maintaining the Court's legitimacy. Each camp might claim that its method facilitates greater judicial modesty than the other.

Specifically, those who favor rules, like positivists and codifiers of earlier generations, seek to limit the exercise of discretion in judicial decision-making, and thus favor the reduction of constitutional propositions as much as possible to claims of fact, not value. They suspect that the context-specific application of standards will lead judges inappropriately to impose their own values. Those who favor standards, in contrast, see their role in constitutional interpretation as akin to that of common law judges, requiring reference to the accretion of past history, precedent, and collective wisdom in order to constrain the inevitable exercise of some contemporary discretionary judgment. Justices who favor a common law approach to constitutional interpretation believe that they will be disciplined from imposing their own values by our traditions, social practices, shared understandings, and the process of reasoned elaboration from such starting points. They believe that it is more arrogant to assert the philosophical or interpretive certainty required by announcement of a single inflexible rule.

Those who choose standards over rules might believe that such a choice, in addition to embodying judicial restraint, promotes judicial legitimacy in several other ways. It might, as a type of alternative constitutional dispute resolution, help to defuse sharp ideological conflict by giving something to each side. Relatedly, it might take steps toward a desired constitutional end-state while minimizing the expressive injury to the losers. Finally, it might seem to facilitate democratic debate and resolution of the matters it leaves unresolved, placing conflict over values more squarely in the hands of the people than of judges. Whatever its jurisprudential or institutional motivation, the choice of standards over rules will register on the political spectrum as unexpectedly moderate or liberal during a period of general rightward shift.

V. The Complexity of Conservative Ideology

A third reason why conservative Justices might appear to vote moderate or liberal is that the very concept of constitutional conservatism is quite complex. A judicial conservative might be thought to favor, at least to some degree, any of the following: 1) originalism; 2) textualism; 3) judicial restraint (deference to legislatures); 4) libertarianism (deregulation); 5) states' rights (decentralization); 6) traditionalism; 7) stare decisis; 8) capitalism; and 9) law and order. These different strands of judicial conservatism may sometimes pull in competing directions, both among Justices, and even within a single Justice across an array of cases. And when one strand trumps others, the outcome of the case may appear surprisingly moderate or liberal.

Such tensions are easy to identify in divided decisions by the Rehnquist Court. For example, adherence to the original meaning of the Constitution may trump deference to the government for sake of law and order. Justices Scalia and Thomas, typically the Court's staunchest advocates of originalism, have sometimes voted with criminal defendants and against the government where they thought that the framers must have meant to forbid modern practices, such as videotaped testimony in child sexual abuse cases or unannounced drug raids.

Original meaning may be at odds with traditionalism. For example, Justice Thomas voted to sustain a First Amendment right to distribute anonymous election leaflets, reasoning that the framers themselves had engaged in anonymous debates over the Constitution, signing their writings with a variety of pseudonyms from "Publius" to the "Federal Farmer." Justice Scalia, dissenting, found the originalist record ambiguous and would have deferred instead to the long tradition and current legislative practice in nearly all states of requiring identifying information in election literature.

Stare decisis may be at odds with any of the other strands of conservatism. The decisive joint opinion in *Casey*, for example, embraced a strong if limited respect for stare decisis, reaffirming *Roe's* central holding without regard to whether it was correct as an original matter. The dissenters, in contrast, saw stare decisis as far too weak to overcome the lack of clear textual or originalist authority for invalidating popularly enacted abortion regulation. Similarly, in Establishment Clause challenges to such practices as official school prayer, invocations of original practices such as George Washington praying at his inauguration have failed to overcome precedents limiting government endorsement of religion.

Some opinions would seem to represent a triumph of libertarianism over textual or originalist literalism or judicial restraint. For example, all the Justices except Chief Justice Rehnquist recently proved willing to invalidate, as an unreasonable search and seizure, state-mandated drug testing for political candidates. In others, strict adherence to text and original meaning may yield to some combination of stare decisis, traditionalism, and a robust view of property rights. For example, Justice Scalia, who typically favors textualist and originalist readings, exemplified this when he wrote an opinion for the Court in *Lucas v. South Carolina Coastal Council*, calling for strict review under the Takings Clause of regulations that sharply diminish property values—even though the Takings Clause says nothing about regulation of property whose title is not transferred to the state, and even though the framers did not envision applying the Takings Clause to such regulations.

These examples could be multiplied indefinitely, but suffice to illustrate that any effort to carry out a program of judicial "conservatism" in constitutional interpretation involves a simultaneous equation with multiple variables. Even a single Justice pegged as a conservative may be pulled in different directions. The outcome of a case, therefore, depends not only upon a Justice's default weighing of these variables, but on the relative strength of each particular ideological pull in the differing circumstances of each case. To complicate matters still further, Justices may agree on a variable but disagree strenuously over its application. For example, consider the dueling originalism that has led the majority and dissent to disagree vigorously as to whether the framers did or did not intend that Congress might employ state officials to administer federal programs, or whether the framers did or did not intend that the Establishment Clause bar only that aid to religion which preferred one sect over others.

Finally, constitutional rights sometimes may undergo what might be called "ideological drift." That is, rights once thought of as having liberal provenance are embraced by conservatives even as liberal attachment to them falters. There is no better recent example than freedom of speech. Free speech rights were traditionally asserted in this century by anarchists, socialists, syndicalists, and communists, and closer to our own time by the pioneers of racial civil rights and opponents of the war in Vietnam. But left-wing support is not always forthcoming when free speech claims are asserted by racist cross-burners, anti-abortion demonstrators, large corporate advertisers, or donors of large sums to political campaigns. In the latter sort of case, liberals often favor government regulation designed to ensure racial dignity, reproductive privacy, or greater equality in the marketplace of ideas, and conservative groups take up the banner of free speech libertarian opposition.

In such circumstances, popular views of the political valence of decisions may lag behind the ideological drift, leading to the perception that conservative Justices have voted "liberal" on free speech, and vice versa. For example, in a recent abortion clinic protest case, the traditionally liberal Justice Stevens voted to uphold all restrictions on the protestors while the historically conservative Justice Scalia would have struck them all down. Similarly, in a recent campaign finance case, the supposedly conservative Justices Kennedy, Thomas, and Scalia embraced vigorously the free speech rights of political parties while several supposedly liberal Justices expressed willingness to allow wide-ranging government regulation of campaign finance. Because the press has an institutional interest in strong First Amendment protection, such decisions are apt to be reported as "liberal" victories for free speech, even if the credit must go to "conservative" Justices.

VI. Conclusion

This essay has suggested three possible explanations—institutional, jurisprudential and ideological—of why a Court moving generally rightward might nonetheless be characterized occasionally by surprising judicial moderation or even a liberal turn. These factors help show why it is so difficult to capture the work of the Court along a single political vector: "sharp right turn," or "the center holds." There is nothing mutually inconsistent among these accounts. Indeed, they may reinforce one another, as when institutional concerns influence jurisprudential orientation. And these accounts help to refute the view, sometimes expressed in popular commentary, that the moderate judicial behavior of the swing Justices on the Rehnquist Court is incoherent or inexplicable. ■

 # The Comparative Context

Compared with judicial institutions in other countries, the United States Supreme Court plays a major role in making public policy. While some view the Court's policy-making activities as necessary and justifiable, others charge the Court with "judicial activism," arguing that the justices should focus on interpreting and applying the law, leaving policy making to Congress, the White House, and the states.

Whatever the merits of this debate, few doubt that the American Supreme Court plays an important role in resolving questions that, in other nations, are left to the legislative and executive branches. In this selection, the political scientist Mark C. Miller uses a comparison between the United States and Canada to examine why an activist judiciary developed in one country but not the other.

Questions

1. What is judicial activism? Why do some suggest that judicial activism is defensible and appropriate while others argue that judicial activism undermines the principles of federalism and the separation of powers?
2. What, according to Miller, accounts for the presence of a more activist judiciary in the United States than in Canada?

12.4 Judicial Activism in Canada and the United States (1998)

Mark C. Miller

The legal systems of Canada and the United States share many common characteristics. Both have their roots in British Common Law. Legal training is similar, and both countries draw their judges primarily from the practicing bar. But despite their similarities, Canadian and U.S. judges have approached their policy-making roles quite differently.

Why? Perhaps the traditional lack of judicial activism in Canada may in part be due to the less political judicial selection system used in that country when compared to the highly public and contested judicial selection processes used for the more activist U.S. courts.

While scholars use the terms judicial activism and judicial restraint often, these concepts can be difficult to define and remain controversial. In general, judicial activism means that the courts are willing to make public policy when the other institutions of government either cannot or will not. In *The Global Expansion of Judicial Power* (1995), Neal Tate and Torbjorn Vallinder define judicial activism as "The transfer of decision-making rights from the legislature, the cabinet, or the civil service to the courts." Judicial activism in the United States also means interpreting the U.S. Constitution with a modern eye and adapting the interpretation of the document for contemporary society.

Judicial restraint usually means that the courts defer to the decisions of other political institutions, and in the United States it also means that the federal Constitution is interpreted as intended by the framers. Some opponents of judicial

---

Mark C. Miller, "Judicial Activism in Canada and the United States," *Judicature* 81 (May–June 1998), pp. 262–265. Reprinted by permission of the American Judicature Society.

activism use the pejorative "judicial legislating" or similar terms to refer to the policy-making activities of judges.

Activism in Canada

Canadian courts have a long tradition of attempting to separate law and politics, and therefore they also have a long tradition of attempting to avoid judicial activism. As Carl Baar stated in *Judicial Activism in Comparative Perspective* (1991), "The judiciary played an important but largely invisible role in the Canadian political system for over a century." And as Peter Russell notes in his 1987 book *The Judiciary in Canada: The Third Branch of Government,* "Canadians are not conditioned to think of courts as part of the political system. . . . The role of the judiciary is perceived as being essentially technical and non-political; it is there to apply the laws made by the political branches of government."

The passage of the Canadian Charter of Rights and Freedoms in 1982 changed the perception and the role of the courts as policy makers. The charter gave the Canadian courts much greater powers of judicial review. Because it included difficult concepts and provisions, the Canadian courts were almost forced to interpret the new constitutional rights contained within it in order to clarify issues of human rights in a complex modern society. After the passage of the charter, the courts in Canada and especially the supreme court became quite activist for a period. But after 1986 it backed away from activist charter decisions. Even though the Canadian Supreme Court has now taken on a policy-making role as it interprets the charter, it nonetheless remains less activist than many courts in the United States.

Judicial activism today still remains foreign to most Canadian judges. In a 1990 study involving interviews with many judges in Alberta and Ontario, Peter McCormick and Ian Greene found little support among Canadian judges for an activist role. As these scholars explain, "Although the interviews clearly suggest that many judges see some law-making as a legitimate component of their duties, this by no means implies that they see this as an activist role for the judiciary in promoting the causes of social reform or political challenge. In fact, quite the reverse is true." For example, of the 51 Alberta judges interviewed, only 11 described their role orientation as activist. In a study published in 1997, Greene, Baar, and McCormick were able to interview 89 court of appeal and supreme court judges in Canada—only two reported seeing their judicial role as primarily "law-makers."

Most of the judges interviewed in connection with this article were certainly uncomfortable with the judicial activist role because they clearly felt that judges should not be policy makers unless absolutely necessary. In fact, most were quite critical of other activist judges in the country. In the Canadian tradition, most of the interviewees articulated a strong belief that political questions should remain separate from legal questions. They also stressed the need for the courts to remain independent from politics. Judges in Canada have generally avoided the public debate on judicial activism that has often occurred in the United States. Thus, even after the enactment of the charter, Canadian judges seem hesitant to take on a judicial activist role.

While judicial activism is a relatively new phenomenon in Canada, most social scientists argue that the U.S. courts have long practiced it. And in recent decades many U.S. courts have become even more activist. According to Larry Baum (*American Courts: Process and Policy*, 1998) from 1960 to 1996 the U.S. Supreme Court struck down 63 federal statutes and 549 state and local ones. These figures are nearly half of the total number of times that the U.S. Supreme Court has struck down legislation throughout its history. Of course, in the United States the lower federal courts and the state courts can also be quite activist.

Court Structure

Although both Canada and the United States have adopted federal systems, the two have structured their courts quite differently. The United States has two distinct and separate parallel court systems—state and federal—sharing the same geographical space. The U.S. Supreme Court's precedents are binding on all courts in both systems, although that court will only hear cases with a significant federal question. Thus the structure of the U.S. court systems is quite complex.

In contrast, the Canadian court system follows a much more unified and singular structure. Minor cases are heard by the provincial trial courts in each province. More serious civil cases begin in superior trial courts located in each province, and each province also has a court of appeal. All judges at the superior court level and above are appointed by the federal government. Since 1949, when appeals to the Judicial Committee of the Privy Council in Britain were finally abolished, the supreme court has served at the apex of this unified pyramid structure.

This rather simple court structure gives the Canadian Supreme Court more ability than the U.S. Supreme Court to increase federal power over the provinces. In interviews, many of the provincial court of appeal judges commented about the power of the Canadian Supreme Court to centralize law in that country. These judges were often concerned that a potentially activist supreme court would increase the power of the federal government over the provinces and the courts located in the provinces. This concern was especially strong in Quebec province, where there is a growing mistrust of federally appointed judges. The court of appeals judges in Quebec feel caught in a difficult position because they serve in Quebec but were appointed by the federal government.

Selection

Judges in the United States are selected using a wide variety of formal selection systems, although it is worth highlighting the fact that each selection system retains a highly political component. U.S. federal judges are appointed for life terms by the president and confirmed by the Senate in a highly political confirmation process. State judges are generally elected in some manner, including retention elections in merit selection states or partisan elections in other states for relatively short terms of office. Thus, in the United States, politics plays a role in the selection of both state and federal judges.

In Canada, all judges at the superior trial court level and above are appointed by the prime minister or the federal minister of justice. The lowest level provincial trial judges are appointed by the provincial cabinets on recommendation of the provincial attorneys general. There is no legislative confirmation process for any of these judges. By tradition, almost all judges in Canada are appointed from the ranks of practicing lawyers or legal academics.

Peter Russell and Jacob Ziegel argue in an influential 1991 *University of Toronto Law Journal* article that, in Canada, "Partisan connections should be irrelevant in identifying the most talented candidates for judicial office." In a study of judicial appointments in Canada, they found that only about half of the federal appointees had any real ties to the prime minister's party, and some of these seemed quite weak. Although these scholars complained about the "patronage" nature of some of the Canadian judicial appointments, in the United States most federal judicial appointees have close ties to the appointing party.

The Canadian judges interviewed for this article prided themselves on not being chosen for their politics. Several went out of their way to note that they were appointed to the superior trial courts by one party and then elevated to the provincial court of appeal by another. They repeatedly stressed how important judicial independence is in the relatively nonpolitical Canadian court system. When asked to state the main differences between judges in the United States and judges in Canada, almost all the Canadian judges interviewed stated that the biggest difference was the political nature of judicial selection and judicial decision making in the United States.

Federalism

Although both Canada and the United States have federal systems of government, the two have chosen very different ways to implement the concept of federalism. At first glance, the division of power between the levels of government seems less vague in Canada than in the United States. The documents that constitute the Canadian constitution, especially the British North America Act of 1867 (after 1982 renamed the Constitution Act of 1867), are much more specific than the U.S. Constitution about which powers are under the jurisdiction of the provinces and which are reserved for the national government. But this clarity may be deceiving. Both societies continue to struggle with the concept of federalism in practice.

Historically, both in the United States and in Canada, the courts have been very active in determining questions of federalism. In the United States, questions of federal constitutional law have occupied the U.S. Supreme Court for almost all of American history. Until very recently, the U.S. courts have generally favored federal power over the states. In the summer of 1997, however, the Supreme Court curtailed the power of the U.S. Congress by declaring that the federal government had no right to require local police officials to perform federally required background checks before an individual could purchase a handgun. It is too early to tell if *Printz v. U.S.* signals a severe shift in the balance of power between the federal government and the states, although it does clearly indicate that the U.S. Supreme Court will not allow federal power to increase without any limits.

Canada also has a long history of debate over federalism, and the uncertainty continues today. As Wayne Thompson notes in *Canada 1996*, "The forces of decentralization and centralization are always at work in Canada." In fact, disagreement over questions of federalism have prevented Canada from becoming a truly sovereign people. As Christopher Manfredi has noted in *Judicial Power and the Charter: Canada and the Paradox of Liberal Constitutionalism* (1993), "The complex realities of the division of powers inevitably meant that the judiciary would be forced to become the 'umpire' of federalism." Because questions of federalism have remained so unsettled in Canada, these issues have often become judicial questions.

For example, in February 1998, at the request of the federal government, the Canadian Supreme Court heard oral arguments on the crucial question of what procedures must be followed if a province attempts to leave the federation. The three specific questions before the court were: (1) Does the Canadian Constitution allow Quebec to secede unilaterally? (2) Does international law give Quebec the right to secede? (3) If there is a conflict between these two sources of law, which one would take precedence?

Since it became the final court of appeal in Canada in 1949, the Canadian Supreme Court has been widely perceived as a centralist force in Canadian politics. With the passage of the Constitution Act of 1982, which included the enactment of the Canadian Charter of Rights and Freedoms, the Canadian Supreme Court was faced with a clear mandate to determine the future of constitutional law and federalism. The charter went into effect despite the objections of Quebec, when the supreme court ruled that provincial consent to the new Constitution Act of 1982 did not require unanimous approval among the provinces. Thus the passage of the charter has increased the power of the courts in Canadian society.

But the effects on Canadian federalism of the charter's passage should not be overemphasized. As Peter Russell has concluded, "Thus far, the Supreme Court's application of the charter has not had the predicted centralizing effects on the Canadian federation. There has been very little of the most obvious form of centralization—that is, the Supreme Court's imposition of *national* standards on provincial legislatures. . . . [In fact], some of the Supreme Court's Charter decisions have actually had a decentralizing effect on policy-making" [emphasis in original]. Although given the opportunity to be activist on questions of federalism, the Canadian courts have generally attempted to avoid the activist role on these issues. In part because Canadian courts have not taken an activist approach, questions regarding federalism in Canada have generally been settled through means other than by judicial decision making.

The Activism-Selection Link

Although there may be some convergence occurring, clearly the courts in Canada are less activist than most courts in the United States. U.S. courts also employ the most politically based judicial selection systems on the globe. Are there links between the judicial selection system and the level of judicial activism in that system? Could it be that the higher the number of political actors involved in the informal judicial selection process, the more likely that judges in that system will be willing to adopt an activist role?

Most of the empirical scholarly work concerning judicial selection processes has focused solely on differences among the formal systems used to select U.S. state and federal judges. But Charles Sheldon and Nicholas Lovrich have argued that scholars should look beyond differences among formal selection systems to examine important differences in the informal procedures and norms used to select judges. In their model, informal judicial selection systems can be compared using the number of participants involved in the initiation, screening, and affirmation stages of the recruitment process. Thus a highly articulated system would have many actors involved in these three stages of judicial recruitment, while a low articulation system would have very few actors involved. Using this model of the informal procedures used for judicial selection, one can begin to draw the links between judicial selection and the level of judicial activism in any legal system.

Among the industrialized democracies of the world, probably England, France, and Japan have the least activist judges. Using Sheldon and Lovrich's terms, these countries also have some of the lowest judicial selection articulation levels. Thus there appears to be a clear link between the articulation level of the selection system and the level of judicial activism in that system.

The U.S. and Canadian judicial systems also illustrate this point. The Canadian court system certainly maintains a very low articulation level because so few actors are involved at any of the judicial recruitment stages. Although the provinces (especially Quebec) would like more say in who is selected as a judge to serve in their province, to date the debate has not revolved around specific judicial appointments. Thus, Canada remains a low articulation system for judicial selection, and its judges practice relatively little judicial activism.

On the other hand, the U.S. generally has a very high articulation system for judicial recruitment because so many political actors (including bar associations, interest groups, political parties, elected politicians, voters, the media, and others) take an interest in who is selected at every level of the judicial recruitment stages. And, of course, the United States has a high level of judicial activism. The link between the number of actors involved in the judicial selection system and the level of judicial activism seems clear.

Although it is more difficult to prove empirically, one could also argue that within the United States relatively different articulation levels among the states' informal judicial selection processes could produce differences in the levels of judicial activism among U.S. state judges. For example, Massachusetts has one of the lowest articulation judicial selection processes in the country, and it has a very low level of judicial activism among judges on its highest state court. On the other hand, Ohio has a very highly articulated judicial selection system, and it has a very activist state supreme court. This pattern appears to hold for various other U.S. state court systems as well.

Clearly, judicial activism is more common and more accepted among American judges. Although the level of judicial activism may be increasing in Canada, Canadian judges still seem uncomfortable with the concept of judicial policy making. Perhaps one reason for this difference is the possible links between judicial activism and the number of political actors involved in the judicial selection system. When comparing court systems in industrialized democracies, the Canadian and U.S. examples seem to point to such a link. ∎

View from the Inside

The inner workings of the Supreme Court of the United States have always been shrouded in secrecy. The justices deliberate and vote in private—not even a secretary or law clerk is present at the judicial conference—and the long process of writing and negotiating the justices' written opinions takes place entirely outside the public view. Leaks of information from inside the Court are exceedingly rare; news reporters, who are briefed routinely on what goes on inside the other branches of government, can do little more than guess at what is happening in the marble temple of justice.

Law clerks—like all other employees of the Court—have traditionally upheld the veil of secrecy. These young men and women, drawn from among the top graduates of the leading law schools in the nation—serve the justices as legal researchers, ghost writers, advisers, and, at times, confidantes. Few have ever spoken out in detail about their experiences at the Court. In 1998, however, Edward Lazarus published *Closed Chambers*, a first-hand account of his clerkship year with Justice Harry A. Blackmun in 1988–1989. Although Lazarus was, in his words, "careful to avoid disclosing information I am privy to solely because I was privileged to work for Justice Blackmun," his book led to considerable controversy. Nevertheless, *Closed Chambers* provides a rare behind-the-scenes account of life at the Court.

Questions

1. Is the secrecy surrounding the Supreme Court necessary or desirable? What accounts for the Court's lack of openness in a political system that values—and usually insists upon—openness in government?
2. What role do the law clerks play at the Supreme Court? Is there a danger that the law clerks will play too great a role, encroaching on the responsibilities of the justices whom they serve?

12.5 Closed Chambers (1998)

Edward Lazarus

L ife at the Court has a distinct rhythm, each term resembling a baseball season. The summer, from the end of June until roughly Labor Day, is the off-season. The Court stands in recess, rendering no decisions except for the rare emergency motion. Most of the Justices leave town for much of this period to rejuvenate and relax.

For the clerks, this is the time for an orientation—to the extent there is one. Immediately upon arriving in July, you begin to get a feel for your co-clerks, the Justice's messenger, and the vitally important secretaries. This group, together with the Justice, constitutes a "Chambers," the Court equivalent of a nuclear family, with all the risk of dysfunction that entails. At best, these are the people you will come to rely on, trust, and even love as you help and support one another through a long year at close quarters. At worst, some become slackers, or rivals, or even enemies to be overcome as you try to do your own work as well as you can. Most Chambers, like most families, find some middle ground.

In the Blackmun Chambers, each outgoing clerk designated two days to train his or her successor. I remember that time as a giant blur, a jumble of shorthand explanations of procedures I couldn't quite grasp, mixed in with a number of "don't worry, you'll figure it out as you go alongs." In quick order, we were trained in the Court's computer system, introduced to its librarians (who double as research assistants), and given a building tour—all of which meant that, after a week, we were on our own yet knew basically nothing except perhaps where to find the two magnificent freestanding spiral marble staircases.

The saving grace for every new clerk was a book called *Supreme Court Practice* (by Robert Stern, Eugene Gressman, and Stephen Shapiro, all former clerks) that each of us kept no more than an arm's length from our desks. *Stern & Gressman*, as it was known, contained just about everything there was to know about the Court's procedures. It explained the basics, such as the fact that the Court hears appeals coming from both state supreme courts and federal courts of appeals (known as circuit courts, which, for their part, review the decisions of federal district courts). It reminded us that the Supreme Court reviews only issues of *federal* law, that the Court agrees to decide only a small fraction of the cases where the parties request review, and that the Court selects which cases to decide primarily to resolve important issues of law and *not* to correct case-specific errors in a lower court's rulings. Mostly, though, *Stern & Gressman* was filled with technical knowledge that only a Supreme Court clerk or practitioner could possibly want to know. In other words, it was our Bible.

In the Blackmun Chambers, we also received a forty-page memorandum, "Helpful Hints for Blackmun Clerks," that explained in detail what our Justice expected of us as incoming cases made their way through the Court's cycle of business. That cycle is triggered when the losing party to a lawsuit files a petition for certiorari (cert.), a formal request that the Court hear the case. If at least four Justices (not even a majority) want to grant the petition, the Court schedules the case for argument. The parties file written briefs; the Justices hear oral argument; then they meet in conference and take a tentative vote. Afterward, opinions are drafted and circulated; revisions are made. Then, finally, the Court announces its decision. At every stage, with the exception of the Justices' private conference, the clerks had some role to play—reading, assessing, commenting, advising—and (in our case) communicating with Blackmun through the impersonal medium of typed "Mr. Justice notes" placed on the top of a file cabinet at the entrance to his inner sanctum.

Nor did all our tasks relate to cert. petitions and argued cases. The Court also handled a steady stream of emergency applications, usually requests for a stay to keep a lower court decision from taking effect. Each Justice was responsible for supervising one or more of the thirteen federal appellate (circuit) courts. Generally, a party seeking a stay would apply first to the appropriate supervising Justice, who then would either handle the application individually, or, much more often, refer it to the entire Court for consideration. Justice Blackmun oversaw the Eighth Circuit (including Minnesota, Missouri, and Arkansas), which meant that many of the stay applications to our Chambers came from death row inmates in Missouri or Arkansas seeking to avert impending executions. Of all the instructions we received in "Helpful Hints," the most detailed and forcefully phrased told us how to process and assist the Justice with these.

By September, we had mastered the basics of our guidebooks, and, after Labor Day, the preseason began. The Justices returned to look over their new clerks. Then they attacked the backlog that had accumulated over the summer: more than 1,000 petitions for cert., whose fate the Justices determine in a single marathon session at the end of September. They also started preparing in earnest for the cases already granted review the previous spring and scheduled to be heard in October.

Opening day is the first Monday in October. At precisely 10:00 A.M., the marshal of the Court solemnly intones the medieval French words "Oyez, oyez, oyez," handed down for over 1,000 years from Norman days through the English common law. And then: "All persons having business before the Honorable the Supreme Court of the United States are admonished to draw near and give their attention for the Court is now sitting. God save the United States and this Honorable Court!" With that, the Justices (always in three groups of three) emerge from behind velvet drapes and take their seats.

The term builds steadily in workload, tension, and fatigue. Opinion assignments pile up in each Chambers as the Court hears and decides cases faster than the written opinions can be crafted. In December, January, and February, the Court hands down its judgments in some relatively straightforward and easily resolved cases. But the big cases, and the close ones, the ones where several Justices forcefully dissent, or where swing Justices straddle the fence and consider writing something of their own, these linger and grow in number, month after month, exerting a viselike grip on all other work that has to be done.

To give some idea of what goes on during the dog days of the term—March and early April—what follows is a list of the functions a law clerk typically performs during this period: drafting majority opinions, drafting dissents, drafting concurrences (opinions that agree with the result reached by the majority opinion but for somewhat different reasons), writing "bench memos" (which help a Justice prepare for a case the Court is about to hear), writing post–oral argument memos (which amend views set forth in bench memos), commenting on draft opinions, dissents, and concurrences circulated by other Chambers, recommending which new petitions for certiorari the Court should grant, and advising on emergency applications, often including last-minute requests for stays of execution.

Juggling these daunting assignments seven days a week for weeks on end produces a mind-numbing exhaustion and also exacts a physical toll. Longtime staffers around the building would joke about the "Blackmun diet," the workaholic's method for shedding pounds. Clerks invented remarkable routines for keeping themselves sharp; one, late at night during the winter months, propped open the security gates on the Court's main floor so that he could run circuits around the building.

As April progresses, some tasks fall away as the Court hears its last set of cases for the term and issues some of the major opinions from cases argued in the fall. The pace of work, however, only quickens. With the exception of a case or two for which reargument might be ordered for the following fall, before recessing for the summer the Court issues opinions in every one of the cases it has heard each term. Most of these opinions, in a weekly cavalcade of major rulings, are handed down in the last two months of the term, with one or two monumental decisions always lingering until the very last day. This rush to the finish generates all the exhilaration of a great pennant race. Then the cycle starts over again.

Within this structure for the term, each week also follows a pattern. I learned to consider Wednesday the first day of the week. Sometime in the middle of the afternoon, without fail, an employee from the Court clerk's office would walk into each Chambers and, with a hair-raising *thwunk*, slam down a large stack of cert. petitions, then give a mildly apologetic shrug and walk back out the door.

These were the so-called paid petitions for certiorari, ones from litigants who could afford their own counsel, court costs, and printing. They came in at the rate of roughly forty per week, neatly bound and color coded (white for the petition itself, red for the response, yellow for the petitioner's reply, and gray if from the United States, regardless of its status as a party).

On Thursdays, another even larger stack would be delivered—the IFP's (*in forma pauperis*), petitions from indigent parties, often prisoners, representing themselves. These petitions were sometimes handwritten, occasionally illegible, and often inscrutable. But from Thursday's pile a number of the Court's landmark cases have emerged, such as *Gideon v. Wainwright* from 1963 (establishing a constitutional right to counsel in state criminal cases), which began as a petition, carefully printed in pencil, from Clarence Earl Gideon, Prisoner No. 003826, serving a five-year sentence in a Florida jail for breaking and entering.

These Wednesday and Thursday deliveries shaped the week because they determined which and how many petitions would be assigned to each clerk. Given the enormous task of selecting anywhere from 80 to 150 cases for full consideration, from what has grown to be more than 6,000 petitions received each year, most of the Justices pool their resources to expedite the evaluating process. Rather than each Justice considering every case independently, a clerk for one Justice in the "cert. pool" circulates an advisory memo to all the Justices in the pool. This "pool memo" summarizes a case and assesses whether it is "certworthy"—that is, whether it raises a sufficiently important and controversial issue to merit the Supreme Court's attention. Although the Justices do not follow the pool memo recommendations slavishly, in practice they carry great weight.

When I clerked, six Justices (Rehnquist, White, Blackmun, O'Connor, Scalia, and Kennedy) participated in the cert. pool. Justices Marshall and Stevens worked with their own clerks to determine independently which cert. petitions merited a grant. Remarkably, Justice Brennan did all his cert. work on his own, with little assistance even from his clerks.

Currently, every Justice except Stevens participates in the cert. pool, and the disappearance of Justices outside the pool has, quite rightly I think, generated concern both inside and outside the Court. As a member of the pool, I well recall how helpful it was to be able to check my judgments in close cases with clerks in the Stevens and Marshall Chambers. And I wonder whether Justice Stevens and his clerks alone can effectively perform this checking function. Others also have questioned whether the Justices have excessively delegated their cert. decisions to whichever clerk writes the pool memo in a given case. In recent terms, Justices Kennedy and Scalia have both proposed reforms adding additional checks to the cert. pool system, but the Court has yet to adopt any major changes.

For a clerk in the pool, which petitions (averaging four per week) you catch in the rotation determines the nature of your week. Some, indeed most, petitions clearly do not raise issues appropriate to Court review, and the pool memo can be finished in a few hours or less. These cases end up on the "dead list," a voluminous roster of cases the Justices won't even bother to discuss at conference. By contrast, writing the pool memo for a petition involving capital punishment (these are specially marked for attention), or for a complex civil case, or for almost any case in which the decision whether to recommend a grant is close, can take a day or even two of nonstop research, writing, and thinking. With bad luck, cert. work might devour most of a week, pushing off the usually more interesting and rewarding work of assisting your Justice with cases the Court is actually deciding.

Cert. work, moreover, cannot be put off for more than a few days because more petitions arrive every week and the pool memos must be finished by 10:00 A.M. of the Wednesday before each of the Justices' biweekly Friday conferences. If your memos are not handed in to the Chief Justice's Chambers by the deadline, your name goes on the "late list," an ignominy calculated to earn the wrath of your Justice not only for your being late but also for the inconsideration you have thus shown (on his or her behalf) to the other members of the Court.

Fridays, at least the Fridays when the Justices met in Conference, were the most suspenseful and momentous days at the Court. At a few minutes to ten, the Justices would begin their perambulations through the plush red-carpeted halls toward the Conference Room located in the Chief Justice's suite directly behind the courtroom. Justice Kennedy, tall and on the lanky side, would fairly bound down the hall, arms swinging. Justice Marshall, old and mountainous, would lumber, wheezing slightly with each labored breath. By 10:00 sharp, they would all have assembled in the wood-paneled sanctum sanctorum for the ritual handshake commencing the Conference. Under the presiding portrait of Chief Justice John Marshall, the Justices would take their assigned seats at the long mahogany table, sharp pencils and yellow pads neatly arrayed at each place; then the junior Justice would shut the door against the outside world.

A few hours later the Justices would emerge, often individually, sometimes in groups of two or three, exchanging a few last words. As they retreated down the red carpet, their gaits would mirror their moods after a morning's decision making. Clerks would gather in doorways to gauge their bosses' success and speculate about which cert. petitions the Justices had granted and how the big cases had come out.

Weekends were quiet around the Court—no tourists or journalists, few secretaries. They were times when you could wander unimpeded through the portrait gallery of former Justices, trading stares with Holmes, Brandeis, Taney, Vinson—the great and not so great of bygone eras—or sit alone in the majestic courtroom, imagining trenchant arguments past and future.

Those oral arguments take place on Mondays, Tuesdays, and Wednesdays for two consecutive weeks each month. Except for a few mornings devoted to handing down decisions late in the term, these argument days, at most forty a term, constitute the sole personal interaction between the Court and the public, including the legal community. As a consequence, they are accompanied by a heightened level of commotion and excitement.

I loved walking from my office into the Great Hall to watch the preargument processional. Kept company by the marble busts of former Chief Justices, lawyers in dark pinstripes and tourists in lesser fashions would line up to pass through metal detectors manned by Court police officers immaculate in their dress blues. Advocates from the Solicitor General's Office (which represents the United States before the Court), some resplendent in morning coats and all solemn in demeanor, would strut past, chests puffed out, in a beeline for the courtroom.

There is something exquisite about the room's proportions, intimate but not cramped, magisterial but not overwhelming. From the pews of the courtroom, the panorama of lush marble, rich drapery, and gleaming appointments inspires an awe heightened by the dignity and ceremony of the proceedings themselves.

The Justices preside from a raised dais behind an imposing, dark mahogany bench. At their feet rest green-and-white china spittoons, relics now used as trash cans. Each Justice has his or her own black leather chair, formerly of varying styles according to a Justice's taste, but now almost uniform, with unnaturally straight, high backs. Rocking and swiveling as is their wont, the Justices look out on law clerks and invited guests to their left, journalists to the right, and counsel for the parties arrayed straight before them at long tables flanking a small lectern. Behind the lawyers sit members of the Supreme Court bar, then the public in pews toward the back. High above the Justices' heads, directly in view, a large frieze depicts a mythological battle between the Manichaean forces of Good and Evil.

The arguments themselves often fail to live up to the atmosphere. Most cases the Court hears involve dry stuff even for lawyers and raise issues that do not lend themselves to exploration in one hour of oral argument. As counsel drones on about some complex statutory scheme better described in previously submitted written briefs, the Justices do not always feign interest. They trade quips and trivia questions with their neighbors or ask desultory questions mainly to stay awake.

But many arguments do stir the blood. For the legally inclined, few sights are more riveting than an immensely skilled, exquisitely prepared advocate threading his or her way through the shark-infested waters of a hard case—parrying questions at every turn, conceding points where possible, standing ground where necessary. While the Court today may not hear arguments like Daniel Webster's in the *Dartmouth College* case of 1819, which, at least according to lore, moved the audience to tears ("It is a small college . . . yet there are those who love it"), the best attorneys can still capture a swing vote in a close case and carry the day. Or they can simply amaze with the agility of their minds.

On the other hand, much of the advocacy before the Court is mediocre, some downright contemptible. I remember one death penalty case where the Court was very closely divided, the outcome clearly in doubt, with the lives of dozens of condemned prisoners hanging in the balance. The lawyer for the defendant simply did not understand that the Court does not respond to pleas for mercy or other emotional arguments that might move a lay jury. It responds to arguments about the meaning of the law—in this case the Constitution—and she gave none.

These are the moments, as a clerk, when you want to jump up, rush to the podium, knock the incompetent lawyer out of the way, and carry on yourself. But you cannot. So you watch helplessly as an attorney, ignorant of potentially winning arguments, faces stony contempt, annoyance, sometimes even ridicule, from the bench. The client, rarely present, pays the price.

On some argument days, most often Mondays, the Court also hands down decisions. Once upon a time, according to a practice long ago abandoned as impractical, the Justices read their entire opinions from the bench. Today, the authoring Justice gives a brief explanation of the ruling. For Justice White, this meant clearing his throat and uttering one unintelligible sentence. Most Justices—especially those with a flair for the dramatic, such as Scalia and Kennedy—seem to revel in the moment and go to some length to make the cases accessible to the lay audience in the courtroom.

I always thought this appropriate. The Justices may discharge in their written opinions what Justice Robert Jackson called their obligation "to do our utmost to make clear and understandable the reasons for deciding cases as we do." Nonetheless, I was struck repeatedly by the symbolic importance of having the Justices meet face to face with even a token representation of "We the People," whose laws and Constitution their opinions define. The Court's decisions, after all, are exercises of enormous coercive power that reorder many, even millions, of individual lives, indeed society itself. The subjects of that authority are entitled, I think, to see the faces behind the printed words.

On rare occasions, public announcement of a decision is accompanied by an expression of extreme disagreement by a Justice in dissent. A few times each term, a Justice will care so deeply about a case and feel so strongly that the Court has reached the wrong result that he or she will follow the announcement of the majority opinion by reading portions of his or her dissent.

Justice Stevens, an extraordinarily courteous man, is among those least inclined publicly to excoriate his colleagues from the bench. Still, he did it severely the term I clerked, when *Texas* v. *Johnson* (the first flag-burning case) was handed down. I doubt anyone who was there has forgotten the moment.

In *Texas* v. *Johnson,* the Court ruled that the First Amendment's guarantee of free speech prohibited the state of Texas from prosecuting Gregory Lee Johnson for "flag desecration" after he burned an American flag as part of a political protest at the 1984 Republican National Convention. At oral argument it had been evident that Johnson's treatment of the flag infuriated Stevens, a World War II navy veteran. He became uncharacteristically testy with William Kunstler, Johnson's flamboyant attorney, who, for his part, was provocatively gleeful about his client's insulting conduct.

At the time, I wondered whether somewhere deep down Justice Stevens ac-cepted the majority's view (axiomatic to almost all the clerks) that, purely as an intellectual matter, Johnson's burning of the flag was a constitutionally protected political statement. But no person, even a supremely rational one such as Justice Stevens, reaches every decision solely by the cold light of reason. And he did not seem to have in this case. As he read his dissent from the bench, Stevens's voice was raw emotion. As he reached the peroration, his face was flush, his eyes just shy of tears.

"The ideas of liberty and equality have been an irresistible force in motivating leaders like Patrick Henry, Susan B. Anthony, and Abraham Lincoln, school-teachers like Nathan Hale and Booker T. Washington, the Philippine Scouts who fought at Bataan, and the soldiers who scaled the bluff at Omaha Beach," Stevens closed. "If those ideas are worth fighting for—and our history demonstrates that they are—it cannot be true that the flag that uniquely symbolizes their power is not itself worthy of protection from unnecessary desecration. I respectfully dissent."

I still feel strongly that the Court majority was right and Stevens wrong in *Texas* v. *Johnson*. But tears do not often well on the high bench, and the purity of Stevens's conviction made an indelible impression. Every night, on the rooftops of the stately federal buildings that line Pennsylvania Avenue, a host of flags are spotlit against the dark sky. When I see those flags now, I'm always carried back to Stevens's speech in the courtroom. I don't look at them quite the same way as before. . . . ■

 Chapter 13

Public Policy

The purpose and function of government is to make policy—that is, to create and implement the rules and programs under which society is to be governed. In a sense, all of the previous chapters have been examining the policy making process: the institutions that interact to create policy and the constitutional foundation on which they operate; the relationship of policy making to public opinion and the electoral process; and the role of nongovernmental actors—like the media and interest groups—in policy development. In this chapter, we turn to examining the total picture.

Political scientists typically divide policy into two broad categories—domestic policy and foreign policy. Domestic policy involves a broad range of issues, including health care, education, the economy, and criminal justice. Foreign policy includes not only diplomacy but also military affairs.

Domestic policy making in the United States has undergone several transformations in this century. The New Deal greatly expanded the federal government's role in economic regulation and social policy making. In the 1960s, Lyndon Johnson's Great Society widened the scope of federal welfare programs, a trend continued under President Richard Nixon. In the 1980s, the election of Ronald Reagan initiated a period of struggle for control over the scope and direction of federal social policy. That struggle has grown even more intense in recent years.

At bottom, the debate over social policy in the United States is marked by a contest between those who believe that the national government should take the lead in solving society's social problems and those who believe that state and local governments and the private sector should carry the load. As for foreign policy, Americans tend to agree on the broad goals the United States should pursue, but frequently disagree on how best to pursue those goals in a complex and often hostile world.

Chapter Questions

1. How have the larger trends and currents in American politics over the past thirty years affected domestic policy? Consider the impact of divided party control of Congress and the White House, increased federal budget deficits, and the conflict between liberal and conservative ideologies.

2. How has American foreign policy changed since the end of the cold war in the 1980s? What goals should the United States pursue in foreign policy, and how should it pursue them?

 # Foundations

Government policy is made by all three branches and is heavily influenced and constrained by public opinion and by the electoral process. The Framers designed a system that prevents any one branch from making policy on its own, and to a great extent the system in fact works just that way. Policy making, in general, involves cooperation, negotiation, and at times conflict among many different players. Nor is that process completed once a policy is enacted into law; the law must be implemented by the executive branch, under congressional and judicial supervision; when necessary, the program must be modified to fit new or unexpected circumstances. Each year the program must be funded through the congressional budget process; periodically, it must be reauthorized by Congress as well.

Political scientists have categorized public policy making along several dimensions; for example, one can look at the various stages of the process, at the different types of policy, or at the different political actors involved. The following selection, by two political scientists, examines public policy making from a variety of perspectives.

Questions

1. "Policies all too often mirror Congress's scattered and decentralized structure," Davidson and Oleszek write. Explain. (Consider the selections in Chapter 9, as well as this one.)
2. Define these terms: *distributive policies*, *regulatory policies*, and *redistributive policies*. What are the defining characteristics of each?

13.1 Domestic Policymaking (1994)

Roger H. Davidson and Walter J. Oleszek

Definitions of Policy

Because policies ultimately are what government is about, it is not surprising that definitions of policy and policy making are diverse and influenced by the beholder's eye. David Easton's celebrated definition of public policy as society's "au-

Roger H. Davidson and Walter J. Oleszck, Congress and Its Members, 6th Edition (Washington DC: CQ Press, 1998), pp. 349–356. Reprinted by permission of Congressional Quarterly.

thoritative allocations" of values or resources is one approach to the question. To put it another way, policies can be regarded as reflecting "who gets what, when, and how" in a society. A more serviceable definition of policy is offered by Randall Ripley and Grace Franklin: policy is what the government says and does about perceived problems. . . .

Stages of Policy Making

Whatever the time frame, policy making normally has four distinct stages: setting the agenda, formulating policy, adopting policy, and implementing policy.

Setting the Agenda   At the initial stage, public problems are spotted and moved onto the national agenda, which can be defined as "the list of subjects to which government officials and those around them are paying serious attention." In a large, pluralistic country like the United States, the national agenda at any given moment is extensive and vigorously debated.

How do problems get placed on the agenda? Some are heralded by a crisis or some other prominent event—the hijacking of a plane by terrorists, the demise of savings and loan associations, or a campaign-funding scandal. Others are occasioned by the gradual accumulation of knowledge—for example, increasing awareness of an environmental hazard like acid rain or ozone depletion. Still other agenda items represent the accumulation of past problems that no longer can be avoided or ignored. Finally, agendas may be set in motion by political processes—election results, turnover in Congress, or shifts in public opinion. The 1994 election results are an example of how the GOP's control of the 104th Congress and its Contract with America drove the national agenda.

Agenda items are pushed by *policy entrepreneurs,* people willing to invest time and energy to promote a particular issue. Numerous Washington "think tanks" and interest groups, especially at the beginning of a new president's term, issue reports that seek to influence the economic, social, or foreign policy agenda of the nation. Usually, however, elected officials and their staffs or appointees are more likely to shape agendas than are career bureaucrats or nongovernmental actors. Notable policy entrepreneurs on Capitol Hill are congressional leaders who push their party's policy initiatives. Speaker Newt Gingrich with his advocacy of a minimalist role for the central government (the "Republican revolution") is a good example.

Lawmakers frequently are policy entrepreneurs because they are expected to voice the concerns of constituents and organized groups and to seek legislative solutions. Politicians generally gravitate toward issues that are visible, salient, and solvable. Tough, arcane, or conflictual problems may be shunned because they offer few payoffs and little hope of success.

Sometimes only a crisis—such as the oil price increases in the 1970s—can force lawmakers to address difficult questions. Yet, despite enactment of legislation designed to ameliorate future energy problems, Americans today are as dependent on imported oil as they were two decades ago. Forecasters predict another energy crisis unless steps are taken to develop alternative fuels, change habits of consumption, and reduce the spiraling demand for oil, especially from the volatile

Middle East. This kind of "creeping crisis" is often difficult for members of Congress to grapple with, in part because of the "two Congresses" dilemma. As conscientious lawmakers, members might want to forge long-term solutions. But as representatives of their constituents, they are deterred from acting when most citizens see no problems with the immediate situation.

Formulating Policy   In the second stage of policy making, items on the political agenda are discussed and potential solutions are explored. Members of Congress and their staffs play crucial roles by conducting hearings and writing committee reports. They are aided by policy experts in executive agencies, interest groups, and the private sector.

Another term for this stage is *policy incubation*, which entails "keeping a proposal alive while it picks up support, or waits for a better climate, or while a consensus begins to form that the problem to which it is addressed exists." Sometimes this process takes only a few months; more often it requires years. During Dwight D. Eisenhower's administration, for example, congressional Democrats explored and refined policy options that, while not immediately accepted, were ripe for adoption by the time their party's nominee, John F. Kennedy, was elected president in 1960.

The incubation process not only brings policies to maturity but also refines solutions to the problems. The process may break down if workable solutions are not available. The seeming intractability of many modern issues complicates problem solving. Thomas S. Foley, D-Wash. (Speaker, 1989–1995), held that issues had become far more perplexing since he came to Congress in 1965. At that time "the civil rights issue facing the legislators was whether the right to vote should be federally guaranteed for blacks and Hispanics. Now members are called on to deal with more ambiguous policies like affirmative action and racial quotas."

Solutions to problems normally involve "some fairly simple routines emphasizing the tried and true (or at least not discredited)." A repertoire of proposals exists—for example, blue-ribbon commissions, trust funds, or pilot projects—that can be applied to a variety of unsolved problems. Problem solvers also must guard against recommending solutions that will be viewed as worse than the problem.

Adopting Policy   Laws are ideas whose time has come. The right time for a policy is what scholar John Kingdon calls the *policy window*: the opportunity presented by circumstances and attitudes to enact a policy into law. Policy entrepreneurs must seize the opportunity before the policy window closes and the idea's time has passed.

Once policies are ripe for adoption, they must gain popular acceptance. This is the function of *legitimation*, the process through which policies come to be viewed by the public as right or proper. Inasmuch as citizens are expected to comply with laws or regulations—pay taxes, observe rules, or make sacrifices of one sort or another—the policies themselves must appear to have been properly considered and enacted. A nation whose policies lack legitimacy is in deep trouble.

Symbolic acts, such as members voting on the House or Senate floor or the president signing a bill, signal to everyone that policies have been duly adopted according to traditional forms. Hearings and debates, moreover, serve not only to fine-tune policies but also to cultivate support from affected interests. Responding to critics of Congress's slowness in adopting energy legislation, Sen. Ted Stevens, R-Alaska, asked these questions:

> Would you want an energy bill to flow through the Senate and not have anyone consider the impacts on housing or on the automotive industry or on the energy industries that provide our light and power? Should we ignore the problems of the miner or the producer or the distributor? Our legislative process must reflect all of the problems if the public is to have confidence in the government.

Legitimating, in other words, often demands a measured pace and attention to procedural details. (Another strategy is to move quickly—before opposition forces can mobilize—to enact bold changes and then work to gain the public's acceptance of them.)

Implementing Policy   In the final stage, policies shaped by the legislature and the highest executive levels are put into effect, usually by a federal agency. Policies are not self-executing: they must be promulgated and enforced. A law or executive order rarely spells out exactly how a particular policy will be implemented. Congress and the president usually delegate most decisions about implementation to the responsible agencies under broad but stated guidelines. Implementation determines the ultimate effect of policies. Officials of the executive branch can thwart a policy by foot dragging or sheer inefficiency. By the same token, overzealous administrators can push a policy far beyond its creators' intent.

Congress therefore must exercise its oversight role. It may require executive agencies to report or consult with congressional committees or to follow certain formal procedures. Members of Congress get feedback on the operation of federal programs through a variety of channels: media coverage, interest group protests, and even constituent casework. With such information Congress can and often does pass judgment by adjusting funding, introducing amendments, or recasting the basic legislation governing a particular policy.

Types of Domestic Policies

One way to understand public policies is to analyze the nature of the policies themselves. Scholars have classified policies in many different ways. The typology we shall use identifies three types of domestic policies: distributive, regulatory, and redistributive.

Distributive Policies   Distributive policies or programs are government actions that convey tangible benefits to private individuals, groups, or firms. Invariably, they involve subsidies to favored individuals or groups. The benefits are often called "pork" (special-interest spending for projects in members' states or districts), although that appellation is sometimes difficult to define. After all, "one person's pork is another person's steak." The projects come in several different varieties:

> Dams, roads and bridges, known as "green pork," are old hat. These days, there is also "academic pork" in the form of research grants to colleges, "defense pork" in the form of geographically specific military expenditures and lately "high-tech pork," for example the intense fight to authorize research into super computers and high-definition television (HDTV).

The presence of distributive politics—which makes many interests better off and few, if any, visibly worse off—is natural in Congress, which as a nonhierarchical institution must build coalitions in order to function. A textbook example was the $1-billion-plus National Parks and Recreation Act of 1978. Dubbed the "Park Barrel" bill, it created so many parks, historical sites, seashores, wilderness areas, wild and scenic rivers, and national trails that it sailed through the Interior (now Resources) Committee and passed the House by a 341-61 vote. "Notice how quiet we are. We all got something in there," said one House member, after the Rules Committee cleared the bill in five minutes flat. Another member quipped, "If it had a blade of grass and a squirrel, it got in the bill." Distributive politics of this kind throws into sharp relief the "two Congresses" notion: national policy as a mosaic of local interests.

The politics of distribution works best when tax revenues are expanding, fueled by high productivity and economic growth—characteristics of the U.S. economy from the end of World War II through the mid-1970s. When productivity declines or tax cutting squeezes revenues, it becomes difficult to add new benefits or expand old ones. Such was the plight of lawmakers in the 1980s and 1990s. Yet distributive impulses remained strong, adding pressure to wring distributive elements out of tight budgets. Even in the tight-fisted 104th Congress, lawmakers in both parties ensured that money would be spent for particular purposes in their districts or states. As one account noted:

> With Republicans cutting non-military spending but protecting the defense budget from reductions, the huge $243 billion Pentagon spending bill this year has taken the place of pork-barrel public works measures of old. Instead of seeking bridges and roads, members of Congress in both parties have been clamoring for defense contracts to protect home-state jobs and businesses.

House GOP freshman John Ensign of Nevada highlighted both the "two Congresses" and the prevailing legislative sentiments toward distributive policy making when he said, "I hate the idea of pork, but if there's a pot of money, I want to make sure that Nevada gets its fair share."

Regulatory Policies   Regulatory policies are designed to protect the public against harm or abuse that might result from unbridled private activity. For example, the Food and Drug Administration (FDA) monitors standards for foodstuffs and tests drugs for purity, safety, and effectiveness, and the Federal Trade Commission (FTC) guards against illegal business practices, such as deceptive advertising.

Federal regulation against certain abuses dates from the late nineteenth century, when the Interstate Commerce Act and the Sherman Antitrust Act were enacted to protect against transport and monopoly abuses. As the twentieth century dawned, scandalous practices in slaughterhouses and food processing plants, colorfully described by reform-minded muckraking reporters, led to meatpacking, food, and drug regulations. The stock market collapse in 1929 and the Great Depression paved the way for the New Deal legislation that would regulate the banking and securities industries and labor-management relations. Consumer rights and environmental protection came of age in the 1960s and 1970s. Dramatic attacks on unsafe automobiles by Ralph Nader and others led to new laws mandating tougher safety standards. Concern about smog produced by auto exhausts led to the Clean Air Act of 1970. And concern about airline delays, congestion, and safety prompted Congress to consider new regulatory controls for the nation's air traffic system. . . .

Redistributive Policies   Redistribution, which visibly shifts resources from one group to another, is the most difficult of all political feats. Because it is controversial, redistributive policy engages a broad spectrum of political actors—not only in the House and Senate chambers but also in the executive branch and among interest groups and the public at large. Redistributive issues tend to be ideological: they often separate liberals and conservatives because they upset relationships between social and economic classes. Theodore R. Marmor described the thirty-year fight over medical care for the aged as "cast in terms of class conflict":

> The leading adversaries . . . brought into the opposing camps a large number of groups whose interests were not directly affected by the Medicare outcome. . . . [I]deological charges and countercharges dominated public discussion, and each side seemed to regard compromise as unacceptable.

Most of the divisive socioeconomic issues of the past generation—civil rights, affirmative action, school busing, aid to education, homelessness, abortion, tax reform—were redistributive problems. Fiscal policy making has taken on a redistributive character as federal expenditures outpace revenues, and lawmakers are forced to find ways to close the gap. Cutting federal benefits and opening up new revenue sources both involve redistribution because they turn "haves" into "have nots." That is why politicians today find budget and revenue issues so burdensome. "I wasn't here in the glory days, when a guy with a bright idea of a scholarship program or whatever could get a few hundred million dollars to pursue it," lamented Rep. Richard J. Durbin, D-Ill. "Now you've got to take from one to give to the other."

Federal budgeting is marked not only by extreme conflict but also by techniques to disguise the redistributions or make them more palatable. Omnibus budget packages permit legislators to approve cuts *en bloc* rather than one by one, and across-the-board formulas (like "freezes") give the appearance of spreading the misery equally to affected groups. In all such vehicles, distributive elements are added to placate the more vocal opponents of change. Such is the unhappy lot of politicians consigned to lawmaking in a redistributive mode. ■

 # American Politics Today

Few public policy issues are as important to Americans of every generation as social security. This combination retirement and insurance system has served Americans since 1935. It is largely responsible for the tremendous reduction in poverty among America's elderly population.

Many Americans have lost faith in the social security system, however. By the government's own admission, the system must be reformed if it is to remain solvent after the "baby boom" generation retires. Some argue that the government should allow workers to manage their own social security accounts, investing their money as they see fit. Others maintain that only modest changes are needed to keep the system intact.

In this essay, the author Dean Baker analyzes and debunks nine "misconceptions" about social security that, in his view, have clouded the national debate on this vital issue.

Questions

1. Why do many Americans believe that the social security program will face a crisis in the next century? How does Baker respond to these arguments?
2. What goals was social security designed to achieve? Evaluate the various reform proposals discussed by Baker in terms of these diverse goals.

13.2 Nine Misconceptions about Social Security (1998)

Dean Baker

1. *The Social Security Trust Fund Is an Accounting Fiction.*

The Social Security tax has been raising more money than is needed to pay for current benefits, in order to build up a surplus to help finance the retirement of the Baby Boom generation. All of this surplus is lent to the U.S. Treasury when the Social Security Trust Fund buys bonds from it. The money is then used to finance the federal deficit, just like any other money the government borrows. The bonds held by the fund pay the same interest as bonds held by the public. These bonds are every bit as real (or as much of a fiction) as the bonds held by banks, corporations, and individuals. Throughout U.S. history the federal government has always paid its debts. As a result, government bonds enjoy the highest credit ratings and are considered one of the safest assets in the world. Thus the fund has very real and secure assets.

It is true that the interest the government pays on these bonds is a drain on the Treasury, as will be the money paid by the government when the fund ultimately cashes in its bonds. But this drain has nothing to do with Social Security. If the Social Security Trust Fund were not currently building up a surplus, and lending the money to the government, the government would still be running a deficit of approximately $60 billion in its non-Social Security operations. It would then

---

Dean Baker, "Nine Misconceptions About Social Security," *The Atlantic Monthly* (July 1998), pp. 34–39. Reprinted by permission of the author, a senior research fellow at the Preamble Center in Washington, D.C. and the Century Foundation in New York City.

have to borrow this money from individuals like H. Ross Perot and Peter G. Peterson and to pay out more interest each year to the people it borrowed from. Therefore, the government's debt to the fund is simply a debt it would have incurred in any event. The government's other spending and tax policies, not Social Security, will be the cause if there is any problem in the future in paying off the bonds held by the fund.

The government bonds held by the Social Security Trust Fund will always be a comparatively small portion of the government's debt, and therefore a relatively minor burden. They will hit a peak of about 14.4 percent of gross domestic product in 2015, whereas the debt now held by individuals and corporations is about 47 percent of GDP. Therefore, at its peak the burden of interest payments to the fund will be less than a third as large as the interest burden the government now bears.

2. The Government Uses Overly Optimistic Numbers to Convince People That Social Security Will Be There for Them. The Situation is Much Worse Than the Government Admits.

Actually, Social Security projections are based on extremely pessimistic economic assumptions: that growth will average just 1.8 percent over the next twenty years, a lower rate than in any comparable period in U.S. history; that growth will slow even further in later years, until the rate is less than half the 2.6 percent of the past twenty years; that there will be no increase in immigration even when the economy experiences a labor shortage because of the retirement of the Baby Boom generation; and that this labor shortage will not lead to a rapid growth in wages. Both possibilities excluded in these projections—increased immigration and rapid wage growth—would increase the fund's revenues. These projections are genuinely a worst-case scenario.

3. The Demographics of the Baby Boom Will Place an Unbearable Burden on the Social Security System.

Those who want to overhaul Social Security make their case with the following numbers: in 1960 there were more than five workers for each beneficiary; today there are 3.3 workers; by 2030 there will be only two workers for each beneficiary. At present the fund is running an annual surplus of more than $80 billion, approximately 20 percent as much as its current expenditures. This surplus will generate interest revenue to help support the system as the ratio of workers to beneficiaries continues to fall in the next century. Also, the fact that workers are becoming more productive year by year means that it will take fewer workers to support each retiree. The United States had 10.5 farm workers for every hundred people in 1929; it has fewer than 1.1 farm workers for every hundred people today. Yet the population is well fed, and we even export food. Rising farm productivity made this possible. Similarly, increases in worker productivity (which have been and should be reflected in higher incomes), however small compared with those of the past, will allow each retiree to be supported by an ever smaller number of workers.

In fact the demographics of the Baby Boom have very little to do with the long-range problems of Social Security. The main reason the fund will run into deficits in future years is that people are living longer. If people continue to retire at the same age but live longer, then a larger percentage of their lives will be spent in retirement. If people want to spend a larger portion of their lives in retirement, either they will have to accept lower incomes (reduced benefits) in their retirement years relative to those of their working years, or they will have to increase the portion of their incomes (higher taxes) that they put aside during their working years for retirement.

This is the main long-range problem facing Social Security. Current projections show that the annual deficit will be 5.71 percent of taxable payroll in 2070, long after the Baby Boom will have passed into history. But the annual deficit is expected to be only 4.44 percent of taxable payroll in 2035, when the worst crunch from retired Baby Boomers will be felt.

Examining just the change in the ratio of beneficiaries to workers overstates the burden that workers will face in the future. To assess the burden accurately it is necessary to examine the total number of dependents—beneficiaries and children—each worker will have to support. It is projected that this ratio will rise from 0.708 per worker at present to 0.795 in 2035. But even this number is well below the ratio of 0.946 that prevailed in 1965. And the fund's trustees project a lower birth rate, meaning that the increased costs of providing for a larger retired population will be largely offset by the reduction of expenses associated with caring for children.

4. Future Generations Will Experience Declining Living Standards Because of the Government Debt and the Burden Created by Social Security.

Projections indicate that workers' real wages will increase by approximately one percent a year. If Social Security benefits are left unchanged, in order to meet the fund's obligations it will be necessary to raise the Social Security tax by 0.1 percent a year (0.05 percent on the employer and 0.05 percent on the employee) for thirty-six years, beginning in 2010. This will be a total tax increase of 3.6 percent, approximately the same as the increase in Social Security taxes from 1977 to 1990.

Even with this schedule of tax increases, real wages after Social Security taxes are deducted will continue to rise. By 2046, when the tax increases are fully phased in, the average wage after Social Security taxes will be more than 45 percent higher than at present. As noted earlier, this is based on pessimistic projections about wage growth.

5. By 2030 Federal Spending on Entitlement Programs for the Elderly Will Consume All the Revenue Collected by the Government.

By far the greatest part of the projected increases in federal spending on entitlement programs for the elderly is attributable to a projected explosion in national health-care costs, both public and private. According to projections from the Health Care Financing Administration, average health-care spending for a family of four in 2030 will be more than 80 percent of the median family's before-tax income. If such an explosion in health-care costs actually occurred, the economy would be destroyed even if we eliminated entitlement programs altogether. If health-care costs in the public and private sectors are brought under control, the problems posed by demographic trends will be quite manageable.

It is very deceptive to combine other spending categories with health care; projected health-care costs by themselves will consume most of the budget. For example, projected federal spending on education, highways, and health care combined should be more than 80 percent of federal revenues in 2030; defense spending plus projected health-care spending should come close to 70 percent of federal revenues.

6. *If Social Security Were Privatized, It Would Lead to a Higher National Saving Rate and More Growth.*

By itself, privatizing Social Security would not create a penny of additional savings. All the privatization plans call for the government to continue to pay Social Security benefits to current recipients and those about to retire; therefore spending would be exactly the same after privatization as it was before privatization. Yet the government would no longer be collecting Social Security taxes. Each dollar an individual put into a private retirement account rather than paying it to the government in Social Security taxes would still be a dollar the government must borrow. Individuals would be saving more, but the government would have reduced its saving (increased its borrowing) by exactly the same amount. Most of the privatization schemes being put forward call for additional taxes and additional borrowing to finance a transition while benefits were being paid out under the old system. Any additions to national savings attributable to these plans would stem entirely from the tax increase. This tax increase would have the identical effect on national savings if it were not linked to privatizing Social Security. In other words, raising taxes is one way to increase national savings, and if we are willing to raise taxes, we need not privatize Social Security.

The fact that individuals might put their savings in the stock market or in other private assets, whereas the Social Security Trust Fund buys government bonds, doesn't affect the level of saving at all. If it did, the government could increase the level of saving in the economy by borrowing money and then investing it in the stock market, or by borrowing money and giving it to individuals with the requirement that they invest it in the stock market. If either step could increase the level of saving in the economy, the government should take it independent of any changes in the Social Security system.

In fact, all else being equal, if individuals invested the money they would otherwise pay out in Social Security taxes, less saving would result, because a large portion of this money would be siphoned off by the financial industry. Currently stock brokers, insurance companies, and other financial institutions charge their customers an average of more than one percent a year on the value of the money they hold. Thus if $1,000 is invested through a brokerage firm for forty years, the investor will have been charged in excess of $400 in fees on the original investment, plus an additional one percent a year on all gains. These fees are a big cost from the standpoint of the individual investor, and a complete waste from the standpoint of the economy as a whole. Meanwhile, the operating expenses of the Social Security system are less than $8.00 for every $1,000 paid out to beneficiaries.

It is easy to see why costs in the private financial sector are so much higher. The private sector pays hundreds of thousands of insurance agents and brokers to solicit business. It also incurs enormous costs in television, radio, newspaper, and magazine advertising. In addition, many executives and brokers in the financial industry receive huge salaries. Million-dollar salaries are not uncommon, and some executives earn salaries in the tens of millions. Privatization would add these expenses, which are currently absent from the Social Security system.

7. If People Invest Their Money Themselves, They Will Get a Higher Return Than If They Leave It with the Government.

This may be true for some people, but it cannot be true on average, for much the same reasons as noted above. Some people may end up big winners by picking the right stocks, but if the national saving rate has not increased, the economy will not have increased its growth rate, and the economic pie will be no larger in the future with privatization than it would have been without it. Thus high returns for some must come at the expense of others. In fact, since the cost of operating a retirement system is so much greater through the financial markets than through the Social Security system, the average person will actually be worse off.

Some advocates of government-mandated saving plans argue that individual investors can get real returns of seven percent on money invested in the stock market (the historical rate of return), and that this would ensure a comfortable retirement for everyone. Certainly people have gotten far better returns in the market in the past few years, but if Social Security projections are accurate, such rates of return cannot be sustained. Profits can rise only as fast as the economy grows (unless wages fall as a share of national income, which no one is projecting). If stock prices maintain a fixed relationship to profits, then stock prices will grow at the same rate as the economy. The total return will therefore approximate the ratio of dividends to the stock price (currently about three percent) plus the rate of economic growth (two percent over the next ten years, but projected to fall to 1.2 percent in the middle of the next century). This means that the returns people can expect from investing in the stock market will be five percent in the near future and 4.2 percent later in the next century. For stock prices to rise enough to maintain a real return of seven percent, price-to-earnings ratios would have to exceed 400:1 by 2070.

8. The Consumer Price Index Overstates the True Rate of Increase in the Cost of Living. Social Security Recipients Are Therefore Getting a Huge Bonanza Each Year, Because Their Checks Are Adjusted in Accordance with the CPI.

There is considerable dispute about the accuracy of the CPI. The Boskin Commission, which was appointed by the Senate Finance Committee to examine the CPI, stated in its final report, in 1996, that overall the CPI had been overstating the cost of living by 1.3 percentage points a year. However, the Bureau of Labor Statistics found that the CPI understated the cost of living when compared with an index that measured the cost of living for the elderly. This is because the elderly spend an unusually large share of their income on health care and housing, which have risen relatively rapidly in price. Questions remain about the accuracy of the CPI, and they cannot be resolved without further research.

However, one point is clear. If the CPI has been overstating inflation, then future generations will be much better off than we imagined. If inflation has been overstated, then real wage growth must have been *understated,* since real wage growth is actual wage growth minus the rate of inflation. If we accept the Boskin Commission's midrange estimate of CPI overstatement, average real wages in 2030 will be more than $54,000 (measured in today's dollars). If the commission's high-end estimate is right, average wages will be nearly $65,000. By 2050 average wages will be at least $82,000 and possibly as much as $108,000.

Another implication of a CPI that overstates inflation is that people were much poorer in the recent past than is generally recognized. This conclusion is inescapable: if the rate of inflation is lower than indicated by the CPI, then real wages and living standards have been rising faster than is indicated by calculations that use the CPI. If wages and living standards have been rising faster than we thought, then past levels must have been lower. Projecting backward, the Boskin Commission's estimate of the overstatement of the CPI gives a range for the median family income in 1960 of $15,000 to $18,000 (in today's dollars)—or 95 to 110 percent of income at the current poverty level.

If the Boskin Commission's evaluation of the CPI is accepted, any assessment of generational equity looks very bad from the standpoint of the elderly: they lived most of their lives in or near poverty. And the future looks extremely bright for the young. Average annual wages in 1960, when today's seventy-three-year-olds were thirty-five, was between $10,006 and $11,902 in today's dollars. Average annual wages in 2030, when today's newborns are thirty-two, will be between $54,000 and $65,000 in today's dollars. Such numbers make it hard to justify cutting Social Security for the elderly in order to enrich future generations, on the grounds of generational equity.

9. Social Security Gives Tens of Billions of Dollars Each Year to Senior Citizens Who Don't Need It. This Money Could Be Better Used to Support Poor Children.

Most of the elderly are not very well off. Their median household income is only about $18,000. However, even if they were better off, it would be hard to justify taking away their Social Security on either moral or economic grounds.

Social Security is a social-insurance program, not a welfare program. People pay into it during their working lives. They have a right to expect something in return, just as they expect interest payments when they buy a government bond. Social Security is already progressive: the rate of return on tax payments is much lower for the wealthy than for the poor. This progressivity is enhanced by the fact that Social Security income is taxable for middle- and high-income retirees but not for low-income retirees. If benefits for higher-income retirees were cut back further, those people would be receiving virtually no return for the taxes they paid in. This would be certain to undermine support for the program.

From an economic standpoint, means testing or any other way of denying benefits to the wealthy would be foolish, because it would give people a great incentive to hide income and thereby pass the means test. There are many ways this could be done. Parents could pass most of their assets on to their children and then continue to collect full benefits. People could move their money into assets that don't yield an annual income, such as land or some kinds of stock. Most of the income of retirees is from accumulated assets, which makes it much easier to hide than wage income. Means testing would in effect place a very high marginal tax rate on senior citizens, giving them a strong incentive to find ways to evade taxes. It may be desirable to get more revenue from the wealthy, but means testing for Social Security makes about as much sense as means testing for interest on government bonds. ■

 # The Comparative Context

In the first two parts of a three-part article, the political scientist Anthony King surveyed five Western democracies—the United States, Canada, Great Britain, France, and West Germany—in an attempt to describe and understand the role played by the government in a number of public policy areas. In the first two parts, King concluded that "the part played by the State [the government] in the United States is certainly greater than it used to be—hence the talk in America of big government—but . . . it is still, for better or worse, much smaller than elsewhere." Public ownership of major industrial enterprises in the United States, King suggested, is a "non-story—of proposals that were not made and of things that did not happen." Governments in the United States play a significant role in the provision of social services, but their role is still small when compared to governments in the other four countries studied. (The only exception King noted is in the field of education, where the role of state and local governments is quite large. The government's large role in education, King concludes, is possible only because Americans understand that "if the State did not supply education, no one else would" and that "education was a field—almost the only field—in which the State could expand without competing, except in a very small way, with private institutions.")*

Without a comparative basis of analysis, it is easy to overstate the concept of big government in America. This is especially true because government's role today is quite large by historical standards. King's argument reminds us that, in comparative perspective, the role of government in the domestic public policy of the United States remains quite low.

King sets out five possible explanations for the smaller role of government in the United States and concludes that only the last—ideas—can provide a satisfactory explanation.

---

*Anthony King, "Ideas, Institutions, and the Politics of Governments: A Comparative Analysis; Parts I and II," *British Journal of Political Science* 3 (1973), p. 302; Anthony King, "Ideas, Institutions, and the Politics of Governments: A Comparative Analysis: Part III," *British Journal of Political* Science 3 (1973), p. 420.

Questions

1. What are some of the ideas that have contributed to Americans' reluctance to allow the role of the state to expand to the levels seen in other Western democracies? Consider in particular the readings in Chapter 5 ("Political Culture and Public Opinion").
2. King notes that education is the one major exception to his analysis. Are there other, perhaps lesser, exceptions? How are these exceptions defended or explained in the American context?

13.3 Ideas, Institutions, and the Policies of Government: A Comparative Analysis (1973)

Anthony King

[Earlier in this paper,] we noticed that the countries have pursued policies that diverge widely, at least with respect to the size of the direct operating role of the State in the provision of public services. We also noticed that the United States differs from the four other countries far more than they do from each other. These findings will not have come as a great surprise to anybody, although some readers may have been surprised—in view of the common assumption that all major western countries are "welfare states"—to discover just how much the countries differ and what different histories they have had.

In any event, it is time now to turn directly to the problem of explanation. Obviously any explanation, were it to account for all of the phenomena we have referred to, would have to be exceedingly elaborate. It would have to encompass a large number of particular events within the five countries as well as the variations amongst them. All we will attempt here is a general explanation of why the United States is so strikingly different. We shall assume that the explanation we need is indeed general: in other words, that the pattern we have observed is not simply the chance outcome of a series of more or less random occurrences. We shall also assume that it is the American pattern, in particular, that needs to be accounted for.

Much of the most important work in the field of public policy in recent years has, of course, been concerned with a very similar problem: accounting for the variations in the expenditure policies of the American states. The writers on this subject have singled out two types of (mainly quantifiable) variable: "political" (e.g. extent of party competition, relationship between governor and legislature, apportionment of legislative districts), and "socio-economic" (e.g. *per capita*

Anthony King, "Ideas, Institutions, and the Politics of Government: A Comparative Analysis: Part III," *British Journal of Political Science* 3 (1973), pp. 409–419, 423. Reprinted with the permission of Cambridge University Press.

income, degree of urbanization, degree of industrialization). They have then gone on, using correlation techniques, to relate these variables to one another and to the variations in policy to be explained. Unfortunately this approach is denied us here, given the problem we have set ourselves. Quite apart from the fact that we are dealing with five units instead of fifty, there is no reason to suppose that any of the expenditures-in-the-states variables is significantly related to any of the differences between the United States and the other four countries. All five are, or have been during much of their recent history, rich, urban, industrial and politically competitive; to the extent that there have been variations in, for example, their constitutions, these variations have not had any discernible bearing on their policies. It is, in effect, as though we were trying to account for the differences, not amongst all fifty states, but only amongst (say) New York, New Jersey, Connecticut, Massachusetts and Pennsylvania.

We must therefore look elsewhere. We shall consider explanations in terms of five possible variables: elites, demands, interest groups, institutions, and ideas. These variables obviously interact with one another, or at least they could. Some examples of such interaction will be noted below, but for simplicity's sake the five variables will mostly be treated separately. . . .

Elites

It could be maintained, first, that government plays a smaller role in the US because *the US, unlike the other four countries, is dominated by an elite which wishes to inhibit the expansion of State activity and succeeds in doing so.* For this proposition to be true, at least one of the following propositions would also have to be true: either America is dominated by an elite whereas the other four countries are not; or the American elite is alone in wishing to limit the sphere of the State; or the American elite is not alone in wishing to limit the sphere of the State but is alone in actually succeeding in doing so. It would also have to be the case that there were in the US factors making for the expansion of State activity, which would have their effect but for the elite's intervention.

Much in this line of argument is not very plausible. America may or may not be dominated by an elite, but, if it is, then so are Canada, Britain, France and West Germany; there is hardly an industrial country anywhere whose power structure has not been interpreted in the style of C. Wright Mills. There is similarly no reason to suppose—on the assumption that all five countries are dominated by elites—that the American elite is somehow more successful than the others in imposing its will, or in thwarting the wills of others; indeed it would be paradoxical to say of an elite that it was an elite but yet could not get its way in matters that were important to it. Nevertheless, there is one element in the elitist explanation—the possibility that the American elite, if it exists, is alone in wishing to limit the sphere of the State—which cannot be dismissed out of hand. We shall come back to it at the end.

Demands

A second possible explanation of the relatively limited role played by government in the US is that, *whereas the mass publics in the other countries have demanded expansions of State activity, the American mass public has not.* In other words, irrespective of whether the United States is dominated by an elite, it may be that little has happened because little has been called for. An alternating rendering of this hypothesis would be that, whereas in any or all of the other countries governments do things whether or not they are demanded, in the US governments act only on demand and, since little has been demanded, little has been done; in other words, public opinion may play a more important part in American political life than elsewhere.

These possibilities raise all sorts of questions, as yet unanswered, in the empirical theory of representation. They also pose a very real problem of evidence: who is to say what the Canadian people wanted in 1917 or the French in the 1920s? All the same, there are a number of points which can be made with some confidence, and, while they should not lead anyone to reject the demands hypothesis outright, they make one wonder whether it can provide more than a very small part of the general explanation we are looking for.

It is hard to think of any act of nationalization in Canada or Europe that took place as the result of widespread public demand for it. The British case is probably typical. Many historians believe that, if anything, Labour won the 1945 general election despite its commitments to nationalization not because of them, and that most voters remained pretty indifferent to the Labour Government's subsequent nationalization measures. Butler and Stokes found in the 1960s that, of a panel of electors interviewed twice at an interval of approximately sixteen months, 61 per cent either had no opinion at all on nationalization or no stable opinion; of the minority with definite opinions, the great majority wanted either no more nationalization or even the denationalization of industries already in the public sector. Yet in 1967 the Wilson Government nationalized the great bulk of the British iron and steel industry.

The only exception to this pattern of indifference/hostility is probably France in 1944–6, where the overwhelming need for national reconstruction and the anti-patriotic aura that private business had acquired during the Occupation seem to have created a climate of public opinion favourable to State ownership. It has been claimed by a French historian that in 1944 "the great majority of Frenchmen were convinced of the economic, social and political superiority of nationalised industry over private industry."

• • •

The explanation in terms of a dominant elite and the explanation in terms of demands are not perhaps very convincing, even on the face of it. Certainly, although much has been written about both elites and demands, neither has often been used for the purpose of explaining variations in policy. The next three lines of argument are, however, frequently advanced, sometimes by different writers, sometimes in combination by the same writer.

Interest Groups

The first of these holds that government plays a more limited role in America because, *whereas in other countries interest groups have not prevented the role of government from expanding, in the US they have*. This argument looks straightforward enough, but it could in fact mean one or more of at least three quite different things. It could mean that interest groups are in possession of more politically usable resources in the United States than in other countries; or it could mean that, although interest groups in most countries are almost equally well endowed with resources, interest groups in America, unlike those elsewhere, have used their resources to keep the State within relatively narrow confines; or it could mean that, although American interest groups have no more resources than other interest groups and do not use their resources for different purposes from other interest groups, they do have the good fortune to work within a framework of institutions that affords them the maximum opportunity to use their resources successfully.

The first of these propositions—that interest groups have more resources in the US than elsewhere—would probably at one time have been widely accepted as true; but the work of Beer and others has made it clear that the conditions under which interest groups can be expected to be strong are to be found in most industrial democracies. The interest groups of Britain, West Germany and Canada have the same sorts of resources at their disposal as those of the United States: leadership skills, knowledge, numbers, access to the media of communication, in some cases, ultimately, the sanction of withdrawing their co-operation. In Britain at least, the major interests are less fragmented organizationally than their American counterparts and succeed in organizing a larger proportion of their potential memberships. In Britain and West Germany, groups benefit from being regarded as having a legitimate right to participate actively in governmental decision making. Only in France do interest groups appear to have considerable difficulty in mobilizing themselves effectively. Since, France apart, American interest groups are not stronger, in this sense, than interest groups in other countries, it follows that the strength of the American groups cannot be used to explain the idiosyncratic pattern of American policy.

The second of the three propositions mentioned above—that interest groups in the United States are more concerned than those in other countries with keeping the State within narrow confines—is worth saying something about, even though there is no comparative literature on the aims of interest groups—indeed precisely for that reason.

Up till now, academic research on interest groups has tended to take groups' perceptions of their own interests as given: a group's beliefs about its interests *are* its interests. On this interpretation, questions about where a group's true interests lie arise only when they are actually raised within the group, by contending factions or by dissident minorities. Even then, the observer usually merely notes the existence of the differences of opinion and does not adjudicate among them; he does not "second guess" the group's leadership or take sides in its quarrels.

This approach may be the only one that can be adopted most of the time; but the attempt to comprehend the behaviour of comparable interest groups across national frontiers exposes a latent weakness in it. Suppose that two interest groups, one in one country, one in another, seem, as regards their material interests, to be in very similar situations: both are faced with a piece of new legislation that may reasonably be expected to affect (say) their incomes or hours of work. Suppose further, however, that the group in one country generally accepts the legislation and tries only to modify it in detail, while the group in the other rejects it out of hand and expends enormous resources campaigning against it. One possible explanation for the groups' discrepant behaviour may be that they possess different information or are making different predictions about the future. Another may be that they find themselves in different tactical situations such that, if either were in the other's position, it would behave similarly. But another possible explanation is that the two groups perceive their interests differently. And they may perceive their interests differently because they have absorbed the values, beliefs and expectations characteristic of the different polities within which they operate. This is too large a theme to be pursued here, but anyone comparing the rhetoric of American interest groups with that of groups in other countries is bound to be struck by what seems to be the American groups' much greater disposition to state their positions in abstract terms and, in particular, to raise, continually, large questions about the role of the State. This tendency probably tells us something about the considerations that American groups have in mind in determining where their interests lie. It undoubtedly tells us a great deal also about the sorts of considerations which the groups believe will appeal to the American mass public and to American decision makers.

The third of the three propositions relating to interest groups suggests that, whatever their resources and their aims, American groups have the great good fortune to work within a framework of institutions that affords them the maximum opportunities for using their resources effectively, especially when what they want to do is prevent things from happening. Since this proposition has more to do with the institutions than with the interest groups themselves, we will consider it in the next section.

Institutions

The classic explanation of the limited role played by the State in the United States as compared with other countries is one having to do with the structure and functioning of American institutions. The contention here is that *the American political system has a number of unusual institutional features, which have the effect of maximizing the probability that any given proposal for a change in policy will be rejected or deferred.* These features include: federalism, the separation of powers between executive and legislature, the constitutional position of the Supreme Court, the part played by committees in Congress, the seniority system in Congress, the malapportionment (until quite recently) of congressional districts, and the absence of disciplined political parties.

To do full justice to this explanation would require a paper much longer than this one. It would also require a great deal of imagination, since this explanation, in an even more demanding way than the others, forces us to try to conceive of what the gross pattern of public policy in the United States would be like were American institutions radically other than they are: it is rather like trying to imagine which of two grand masters would win a tournament if they played not chess or even checkers but croquet. This explanation also differs completely from the others discussed so far in that, whereas in the case of elites, demands and interest groups we were arguing that the US does not differ in most material respects from the other four countries, in this case there can be no doubt that political realities as well as constitutional forms in the US are quite unlike those in Canada and western Europe.

The question, then, is not whether America's institutions differ from the other countries' but whether these differences can account for the observed differences in their patterns of policy. There would seem to be three reasons for supposing that they cannot—at least not on their own.

First . . . it has never seriously been suggested in the US that certain tasks undertaken by governments in Canada and Europe—for instance, the operation of railways and airlines—should also be undertaken by government in America. Suggestions of this kind have occasionally been made but almost never by major national leaders or parties. And this fact seems hard to attribute to institutional resistances. Of course politicians often refrain from putting forward proposals because they know they have no chance of success; possible courses of action may not even cross their minds for the same reason. But it is very hard to believe that American political leaders have consistently, over a period of nearly a hundred years, failed to advance proposals which they might otherwise have advanced simply or even mainly because they feared defeat as the result of obstruction in the House Rules Committee or an adverse ruling by the Supreme Court. It seems much more probable that politicians in the US have not advanced such proposals either because they did not believe in them themselves, or because they believed that other politicians did not believe in them, i.e. that they could not obtain adequate majorities in the various governmental arenas.

Second, in comparative perspective, even reformist Congresses and Administrations, like those of Franklin Roosevelt and Lyndon Johnson, appear as remarkable for what they have not done as for what they have. Only small excursions have been made into the field of public enterprise; and, among the social services, Medicare is only the most conspicuous instance of State provision having been introduced in the United States on a relatively limited basis although substantially more developed programmes had already been in existence, sometimes for many years, in other countries. This apparent reluctance on the part of even reformist majorities to expand the role of the State very far cannot be accounted for in institutional terms.

Third, the institutional obstacles, although they undoubtedly exist, can be surmounted. One of the striking things about the American experience is that almost all of the major innovations in the policy fields we have been discussing have been concentrated in a small number of Congresses: Roosevelt's first three, and the 89th elected with Johnson in 1964. And what distinguished these Congresses was not the absence of procedural obstacles (although minor procedural changes were made) but the presence of determined reformist majorities. In 1935 the Social Security Act passed both houses of Congress in under six months; in 1965 Medicare, having been debated in one form or another for nearly twenty years, was enacted in under seven months. The Social Security Act passed the House of Representatives by 371 votes to 33, Medicare by 315 votes to 115. When the will to surmount them is there, the institutional obstacles do not seem so formidable after all.

These points need to be qualified. For one thing, although the obstacles usually referred to—federalism, the separation of powers, and so forth—are not insuperable, it may be that other institutional factors—for example, the structure of American political parties or the expensiveness of political campaigns—result in the election of Congresses and Administrations (especially the former) that are less willing than the electorate to envisage the State's playing an expanded role. For instance, as late as 1961 the congressional liaison staff of the Department of Health, Education, and Welfare reckoned that Medicare still could not command a simple majority in the House of Representatives even though the evidence suggested that public opinion had supported Medicare or something like it for many years. For another, it would be wrong wholly to discount the role played by the Supreme Court prior to 1937. Although not entirely consistent in its judgments, the Court repeatedly struck down legislation that offended against the canons of *laissez-faire:* in 1905, a New York statute regulating working hours in bakeshops; in 1908, a federal law prohibiting "yellow dog" labour contracts (in which workers bound themselves not to join trade unions); in 1918 and 1922, two federal Child Labor Acts; in 1923, a District of Columbia minimum wage law; and so on. The belief that the Court would strike down other similar pieces of legislation undoubtedly prevented many of them from being considered in the first place.

These qualifications are important. Nevertheless, it seems pretty clear that, for the three reasons given, the institutional explanation by itself is not enough. To the extent that institutional factors operate, they must, it seems, operate in conjunction with others.

Ideas

The time has come to let the cat out of the bag—(especially since most readers will have noticed that it has already been squirming for a long time. If the argument so far is correct, it follows that the most satisfactory single solution to our problem is also the simplest: *the State plays a more limited role in America than elsewhere because Americans, more than other people, want it to play a limited role.* In other words, the most satisfactory explanation is one in terms of Americans' beliefs and assumptions, especially their beliefs and assumptions about government.

There is no need to go into detail here about what these beliefs and assumptions are. They can be summarized in a series of catch phrases: free enterprise is more efficient than government; governments should concentrate on encouraging private initiative and free competition; government is wasteful; governments should not provide people with things they can provide for themselves; too much government endangers liberty; and so on.

Obviously many Americans' political beliefs are much more elaborate and subtle than such phrases imply. Obviously, too, not all Americans believe all of these things. The central point is that almost every American takes it for granted that the State has very few—and should have very few—direct operating responsibilities: that the State should opt "for the role of referee rather than that of manager." If a proposal is made in the United States that the State should not merely supervise the doing of something by somebody else but should actually do it itself, the onus is on the proposer to demonstrate that the case in favour of State action is simply overwhelming. It has to be overwhelming since Americans, unlike Europeans, are not accustomed to a high level of governmental activity and since it will simply be assumed, probably even by the proposer himself, that the *a priori* objections to State action are exceedingly powerful. It is against this background that organizations like the AMA practically always bring forward highly general anti-State arguments against the most specific proposals entailing an expansion of the government's role. . . .

The contrast between the United States and our other four countries is not complete: most Canadians probably make the same sorts of assumptions as Americans about the role of the State, and the Conservative Party in Britain has a strong bias in favour of the private sector. But the contrast is very great nonetheless. Certainly it is more than great enough to account for the policy divergences we have observed. Not only are social democrats in Canada and Europe committed to making extensive use of the machinery of the State: equally important, conservatives in the other four countries, as we have seen, are also not consistently anti-Statist in attitude; on the contrary, they often express a highly exalted view of the role of the State in economic and social life. It was not a socialist but a British Conservative MP who said: "In many respects . . . the individual is as much derived from the State as the State is from the individual." It was not a socialist but de Gaulle who said: "It is to the State that it falls to build the nation's power, which, henceforth, depends on the economy."

• • •

. . . There is nothing new, of course, in our assertion that a limited conception of the role of government is a central element in American political thinking: every textbook has a paragraph on the subject. There is nothing new either in our saying that Europeans and even Canadians do not share this conception to anything like the same degree—if they share it at all. What probably is new in this paper is the contention that these differences in beliefs and assumptions are crucial to an understanding of the distinctive pattern of American policy. It is our contention that the pattern of American policy is what it is, not because America is dominated by an elite (though it may be); not because the demands made on government are different from those made on governments in other countries; not because American interest groups have greater resources than those in other countries; not because American institutions are more resistant to change than those in other countries (though they probably are); but rather because Americans believe things that other people do not believe and make assumptions that other people do not make. More precisely, elites, demands, interest groups and institutions constitute neither necessary nor sufficient conditions of the American policy pattern; ideas, we contend, constitute both a necessary condition and a sufficient one. ■

 # View from the Inside

Under the Constitution, the president is the commander in chief of the armed forces of the United States. In planning military operations, however, the president must rely heavily on the advice of his military advisers, particularly the chairman of the joint chiefs of staff. Although the president retains the final authority to decide when to commit American soldiers to battle, these military advisers have great influence in every area of operations—from identifying threats to detailed operational planning. In this excerpt from his autobiography, General Colin Powell—who served as President George Bush's top military adviser—recalls the planning and execution of the 1989 invasion of Panama, which resulted in the capture of General Manuel Noriega, the Panamanian strongman who was wanted in the United States on drug-trafficking charges.

Questions

1. Evaluate the balance of power between the president, his civilian advisers (including the secretary of defense and the national security adviser), and his military advisers (especially the chairman of the joint chiefs of staff). Does the system, as illustrated here, put into practice the idea of civilian control over the military?
2. In what ways did General Powell not only advise on military aspects of the operation but also contribute to determining the broad outlines of American policy toward Panama? Is such a role for the chairman of the joint chiefs of staff desirable or undesirable? Why?

13.4 "Mr. Chairman, We've Got a Problem" (1995)

Colin Powell

I was sitting in the study [of my quarters at Fort Myer] on Saturday evening, December 16, 1989 when I got another call from [the Joint Chiefs operations officer] Tom Kelly. "Mr. Chairman," Kelly said, "we've got a problem." As usual, the first details were sketchy. I learned only that a U.S. Marine had been shot in Panama. Soon afterward, I was informed that four officers in civvies had driven into Panama City for dinner, where they ran into a roadblock near PDF headquarters. It was Panama's annual armed forces day, and I suspect that a lot of the PDF soldiers had been drinking and carousing. At the roadblock a group of these soldiers tried to yank the Americans from their car. The driver hit the gas and started to pull away. The PDF fired, and Marine Lieutenant Robert Paz was hit and died soon afterward.

The situation grew worse as the night wore on. A Navy officer, Lieutenant Adam J. Curtis, and his wife, Bonnie, who had witnessed the shooting, were detained by the PDF and taken to a police station for interrogation. Curtis was roughed up and threatened with death. Mrs. Curtis was forced to stand against a wall while PDF soldiers pawed her until she collapsed.

I reported all this to Cheney, and we considered whether we had an unignorable provocation. He informed the White House, and a meeting was set with President Bush for the next morning.

That Sunday was hectic. I went first to the Pentagon to check with Thurman* on Saturday's events. Although our officers had taken a wrong turn and had blundered into the roadblock, the PDF's behavior was still inexcusable. Moreover, the shooting represented an increasing pattern of hostility toward U.S. troops. "How's Blue Spoon proceeding?" I asked. "Rehearsed and ready to go," said Max. I called the leaders of the Transportation Command and the Special Operations Command and told them to be ready to move, then went to Cheney's office for a 10:00 A.M. meeting. In the room were Paul Wolfowitz, undersecretary of defense for policy; Pete Williams, the assistant secretary for public affairs, in my judgment the best in the business; and Bill Price from the NSC. We went over the options. By the time Cheney ended the meeting, Wolfowitz and Price were still not sure we had a "smoking gun" justifying military intervention. Cheney asked me to stay behind. When we were alone, he asked, "What do you think?"

"Max and I both believe we should intervene to protect American citizens," I said. "Besides, Noriega's not a legitimate leader. He's a criminal. He's under indictment." I told Cheney, however, that I wanted to hold off my final recommendation until I had a chance to talk to the chiefs.

"Okay," Cheney said. "I'll set the meeting with the President for this afternoon."

Panama was the first major foreign crisis of the Bush administration. It also presented the first serious test of the chairman's new role under Goldwater-Nichols. In the past, the chiefs had voted to achieve a consensus that the chairman could carry to the Secretary of Defense and the President. Now, I was the principal military advisor. The chiefs had great skill and experience. They were the ones who provided the trained and ready forces to the CINCs. I was not likely to ignore their wisdom. But now, as chairman, I was no longer limited to a messenger role.

Back at my office I asked Tom Kelly to have the chiefs meet me at Quarters 6 at 11:30 A.M. I did not want all that horsepower coming to the Pentagon on a Sunday morning. They were sure to be spotted by the press, setting off all sorts of alarms. Soon they began arriving from church and home. I made coffee, and we sat down in the library on the first floor. "Sorry you lost a man," I said to Al Gray, the Marine Corps Commandant. Gray nodded grimly. Tom Kelly and Rear Admiral Ted Sheafer, my intelligence officer, briefed the chiefs. After we had talked over the military options, I gave them my judgment. "Paz's killing can't be overlooked. Blue Spoon is a good plan. We're ready, and I think we should go with it. But I want your views."

Carl Vuono, the Army Chief of Staff, Carl Trost, the Chief of Naval Operations, and Vice Chairman Bob Herres all agreed. Larry Welch, the Air Force Chief of Staff, still debated if we had sufficient provocation, but soon concurred. Al Gray wondered if we needed to move as quickly as Blue Spoon required. Al knew that the plan, as it stood, contained only a minor role for the Marines. He

---

*General Max Thurman was commander in chief of U.S. forces in the Southern Command, which included Panama.

wanted time to bring Marine amphibious units to the party. "Al," I said, "Max has a solid plan, ready to go, and we're not going to delay it or add anything unnecessary." Al understood, and in the end, Blue Spoon had the unanimous support of the chiefs.

It was a strange time to plan for war. Sunday afternoon, December 17, I was hurrying down a festively decked corridor of the White House, Tom Kelly at my side, lugging his map case, when our way was blocked by Christmas carolers in eighteenth-century costume. We shook hands with them, exchanged holiday greetings, and continued on up to the Bushes' private apartment on the second floor.

The President was sitting in his pensive pose, slouched, chin resting on his chest, chewing his lower lip. He wore slacks and a blue blazer with red socks, one marked "Merry" and the other "Christmas." He had called in Dick Cheney; Jim Baker, now Secretary of State; Brent Scowcroft and his deputy, Bob Gates; and Marlin Fitzwater, the press secretary. John Sununu was not present, which promised a little less blindsiding.

Cheney led off with a review of what had happened in Panama and described our proposed response in general terms. He then turned the stage over to me to explain the military plan. Tom Kelly uncovered his maps, and I began to brief, using a pen-sized laser pointer that threw a beamless red dot on the map. The disembodied dot seemed to amuse the President.

Except for Cheney, the others were hearing an expanded Blue Spoon plan for the first time. I started off with our prime objective: we were going to eliminate Noriega *and* the PDF. If that succeeded, we would be running the country until we could establish a civilian government and a new security force. Since this plan went well beyond "getting Noriega," I paused to make sure that this point had sunk in, with all its implications. No one objected.

I went into the military details. We would use the forces in place, which we had been quietly beefing up to a current total of thirteen thousand troops. That number, however, was not enough. Thurman and Stiner had a strategy to strike at every major PDF unit and seize all key military installations. Army Rangers would parachute onto the main barracks at Río Hato, west of Panama City, and take out the PDF companies used to put down past coups. Our Air Force's new F-117A Stealth fighter would be employed for the first time in combat to support the Rangers. Paratroopers of the 82d Airborne Division would fly in from Fort Bragg and drop on objectives east of the city. More infantry from the 7th Infantry Division would be flown in from Fort Ord, California, to extend our control of the country and to help restore law and order. U.S. troops already stationed in Panama would seize the Commandancia and objectives in the city proper; and Navy SEALs would take the airfield where we knew that Noriega kept his "getaway" plane. Special Forces units would search for him, a tough assignment, since we had not been able to track him day to day. A Marine company in Panama was set to secure the Bridge of the Americas over the Panama Canal, and the Delta Force had the mission to rescue Kurt Muse, the CIA source held in Modelo Prison across the street from the Commandancia. The Blue Spoon force would total over twenty thousand troops. I predicted that within hours of H-Hour, Noriega, captured or not, would no longer be in power and we would have created conditions that would allow the elected Endara government to come out of hiding and take office. I finished my briefing pointing out that "the chiefs agreed to a man." Then the questions began flying.

George Bush sat like a patron on a bar stool coolly observing a brawl while his advisors went hard at it. Brent Scowcroft's manner had an irritating edge that took getting used to, but his intelligence was obvious and his intent admirable. He wanted to leave the President with no comfortable illusions: "There are going to be casualties. People are going to die," Scowcroft said. The President nodded, and let the debate roll on.

Jim Baker believed we had an obligation to intervene; that was why we maintained military forces to meet such obligations. He could not resist mentioning that the State Department had urged intervention for some time. Scowcroft kept my feet to the fire. "Suppose we go through all this and we don't nab Noriega? That makes me nervous." That was possible, I said, since we did not know where he was. Suppose he escaped into the jungle? That too could happen, and it was an easy place to hide. Brent hammered away at casualties. Numbers, he wanted. Numbers. I said I could not be specific. Obviously, people were going to get hurt and die, soldiers and civilians, I said. A lot of real estate was going to be chewed up. We could anticipate chaos, especially in the early stages.

The key issue remained whether we had sufficient provocation to act. We had reasons—Noriega's contempt for democracy, his drug trafficking and indictment, the death of the American Marine, the threat to our treaty rights to the canal with this unreliable figure ruling Panama. And, unspoken, there was George Bush's personal antipathy to Noriega, a third-rate dictator thumbing his nose at the United States. I shared that distaste.

The President himself pushed me on casualties. "Mr. President," I said, "I can't be more specific."

"When will we be ready to go?" he asked.

"In two and a half days," I replied. "We want to attack at night. We're well equipped to fight in the dark, and that should give us tactical surprise."

The questions continued, thick and fast, until it started to look as if we were drifting away from the decision at hand. I could see Tom Kelly, in his first meeting with this group, growing uneasy. But then Bush, after everyone had had his say, gripped the arms of his chair and rose. "Okay, let's do it," he said. "The hell with it."

• • •

As D-Day approached, I told Tom Kelly to make sure Cheney got every scrap of information about Blue Spoon. I still preferred to brief the Secretary myself, or at least be present while he was briefed. But over the next feverish forty-eight hours I would not have time, and after our recent discussion I certainly did not want Cheney to feel cut off from any source. He began vacuuming up data. How many men in a squad? What equipment do SEALs carry? Why do Rangers jump from five hundred feet? He wanted to have it all by H-Hour, and I understood why. When the dust settled on this invasion, I would still be an advisor; but he and the President would have to bear the responsibility.

In one of my several phone conversations with Max Thurman, I mentioned that Blue Spoon might be fine as a code name to hide an operation, but it was hardly a rousing call to arms when the time came to go public. You do not risk people's lives for Blue Spoons. We kicked around a number of ideas and finally settled on Max's suggestion, Just Cause. Along with the inspirational ring, I liked something else about it. Even our severest critics would have to utter "Just Cause" while denouncing us.

War planning is a mosaic of thousands of troubling details. The weather was turning bad, and icing conditions stateside were going to affect our ability to assemble the required airlift. Rules of engagement, the instructions to our troops as to when they could use deadly force, had to be approved. I had to tell Thurman to change the F-117A target list. We did not want to bomb Noriega's country villas in the hope he might be there and end up killing maids and children instead.

The last night before the invasion, sitting alone in the dark in the backseat of my car on the drive home, I felt full of foreboding. I was going to be involved in conducting a war, one that I had urged, one that was sure to spill blood. Had I been right? Had my advice been sound? What if the icy weather in the States hampered the airlift? How would we then support the troops already in Panama? What would our casualties be? How many civilians might lose their lives in the fighting? Was it all worth it? I went to bed gnawed by self-doubt.

When I got to the Pentagon early on Tuesday morning, December 19, I found that my Joint Staff, under its able director, Lieutenant General Mike Carns, and Max Thurman's SOUTH-COM staff in Panama were on top of things. Army Lieutenant General Howard Graves was skillfully merging our military plans with State and NSC political and diplomatic efforts. All loose ends were being tied up. We were "good to go." My confidence came surging back. My worries vanished, and I entered the calm before the storm.

That afternoon, with the country going to war in less than ten hours, I had a student named Tiffani Starks in my office asking me to explain why I had chosen a military career. The conversation was part of the girl's high school project to interview a "famous person." Earlier, I had had lunch with Thomas P. Daily, an Annapolis midshipman, the payoff after my losing a bet on the recent Army-Navy football game. I went through these innocent encounters as scheduled to make my day look normal and thus protect the security of Just Cause.

After talking with Miss Starks, I slipped off to the White House for one last meeting. Jim Baker and the State Department had worked out a plan to spirit Endara from his hiding place just before H-Hour to Fort Clayton, home to U.S. Army South, where he would be sworn in as president. We did not yet have Endara's agreement to the plan and would not know if he would go along until later in the evening. Endara's participation was the last check-off point before the invasion. If we did not have him on board, President Bush would have to decide whether to go ahead without him or to abort the mission.

What about Noriega? the President kept asking. Were we going to nab him? Was this operation going to be branded a failure if we could not deliver Noriega's head? "Mr. President," I said, "we don't have any way of knowing where he'll be at H-Hour, but wherever he is, he won't be El Jefe. He won't be able to show his face." I also cautioned against demonizing one individual and resting our success on his fate alone. Still, a President has to rally the country behind his policies. And when that policy is war, it is tough to arouse public opinion against political abstractions. A flesh-and-blood villain serves better. And Noriega was rich villain material.

• • •

. . . [M]ost of the fighting was over, except for scattered skirmishes with the Dignity Battalions. Noriega, however, still eluded us. We brought in more infantrymen from the 7th Division to comb the countryside and run down the remainder of the PDF. These troops went from town to town shouting "boo," which convinced the once feared PDF detachments to surrender. We packed Panama City with more troops to maintain order. We put up temporary housing for Panamanians displaced by the fighting and fires that had burned down several blocks, particularly around the Comandancia.

President Endara had been sworn in a few hours before H-Hour and was now in the Presidential Palace. Twenty-four Americans gave their lives in Panama to achieve this victory for democracy. My private estimate to Cheney had been that we would lose about twenty troops. Our armed forces had acquitted themselves superbly, although we had made some mistakes. We did not plan well enough for reintroducing civil government. Our press arrangements produced recriminations on both sides. We were slow in getting the press pool to Panama and to the action. Pete Williams, the Defense Department spokesman, tried to compensate by sending a commercial airliner to Panama loaded with a couple of hundred reporters whom we could not properly accommodate. Consequently, the press ate us alive, with some justification. In the future, I knew, we needed to do a far better job.

Yet things had happened on the press side during Just Cause that tested to the limit my customary support of the media. On the second day of the invasion, I watched President Bush during a televised press conference. He was visibly upbeat after the quick success of Just Cause. The President could not know that as he was giving occasionally smiling answers to reporters, the networks were simultaneously showing on split screens a transport plane at Dover Air Force Base, Delaware, unloading the bodies of the first American casualties. The effect was to make the President look callous. Sensational images, but cheap-shot journalism.

I was angered when the press started trying to direct the war as well as cover it. Near the center of Panama City stood a radio tower. Every armchair strategist knows that you have to knock out the enemy's capacity to communicate. And look at that, the U.S. military had foolishly left this transmitter operating, broadcasting prerecorded Noriega propaganda. The White House started taking flak from the press over the still-standing tower. And I started taking flak from Brent Scowcroft. I told him that the tower was not bothering us, and we did not yet have troops in that part of town to take it. We did not want to knock the tower down anyway, because President Endara would need it in a day or so. No dice. The press heat was too great and the tower had to go. I told Thurman and Stiner to destroy it. They were mad as hell at being overmanaged from the sidelines and for being ordered to take a pointless objective. But soon, Cobra attack helicopters were shooting missiles at the girders, not unlike my old Vietnamese buddies shooting down trees with a rifle.

After the first night at the crisis center, we were back in our offices. I got another call at the Pentagon from Brent Scowcroft telling me that several correspondents were trapped in the Marriott Hotel in Panama City. "We've got to put troops in to rescue them," Brent said.

"They're in no danger," I pointed out. "I've checked the situation. They're safe in the basement of the hotel. The fighting will soon sweep right past them."

I thought I had convinced Brent until I got a second call. He was taking terrific pressure from bureau chiefs and network executives in New York. "We've got to do something," he said.

"We shouldn't do anything," I reiterated. "We've got a perfectly competent commander on the ground. He's got a plan, and it's working." Were kibitzers supposed to direct the fighting in Panama from executive suites in Manhattan? I reminded Brent that there were 35,000 other American citizens in Panama, and we were trying to ensure the safety of all of them. Only a few minutes passed before Cheney called. There was no discussion. Do it, he said. No more arguments.

Again, I reluctantly called Thurman and Stiner. "I hate to tell you this," I said as I explained the situation. "But get those reporters out, and I'll try to keep Washington off your backs in the future." Stiner sent in units of the 82d Airborne to storm the Marriott. On the way, they ran into a stiff firefight. We got the reporters out, but the 82d took casualties, three GIs wounded, one seriously, and a Spanish photographer was killed by American fire while covering the rescue.

I told Cheney that I did not want to pass along any more such orders. "If the press has to cover a war," I said, "there's no way we can eliminate the risks of war." Cheney called Scowcroft and asked him not to issue any more orders from the sidelines. This was a new, tough age for the military, fighting a war as it was being reported. We could not, in a country pledged to free expression, simply turn off the press. But we were going to have to find a way to live with this unprecedented situation.

Early on Christmas Eve, I was in my garage trying to relax by pulling the engine on one of my Volvos when my cellular phone started ringing. My exec, Tom White, was calling with the news we had been hoping for. I let out a whoop and a holler and ran back into the kitchen. "They found Noriega!" I shouted to Alma. Our troops had been searching for him for days in hideouts and hinterland villages. We had missed him on the first night while he hid in a whorehouse. Noriega had just sought sanctuary, Tom had told me, in the Papal Nunciatura in Panama City. He had called the papal nuncio, Monsignor Sebastian Laboa, and asked to be picked up in a Diary Queen parking lot near San Miguelito. There the strongman was found waiting in a dirty T-shirt, shapeless Bermuda shorts, and an oversize baseball cap pulled low over his all too recognizable face.

My relief was even greater ten days later on January 3, when Monsignor Laboa persuaded Noriega that the game was up and that he should turn himself over to the Americans. The Vatican looked on Noriega as an accused criminal with no legitimate claim to political asylum. As soon as the Panamanian people learned that Noriega was in U.S. custody, they started dancing in the streets. Until then, they had been afraid that he might yet return to power.

I flew to Panama in early January for a firsthand look and to visit the troops. While with the 82d Airborne, commanded by Major General Jim Johnson, I was carried away. "Goddam, you guys did a good job!" I said. Fred Francis of NBC caught my outburst on camera, and I made the evening news. Anyone fearing a moral decline in this country may be heartened to know that the Joint Staff mailroom was soon flooded with complaints about the chairman's language.

Our euphoria over our victory in Just Cause was not universal. Both the United Nations and the Organization of American States censured our actions in Panama. Reports circulated of heavy civilian casualties. Some human rights organizations claimed that the invasion had resulted in thousands of Panamanians killed. At the time, Max Thurman's SOUTHCOM staff estimated Panamanian casualties in the low hundreds. Subsequently, the House Armed Services Committee carried out a thorough investigation, which estimated that three hundred Panamanians were killed, of whom one hundred were civilians and the rest members of the PDF and the Dignity Battalions. The loss of innocent lives was tragic, but we had made every effort to hold down casualties on all sides.

A CBS poll conducted soon after the installation of President Endara showed that nine out of ten Panamanians favored the U.S. intervention. President George Bush had been vindicated in a bold political decision. Generals Thurman and Stiner and all the troops under them had achieved a victory for democracy with minimal bloodshed. The American people supported the action and were again proud of their armed forces. We had a success under our belt.

The lessons I absorbed from Panama confirmed all my convictions over the preceding twenty years, since the days of doubt over Vietnam. Have a clear political objective and stick to it. Use all the force necessary, and do not apologize for going in big if that is what it takes. Decisive force ends wars quickly and in the long run saves lives. Whatever threats we faced in the future, I intended to make these rules the bedrock of my military counsel.

As I write these words, almost six years after Just Cause, Mr. Noriega, convicted on the drug charges contained in the indictments, sits in an American prison cell. Panama has a new security force, and the country is still a democracy, with one free election to its credit. ■